# Revolution and Foreign Policy in Nicaragua

# About the Book and Author

Since the revolution in 1979, Nicaragua has faced economic dislocation, a growing debt, chronic hard currency shortages, a counter-
revolutionary war, economic and diplomatic pressure from the US,
and regional isolation.  In spite of these challenging problems, the
Sandinista leadership, maintaining a broad array of international
contacts, continues to pursue an activist foreign policy and to explore new avenues through which to promote regional peace.  In this
volume, Dr. Vanderlaan analyzes the domestic and international determinants shaping revolutionary Nicaragua's foreign policy within the
broader theoretical contexts of Latin American foreign policy, revolutionary transformation, and the politics of dependence.  In the domestic sections, she investigates the influence of *Sandinismo*, nationalist
pragmatism, and economic underdevelopment.  Turning to international
constraints on policy, the author details the ideological, economic,
military, and diplomatic dimensions of US-Nicaraguan   relations;
discusses the roles played by Central and South American states in
shaping FSLN policy; and examines Nicaragua's ties to the Soviet Union
and Cuba.  Finally, the author examines the Sandinista record and
discusses the contributions and limitations of the Nicaragua model.

Mary B. Vanderlaan is assistant professor of political science
at Hartwick College.

# Revolution and Foreign Policy in Nicaragua

## Mary B. Vanderlaan

Westview Press / Boulder and London

*Westview Special Studies on Latin America and the Caribbean*

---------------------------------------------------------------------------
This Westview softcover edition was manufactured on our own premises using
equipment and methods that allow us to keep even specialized books in stock.
It is printed on acid-free paper and bound in softcovers that carry the
highest rating of the National Association of State Textbook Administrators,
in consultation with the Association of American Publishers and the Book
Manufacturers' Institute.
---------------------------------------------------------------------------

Published in 1986 in the United States of America by Westview Press, Inc.;
Frederick A. Praeger, Publisher; 5500 Central Avenue, Boulder, Colorado 80301


Library of Congress Cataloging-in-Publication Data
Vanderlaan, Mary B.
    Revolution and foreign policy in Nicaragua.
    (Westview special studies on Latin America and the
Caribbean)
    Includes index.
    1. Nicaragua--Foreign relations--1979-
I. Title.   II. Series.
F1528.V36  1986      327.7285        86-1650
ISBN 0-8133-7053-1


Composition for this book was provided by the author.
This book was produced without formal editing by the publisher.

Printed and bound in the United States of America

∞   The paper used in this publication meets the requirements of the
    American National Standard for Permanence of Paper for Printed
    Library Materials Z39.48-1984.

6  5  4  3  2

To those who struggle
for peace and human liberation
in an interdependent world

# Contents

# List of Illustrations

# Acknowledgments

I have many people to thank. Numerous individuals and organizations - not all of whom I can mention here - assisted me in obtaining contacts, interviews or data during research trips to Nicaragua, Honduras and Costa Rica in 1982, 1983 and 1985. My gratitude to Vicky Furio and Phil McManus. In Nicaragua I received invaluable assistance from Noel Corea, Margarita Clark and others of the Associacion Sandinista De Trabajadores De La Cultura; from Martin Vega at the Foreign Ministry; and from the staffs at: Comite Evangelico Pro Ayuda al Desarrollo, Instituto Historico Centroamericano and Centro Ecumenico Antonio Valdivieso. In Honduras and Costa Rica I benefitted from the cooperation of several governmental, popular and church organizations. In Costa Rica, the staff and social scientists at Departmento Ecumenico de Investigaciones provided warm atmosphere and helpful contacts. I have incurred a debt to many willing informants in the region. Officials at the US Embassies in Nicaragua and Honduras graciously granted interviews.

Travel and manuscript preparation support were provided by grants from the Dean's Office of Hartwick College in 1982 and 1986; grants from the Hartwick College Board of Trustees in 1983 and 1985 supported field research and library work. College and departmental support for a half-year sabbatical leave in 1985 allowed me to complete the major portion of the manuscript. My secretary Jan Stankiewicz and displaywriter operator Wendy Hunter invested more hours than they care to remember typing several drafts of the chapters. I deeply appreciated their energies and proficiency. Students Wanda Haxton, Marion Magill and Cynthia Van Zelm eagerly assisted in library work and proofreading. My gratitude to these colleagues.

I am especially indebted to fellow academicians and researchers who read portions of the manuscript and offered valuable criticism and insight: John Booth, John Buchanan, Mary Jo Dudley, Walter LaFeber, Carl Meacham and Tom Walker. Their time and counsel affirmed me in my work. Finally but never least, my deepest thanks to mi companero, Al Meyering, for his unending patience and loving support, and, to my dear friends and family who provided encouragement and space.

*Mary B. Vanderlaan*

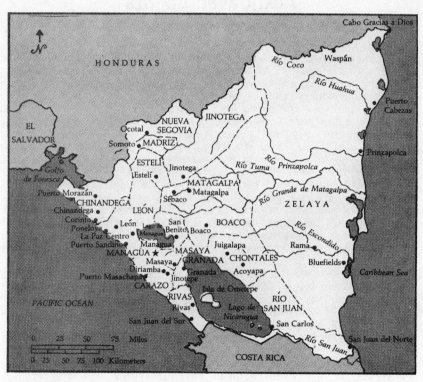

Nicaragua

Source: Thomas W. Walker, Nicaragua: The Land of
Sandino (Boulder, Colo.: Westview Press, 1981), p. xx.

# PART 1

# Introduction

# Introduction

For many Nicaraguans the Sandinista-led "Triumph" over dictator Anastasio Somoza Debayle in July, 1979 marked the beginning of a new chapter in the historic struggle against foreign domination and political-economic dependence. While the immediate object of hatred for a majority of Nicaraguans in the late 1970s was US-aligned President Somoza, the FSLN--the Sandinista Front for National Liberation--claimed its origin in the struggles of Agusto Cesar Sandino against US Marines in the 1920s and 1930s. The Frente Sandinista pledged to carry out a popular political and socioeconomic revolution in "Nicaragua Libre" which incorporated objectives of pluralistic politics, a mixed economy and international non-alignment. Rejecting the Somoza foreign policy model of facilitating the United States' regional initiatives and of bowing to assertions of a special US prerogative, the nationalist FSLN called for an end to US interference in Nicaragua and for international relations on the basis of mutual respect.

The Sandinista revolution was, among other things, a reaction to the history of United States-Nicaraguan relations. The US Marines--Sandino's "Yanquis"--figured prominantly in that history. Sent by Washington to impose its brand of "civility," to replace an uncooperative bourgeois faction with a more cooperative one or to crush popular revolts, the marines landed in Nicaragua in 1893, 1894, 1895, 1896, 1898, 1909, 1912, and 1925. In 1912 and up to 1925 a garrison of about 100 marines was stationed in Nicaragua. In 1925 many more marines occupied Nicaragua to quell a civil war after US Secretary of State Frank Kellogg warned of a threat of "Soviet Bolshevism" there. Popular guerrilla uprisings against US domination led by General Sandino thereafter were viewed as a threat to US interests--e.g. under the Bryan-Chamorro Treaty of 1914 Nicaragua had ceded to the United States a long-term option to construct a canal through Nicaraguan territory. Nicaraguan territory also constituted the heartland of what the United States considered its "soft underbelly" region. Political conformity and stability there was assumed to be in the US national interest. The marines' struggles against Sandino's forces from 1927 to 1932, in fact, constituted the United States' first counterinsurgency war in Latin America. That war included the aerial bombardment of Ocatal in 1927, a battle in which 300 Nicaraguans died.

Before the marines were recalled from Nicaragua in 1934 under

4

FDR's Good Neighbor Policy they trained and armed a surrogate force--the Nicaraguan National Guard, under the direction of General Anastasio Somoza Garcia. It was Somoza's Guardia which assassinated General Sandino in 1934 as he left a dinner meeting with Somoza, and, after he had laid down arms. And it was the Guardia which was to symbolize for Nicaraguans both the ruthlessness of the Somoza family and that family's link to the United States. For 46 years the Guardia was key to the Somozas' power. During that period the Untied States trained and equipped the military force which the Somozas used to silence political dissenters. Indeed, bolstered by US support the Somoza family dominated Nicaraguan politics until 1979.

Nicaragua's role in the informal alliance with the United States, meanwhile, was to play the reliable ally--in UN voting, in providing staging areas for CIA assaults against Guatemala (1954) and Cuba (1961); in operating as the backbone of the 1960s regional anti-communist alliance (CONDECA); in acting as the lynchpin in CONDECA's system of repressing regional popular movements; and the like. The United States' interests in Nicaragua historically were defined more by strategic than economic concerns.[1] Nicaragua nevertheless supplied raw materials and markets for the United States through the 1970s. Moreover, import/export and tax incentives, as well as the secrecy of economic operations there, both allowed US companies to control the bulk of all foreign enterprises in Nicaragua and allowed the Somoza clan to continue its own capital accumulation.

Yet, despite the United States' post-World War II emphasis on order and the Somoza government's attempts to eradicate the nationalist, anti-imperialist legacy of Sandino's early struggles, smaller-scale popular uprisings continued into the 1950s and 1960s.[2] In 1962, Carlos Fonseca Amador, Tomas Borge Martinez and others created the FSLN in an attempt to present a coherent political and economic response to Somocismo. In 1969 the Frente distributed a political program which became a working basis for the broader FSLN political organization that emerged during the period of guerrilla struggle in the 1970s.[3] More importantly, the anti-imperialist tradition of Sandino and Nicaragua's post-World War II role as facilitator of the United States' East-West-inspired policy for Latin America had become sources of an alternative vision for Nicaragua in the region and in the world.

At the same time that the new Sandinista government was introducing its alternative vision for Nicaragua's foreign and domestic policy, however, superpower tensions were also increasing. The Cold War was heating up. Not only had Soviet and Cuban activism in Africa in the mid- to- late 1970s convinced many in Washington that the Soviets had used detente to forward their own interests in the Third World, but the late 1979 Soviet invasion of Afghanistan also spurred the emergence of both a newly viable conservative bloc on Capitol Hill and new suspicions about Soviet intentions. The resurgence of anti-communist, bipolar conservatism in Congress in the late 1970s, for example, was reflected in heated Senate debate over the Panama Canal Treaty, in Senate objections to the (ill-fated) SALT II Treaty and in significant Congressional resentment over the 1978 formal recognition of China. The fall of the Shah in Iran, the Carter Administration's sudden notice of a Soviet combat brigade in Cuba and the Ogaden Desert war between Ethiopia and Somalia, among other things, contributed to the growing assessment after 1978 that detente was dead and a new Cold War had begun. Candidate Ronald Reagan and the Republican Party declared as much in 1980. The Nicaraguan revolution was portrayed as an example of expanding Soviet influence. President Carter himself, meanwhile, left behind his earlier regionalist worldview for the bipolar, globalist view of National Security Advisor Zbigniew Brzezinski.

Carter's rethinking and domestic political pressures from the right shaped a wary US reaction to the Sandinista victory in Nicaragua. But it was the election of .conservative Reagan in 1980 that signalled a sharper turn in US foreign policy toward themes of bipolarism, anti-communism, and "rolling back" Soviet influence. (These issues are discussed in detail in Chapter 5.) Consistent with this worldview, the Reagan Administration in early 1981 declared events in Central America to be "textbook cases" of Soviet expansionism. It was in this superpower context, then, that the FSLN had to carry out its revolution. And it was this US posture which was to shape prospects for the survival of the Nicaraguan model of development.

THE BOOK'S FOCUS

In the chapters that follow I examine both the FSLN's alternative foreign policy vision and the critical contexts--domestic and foreign--within which the revolutionary government worked to devise and implement specific foreign policies. Following Coleman (1984), foreign policy is viewed as a state's attempts to cope with its international environment. It does so either by influencing the environment in a positive way so that the environment can be used to pursue the state's national goals, or, by rendering the environment less threatening, thereby eliminating some of the obstacles to pursuing state objectives. To the extent that they both generate demands upon and are facilitated and affected by foreign policies, domestic policies are an important dimension of foreign policy. Thus, in shaping a new independent foreign policy for Nicaragua the Sandinistas were constrained by domestic and international constituencies and realities. These realities both limited policy options and interacted to shape the Sandinista worldview. Although Nicaragua's revolutionary leaders demonstrated an ideological commitment to structural change, both domestic and foreign pressures regulated the nature and the pace of that change. As we might expect would be the case for a small, dependent state, the Nicaraguan government has had to tailor its committments and accommodate realities and immediate necessities. A salient feature of Nicaraguan policies in the early 1980s has been the necessity of finding some balance between generating and holding support abroad and holding to or altering its plans for structural change in internal structures and in external linkages. A major factor for any poor state in wooing political or material support from abroad is the ability to demonstrate economic, political or social viability at home -- another example of the internal - external linkage (e.g. Rosenau, 1980; 1981).

Domestic contexts and determinants of policy are considered in Part Two. I also discuss how external actors maneuvered to affect domestic political dynamics and, in turn, revolutionary Nicaragua's image in the world. External pressures, demands and opportunities affecting Sandinista foreign policy are analyzed in Part Three. There I consider the key role played by US policy and the additional pressures and opportunities flowing from European and Latin American reactions to the revolution. In Part Four I examine patterns in Nicaragua's international relations and military-security policy.

It has not been the purpose or intent herein directly to compare pre- and post-revolution foreign policy. Nor do I undertake an examination of institutional or structural mechanisms of foreign policy-making as such. Rather, my purpose has been to examine patterns in post-1979 foreign policy and to illuminate key determinants of those policies. Considering policy as a function of the dynamic interaction of internal and external determinants with leadership orientations distances the analysis somewhat from the limitations imposed by ideological conceptualizations of the regime under study. Contrary to prevailing theories emanating from Washington regarding the "dogmatic," "Marxist-Leninist" character of the Sandinista government, for example, this study suggests that Sandinista foreign policy into the mid-1980s, though it reflected a political will to break traditional patterns of subservience to the local hegemon, is more$_4$ accurately characterized as pragmatic, flexible, and responsive.

Because the United States, in light of the Sandinista revolution, quickly came to define its interests in the region and vis-a-vis Nicaragua in broad terms, the US role in shaping the FSLN's opportunity structure in international relations was also great, even predominant. US Nicaragua policy under the Reagan Administration, motivated by an ideological agenda of "rolling back" (i.e., rather than "containing") socialist--read communist-- experiments in the Third World, was designed precisely to undermine the survival of the FSLN regime, and thus, of the Nicaraguan example. Much attention, therefore, is given to domestic, regional and global dimensions of US policy. Similarly, much attention is given to the ways in which Sandinismo and immediate concerns about survival have competed and/or interacted to shape Nicaraguan foreign policy options.

Finally, this book also provides a case study of the limitations, pitfalls and opportunities encountered by small states interested in forging new international relationships or addressing dependence in an incipient multipolar global setting. Nicaragua's attempts, successes and failures at promoting alternative linkages, its reliance upon and appeal to Third World solidarity and its willingness to bear the costs of policy independence, and the like, have established revolutionary Nicaragua as something of a test case for Latin American and other underdeveloped states. It is the context of Latin American foreign policies and small state dependence into which this study of Nicaraguan foreign policy is placed. I begin with that theoretical focus.

NOTES

1. This is especially so from a comparative perspective on where the United States was accumulating wealth in Central and South America. Unlike in Guatemala, Honduras, Chile or Brazil, for example, there was no American Sugar Company, no ITT, no United Fruit Company monopoly, or no Standard Oil in Nicaragua. Compared to situations in El Salvador and Guatemala, few US companies operated in Nicaragua. Rather, by the 1970s in Nicaragua the Somoza family was the economic power and the near monopoly in many sectors.

2. For example, see Edelman, 1985. Instances of anti-dictatorial, anti-Somoza or anti-imperialist uprisings in the 1950s occurred in 1954, 1956, 1959 and from 1958-1963. Many of these revolts were led or organized by veterans of Sandino's guerrilla army.

3. For a discussion of the early organization or evolution of the FSLN see George Black (1981) or John Booth (1982).

4. The Reagan Adminstration's language of crisis and immediacy, its East-West posturing, its rhetoric and hyperbole regarding Sandinista Nicaragua and its institutionalized campaign of misinformation regarding Nicaragua from 1983 onward created an atmosphere of polarization on Nicaraguan issues at home and abroad. That polarization likewise affected the academic community in the 1980s though, I believe, to a somewhat lesser degree. While the US administration was successful in many quarters in shaping attitudes about the Nicaraguan revolution, this work is not intended or designed as a refutation of Reagan Administration claims about the FSLN's foreign policy motivation or direction. Hopefully, this study rather points up the hazards of simple political characterizations of complex processes. It remains a feature of partisan politics and heated debate, of course, that multifaceted realities are reduced to pithy labels or assessed according to narrowly perceived historical "lessons."

# 1

## Nicaraguan Foreign Policy:
## A Theoretical Focus

> A country that wants to call its own shots, that wants to
> develop its own foreign policy can be a very bad example.
>
> Foreign Minister Miguel D'Escoto
> March, 1982

Any analysis of revolutionary Nicaragua's foreign policy must
be set into the broader contexts of 1)Latin American politics and
foreign policy in a post inter-American security era, and 2)small
states' dependence, underdevelopment and search for survival
strategies in international relations.  Changes in United
States-Latin American relations, say from the 1950s and 1960s to the
1970s and 1980s, and particularly for Central America and the
Caribbean, may be more changes in degree than of kind.
Nevertheless, factors such as the decline of global bipolarity and
the growing role of European, Asian and Third World states as
international actors have led to a waning of US hegemony and to new
foreign policy strategies in the region.  Although US policy and
behavior remains as probably the single-most important consideration
among Latin American foreign policy decision makers, global power
shifts and Third World interests in economic development, national
survival and security have led to small states' concerns with
increasing maneuverability vis-a-vis larger, more powerful states.
These small and often underdeveloped states seek to gain sovereignty
or increased independence by reducing economic and political
dependence on external actors.

Because Nicaragua's foreign policy after July, 1979 has been
shaped by these historical realities and has paralleled the policy
aspirations of other small states seeking to address conditions
imposed by underdevelopment, it is useful briefly to review and
characterize the trends in Latin American foreign policies
generally[1] before discussing Nicaragua's policy in particular.

THE LATIN AMERICAN CONTEXT:  WANING US HEGEMONY

The fifteen year period in US-Latin American relations from
1945 to about 1960 has been characterized as the inter-American or

hemispheric security era.  In this Cold War period of global bipolar
politics the United States acted on the hegemonic presumption that
it had the capacity and the duty to determine the general course of
events in Latin America.  This presumption, moreover, was predicated
on the notion that the pluralistic democratic tradition of Western
humanist  government  would  be  a  natural  outgrowth  of
self-determination or political development in Latin America -- a
notion that happened to ignore the actual Latin American perspective
that  "...freely competing factions all too often seems a choice
between chaos and privilege...."  Indeed, "For 150 years Latin
American governments have endeavored not to balance competing
centers of power, but either to integrate them or to eliminate them
in  the  name  of  collective  harmony.  This  enduring  effort
characterizes regimes both benign and arbitrary, civilian and
military, rightist, leftist or centrist" (Dealy, 1985: 108, 110).
This corporatist belief, as Dealy points out, predates the
contractarian conception of John Locke, and, in contrast to US
political theory, encourages governments "...to intervene actively
on behalf of the community..." (p. 111).  Individual rights must be
limited by the state's need for public order.  Thus, contrasting
political conceptions between North and South America should have
suggested to North American policy makers that Latin American
political structures would not easily conform to the US model.

Yet, few Latin American, European or other states had the
post-war ability to challenge the United States which was at the
zenith of its power.  Although the objectives of Latin America and
the United States were every year more incompatible -- the Latin
American states were concerned with socioeconomic growth, presaged
by deeply rooted political and social changes, while the North
Americans were concerned about the expansion of communism -- US
predominance and economic strength meant that North American
concerns would delimit inter-American relations.

As Latin America was pulled further into the financial order of
the local superpower through direct US investments and economic aid
in the early 1950s, the United States pushed for and got Latin
American compliance in the creation of several hemispheric security
or security-facilitating organizations as a first order of post-war
business.  In 1947 the Rio Treaty for mutual defense created the
mechanism  for  a  multilateral  military  response  to  any
"extra-hemispheric" threat against one or more member states.  In
1948 the Organization of American States (OAS) was created to
promote  economic  cooperation,  regional  problem-solving,
representative democracy, and complete non-intervention in each
others' affairs.  In practice it meant, for at least the 1945-1960
period, US diplomatic supremacy in the hemisphere, in addition to
its economic and military supremacy.  It also meant 20 Latin
American votes cast with the United States' at the United Nations.
In 1950 the Mutual Security Act paved the way for the stationing of
United States military groups throughout most of Latin America for
the purposes of advising, training and arming the continent's armed
forces.  This large US military presence was to be significant in
shaping US-Latin American relations in the next decades.  A national
security doctrine, heavily influenced by US anti-communism, became
popular and indeed became an identifying ideology among traditional

Latin American militaries which so often wielded the dominant power in Latin American states. Meanwhile, US-dominated lending institutions, like the World Bank, the Inter-American Development Bank and the International Monetary Fund, provided access to loans and grants for economic development. Thus was a continent anxious for development kept within the sphere of influence which the United States had carved and shaped from the 1800s onward. For example, Central America was often referred to as the United States' "backyard." And so the stage was set for future US definitions of its national security interests in the hemisphere.

. The United States soon realized, however, that collective action in support of or in deference to US policy objectives for the hemisphere could neither be assumed nor easily organized. The Latin American states, wanting to overcome the legacies of European colonization and North American neo-imperialism, were primarily interested after World War II in spurring economic growth, industrialization, and agricultural modernization. OAS members generally did not perceive communism as the paramount political problem or security threat -- though some used anti-communist arguments to win or maintain US military aid or to repress popular opponents -- and many were critical of US actions against reformist and popular movements such as those in Guatemala (1954), Cuba (1961), the Dominican Republic (1965), and Brazil (1964). A disjuncture of interests between the Latin Americans, concerned about economic development, and the United States, concerned about ideological nonconformity, created obstacles to hemispheric dialogue.

President Kennedy's program for Latin American development in the early 1960s, the Alliance For Progress, seemed to epitomize the differing conceptions between North and South of the problems to be addressed and the solutions to be employed. While the stated objective of US policy was to eliminate the attractiveness of communism -- the spectre of Castro's Cuba figured importantly in US thinking after 1959 -- by eliminating hunger, poverty and illiteracy, the US spent as much energy on and had greater success in establishing national counterinsurgency organizations and longer-term patterns of military interaction (e.g. in training armed forces in guerrilla tactics and mob control). In the 1960s, a wave of intelligence officers, military and technical advisors, and multinational business representatives swept over the Southern continent, promoting US interests and North American definitions of development with security. Meanwhile, political problems beset the Alliance: misunderstandings occurred over whether the aid came before or after states met the political and social conditions placed on it, and, over who would administer the funds and the granting processes -- Washington or Latin American economists. Moreover, Peru, Argentina, and later, Honduras, Brazil and the Dominican Republic ignored Washington's demands for free elections, producing another set-back and eventually contributing to the practical demise of the Alliance under President Johnson.

While the North Americans cited the success of the Alliance For Progress -- no other nation in the hemisphere had gone the way of Cuba -- South Americans reiterated a wariness about US intent in Latin America and could point to few economic successes in terms of

12

greater economic sovereignty, lessened economic dependence or firmer
bases for sustained economic growth. Over time a newer
consciousness of North-South conflict, especially in the economic
sphere, took the place of the historic theme of hemispheric common
interests and futures. Many South American states, save Chile and
Argentina, for example, increasingly identified with fellow poor,
Third World states which were reacting to years of foreign dominance
by experimenting with strategies of defiance and autonomy. Although
less true of the more underdeveloped, more dependent Central
American and Caribbean states -- which had been repeatedly
penetrated by US armed forces during the 1800s and 1900s and where
traditional political elites, bolstered by the US presence and their
own militaries, maintained highly inegalitarian repressive orders --
by 1960 Latin American states generally had moved to a post
inter-American security era in relations with the United States.
Even in Central America the traditional orders, characterized by
unholy alliances among the aristocratic, military and Catholic
Church elites, were beginning to disintegrate under international
and domestic economic and political pressures. Varying
manifestations of Latin American nationalism, stemming from tensions
inherent in processes of socioeconomic and political change,
appeared across the continent from the 1930s onward: antiyanquismo,
nativism, economic nationalism, military socialism, revolutionary
nationalism, and the like. Dating from the late nineteenth century,
this anti-Americanism and Southern nationalism became sustained
during the period of US economic and military intervention in
Central America and the Caribbean (Atkins, 1977: 37).

Together with other changes in global politics in the last
decades, such as superpower nuclear parity, economic and political
rifts in both the traditional Eastern (Moscow-centered) and Western
(Washington-centered) alliances, the resulting growth in the number
of competing world power systems and the organization of Third World
forums, the continent-wide doctrine of developmentalism (read
economic independence) in Latin America was imposing limitations on
traditional US foreign policy tools.² For example, whereas in the
1950s nearly all Latin American states had military links (aid,
training) to the United States, military assistance programs had
decreased significantly by 1979. In the 1968 to 1978 period, US
arms accounted for only 15 percent of Latin American and Caribbean
arms purchases, as Israeli, European and several Latin American
states (Brazil, Argentina) took over this market. By the mid-1980s,
90 percent of Latin American arms purchases were from non-US
sources. (As we shall see, however, US military assistance programs
in Central America expanded significantly in the 1980s.) Moreover,
the Latin American militaries' traditional adherence to a national
security doctrine -- inspired by US anti-communism and implemented
through acts of repression against popular dissent -- was
increasingly being challenged as South American states, in
particular, moved to replace powerful militaries with civilian
regimes.

Similarly, in the areas of aid, investment and trade US
latitude for influence, rather than increasing, was actually
diminishing in some ways. Bilateral economic assistance distributed
through the US Agency For International Development (USAID) was

considerably lower in the 1980s than in the 1960s, while the presence of Latin American, European, Asian (especially Japanese) and Eastern bloc donors increased notably. US investment in Latin America by 1984 represented about 17 percent of all overseas investment (such investments made up only 5 percent of total US investment). Moreover, under 10 percent of new US foreign investment after 1960 was in Latin America, owing to such factors as Latin American measures to reduce the political and economic roles of US corporations in their small economies, their efforts to gain control over major local resource industries such as in oil and mining and the attractiveness to US companies of Asian investments. At the same time, foreign investors attempted to reduce risk where political stability appeared to be threatened by growing class conflict in highly inegalitarian societies. Figures on imports and exports confirm a picture of declining US economic interests and influence in Latin America. Slater (1984) notes that whereas total US trade with the rest of the world is about 8 percent of GNP, within that, exports to Latin America are about 14 percent and imports from the region were about 14 percent of total US imports in 1970 (down from 24 percent in 1960).

Even though traditional foreign policy tools of US economic clout were declining and regional powers like Mexico, Venezuela, and Brazil were increasing their hemispheric influence, US interests in Latin America -- and, in practical terms, how the United States defined its regional security interests -- did not appear to be declining. Mexico, with its oil, was one of the United States' largest trading partners, and because they were regional powers, relations with Venezuela, Brazil and Argentina were important to the United States. Adding to US regional interests, much of the its oil was refined and shipped through the Caribbean. Moreover, while the United States had trade imbalances elsewhere, it had advantageous balances with Latin American states. A large portion of US exports to the Third World went to the region. US banks, meanwhile, had increased their exposure in Latin America.

Undoubtedly more important in shaping US Latin American policy after 1979, however, was the fact that, as I noted earlier, a number of international events in 1978 onward had sparked a new level of Cold War hostilities and suspicions between the United States and the Soviet Union. The events encouraged renewed bipolar analysis of US security interests and foreign policy objectives. Washington reemphasized security interests and US influence in the "soft underbelly" Caribbean region as popular and revolutionary movements in Nicaragua, Grenada and El Salvador made headlines and as events in the US "back patio" were interpreted in the foreign policy sector as explosive. US domestic politics and world politics became increasingly polarized. Many in Washington argued during the 1980 presidential campaign, for example, that President Carter had, in effect, "lost" Nicaragua and Iran, that a "Vietnam Syndrome" had left the United States "fearful of the use of power," and that American power and prestige could be restored to traditional levels through new, tough policies. According to a resurgent conservative bloc in US domestic politics, the United States could reverse the trend of waning world and hemispheric influence through the use of force if necessary. Soviet world influence could be rolled back by a newly determined America. In this view, US dominance over the Western Hemisphere as it was manifested in the post World War II era was the normal -- and the desirable -- state of things. It was this worldview which, under Ronald Reagan's leadership, was to shape US responses to the Nicaraguan revolution in the 1980s.

Political events in the Central American - Caribbean area after 1978 nevertheless highlighted the geostrategic and changing-power-relations themes discussed earlier. States in the region were searching for new economic and political relationships in the international arena as US hegemony declined. In fact, the searching itself was both the product and cause of socioeconomic and political turmoil, turmoil heightened by the reality that, relative to its power in South America generally, US power in Central America was still significant. In the larger contexts of weakened hemispheric influence, the proliferation of world political powers, a persistently independent Mexican foreign policy, polarization over US-Latin American policies (emergent from the Panama Canal Treaty debates in Congress) and a growth in Cuban prestige among Latin American states, the United States saw dangerous implications in regional events for its position vis-a-vis small states and for its Caribbean security interests generally.

The events surrounding the Nicaraguan revolutionary "Triumph" in July, 1979 pointed up the urgency and the inevitability of all these themes for United States foreign policy.[3] While the United States worked through various channels in 1979, including talks with Somoza and his bourgeoisie opposition, to block the FSLN from coming to power -- the United States preferred a coalition government for post-Somoza Nicaragua in which the Sandinista Front would be a minority voice -- it was the Latin American states which held the political initiative. In May (1979) Mexico broke diplomatic relations with Somoza and in June Bolivia, Colombia, Chile, Ecuador and Peru (the Andean Pact) legitimized the Sandinistas' struggle, declaring "a state of war" in Nicaragua and characterizing the struggle as one in pursuit of freedom and justice (NYT, 6-18-79). Thus encouraged, many states in Latin America increased their aid to the FSLN, Cuba among them. Similarly, a US initiative to send a multilateral "peacekeeping force" to Nicaragua, in effect to deny the FSLN complete military control after Somoza's fall, was blocked at the June OAS conference by traditional US allies: Panama, Costa Rica, Mexico, the Andean Pact (Chile abstained) and others.

The OAS resolution calling for the installation of the FSLN-appointed junta and for non-intervention in Nicaraguan affairs represented another break in the traditional role of the OAS as a proxy for US policy objectives. Reacting with alarm, national security managers in Washington let it be known that unilateral intervention was "not inconceivable", and, that it feared another Cuba and an extension of the Soviet bloc. The 82nd Airborne Division, effective in the Dominican Republic in 1965, was placed on alert. The diplomatic activities and political assertiveness of the Latin American states in support of revolutionary nationalism in Nicaragua, however, significantly increased the costs of any unilateral US military action there. The July 19 Triumph in Nicaragua signalled the end to direct US control over Nicaragua and a dramatic decline of hegemony over Central America. But it also pointed up the growing independence of Latin American foreign policies and the constraints they were increasingly placing on US action.


THEORETICAL FOCUS

Latin American Foreign Policy:   The Recent Literature

The Nicaraguan revolution in 1979 occurred about a decade after scholars began documenting shifts in Latin American foreign policies away from the patterns imposed by US hegemony in the inter-American security era. Scholars have noted that Latin American global and domestic politics represent more than a search for greater independence. Their politics also reflect an interest in structural (economic and political) changes both to accommodate the mass mobilization of peasants and workers and shifting class alliances among traditional political forces, and to break patterns of chronic underdevelopment and dependence. Indeed, the current Latin American social and political dialectic gives background to the long-term revolutionary process initiated in Nicaragua toward a socialist transformation based on nationalist and egalitarian objectives. As Stavenhagen (1981: 218-219) points out: "Rarely in history has there existed over an entire continent, as there currently is in Latin America, such a generalized awareness among the most diverse social groups as to the necessity of carrying out major modifications of the political and social structure."

The fields of Latin American and comparative foreign policy, moreover, yield broad theoretical guidance for a consideration of revolutionary Nicaragua's foreign policy even if few other small, dependent states overtly pursue all-encompassing structural change. That is, although policy will reflect the uniqueness of the Nicaraguan situation after the war of liberation, policies will also share characteristics with other states at a similar economic level or in a similar international setting. The consensus among observers and scholars that there is nothing to suggest that "...underdevelopment, internal polarization and external dependence can be maintained indefinitely...", leads to a concern with the domestic and international "...obstacles, contradictions, tensions and conflicts..." (Stavenhagen, 1981: 219) that will be encountered in the process of change. The Nicaraguan case exemplifies the fact that despite external pressures on or counterinsurgency campaigns within the Latin American states, the revolutionary model of social change has not been abandoned. Yet no single model of change could address the varying situations among Latin American states. The search for new strategies of implementing change in the context of dependence continues. Foreign policy strategies become central to the struggle to escape underdevelopment and dependence.

The literature on Latin American development and foreign policies suggests important departures for a study of Nicaraguan foreign policy, for example, highlighting major determinants of and constraints on policy in small and traditionally dependent states. Scholars suggest that economic level, the drive to develop, the choice of development models and the extent of state economic dependence on the United States are critical determinants of Latin American foreign policy.[4] As the case of revolutionary Nicaragua demonstrates, concern for state security and perception of external threats are also important factors which help shape both internal institutions and policies and external linkages. In this way, and especially in the case where a small state faces clear external threats to its economic and political survival, domestic policies are one dimension of foreign policy. For the small, dependent states, moreover, elites' orientation, resolve and evaluation of the dependent relationships in the context of national development goals are vital aspects of the conversion process bringing dependency to bear on decision making. Thus Ferris (1981) notes that although dependency establishes limits on policy choices, Latin American governments have substantial latitude in foreign relations within those limits. Dependence does not preclude foreign policy variations and in poor, weak states, for example, opinion leaders' optimism and faith in human potential can yield a strength or capacity not predicted by objective realities. States can maintain or improve their economic standing through support of policies which uphold the status quo and/or do not challenge the dependent relationship with the local metropole (the source of capital formation), thereby winning aid and other supports in the short term. Or, they may work to change the international economic structure through alignment with Third World movements. But, both tangible state capacities or relative power and the intangibles of leadership and national determination affect policy choice of means and ends. Widespread popular mobilization in Nicaragua during and after 1979, for example, though it generated many political demands also provided support and momentum for fundamental change in a poor country facing seemingly insurmountable economic problems.

Leaders' visions for the future and their selection of broad development strategies directly shape the state's foreign policy, just as foreign policy is a central tool in reducing dependence or meeting other long-term objectives. With this in mind, Stavenhagen (1981: 219-21) envisions three alternative models for the future of Latin America: the continuation of dependent development or "governing against the people"; the pursuit of an autonomous capitalist development or "governing without the people;" and revolutionary socialism.[5] Since the first two alternatives preclude structural change necessary to uprooting dependence, Stavenhagen argues that the third alternative is the only positive alternative to underdevelopment. However, he argues that there will necessarily be a transition period between the reality of dependent underdevelopment and socialism in the future, a period for which there is no recipe, but during which a regime must confront and adapt to contradictions between socioeconomic change and the world capitalist system. In fact, it appears to be just such a period that Nicaragua has entered since the revolution and the Sandinistas' philosophical rejection of dependent development. Along with other dependencia writers Stavenhagen stresses the role of inter-state relations in dependency reversal,[6] thereby once again directing interest toward foreign policy as a tool for change.

Similarly, Coleman and Quiros-Varela (1981), contending that political leaders in Latin America are judged by their ability to establish and reach goals for economic transformation, argue that there is a direct relationship between a state's development model and its foreign policy behavior. In an analysis that builds on Stavenhagen's alternative futures, these authors argue that conventional development strategies in Latin America imply close ties with developed, capitalist powers and a relationship of dependent development and alignment with the United States. Reformist strategies, possible in democratic or authoritarian Latin American regimes, employ a foreign policy of capital generation and search for national autonomy, accomplished by tactics of presenting the regime to the West as the "last alternative to a thoroughly Marxist regime" and to the socialist world as a progressive, national-populist regime. Finally, revolutionary strategies reject piecemeal reforms for simultaneous attacks on "economic dependence on the hegemonic capitalist power" and on internal colonialism through centralized political direction, an attack on private property and a demobilization of "those who bear the costs of redistributive activity" (p.48-53). Agreeing that policy will depend on elite orientations, e.g., their development model, these authors conclude that since attempts at reducing or reversing dependence will carry heavy punitive costs, the only policy alternatives appear to be assistance from the socialist bloc or the spreading out of dependence through developing relationships with a wide variety of capitalist and non-capitalist states.

Following Coleman and Quiros-Varela and others, foreign policy -- for developed and underdeveloped states alike -- can be used both to shape the external environment and to facilitate domestic policy objectives. Domestic politico-economic reorganization in the small, dependent state may render the state less manipulable by external actors or systems, though tested models or successful strategies have not clearly emerged in the Third World to date. In the process of change, foreign policy may be used as a tool in rallying national integration, domestic mobilization and popular support as the public is educated to the link between underdevelopment and external hegemony. In short, a study of foreign policy in a small, dependent state must include consideration of all policies aimed at coping with the external environment and of both domestic and international factors affecting the prospects for political and economic development in those states.

## Latin American Foreign Policy Characteristics

Certain common patterns of interests and tactics have appeared in Latin American foreign policies during what I have referred to as the post inter-American security era. As I mentioned earlier, Latin American states have shown a renewed, and at times fierce, interest in achieving independence or sovereignty from all outside powers. This drive for independence is in large part a reaction both to histories of US and European penetration of and dominance over Latin American societies and to more recent Third World actions to develop potential bargaining positions within the world political economy. Indeed, the struggle for greater automony coexists with Latin American recognition of increased regional and global interdependence of states and the growth in potential for Third

World solidarity. Interdependence on other small, poor states, say within Latin America, is often considered to be less costly than the more unequal relationships between Latin America and northern industrialized states.

Latin American states across the political spectrum have attempted to enlarge the room for maneuvering vis-a-vis the United States, for example, to win military or economic aid from el Norte while minimizing direct US influence over their domestic politics. Most of the Latin American states in the last decades have experimented with levels of defiance in the face of US influence and of autonomy from Washington's continental or local objectives. Examples abound from the Alliance For Progress decade and from the period of Carter's human rights policies in the late 1970s. Such strategies of independence are pursued on a continuing basis in Latin American states today, though with varying degrees of determination and success. Former Costa Rican President Daniel Oduber (1985: 146), for example, argues that "...it is impossible to assume that Latin American nations will place US interests above the national interests of individual Latin countries....The solid bloc of the post-war period is now finished; the Malvinas War [between the United Kingdom and Argentina in 1982] was proof of that." Commenting on US policy directions in Central America in the mid-1980s, Oduber reflected the views of many Latin American leaders:

> Terms of trade, external debt, migration policies, scholarships, technology transfers, and investment policies that respect each country's characteristics and institutions will do more for stability and peace than any military solution--which inevitably leaves resentment, instability and continual struggle.

Certainly the larger, more industrialized states such as Brazil, Venezuela, Argentina, and Chile have greater real potential for increased autonomy across an array of issues. But state determination to achieve greater independence is not always rooted in objective capabilities.

A second common interest pursued through the foreign policies of Latin American states is building stronger, more self-reliant and less dependent economies. As with attaining the goal of increased independence, attaining this goal too is limited by the present structure of the global political economy -- characterized as it is by: huge rich-poor gaps among states; the predominance of northern capitalist states in world markets, technology, communication and the like; and the real economic dependence of Third World and peripheral states. Nevertheless, the Latin American states' foreign policies can generally be characterized as searching for strategies and employing tactics that minimize vulnerabilities to external control.

While there is little agreement in the theoretical literature about how or whether dependence can be reversed, most states are clear about the immediate causes and effects of underdevelopment and dependence in their economies. Many Latin American states, including Nicaragua, have had very open, penetrable economies, made even more so by their historic agro-export development models. Trade dependency brought on by high export product concentration, a geographic concentration in export destination and in sources of supply, and a high ratio of exports to GNP has been a feature of these economies. This pattern has been complicated by unequal bilateral relationships where the smaller state is of little or low salience to the larger state as a trade partner. The larger state in this relationship, however, is often a vital partner for the small state -- e.g., the historic pattern of Nicaraguan-US relations -- and the small state's effectiveness often depends on governmental or business constituencies in the more powerful state. Strengthening the local economy and raising the level of economic or social opportunities for citizens, in other words, is not only important for its own sake, but is also necessary for building internal support for domestic and foreign policies. Building broad support at home and fanning the flames of nationalism when local objectives clash with those of the local hegemon yields a base of strength or resilience essential to an otherwise (relatively) powerless state.

Much of the task of economic development for Latin American countries has been to work toward local development goals without appearing to challenge or undermine the interests of the United States. Yet the intent for some time has been precisely to limit the United States' influence in the local economies. This struggle for greater self-reliance points up again how, especially for poor, relatively powerless and internationally penetrated states, domestic and foreign policies are linked. Foreign policy is an important tool in and the best hope for attaining domestic goals. Yet, as Atkins (1977: 49) characterizes the continuing Latin American dilemma: "...how are nations to improve their capability position and modernize their societies while preventing inordinate influence in their economies and political systems?"

Tied in with these two Latin American interests are several others, namely, achieving greater international prestige or respect and, for some, (e.g., Mexico, Brazil, Venezuela), seeking global or regional leadership positions. Again, these interests have roots in common histories of foreign domination and suppression of local identities or interests. But they also reflect the waning of US imperial power in the Western Hemisphere, an ideological change toward a Third World stance and a collective psycho-social need to assert control over one's own destiny. It is interesting to note in this context the important leadership role played by Latin American states on the Third World's behalf in calling for the New International Economic Order (NIEO) in the 1960s and 1970s. Moreover, both recent Latin American political initiatives, such as independent voting at the UN and the OAS, regional debt seminars, and the Contadora peace process in Central America (to name only a few) indicate new levels of regional confidence and a growing ability to manipulate changing world power divisions.

## Latin American Foreign Policy Tactics

Similarities among Latin American foreign policies also appear in the tactics employed to secure their interests and to strengthen state influence capacity. I will discuss briefly state policy behavior in the post-security era, behavior one author has characterized as "pragmatic opportunism" (Milenky 1977:95). In brief, states are increasingly interacting and conflicting with regional neighbors, playing roles in international bodies, trying to play off the superpowers, seeking new trade partners and expanding state control over the economy.[8]

The Latin American states have used foreign policy means which are similar to those of other small states interested in minimizing the effects of relative powerlessness (or, low influence capacity) in the world arena. One tactic that has proven useful in providing both leverage with the North and forums for discussing common problems is joining international organizations and acting in concert with like-minded or like-situated states. The opportunities afforded by such organizations as the United Nations, the Non-Aligned Movement, the Economic Commission for Latin America and regional market pacts are important to these poor states. For example, although the non-aligned states cannot generally meet their own needs for trade, technology and capital, they are able, acting in association, to maximize their scarce resources, to bring pressure for reform of the world economic system, to express regional interests and identifications, to promote national development through joint projects and to practice a (limited) separate existence apart from the realm of political-military superpower confrontation.

For the Latin American states, multilateral diplomacy and bloc bargaining thus yields room for maneuvering vis-a-vis the local hegemon -- the United States -- and other more powerful nations, while it facilitates the continuing evolution of Latin American foreign policy perspectives toward a North - South orientation and away from an East - West orientation. The growing recognition in Latin America of the potential for greater individual and bloc influence through collective action is seen in the fact that most all of the states are currently working within the Non-Aligned Movement either as full members, as participants with observer status or as petitioners for full legal states. Interestingly, the largest number of Latin American states, including Nicaragua after the Triumph, joined or petitioned the Movement in 1979 during the institutional presidency of Fidel Castro.

This, of course, is not to say that there is full issue or ideological consensus among the Latin American states. Inter-state tensions have appeared due to the current energy situation (from oil booms to oil gluts), to philosophical differences on world political issues such as the Middle East and relations with the Eastern bloc and over the efficacy of resource diplomacy (such as the use of cartels or of confrontation with the United States). Moreover, military governments facing popular opposition movements are apt to align more closely with the United States, given its traditional interest in the maintenance of stability, and to enunciate a national security doctrine replete with charges of foreign communist aggression. Nor is this to say that individual state diplomacy is becoming unnecessary. Important bilateral trade, technology, investment, and aid negotiations with industrialized northern states go on. Individual negotiation and weak-state strategies of pragmatic opportunism will regularly be coordinated with the state's participation in multilateral forums.

Yet these states are also increasingly aware of each other as important factors or partners in foreign policy, especially with regards to economic power. Therefore, as Milenky (1977:94) points out, competition among Latin American states for manipulating the instruments of collective solidarity will be intense. And, "...multilateral diplomacy directed primarily towards extra-regional targets, supplemented by intra-regional action but frequently disrupted by competitive struggles among leading nations, will be a central feature of the Latin American region."

A second but corollary foreign policy tactic has been the promotion of international law, non-intervention and peaceful, negotiated settlements of disputes. Being all too aware of their position of comparative military and economic weakness, the Latin American states have turned in addition to appealing to moral principals and humanitarian sentiments in international relations. (An early example of the Latin Americans' greater predisposition to yield to international norms was their decision to join the League of Nations after 1919 while the United States rejected membership.) For poor states whose first concern is economic development, security obtained through international recognition of sovereignty, non-intervention and diplomacy is much preferred to huge military outlays or an industry geared to defense. In dealing with a hostile superpower, moreover, world opprobrium is an important factor delimiting the superpower's actions vis-a-vis the small state. Just such an example is presented by the reaction of Latin America and European states to US Central America policy after the Nicaraguan revolution.

Another foreign policy tactic common to the Latin American states is the broadening of international contacts for purposes both of lessening the potential for (traditional) US hegemony and of escaping the pressures of superpower conflict and East - West side-taking which typified politics in the inter-American security era. At the same time, however, a number of states such as Peru, Argentina, Mexico and others have managed to play on superpower rivalries to get benefits and negotiating room from both, while staying non-committal and even enunciating non-alignment. (Historical realities were to make such an option difficult for Nicaragua.)

Most Latin American states have broadened trade, aid and diplomatic ties to include sizable relationships with Western Europe and the EEC, Japan, Canada, Asia, the Eastern bloc and other Latin American states. The overall impact has been a diversification of their dependence, a lesser potential for any one state to exert an inordinate influence over the local economy or domestic politics, and a greater feeling of independence, even if actual independence has not been enhanced. In fact, although international contacts have been broadened and though Latin America has increased its international presence, new contacts may not always represent more equitable, balanced or symmetrical relations.

An important historical example of unequal interdependence between North and South American states was the security dependence of Latin American states on the United States, and, the United

States' activities designed to encourage or expand that dependence. The United States traditionally was interested in eliminating extra-hemispheric ideologies or economic influence while overseeing the stability of pro-US regimes. Therefore, successive US administrations not only acted to provide broad military assistance programs, including officer training and mob-control (and later, counterinsurgency instruction), but also sought to assure proper national priority-setting by working to shape Latin American budgets. (These same objectives and methods characterized US policy in the 1980s in Central America, the region in which the United States was most willing to interject its military power.) Many Latin American governments, on the other hand, accepted or sought US security assistance along with economic assistance as the best means for maintaining power in the face of growing class antagonisms which accompanied economic development. Though both actors benefitted from the relationship, the greater dependence of the Latin Americans and their eventual dissatisfaction with inordinate US political influence led to an interest in strategies which would increase their autonomy. For the FSLN in Nicaragua, military dependence on the United States was a priority concern.

Because of their increased global contacts, Latin American states today are much less trade or security dependent on the United States. Though the United States continues to exert considerable military prerogative over the continent in general, it is no longer possible to explain the foreign policies of Latin American states simply by looking at relations with the United States. Having alternative sources, markets and allies gives the small state greater room for independence than in the situation where contacts are few and unbalanced. As one scholar put it: "If power lies in not having to give in, it may be exerted in a particular situation somewhat independently of the ranking of two contending governments in someone's power calculations" (Fox, 1977: 3).

## Addressing Dependence

Diversifying their dependence has become a popular foreign policy tactic among poor Latin American states, in part because of the greater psychological feeling of independence afforded by such a policy. As the case of revolutionary Nicaragua demonstrates, diversifying dependence has been accepted as an enabling step in the process of increasing state independence. That is, many view economic dependence itself as an intractable problem unless major structural changes occur in the world political economy and between metropole (central, capitalist) and periphery (underdeveloped) states. Yet diversifying or spreading out dependence blunts some of the effects of dependence by yielding a little more self-reliance and local control over resources or national surpluses. Dependence is mitigated to the extent that the small state can create or take advantage of opportunities for maneuvering around or negotiating with larger states on whom they rely for important exchanges.

Although there have been dramatic changes in US-Latin American relations, the success of Latin American, and especially of Central American, foreign policies still depends to a significant degree on how the United States responds to them. Foreign policy choices of

economically dependent Latin American states are limited by the
United States' definitions of its own interests and the resulting
level of United States policy activeness in the region. In the
cases where the United States takes special notice of local events
because they challenge traditional patterns, the maneuvering room
afforded the small state by linkages to other states may be lessened
as Washington applies pressure on both that state and its supporters
in and out of the region. This reality and its implications is a
central theme in the study of revolutionary Nicaragua's foreign
policy.

How to achieve dependency reversal, on the other hand, or,
whether dependency is reversible in the present world economy are
questions debated in political science.[10] As Munoz (1981) notes,
there are few agreements among theorists about concrete strategies
of dependency reversal or building self-reliance. Most writers do
define the process as encompassing not just the economic sphere, but
also the social, political, cultural spheres, and, as proceeding at
both the domestic and international levels. Dependency reversal
therefore, would necessitate both domestic structural changes, for
example, in the distribution of power and benefits, and changes in
the nature of external linkages, for example, away from unequal
relationships. Many loosely equate dependency reversal with
self-reliance and a transition to socialism.[11] The attitude that
emerged in revolutionary Nicaragua was that although it might never
be able to achieve a totally self-contained economy, there was
certainly much that could be done in the international arena to
increase its political sovereignty.[12]

But both domestic economic forces, empowered by the proximity
and interest of the local hegemon, and international factors worked
in the short-term to limit and threaten the transformation process.
Indeed, the case of Nicaragua has held world attention because it
was a rare example of an underdeveloped dependent state, in close
proximity to the regional hegemon, which was: asserting
independence; initiating a moderate transition toward nationalist
socialism incorporating a private sector; enunciating goals of
non-alignment and greater self-reliance; and actively pursuing these
things at both the national and international levels. Revolutionary
Nicaragua's foreign policy was intended to be, at once, a reflection
of the general development model pursued by the new leaders and an
enabling device for that transformation process.

However, both the preferred development model and its
accompanying foreign policy were among the alternatives for Third
World development considered by the United States to be
unacceptable. The local superpower historically allowed only those
models of change in Latin America that preserved the monopoly of
capitalist structures and an active, "independent" private sector.
The post-Triumph economic program in Nicaragua called for a mixed
economy where private property rights were to be protected. It
utilized incentives for private sector production. Sandinista
leaders, meanwhile, negotiated with foreign firms to encourage them
to stay in "Nicaragua libre" (see Chapter 3). At the same time,
central government agencies planned for increasing the access of the
poor majority to social benefits and political voice. They sought
to make a larger share of the national economic pie accessible to

the poor. The development model of dependent capitalism was to be replaced by a Nicaraguan mixed-economy socialism. Nicaraguan economist and Jesuit priest Xabier Gorostiaga explained the new balance sought between the public and private sectors in revolutionary Nicaragua which would assure that basic human needs would have priority over private accumulation:

> Our strategy differs from other models of economic development whose first priority is to establish a model of accumulation. Our first objective is to satisfy the basic needs of the majority of the population. This creates a new logic which we call the 'logic of the majority.' i.e., the logic of the poor. Instead of organizing the economy from the perspective and interest of the top 5 percent, as was done during the Somoza dynasty, we are trying to organize the economy from the perspective of the majority (BI, 10-17-83).

Thus, the confrontation that quickly emerged between Nicaragua and the United States after 1979 exemplified the struggle and resistance, predicted by Third World and development theorists, that is inevitable when global capitalist structures, northern economic dominance, and superpower hegemony or bipolar politics are challenged. It also exemplified contrasting views of what representative democracy meant in terms of political structures. This struggle was additionally exacerbated by increasingly tense superpower relations on the global level.

## NICARAGUAN FOREIGN POLICY OBJECTIVES

> I stood back to back with the US and gave my friend and ally all the support I could muster....(No) president anywhere supported the policies of the United States more devoutly than I did. The record will show that no such loyalty existed anywhere.
>
>                    Anastasio Somoza, 1980
>                    Nicaragua Betrayed

The revolution in Nicaragua was at once a rejection of Northern imperialism, economic dependence and the Somoza model of economic development. It represented the adoption by new power-holders of an alternative set of policy prescriptions for overcoming obstacles to self-determination and sovereignty. The new government enunciated aims of recreating the relationship of Nicaragua to the world political economy, thereby facilitating over the longer-term a restructuring of society and polity at home following the principles of popular hegemony, national unity, increased self-reliance and economic development. In the international arena the Frente (the Sandinista Front) pledged to make policy based on the broad principles of national sovereignty, non-alignment with Third World solidarity, a preference for a North-South perspective and an internationalism of active participation and wide diplomatic exchanges, i.e. across all ideologies.

The orientation of the nationalist, socialist FSLN represented a response not only to Nicaragua's past and present dependent, agro-export status or to its poverty in relation to other continental South American states. It was also a response to the historical dominant linkage to the United States, consolidated as it was through overt US military interventions and economic, military and political support for the Somoza dynasty in this century. Indeed, the Sandinistas had always considered that the struggle was being waged as much or more so against US hegemony as against the Somozas. Once in power the FSLN made it clear, in words and in actions, that it would distance Nicaragua from the United States. In their view, US-inspired policies in Nicaragua and Nicaraguan complicity in US policy had hurt Nicaragua's real interests, had injured Nicaragua's national dignity and had greatly narrowed Nicaragua's development alternatives (Booth, 1982: 211). Though the Sandinistas wanted to maintain relations and links with the United States, they sought to reduce its broad influence over Nicaraguan policy. An early gesture important for its symbolism, therefore, was Nicaragua's withdrawal within weeks after the July 19 Triumph from the Central American Defense Pact (CONDECA), a pact established under US security auspices in the 1960s and concerned with stemming perceived communist threats to the region. To the Sandinistas, the pact was another instrument of US imperialism (NYT, 8-9-79).

According to FSLN officials, this distancing was not to include other democratic or industrialized states, nor did it represent a rejection of Western or Northern relations. For example, the 1979 "Program of Government" called for "solidarity with the democratic states of Latin America and the rest of the world." Speaking in early 1980, Junta member Sergio Ramirez Mercado expressed the Sandinistas' awareness of the role Nicaragua was playing as "a test case for Latin America": "It was in those days of struggle that a new kind of political behavior emerged. That framework of democratic support for the Nicaraguan Revolution made us realize that we could form a bloc of democratic unity opposed to the interests of imperialism" (quoted in Black, 1981: 304). Nicaraguan leaders hoped to keep the support of Latin American, Western European and other states that had aided the FSLN through a variety of means during the struggle against Somoza. The young fighters-turned-leaders had learned that the capitalist states were not always uniform in their political perspectives, that policy rifts with the United States often occurred among these states and that an informal anti-imperialist bloc might be possible, involving also such democratic Latin American states as Venezuela and Mexico. These ties were also considered important for the pause they would give to any Washington plans to subvert or overturn the new regime. Observing early FSLN behavior in foreign relations, Black argues: "...the wisdom of Nicaragua's foreign policy has been to accept foreign support from whatever the source, while remaining lucid about the widely differing motives which underlie each country's solidarity and turning them to Nicaragua's advantage" (1981: 300).

The Sandinista leadership's ideological rejection of political and economic dependence and of an agro-export model of growth resulted in the enunciation of foreign policy objectives of self-determination and non-alignment. These would be accomplished

Table 1.1
Nicaraguan Foreign Policy Objectives
_____

_____

SOVEREIGNTY
SELF DETERMINATION
NATIONAL DEFENSE & NON-ALIGNMENT

Longer Term Goals

1. Formation of Sandinista People's Army, Sandinista
   Police, Popular Militia
2. Membership in the Non-Aligned Movement
3. Systematic support for peace in international forums
4. Membership as observer in Socialist International
5. Maintenance of diplomatic relations with a broad
   spectrum of nations
6. Stability in international commercial relations
7. Diversification of financial dependence and
   maintenance of varied bilateral and multilateral
   financial aid sources

International Behavior

1. Non-aligned voting pattern in United Nations
2. Support for national liberation struggles in the Third
   World; condemnation of colonialism, neo-colonialism,
   apartheid, Zionism, and all forms of racism
3. Support for a New International Economic Order (NIEO)
4. Maintenance of past diplomatic relations without
   breaking with any country
_____

Source:   "The Philosophy and Politics of the Government of
          Nicaragua"  Managua, March 1982.

through what the Foreign Ministry considered a "principled yet
pragmatic disposition" (Bendana, 1982: 326), a phrase suggesting the
leadership's awareness that real constraints would mitigate against
attaining any rigid ideological program.   Under broad banners of
Sandinismo, egalitarianism, socialism, democracy, and sovereignty,
revolutionary Nicaragua moved through a definitional period as
leaders attempted to consolidate the immediate gains of the
revolution while also delivering on its promises.
    According to Foreign Minister Father Miguel D'Escoto Brockman
(1983:15), Nicaragua's foreign and domestic policy goals grew out of
"the four pillars of Sandinism": democracy, Christian values, social
justice and nationalism, where nationalism meant developing a system
which addressed specific needs arising from Nicaragua's historic
situation:

    We are not talking about chauvinism here, but about a
    nationalism that is manifested in the will of our people
    to regain sovereignty, to determine our own destiny, even
    to have the right to make our own mistakes and learn from

them, and to determine what system of government we will opt for to best meet the needs of our people. Sandinism is not nationalistic in any sense that leads us to believe that we have discovered a formula that is good for any other country. We believe that, just as we are looking for our own way, every other country has to look for its own way. This is why for us it seems strange that we might be intent on exporting our revolution. A revolution is not an exportable item.

Defense. It is clear that two goals in particular were prioritized in the first period after .the July 19, 1979 military victory over Somoza. One objective was to restore Nicaragua's economy in a way which reorganized society's opportunity structure, thereby facilitating structural and economic change dictated by a "logic of the majority". A second goal, according to foreign policy officials, was to "neutralize interventionist sectors in the United States and elsewhere which were intolerant of pluralism and prone to confuse a peoples' will to independence with international communist conspiracies" (Bendana, 1981: 323). As another Sandinista government official put it in 1980 during a discussion of Nicaragua's search for international understanding and diplomatic-political support:

We know who our natural allies are. But we also know who the friends are that we need. The biggest single threat we face is military intervention from the north. If that looks like happening, all the left wing support in the world won't prevent it. But with friends like Mexico, the EEC, even the USA itself...well, that would be a different story (quoted in Black, 1981: 300).

A principal concern of the new leaders, thus was gaining time for the revolution to develop, especially given the United States' historic hostility to political initiatives in Latin America which it did not control. Foreign Minister D'Escoto stated the FSLN position clearly when he addressed the UN General Assembly in October, 1980, just over a year after the Sandinistas came to power: "We wish to be friends [with the United States] but we will never sell out, nor will we ever compromise in our sacred task of building a new, free, and sovereign Nicaragua."
Wary of the possibility of international hostility toward the revolution -- spearheaded, it was feared, by anti-revolution, conservative forces within Washington -- and with knowledge of the United States' role in trying to keep them from power in the 1978-1979 period, the Sandinistas early on decided to mobilize a peoples' army, police force and militia under Sandinista control. The aim was both to reduce national security dependence on foreign military technology and to mobilize skilled cadres for meeting national development needs (see Chapter 8). The Somoza model of relying principally on the local hegemon, and later, on newer small arms producers like Argentina and Israel for military hardware and training was rejected in favor of a policy aimed at greater security self-reliance through popular mobilization. In concert with

28

strategies and tactics used by other small Latin American states, moreover, Nicaraguan leaders sought security through expanded international contacts and membership in a variety of international forums. As one of their first pieces of business, the Sandinistas were interested in building up a defense structure not beholden to either the local hegemon or to any constituted military bloc. Despite the technical problems related to standardization inherent in obtaining weapons from a number of sources, the Frente sought initially to win military aid from a variety of Western and Third World sources. As I detail in Chapter 8, however, US policies were to be significant in encouraging Nicaraguan reliance on Soviet military aid in the 1980s.

Economic Reorientation. Regarding the priority economic concern, Sandinista leaders oriented foreign economic policy toward diversifying trade and markets, as well as sources of imports and technology, in an effort at breaking the extensive, monopolistic commercial network of Somoza's time and achieving national autonomy in the foreign trade sector. While diversifying its economic dependence, Nicaragua would also link agricultural and industrial policy, attempting to break with the inherited industrial model of import-substitution industrialization which relied on imported machinery and inputs. The Ministry of Foreign Trade was given authority to direct, plan and organize foreign trade through the organization of semi-automomous export enterprises, with the goals of benefitting a majority of the people and keeping export earnings within the national economy (Ministry of Foreign Trade, 1984). Arguing that foreign trade during the Somoza dictatorship was "designed to maintain the exploitation of the majority of the population," the new leaders sought, in addition, to increase foreign exchange by expanding and diversifying exports; to restrict luxury imports; to seek favorable credit lines from countries which did not impose conditions; and to sign medium and long-term agreements which would allow resource planning. The Ministry's function was to "rationalize" trade, and in so doing, to reduce Nicaragua's dependence on US financial institutions and corporations -- a legacy of US political leverage which the new government saw as a critical obstacle to Nicaraguan development. The Sandinistas pledged to balance ties by establishing links with the United States, other capitalist industrial states, the Third World and the socialist states--the so-called "walking on four legs" policy.

A first objective, then, was to diversify dependency on the assumption that numerous foreign decision arenas and a variety of markets were preferable to financial dependence on decisions made in one or two foreign countries. With diversification a smaller sector of the domestic economy would be affected by any single foreign decision. Opportunities for politically motivated economic blackmail by foreign governments would be reduced. The tactic of diversifying dependency, however, also reflected an awareness of the difficult if not impossible goal of actually reversing dependence in the short term.

On a broader level, officials repeated concomitant commitments to plural politics, a mixed economy, international non-alignment and what Commandante Jaime Wheelock Roman (1983) referred to as the "gradual process of transformation" in Nicaragua. The Nicaraguan model, according to former Junta member and later Vice President Sergio Ramirez (1983:215), was a "national project", a "genuine project of a sovereign revolution" which:

> ...emerges from the long period of US domination in Nicaragua, a domination that was political, economic, and even military as well as social, ideological, and even cultural. It is in the face of this domination that our model responds and establishes a vital necessity that independence be our own model, and together with this national independence, the recovery of our natural resources and of the will to develop an economic project that while transforming the nation, will give us the possibility not only to generate riches but also to distribute them fairly.

Nevertheless, the Sandinistas very soon began experiencing the political repercussions of their economic decision; in particular, the United States was prepared to impose heavy costs against a regime with an historically "non-conformist" political stance.

Accomplishing new economic objectives required wide-scale population and resource mobilization as well as education programs preparing citizens for hardships ahead and building popular support for the Sandinista program. In the new government's view a key objective of political education was to highlight the linkages between Nicaragua's domestic economic hardships and the world economy, represented by the historic relationship of dependence on the United States. Similarly, the FSLN leadership was keenly aware of the interaction and interplay between domestic and foreign policies; activities in each sphere could produce opportunities for or limitations on policy in the other. Because it could forward development goals, foreign policy in Nicaragua was viewed as a facilitator of domestic policy. Economic transformation and the consolidation of the revolution at home would be spurred as external linkages and influence capacities were changed. Conversely, domestic realities or policies both constrained foreign policy choices and influenced foreign reactions to the revolutionary government.

## Nicaraguan Foreign Policy Strategies

If the exact nature of the nationalist, mixed-economy model implied by Sandinismo was not clear, several enabling foreign policy strategies were adopted in the immediate post-Triumph period: joining the Non-Aligned Movement and demonstrating solidarity with a Third World stance, and, seeking political support, diplomatic exchanges and aid from all states sympathetic to or respectful of Nicaragua's revolution. As Foreign Ministry official Bendana (1981: 326) put it, "The Sandinista commitment to political pluralism at home found its counterpart in a foreign policy seeking to maintain friendly relations with as many countries as possible". Early government statements of philosophy stressed a willingness to maintain relations with any country interested in doing so within a framework of mutual respect and cooperation, to establish relations independent of states' economic, political or social regimes and in particular to maintain relations with all countries of Latin America. No little thought was given to the increased world visibility and influence capacity accruing from such a stance. Moreover, the diplomatic and political space afforded by solidarity with the Non-Aligned Movement was recognized as an important means for avoiding the international isolation Cuba faced after its revolution in 1959. Thus, from the beginning the FSLN expressed deep concern about the security of its nationalist movement in view of the United States' scepticism and interpretation of non-alignment as furthering the USSR's global agenda.

Figures on diplomatic relations in the first year after the Triumph reflect the priority placed on increasing Nicaragua's visibility: Somoza's government had diplomatic relations with 43 governments -- all US-aligned -- which also had embassies or legations in Managua in 1967 and 1968. By 1976 official lists noted relations with four additional governments, although these did not have representatives in Nicaragua. By contrast, in the first year after the Triumph, the Sandinistas had maintained relations with nearly all these governments and had diplomatic relations without in-Nicaragua foreign representation with another 13 states.[13] In the initial revolutionary period, in other words, Nicaragua had increased the number of formal diplomatic relations by 75 percent and had also spread those relations to include non-Western and Socialist governments. By 1985, Nicaragua had increased its formal relations by nearly 300 percent; the Sandinista government had established diplomatic relations with 112 states. (The economic and political dimensions of these relations are explored in Chapter 9.)

Central to the Frente's new foreign policy was another strategy to facilitate the longer-term goals of reduced dependence on the United States. In September, 1979, within two months of Somoza's overthrow, Nicaragua joined the Non-Aligned Movement--meeting then in Havana under Fidel Castro's Chairmanship--thereby signalling a break with Nicaragua's past alignment and casting Nicaragua's lot with the underdeveloped states. Appealing for "disinterested help", Junta leader Daniel Ortega Saavedra publically detailed Nicaraguan foreign policy for the first time:

> We are joining the Non-Aligned Movement because...we see in it the broad organization of Third World states that are playing an important role and exercising a growing influence in the international sphere, in the struggles of people against imperialism, colonialism, neocolonialism, apartheid, racism, including Zionism, and every form of oppression. Because they are for active peaceful coexistence, against the existence of military blocs and alliances, for restructuring international relations on an honorable basis, and for the establishment of a new international economic order....In the Sandinista revolution there is not any alignment; but an absolute and consistent support for the aspirations of peoples who have achieved independence or are struggling to do so. That is why we are non-aligned (quoted in Borge, et. al. 1982: 45).

Although Panama and other South American states were already members, Mexico, El Salvador and Costa Rica held observer status and Honduras was waiting for the same, the United States looked slightly askance at the Nicaraguan move. Nor did Washington lend credibility to Nicaragua's pledge to refrain from any bloc alignment. To Washington, the movement's anti-imperialist position and Castro's current leadership meant Nicaragua was leaning toward a pro-Soviet stance. This perspective followed from the United States' historical view of Third World nationalism and its underestimation of the intensity of the drive for independence. In procrustean fashion, the United States -- and especially under Ronald Reagan -- preferred to view world events through an East-West prism or as a zero-sum game. Movements or events not clearly in the immediate US interests were assessed as events that could potentially further the Soviet Union's interests. Third World nationalism and accompanying struggles for independence which the Non-Aligned Movement represented had not had credibility or legitimacy in Washington decision-making circles. Nor had the implications for the United States of disregarding Third World claims been examined. It was just this larger issue, again, that made Nicaragua after 1979 a test case for Latin America and for how the United States would address small state nationalism in an increasingly multipolar, interdependent world.

To FSLN leaders, this move and others were assertions of Nicaraguan sovereignty and independence from US dictates. The assertion of independence, of course, was later to haunt the Sandinistas. In late 1982, Foreign Minister D'Escoto explained US hostility against Nicaragua by noting the distance Nicaragua had gone since 1979 toward defining its own foreign policy positions:

> When the Sandinista Revolution triumphed, Nicaragua did not have what would normally be understood as a Chancery. Evidently it was not necessary that there be one, since all the fundamental decisions that had to do with the establishment of relations, the type of relations with different countries, the positions to be adopted in sub-regional, regional or world forums, all these decisions were made by the State Department or in the US Embassy in Managua. Today and since July 19, 1979, this ignominious situation has changed in a radical way (IHCA, January, 1983).

## CONCLUSIONS

I have suggested several overlapping contexts for the study of revolutionary Nicaragua's foreign policy. A redefinition of their interests in a post-hemispheric security era has led Latin American states generally to employ tactics that both reflect and accelerate a waning of US political hegemony in the region. Though Nicaragua differs from all other Latin American states, save Cuba, in that it 1)changed foreign policy direction by means of a revolution and the establishment of new domestic institutional practices, and 2)openly proclaimed a policy of reducing the United States' influence in its affairs, other Latin American states pursue broadly similar objectives. Regardless of its revolutionary rhetoric, moreover, how rapidly or successfully Nicaragua will attain its goals will depend on the interplay of domestic and external factors (linkage theory), such as its economic dependence and US reactions to the new regime, just as such factors constrain other Latin American foreign policies. In fact, the nature of the revolution itself was being shaped by international factors, including a hostile US stance. Nevertheless, all these states continue to seek greater independence from the United States, a firmer alliance with other Third World states and greater economic self-reliance or self-propelled growth. Meanwhile, however, the United States was to demonstrate in the 1980s that it would resist challenges to its traditional hegemony, that it continued to define its interests broadly in Central America (especially), and that it remained prepared to employ its formidable military might in attempts at re-establishing its political prerogative.

While much has been written since 1979 comparing the Nicaraguan revolution to events in Cuba in the early sixties, less has been written about the growing recognition among all Latin American states, including Cuba, of their common situations in the world political economy and vis-a-vis the United States. Indicative of this Latin American perception are the growing ties between Cuba and governments on the continent, the growth of intra-regional aid and trade and revolutionary Nicaragua's emphasis on Latin American solidarity. Thus, it is important to note the differences in the historic hemispheric and global contexts between the Cuban and Nicaraguan revolutions, separated as they are by twenty years. The foreign policy objectives enunciated by revolutionary, socialist-minded leaders in Nicaragua after 1979 were substantively similar in many ways to those already being pursued, though perhaps with less rhetorical fanfare, in other South American countries. US potential for power and influence on the continent had narrowed, just as the world was increasingly multipolar in the twenty years since Fidel Castro's ascendence to power. The Fidelistas faced a Latin America heavily influenced by the United States and in the throes of anti-Communist, anti-Cuban counterinsurgency preparations. Anti-insurgency mindsets encouraged traditional military regimes. Moreover, there were many more alternative aid/trade/credit sources open to Nicaragua -- in Western Europe, Canada, Japan, the developing Third World and within the socialist bloc -- than were open to Cuba in the 1960s, especially after the United States had made clear its Cuba policy.

For this reason, Nicaragua was considered by many to be a test case, both for Latin America and its "inevitable revolutions",[14] and, for the Third World generally, interested as it is in non-alignment and "third ways" (i.e., outside the influence-realms of both superpowers). Nicaragua's revolution offered a model of "democratic socialism" where a "popular hegemony" would operate in a system of political pluralism and a mixed economy. It was thus seen by many Latin Americans as opening the possibilities for a moderate model of structural change more appealing than the politically-closed and Soviet-dependent Cuban model. In addition, Nicaragua exemplified the possibility of mobilizing a population for revolutionary change in an area that had been most affected by US domination and imperialism. For the same reasons, and because of the global power shifts discussed earlier, the United States was to find it more difficult in the 1980s to garner international or hemispheric support for isolating this Latin American revolution. The very survival of the revolution into the second half of the 1980s attests to this fact. Moreover, the Sandinistas seemed to recognize early on that the revolution's survival might well depend on how important this experience was to other Latin American states and, on whether the appeal of their model would lead to Latin solidarity, however costly that became in the face of a hostile United States. While the FSLN counted Latin American support as crucial to the revolution's survival, the Frente was also not naive about the depth of US-Latin American ties and the costs of restructuring them in a context of economic decline, rising debt levels and US pressures to reinvigorate hemispheric security. The Sandinistas would make concerted efforts to win broad Latin American diplomatic, political and economic support.

Nicaragua was a test case in another sense as well as its leaders searched for ways to reduce dependency from a position of economic underdevelopment. Indeed, this situation and the proximity and history of influence by the local superpower point up the central point of departure here ·-- to consider how domestic and international constraints shaped and influenced the Sandinistas' ideological orientation, Nicaraguan objective realities, and, in turn, Nicaragua's international policies. In the following chapters I focus on the interaction of domestic and international factors (demands, constraints) in their impact on Nicaragua's foreign policy behavior. This allows a consideration of the complexities faced by an underdeveloped state with great determination (though with few resources) to achieve greater independence and sovereignty where the local hegemon feared such an example and labelled it ideological (other-bloc) aggression.

NOTES

1. For a more complete review of US-Latin American relations see Atkins (1977); Schulz and Graham (1984); Foreign Policy Association (1979); and Lieuwen (1967).
2. This discussion draws especially from Stepan (1981) and Slater (1984).
3. Stepan and Black (both 1981) relate these events in greater detail. See also Chapter 5.
4. For a broader discussion of these issues see: Coleman and Quiros-Varela; Poitras; Stavenhagen; Ferris; Braveboy-Wagner, (all 1981); and Tancer (1976).
5. Stavenhagen uses the term revolutionary to refer to changes in class and production systems rather than to the methods of taking power (p.221).
6. For example, see Tinbergen, ul Haq, Hall and Blake, et. al. in Munoz (1981).
7. In this section I draw from Cochrane's (1978) useful review of major works of the mid- to late 1970s on Latin American foreign

34

policies and from Milenky (1977); Munoz (1981); Nef (1984) and Ferris (1981).

8. For case examples and further discussion see Ferris and Lincoln (1981).

9. As van Klaveren (1984: 7-9) points out, dependency theory offers only very general guidance to a study of foreign policy for several reasons, among them: 1)politics are not dependent on each other the same way that economics are; and 2)while foreign policy theory views the state as an actor, dependencia focuses more on relationships between the global capitalist system, an aggregate unit, and the disaggregate dependent society.

10. For a helpful overview of dependency literature and traditional dependencia analyses, see Heraldo Munoz (1981). Munoz presents a sampling of current literature on strategies for addressing dependence.

11. Theorist Immanual Wallerstein (e.g., 1981) argues that socialism involves the creation of a new kind of world system and cannot be equated simply with state ownership or self-reliance. Until a new world system emerges, in this view, we continue to live in a capitalist world economy. While there may be changes in this system, socialism in one state, or, solving dependency within a capitalist context is impossible. His views reflect the lively debate among dependency theorists generally.

12. Some of the strategies for dependent, small states discussed in the literature include: 1)collective bargaining with the industrialized capital centers for a New International Economic Order (e.g., ul Haq, 1981); 2)working from a management-scientific approach on a centralized world level to address underdevelopment and other international socioeconomic problems in our interdependent world (Tinbergen, 1981); 3)implementing a "revolution of being" -- to replace the historically dominant "revolution of having" and the "anti-values" of capitalist and Stalinist societies -- where humanistic values color a process of continual social construction (Lagos, 1981); and 4)pursuing self-reliance at local, regional, national and world levels by regaining control over resources and encouraging creativity, processes that will entail new external links of cooperation as well as struggle and resistance, and that will involve both national independence and interdependence (Galtung, 1981).

13. Figures are from Europa Yearbook, 1967-1983 and the Ministry of Foreign Commerce, 1985.

14. This is a reference, of course, to Walter La Feber's work.

# PART 2

# Domestic Constraints
# on Foreign Policy

# 2

## Sandinism and Nicaraguan Political Structures

We would like to challenge the international community so
that they don't lose themselves searching for precise
ideological definitions of a process as complex as ours;
we would like to challenge them to evaluate and analyze
the actions of our process over the past six years, its
underlying values and principles and then judge if it can
be labelled a "communist terrorist menace." Or rather, if
our process shouldn't be considered an attempt to
assimilate humanity's historical experiences as a means to
simultaneously achieve social change and democracy,
learning from the errors and successes that the people's
collective memory has bequeathed to us.

> FSLN Political Coordinator Bayardo Arce
> February, 1985

Considering Nicaragua's foreign policy as the result of a
dynamic adaptation process where internal and external factors
constrain policy frees the analysis from the conceptual narrowness
that accrues from attempts to label processes as ideologically left
or right. In addition to the ideological perspectives of the
revolutionary leadership, domestic factors such as the cultural and
religious heritage of Nicaragua, the legacy of Somoza's regime, the
economic situation of the small country and the political experience
of the Nicaraguan people also shaped the course of the revolution.
In fact, these variables and others, such as Nicaragua's
geostrategic location in the "back yard" of the United States,
greatly influenced the political perspectives, framework and goals
of the Sandinistas through their formative years since the creation
of the Frente Sandinista de Liberacion Nacional (FSLN) in 1961.

SANDINISMO

Factors Shaping Sandinista Thought

Sandinista political philosophy did not emerge from a vacuum,
nor was it completely defined, teased out in its socioeconomic
context or set on an absolutist, dogmatic course toward well-defined

37

ends. Local, regional and world circumstances imposed some policies on the FSLN. Certain attributes will continue to shape the political environment in Nicaragua, among them Latin American political culture, the strength of Catholicism, Western cultural influences, and widespread politicization since 1979. Moreover, the revolutionary agenda required strong popular support at home if it was to be pursued effectively. Popular support is especially important to decision-makers who envision new socioeconomic structures and external relationships. The Nicaraguan social, historical and cultural contexts were significant in shaping opportunities for and the nature of citizen support for government policy. As such, socio-cultural characteristics presented constraints within which the leadership had to work in forging domestic and foreign policy.

Latin Political Philosophy. North and South American conceptions of government and of individual rights or responsibilities differ in a significant way that also has implications for how each defines optimal political development. For example, a major rationalization given for US policy toward Nicaragua during the Reagan Administration was that emergent political structures were undemocratic and "totalitarian." In traditional Latin American political philosophy and following Rousseau's thought, "community flows from unanimity." Quoting again from Dealy (1985: 109-111): "Unlike liberal democrats who believe that the general welfare unfolds and advances by protecting a large number of different groups, those both in and out of power in Central America agree that particularistic and opposing factions invariably disrupt public order and are insufficiently restrained by countervailing power centers...." In this view political consensus and unity allowed public order, while the near universality of the Spanish language and Catholic faith in South America gave added impetus to the notion that that consensus was possible and desirable.

Although some governments in Latin America adopted constitutions similar in language and structure to the US Constitution, a predominant practice among Latin American states was -- with varying levels of determination, violence and attentiveness to law -- to demobilize, intimidate or erradicate the opposition and even incipient opposition groups. A traditional Latin American political practice has been to control the means of power and to guard them against opposing groups. Diversity was often viewed as an opening for anarchy; the preferred method of governing involved a fusion of the masses, the government, its policy and the "national spirit" into a "single united body" representing the collective interest (Simon Bolivar's conception). Individual rights were not absolute or inalienable, but were relative to the common rights, values and security of the state.

Sandino's Legacy. Sandinismo in some ways continued this tradition while mixing it with nationalist, anti-imperialist sentiment and socialist thought. Understanding these traditional conceptions of government and how they differ from Western, liberal thought, then, yields at least partial insight into the animosity that quickly emerged between Washington and Managua. The Sandinistas interpreted Washington's view of pluralist democracy as representation guaranteed by and for the wealthy. Using revolutionary and Marxist rhetoric, the FSLN asserted a right to sovereignty, an end to the United States' predominant influence in Nicaragua's foreign affairs and the freedom to put into practice a different vision of democracy -- one that incorporated social and economic requisites and that considered the well-being of the corporate body politic.

Augusto Cesar Sandino's struggle in the 1920s and 1930s left a strong nationalist legacy in Nicaragua, which continues to spur anti-imperialist and anti-dictatorial sentiment among Nicaraguans. Even after Sandino's death in 1934 there were armed uprisings -- for example in 1937, 1940, 1948, 1954, and twenty times between 1958 and 1963 -- against the Somozas and their brand of brutal dictatorships. A large number of these movements were organized and led by former soldiers of Sandino. All of the incidents reflected continuing hope for Sandino's vision of a nationalist, popular alternative to United States-supported government in Nicaragua. Sandino became a mythical peasant hero in Nicaraguan popular culture. For their part, after killing Sandino the Somozas also tried to snuff out Sandino's memory.

During a nationalist upsurge in the 1950s, Carlos Fonseca Amador purposely set out to develop a "national revolutionary ideology" by culling from Sandino's writings and interviewing Sandino's contemporaries and compatriots of the 1930s. A Marxist, Fonseca sought to build a coherent, nationalist ideology firmly rooted in the Nicaraguan experience of national resistance and the search for social justice. Such a theoretical program would include prescriptions for political practice and popular mobilization and be broad enough to take the place of Somocismo. Sandinismo was "...at once political mythology and a theoretical framework, a strategy and a program to guide the Nicaraguan revolution..." (Armstrong, 1985: 19).

The Church. Other socio-cultural factors constrained revolutionary policy and the extent to which the new domestic and foreign policy agenda would be supported. A powerful social institution influencing and defining the path of the revolution was the Catholic Church, to which 85 percent of the Nicaraguan people claimed membership.[1] The growth of a "Liberation Theology" and the organization of Christian Base Communities -- Bible study groups which proliferated among the poor as literacy grew--led to the involvement of many church people as mobilizers and fighters during the insurrectionary period (see Dodson and Montgomery, 1982). Catholic political and social influence and participation continued after the Triumph with a number of priests working in top government posts. For example, Father Miguel D'Escoto served as Foreign Minister; the Cardinal brothers, Ernesto and Fernando, served respectively as Culture Minister and Education Minister. In addition, direct church group representation was guaranteed in the Council of State, the advisory, legislative body that functioned under the FSLN Junta prior to elections in 1984. Moreover, the Nicaraguan Bishops and the Nicaraguan Archbishop (who became a Cardinal in 1985) used thinly-veiled pastoral letters and weekly sermons to express the hierarchy's views of new policies. Radio Catolica, a non-government Catholic station continued to operate

under the revolutionary system, offering at times blistering
critiques of particular policies and warning about the evils of
aligning the revolution with what the hierarchy came to see as
unreconstructed Marxism. Though it was harassed by the government
in early 1986 for what the FSLN labelled irresponsible behavior, as
an institution Radio Catolica continued to air the hierarchy's
opinions.

A major concern of the traditional hierarchy was the loss of
its authority during the inevitable democratization of church
structure that accompanied the revolution in Nicaragua. The
decisions of recent Latin American Bishops' conferences, such as
those at Medellin in 1968 and Puebla in 1978, to work against
institutionalized social injustice and to show a preferential option
for the poor were pursued by many Nicaraguan priests who were
encouraged by the revolution's emphasis on popular participation and
the empowerment of the oppressed. Such change, however, directly
challenged the hierarchy's historical prerogative and led to worries
not only about the loss of its authority, but also about an
over-identification of parishioners with secular programs and
revolutionary ideology. Such critiques, in fact, led to
church-state tensions and to a series of dialogues between the FSLN
government and the Catholic Church hierarchy (see Chapter 4).

The significance of active Catholicism for the revolution
existed not only in its differentiating the Nicaraguan Revolution
from the Cuban experience and model, but also in its teaching --
especially since Bishops' conferences at Medellin and Puebla --
regarding the worth and dignity of all, a preferential option for
the poor, the importance of creating social justice on earth, and
the efficacy of the community of believers in shaping political and
social realities. Increasingly, the Latin American Catholic Church,
through its ministry and its organizations (e.g. the communidades de
base) taught values of participation, self-worth, dialogue and
debate. Characteristic of this recent attitude toward politics and
"being in the world" was Nicaraguan Archbishop Obando y Bravo's
support for the taking up of arms in the late 1970s, and, the more
current, rigorous debate within Catholic and Protestant Churches in
the mid-1980s over the direction of the revolution. (Although
Obando opposed Somoza, he did not support the FSLN.) While the
Catholic Church experienced tensions between the hierarchy--which
was sceptical about the continued openness of the FSLN
government--and a popular church in full support of the Sandinista
regime, it was nonetheless true that the church continued as a
powerful social force for pluralism.

Supporting the view that religion became an essential feature
of the revolution, many Nicaraguan church leaders interviewed in
1982, 1983 and 1985 spoke of a new growth in religious
identification and activity, a government which generally encouraged
their work, and a new social tolerance not experienced during
Somoza's time (author interviews). An important day-to-day social
reality was the blending of religious faith with political
activeness where church and government organization often worked in
conjunction. For some Nicaraguans, the religious and political
"awakenings" occurred simultaneously and were one reality, one
revolution. For others, the church of the hierarchy, especially

after 1983, became an important forum from within which to call for policy changes. And for others, the hierarchy's scepticism about the revolution motivated a decision to leave the church. The important point is that contrary to the experience in Cuba, in Nicaragua the bishops took the option of being an active influence on political and social life. In Cuba the church hierarchy opposed the revolution and many clergy exiled themselves, thus ensuring that the church would have no influence over the course of Cuban events into the future.

The activeness and social legitimacy of a newly-democratized church in Nicaragua, where lay members took on larger roles in the operations and practices of the church, also influenced pluralistic institutions and worked against closed, cooptative or authoritarian decision-making structures. Citizen demands and supports emanating from religious commitment worked through highly valued church organizations to influence government direction.

<u>Politicization</u>. Prior to 1979 most Nicaraguans had been disenfranchized, repressed and socialized to accept political apathy and fraudulent elections. The revolution, however, sparked new pressures for a responsive political order. Widespread popular involvement in the war, the creation of citizen organizations after 1979, popular education campaigns after the Triumph and the acknowledged populist nature of policies implemented after 1979 expanded both the relevant political strata and the political arena in Nicaragua. In the context of expressing US concern about the pervasiveness of FSLN organizations, then-US Ambassador Anthony Quainton in 1982 and 1983 commented on the high levels of active participation he observed in his travels around the country (author interviews). Another long-term US observer of post-1979 Nicaragua, a resident of Managua, argued in 1982 that:

> A great majority, 75-80 percent, of the population are for the revolution. The revolution is for the poor, to benefit the poor. As peasants in Central America, these know they're living in a priviledged place. There is grumbling here. But the grumbling is from people who know the revolution is for them and its good grumbling; they realize they can grumble now. They demand things. But at the same time they know that what the government can do economically is limited (author interview).

More so than in Cuba, the masses in Nicaragua were central to the struggle against the old regime. The broad class alliance that finally pushed over the Somoza regime ensured that no one narrow class vision would determine the final characteristics of the socialist-oriented, nationalist revolution in Nicaragua. Whereas the government, through mass organizations, encouraged and cajoled grass roots initiative and participation, it also encouraged the development of sub-group interest aggregation. Organizations representing women (AMLAE), youth, labor, non-FSLN parties, and the like defined their interests and lobbied their causes in the Council of State and other forums. The FSLN government recognized the importance of popular power as a motor of the revolution and of the consolidation process. In general, the revolutionary leaders

42

"...struggled to safeguard an institutional arrangement which provided a balance between revolutionary and non-revolutionary groups." Nor was there always agreement between Sandinista organizations and the Sandinista National Directorate (Azicri, 1981: 354).

Popular support was also essential in the face of bourgeois organization to oppose and thwart government programs; it became more important as that opposition was aided by outside powers in creating incidents of military and economic sabotage against the revolutionary government. As Tomas Borge, Interior Minister and founding member of the FSLN, challenged in 1982: nowhere else in Central America could the government safely hand out guns to its own people lest the guns be turned against it (author interview). As contra attacks stepped up in 1984, so too did requests from campesinos in the countryside for guns to defend their communities. By mid-1985 nearly 300,000 rifles had been handed out to rural inhabitants. The government stepped up land reform and land entitlement in order to give more campesinos and peasants a vested interest in national or territorial defense.

Needless to say, the United States viewed mass mobilization in Nicaragua as a method for political control, not a legitimate form for citizen participation. Because the United States considered the well-being of the Nicaraguan bourgeoisie private sector to be the bell-weather of its own economic and political interests, Washington worried about the shrinking share of political power held by this group (see Chapter 4).

Ties to the West. Other domestic factors influencing participatory institutions in Nicaragua were its historic ties to the West and to the United States and its geographical location. As Foreign Trade Minister Cuenca noted in a 1985 interview about Nicaragua's social, economic and psychological identity: "Nicaragua is not an island...We locate ourselves in the Western Hemisphere." These forces produced pressure for an internationally cooperative political system. Just as Nicaragua had a US-tooled economy, one tied historically to the United States through economic exchanges, so too were Western values and tastes transmitted over the years. In revolutionary Nicaragua of the mid-1980s, US popular music was heard alongside folk and revolutionary music on the airwaves; US clothes and luxury products were sought after and there was a demonstrated affinity for the people of North America. The ideals of the US Founding Fathers were discussed among the Sandinistas along with Marx's tenets. In the context of US hostility toward the revolution, this culminated in something like a love - hate relationship toward the United States. Similarly, though the Nicaraguans appreciated and its leaders sought signs of support from the other superpower, the USSR, during a time, as they saw it, of a potential invasion from the North, the deeply religious Nicaraguan people rejected atheism or any government attempts to curb religious freedom. Despite hostile feelings toward the Reagan Administration and its philosophy, it was no less true that Nicaragua's historical and cultural affinities to the West would be manifested in attitudes about future international relations. It is interesting, and probably telling for future policy, that Nicaraguans, including FSLN leaders, made a point in discussions and interviews to separate the

Reagan Administration from the American people and their system generally.

The point of this introductory discussion has been to suggest the importance of social and cultural contexts for defining the level and nature of popular demands placed on Nicaraguan leaders. These factors were long-term and definitional in the sense that they characterized the role and vision of the Nicaraguan people. To the extent that they influenced the policy and institutions of the new government, they were forces for a responsive, participatory system. The degree of such influence in the future will undoubtedly be determined by the dominant party's (the FSLN's) conceptualization of itself as the vanguard of the people and the degree to which tolerant rather than rigid attitudes toward dissent are institutionalized as the revolution evolves. But political or social organizations at odds with traditional norms or culture could not easily be sustained over the long term. Yet, to the extent that the United States used domestic opposition groups to undermine the FSLN, the Frente was encouraged to close opportunities for political diversity and to retain hegemony over the central means of power. Sandinista institutions evolved in a precarious regional and international security setting. Despite internal and external (economic, military) pressures on them, the Frente nevertheless left open significant avenues for influence from non-FSLN groups. Six years after the revolution the Sandinistas were negotiating with opposition parties in a parliamentary system to write a new Nicaraguan constitution.

In general, Nicaraguan socio-cultural realities would undoubtedly produce latent and explicit pressures for a foreign policy of normalized relations with the United States and strengthened ties to other Third World and developing states. The nationalist furor aroused by the revolution created a force for a Nicaraguan-centered and defined development strategy and sparked antipathies against domineering foreign influence.

## An Overview of Sandinista Philosophy

The broad-based alliance politics the FSLN sought to forge -- for practical if not for ideological reasons -- led them to promise guarantees of participation to all who upheld the ideals of the revolution. It also led them politically to demobilize the small economic and political sectors that hoped for a return--albeit within a liberal democratic orientation in the post-Somoza period--to the capitalist-oriented system which existed prior to the revolution. The FSLN thereby made clear that neither a return to Somoza-type politics nor a resurrection of the US-inspired development model pursued under Somoza would be acceptable political options in the revolutionary period. Although there were similarities, the Sandinista model also differentiated the Nicaraguan process from those in Cuba and in Africa during the mid-to late 1970s that depended upon more highly centralized structures with a single charismatic leader. These systems quickly turned to command economies and displayed a greater willingness to employ coercive methods.

Still within traditional Latin American political philosophy, the Sandinistas envisioned consensus, national unity politics. The FSLN was to act as vanguard of the people to interpret and plan the political economy according to what was necessary to enhance the basic well-being of the majority -- the poor workers, campesinos and peasants of Nicaragua. Although the Sandinistas as the vanguard party defined and promoted the "revolutionary project" -- defined as popular, democratic and anti-imperialist -- their position was that all classes, including the bourgeoisie, could participate as long as they accepted these tenets of the revolution and subordinated their interests to the "logic of the majority." Thus the revolution was to be both political and social; both the power holders and the economic structures of the "institutional pyramid of organized class power" would be changed (see Coraggio and Irvin, 1985). In the words of a Latin American Studies Association report (LASA, 1985:41), "Economic elites can survive in the new system, and even make private profits, if they recognize the interests of the majority population and collaborate with the state in meeting the majority's needs; but they will no longer be allowed to rule."

Typical of other Third World states, the Sandinistas aimed for a political-economic model that avoided the historically-proven defects of sweeping theories of central planning and price-setting, national ownership or strict egalitarianism. But the US model for Third World development -- developing productive forces through unrestricted private (usually foreign-controlled) enterprise and evoking patience until benefits trickled down to the masses -- was also rejected as a system that produced a few wealthy and many oppressed people. The FSLN believed that the petit bourgeoisie (small private owners and producers) and the peasants could be the principal motors of development in the context of Nicaragua's dependent, semi-capitalist and poor society. One indicator of its independence from Moscow-oriented or orthodox strategies was the FSLN's use of texts written by Fonseca, Jaime Wheelock (Agriculture Minister) and Humberto Ortego (Defense Minister) for the political education of FSLN party cadres (Edelman, 1985: 42). Nor did FSLN economic policy or patterns of international relations conform to such orthodoxy (e.g. see Chapters 3 and 9).

While insisting on broadening the potential for central economic coordination in pursuit of development and security goals, the Sandinistas still made many concessions and provided major production incentives to the business class. The FSLN was not radically anti-bourgeoisie; expropriations in general were limited to lands and firms being decapitalized, while the bulk of the productive sector was left in private hands (see Chapter 3). As Harris (1985: 6) notes: "The Sandinista concept of popular hegemony can be contrasted with the Marxist-Leninist concept of the dictatorship of the proletariat. As used by the Sandinistas, popular hegemony does not refer to the dictatorship of one class over another, but to the predominance of the interests of the popular majority over those of the privileged minority who benefited from the exploitation and oppression of the Somoza dictatorship...."

The elimination of the private sector was not a part of the "revolutionary project," although tensions between the FSLN's vision of structural change and the reality in Nicaragua of a market-oriented productive sector were inevitable during the gradual

transition to socialism envisioned by the FSLN. The business class
remained sceptical about the Sandinistas' commitment to maintaining
a private sector within its proposed model of Nicaraguan socialism
despite the fact that the FSLN continued to voice this commitment
and to offer economic incentives to the private sector.

Indeed, political tensions were bound to accrue from the
broad-based alliance that emerged under the direction of the FSLN
(whose fighting forces and mass support were predominant). This is
so simply because some of those in the anti-Somoza camp supported
wide-ranging social transformation and others, primarily the
bourgeoisie, did not. The Sandinistas saw as necessary to the
revolution's consolidation the creation of new socio-political
institutions, such as trade unions, defense committees, popular
organizations, etc., which would guarantee the majority poor the
decisive voice within a revolutionary alliance (Coraggio and Irvin,
1985: 25). Because: 1)the bourgeoisie's traditional privileges of
power and prestige were being narrowed by FSLN policies of popular
mobilization and central government control over much of the
nation's economic surpluses; 2)the United States had given aid and
moral support to this sector since the revolution; and 3)many in the
popular sectors demanded a faster pace of change, the Sandinistas
were involved in continuous consensus-seeking "national dialogues"
and inter-group mediation after 1979. That process did not
eliminate fierce political debates within Nicaragua, however. In
the absence of historic experience with open political competition
and compromise, debate was marked by mutual distrust and intolerance
on all sides.

Pluralism. The nature and form of pluralism in Nicaragua
continued to evolve and to be shaped by Sandinista thinking, by the
interaction of social and economic sectors and by international
factors such as US support for counter-revolutionary groups and
sabotage activity. In fact, United States hostility, and, FSLN
attempts to counter US charges and maintain sizeable international
support have indoubtedly been the most significant realities
influencing both Sandinismo and Nicaraguan political structures
since 1979. An example of this process is seen in the timing of an
analytical, philosophical speech on the nature of Sandinism given by
FSLN ideologue and political coordinator Bayardo Arce in February,
1985. In that speech Arce characterized Sandinismo as the result of
a convergence of three ideological currents that also shaped the
historical potential for revolution in Nicaragua: Third World
nationalism, post-Medellin Latin American Catholicism and
non-doctrinaire, antidogmatic Marxism (BI, 3-7-85). Stressing the
Latin American context of the revolution, Arce likened it to
Bolivarism:

> An alternative view [i.e. to the United States'
> 'neo-Monroe, imperial vision' for Latin America] exists
> that is rooted in the history and experience of the Third
> World, particularly Latin America....We are concluding an
> anniversary of the Sandinista struggle which is also
> Bolivarian. That is the essence of our historical roots:
> a deep Latin American alignment. Since July 19 [1979], we
> are no longer a banana republic, no longer somebody's

backyard. We are not part of any bloc but rather, part of
a humanity...that is struggling to transform relationships
of dependence and submission into relationships of
friendship and solidarity, respect and mutual cooperation,
so that we can leave behind underdevelopment while
preserving our freedom.

   The international context clarifies the importance of the
speech. It came as the Nicaraguan leaders were launching a renewed
diplomatic drive to garner international support in the aftermath of
an intensive rhetorical and diplomatic campaign by the United States
to discredit as a "sham" the November, 1984 Nicaraguan elections.
Waging its own campaign against the FSLN at home and abroad, the
Reagan Adminstration labelled the Sandinista government
Marxist-Leninist, totalitarian, communist, Stalinist and repressive.
Indeed, US officials in early 1985 repeatedly levelled these charges
-- ignoring the positive election reports from international
observers -- in efforts to shape opinion prior to Congressional
votes on new US funding for the anti-Sandinista contras. In
Managua, the Sandinistas were disheartened by a poor turnout of
international representatives at President Daniel Ortega's
inauguration in January. The Frente was therefore determined to
make an all-out effort to counter a new level of US hostility and to
glean support -- in the form of aid or official statements or visits
-- from West Europe and Latin America. Although the Sandinistas had
always sought and, for the most part, had received Latin American
support, given US moves and the "hellish" nature of the Nicaraguan
economy (President Ortega's characterization) at that time, Arce
gave particular emphasis to Sandinismo's ties to Latin American
experience and independence movements. By 1985, in the face of US
regional militarization and talk of an embargo or an invasion, the
FSLN had come to assess Latin American alignment and support as a
sine qua non for the defense and survival of the Sandinista
revolution.
   Arce sought to evoke Latin American solidarity as he also
placed the Nicaraguan revolution in the historical context of the
search for Latin American sovereignty. However, the speech was also
a defensive effort to counter US-projected images of a dogmatic,
Soviet-aligned revolution. Continuing the drive, Vice-President
Ramirez toured Western Europe and President Ortega presented the
United States and Contadora with a new peace initiative in the weeks
after this speech.
   Although the revolutionary process was yet evolving, it was
clear that the Sandinsitas had established a system of participatory
politics that differed from Western, liberal conceptions of
democracy. In the Sandinistas' collective vision of government,
political and economic equality were naturally related. Moreover,
in this view human potential could be and should be developed; the
Nicaraguan people, driven to apathy under Somoza, could be
socialized through participation in mass organizations, community
projects and government-sponsored social programs. Contrasting
their model of democracy with the US model, Nicaraguan leaders
argued that Western liberalism, and certainly as it was manifested
in Somoza's Nicaragua and other areas of Western-influenced Latin

America, simply protected individual rights of the privileged classes, failed to afford opportunities to out-classes, and thereby blocked real social change. Foreign Minister Miguel D'Escoto (1983: 15) echoed this attitude when he offered a definition of democracy in Nicaragua:

> This democratic aspiration is not to be confused with an aspiration to have just the formality of democracy; we are talking about real participation. We are quite aware that democracy entails social democracy, economic democracy, political democracy and many rights, such as the right to work, to a family wage, to learn to read, to write--all those different rights that provide us with an opportunity to participate and not be manipulated. We are moving in every direction to develop our new democratic Nicaragua. We are not going to fall to what Somoza did. He tried to give a shellac of democracy by having controlled elections from time to time so that the United States could say his regime was democratic.

The young, generally well-educated Sandinistas argued for a democracy befitting Nicaragua's history and rejected the US model due to what they saw as the "...sad record of formal liberal democracy in promoting social justice elsewhere in Latin America" (Walker, 1981: 102). To the Sandinistas, elections tended to breed personalism, broken campaign promises and an avoidance of tough decisions on policies of austerity that might alienate voters. Just such events related to the introduction of Western liberal forms in Bolivia and Mexico had turned those revolutionary settings into populist and directionless regimes. The FSLN voiced a preference for a social, economic democracy built from below through mass mobilization in support of structural change. Being all too aware of Washington's economic and political destabilization campaigns against other reformist or revolutionary Latin American states and movements, the Sandinistas were sceptical of elections which could be, especially in a poor and vulnerable state, easily manipulated by external actors. The FSLN as vanguard hoped first to introduce and develop new institutions under popular hegemony and then to hold elections to consolidate and give further shape and legitimacy to the revolutionary process. As O'Shaunessy (1985: 5) points out: "The biggest risk of the liberal model to a late-developing, dependent Third World nation such as Nicaragua is the encouragement of competition, not consensus, among groups and individuals. This risk is especially compelling when that nation is located geographically within the 'national security' zone of a hostile superpower."

Pluralism in Nicaragua, therefore, was to be structually limited by popular hegemony and a collective vision.[2] But no group qua group was to be excluded, save those that took up arms against the government. Through 1985, political pluralism thus defined was maintained in Nicaragua and was reflected in the existence of opposition parties, multiple independent radio stations, labor union competition, vocal and hostile church groups, opposition meetings and conventions, and the like. Opposition and dissent could be heard and seen within Nicaragua; opposition structures were not systematically eliminated despite the war-time State of Emergency restrictions such as prior censorship of the print media. On the other hand, in the context of heightening counter-revolutionary activity against Nicaragua, the FSLN found it increasingly difficult to distinguish legitimate domestic political opposition from counter-revolutionary activity aimed at overthrowing them. In this atmosphere, political debate was difficult and highly charged and led to lapses when the FSLN government directly and indirectly harassed opposition groups and jailed political opponents for, (usually) brief periods of time (e.g. NYT, 6-30-85).

## FSLN Reactions To The Opposition

Finding a balance between tolerance and repression in the context of broad structural change and challenges to national security (stemming from the contra war) resulted in instances of suppression of dissent. In a period of economic exigency, the Sandinista government pursued both national defense and its revolutionary agenda of socioeconomic transformations and national reconstruction. Meanwhile, the FSLN was instituting itself as the hegemonic party in Nicaragua and pledging power to its social base -- the peasants and workers. Moreover, in an atmosphere from 1984 onward in which internal opposition groups were being polarized over the issue of whether they would work within the system or join those who hoped to overthrow it with arms, it became difficult for government supporters to assess the intent, purpose or motivation behind opposition statements and moves. There was much suspicion operating among all the political organizations and tensions were heightened by the fact that the United States worked to influence what opposition groups it could through various channels, such as its embassy in Managua. At other times the FSLN purposely blurred these distinctions in order to discredit and intimidate the domestic opposition. The FSLN openly assailed critics among the bourgeoisie as agents of the CIA or as complicitors in contra efforts. For example, La Prensa, the opposition newspaper, became La PrenCIA in the state paper. The FSLN fostered an us-them mentality in speeches and through the Sandinista media. A La Prensa writer complained in 1985 that the label "contra" in Nicaragua no longer referred only to Somocistas, but to anyone criticizing the FSLN: "Contra means many things in Nicaragua: La Prensa workers, campesinos who are against the FSLN and Miskito Indians who were butchered" (author interview). Those most apt to suffer such harassment were the business bourgeoisie, the former economic elites and power holders, and those who publically argued that Sandinismo was inimical to Catholicism. Several business leaders, for example, had land or factories expropriated for reasons that were unconvincing and which appeared to be excuses for political retribution. In 1985, for example, a portion of the land of a vocal business critic, Enrique Geyer Bolanos, was confiscated to become part of an FSLN land reform program in the area around Masaya. Commandante Wheelock argued that the confiscation was in response to Bolanos' refusal to negotiate with the government regarding the status of that land. The business sector remained unconvinced. On other occasions, Sandinista youths or turbas broke up opposition political meetings with stones and physical assaults. On some occasions, the FSLN condoned this behavior rather than trying to stem it. Other government critics have said they were briefly jailed, interrogated and warned against political activity. There were also several documented charges of disappearances, although the FSLN government allowed a number of independent investigations into its prison system. Though church leaders were largely immune from direct harassment, the FSLN attempted at times to limit church-sponsored gatherings on the grounds that they were blatantly political and undermined support for government policy (see Chapter 4). On similar grounds the Sandinistas expelled ten foreign priests from Nicaragua in 1984 and closed down an unauthorized church publication in late 1985.

In a situation of military and economic crisis, the Sandinistas clearly narrowed the space for political maneuvering. Their proclivity to do so in response to security concerns became evident again in October, 1985 when the FSLN government tightened the State of Emergency restrictions that had been loosened during the 1984 electoral period. Citing the hardening position of Washington and presenting evidence that the CIA and the contras were beginning a new campaign to create an internal front and urban terror inside Nicaragua, the government suspended the rights to free expression and assembly, the right to strike and many guarantees for defendents. Habeus corpus, which had originally been suspended, was restored two weeks later (see also Chapter 8). While the new restrictions were only selectively enforced into 1986, the suspension decree opened the possibility for greater crackdowns on the opposition when or if the contra war escalated. According to Vice President Ramirez, restrictions would affect only those involved in "conspiratoral activities" against the revolution and public order; the national discussions regarding the new constitution would "in no way be suspended" (IHCA, October, 1985).

Independent observers argue that press censorship was the point on which the FSLN was most vulnerable internationally and that the imposition of press controls in March, 1982 turned out to be a major error in Sandinista judgement, not justified by the military situation at that time (LASA, 1985: 30). To the FSLN, however, La Prensa was a mouthpiece for the Reagan Administration: "A country at war cannot allow a newspaper which is the instrument of the enemy to publish its opinions freely" (Vice President Ramirez, quoted in LASA, op. cit.). And, as the LASA report (p. 31) notes, "La Prensa is unremittingly hostile, though not openly subversive, in virtually every article and self-censors any news which reflects favorably on the FSLN." Although La Prensa, effectively the only opposition newspaper, was censored, the FSLN controlled only 16 of 39 radio stations, none of which was regularly censored. During the 1984 electoral campaign Sandinista television carried uncensored debates among contending parties; each party received 22 hours of free and uninterrupted TV time (15 minutes per day in prime time) and 44 hours of free time on the 16 state-run radio stations. The political messages of the opposition parties were clearly heard by Nicaraguan voters. Similarly, despite the tightening of the State of Emergency in 1985, alternative or non-FSLN opinion continued to be aired in Nicaragua. Government opponents continued to hold press conferences and material censored from La Prensa continued to be privately circulated and displayed on a billboard in front of the newspaper's Managua offices.

Independent unions continued to exist and make demands in the workplace, although membership in FSLN-affiliated unions appeared to be the choice of the bulk of unionized workers. In 1985, 1,099 unions and locals existed in eleven central workers organizations. Five of these organizations were not affiliated with the FSLN; out of a nation-wide union membership of 227,931, 4 percent (8,361) belonged to these five federations (BI, 2-7-85). More significant was the fact that worker input and increased worker control continued to be part of the Frente's program; institutionalized channels existed for the expression of workers' views and complaints.[3]

The context of human rights abuses in other Central American and Third World states gives some perspective to the situation in Sandinista Nicaragua. While the FSLN did not fully tolerate political dissent, it also had not been guilty of the government-sponsored village massacres and routine disappearances of the politically active and non-active alike in El Salvador and Guatemala between 1979 and 1985 or in Brazil, Argentina and Chile a few years earlier. The Frente, in one of its first acts as a government, abolished the hated capital punishment law of Somoza. This meant that captured Guardia members--the enforcers of Somoza's authoritarian and brutal rule--would be imprisoned rather than killed, the punishment many Nicaraguan people preferred for their oppressors. Although several instances of summary and unofficial executions of Guardia members came to light -- executions carried out by liberation fighters or citizens not under the FSLN's command and during the time of social upheaval shortly after the July 19 victory -- the Frente's attempts centered on keeping angry masses from taking retribution. By 1982 the government human rights commission had put lawyers to work reviewing the cases of the captured Guardia so that shortened sentences could be given those whom had not committed (documented) atrocities against the people. Nor has the FSLN practiced systematic terror or explicitly developed mechanisms of suppression. The Frente has shown a high concern for world opinion regarding its human rights record and has commented on and investigated charges brought against it. (I discuss the Miskito Indians issue in Chapter 4). Revolutionary Nicaragua, in other words, had not experienced the repression that accompanied social and economic change in many other Latin American countries.

Viewing the whole system as it had emerged to that point, Latin American historian, Luis Hector Serra (1982: 111) characterized the Sandinista Revolution as one in which "an original and valuable form of democracy" befitting Nicaragua's historic circumstance was being developed. The mass organizations were "principal channels and practical schools of an original democratic system created through trial and error." Social and political organization in cultural and economic spheres had invited broad, though often tense, public discussion on a full range of issues and made room for the future of a new kind of participatory democracy within the Latin American context. Despite the war-time State of Emergency, public debate remained a feature of Nicaraguan politics in the mid-1980s. Contradiction also characterized political development; as rights restrictions were being tightened in 1985, measures were also being taken to introduce local elections and to broaden participation in neighborhood organizations.

It is somewhat surprising that the opposition was allowed to operate at all in Nicaragua. The clear purpose of the United States and of the armed and unarmed opposition it supported was the overthrow of "the present structure" in Nicaragua (as President Reagan put it in 1985) and the replacement of the revolutionary process by a pro-US, capitalist government. Few other governments that censor information face such an immediate threat or one posed so blatantly by a superpower. Yet, an important motivation continued to exist for the Sandinistas: FSLN leaders claimed that they were attempting to create a new, humane, non-aligned, pluralistic and democratic model of development for Latin America and the Third World. They had pursued international support evoking these principles. They would therefore be held responsible for the policies they employed as well as for carefully defining citizens rights in the new constitution -- even if making rules for peace-time during an emergency period seemed difficult. For Nicaragua, such a crisis atmosphere had existed practically since the beginning of the revolutionary process.


POLITICAL STRUCTURES

The Sandinistas moved quickly after the overthrow of Somoza to take charge of the coercive apparatus of the state, the army and the police, and to establish themselves as the governing authority. While they were aware of the importance of bourgeoisie and middle class representation at top governing levels -- these groups had helped in the final overthrow of the US-backed dictatorship and controlled future economic production -- the Sandinistas were basically unchallenged in 1979. No other political group had either enough popular support or a political program or organization for rebuilding Nicaragua after the war (see Black, 1981; Walker, 1981; Booth, 1982). The FSLN, meanwhile, had a coordinated organization of politically committed cadres as well as the political momentum once Somoza and the Guardia fled the country in July, 1979. While a few of the Commandantes openly preferred Leninist political organization and all of the leaders spoke boldly of revolutionary changes, often employing Marxist rhetoric, the organization and practice of the new government proved to be flexible, conciliatory, pragmatic in economic policy and responsive to domestic and international events. In a position to do so, the FSLN did not choose a 'maximalist' plan of nationalizing all means of production, assuming full power or erradicating potential opposition in an all-out effort to transform Nicaragua according to a fixed model of socialism. As I noted in Chapter 1, the two immediate concerns were the defense and consolidation of the revolution and economic reconstruction.

According to the earliest available internal working document of the FSLN (FSLN, 1979), immediately after the July 19 victory the

Sandinistas defined their political tasks and tactics as:
developing favorable conditions for later socioeconomic
transformation; channeling democratic, progressive and revolutionary
forces against the "enemies of the revolution"; uniting all national
sectors around the defense of the revolution; isolating any
counter-revolutionary opposition; drawing politically active forces
under the leadership of the vanguard FSLN; and educating the masses
to make them the driving force of the revolution (p. 9, 23-24). The
document, a result of the first national meeting of FSLN cadres in
September, 1979, gives insight into the Sandinistas' first impulses
and assessments of their vulnerability after routing the Somoza
regime from power. In it the FSLN defines the revolution's enemies
as 1)the "traitorous bourgeoisie" -- those who were disinvesting,
decapitalizing their business concerns or leaving the country, and,
who had had contacts with the US government in the latter's attempts
to keep the FSLN from power; 2)the "far left" which had already
inspired anti-Sandinista incidents in Nicaragua; and 3)the "vestiges
of Somozism" -- both Somoza supporters and corrupt practices that
had become the norm in many spheres of economic and political life.
The allies of the revolution, meanwhile, were the workers, peasants
and petty bourgeoisie who identified with the revolution and its
blueprint.

Apart from this discussion of polar politics, however, the FSLN
emphasized the importance of "political realism" and the practical
necessity of gaining support among the middle-income population
strata. Looking into the future, the Sandinistas acknowledged that
as their "...approach becomes institutionalized, it is going to give
rise to contradictions, manifestations of which are already
beginning to surface" (p. 15). Because they were expecting and
already getting opposition from the traditional financial elite, the
FSLN spent considerable time at this strategy session weighing the
problem of factions or splinter groups within the FSLN, calling for
discussion and unity under one banner, establishing mechanisms to
"foster group debate" and "settling differences and thus
strengthening the vanguard" (p. 38-41).

Similar to the experience in other Latin American systems with
a dominant, government-sponsored party, in Nicaragua after 1979 the
distinctions between the state and the FSLN party were blurred.
Immediately after the overthrow of Somoza and in the wake of mass
destruction after the war, a five-member Junta ruled Nicaragua by
consensual decision-making under emergency powers. Decisions of the
Junta, made up of two business class representatives and three top
Sandinista leaders, were unappealable. This body later was replaced
by the three-man Junta made up of: Daniel Ortega Saavedra,
Sandinista commandante and Junta leader; Sergio Ramirez Mercado, a
writer and Sandinista party member; and Rafael Cordoba Rivas, a
member of the Democratic Conservative Party, a reformist splinter of
the traditional Conservative party. The Junta ruled Nicaragua in
consultation with the FSLN National Directorate and the advisory,
co-legislative Council of State until January 1985. The Council of
State, a corporatist structure guaranteeing the representation of
social, political, religious and economic groups (i.e., not
electoral districts), debated policy initially set out by the Junta
and the Directorate, and, initiated legislation. The Junta, though

it proved to be sensitive to expressed concerns, had final legislative authority to announce national unity policy. In January, 1985, the Junta and the Council of State in turn were replaced by the directly elected president, vice president and constituent National Assembly. Given its polling of about two-thirds of the votes in 1984, the FSLN continued to dominate in top government posts; the FSLN Directorate directly consulted with and advised President Ortega.

After 1979 the FSLN took the role of vanguard, setting out guidelines and parameters for the revolution. On another level, policies were implemented through the FSLN-headed ministries and autonomous agencies and it was at this level that technical experts and life-long--and many non-FSLN bureaucrats--had extensive influence. In a political economy so underdeveloped and in the throes of fundamental change, some of the planning went on in the field and according to immediate needs. As Planning Minister Henry Ruiz complained early on (Booth, 1982: 184ff.), there was not as much direct popular influence as he had hoped would shape revolutionary policy. Sandinista leaders, facing difficult development issues with minimal resources, and, trained in command and leadership roles during the struggle against Somoza, were not reluctant to employ command models in establishing national goals, priorities and the framework of national political debate. There was Sandinista television and a Sandinista army in the new Nicaragua rather than Nicaraguan state television or a politically-independent Nicaraguan army, although the latter issue was widely addressed in national, all-party dialogues and may well be changed in time. This fusion between a hegemonic party and the state was reinforced or made possible by the reality that most FSLN members also led mass and community organizations such as the neighborhood Sandinista Defense Committees (begun during the insurrectionary period), labor unions, and womens, youth and other groups. Moreover, similar to political reality in Mexico, for example, FSLN militants (cadres with fighting experience and proven political loyalties) who held government posts in effect gave the FSLN de facto control over the state bureaucracy and the security forces -- the police and the army (LASA, 1985: 16). At the same time that he spoke as president of the country, Daniel Ortega also spoke as a member of the FSLN National Directorate. The nine Commandantes on the Directorate -- the top commanders in the war against Somoza -- have directed major ministries of government since 1979.

While there were state-controlled organizations similar to those in many development-oriented countries to mobilize people in support of government programs, and while groups that did not support the revolutionary process often had their government support withdrawn or faced harassment, opposition groups both functioned and drew limited support in Nicaragua (NYT, 3-23-85). As a group of Latin American scholars (LASA) noted in their report on the status of Nicaraguan politics, five years after the Triumph there continued to be a substantial amount of "noise" in the political system from the top level on down.

There were limits to the control of the FSLN. Moreover, several factors worked to encourage decentralization and regional or local influence. Realities such as the widescale, popular and cross-class participation in the insurrection; the emergence of newly politicized, efficacious and politically-skilled masses; the critical importance to economic recovery of the cooperation of the business bourgeoisie; and the implementation of revolutionary policies led to new class and sectoral animosities. Although the Sandinista National Directorate directly or indirectly gave prior approval to major decisions or policy agendas, much debate and bargaining took place in legislative, advisory and mass organization forums in efforts at consensus. In the process of policy implementation, moreover, government officials often ended up ajudicating between classes and groups. FSLN officials often had to restrain popular and spontaneous efforts to change the existing class balance of power, such as during unauthorized factory or land takeovers, in periods of new wage demands or strikes, and the like. Fagen (1983: 126) gives the example of Ministry of Labor employees, many of whom also served under Somoza, ajudicating confrontations between newly organized peasants and rural workers -- the FSLN-led Associacion de Trabajadores del Campo, ATC -- and large landowners. (Other examples are noted in Black, 1981; Walker, 1982; and Colburn, 1984). Constituent demands, practical necessities, and most of all, necessities of production and survival, informed new policies.

Contributing to the difficulties encountered by the Sandinista regime in translating revolutionary goals and political hegemony into coherent, positive change at the grassroots were the shortage of technically-trained personnel and bureaucrats in Nicaragua, the multitude of Somoza holdovers who were not turned out of their jobs as a matter of course and the thinly-staffed government ministries with their very limited resources. Not only was the state's fiscal and technical capacity outstretched by the large number of development projects underway into 1983, it was also true that not all government personnel were in agreement with FSLN policies. Sandinista hegemony did not always lead to centralization; the FSLN soon realized the practicality of local control, input and resource mobilization. FSLN majoritarian status did not always translate into economic or political control.

Nevertheless, due to the success of the FSLN's committed cadres and professionally trained organizers at building a base of support throughout the country -- through the organization of neighborhood and regional groups, comites de base, and a host of other organizations, and, through the provision of such new government services as education, health care and literacy training -- the Sandinistas acquired a dominant influence in Nicaraguan public life and a major advantage over other political movements in terms of organizational breadth and ability to mobilize support.[4] That is, "unlike the Somozas, who had based their power in a corrupt, foreign-trained military establishment and in a small internationalized economic elite, the Sandinistas drew their strength - and their revolutionary mandate - from the mass of the people" (Walker, 1982: 20).

## Political Institutionalization

Political development in revolutionary Nicaragua included the institutionalization of a participatory model and movement toward the original objectives of a mixed economy, political pluralism and non-alignment. This development is evidenced among other things by the 1984 electoral process and the constitution-writing process of 1985-1986. The Sandinistas, rather than ruling by decree or without appeal processes, preferred in general to introduce legislation for discussion or to address problems through "national dialogue" sessions with affected groups. The Sandinista leadership put a high priority on maintaining dialogue with critics at home and abroad. The FSLN made concessions and withdrew controversial proposals in the interests of preserving a credible domestic opposition and the practice of dialogue toward consensus. They did not insist on winning on every point. This approach to governing was institutionalized into the electoral process; after more than a year of studying world electoral systems, a commission from the FSLN and the Council of State chose a proportional representation system in order to ensure political space for non-Sandinista parties that as yet had not built sizeable organizations. Prior to the November, 1984 election Sergio Ramirez reflected FSLN thinking:

> There is a dominate party here -- the FSLN. We can't change that overnight. Political equilibrium cannot be created artificially. We are having elections here, hardly five years after a revolution; a true political earthquake....I can't say we have a balanced political equation here. These [opposition] parties are very small parties. To us the real danger was that these parties would not poll enough votes to gain a seat in the National Assembly, and would simply disappear. That's why we chose a proportional representation system....Our goal is to open a political space for the future (LASA, 1985: 31).

Such a space was in fact opened: the opposition won about 33 percent of the votes--29 percent went to parties to the right of the FSLN and 4 percent went to three parties to the left of the FSLN--for a total of 35 seats (36.5 percent) out of 96 in the National Assembly.[5] That was enough to deny the Sandinistas the two-thirds majority they would need to control the constitutional-drafting process after 1984.[6] All but two of the opposition members to the Assembly, moreover, were elected on platforms that recognized the capitalist nature of the economy and indicated concerns for the preservation of the private sector and the maintenance of the mixed economy. Based on party platforms, the results also indicated that: a number of voters placed some of the blame for the poor economy and for the military draft on the FSLN; a significant portion of the voters wanted a state – military separation and an FSLN dialogue with the contras (a position the FSLN consistently rejected); and some voters were not comfortable with the relationship between the mass organizations and the FSLN. But more important than the differences in issue positions was the fact that they were expressed legitimately in an incipient electoral process rather than through decapitalization or support for the counter-revolutionaries. At the same time, however, precisely because the elections contributed to the consolidation of the leadership role of the FSLN within yet undefined pluralist structures, they served to heighten domestic and international tensions for Nicaragua. A new system with guarantees for the representation of dissent and opposition was being developed during a period when Nicaragua was at war with US-backed rebels and was suffering an economic emergency. That reality also signalled the delicacy of the political development underway in Nicaragua in the mid-1980s.[7]

Judging by the Assembly debates during the process of drawing up the General Statutes of the National Assembly in 1985, the FSLN had a legislative predominance in the task of constitution writing, but not political clear sailing. Much lively debate occurred during the Statutes-writing phase and FSLN-aligned representatives did not always vote with the FSLN party position. Twenty FSLN representatives, in fact, were not FSLN party members and the variation in their occupations and socioeconomic backgrounds suggested the probability of independent thinking in the future. However, the degree to which these representatives would feel free fully to reflect their home or territorial constituencies' interests remained to be seen. In this context, it is important to keep in mind the absence in Nicaragua of a tradition of an accountable legislature or of long-held expectations or norms of honest, open government. Local observers expressed concern, for instance, about the degree of public confidence in government institutions. To a large extent it was up to those working in these new political institutions to establish their credibility and usefulness. Sandinista officials acknowledged that historic responsibility.

Unless major changes came about from the new constitution, the Nicaraguan president, along with selected advisors, would have nearly complete power over the direction of foreign policy. The legislature, in the meanwhile, had the right to disclose and report on that policy, while it could regulate the behavior of foreign investors in Nicaragua. Again, the extent and nature of these powers as well as the president's had yet to be finalized and tested against reality. The difficult task was establishing legislation and norms which would be relevant both to the economic and military crisis facing Nicaragua in the mid-1980s and to peacetime. The multiple critical contexts and the immediacy of the crises defining this period of political institutionalization presented severe constraints on the development of open political structures.

In the near term it was clear that the FSLN National Directorate would continue to guide policy. The constitution-drafting process was organized by the work of various committees assigned to consult with 1)the full range of political groups or sectors inside Nicaragua[8] and 2)foreign legislative and juridical groups -- a task accomplished by an Assembly committee's travel to Latin American, Western European and Eastern European states. An all-party, FSLN-dominated Special Commission which reflected the seven Assembly parties in proportion to seats held was appointed to write a first draft of the constitution. That draft was presented to the full legislature in February, 1986. During 1986 the draft was presented at open town hall meetings (<u>cabildos abiertos</u>) where interested citizens were invited to debate the draft or offer alternating proposals. Within the United States, the fact that political consolidation was proceeding in Nicaragua without political instability or major political disaffection led to even greater determination among conservatives to destroy this example.

## Remaining Questions

Major questions about the development and future of pluralism in Nicaragua remain for second half of the 1980s. Would regular elections, the legal status of all parties, guarantees for all political actors and power-sharing be protected under the constitution and in practice? Would the law provide for decentralization, checks on bureaucratic tendencies, respect for private property and legitimate criticism? How would the issue of FSLN - state separation be addressed and what would be the relationship of the mass organizations to the FSLN?

By the mid-1980s it was clear that a key political tension within Nicaragua, and on another level, between the United States and Nicaragua, was that which resulted from the tensions between the two models of democracy offered by Sandinismo or "participatory democracy" on the one hand, and, by the United States and the business classes and major opposition parties in Nicaragua on the other. The contra war, meanwhile, exacerbated these tensions, increased the Sandinistas' suspicions of opposition groups, led to bureaucratic shrinkage of power under greater FSLN dominance and threatened to provide a justification for Leninist tendencies already preferred by a minority sector within the Sandinista Frente. The room for national debate about the proper development of Nicaraguan democracy was being narrowed, despite the fact that creditable national elections were held and a voice for opposition groups was upheld. If the FSLN was to be, as a matter of political reality, the dominant political force or, indeed, the vanguard of the revolution, how tolerant and responsive would it be to out-groups as it defined the framework for the transition to Nicaraguan socialism? What mix of participatory models would evolve in the revolutionary process?

Despite US claims to the contrary, in the mid-1980s these were yet open questions. Nor had the Soviet bloc or the FSLN's legislative opposition identified with the United States' view of Nicaraguan processes. According to a communist bloc envoy in Managua in 1985, "This is hardly what we would call socialism. It is much too undisciplined, much too chaotic." An opposition Nicaraguan economist, reflecting distrust of FSLN intent claimed, "The Sandinistas have a socialist mentality and a long-term plan to go with it, but they haven't really put it into practice yet. They are like Catholics who profess religion but still lapse into sin." Undoubtedly closer to a realistic assessment of Nicaraguan politics in the mid 1980s, a Latin American diplomat in Managua characterized the government as a hybrid regime that is "a peculiar creature that is neither fish nor fowl" (NYT, 3-23-85).


## INTERNAL POLITICS AND FOREIGN POLICY

The structure of politics in Nicaragua had implications for

Nicaragua's relations with other states not only because revolutionary Nicaragua was seen as a test case for Latin America, but also because it had an underdeveloped economy dependent for survival on broad international support. In later chapters I discuss the United States' concerns about the kind of political regime that emerged in Nicaragua and the implications for Nicaragua of the United States' judgement. Washington rejected the FSLN's conceptualization of Sandinista democracy, coupled as it was with anti-imperialist, non-aligned and socialist objectives. Although the United States made attempts after 1979 to influence the course of Nicaraguan politics by shoring up the small business class with direct and clandestine aid, it became clear by 1982 that the Unites States, accustomed to greater political control in the region, preferred not to work with the Sandinistas but to force them out of office. This made aid, trade and support from other states all the more important to the revolutionary government.

Few other states in the world subscribed to the United States' theory of the root cause of social unrest and instability in Central America: that Soviet, communist and expansionist forces were at work there. Nevertheless, given the interests of other potential partners in Latin America, Western Europe and elsewhere, political structures in Nicaragua would figure in these relationships as well. Latin American states were increasingly concerned with both democratic or pluralist structures and greater independence from the traditional continental power, something that might be achieved though pragmatic economic development models that did not require alignment (or increase dependence). These states were interested in Nicaragua making advances in these directions. Although the Western European states preferred not to antagonize the United States, they were also interested in Nicaragua developing non-aligned and democratic, even if socialist, politics. A closed regime intolerant of its opposition and insensitive to its foreign partners' interests would not be able to woo such important and necessary international support.

The organization of Nicaraguan domestic politics was important to the success of its foreign policy in another way as well. In order to pursue the fundamental structural changes laid out after the revolution, and, to mobilize the energies and resources necessary to move Nicaragua closer to self-reliance, the FSLN would need the voluntary cooperation and moral support of the Nicaraguan people, and especially of those who owned the means of production. Choosing a mixed economy over a centralized, command model and a political structure where the dominant political movement negotiated with out-groups meant also that the FSLN had to employ dialogue and concessions as it acted as the vanguard for the majority poor. Reducing Nicaragua's dependence, for example, meant eating more locally grown, traditional foods rather than imported foods and reducing or eliminating "luxury" imports from abroad. For many people it meant sacrifices and changes in life styles. Again, domestic and foreign policies were intertwined in the revolutionary process. Crucial to keeping the bulk of public support, then, was maintaining a political system considered to be at least minimally legitimate or reasonable and responsive. The tensions inherent in working out policies with the internal opposition is a subject taken up in the next two chapters.

NOTES

     1. For an indepth consideration of the role of the Catholic Church in the revolutionary process see: Dodson and Montgomery, 1982; Cesar Jerez, 1984; Hynds, 1982; Lernoux, 1984; and Dodson and O'Shaunessy, 1985.
     2. In all democratic systems there are certain structural limitations on participation and the nature or extent of democracy. For a more complete discussion of democracy in Nicaragua see, for example, Coraggio and Irvin (1985), O'Shaunessy (1985), and Walker (1985).
     3. The FSLN did not practice full tolerance regarding labor indiscipline and independent unions when these led to strikes or demands that created obstacles to increased production--a Sandinista priority. In July, 1981, strikes were outlawed along with seizures and work stoppages. (The right to strike was reinstituted in 1984.) In another incident, six leaders of a Corinto dock workers union were arrested in June, 1983 when they tried to take their union out of the central Sandinista workers' union (CST). In early 1986 the FSLN told a non-FSLN union it had to suspend publication of its often-critical newsletter.
     4. To become an official member of the FSLN organization one had to have organizational sponsorship from any of a number of FSLN-supporting groups and work for the party for 6 to 12 months. Members were required to pledge 4 percent of their incomes as party dues. According to FSLN officials, these dues (not state monies) paid for FSLN expenses.
     5. A number of foreign independent observers and organizations reported that the elections were clean, honest and fair. The Latin American Studies Association report (LASA, 1985) gives detailed coverage of issues surrounding the election, investigates the charges of US and domestic critics and reports electoral results. In stark contrast to contemporaneous elections in El Salvador, Guatemala, Mexico and Brazil, for example, there were not broad or confirmed charges of ballot-box stuffing, voter intimidation, voter reprisals or electoral violence in Nicaragua in 1984.
     6. A 60 percent rule was later adopted, though this did not translate directly into FSLN legislative victories. The climate of debate was often tense as small parties maneuvered to stall the writing process (e.g. IHCA, March, 1986). The FSLN representatives worked hard to create consensus articles.
     7. Party representatives reflected confidence in the new, if tenuous and yet untested, legislative system. A representative of the largest opposition party, the Democratic Conservative Party (PDC), pledged to check FSLN policies: "We will fight any proposal that is Marxist in nature or limits people's freedom to produce and sell as they please. There will never be another Cuba here, never." Sandinista official Rafael Solis Cerda acknowledged an active opposition: "We'll have to take into account that we have problems and dissent" (NYT, 11-18-84). Other FSLN officials asserted that in the post-election "second phase" of the revolution, a key objective

would be to provide incentives and security to the private sector.
All but the bourgeoisie opposition groups decided to work within the
system.
    8.   The organized business bourgeoisie (CDN-LaPrensa) and
Catholic Church hierarchy groups voluntarily abstained from the
consultation process.  These groups decided during 1984 to pin their
hopes on the armed counter-revolutionaries.  While they publically
and consistently opposed the FSLN-led political consolidation
process after the 1984 elections, these groups were not united and
did not offer a public or coherent political program to compete with
that of the FSLN.  (See Chapters 4, 6).

# 3

## Economic Realities and Constraints

We are a poor underdeveloped, small country. We will be forever dependent. The only way of getting some flexibility is to diversify our dependence and increase our international relations. This is not easy to carry out. It implies a lot of changes in technology. It takes time.

Priest, Economist Xabier Gorostiaga
1981

Nicaragua's position in the global economy as a dependent state will be determinative for its behavior in international affairs well into the future. Movement toward a less dependent, more stable economy was necessary for the consolidation of the revolution and maintaining popular support at home -- recall the Sandinista priority of rebuilding the economy and delivering on the promises of the revolution. But economic development was also necessary for long-term state legitimacy and security given Nicaraguan realities and the external constraints the new government faced.

THE HISTORICAL SETTING

The Sandinista emphasis on implementing a new model of economic growth is best understood in the contexts of Nicaragua's economic history and conditions at the time of the Triumph. As LaFeber (1984) and others (Cruz, 1984; Feinberg and Pastor, 1984) have noted, Nicaragua and other Central American states had experienced spiralling growth rates and economic expansion in the pre- and post-Alliance For Progress era and during the heyday of the Central American Common Market. For example, in the 1950s and 1960s Nicaragua had among the highest of Latin American growth rates; exports were diversified and expanded to five principal commodities (sugar, cotton, beef, coffee, fish); manufacturing increased by 10 percent; and GNP rose 23 percent in the 1960-70 period (Cruz, 1984: 99). However, these statistics did not reflect the growth in concentration of wealth, in middle class frustration and in unemployment which resulted from the introduction of mechanization in industry and agriculture, and, which was complicated by illiteracy. Nor did the statistics reflect either the social life

61

conditions of the majority poor or the Somoza family's predominance within the Nicaraguan economy. While Somoza and his <u>Guardia</u> funnelled the nation's capital and savings into secret foreign bank accounts, only 2 percent of rural dwellers had access to potable water; only 28 percent of Managua's residents had access to sewers; and landlessness grew as a result of land and tax reforms (LaFeber, 1984: 62). Meanwhile, Somoza's efficient and brutal <u>Guardia</u>, in neo-fascist fashion, forced a calm among the populous; political discourse was sterile at best and class-based political organizations were repressed.

Nicaragua's dependent status was a function of its historical export-led model of growth, characterized as it was by investment, trade, aid-credit and debt ties with the West -- and the United States in particular -- during the Somoza years. Indeed, after World War II Nicaragua had linked its economic growth to an expansion of markets for its traditional export items in the industrialized world (Conroy, 1985a: 41). The external sector accounted for about 35 percent of the national product in the late 1970s, suggesting the extent to which primary exports and trade were the dynamic elements in the economy (Cruz, 1984).

While export products remained very important to the entire economy they were also extremely vulnerable to fluctuations in both domestic production and world market pricing mechanisms. Moreover, Nicaragua's primary product export sector focused and relied heavily on the United States. Maintaining growth required a healthy and expanding export sector under favorable pricing and export-import balances--conditions that were not to be experienced in the 1960s and 1970s. According to the Economic Commission for Latin America (ECLA), the level of Nicaraguan exports was tied directly to its rates of economic expansion, capital accumulation, investment and employment, as well as to its capacity to maintain imports (Conroy, 1985a: 41; Fitzgerald, 1982). Poor performance in the export sector, in other words, meant almost certain economic contraction or stagnation.

Other factors worked to deepen Nicaragua's external dependence: patterns of financing government deficits by borrowing abroad; reliance within the national banking system on foreign borrowing; and "a chronic imbalance in trade relations that required continual compensatory capital flows and/or foreign borrowing" (Conroy, 1985a: 39).

## CACM-Based Development

A number of events during the 1960s and 1970s which were related to the economic system and model established by the US-inspired Central American Common Market (CACM) led to economic decline in Nicaragua by the late 1970s. The CACM's objectives of expanding the regional market and encouraging industrialization were met and produced impressive growth rates for a number of years. However, weaknesses in the system led to a negation of economic development in the longer term. For one thing, the pact did not protect the market from non-regional capital investment. Soon many new foreign finishing or tertiary industries for semi-manufactured products appeared, taking advantage of low internal tariffs, low wages, and the like. As a result, indigenous manufacturing capacity did not increase. Second, the economic model's emphasis on import-substitution industrialization led to import-intensive manufacturing -- machinery, spare parts and semi-processed goods were needed for this industrialization and were imported primarily from the United States. This in turn led to high extra-regional import bills, despite the fact that the import bill for consumer goods was decreasing (Barry, et.al. 1982: 35). The result was greater trade deficits at a time when external demand for primary exports was also declining. Regional demand for consumer goods, meanwhile, was tapering off due to the skewed income distribution fostered within the Central American states by the CACM system.

Other structural changes moved Nicaragua further away from long-term, indigenous development. Such development might accrue, for example, from the capacity to be self-sufficient in food or from industrialization strategies cognizant of local resources and needs and geared toward internal dynamism rather than external financing. In Nicaragua, the expansion of industry was accompanied by a severe decline in the contribution of agriculture to gross domestic product. The agricultural share of GDP dropped from 45.8 percent in 1950 to 23.4 percent in 1960. Meanwhile, industrial growth did not result in job creation in the industrial sector: as a share of total employment, employment in industry grew only 0.3 percent from 1950 to 1963 and another 0.3 percent by 1971 (from 11.4 percent in 1950 to 11.7 percent in 1963 and to 12 percent in 1971). By 1977, the peak year in economic activity prior to the revolution, this figure had grown only by 3 percent to 15 percent (Brundenius, 1984: 7). With little government concern in the Somoza period for employment or land reform programs -- let alone social welfare planning -- the growing pool of migrant laborers became self-employed or underemployed. They were thereby further removed from any benefits accruing from Nicaragua's externally-oriented industrialization.

Without central (CACM) planning of regional industrialization, moreover, the bulk of foreign investment went to El Salvador and Guatemala. This left Honduras and Nicaragua hurt most by a system which also primarily benefitted the incipient national bourgeoisie in each country -- a group tied to the multinational corporations (see Barry, op,cit; Brundenius, 1984: 5-15).[1]

From 1959-1979 the incipient industrial sector in Nicaragua ate up twice as much foreign exchange as it generated. This sector, and an enormous service sector which grew up in Managua to support it, largely lived off the profits earned by coffee and cotton exports to extra-regional countries (IHCA, December, 1983). While the Somoza government borrowed and sought foreign financial assistance or direct investment to offset the widening gap between foreign exchange earnings and the demand for foreign exchange (e.g. to finance imports), the private sector failed to establish a pattern or tradition of capital investment (Conroy, 1985a: 41; LASA, 1985: 18).

Despite its centrality to the Nicaraguan economy, too little attention was given in the 1970s to export crop planning. In 1970, for instance, in efforts to expand export earnings, cotton planting was extended to marginal lands. This led, however, to lower per

acre production. Especially after 1974, production costs rose more
than the price of cotton; the 1973 oil crisis created higher costs
for machinery, fertilizers and pesticides needed in cotton
production. By 1977-1978 producers were deciding to use their land
for other products and the government stopped its financing of new
planting (IHCA, op.cit.). Cotton production fell and affected
production capacity and trade imbalances into the 1980s.

Thus, due to lowered demand, the saturation of the small local
market, the external shocks due to the oil crisis, the uneven
national benefits from regional integration, the growing
restrictions and higher interest rates on foreign assistance or
borrowing and the like, the CACM began rapidly to decline. By 1975
only Guatemala held regional trade surpluses and by 1980, after a
year's effort at economic reactivation by the revolutionary
government, Nicaragua's regional deficit stood at $225 million
(Brundenius, 1984: 15). During the 1970s, moreover, Nicaragua's
economic activity slowed and its trade imbalance grew. This was due
in part to the fact that Nicaragua had sold the bulk (76 percent) of
its manufactured products to other CACM states, countries which were
also experiencing economic slow-downs and were unable to present a
growing demand. Meanwhile, Nicaragua's food import bill, especially
vis-a-vis the United States, was growing. This came at a time when
Nicaragua was exporting food (e.g., beef) and when the government
was not effectively seeking new export markets. According to
Cambridge economist and FSLN economic advisor E.V.K. Fitzgerald, by
1979 Nicaragua had barely begun the phase of import-substitution
industrialization that most other Latin American states had already
passed through (LASA, 1985: 18).

## The Economic Situation At The Time of the Revolution

Following from the CACM model of growth and the resulting
structure of Nicaragua's economy -- open to outside manipulation and
featuring a small internal market -- Nicaragua's public debt grew by
a factor of 59 in the 1960-80 period (Barry, et.al., 1982: 47).
Again, in the period of the 1970s the contradictions of the
agro-export led growth model were coming to bear. According to the
World Bank in 1981, Nicaragua's public debt as a percent of GNP grew
from 20.6 percent to 62.9 percent between 1970 and 1979. The United
Nations Economic Commission on Latin America reported that Somoza
had deliberately designed Nicaragua's debt to private banks -- 70
percent of the total debt, of which 75 percent was owed to US banks
-- so that "most of it could be drained from Nicaragua rather
than being invested there" (Jonas, 1982: 383). By the time of the
July 19 Triumph, Nicaragua's debt stood at $1.65 billion, of which
$618 million -- more than the total of Nicaragua's exports -- was
due by the year's end.

The fact that the FSLN leaders in an early foreign policy
decision took on and renegotiated Somoza's debts is made more
interesting in light of the fact that the national treasury held
only $3.5 million--or one day's worth of imports--at the time the
FSLN took power. Nor did the pattern of falling prices for exports
and rising prices of imports appear to be changing. For example,
from 1981 to 1982 export prices showed the following declines:

cotton, 14 percent; coffee, 4 percent; gold, 31.8 percent; and industrial goods 7.5 percent (on average). This reduction in prices for Nicaraguan exports on the world market accounted for a loss of $246 million in earnings in 1982 (Ortega, 1983). According to ECLA figures, over the five-year period to 1985, market prices for Nicaragua's principal exports fell, in some cases, to below 1950 prices and, in other cases, to below production costs. For example: sugar and banana prices averaged a 32 percent decline in this period; wheat, beef and corn prices declined 24 percent; metals and minerals showed a 23 percent decline; and agricultural and raw material commodity prices fell 16 percent (BI, 3-21-85).

War damage added to Nicaragua's economic plight. The costs of the war included: 50,000 dead; 100,000 wounded (and, requiring long-term care); tens of thousands orphaned children; $200 million in cotton exports lost; nearly $500 million in infrastructure damage; and $1.5 billion in capital flight, attributable mainly to the Somoza group. Unsown crops, a 25 percent reduction in cattle herds and rural dislocation, meanwhile, produced severe food shortages. Industrial production came to a standstill. GDP was down 24 percent in 1979 and inflation stood at 80 percent (Fitzgerald, 1982: 207; Barry, et. al., 1982).

The economic task the FSLN faced in 1979 was staggering. Addressing these realities in a way that worked toward changing the historical external and internal economic relationships developed since World War II became a top Sandinista priority. The Sandinista leadership promised a new foreign policy to facilitate Nicaraguan-centered development where capital accumulation was structured to meet the needs of the majority poor and did not deepen Nicaragua's dependence. Development, in other words, would be based on the "logic of the majority." As a beginning, the Frente expropriated the Somoza family holdings as "the people's property" and nationalized the (Somoza-depleted, nearly bankrupt) financial institutions and insurance companies.

Socioeconomic divisions in the populace created another set of strains. Many in the bourgeoisie industrial sector adopted a wait-and-see attitude; they were reluctant to utilize profits for reinvestment or expansion, given a new regime and the continued decline in both CACM exports and the importation of equipment goods. The landed bourgeoisie largely owned and controlled the country's export means of production. The level of future export earnings was primarily in the hands of the bourgeoisie sectors and depended upon their willingness to plan, harvest or produce. In fact, the great majority of all productive assets in Nicaragua were in private hands. Meanwhile, workers who had experienced a wittling of wages due to inflation since 1976 were joined by the under- and unemployed in presenting new wage demands on the Sandinista government. While the FSLN called for austerity and no new wage increases -- in return for more employment, social wages and price-subsidized basic needs -- this call for patience and emphasis on the public good worked better in the public than in the private sector where workers were contributing in part to the savings of the wealthy. Those in the rural areas, on the other hand, presented the real test for the success of the revolution. It was in the rural areas that Nicaragua's most extreme poverty existed historically and it was

from there that the nation's greatest wealth came. Ninety percent
of Nicaragua's foreign exchange earnings were derived from
agriculture and 70 percent of the population earned their living off
the land (Colburn, 1984: 103).

The economic situation, in brief, was complex and required
delicate handling for any group wishing to maintain popular and
international support. The Sandinistas had organized and
facilitated popular mobilization; now they had to deliver on their
promises of change within a context of scarcity and of withdrawal or
retraction among those who owned the means of production. At the
same time that they were encouraging a reduction in class behavior
among the bourgeoisie in the interests of a viable mixed economy,
the Sandinistas had increased class consciousness among campesinos,
peasants and workers in the interests of consolidated, long-term
support for structural change (see Chilcote and Edelstein, 1985).
The resulting socioeconomic dynamic led to apparent policy
inconsistencies and to criticism from the Nicaraguan left and right.
The Sandinista concepts of "popular hegemony" and the "logic of the
majority," business class nervousness about its political future
and US overtures to this class all contributed to a determination by
the FSLN that "...the management of scarcity in favor of the classes
populares cannot be left to the vagaries of the market or to
capitalists large or small" (Fagen, 1983: 151). As domestic
economic crises mounted, pushed along by US economic aggression, the
FSLN came increasingly to determine production priorities, pricing
and distribution. The government also had to increase capital
investment by the public sector to make up for the lack of private
sector investment. By 1985 approximately 22 percent of the national
budget went to capital investment, compared to 5 percent under the
Somoza regime; the public sector accounted for 75 percent of new
investment for production (LASA, 1985: 18).

Thus, the class nature of the revolution also deepened, and the
economy, though with a preponderant private sector, moved in a
direction away from a market orientation. To the extent that the
bourgeoisie would not play its assigned role in the Sandinistas'
mixed economy model, the FSLN government expanded its own role in
running the economy. Critics in the United States, meanwhile, were
quick to label the process Soviet-inspired communism.[4]

## SANDINISTA ECONOMIC POLICY

As they defined the path of the revolution, Sandinista leaders
had to balance competing forces in the domestic environment,
adapting demands from the domestic business bourgeoisie and
international financiers with demands from poor urban workers, rural
campesinos and peasants. The Frente's conceptualization of a mixed
economy development strategy envisioned four key sectors: a private
sector of traditional businesses; a state sector based principally
upon the expropriation of Somoza's properties; a sector of peasants
and artisans; and a cooperative production sector (e.g. see Conroy,
1985b). Foreign policy makers faced the added task of adapting
internal and external demands. Sociologist Pablo Gonzales Casanova
(1984:221), reflecting the sentiments of the FSLN, identified a

major issue for anti-imperialist revolutionary movements in Latin America:

> From a global or national point of view, the major weakness lies in the urgency of satisfying the needs of the majority with production systems for the minority, within an international capital goods and financial market that is generally unfavorable and that is strong enough to apply economic, political, ideological, and military pressure on popular governments that constitute a serious threat to the continuity of colonialist methods of accumulation.

## Pragmatism and Production

Early FSLN policy reflected a pragmatism in the economic sphere and a recognition of the importance of small and medium-sized capitalists (rural and urban) in reconstruction, spurring production and building national unity. Nicaragua's economic program, despite revolutionary rhetoric, was not unlike development programs in other Third World states which sought to incorporate newly politicized campesinos and workers into social and political structures which addressed the needs of these majorities. The development model guiding the Sandinistas gave priority to orienting production to meet domestic needs, while developing and utilizing local resources. It sought economic change that went beyond simple redistributive programs actually to address conditions of economic vulnerability. FSLN economic policy was based on the assumption that: "Reducing vulnerability to changes in external economic conditions is necessary to ameliorate the instability that is characteristic of monocultural economies. Reorientation toward self-sufficiency...provides some insulation from negative shifts in the terms of trade and from the leverage of trading partners" (Chilcote and Edelstein, 1986: 95).

Guaranteeing private property, bowing to the great number of Nicaraguans who identified with "middle class" values, and maintaining adequate margins of profits for exporters, the FSLN promised a mixed economy with a gradual period of transformation away from the externally-oriented economic model of pre-revolution days. Land reform, health and literacy, labor organizing and crop diversification programs, among others, moved forward, following from the "logic of the majority." In order to address immediately the needs of the poor, meanwhile, the FSLN government after 1979 subsidized not only the price of basic food commodities such as sugar, milk and grains, but also that of public transportation and social programs. These subsidies increased over time until 1983. For example, in 1983 total subsidies were up 35 percent and government spending on social programs was up 23 percent over the previous year. While inflation was running at 25 percent, the public experienced only a 9 percent increase on such items as rice, beans, coffee, eggs and milk.[5]. Reflecting social priorities, the price of some non-essential goods in turn went up by 60 percent (CAHI, 5-20-83). By 1983, however, reductions in social investment were becoming necessary due to increased defense costs and economic losses from US-backed counter-revolutionary attacks from Honduras and Costa Rica. Economic austerity and defense were becoming the watchwords. In February, 1985 emergency economic measures were announced that reduced or eliminated earlier subsidies and put the economy on a war-time footing. From 1983 onward, in other words, the path of the revolution, was clearly being shaped by US economic and military policy which exacerbated the already austere economic outlook. (I take this up in detail in later chapters.)

The Sandinista attitude toward the bourgeoisie private sector -- i.e., as opposed to the private sector made up of small producers and new small landowners, whose interests were different from and opposed to those of the monied private sector -- was that as long as they produced and did not challenge the authority of the revolution, they would not lose their holdings. Likewise, they would receive needed foreign exchange. According to Central American Monetary Council figures for the period 1980 to 1984, the Nicaraguan private sector did compare favorably with other Central American private sectors in terms of the amounts of money or credit (in Central American dollars, per capita) made available for business use. Whereas the average 4-year figure for Nicaragua was 559, figures for neighboring states were as follows: Costa Rica: 324; Guatemala: 208; Salvador: 219; and Honduras: 231 (Ministry of Foreign Trade; author interview, 1985). While FSLN officials claimed there was no political program to eliminate the private sector, however, they warned the bourgeoisie not to expect being allowed to reverse the revolution's achievements or to regain political control.

The FSLN guaranteed continued private ownership of productive holdings and defined the private sector's role as supporting the state-regulated economy. The private sector's participation in the GNP by late 1983 stood at 55-60 percent, though this figure overestimated the private sector's actual economic (or political) power. This was so due to the restrictions put in place by the Sandinistas. Businesses were not free to raise or lower wages or fire workers. Regulations operated in the buying of raw materials and the importing of materials (Gilbert, 1985). The FSLN initiatives led business groups to protest what they saw as their inalienable rights "to dispose freely of the fruits of our labor" (La Prensa, 1-21-83). These groups charged that they were being reduced as owners to "being the administrators of our own enterprises (NYT, 12-31-81).

Such tensions reflected the fact that to 1986 the Sandinistas had not confronted the problem of how to obtain bourgeoisie support for the revolution's development strategy without giving that sector a sizeable political role. Fearing its own political emasculation, the monied private sector sought to export its capital. As Farer (1985) points out, Castro solved this problem in Cuba through draconian regulatory measures and by completely socializing the economy. There, Soviet aid blunted the costs and dislocations of the switch-over, while support from the Cuban underpriviledged classes accrued from programs redistributing the wealth. In Nicaragua, such methods and goals were rejected for a mixed economy model better suited to Nicaraguan realities. But again, "popular hegemony" relegated the bourgeoisie to production support--not majority political--roles. This contradiction was to remain as a significant political problem. The situation was clearly exacerbated by a hostile US stance. As the counter-revolutionary backlash developed and was increasingly centered in Washington, the FSLN also became increasingly mistrustful of the motivations of the pro-US Nicaraguan bourgeoisie. As a result, the political space for this group was also significantly narrowed by FSLN-enforced civil rights restrictions and national security measures.

The FSLN pursued policies aimed at diversifying economic dependence and linking the industrial and agricultural sectors. Their purposes included reducing Nicaragua's dependence on imported production inputs and developing a more self-contained industrial capacity. In the context of scarcity and austerity, FSLN policy sought to control traditional consumption patterns of the monied classes in the interests of the poorer classes; economic surplus was invested with the goal of developing a more rational pattern of imports which would protect the standard of living of the majority poor.

The principles upon which the process of industrial transformation in Nicaragua was to be based included 1)promoting agricultural productivity and self-sufficiency; 2)giving priority to the production of basic consumer goods; 3)improving links between the industrial and the agro-industrial export sectors; 4)promoting new export industry based on domestic raw materials; 5)promoting spare parts and inputs industries; and 6)promoting construction industries to support infrastructure development (e.g. see Brundenius 1984). Along with agricultural and land reform programs, these objectives constituted essential features of the FSLN's development model.

Regarding the CACM, the FSLN expressed hopes for its revitalization but wanted it restructured away from "traditional subservience" to multinational corporation interests, toward an orientation to popular and regional interests. In the FSLN view, this would also lessen the vulnerability of the revolution to the use of trade and credit restrictions as instruments of political pressure (Bendana, 1982: 324).

Just how successfully these principles could be pursued in the context of trade imbalances, external aggression and competition between immediate needs and the requisites of longer-term growth depended on FSLN creativity, levels of popular support and international willingness to provide aid. In the first years of the revolution a number of factors contributed to a disappointing performance in the external trade sector: destruction and dislocation from the war; the decline of the CACM generally and as a market for Nicaraguan goods; the decline in world demand for traditional Nicaraguan exports; and unfavorable terms of trade resulting from a 12.4 percent decline in traditional export commodity prices between 1981 and 1983 alone (Brundenius, 1984:23). From 1985 onward, moreover, defense requirements dictated priorities.

## Agriculture

In the economic sector closest to the lives of most Nicaraguans, the FSLN pursued projects which increased traditional export production, regulated the use of foreign exchange earnings, encouraged the sowing of crops for local consumption and provided land to the majority landless. Capital investment in agriculture increased in the years after the Triumph. In 1981, for instance, 34 percent of the national budget went to capital investment in agriculture, up from 15 percent in the previous year (LAWR, 8-29-80). The national bank encouraged traditional export crop production through credits and financing for the small producers -- private individual holdings and peasant cooperatives -- which produced 75 percent of the coffee, 77 percent of the cotton and 90 percent of the sesame seeds for export. The number of small farmers receiving bank credit for planting these crops increased from 20,000 in 1978 (the last full year of Somoza's rule) to 75,000 in 1981; the program budget increased from 91 million Cordobas to 1 billion Cordobas in the same years. Small farmers in agricultural cooperatives or those working individual farms were also given preferential loan interest rates over those available to medium and large producers (IHCA, December, 1983; author interview, Ministry of Foreign Trade, 1985).

New crop projects were begun to expand local production of locally consumed and exported foods and other basic commodities. In 1983 a project was begun with a $375 million investment which would eventually employ 65,000 agricultural workers in 38 new agricultural efforts, including 7 poultry farms, 3 rice schemes, 2 dairy farms; 2 African palm projects and 4 coconut oil projects (LAWR, 9-16-83). Another effort focused on development of the Atlantic Coast and non-traditional crops; palm, cocoa and rubber trees would produce materials normally imported, while basic grain and irrigation projects would bolster local food supplies (LARM, 5-6-83). The broad land reform program, moreover, brought many more people into the sector producing crops for export and increased the amount of land under production.[7]

The agricultural policy that had the greatest implications for export earnings and international trade activity was that regarding two of Nicaragua's strongest foreign exchange earners, cotton and coffee. While the production of these crops symbolized the displacement of campesinos from land and years of exploitation of the rural work force -- symbols of dependence and poverty for many Nicaraguans -- the Sandinistas saw no alternative to prioritizing their continued development. In 1983 a program of coffee renovation was begun which would replace the coffee plants on 5 percent of coffee land per year with disease resistant seeds that afforded a higher yield (LARM, 2-18-83). By developing coffee production, the leaders hoped to finance national reconstruction and repayment of inherited and new debts (CAHI, op.cit.). A one-hundred weight of coffee sold in 1983, for example, for $120 (US) and needed only $10 in foreign inputs. The net output of an average manzana (1.73 acres) of cotton brought $480 and therefore, like coffee, was also highly productive. In 1982 coffee made up 30 percent and cotton accounted for 21 percent of the total value of all Nicaraguan exports, together yielding about $240 million in foreign exchange that year. In addition, about 30 percent of all planted land was planted in coffee and cotton and the harvest periods were a most important employment source. At the same time, cotton and coffee

were nearly invulnerable to US economic pressures; only 17 percent
of these crops traditionally were sold to the United States. The
importance of this factor to Nicaragua's economic survival became
very clear in May, 1983 when the United States, for political
reasons (and in violation of the international General Agreement on
Trade and Tariffs -- GATT), cut its sugar quota to Nicaragua by 90
percent. Two-thirds of Nicaragua's sugar, or about $15 million
worth per year, traditionally had been sold to the United States.

The combined effects of Sandinista policies -- from land reform
to rural investment -- worked to cement rural support for the
revolution at levels generally greater than support in urban areas
where austerity measures and goods shortages had greater impact.
But it had also become clear by 1983 that, due to growing economic
and military pressures being exerted on the country by the United
States, government energies and national resources would be
increasingly directed toward defense and managing financial exigency
-- not toward rural or agricultural development as such. As I point
out in Chapter 6, US policy and contra operations aimed explicitly
at undermining the Sandinistas' urban and rural development strategy
and their foreign exchange potential.

## Maintaining Foreign Exchange Levels

The Frente did not have tested foreign models or a large
academic literature to consult which addressed the complexity of
Nicaragua's economic situation -- agricultural exports were the
nation's "heavy industry" and foreign financial dependence was
great. The Sandinistas, interested in adapting policy from
socialist and social democratic experience, recognized that the
export sector both held the greatest potential for economic surplus
within the society and had been the central feature of the Somoza
model of export-led development (Conroy, 1985a: 39, 46). It had
been the vehicle for the insertion of foreign capital into
Nicaragua's economy. Additionally, the export sector was a crucial
element in Nicaragua's dependence on the United States. This link
in turn provided the United States and domestic opponents of the
revolution important leverage over Nicaragua's financial and
political future. Thus, even as the export sector was bolstered,
foreign economic policy aimed to diversify trade relations and find
additional markets and sources of imports. The Sandinistas hoped
thereby to reduce Nicaragua's dependence on structures dominated by
the United States and US banks and corporations (Bendana, 1982:
324). Similarly, in response to World Bank suggestions that to
receive loans Nicaragua should enter agreements with the IMF or
present an acceptable program of economic stabilization, Central
Bank President Figueroa stressed the Sandinistas' commitment to
"...an economic program worked out by Nicaraguans...that will not
affect the majority of people in a detrimental way" (CAHI,
11-5-82).

The logic of the market called for investing where there would
be a profitable return. In Nicaragua that meant the export crop
sector. It was this sector that could earn badly needed foreign
exchange. The profit-oriented strategy, however, conflicted with
another development goal, that of improving Nicaragua's capacity to

feed itself and to make a basic healthy diet available and affordable to all Nicaraguans. Trying to accommodate these things, the FSLN divided investments between crop development for domestic consumption and expansion in export crop production, while cutting back luxury imports and otherwise controlling the available foreign exchange.[9] The policy also required reassuring large- and medium-sized private producers, who were in control of the bulk of export production, that laborers, financial credits and profits would continue to be available to them. And this requirement, in turn, did not always mesh with FSLN policies of land reform, improvement in the working conditions and livelihoods of the poor, and the like. Fitting revolutionary goals to economic and social realities in Nicaragua promised to make policy-making interesting and to generate tensions, inconsistencies and criticisms.

## Export/Import Strategies

In order to control and encourage Nicaragua's economic surpluses according to the "logic of the majority" the FSLN government nationalized external commerce, replaced the large producers as the middle-men in marketing and established the National Financial System for controlling foreign exchange and distributing production credits. Before 1979, for example, four export houses controlled cotton exports and captured the profits; the large producers acted as the marketing middle-men and earned the surpluses even though the small and medium-sized producers had been the most productive, dynamic element in the cotton sector (e.g. Ministry of Foreign Trade, 1984). For these small growers, FSLN policies made little difference; the government simply replaced the wealthy class as marketer. Small domestic producers were not required to sell their crops to the government, but the government did guarantee both floor prices for commodities (regardless of the world price) and foreign exchange for production imports. Land reform, credit and loan programs, meanwhile, benefitted the small and medium-sized farmers at the expense of the large, less productive and efficient growers who now had to compete with small producers.

While about 40 percent of Nicaragua's GDP was controlled by the public sector, this sector accounted for only a quarter of agricultural export production. The importance of agricultural exports to total Nicaraguan exports explains the FSLN's determination to regulate the export sector, a most important source of foreign exchange. In 1981, for example, five agricultural products accounted for 72 percent of Nicaraguan exports. While the state sector accounted for 28 percent of all agricultural export production in 1984-1985, small-scale private producers accounted for 30 percent and large-scale private producers contributed 42 percent. Private producers contributed 72 percent of agricultural exports (author interview, Foreign Trade Minister Alejandro Martinez Cuenca, 1985). Thus:

The private control of export production forces the Sandinista government to face the stiffest test of its resolve to maintain private production in the majority of

> the economy. The conflict is theoretical as well as
> practical. The urgent need to expand export
> production...has led the government to introduce
> preferential treatment for those producers, including
> special access to foreign exchange, reductions in the
> original highly progressive export taxes and reduced
> interest rates (Conroy, 1985a:48).

The government negotiated with private producers by sectors,
with cotton or coffee producers for instance, and through industrial
production agreements that essentially established contracts between
government and producers regarding production quotas and commodity
prices (see Gilbert, 1985: 19). To encourage exports the
Sandinistas offered unparalleled production incentives such as
changing the base for export taxes and establishing a system for
allocating dollar payments for export earnings that gave producers a
larger-than-the-official exchange rate for a portion of their
earnings. For example, from 10-40 percent of the proceeds from
sales would be in Central Bank certificates that paid 27 Cordobas to
the US dollar rather than the official rate of 10-1 on the parallel
exchange market. The greatest incentive under this system went to
manufacturing, where 40 percent of earnings were paid in these
certificates; for cotton the figure was 28.5 percent; for meat
exports: 25 percent; for sugar exports: 10 percent; and other
agricultural products: 30 percent (LARM, 4-30-82). Funds for
export promotion went mainly to cotton (51 percent); remaining funds
went to sugar, beef and other traditional export items (LAWR,
12-17-82). There were also selective taxes on foreign exchange
purchased for imports. Together these measures amounted to a
partial devaluation of the Cordoba, something the business sector
had been pressing for. Unofficially, the government claimed that
the State of Emergency, implemented after March, 1982, interrupted
plans to give more concessions to the bourgeoisie private sector and
to the "right-wing" political opposition.
    Meanwhile, state agencies had a preponderance of control over
export marketing: the National Agrarian Reform Institute (INRA),
for instance, ran 5 of 6 sugar mills in Nicaragua (LAWR, 8-29-80).
The Foreign Trade Ministry itself by 1985 controlled approximately
75 percent of exports; seven semi-automous enterprises managed the
other 25 percent. The enterprises bought directly from producers
and sold directly to the international market (Foreign Ministry,
1984; author interviews, 1985), and in the process presumably
developed their own interests, methods and influence over government
policy.
    Import policy gave priority to machinery and oil, items which
increased Nicaragua's productive capacity and helped peasants and
farmers. Such priorities also meant austerity in private
consumption. From 1978 to 1982 the import of capital goods for
industry rose 45 percent while in the same period capital goods
imports for agriculture rose 94 percent in dollar terms. Consumer
goods imports, meanwhile, rose only 8 percent overall. The import
of alcohol and "luxury" food goods dropped 43 percent. Similarly,
the importation of private automobiles fell 62 percent and
statistics on home appliances, furniture and carpet showed a 45

percent drop. Reflecting the "popular hegemony" principle, the importation of basic food products such as grains, milk, poultry, eggs, vegetables and the like rose 27 percent in the 1978-1982 period. The importation of health equipment was up 41 percent (CAHI, 2-6-84). While there were 4000 registered importers in Nicaragua by 1985 according to the Foreign Trade Minister, the government or state enterprises controlled about 40 percent of total imports.

The Nicaraguan opposition newspaper La Prensa argued that the notion that there was such a thing as luxury consumption was "exaggerted and highly erroneous;" La Prensa advocated that production decisions be left to individual liberty. Motivated by similar interests, the bourgeois private sector represented by COSEP (a private enterprise group that had become a forum for political opposition to the Sandinistas) argued that import taxes worked to impede the ability to re-equip manufacturing. Although bourgeoisie groups were bitterly condemning government policy, businesses using local raw materials were reportedly thriving in the new system (e.g., LARM, 4-30-82).

## The Debt Issue

Not only had the Somoza family business and the Nicaraguan state financial system come to rely on external financing, loans and accumulating debts, the small business bourgeoisie and the traditional landed elite had also become accustomed to relying on bank loans for capital expansion (i.e., rather than investing their own profits). Many of these profits went to overseas bank accounts, for homes in the United States, or for other luxery expenditures. While domestic production and world prices were good and while the CACM system was yielding positive economic growth statistics, debt repayments continued and new loans were awarded. The cycle began to slow in the 1970s, however, when falling world commodity prices met higher oil and production costs and when loan monies and easy terms were becoming harder to find. In July, 1979 the Sandinistas inherited from Somoza a national debt of $1.65 billion and a $3.5 million national treasury. Export prices were continuing to decline. The economic outlook was grim. There was significant pressure on the new leaders to renounce Somoza's debt: to Nicaraguan workers and poor campesinos the debt represented Somoza's repression and the base of the wealthy elite's consumption; to others, paying the debt off meant paying for the war machines Somoza and the Guardia had used against them. Not a little attention -- at home and abroad -- was turned to how the Sandinistas would address the issue of Nicaragua's standing debt.

In a practical move taken to keep Western credit lines open and to evoke world trust in their new and untested leadership, the FSLN met with the state's creditors and renegotiated the debt. In late July, 1979 Sergio Ramirez announced that the new government would honor all but two debts left over from the previous government: a $4 million debt to Israel and a $3 million debt to Argentina--debts which represented arms sales to Somoza in the last two months of fighting (NYT, 7-27-79). In November, 1979 while in Belgrade, Yugoslavia for meetings of the Non-aligned Movement, Sandinista

official Alfredo Cesar announced that Nicaragua had rescheduled its
debt with the Inter-American Development Bank and the World Bank,
and, that talks with other creditors were underway. According to
Cesar "...people are understanding of our situation," (NYT,
11-28-79). Yet, Cesar made clear that the FSLN was trying, as a
matter of principle, to get out of the cases where creditors had
apparently condoned corrupt practices of Somoza. Nor did the
Sandinistas want new loans to pay for the old.

In a major early foreign policy experience for the Sandinistas,
the FSLN negotiated an agreement with ninety creditor banks in
September, 1980. After nine months of inter-party talks, and
managing to keep the IMF out of the agreement (the Sandinistas did
not want to get involved in an IMF-designed austerity program which
would contradict the aims of the revolution), the Sandinistas gained
a 5-year grace period on the repayment of $582 million due
in 1980. Repayments would be at commercial rates over a 12-year
period. The FSLN agreed to pay Somoza's debt at regular rather than
at concessionary rates (Jonas, 1982: 383-386). The Sandinista
goverment would be financially obligated to the major world banks
for many years to come. While the Sandinistas had deliberately not
"gone the way of Cuba" by renouncing the debt and turning to the
only other alternative financial source -- the USSR and the Eastern
bloc -- they were also quite aware of the role of transnational
capital in squeezing the reformist and socialist Allende government
in Chile in the early 1970s.

The debt renegotiation process, therefore, was a bitter pill
for Nicaragua's new leaders. Yet, addressing the debt became a
commitment the Frente was to work hard to meet. Motivations for
doing so were also to expand. First, the Sandinistas were anxious
not to provide the counter-revolution with another avenue of
rationalization for undermining their rule. Moreover, the FSLN
objective of a mixed economy required the participation of the
private sector; private sector support was one criterion Western
creditors often applied on new loans. It was also this group which
had ties to international capital. Additionally, not only were
Eastern bloc aid offers limited, but economic and political factors
also reduced the feasibility of drawing on Eastern bloc credits (see
Chapter 9).

Servicing the debt put severe constraints on the revolution.
In 1981, for example, 40.1 percent of Nicaragua's export earnings
went to external debt servicing. Repayment on US loans was due on
top of that. By the end of 1981, the FSLN had to reschedule 93
percent of its multilateral and commercial loans (Barry, et.al.
1982: 219). By June, 1983, the Sandinistas owed $900 million to 117
private banks and asked for a postponement of $140 million due
before December, 1984 (NYT, 6-15-83). Yet, despite the burdens debt
servicing caused, the government did not miss a payment until March,
1983. After that, the Sandinistas continued to scramble to work out
agreements with creditors of all types. They continued to make
token payments on arrears (e.g., LAWR, 2-15-85). But the FSLN was
working in contexts of direct US political pressure on the loaning
agencies, and, of direct military aggression and deepening economic
crisis at home. By mid-1985, Nicaragua's debt, most of it incurred
to pay for oil or to maintain agricultural production, had gone up

$2.5 billion since 1979 to about $4.2 billion. The interest payment
due on the debt at that time, $400 million, was equal to one year's
export earnings.

In June, 1985 Central Bank President Joaquin Cuadra and
Finance Minister William Hupper reached an agreement with the
Committee of Creditor Banks--130 private banks from the United
States, Japan, Western Europe and Canada--to reschedule and extend
payments on the $1.5 billion private bank debt. New meetings were
scheduled for 1986. Recognizing the Sandinistas' political will to
honor its debt within the context of its economic capacity, creditor
banks required Nicaragua to show its good faith by paying $15
million by June, 1986 (BI, 6-20-85). To the extent that the banks
were willing to cooperate with the Sandinista government to
establish easier repayment terms, they--and the multinational
corporations which continued to do business in Nicaragua--were more
pragmatic than the Reagan Administration which had decided to
isolate Nicaragua. But the financial community also feared the
instability or investment and market losses which could result from
US policy, and, which might threaten other economic arrangements
among other debt-ridden Latin American states (e.g. IHCA, July,
1985). As I discuss in Chapter 9, Sandinista Nicaragua had become a
leading voice for a unitary continental approach to the Latin
American debt issue. While the issue became increasingly
politicized in the 1980s, Nicaragua, Peru, Cuba and other states
were calling for achieving a broad debt moratorium and for
prioritizing payments to banks open to guaranteeing development
credits.

The Sandinista government, meanwhile, continued its discussions
with other creditors, kept up principal payments on an old IMF debt,
made every interest payment from 1980 to 1982 and maintained links
to the World Bank. The largest portion of Nicaragua's debt, in
fact, was owed to regional creditors--Nicaragua was not only
indebted to its CACM neighbors, but also had a $1 billion oil debt
with Mexico and Venezuela. The bulk of its debt, in other words,
was with the Western world. The FSLN, by choosing to remain on good
terms with each of their creditors, was also required to operate
within the financial expectations of that community.


A RADICAL PROGRAM?

The economic program pursued by the Sandinistas has been
pragmatic rather than dogmatic in confronting Nicaraguan dependence,
debt, infrastructure destruction and dislocations stemming from the
revolution's socioeconomic programs. Sandinista economic policy has
been heavily influenced by 1)a determination to avoid economic
disruption and 2)concerns for the economic and political survival of
the revolution. While there was no precise model for the process of
economic, social and political transformation, the FSLN attempted to
create policy in line with their conception of popular hegemony and
Nicaraguan realities. Yet, when policies aimed at social
restructuring threatened economic disruption or Nicaragua's ability,
for example, to stick by its commitment to service the debt, the
FSLN often asked cooperation, continued productivity and sacrifice

from groups awaiting the promises of the revolution.

As Colburn (1984: 106-107) demonstrates through his study of the rural labor situation, the FSLN moved over time away from emphasizing unnecessary poverty of the masses to arguing for austerity. Rather than promoting labor militancy, the FSLN encouraged labor discipline. As Daniel Ortega and Victor Tirado told strikers at a plywood factory in October, 1979: "The old systems of struggle are not appropriate in this historical moment. If a policy of restraining or limiting salaries exists it is because the situation necessitates it. The workers at Plywood should know that they are already in control" (quoted in Colburn, op.cit.).

Again with economic stability in mind, the Sandinistas negotiated with US and other foreign companies to get them to stay on after the government changeover. The FSLN repeatedly voiced an interest in working with foreign companies so long as their[10] operations were not exploitive of Nicaragua's people or resources. But again, US pressure came to bear. Standard Fruit of the United States, for instance, broke a contract with the Sandinista government and left the country after coming under pressure from the US government not to do business with the FSLN. The FSLN rejected a strategy of nationalizing foreign investment, although by 1986 a new investment code had not yet been formally announced. In the absence of a formal code, government regulations on foreign companies tightened after 1982 and as exigency came to define the national economic situation. By 1985 government policy disallowed the repatriation of profits, set a 50 percent tax on profits (the same rate applied to domestic businesses) and required that all profits be deposited in the Nicaraguan Central Bank. There were no restrictions, however, on the percent of foreign ownership allowed in any business operation in the country, a regulation commonly employed in Third World states. Import/export regulations and labor codes, meanwhile, applied to foreign- and domestic-run operations alike. Dislocations and shortages due to the war and/or government workplace reforms similarly affected all business operators in Nicaragua: transportation of products for exports was often delayed; import permits (e.g. for raw materials) were prioritized by the Central Bank according to defense requirements; draftees' jobs had to be kept open and their pay had to continue while they performed military service; government pay categories (e.g. insuring equal pay for equal work) had to be adhered to; et cetera. Yet, despite these conditions, businesses could make profits. As in many other areas of Nicaraguan life, however, foreign economic and military hostility was taking a toll on productivity and straining economic relations; uncertainty over the future of the conflict or the prospects for peace lead to uncertainty concerning how economic transactions might be regulated in the future.

The Sandinistas had also been students of Latin American history and clearly attempted to avoid the lessons of Chile -- where the middle class sectors (with outside help) effectively subverted structural reforms[11] -- and of Cuba -- where a lack of broad foreign support and conducive international conditions led not only to dependence on "the other" super-power, but also to the adoption of a centrally planned, public sector economy. Rather, FSLN economic policy was consistent with traditional Latin American, structuralist

Table 3.1
Rates of Economic Growth in Latin America, 1983

| Latin America | -3.3% | Costa Rica | -0.5 |
|---|---|---|---|
| Guatemala | -2.5 | Panama | 0.5% |
| El Salvador | -1.5 | Mexico | -4.0 |
| Honduras | -0.5 | Venezuela | -2.0 |
| NICARAGUA | 5.0 | Cuba | 4.0 |

Source: ICAS, February, 1984 (ECLA data).

thinking and followed a number of policies advocated for Latin America by earlier US administrations (see Conroy, 1985b). The Nicaraguan model, though it was rejected by those who subscribed to conservative and orthodox laissez faire economic perspectives, held out hope for underdeveloped states looking for modes of economic organization that addressed conditions of dependence, inherited agro-export economies and externally-oriented structures.

While the Sandinista government was generally unwilling to compromise its long-term socioeconomic goals, the evolution of its economic policy and behavior was marked by pragmatism. Despite the dislocations which were the by-product of the economic transformation process and US economic hostility, Nicaraguan economic performance was notable, especially when compared to that of Central and Latin American states in the same period. For example, while Nicaraguan economic growth from 1979 to 1984 exceeded 22 percent overall and 7 percent in per capita terms, in the same period Central American average economic growth was -5.7 percent in aggregate terms and -14.7 percent in per capita terms (Conroy, 1985b:220). Nicaragua's performance as measured by GDP from 1980 to 1983, moreover, was among the best in Latin America according to UN Economic Commission for Latin America (ECLA) statistics for the continent. In 1983, for example, though Nicaragua faced mounting contra attacks and increasing external economic pressures, Nicaragua's 5 percent growth rate was the highest in all Latin America (see Table 3.1).[12] The continents' economic growth rate averaged -3.3 percent in 1983.

By mid-1983 and into 1986, however, the Nicaraguan economy was being shaped principally by US military and economic policy and the need for survival policy-making. Without the economic means to maintain their economy, the Nicaraguans again depended on a foreign policy capable of winning enough international support to sustain the revolution. (I take this up in Part Four). In 1984, 50 percent of crops sown for local consumption were lost due to contra sabotage -- the contras were more successful in economic terms than in military or political terms -- and in August, the prices of basic foodstuffs were doubled to reduce government outlays for subsidies. Taxes on non-essentials like soft drinks and beer rose sharply. Currency exchange restrictions were tightened and goods shortages became greater (LASA, 1985). The 1985 budget ceiling was placed at $2.8 percent billion, at least 40 percent of which would be allocated for defense. Health, social services and subsidies for contra victims were the next highest priorities (BI, 1-10-85). Money for education was sharply reduced.

By 1984, public discontent had risen noticeably, with complaints centering on austerity measures, resulting goods shortages and the military conscription law which was implemented in 1983. Yet the fact that the FSLN retained a 63 percent showing at the polls in November, 1984 suggested that most Nicaraguans did not assign the bulk of the blame for economic hardship on the Sandinista government itself. Speaking at the time of the sixth anniversary of the revolution, Interior Minister Tomas Borge took note of key ingredients -- popular will and a future-orientation -- in maintaining a beseiged revolution:

> We still haven't met many economic goals. We haven't constructed buildings, only a few roads and a few hospitals. We're still in the stage of social underdevelopment. We're going through a severe economic crisis, that is clearer than the bright face of the moon....But we have had an extraordinary success. Besides planting some corn and a lot of cotton, we've planted and harvested hopes. The Nicaraguan people have confidence in their revolution. In such a poor country, harassed by problems, with an acute housing problem, how can it be explained that given all this, the people are on this side of the fence? (BI, 7-4-85)

Nevertheless, economic hard times were to continue. In a mid-1985 interview, President Ortega noted that inflation that year was running at 125 percent (NYT, 7-18-85). According to Ortega's February, 1986 address to the National Assembly, 1985's inflation actually reached 300 percent. Using frank language about economic shortcomings and bureaucratic failures, Ortega returned to themes of determination, vigilience and national unity.

The austerity measures announced in February, 1985 aimed to reduce "...the gap between the real purchasing power of the Cordoba and the Nicaraguan economy's production capacity..." by "...cutting government spending, increasing wages for production and other salaried workers, and eliminating speculation with prices....." They also aimed at restructuring and reducing the overall demand of goods. The FSLN, in brief, put the economy on a war-time footing in order to convert surplus capital into "...salaries for workers, goods, money and resources that will ensure the military defense of the revolution." In addition to the measures introduced earlier, such as the elimination of food subsidies, the austerity program reduced public works, froze government hiring, called for a review of all government programs and gave "...unrestricted support for defense-related needs and health care." It increased incentives to export production and encouraged domestic production over importation (BI, 2-14-85).

Unlike orthodox austerity programs such as those of the IMF, however, the FSLN measures did not eliminate those programs which

provided a social wage to the neediest peasants and poor workers.
IMF agreements typically required sharp reductions in budget
deficits, higher prices for government services, lower wages and
higher local interest rates. Moreover, it is important to make this
comparative note: undoubtedly because the Frente manifested a real
policy concern about the effects of austerity on the majority of
poor Nicaraguans the popular riots, mass unrest and general
instability that accompanied austerity programs in other Latin
American states in the 1970s and 1980s did not surface in
revolutionary Nicaragua. Nor did the Sandinistas establish a
pattern of brutal coercion or violence to enforce austerity
measures, patterns typical of many other economically-pressed Latin
American countries.

US-funded and directed contra attacks by this time had cost
Nicaragua several hundred million dollars in lost exports and
production (about one-quarter each of its exports and GDP), and had
resulted in the destruction of production machinery, infrastructure,
farms, schools, and clinics. About 8,000 Nicaraguans had lost their
lives. US economic pressure on banks and international lending
agencies, meanwhile, had blocked credits and about $423 million in
bilateral and multilateral loans--all of which had been approved at
the technical level--between 1981 and mid-1985.[13] (I discuss US
economic and military aggression in detail in Part Three.) In
attempts at further isolating the Sandinistas, the United States
announced an economic boycott on Nicaragua on May 1, 1985.
Nicaragua would have to find alternative sources of spare parts for
its largely US-tooled economy and redistribute the 18 percent of
trade Nicaragua still did with the United States. (The United
States was Nicaragua's largest trade partner at the onset of the
embargo.)

Given the broad impact of US policy, the Nicaraguans lowered
their expectations for year to year economic growth and planning for
what economist Fitzgerald has described as a "passive transition,"
where planning was replaced by "doing what you can get away with."
Nicaragua had been pursuing development policies using external
financing, incentivizing exports and expanding domestic food
production -- policies not much different from those promoted by the
World Bank. By 1984, however, US policy, had fairly successfully
undermined Nicaragua's economic program by attacking the Achilles
heel of each element in Nicaragua's economic efforts. Nicaragua was
left to depend on trade credits and bilateral finance where it could
get it, even if this meant retooling to maintain production.
Nicaragua's choice of technology was conditioned by its sources of
credit (see Chapter 9).

The US government explained Nicaragua's economic situation by
indicting the FSLN for "radical statist" policies and economic
mismanagement. The US popular press followed suit with headlines
like "Strict import controls...have created havoc with commerce"
(NYT, 12-31-81), "Growing bureaucracy has made simplist business
transactions a wrestling match with red tape" (LAT, 8-17-83) and
"Nicaraguan economy in tailspin" (MH, 7-11-83). Yet, economic
statistics reflect a surprisingly healthy performance between 1980
and 1983. With increases in area planted, with harvests up and
despite a drop in coffee production after a record crop in 1982,

Nicaraguan agriculture grew 15 percent in 1983.  Increases in crop
production for domestic consumption by 1984-85 (i.e. over 1977-78
levels), such as those in corn, sugar, beans (each up 30 percent),
rice (up 100 percent) and eggs (up 50 percent) also supported higher
levels of local consumption of meat, beans and sugar.  In fact,
demand outstripped production, while rationing introduced under the
austerity program worked to increase demand even further.  In terms
of social consumption, medical consultations were up by a factor of
three and school attendance more than tripled (figures are from
Fitzgerald).  In contrast, middle class consumption fell as
redistributive and social entitlement programs restructured access
to production.

Despite war damage and other obstacles, production had
recovered remarkably.  In addition, because Nicaragua could show
successes, foreign donations and aid continued, though much of it
was in the form of soft loans and credits which ultimately added to
Nicaragua's long-term debt (see Chapter 9).

These and other aspects of the Nicaraguan socioeconomic process
during the early years such as Sandinista pragmatism and labors'
continued productivity, suggest that in the absence of hostile US
policy, the Sandinistas' economic strategy could have been quite
successful in rebuilding the country, in addressing its debt and in
expanding bases for self-sufficiency (see e.g., Conroy, 1985b;
Harris, 1985; Brundenius, 1984).  The Sandinista program of
political economy could well have become a working example for other
poor states interested in addressing underdevelopment and huge
rich-poor social gaps through mixed economy -- rather than command
economy -- models.  As it was, Nicaragua's growing oil debt and
trade deficit, its chronic hard currency shortages and Washington's
embargo and support for the contras combined to create economic
crises in Nicaragua.  True to its purpose, US policy worked to make
the Nicaraguan revolutionary example appear economically unviable
and unworkable.  US meddling in Nicaragua's internal politics, for
example, is explored in the next chapter.

One major tactic employed by the Sandinista leadership in
attempts to keep the revolution alive was keeping Nicaragua visible
and in the world spotlight.  Non-alignment and internationalism were
complimentary policies rigorously pursued by the Frente.  They paid
off, in part, by raising the political ante for an administration in
Washington which aimed at eliminating the Sandinista challenge to
its historical prerogative.


NOTES

1.  By 1980, 41 percent of the people living in Central America
did not have finances to cover even most basic nutritional needs; 64
percent were living in extreme poverty, unable to afford basic needs
(Brudenius, 1984: 13).

2.  Large and medium-sized properties dominated the
agro-pastoral sector in Nicaragua:  1.5 percent of land-owners, the
large owners, controlled 41.2 percent of total agricultural area
(latifundia) and another 20.3 percent of landowners, the
medium-sized owners, occupied another 41.1 percent of this land.

The remaining 78.2 percent of landowners shared 14.7 percent of the land (minifundia). While large and medium-sized owners used modern technologies and were oriented to the world market, the small holders used inferior equipment to grow beans, maize and rice for internal consumption, (see Weber, 1983: 123).

3. According to the FSLN's 1980 Program of Reactivation, public and private contributions to the Gross Domestic Product broke down as follows in 1980:

|  | % Public | % Private |
|---|---|---|
| Agro-pastoral | 20 | 80 |
| Industry | 25 | 75 |
| Construction | 70 | 30 |
| Mining | 95 | 5 |
| Services | 55 | 45 |
| Trade | 30 | 70 |
| Transport, Communications | 60 | 40 |

For more indepth analyses of the Nicaraguan economy since the revolution see Gilbert (1985); Latin American Perspectives (Winter, 1985); Conroy (1985a and 1985b).

4. This is so despite the fact that both in terms of the size of the public vs. the private sector and of government regulations over economic activity, Nicaragua did not differ much from other Latin American states-- or other Third World states--facing similar obstacles to development. Undoubtedly what raised the ire of US officials vis-a-vis Nicaragua was the FSLN's talk of Nicaraguan socialism and of greater independence from the United States. Several of the nine Commandantes in the National Directorate were frank about their Marxist-Leninist leanings. These things, rather than actual policies or events in Nicaragua, appear to explain the level of US hostility (see also Gilbert, 1985).

5. A comparison of a basic consumer's goods basket of 21 essential items across Central America showed the following increases in domestic consumer's prices in those countries between January 1982 and January 1983: Costa Rica: 102.7 percent; El Salvador: 24.1 percent; Guatemala: 20.4 percent; Honduras: 28.6 percent; and Nicaragua: 11.1 percent. Although each economy was suffering price increases in daily life essentials, the impact of increases on Nicaraguans was minimized by government subsidy policy (ECLA figures cited in CAHI, 5-20-83).

6. This would be a long, difficult process. For example, in 1982--three years into the revolution--Nicaragua spent $218 million of its foreign exchange for inputs, spare parts and machinery for an industrial sector that produced only $100 million in export earnings. In fact, industrial production went down 5.6 percent in 1982 due to dislocations and destruction left from the war of liberation; a lack of business confidence; economic restructuring; and the like. (CAHI, 12-13-83).

7. For a discussion of land reform in Nicaragua after 1979 see CAHI, 1-13-84; LASA, 1985: 13; IHCA, December, 1983; Collins, 1982; and Colburn, 1984. Of Nicaragua's 7 million acres of agricultural land, 4.4 million acres were in private hands and 2.6 million acres were in the hands of the public sector. It was this

latter sector which was involved in land distribution programs. By the end of 1983 the share of agricultural land held by the largest owners had declined 41 percent to 12 percent. The land held by the smallest individual landowners had increased 65 percent since 1978. Yet, by 1985 only 35 percent of Nicaragua's arable land had been affected by land redistribution. About two-thirds of the affected land was thereafter farmed by individual peasant proprietors. Remaining lands were divided between large state-owned farms and agricultural coops of individual peasant families (LASA, op.cit.; author interviews, Nicaraguan Institute of Agrarian Reform [INRA], 1983, and 1985; Foreign Trade Ministry, 1985).

8. World Bank and IMF austerity plans generally stressed a reduction of government outlays for social services, basic needs subsidies, etc. This contradicted the purpose behind the FSLN's "logic of the majority."

9. By May, 1983, Nicaragua had begun 31 new agricultural and agricultural-export projects through co-investment and cooperative projects with other governments. In 1982 the production of sugar, coffee, pork, poultry and eggs had reached record levels, and beans and rice were at their highest levels since 1976. This domestic production helped reduce Nicaraguan imports by 22.4 percent in 1982, although the trade deficit remained high at well over $300 million (CAHI, 5-20-83).

10. According to officers from some of these companies, the FSLN made most of the concessions in these talks. One foreign operation--a gold mine--was nationalized in 1979, however, apparently because it symbolized to the Sandinistas decades of foreign exploitation of Nicaraguan resources. The Neptune Mining Company of New York (52 percent of which was owned by the American Smelting and Mining Company) and the Nicaraguan government agreed to arbitration on tax and accounting questions in 1982. Nicaraguan leaders agreed to pay the company $3.7 million plus interest over a six-year period for minerals seized during the nationalization process (Audett and Kowalewski, 1983).

Information for this section was drawn from interviews with officials at the Nicaraguan Foreign Trade Ministry and the US Embassy, Managua, 1985.

11. See Stavenhagen (1981: 218).

12. For a refutation of the Kissinger Commission's thesis that Sandinista Nicaragua's economic performance was dismal and bore all the negative experiences of "Marxist-Leninist" models, see Conroy (1985b).

13. These figures and other comments credited to E.V.K. Fitzgerald in this section are from his oral report on the Nicaraguan economy presented at the Latin American Studies Association meetings in Albuquerque, New Mexico on April 18, 1985. Dr. Fitzgerald has been senior economic advisor to the FSLN since shortly after they came to power in 1979.

# 4

## The Domestic Opposition
## and External Actors

Internal and external determinants of foreign policy may not always be easily differentiated for their effects on policy due to the interaction or linkage between these factors. Particularly in the case of the poor, economically penetrated state or in the case of military aggression on the small state by a larger power (i.e., short of declared war), external actors will greatly influence the course of events through their influence upon or their interaction with local constituent or power groups. Economic dependence is the result of, among other things, the linkages between external (political and) financial actors and core groups in the world economic system and internationalized elites or bridgeheads in the dependent society. This linkage is based on the coincidences of interests between local dominant classes and international actors, although in Latin America these interests or their policy implications are increasingly being challenged by local, historically dominated groups. The linkage is reinforced by the history of long-standing relations between the hegemonic power--the local superpower-- and the dependent state.

In Nicaragua, the United States had established political and military dominance over the dependent society through both military interventions and occupations--in 1909; from 1912 to 1926; and from 1926 to 1933, to cite the most recent direct US actions. Washington had also politically manipulated the Liberal and Conservative parties, the poles of political activity during the period. In the Somoza years after 1933, the United States exerted political influence through military aid and relations with the Somoza family as well as through financial and corporate channels. The US Embassy in Managua was a major conduit for cementing these ties and directly expressing US interests.

The coming to power of the Sandinistas signalled the end of this special relationship and the end of a foreign (or domestic) policy that would necessarily be identified with the interests of the dominant economic classes. The geographical and historical proximity of the local superpower, however, meant that the abrupt change of direction under the Sandinistas--considered by Washington to be a direct challenge to the traditional US prerogative in the area--would be resisted or undermined. This proximity encouraged the resistance of the Nicaraguan business bourgeoisie to the revolutionary project of structural change. Washington's rejection of the revolution's methods and goals gave the local bourgeoisie little reason to attempt a coming-to-terms or an assimilation into the new mixed-economy, nationalist model of the FSLN. Meanwhile, the local superpower also sought out other in-country constituent groups to use or manipulate in its efforts at undermining the revolution "from within." The Atlantic Coast Indians, and in particular, the Miskito Indians with their long history of resistance to any Managua "Spanish" government, became such a proxy group for the United States from 1981 onward. Similarly, the Reagan Administration and conservative and right-wing groups in the United States made attempts to bolster the political and social standing of the Nicaraguan Catholic Church hierarchy--a group opposed to the Sandinistas.

Another type of internal - external linkage that became relevant to the Sandinistas' effort to project a positive regime image to international supporters--one aspect of any state's foreign policy--was the relationship among the Vatican, the Nicaraguan Catholic Church hierarchy and the Sandinista government. Both the Frente and the local church hierarchy took their cases to Rome for mediation or for approval and both El Papa's 1983 visit and his statements regarding Central American and liberation theology, at least indirectly, influenced the course of Nicaraguan revolutionary politics. US political forces also played on church-related issues and on the issue of "religious persecution" in pursuing broader US objectives. They thereby further exacerbated the strain in church and church-state relations. Within the United States, however, the opposition of major church organizations and other groups to US Nicaraguan policy robbed the Reagan Administration of the public support it needed to act more directly against the Sandinistas.

In this chapter, then, I discuss the role of external actors in influencing local constituent groups, and, the impact of these local political opposition sectors in affecting the Sandinistas' perceptions, international policy options and behavior.


THE NICARAGUAN BOURGEOISIE

Competing Perspectives

Although some in the traditional (landed) elite class and many in the newer monied middle class joined in the insurrection to oust Somoza, few from the old or newer bourgeoisie supported a revolutionary program that would over time narrow its political and financial pre-eminence.[1] Arguing that the existence of the private sector would be guaranteed, the Frente pledged that the state sector would be clearly delimited. However, the private sector was publically warned not to expect a share of political power; its role in the new Nicaragua was to help in reconstruction and economic development. Having no illusions about the inevitable clashes between its anti-imperialist and nationalist - socialist perspective and the goals of the bourgeoisie to preserve its own privilege in the post-"Somoza mafia" period, the FSLN used its political hegemony to restructure the economy. The Frente nationalized banks, trade and credits and by so doing reduced the economic options of the business class. In July, 1981 and giving expression to frustration with the private sector's poor economic performance, the Sandinistas introduced: a stringent law against decapitalization; an agrarian reform law; a decree expropriating thirteen major private firms; and a law allowing the expropriation of property owned by business people who were out of the country for more than six months. At the same time Daniel Ortega vented some of the Junta's anger with a reluctant business class, denouncing "...unpatriotic investors and producers who have decapitalized factories and farms, who in 1978 under Somoza invested 1,260 million cordobas and now hardly manage to invest 589 million cordobas." Implying that the business sector was trying to force its will on the country, Ortega charged: "This is a private sector that is consciously playing with fire, that wants to destroy popular power to impose the power to rob and oppress the workers" (quoted in Gilbert, 1985).

The actual economic situation suggests that the businessmen often reacted to the _Frente_ more on the basis of its language than on the basis of actual regulations or laws (e.g. see Gilbert, 1985). Official policies appeared to be designed to maintain room for business profits to the extent that, as Fagen (1983: 132) argues, decisions not to participate in the Sandinista program could clearly be seen as motivated by class interests and a political intent to undermine the new state.

The bourgeoisie perspective was that the _Frente_ could not be trusted and that its long-term objective was to establish a Marxist-Leninist, communist state in Nicaragua. For them, the economic and political future under "popular hegemony" was uncertain at best unless the revolutionary program was replaced by a (Western-oriented) democratic, pluralist, and capitalist system. This group, which had been in direct dialogue with the FSLN through the US Embassy both before and after the July 19 Triumph, was greatly encouraged by the election of Ronald Reagan in November, 1980 and his well-publicized distaste for the Nicaraguan revolution. By that time, moreover, a bourgeoisie coalition of opposition to the government was operative, consisting of middle class bourgeoisie, the publishers of the newspaper _La Prensa_, the Catholic Church hierarchy and the bourgeoisie political parties.

It was not long before open antagonism surfaced between the FSLN government and the private sector. A number of clashes occurred, for example, between workers--who expected immediate improvements in their living and work conditions after the revolution or who wanted their own land on which to produce--and the land or factory owners and managers (e.g. Colburn, 1984). While the FSLN did not condone or encourage spontaneous work stoppages or property seizures, it also did not have the full administrative capacity to stop them. Using negotiation, calls for sacrifice and patience, arrests and punishment, and new labor regulations, the FSLN attempted to address the situations as they arose. In some instances and when it was in a position to do so, the _Frente_ sided with those making up the social base of the revolution--the poor peasants. New small farmers, meanwhile, were organizing politically in support of the FSLN and were receiving advantageous farm credits. Land ownership structures were changing due to agrarian reform. Such events in turn led the business sector further to distrust the

government's expropriation policy and to interpret poder popular as
an undermining of its' and management's authority in the labor
arena.
   In May and June of 1980 an armed clash occurred between the
FSLN police and one group from the business opposition--the
Democratic Action Front (FAD)--which had begun a program of armed
harassment of the FSLN.  FAD drew its members from those same
business bourgeoisie groups which the United States had
traditionally encouraged with financial and political support.  In
June, FSLN police broke up FAD by force and arrested some of its
leaders.  Another leader, Jorge Salazar, died in a shootout with
police.  Salazar had led the traditionally powerful Union of
Nicaraguan Agricultural Producers and had served as vice-president
of the central business organization, the Superior Council of
Private Enterprise, (COSEP).  Investigations uncovered an arms cache
and links between FAD and ex-Guardia members in exile in Honduras.
Beyond heightening tensions between the Frente and the business
opposition, this incident also increased the Sandinistas' concerns
about a counter-revolutionary organization linking the internal
opposition to Somocista counter-revolutionaries based in Honduras
and Miami, as well as to the US government.  This same suspicion led
the FSLN in early 1983 to occupy and take over the Coca Cola plant
in Managua on the charge that its owner and manager, Adolfo Calero
Portacarrero, was using company profits to fund the Honduran-based
FDN contras, a charge given legitimacy by Calero's assumption of a
top FDN position shortly thereafter.
   Despite these and other instances, the FSLN continued to assert
its support for a mixed economy model of development:  "We want to
create a country where social classes can coexist.  The bourgeoisie
has its future guaranteed in this country as never before....We have
never wanted to get rid of the bourgeoisie.  We do not want to do it
now.  We are not going to do it" (Commandante Bayardo Arce, MH,
8-14-83).

The US Role

   The United States had not been sitting idly by waiting to
assess the true nature of the Sandinista revolution; traditional
forces having labelled it as inimical to US interests, plans for
overt and covert actions were set in motion during the Carter
Administration as early as 1978 to enhance the political fortunes of
the middle class business sector in Nicaragua.  In addition to
clarifying the nature of pressures operating on the FSLN government,
then, consideration of the US role also provides a broader context
for viewing the FSLN - business sector relationship.
   The Washington foreign policy community saw a healthy private
sector as the means to the United States' brand of political
pluralism and to the continued integration of Nicaragua into the
capitalist world economy.  For example, a US Embassy official in
Managua referred to COSEP (the Nicaraguan bourgeoisie's council) as
the bellweather of the United States' role in Nicaragua.  In the
rating of embassy assignments, the embassy in Nicaragua was moved
from the lowest to the highest rating after the FSLN Triumph.  The
Carter Administration signed a finding that US interests were at

stake and authorized the CIA to fund "friendly" groups in Nicaragua such as unions, newspapers, political parties, and individual business people. A later New York Times report confirmed that the Reagan Administration had inherited a CIA program with a budget in the low millions which involved mainly sending money to "moderate elements." Besides these unspecified covert funds, the United States during the Carter and Reagan Administrations sent money to these same sectors through AID (Agency for International Development) pipelines and programs, disregarding its earlier policy in Nicaragua of not giving funds to expressly political groups. Monies distributed through the US Embassy went to COSEP and its affiliated organizations and to other groups in political opposition to the FSLN.

The aid program under Carter followed the reasoning of men like Assistant Secretary of State for Inter-American Affairs Viron Vakey. He testified to the House in late 1979 and early 1980 on the issue of a $75 million reconstruction aid package to Nicaragua that increasing the business sector's capacity to operate was the United States' best leverage to insure moderation in Nicaragua and to reduce the influence of the USSR or Cuba. The testimony of another witness, a former CIA operative and regional consultant, Dr. Cleto Di Giovanni, on the other hand, presented a preview of what would become policy under Reagan. Di Giovanni argued, in effect, that the FSLN was Marxist and that the United States should withhold aid at that time to prepare for later taking advantage of "disenchanted elements" in Nicaraguan society when the credibility of anti-Communist, Nicaraguan exile forces became established (House Committee on Foreign Affairs, 1980). Indeed, AID monies in this period went to the opposition paper La Prensa--undoubtedly in addition to covert funds--and to the Social Action Committees of the Moravian Church, the church of the Miskito Indians (McConnell, 1983). These and other aid links were to come under greater FSLN suspicion in 1982 as US-sponsored hostilities against Nicaragua--involving former National Guard members, Miskito Indian fighters and other political opponents to the FSLN--became public knowledge.

The structure of the $75 million aid package approved by Congress for Nicaragua in 1980 made US concerns about the revolution clear. It allocated 60 percent of the funds for the private sector (for purchases from US companies) and included another $5 million grant which provided operational and scholarship funds for groups which also happened to be in political opposition to the revolution. Although the Reagan Administration, upon coming to office, cancelled the last $15 million installment of that loan, it did not dismantle the covert programs which aimed to bolster the private sector, the Catholic Church, and their organizations. President Reagan kept the overt AID grant monies for the private sector--a portion of the $75 million loan--intact. The FSLN, however, suspicious about US intentions vis-a-vis Nicaragua, stopped this money from coming into Nicaragua in late 1982, charging that it was being used to undermine the revolution and to sponsor groups with counter-revolutionary intentions.

In the face of US pressures -- such as attempts by the United States to foment discontent through the US Embassy--the FSLN became less willing to cede political space to its domestic opponents. As one FSLN official put it in 1981: If the Reagan Administration forces us to the wall, either directly or through their class surrogates who surround us, we will have no choice except to go on a war footing. And if we do, its questionable whether we will be able to create the political and pluralist space which many of us hope this revolution will have (quoted in Fagan, 1983: 137). By 1982, moreover, some in the business sector began to feel that hostile US rhetoric and actions were counter-productive to preserving a society with pluralism. For example, an editor at La Prensa labelled Reagan policies "stupid" and cited them as the cause of a harder FSLN line (NYT, 2-15-82). When Nicaragua's Ambassador to the United States, Fiallos Navarro, resigned in December, 1982 he also decried US policy in support of the contras and stated that the revolution was irreversible (NYT, 12-13-82).

In order to assauge the bourgeoisie's concerns and encourage continued production, the FSLN held a number of national dialogues with the business community and the parliamentary and non-parliamentary opposition political parties during the 1984 electoral period and into 1985. The FSLN wanted to maintain channels of access to the productive sector even though it had shown its determination to maintain political hegemony over this class. But it was also clear by 1984 that the Catholic Church hierarchy had become the leading voice of opposition to the Sandinistas, for a variety of reasons. A number of business leaders had exiled themselves to the United States, Costa Rica and elsewhere and other leaders quit Nicaragua in 1982 and 1983 to join the US-sponsored contras -- among them Alfonso Robelo and Adolfo Calero. These moves were spurred by the loss of the bourgeois private sector's political and moral legitimacy--in the eyes of many Nicaraguans--after the Salazar affair and several other incidents. But this sector was also frustrated watching its political fortunes decline under popular hegemony. Economic austerity, the contra war and the limitations on non-essential imports, in addition, reduced the standard of living to which this sector was traditionally accustomed. The national military and economic situation also led to reduced space for political criticism.

The United States, meanwhile, worked through the domestic and the external (contras) opposition to further undermine the political system in Nicaragua. The United States played on fears that the FSLN would be successful in further institutionalizing the revolutionary system through legitimizing elections. By 1984 and 1985 a process of polarization and political radicalization was well underway among business and other opposition sectors. Whereas in 1982 some in the bourgeoisie had called on the US to temper its hostility, by 1984 some in this sector privately and others openly supported the intent of US policy and tied their futures to the success of that policy. As US hostility against the Sandinista government increased, and, as the Reagan Administration interest in undermining that government became clearer, the pro-US sectors also showed less interest in finding a modus vivendi with the FSLN.

## The US and Nicaragua's 1984 Election

It is important to clarify the key role played by the United States in 1984 and 1985 in shaping the internal and external opposition to the Sandinistas. This critical period represented a watershed for both US-Nicaraguan policy and for the Sandinista revolution. For both countries it was an election year, and for both countries the US-sponsored contra war was at a critical juncture. From the perspective of US policy, the contras had not shown decisive capabilities--they had not taken a city, let alone a large territory; Congress had shut down contra funding in August, 1984, while a new vote scheduled for early 1985 presented the administration with another opportunity to meld support for its Nicaragua policy. Moreover, in efforts at winning a policy consensus among the public and Congress, the administration had to present the Nicaraguan elections as a "sham" and the FSLN government as illegitimate and Marxist-Leninist ("totalitarian"). A major policy path being pursued at this time by the administration--as an alternative to Congressionally unpopular covert aid to the contras--was uniting and legitimizing the Honduran-based FDN contras and the Costa Rican-based ARDE contras, linking them with prestigious (Nicaraguan) civilian political opponents of the FSLN based in and out of Nicaragua, and then openly funding this "government-in-exile"(see Chapters 5 and 6).

From the Sandinistas' perspective, the contra war and US economic aggression by 1984 had brought the Nicaraguan economy to its knees. A major new political offensive was necessary to recapture international support and to eliminate any excuse for US military intervention. Similarly, a new military effort was necessary to crush the contras. Besides expanding its military capacity against contra incursions through a military draft and improved training, in early 1984 the FSLN announced a series of political initiatives, including presidential and parliamentary elections scheduled for November 4, 1984--two days prior to US presidential elections. The Sandinistas saw the elections both as further institutionalization of the revolutionary process and as a defensive move against the US charge that the FSLN was an illegitimate government without popular sanction. The elections were to serve both as a move toward political consolidation of the revolution and as a major foreign policy initiative. Moreover, the Frente saw the current period of economic and political crisis as the time for the domestic political opposition to, in essence, either fish or cut bait: to show its patriotism by working, competing and dialoguing within the revolutionary process; or otherwise, to resign itself to having no organized political voice in Nicaragua if its political intentions aligned it with elements attempting to change the system by force. The FSLN wanted to consolidate revolutionary achievements up to that point, gain legitimacy for new permanent political institutions and move into a "second phase" of the revolution. More significant to the Sandinistas' concern for the defense of the revolution, the electoral period served to mark the battle lines among the contending political (and military) forces in and out of Nicaragua, to clarify the political positions of domestic opposition groups and to demonstrate the role of the United States in shaping the internal political climate for the Sandinistas.

The positions and activities of the internal opposition and the external counter-revolutionaries are illustrative of how, during the 1984-1986 period, the United States both manipulated the image of Nicaragua in the international arena and worked to prepare the way for ousting the Sandinistas' from power. Pursuant to its objective of presenting Nicaragua's elections as fraudulent, the United States pressured the Western-oriented opposition parties to withdraw from the campaign and/or to demand that the FSLN negotiate with and allow the participation of the armed contras, an event which would thereby legitimize the contras as power-contenders in Nicaragua. For example, Conservative Party leaders charged that in July, 1984 US Ambassador Harry Bergold offered them "operational funding" if they would turn down campaign monies -- monies offered by the Nicaraguan government to all the parties under the electoral law -- and pull out of the electoral process.[2] According to other sources, the US Embassy employed several avenues in attempts to deprive the Sandinistas of electoral competition (e.g. LASA, 1985).

The participation of one candidate in particular--Arturo Jose Cruz--was presented by the United States as a key to the legitimacy of the election process. Arturo Cruz, a friend of Eden Pastora and Alfonso Robelo (who were both with the armed rebels by 1982) had served under the Sandinistas as the director of the Central Bank and then as Nicaragua's ambassador to the United States until he became disenchanted with the direction of the revolution in 1983. Cruz had earlier worked as an economist for the OAS and had lived in Washington for nearly thirty years; he was one Nicaraguan American policy-makers knew and trusted. To the Reagan Administration, Cruz was a respectable alternative to the FSLN and was a man known and liked by the US Congress. For the purposes of US policy, Cruz was a friend around whom a post-Sandinista government could be formed.

While Cruz had not lived in Nicaragua for many years and was not politically active there, he came back onto the Nicaraguan scene in 1984 when one group from the domestic opposition sought him out as its presidential candidate. That group, the Coordinadora (CDN), was an alliance of three small Western-oriental parties and their business and labor affiliates. Members of the CDN -- for example, COSEP, the bourgeoisie business sector -- were precisely the people the United States had kept contact with since the days of Somoza's political demise. As a US Embassy source in Managua put it in 1985: "Our contacts with [the domestic opposition] are very good--too good" (author interview). And it was this group that was most vehemently opposed to a system based on popular hegemony. Nevertheless, although the CDN had contacted Cruz about being its candidate, it waivered on the issue of whether or not to field a candidate or to take its chances against the FSLN and other opposition candidates, thereby lending credibility to the election process.

As one major component of the Coordinadora, the bourgeoisie sector represented by COSEP opposed both participation in the elections and any accommodation between the Frente and its domestic opposition. Giving further evidence of its hardening position, COSEP blamed Sandinista economic mismanagement for the economic

situation and business' lack of investment confidence. Downplaying
the role of US economic and military aggression, the CDN-COSEP group
reflected the stance assumed by the Catholic Church hierarchy (i.e.,
by a majority of the bishops) of not acknowledging or condemming US
policy aimed at undermining the FSLN government.  The bourgeoisie
joined the church and the United States in 1984 onward, calling upon
the FSLN to dialogue with the armed opposition under the mediation
of the church--a dialogue the FSLN at that time saw as treasonous, a
capitulation of its sovereignty.

Cruz himself took up this position in July, 1984 saying he
would not participate in November unless the Frente agreed to a
cease-fire, talks with the contras and guarantees of freedom to
campaign throughout the country.  In August--in a move that aimed at
painting the contras as reasonable people, at lending increased
world attention to Cruz's (i.e., the bourgeoisie's) political
fortunes, and at forwarding US objectives at the same time--Adolfo
Calero of the Honduran-based FDN (Nicaraguan Democratic Front, the
largest contra group) announced, and Cruz then reported, that the
FDN would not insist on talks with the FSLN, but that it would abide
by any accord between the Nicaraguan government and the domestic
opposition.  The FDN promised a cease-fire if, among other things,
"serious talks" were underway, if the FSLN released political
prisoners and if it allowed foreign observers to monitor the
November elections (NYT, 8-16-84).  The FSLN interpreted the FDN
position as mere political posturing.  Among domestic critics, Cruz
was the best known internationally.  Yet the domestic opposition was
not united; nor did the bourgeoisie CDN-La Prensa group have broad
backing in Nicaragua.

In the next weeks, ignoring the dates for legal registration of
candidates and again taking actions that also couched US objectives,
Cruz and the CDN introduced a series of conditions for their
electoral participation.  They initiated a campaign to win
international support for their cause.  In fact, Cruz visited
Ecuador, Venezuela, Costa Rica, Colombia and El Salvador in
September and returned to Nicaragua saying all these governments
shared his dissatisfaction with the FSLN.  According to Cruz, these
states supported his cause and feared that there would be a "crisis
with all of Central America" if the Sandinistas remained in power
(NYT, 9-14-84).  Cruz's posturing was thus consistent with US
strategy for winning contra funding from Congress--i.e. winning
regional support for US policy or, at least, regional condemnation
of the Sandinistas.

What was notable about the CDN demands was that 1)they
reflected all of the concerns the United States had raised about the
revolutionary process and the conditions the United States had
placed on improving relations with Nicaragua, and 2)they proposed
changes so sweeping that, if conceded, would amount to a dismantling
of the revolution by the revolutionaries.  The CDN conditions
included:  that the FSLN hold a national dialogue with the CDN and
others to establish a new electoral law and a later election date;
that the FSLN end the military draft, allow complete press freedom
despite the military emergency and establish local political
automony; that the army and police be separated from FSLN control;
that government support for Sandinista mass organizations be

terminated; that the government halt the expropriation of farms and businesses; and that voting booths near military installations be moved. A number of the conditions challenged the very philosophy and structures of the revolution, or, policies adopted for its defense. Given the CDN's international links, the United States' promotion of the CDN's cause and the focusing of the CDN's campaign on the world front rather than on the Nicaraguan political scene (where neither the CDN nor Cruz had broad mass support), the FSLN was necessarily cautious in its response, taking care to protect its own international image. Aware of the United States' posturing on this issue, the Frente announced that Cruz could register beyond the deadline and it yielded on important issues that did not challenge its sovereignty: moving voting booths, significantly widening press freedoms, allowing the opposition to inspect vote lists and welcoming foreign observers to monitor the elections. However, the CDN refused to say whether it would participate in November. While the United States and COSEP pressured Cruz and the opposition parties not to run, President Betancur of Colombia, the Mexican government and the Socialist Internationale (SI) tried to mediate a settlement between Cruz -- who had indeed gained the world media attention -- and the FSLN, hoping thereby to pave the way for his participation in the election. As late as one month before the elections, the FSLN and Cruz were in contact through mediaries to find a solution. This was, in fact, a tribute less to the determination of the contending parties than to international groups (outside the United States) interested in a political settlement of Nicaragua's conflict.

## Political Polarization: The Legal and Illegal Opposition

While the FSLN had significant motivation for reaching some formula for the CDN's participation and for offering concessions to Cruz, there was reason to be suspicious about the sincerity of Cruz and the CDN during this period. CDN statements, its negotiating position and its eventual refusal to participate suggest that the broader aim of the Coordinadora, in conjuction with US policy, was to discredit the FSLN internationally. CDN officials in August and September had said their purpose was to discredit the elections and to force the FSLN, under international scrutiny, to make political concessions before a national political contest where the people would decide political fates. Some CDN leaders went so far as to say that what they really needed to discredit the FSLN was "Arturo in jail". Cruz himself argued that the CDN was the only legitimate Nicaraguan opposition to the FSLN and that the election would be legitimate only if the CDN participated. Meanwhile, La Prensa, whose editors were aligned with the CDN and COSEP, portrayed the non-FSLN, democratically-oriented parties as Sandinista collaborators for staying in the race. Ultimately, deciding not to participate meant that Cruz's popularity in Nicaragua would not be tested. Apparently sensing by September that they would not do well electorally, CDN officials expressed the hope that economic conditions would "tip the balance" in their favor in 1985 (NYT, 8-26-84).

Its political position served to align the CDN with the

principal US policy thrust at the time--to legitimize the military campaign of the counter-revolutionaries. Indeed, this tie to the contras was openly confirmed in the months prior to and following the November elections. On October 30, after a meeting with US Secretary of State George Shultz, Arturo Cruz emerged saying "The contras are our esteemed fellow citizens who chose the route of war" (LASA, 1985: 28). Earlier in 1984 Cruz had told Congress that support money for the contras should be continued so long as the FSLN was obtaining military aid from the Soviet Union and Cuba. In 1985 Cruz lobbied Congress for contra funds and in February personally visited contra camps in Honduras and Costa Rica. Lending evidence to the FSLN argument that Cruz had now become the link between the domestic CDN and the armed counterrevolution, Cruz, in a speech aired over Radio September 15 from Honduras, said he had come to the camps as a symbol of unity. He praised US policy and the heroism of the FDN fighters and called on God to go with them into battle. FDN (contra) leaders meanwhile announced unity agreements which had been proposed and arranged by the United States (CAHI, 3-12-85; BI, 3-21-85). Nevertheless, in order to win international support in the future, the United Nicaraguan Opposition (the contras and CDN) would have to convince the world that theirs was a uniquely Nicaraguan organization, that it had a broad base of support inside Nicaragua, and that it had a democratic agenda under a united leadership. On those terms, US officials hoped, other states might be convinced to join the United States in challenging the sovereignty of the FSLN. This, however, would prove to be an impossible political task.

That the principal Coordinadora players (including the La Prensa group) had explicitly moved to separate themselves from the legal political or parliamentary process in Nicaragua, as well as from other political opposition groups in Nicaragua which had chosen to work within the system, became clear during the first half of 1985. By that time their actions indicated they had given up on reform or compromise through political dialogue. In 1985 CDN leaders worked essentially in tandem with US policy objectives in an effort to forestall peace initiatives (such as Contadora) which recognized the FSLN as a sovereign government, to legitimize the contras, and to sell its political wing--made up of the old business bourgeoisie leaders--as the rightful heirs of the Triumph and the only hope for a democratic future. The lines between the non-parliamentary opposition (CDN) and the contras on the one hand and the FSLN (especially) and the parliamentary opposition (to an extent) on the other were being clearly drawn. In January, 1985, for example, an FDN radio broadcast from Honduras rejected..."pacifist speculations which go against the interests of the Nicaraguan people. We will never accept any peace drawn up behind our backs under which the present Sandinista government remains in power in Nicaragua" (NYT, 1-10-85).[3] The Sandinistas in turn condemned the contras and labelled the non-parliamentary (the extra-legal) political opposition as a right-wing group that could only say what it did not want--revolutionary change--while hiding its true objective of overthrowing the Nicaraguan government.

Another event in February, 1985 demonstrated the chasm between the Frente and the business bourgeoisie and the hardening demands of

CDN members. It also displayed the determination of the Sandinistas to maintain communication with this (non-parliamentary) sector despite its own assessment that COSEP and the CDN had thrown their lot in with the counter-revolution. In a four-hour government-initiated national dialogue with President Ortega and FSLN officials, Enrique Geyer Bolanos, president of COSEP, presented the bourgeoisie's position to the government in the form of five bottom-line demands (BI, 2-28-85; CAHI, 3-5-85). The demands reiterated Cruz's conditions and included the US, CDN, and Catholic hierarchy demand that the FSLN politically recognize and negotiate with the armed rebels. Such talks were to be held under the auspices of the Nicaraguan Bishops' Conference or the Latin American Bishops' Conference (CELAM), a group currently under the leadership of conservative bishops. Because Contadora (the Latin American peace initiative) was stalled at that time, this call for talks with international guarantees took on some legitimacy even though it purposely discredited the internal economic dialogue that the Frente had reinitiated with local producers--the bourgeoisie--after the elections.

While the government-private sector meeting served to reaffirm the desire of many business people to stay and produce in Nicaragua under some guarantee of a future for the private sector and with some privileges restored, it also renewed the FSLN's fears that at least part of this sector was closely aligned with external forces set on its overthrow. Yet, as in the second half of 1984, the Frente expressed a willingness to pursue solutions with the bourgeoisie in each of its five major contention areas, save on the final point. Indeed, the FSLN took pains after the elections to re-publicize its commitment to the survival of a mixed economy as a matter of internal, historical and geographical necessity, pledging "...to provide incentives and security to the private sector" (Agriculture Minister Wheelock, quoted in LASA, 1985).

The depth of inter-party mistrust and the political alignment of the CDN and COSEP leaders with the contra effort blocked any genuine dialogue between these groups. Clarifying the nature of political pluralism in Nicaragua under the Sandinistas, President Ortega set the limits for the opposition: "As long as these groups do not identify with, take the position of or join the mercenary forces who assassinate our people, they will have the opportunity to work politically in this country" (BI, 3-21-85). In fact, business organizations continued to meet and publically criticize the FSLN. And, not all business people were ready to capitulate to an overthrow strategy: whereas Bolanos of COSEP--who was a former advisor to Arturo Cruz--was calling the Frente's refusal to talk to the rebels "a strategy of war and holocaust" (effectively the United States' position), other businessmen expressed the attitudes of many who opted to work within the system and to dialogue with the Sandinistas: "We have our own ideas and we won't give up" (NYT, 3-31-85).

## The United Nicaraguan Opposition

As opposition rhetoric concerning Nicaragua continued to heat up from early 1985 onward, Reagan Administration policy revolved around forging unity among military and civilian opponents to the FSLN, among them Cruz, Pedro Joaquim Chamorro--the La Prensa editor who had left Nicaragua late 1984, and others. The objective was to create a "democratic coalition" or a potential government-in-exile to which overt monies and recognition could be given. This process would be in lieu of "covert" funds for a not-so-secret war against Nicaragua, an effort from which Congress had wearied. The exiled civilian opposition, with ties to both in-country CDN leaders and the bourgeoisie-turned-guerilla fighters (Calero, Robelo, etc.), began working with US officials to draft a democratic program for Nicaragua which could be publicized and used as the basis or rationale for open US backing when conditions were ripe. While Cruz and Chamorro, identified by the United States as key private sector democrats, were positioning themselves closer to US policy and the armed counter-revolution by touring the United States and Western Europe with requests for money and political support, the other task--uniting the contra groups under one coordinated body--proved more difficult. Pastora's continued refusal to tolerate the Somocista Guardia element in the FDN, and, political differences among the opposition leaders complicated the process. While ARDE's Alfonso Robelo had joined the Honduran-based FDN and Adolfo Calero under great US pressure in 1984, Pastora had consistently resisted. The other anti-Sandinista leaders decided to move ahead under the banner the United Nicaraguan Opposition without this one-time popular revolutionary hero.[4]

In March, 1985 the various opposition leaders--excluding Pastora and Brooklyn Rivera, a Miskito leader who was holding his own talks about a cease- fire and autonomy plan with the FSLN--signed a document in San Jose, Costa Rica introducing themselves as a united democratic front and posing an ultimatum to the Sandinistas. The Frente's last chance for coming to a "peaceful solution" with their opponents would expire April 20, 1985. If the Sandinistas did not agree to talks under the document's conditions by that date, Calero challenged, the "...coalition will dedicate [themselves] to an all-out effort, political, diplomatic and armed, against the Nicaraguan government. The Sandinistas can come to the bargaining table by invitation or they can come by force" (NYT, 3-20-85). The conditions, similar to those pressed earlier by Cruz and the CDN, included a dissembling of the current Nicaraguan political system--for example, the National Assembly, the military structure and electoral laws would be dissolved.[5] This was the first time since 1981 that the United States was able to cajole the bulk of the exiled civilian and armed opposition formally to join--even if tenuously after many years of leadership squabbling--and to sign a document proposing a post-Sandinista government structure. The move were also designed to put pressure on the "loyal opposition" inside Nicaragua and to present to Congress a potential alternative to covert contra funding.

Back in Managua, the San Jose events led the Interior Ministry to direct CDN members to cut their ties with Arturo Cruz and Pedro Chamorro or "suffer the consequences" (NYT, 3-10-85). The fact that, as a US Embassy analyst in Managua confirmed, the CDN was politically aligned with the external, armed opposition, had many ongoing ties with the external opposition and saw themselves merging with UNO at the appropriate time, made the _Frente_ suspicious of any political move by this non-parliamentary opposition. CDN leaders in Nicaragua, however, denied any links to the contras, saying Cruz had signed the document as a private citizen and that their's was a "civil struggle within the political system." The FSLN, nonetheless, accused the CDN of plotting with Cruz and the CIA to provoke the Nicaraguan government into arresting Cruz or, alternatively, to make an attempt on Cruz's life, blame the FSLN, and thus spark an international event discrediting the Sandinista government (_BI_, 3-8-85). To preclude such an occurrence, the FSLN barred Cruz from returning to Nicaragua, where he had planned to brief the domestic opposition on the San Jose document.

US-inspired events had again created a situation in which the FSLN felt compelled to tighten the reins on its opposition. Later the same month another US move fired the Sandinistas' sensitivity to its internal political opponents. The Reagan Administration's National Endowment for Democracy gave _La Prensa_ a $100,000 grant to guarantee the existence of this impoverished press. The political importance of this move rested not only in the relatively hefty-size of the grant, but on the fact that _La Prensa_ supported and repeatedly printed Reagan's charges against the _Frente_. Moreover, while the Reagan Administration ignored press censorship in ally Latin American and Third World states, censorship had been an important issue used in rationalizing US policy against the FSLN. Not so ironically, the grant was given at a time when Nicaraguan government officials were talking to the _La Prensa_ group about easing censorship or removing it altogether. No doubt, both governments' moves had been motivated by the 1985 debate over contra funding in the US Congress.

## A US Peace Offer

Although the San Jose document-signing event was touted by the Reagan Administration, it was not effective in turning the tide against the Sandinistas either in Congress or among other countries. With Congressional leaders promising a rejection of the President's request for renewed military funding and Costa Rica's refusal to allow the newly-united contras permission to remain in Costa Rica or hold a press conference after the two day opposition meeting, President Reagan tried another highly publicized tact in April, 1985 intended to gain momentum for administration policy. Reagan announced a "peace plan": the United States would stop military aid to the contras and call a cease-fire if the FSLN would negotiate with the rebels by June 1, under the mediation of the Catholic hierarchy. The FSLN should agree to hold new internationally-supervised elections, end "repression" of the press and church, send home its Eastern bloc advisors, reduce the size of its army, etc.--demands paralleling those made earlier by the opposition and which the FSLN had already rejected on the grounds of national sovereignty and US imperialism. Under the plan, if the FSLN did not comply the United States would use the $14 million request already presented to Congress to renew military aid to the contras.

As one senior administration official put it at the time, these were conditions that were "utterly impossible" for the Frente to accept; Reagan officials were making foreign policy based purely on domestic political considerations. The Reagan "peace plan", in fact, turned out to be another move accepted neither by Congress nor by foreign governments such as the Contadora states.[6] Nicaraguan Foreign Minister D'Escoto seemed to size up the ultimatum as many saw it: "Ronald Reagan has said drop dead or I'll kill you." Secretary of State Shultz wasted no time in replying, "We'll give them a little more time to think it over" (NYT, 4-7-85). Shortly thereafter reports began circulating that US officials were openly discussing invasion plans. Meanwhile Shultz and others told Congress that if the contra effort failed, there was a real possibility that US troops would have to be used against Nicaragua.

At the same time, the administration continued its campaign to shore up the international image of the contras, urging them to establish a code of conduct and draft a document affirming democratic goals and civilian control over the fighters. These US efforts continued into 1986; but, lingering leadership disunity, poor performance in the field and reports of contra abuses and scandals also continued seriously to affect the US contra program.

In Sum. This rather detailed account of events surrounding the 1984 Nicaraguan election and the months following demonstrates how closely linked were internal and external factors operating on Nicaragua's domestic and international political environment, and, on Sandinista policy options. US actions led in 1984 onward to tense domestic politics in Nicaragua and to a clear polarization between supporters and opponents of the revolutionary process. Among the supporters of the system were those who wanted at least to share power with the Frente, if they could not win the votes to replace it; who wanted some revolutionary programs reformed or legally checked; or who openly embraced the structural changes accompanying the revolution and FSLN rule. The opponents were those who had rejected the premises upon which the revolution was based; had rejected popular revolution as inherently Marxist, totalitarian and brutal; or had decided to hold out for and work to facilitate a US-supported over-throw of the Sandinistas, the implementation of a pro-US regime and a restoration of their pre-revolution class and power positions. The opponents, some of whom had earlier been part of the "loyal opposition," were forced by events in the electoral period to make a decision regarding their stance toward US policy and the contras. US policy gave no room to non-FSLN parties who chose to work within the revolutionary system.

While these events may be interpreted as a policy failure on the part of the United States--most groups which had problems with FSLN rule nonetheless chose to work within the system as it had evolved, and, soundly rejected both heavy-handed US interference and US support for the contras--the events also produced increased pressure on the FSLN in the international arena. This had been another objective of US policy-makers. In the world spotlight because of broad interest in the first Nicaraguan elections since the revolution, and because of US charges of a fraudulent, undemocratic election process, the Sandinista government was forced to expend great energies explaining its electoral system and political practice to visiting groups and aid-giving countries.

Much political energy was spent defending the Nicaraguan process against increasingly hostile charges from a Washington administration intent on investing political capital to show the elections to be a "sham", or, insignificant to the future of politics in Nicaragua. Indeed, a number of governments held back on commitments to the Nicaraguans in 1984 preferring to await the results of the election period and assessments of its fairness. Nevertheless, the FSLN demonstrated a capacity for flexibility and pragmatism in addressing opposition demands in this period. Most importantly for the Frente's international image, the Sandinistas were able to conduct elections--assessed by independent groups as the cleanest in Nicaraguan history--in the midst of national economic, political and military difficulties which were clearly being fueled by the local superpower.

The heightened political polarization within Nicaragua, inspired largely by US maneuvering from mid-1984 to mid-1985, was manifested in late 1985 and 1986 in an increasingly confrontational stance on the part of both the Catholic hierarchy and the CDN-COSEP-La Prensa bourgeoisie. Again taking cues from uncompromising anti-Sandinista rhetoric in Washington, the traditional monied class in Nicaragua openly taunted the FSLN, provoked government responses and tested emergency restrictions. For example, as part of a broad effort to tighten its national ranks, COSEP planned for a convention in Managua "dedicated to the memory of Jorge Salazar"--an early anti-Sandinista conspirator (LNSN, January, 1986). An affronted FSLN banned the meeting. In conjunction with the bolder political role being played by the church hierarchy in this period, the Sandinistas perceived the bourgeoisie's activities as contributing to the possibility or creation of an internal front which could be manipulated by the United States as part of its counter-revolutionary activities. The October, 1985 broadening of the national emergency must be seen in this light.


## THE MISKITO INDIANS

> The Somoza dictatorship never made the slightest effort to bring education or health to [the Atlantic Coast] population. Tuberculosis decimated lives and illiteracy blotted out minds. Neglect was the policy toward the Miskitos. We wanted to resolve this historic backwardness, having a great deal of will, but with little knowledge. We committed errors, many errors, many times no account was taken of the cultural particularities of the Miskitos....Such errors were committed in good faith; they were taken advantage of by the bad faith of the counter revolution.
>
> Tomas Borge, Interior Minister
> 1984

Another constituent group in which the United States took interest in efforts to promote the idea of an indigenous groundswell against the Sandinistas and to discredit the FSLN internationally was the Atlantic Coast Indians, approximately ten percent of the total Nicaraguan population. In 1981 onward, US policy included 1)propogating misinformation about the FSLN's relationship with the costenos as part of a wider anti-Sandinista campaign and 2)playing on historic Indian animosities toward the "Spaniards" in Western Nicaragua in order to recruit counter-revolutionary fighters for its covert operations against revolutionary Nicaragua.

## Atlantic Coast History

The swampy and tropical forest Atlantic Coast region--actually the Department of Zelaya, sub-divided into Zelaya Norte and Zelaya Sur--makes up the eastern half of Nicaragua's territory and is home to six different ethnic and language groups. Among these the Miskitos, numbering about 67,000 in 1981, constitute the predominant ethnic minority. The Atlantic Coast was never effectively incorporated economically or politically into the official Nicaraguan state; its isolation was maintained by the Somozas, who nonetheless managed to reap financial reward from the region's natural wealth. Differentiated ethnically and historically from Western Nicaragua, the Atlantic Coast Indians had stronger cultural, church and economic ties to US church and corporate sectors than to any Managua government. Accustomed to years of paternalism on the part of the Somozas (who gave money gifts to the Miskitos' Moravian Church), US corporations and US church organizations, the Miskitos came to identify with their foreign employers and external cultural - economic systems. Little concept of Nicaraguan nationalism existed among the costenos, for whom the village was their nation. The coastal populations were socialized early on to foreign influence and control: the British arrived in 1560, followed by German missionaries of the Moravian Church by 1850. US economic activity, introduced shortly thereafter, soon comprised about 90 percent of all coastal commerce. While British influence appeared mainly in language and social structural practices, the Moravian Church and its teachings became the unifying factor among regionally dispersed Miskito villages. At a time when US economic penetration had already transformed Mosquitia into an export enclave--where profits were expatriated by corporate investors rather than being reinvested in infrastructure or for development--US church groups took the responsibility for the Moravian mission in 1916. Indeed, it was not until 1974 that the administrative structure of the church was entirely in indigenous hands (CIDCA, 1984: 13). At the center of community life, the church maintained strong links to US groups and church teachings were also heavily influenced by US sentiments and visions. For example, the strong anti-communism that took root among the Miskito Indains and other costenos in the context of US paternalism was a convenient entree for anti-Sandinista contra recruiters in 1981 onward who also played on historic suspicions of the Managua government.

On the economic side, meanwhile, by 1930 and due to its status as an export enclave, the Atlantic Coast (Zelaya) was in a state of constant depression and was even more underdeveloped and dependent than Western Nicaragua under its various US-supported administrations. Having no resources or authority to build their own industry or other bases for a self-reliant economy, Miskito workers often left their villages for meagre wages in the few commercial and mining centers. Those left behind in the undeveloped, less-than-fertile, rural areas cultivated food crops, sold small surpluses, but also soon became dependent for food, clothes and supplements from their Western benefactors. Local petty bureaucrats politically administered the territories, while a pattern of class and ethnic domination created an internal colonialism that put the Miskitos under English-speaking, lighter-skinned Creoles and relegated them to the lowest skill-requiring jobs (CIDCA, op. cit., 15; Bourgois, 1985: 211). The Somozas, who bought some support in Zelaya through their charity donations to the Moravians, and the National Guard were not very active in Zelaya, even though Sandino had recruited some fighters and support there in the 1920s and 1930s. Interestingly, Sandino's movement represented the first nationalist, political linkage between the Western and Eastern territories within Nicaragua.

## The Revolution and the Miskitos: "Awakening the Giant"

The Sandinistas' original goals regarding the Atlantic Coast peoples--goals set forth in their original 1969 political program--were to end their exploitation, develop agriculture, fishing, forestry and the like, end years of racial discrimination and stimulate the development of local culture. In short, the Frente wanted both to develop the resource-rich Atlantic Coast and to integrate Zelaya into the Nicaraguan political economy. After 1979, studies were being done by new government ministries to assure culturally appropriate and economically feasible development projects for the Zelaya Department. It was the Sandinistas' intention to incorporate these peoples as equal citizens and to integrate the Atlantic Coast economy into the Nicaraguan political economy through the revolutionary program. Having little experience with the coastal people and having done essentially no political work in Zelaya as they had elsewhere in Nicaragua since the 1960s, however, the FSLN had not predicted the levels of apprehension, suspicion and outright hostility they met when they went with enthusiasm to bring the revolution to the Zelaya. Differences in cultural, historical and world views between the FSLN and the costenos actually assured animosities between these groups.[8] Although it is probable that those differences could have been worked out over time among FSLN, Moravian Church and local leaders, US policy aimed instead at creating an armed confrontation between the Miskitos and the Sandinistas.

## The Miskitos in US Policy

Aided by its experience with and research analyses of ethnic minorities as agents for its policy in other parts of the world, the United States under the Reagan Administration was quick to manipulate local suspicions and grievances to forward US policy objectives vis-a-vis Managua. A major opportunity to discredit the Sandinistas' world image came in January, 1982. At that time the

FSLN, as a part of its military-security policy, acted quickly to evacuate Miskito communities from the Rio Coco (Nicaragua's river border with Honduras).  The area had been under attack and recruitment pressures for some time by counter-revolutionary forces based in Honduras.  In fact, the United States, with the help of the Honduran military, had worked through a self-appointed, self-exiled Miskito leader named Steadman Fagoth[10] to organize the "Red Christmas" contra military campaign in late 1981.  The purpose of the campaign was to recruit Miskito fighters and, with other Somocista forces, to take control of a large portion of northeastern Nicaragua (Mosquitia).  According to the plan, Washington would then insert a government-in-exile which it would officially recognize. Ill-conceived and without the popular support it would have required, the CIA plan ultimately failed.

The FSLN, nervous about counter-revolutionary movements, and especially in an area that historically was not well integrated into the Nicaraguan state, also expressed concern for the lives of the villagers.  But with state security the primary concern, the Frente relocated 8,000 Miskitos who eventually agreed to the move inland. Another 10,000 Miskitos crossed over into Honduras to escape the FSLN and contra fighting. To ensure that the Indians did not return to the area and that the evacuated villages would not be used as camps by the contras, the Sandinista army was ordered to destroy at least fifty Miskito settlements and towns.  Later in 1982 other Indians were moved by force out of combat areas. Inter-party suspicions grew as a small number of Moravian religious lay leaders and several thousand Miskito peasants joined contra forces and set up camps inside Nicaragua that were coordinated and supplied by the CIA under the local leadership of Fagoth and the FDN (Honduran-based contras).

Tensions increased when in March, 1982 it became public knowledge that the Reagan Administration had formally approved financing for these and other paramilitary forces whose purpose it was to use military means in pursuit of five major objectives: 1)blocking the delivery of social and economic benefits to the Atlantic Coast peoples; 2)blocking ideological change in the direction of support for the revolution; 3)terrorizing those who refused to join the contras or who worked with government programs; 4)sabotaging the economy and 5)undermining the costenos' faith in the government's ability to protect them.  In Managua, the FSLN reacted to this security threat by declaring a military State of Emergency.

Sandinista Human Rights Abuses.  In this context of FSLN security concerns and an escalating contra campaign, there were incidents of human rights abuses--such as beatings, detentions and some killings--carried out by FSLN military against Miskitos.  Human rights investigators later documented that these abuses occurred mainly between July and October, 1982 and near where contra camps were discovered, but that "Measures subsequently taken by the Nicaraguan government to curtail mistreatment of innocent civilians demonstrate that such incidents did not and do not reflect government policy" (CIDCA, 1984: 4).  Many abuses were reportedly carried out by young FSLN militants who were not properly supervised or were motivated by historic racism.[11]  The American Indian

Movement (AIM), whose delegates investigated the relocation situation in late 1981, supported the FSLN evacuation effort and charged that the real danger to the Miskitos came from US CIA regional activities (McConnell, 1983). For example, not only were Miskitos literally being caught in the contra-FSLN cross-fire, but other Indian villages which supported the FSLN were being destroyed or besieged (with deaths resulting) by contras trying to increase their recruits. Similar reports by on-the-scene Moravian Church and political representatives confirmed that no massive abuse occurred at the time of the relocation and that many Indians were relieved to escape the attacks occurring in the frontier region. In the Spring of 1984, the Americas Watch rights commission concluded that rights abuses against the Miskitos had ended, but that problems at detention centers still existed (NYT, 5-6-84). In its 1985 report, Americas Watch reported "important improvement", noting that the Nicaraguan government "has demonstrated sensitivity to criticism of human rights abuses...and had taken measures that directly respond to those criticisms." The Inter-American Human Rights Commission also concluded in early 1985 that Nicaragua had complied with the majority of its recommendations to improve the Miskitos life situation--for example, having to do with facilitating their repatriation to traditional lands and reviewing the sentence of those jailed. Due to "circumstances beyond Nicaragua's control", however, the Commission reported that it could no longer mediate the Miskito situation to a "friendly settlement". The reference was to United States' support for counter-revolutionary groups attacking from Honduras and Costa Rica. A number of international and US human rights monitoring and reporting groups, then, had investigated the Miskito situation, had mediated between the FSLN and the Miskitos and noted that Washington's counter-revolutionary activities greatly exacerbated the situation. None found evidence of mass killings, genocide or systemmatic Nicaraguan government abuse practices.

US Misinformation. The resettlement and human rights issues became central, however, to the United States' misinformation campaign against the revolutionary government in early 1982, a campaign effective in shaping the Sandinistas' international image and in spreading distrust about the Frente's versions of events. In January, 1982 the US State Department announced that 170,000 Miskitos had fled the border zone and in a television interview the United States' UN Ambassador, Jeane Kirkpatrick, said that 250,000 Miskitos had been herded into concentration camps by the Sandinistas. (Recall that the official Miskito population in 1981 stood at 67,000.) Steadman Fagoth, who was working with the FDN and the CIA, announced around the same time that the Frente had murdered 400 Miskitos, that 3,500 were missing and that others were force-marched to concentrations camps. The Washington Post reported an alleged massacre of 200 Indians. And, then-US Secretary of State Alexander Haig, at a news conference, showed a photo from the French magazine Le Figaro which he said showed the Frente burning the bodies of Miskitos they had killed. President Reagan, disregarding heavy death-squad activity in El Salvador and Indian massacres in Guatemala, called the FSLN the worst violator of human rights in Central America.

As it turned out, the United Nations, the Honduran government and Amnesty International all confirmed that no massacre had taken place. The Le Figaro photographer responded to Haig's charge that the photo had been taken in 1978 of the Red Cross burning the bodies of Nicaraguans who had been killed by Somoza's National Guard. In addition, CIDCA (1984: 7) later documented the FSLN's version of the relocation process in early 1982 that children, pregnant women and elderly were airlifted, that no one had been killed by the FSLN on the trek and that new farming areas, not concentration camps, had been the destination. (CIDCA and other groups did not absolve the Sandinistas of all abuses in 1981 and 1983.) The Executive Director of the North American Moravian Church's Board of World Missions, meanwhile, asked Americans to lobby against Reagan's policies of sending arms and recruiting Indians and the Moravian Church of Nicaragua sent the US Congress a letter in 1983 to the same effect, linking US policy to the misery of the Miskitos. By that time, however, the facts had become a casualty to a constant stream of allegations against the FSLN from the United States and President Reagan. The "Miskito issue" lingered for years as a blot against the revolutionary regime. The FSLN, in turn, had to expend much energy defusing these issues in Latin America and Western Europe and to US visitors.

To return to the larger point, an external actor used indigenous groups to narrow the international (and domestic) operating space for the Sandinistas and thereby also directly shaped the Frente's thinking on security and military matters. The larger US goal was to undermine the revolution itself; nor did US policy reflect a sincere concern about the well-being of the ethnic minorities themselves. Instead the United States cultivated its contacts on the Atlantic Coast for strategic, military purposes. For example, US AID monies in the 1979 to 1982 period went to fifty Moravian Church "locals" with whom then-US Ambassador Lawrence Pezzullo said he was in "close communication" (Mc Connell, 1983). Further, a $300,000 AID grant for fiscal year 1982 was earmarked for agricultural cooperatives. But a small number of Moravian pastors used organizational funds to assist Miskito contra fighters in doing political work, recruiting and training. One result of this connection--direct and indirect--between US officials, the Miskitos and the contras was that the FSLN militarized the Rio Coco area in late 1981 and arrested ten Moravian clergy in February, 1982.

More effective linkages existed directly between the CIA and the Miskitos and through Steadman Fagoth, who coordinated with both the CIA and Honduran officials.[12] Under the cover of joint (and later, continuous) US-Honduran military maneuvers from 1982 onward, moreover, the United States moved heavy weaponry and supplies to the Miskito fighters, who nonetheless were reported to be rather undisciplined, ineffectual combatants. By 1982, direct CIA involvement with the Miskitos and a higher level of sophistication in weaponry lead to increased pressures on Miskito communities and to polarization as people had to decide to join the contras, support the Sandinistas or flee to refugee camps in Honduras.

## FSLN Policy Regarding the Atlantic Coast

Given the events in the Atlantic Coast region, the Sandinistas had to develop a new Atlantic Coast attitude and policy in 1982 onward that would effectively meet the demands of a polarized, partially-militarized, partially-exiled indigenous population. The Frente sought also to pacify the Miskitos. This had become a matter of national defense. And, the time was right--the Miskitos had split in 1982 into several factions with different game plans. While Fagoth was identified with the cause of the FDN and was supported by the United States, Brooklyn Rivera first joined the ARDE contras (under Pastora) in Costa Rica, but by 1984 appeared willing to negotiate a solution with the FSLN (see Chapter 6). This position was spurred, according to Rivera, by his determination that the US-FDN-ARDE cause was inimical to Indian interests. According to Rivera, "Robelo told me clearly that he will oppose, always, our demand of land and our automony, that while he is a leader in Nicaragua, he will oppose us strongly. So what would be the hope for the Indian people in the future if the contra would take power?" (BI, 2-14-85).

Insisting on the maintenance of a sovereign Nicaragua, a single nation territorially and politically, the Frente promised in its declaration on indigenous communities in 1981 to guarantee and give titles for the communities' lands within the context of national economic development. The Miskitos' long-standing demands for regional autonomy, however, took on an added sense of urgency in the context of the war and constant US-sponsored military maneuvers near the Nicaraguan border in Honduras. Yet, in 1982 the Frente had publicly admitted that it had moved precipitously against the Miskitos by arresting their leadership, treating church leaders with suspicion and unilaterally planning their integration into the larger Nicaraguan polity. At that time the Sandinistas began studying federal structures which would allow local political and economic autonomy, with Managua retaining sovereignty in matters of defense, international trade and foreign policy. In a test of their flexibility, the FSLN, under Deputy Interior Minister Luis Carrion, began autonomy talks with Miskito contra leader Brooklyn Rivera (of Misurasata) in 1984 and with local and regional indigenous groups in Zelaya Norte and Zelaya Sur. In late 1983, in another move aimed at pacifying the militant Miskitos, the Frente had issued an amnesty for Miskito prisoners and for fighters who would lay down their arms. In early 1985, the prisoner release and amnesty for Miskito fighters was extended, leading an Anglican Minister from Zelaya Sur, Juan Ordonez, to comment: "The Sandinistas have matured a lot since they took power" (BI, 6-20-85).

But the Miskito question for the FSLN was more complex than pacifying a sub-population through direct negotiation and compromise. Beyond the issue of the immediate defense and security of Zelaya was the Miskito demand for a separate autonomy in alliance with rather than being integrated into the revolutionary state, the FSLN's initial vision. The FSLN had good reason to worry that external powers would always try to take advantage of this situation. Moreover, the issue of the Miskitos gaining some kind of territorial autonomy in Nicaragua raised the spectre for other Latin

American states of indigenous peoples demanding similar guarantees. No other Latin American government had conceded this kind of regional political autonomy. The FSLN, however, was forced to address the historic demands in a situation of military emergency. The Frente's bottom-line position was that the sovereignty of one Nicaraguan state under the central revolutionary government be maintained. Yet, the FSLN understood that government from Managua was not viable as the only form of authority. A need existed for a new relationship between the government and the region, despite fears reiterated by Carrion that the United States might try to manipulate autonomy--to break off the area as a foothold in Central America. Separatism had been an issue used by the United States and Fagoth; as such, the FSLN saw it as an artificial demand, one made in Washington and without historical roots in Nicaragua.

In late 1984 and 1985 the Sandinistas took the public position that some autonomy agreement was the responsibility of the revolution vis-a-vis the eight million indigenous peoples in Latin America; the Frente placed the Miskito issue within the total picture of social justice in Nicaragua and thus again trumpeted their revolution as a model for other states. The struggle of indigenous peoples was subsumed into the total revolutionary struggle.

Although talks were on-and-off between Rivera and the FSLN, Rivera agreed not to join with the CIA and acknowledged that Indian issues could only be addressed within the context of the revolution. When Rivera began bulking in the talks in 1985, and as Fagoth remained with the armed contras, many Miskito groups essentially rejected both men as representative of Miskito interests and began negotiating with the Frente directly. Through 1985, local leaders and activists in Zelaya Norte and Zelaya Sur met with an FSLN commission under Luis Carrion and later, Interior Minister Tomas Borge, in their churches and work places to debate the nature and form of Atlantic Coast autonomy. In the second half of 1985, Miskitos began moving back to their traditional homeland around the Rio Coco with the FSLN's blessing and pleas for international resettlement aid. Belgium, Sweden, France and others responded.

In sum, the United States' policy vis-a-vis the Miskito population had begun to unravel at least by 1983 when it became clear to many Miskitos and international human rights groups that US policy was detrimental to Indian interests. During 1985, moreover, the majority of Miskitos demonstrated a clear preference for working out a political solution with the Sandinista government. In early 1985 Sandinista and Miskito rebel leaders--who now had a harder time recruiting Indian combatants--worked out a cease-fire arrangement for much of the Atlantic Coast region. The Sandinista army withdrew its units from Miskito villages and allowed the Indians--including rebel leaders--to return and resume controlling their own affairs. Although several violations of the truce were reported by both sides in the next year and while the FSLN government remained concerned that anti-revolution or separatist rebels might renew military operations, a shakey cease-fire was holding into mid-1986. While the United States initially scored a propaganda coup against the FSLN, the FSLN's instincts for survival and flexibility, along with international support and attention,

allowed it to move the issues into negotiations. The FSLN appeared
to score its own coup, in fact, by identifying the cause of
indigenous peoples with the revolution and offering itself as a
model for Third World states facing similar indigenous populations
in the national context of dependence. In practical and immediate
terms, however, the Frente sought a national structure that afforded
increased security.

THE CATHOLIC CHURCH

Because of its importance in the lives of most Nicaraguans, and
given its international structure, the Catholic Church has been
another channel through which external actors have tried to
influence the course of the revolution in Nicaragua. In this
section I briefly examine the potential for external influence,
potential created again both through the existence of common
interests that linked domestic and foreign groups and by the FSLN's
sensitivity to church issues and criticisms. Without giving full
analysis or discussion to the issues that have festered between the
Catholic hierarchy and the FSLN, I outline the central concerns of
each major party to illuminate where and why external actors have
exerted influence, directly and indirectly, through and upon the
Nicaraguan Catholic Church. Once again, the United States
government and US groups figure prominently. But the Vatican and
regional church organizations have also influenced the Nicaraguan
hierarchy during the post-1979 process of transformation in
Nicaragua.

The Church Hierarchy's View

    The Catholic Church in Nicaragua--and in Central America
generally--is a complex and ideologically divided organization which
interacts with the people and with government at a number of
levels.[13]  Church and FSLN organizations and officials in Nicaragua
have contact or interact, for example, in community or development
projects and at local, regional and national levels. But tensions
between the FSLN and the Nicaraguan Catholic Church--more accustomed
to a fatalistic and passive body of believers--have surfaced,
particularly in Managua, as many priests and nuns used the vehicle
of the revolution to implement the Medellin (1968) and Puebla (1978)
Latin American church calls for a ministry to the majority poor and
oppressed. This "liberation theology" was spreading in popularity
in Latin America in the 1970s and 1980s and was being met with
increased concern and scepticism in Rome. It was most fully
articulated in Nicaragua where a theology of liberation was
invigorated by a revolution based on the "logic of the majority."
In Nicaragua, the traditionally conservative hierarchy had to
confront both a government that employed Marxist concepts and
priests who were political activists on behalf of their
parishioners. This, during a period within the Catholic Church
world-wide in which liberation theology was often being challenged
or warily tolerated.[14]  The situation was ripe for tensions between
both domestic and international religious and political leaders.

Whereas the majority of Nicaragua's ten bishops supported Archbishop (later, Cardinal) Obando y Bravo's fears that the revolution had undermined and would continue to undermine the authority of the official church hierarchy, the majority of the priests and nuns in Nicaragua were foreign, felt loyalty as well to their own orders and were somewhat less sympathetic to concerns of the local bishops. Many of these, including the bulk of the eighty-six North American Catholic religious, had been in support of the Sandinista revolution, as had the independent Maryknoll, Dominican and Jesuit orders (CARIN, November, 1984). These groups tended to support the "popular church" or the "church of the poor" by ministering to the communidades de base (Christian base communities) and working in support of government programs. The tension between the traditional church and the popular church of liberation theology was exacerbated by the presence of four Catholic priests in top government posts after 1979. For example, Miguel D'Escoto, a Maryknoll priest, accepted the post of Foreign Minister.

While the body Catholic in Nicaragua had come to be split about evenly between the "church of the hierarchy" and the "popular church," there were three discernible streams of thought within the Central American church on the "spectre of communism" issue as it has been pursued with new vigor since 1979 by the United States and its regional allies (LAWR, 9-9-83). The anything-is-better-than-communism (read Marxism) group is numerically the smallest but holds probably the greatest power and money influence; its ties historically are to the traditional elite classes. A second group supports neither communism nor the United States' regional militarization, but instead looks hopefully to an electoral (Western, pluralist) solution to regional instability—a political practice, however, with no tradition regionally. This group may be the largest group, and, when pressed, prefers alignment with US solutions over Marxist influence. A third group is willing to run any risk to end social injustice, even if it means socioeconomic dislocations and challenging the church hierarchy or the church's traditional clientele. This group is animated by the communidades de base and has often refrained from even legitimate criticisms of revolutionary activity. Not surprisingly, these streams of thought within the Catholic Church parallel hemispheric and extra-hemispheric political positions on the Central American situation and events in Nicaragua after 1979.

The Nicaraguan church welcomed Somoza's overthrow and indeed had given its blessing in this instance to the taking up of arms as the only remaining means to ending Somoza's brutal rule. In November, 1979 a pastoral letter from the bishops had endorsed the FSLN's plans for a transition to Nicaraguan socialism, a sovereign Nicaragua free of outside control and an end to capitalist dependence (see e.g., Dodson and Montgomery, 1982). However, by 1982 it was clear that the church hierarchy did not subscribe to the projecto politico of the Sandinistas as it had unfolded. Nor had the Nicaraguan bishops fully accepted the mandates of Medellin and Puebla.

Archbishop Obando's preferences for post-Somoza politics were for a "third way" between leftist and rightist solutions; he hoped for politics along a Western, capitalist, Christian Democratic model and was theoretically and actually allied with the political objectives of COSEP, the Nicaraguan Social Christian Party and later the CDN.[15] After its fact-finding trip in 1981, for example, the Pax Christi international human rights group gave its assessment of church-state relations in Nicaragua, noting the political (not theological) nature of the antagonisms:

> The church of the political opposition seems to us to be almost exclusively linked to the party politics of the Social Christian Party and to [COSEP] headed by Alfonso Robelo. It also plays an important role in the American strategy aimed at destabilizing and overthrowing the revolution....The interwoven relations between the hierarchy and the political opposition have been growing considerably. As a result, Archbishop Obando was given a more and more political role. In the opposition newspaper, La Prensa, he is almost daily played off against the FSLN. Although the bishops accuse the FSLN of 'politically instrumentalizing' the Christians, they themselves are, in no modest way, instrumentalized by the opposition....(quoted in Hynds, 1983: 7).

Besides being used by the political opposition the hierarchy itself did a number of things that were seen by some observers as explicitly political and as constituting persecution by the hierarchy of religious who were identified as supporters of the revolution. A 1984 US National Council of Churches report of a fact-finding trip looking into church issues in Nicaragua concluded that it found no evidence of systemmatic, government-supported persecution of the church (Catholic or Protestant). However, it reported numerous examples of the transfer or forced isolation of priests and communities sympathetic to the FSLN. Numerous religious, priests, nuns and lay workers were removed from duties or sent abroad by the hierarchy, in what the US NCC saw as another form of religious persecution.

Moreover, the NCC cited what it saw as the most fierce form of religious persecution taking place in Nicaragua: US-backed counter-revolutionary forces regularly targeted for attack churches and church leaders with a commitment to the poor. Similar stories of congregations disbanded, churches destroyed, and church- and government-related development workers killed by the contras were reported by Catholic and Protestant church groups in Nicaragua.

## The Hierarchy in Political Opposition

As the Frente initiated structural change and as bourgeoisie opponents of the FSLN identified increasingly with US policy or the armed counter-revolutionaries, the hierarchy too became more politically vocal and hardline. It indicated an unwillingness to dialogue or negotiate differences with the FSLN. The church hierarchy's position was that there was no historical precedent for, and therefore little hope of, a collaborative relationship between the Catholic Church and a leftist, revolutionary state. To the bishops, revolution meant persecution of the church. This was an historical inevitability. Therefore, actual events in Nicaragua mattered little. Thus, by 1984, as the bourgeoisie opposition exiled itself or lost political credibility within Nicaragua (as a result of its identification with US policy, and, as pressure on Nicaragua from the United States mounted), the church hierarchy, and Archbishop Obando y Bravo in particular, came to assume the leadership of anti-Sandinista opposition in Nicaragua (e.g. Dodson and O'Shaunessy, 1985).

The result of five years of mutual distrust between the hierarchy and the Sandinistas was that during the 1984 election year, Obando, though he avoided overtly partisan activity, strongly supported the CDN's political objectives in his sermons and statements, all of which were reported in-depth in La Prensa. He thereby gave important sustenance to opponents of the Frente (e.g. NYT, 10-25-84; 11-18-84). For instance, Obando led the criticism of the 1983 military draft law, repeatedly questioned the legitimacy of the FSLN government, and argued that the Frente was not seriously seeking peace in Nicaragua. Meanwhile, Obando refused to acknowledge the US role in the contra war, or, the suffering resulting from contra attacks. In mid-1984 the US and other media reported meetings between Obando and US businessmen. Obando sought financial support for his plans to create church-sponsored neighborhood groups to compete with the FSLN's CDSs. Similarly, Obando sought to enlist the support of external church sectors, like the Vatican itself, regional church bodies such as CELAM (the Latin American Conference of Bishops) and US churches, in his condemnation of the FSLN. By so doing, Obando enlarged the scope of the church-state conflict in Nicaragua and squarely placed it in the international political arena.

Another major turning point in terms of the hierarchy's identification with the political program of the United States, the CDN and the contras came in the bishops' 1984 Easter letter to the people of Nicaragua, published after a brief delay by the FSLN in La Prensa and the pro-government papers. Entitled a "Pastoral Letter on Reconciliation", the Easter letter laid the blame for the war situation in Nicaragua on internal causes, rather than assessing blame against the hostile designs of the United States. It called for government talks with the contras whom the FSLN viewed as merely proxies for the US cause. (The FSLN position was that it would talk only to the force behind the contras--the contras' "boss", the United States.) The letter, meanwhile, did not acknowledge the FSLN's December, 1983 amnesty (reconciliation) offers to the contras, it ignored direct US military involvement against Nicaragua -- such as the mining of the harbors -- and it indicted the revolution for spreading a materialist ideology that repudiated the church.

The FSLN and a broad cross-section of the Nicaraguan people saw the letter as partisan and provocative rather than as a genuine call for reconciliation. Worse, the church, which argued traditionally that it be separate from politics, was again seen as squarely having taken sides with CDN and US policy objectives and against the revolution and the FSLN. The effect in Nicaragua was further to polarize church and government communities, making any negotiations much more difficult. Political lines had been drawn. As the Latin

American Studies Association report concluded in 1985 about prospects for reconcilation between the church and the Frente: "There are elements of the church hierarchy--including, perhaps, the Vatican--who view the FSLN government as a weak, unstable regime; a regime without a future. So why should they waste time negotiating with it? Until the church hierarchy recognizes that the revolutionary process here will endure, the prospects for reconcilation are poor" (LASA, op.cit.: 41).

Similarly, the United States exacerbated and sustained the church-state confrontation by making clear both its view that the revolution was reversible and its readiness to assist groups in undermining the process. Indeed, the Vatican and the Nicaraguan hierarchy appeared over time to adopt the position that with the United States' help, the revolution could be reversed. In any case, these church sectors had decided that they could not or would not oppose US aims vis-a-vis Nicaragua.

## The FSLN View

In its "Document on Religion" of October, 1980, the FSLN reaffirmed its "commitment to religious freedom and respect for the religious sentiments of the Nicaraguan people." The nine-point document emphasized that religion and public profession was a right of conscience for all citizens and that in recent Nicaraguan history Christians and the institutionalized churches had acted as forces for justice.[16] Moreover, the document defined the FSLN government as a lay government which should not participate in church discussions; religion was left as a matter for the churches. This document reflected the reality 1)that the church had influenced the development of the FSLN and the broad alliance front against Somoza and 2)that the Sandinistas were aware of and sensitive to the importance of the churches' role and influence in both international and domestic affairs.

In deference to the role played in the insurrection by church members and clergy and cognizant of the importance to the revolution of support from church sectors, the Sandinistas in 1979 asked four Nicaraguan priests to serve in social and foreign policy posts in the revolutionary government. While the traditional church in Nicaragua, the hierarchy, frowned on the priests' participation and called on the Vatican to act, the Foreign Minister, Father Miguel D'Escoto (1983: 18) explained his participation as a way to promote Christian values during the process of social transformation. The priests in government represented the progressive element of the church (those committed to the Medellin and Puebla mandates) which sought to democratize its structures, make the church more relevant to the lives of the majority poor and empower, politically and economically, the traditionally oppressed. In this view, there was no contradiction between the revolution and Christianity. The Archbishop group, while it stood fast against Somoza in the insurrectionary period and had a commitment to increased social justice in Nicaragua, nevertheless was suspicious both of socio-political initiatives that required structural change or that challenged the prospects, ideological assumptions or international alignments of the church's traditional elite constituency. The hierarchy was similarly suspicious of what it saw as the corollary implications of liberation theology: a dissemination of power and initiative downward.

Clashes--mainly rhetorical but including incidents between Sandinista militants and hierarchy supporters--began when the hierarchy became critical of the FSLN's use of Marxist rhetoric and symbols and of its widespread mobilization and politicization of the Nicaraguan people, processes actually well underway by the time of Somoza's overthrow. Differences among and between church and Sandinista groups over ideological perspective and over the revolution's goals and character fueled feelings of uncertainty and mutual mistrust. In an atmosphere of FSLN experimentation with a nationalist, mixed economy development model, the formation of class (bourgeoisie) opposition, and increasingly intense US hostility after Ronald Reagan's inauguration, relations between the church hierarchy and the state also became highly charged. On the international level, the Reagan Administration began citing "persecution of the church" as one justification for its hostile policy vis-a-vis the Sandinistas.

## The Bases of FSLN Suspicions: US-Church Links

Much of the FSLN's nervousness about (traditional) church sectors or the Nicaraguan Catholic Church itself becoming direct or indirect agents of US policy was based on knowledge of earlier experience in Latin American history. The CIA had used religious groups for its own purposes on a number of occasions--for example, in Brazil and Chile--and had contributed to divisions and persecution within the Catholic Church by financing conservative church groups and training police in anti-subversion techniques. Latin American governments' suspicion and persecution of clergy involved with liberation theology and social justice issues among the poor (especially in the 1970s and early 1980s) was indirectly encouraged by anti-revolution and anti-subversion rhetoric in the United States. For example, shortly after the Latin American Bishops meeting at Medellin in 1968, Nelson Rockefeller--the governor of New York who had national aspirations--had warned of the potential for subversive penetration in the region under the guise or practice of liberation theology (e.g., Lernoux, 1982). Reagan Administration supporters also took up this theme.

FSLN suspicions of the church hierarchy's objectives grew as links between the bourgeoisie and the church and US policy were first assumed and then became clear in 1983 and 1984. Obando's public affinity for US-inspired political models led the FSLN to believe that the hierarchy might become a channel for US subversion. In one instance, the government presented evidence--rejected by Obando--that a priest close to Obando was trafficking in weapons for the counter-revolutionaries. During 1982, the Frente charged politically conservative evangelical sects operating in Nicaragua with launching a "silent invasion" in conjunction with the CIA. More reticent at that time about making similar charges against the Catholic hierarchy, the FSLN was yet convinced that potential for such links existed among conservative Catholics who tended to be wealthy, from the bourgeoisie class, Western-oriented and pro-US.

Suspicions about a US design to encourage Catholic disenchantment towards the revolution were reinforced in 1982 when the State Department and its Assistant Secretary of State for Human Rights at that time, Elliot Abrams, leveled charges of religious persecution against the FSLN and called on US bishops to speak out against the FSLN in Nicaragua (WP, 8-21-82). Inside Nicaragua, the political opposition--namely the La Prensa-bourgeoisie private sector group--kept this US charge alive by hailing the Archbishop as a "martyr" and a "prophet." Political divisions between the FSLN and the hierarchy sharpened, while theological discussion within the church was effectively coopted by the hierarchy.

By 1984 and after the Bishops' Easter Letter on Reconciliation, the FSLN openly labelled the hierarchy traitorous and in collusion with a "plan of internal destabilization" (NYT, 4-26-84; 5-8-84). In the Frente's view, the church was using religious symbols and authority during an electoral period for political purposes and in support of the US-aligned CDN. The FSLN placed further restrictions on religious rallies which might be used for political ends and expelled ten foreign priests from Nicaragua in mid-1984 when these restrictions were ignored. The FSLN move was roundly criticized in the international media, by several Latin American states and by the Vatican. Several incidents in 1984, then, caused church-states relations to sink to their lowest level.

In the broader context of strained relations with the COSEP-CDN opposition, intense US military and economic aggression and defense concerns, the FSLN wanted to mend fences, or appear to do so. It stressed once more the idea of national unity talks. To that end, the FSLN renewed earlier efforts to initiate a dialogue with the hierarchy. At the same time, a government delegation travelled to Rome for discussions with the Vatican on church-state relations in Nicaragua. While relations remained tense through 1984, at the end of the year the church agreed to new talks. After a four-hour private meeting between President Ortega, other FSLN people and church officials, including Obando, the creation of a joint commission to define, study and propose solutions for points of conflict was announced.

Talks in 1985 nevertheless produced little movement toward mutual trust, but instead reflected the fact that a lowering of church-state tensions in Nicaragua was ultimately dependent upon a coming-to-terms among the major contending parties--the United States, the contras and the FSLN--and between competing world-views. The church hierarchy had demonstrated its determination not to make a separate peace with the FSLN, but to pin its hopes on a regime change facilitated by the United States and the contras. Yet, for both parties the existence of a forum for dialogue was useful in itself. From the Frente's perspective, such dialogue was important for its image at home and abroad as well as for national unity. It was also the case that some in the FSLN still held hope of finding a modus vivendi with the church hierarchy that would effectively neutralize the church as a political actor in the FSLN - United States stand-off.

Now-Cardinal Obando tried to present himself as a neutral actor and potential disinterested mediator in 1985. Regular meetings with government officials added some legitimacy to this image and to the idea that the hierarchy could mediate any FSLN - contra talks in the future. Yet, while he claimed to support the need for sincere dialogue between the FSLN and the contras, he also continued to give moral and religious sustenance to the armed opposition. For example, during a US stopover in Miami in May--Obando was returning from his investiture in Rome--the new Cardinal held a mass for exiled Nicaraguans and contra leaders. Contrary to the image of a neutral hierarchy, moreover, Obando and a majority of the Nicaraguan bishops continued to support US objectives for Nicaragua without condemning the US role in the contra war. More disturbing to the FSLN, in the second half of 1985 and into 1986 Obando undertook a widely-publicized tour of Nicaragua during which he used thinly-veiled ecclesiastical language to condemn the military draft and the revolution itself. The Cardinal discouraged participation in the secular revolution; similarly he appeared to many Nicaraguans to be exhorting young men to resist the military service law. Again, the Sandinistas charged Obando with counter-revolutionary sympathies and political interference.

## External Actors

The US. Though it is difficult to document direct links or coordination between the US government and the Nicaraguan church hierarchy, there are indications that the hierarchy played a role in the Reagan Administration's strategy to destabilize the Sandinista regime. For instance, US AID monies were channelled to the church hierarchy for its programs during 1981 and 1982 until the FSLN disallowed this flow of money for political reasons. Moreover, regular contacts existed between US government officials and US businessmen and Archbishop Obando. For example, Kissinger Commission members spent as much time with Obando and church officials on their 1983 fact-finding trip to Nicaragua as they did with Nicaraguan government officials. The US Embassy regularly scheduled meetings with hierarchy officials for visiting Congress-persons and for President Reagan's second roving Ambassador for Central American issues, Harry Schlaudeman. The Nicaraguan Catholic hierarchy, in other words, had open lines of communication to US policy makers.

Symbolic of its support for the hierarchy's stance vis-a-vis the FSLN and the revolution, the Reagan Administration repeatedly used charges of Sandinista persecution of the church in its wider misinformation campaign against the revolutionary government. In 1985 and when US - Nicaraguan relations were at their lowest since 1979--the United States had broken off bilateral talks, had officially imposed an economic embargo and had labelled Nicaragua a terrorist state--President Reagan sent a warm congratulatory note to the newly consecrated Cardinal Obando.

Common political and economic perspectives tied the Nicaraguan hierarchy to both the Reagan Administration and to US groups of similar ideological persuasion. In its 1980 campaign issue-position papers (referred to in Central America as the Sante Fe Document), the Reagan election team directly linked the well-being of the traditional Catholic Church in Latin America to the well-being of capitalism and liberty there. The document defined political liberty as "private property and productive capitalism," and argued that any other conception of liberty--such as the FSLN's in Nicaragua--was "... less Christian than Communist": "The United States must seize the ideological initiative....The war is for the minds of mankind. Ideo-politics will prevail...." It added, "US foreign policy must begin to counter (not react against) liberation theology as it is utilized in Latin America by the 'Liberation Theology' clergy. The role of the church in Latin America is vital to the concept of political freedom."

Acting out of similar conceptualizations, two conservative US groups that supported President Reagan's Central American policy and wanted to combat the "evils" of liberation theology--the Institute on Religion and Democracy (IRD) and the Heritage Foundation--began public education campaigns in 1981 portraying the Sandinistas as repressors of the church and of Obando in particular. In 1982, for example, the IRD brought Obando to the United States to honor him with a special award. (Recall that the COSEP-CDN-La Prensa groups inside Nicaragua at this time were calling Obando a "martyr.") Financial aid also flowed to the hierarchy from these and other groups. In 1984 the IRD gave the hierarchy a $40,000 grant for its "pastoral work" in 1984.

Conservative US business groups also provided moral support and direct aid to the Nicaraguan church hierarchy, often with the intent of helping to weaken the FSLN and offer alternatives to its rule. For example, officials of the W.R. Grace Company, who in 1983 took the public position that the United States should openly invade Nicaragua to prevent another communist state on the Cuban model, met with Obando in 1984 (NYT, 12-12-84). The discussion focused on forwarding the Archbishop's plans to create community and neighborhood organizations to compete with FSLN organizations. Leadership and religious training was planned to counter the FSLN's "Marxist-Leninist" drift. Obando, according to an internal Grace Company memo, had organized a group of concerned Nicaraguan citizens and now requested money and technical aid such as films and film projectors, which could be carried into Nicaragua "without any problem".[17] As Obando had expressed on other occasion, he feared that uneducated Catholic Nicaraguans might not see the anti-church implications of the Sandinista revolution. His overall purpose, however, seemed more political than theological. Again, the hierarchy, with the United States, believed that the revolution was reversible.

As polarization occurred within Nicaraguan political groups, the church hierarchy emerged as the leading voice of political opposition; the church had become a competing power center. Given its position of traditional moral authority in Nicaragua, the Nicaraguan church hierarchy was a natural channel for US influence and image-management efforts. Since 1981, the Reagan Administration had effectively encouraged and played on internal church conflicts and church-state conflicts in efforts at neutralizing or isolating progressive church forces in both Nicaragua and the United States. But the persecution-of-the-church issue had also been an important rationale offered for the United States' anti-Sandinista policy, a rational that obfuscated both the existence of divisions within the

Nicaraguan Catholic church and the explicitly political nature of
the hierarchy's opposition to the FSLN.

It is important to note, however, that US reactions to the
revolution were not monolithic. Nor did anti-Sandinista campaigns
by the administration or conservative US groups go unchallenged.
President Reagan's Central American policy and especially his policy
toward Nicaragua had come under sharp attack and opposition from
mainstream US church denominations, national organizations and local
churches by 1982. The national bodies of the Lutheran, Mennonite,
Unitarian, Presbyterian, Episcopal, Methodist, American Baptist, and
Catholic bishops passed statements condeming US policy as a "policy
of death" in each year after 1982. In October, 1985 the US Bishops'
Conference called on Congress to legislate "the broadest possible
prohibition" on aid to the contras and condemned Reagan
Administration policy as "incompatible with our commitment to
Contadora" (IHCA, November, 1985). (Similarly, the Latin American
Council of Churches and church groups from Europe had both condemned
US Nicaragua policy and sent aid donations to Nicaragua.) Major US
church groups not only mobilized opposition to Reagan's policies,
but also actively lobbied the administration and Congress to pursue
negotiations in both Nicaragua and El Salvador. National church
organizations and local churches, in fact, represented an important
core of US public opinion against Central American policy. (Into
1986 US public opinion was running over 65 percent against Reagan
Administration policy of supporting the contras.) These expressions
of opposition to US government policy served to delegitimize the
administration's efforts vis-a-vis the contras and CIA regional
activities and were partially manifested in Congressional
unwillingness continuously to fund these activities.

CELAM and the Vatican. Other (non-US) external actors with
international influence also pressured the Sandinistas. In the late
1970s the Latin American Conference of Bishops, CELAM, had come
under the direction of Colombian--the only Latin American church
group not officially accepting the Medellin document--and
conservative bishops. This group had less influence in the large
Latin American churches (such as Brazil's) and thus focused much of
their attention on Central America where the traditional church was
stronger (e.g., Lernoux, 1984: 139). Sceptical of liberation
theology and preferring US-inspired political systems, CELAM's
official view of revolutionary Nicaragua was that it was dangerously
tied to the USSR and Cuba and was close to Marxism; the revolution
was judged to be inimical to the church's long term interests. A
CELAM report in 1982 accused Christians supporting the revolutionary
process of socio-political reductionism, political manipulation of
the faith, undermining church unity and insubordination to the
church hierarchy (Hynds, 1982: 9). Citing no direct or verifiable
evidence of its claims, CELAM nevertheless gave money to support the
hierarchy's new pastoral programs which were directed by loyal
priests. CELAM continued to use its influence in international
church circles to discredit the FSLN regime and to encourage the
disenchantment of the Nicaraguan hierarchy with the Frente.

The Vatican displayed greater reluctance to side publically
with the hierarchy or the FSLN and the popular church. Calling for
church unity, obedience to the hierarchy and hierarchy sensitivity

to the grassroots members' needs, Pope John Paul II in 1982 did not publically support the Nicaraguan bishops' harsh criticisms of the FSLN, but called for a dialogue between the church and the state in search of reconciliation. While the Pope's position on issues of priests in government and liberation theology left him closer to the Nicaraguan hierarchy's (and CELAM's) position, El Papa nevertheless stressed dialogue. He refused to endorse US policy vis-a-vis Nicaragua or publically to challenge the legitimacy of the FSLN regime, something Obando did repeatedly.

Both the Sandinistas and the hierarchy continued to seek the Vatican's support, advice or mediation between 1980 and 1986. On five occasions, the Frente sent high-level delegations to Rome to present to the Vatican its case regarding priests in government and other conflicts with the hierarchy: in October, 1980; in July, 1981; in April, 1982; in September, 1984 and in June, 1986. Though the Vatican assured the church hierarchy that it would not make an agreement with the Sandinistas without the hierarchy's approval, the Vatican through its Secretary of State Agostino Cardinal Casaroli did spend about a week in talks with FSLN delegates on each of their visits (CAHI, 8-27-84; NYT, 9-13-84). In 1986 the Pope met with Vice President Sergio Ramírez. On other occasions Archbishop Obando travelled to Rome, and, after the 1984 Easter Letter controversy, Obando was called to Rome by the Pope for consultations. While much of the talk and mediation by both sides with the Vatican centered on the issue of priests holding political office, the FSLN worked hard to defuse its tense relations with the church as a matter both of practical politics and national defense.

Events suggest that Pope John Paul, while he still refused to take sides publically--for instance, he issued an immediate and sharp denial when President Reagan in April, 1985 told the media that the Pope supported US policy on Nicaragua--by 1984 and 1985 he actually encouraged Obando to maintain his vocal opposition to the FSLN government. Conservative groups within the Nicaraguan church and hierarchy and the Reagan Administration had been working for some time to influence the Vatican to condemn the Sandinista government. For example, in its background briefing paper for the Pope prior to his 1983 Nicaraguan visit, the conservative branch of the church outlined the evils of Sandinismo and presented a strategy for confronting it. The paper asserted: that the FSLN was Marxist-Leninist and as such sought the destruction of the church; that no available evidence indicated that this was not the case or that the Frente would change; that the FSLN would see any concession by the church as a weakness and become more aggressive; that the church should not trust the Frente; and that the Pope should publically embrace the "extremely popular" Archbishop Obando. The Pope was encouraged to coordinate strategy with the Nicaraguan hierarchy and Catholic officials who had experience with communism. Churchmen who opposed Obando, it was recommended, should be removed from their offices.

In the same period, Reagan envoy Vernon Walters flew to Rome to brief the Pope on Central America, and, presumably, to justify US policy in the region. These briefings undoubtedly shaped the Pope's perspective on the revolution in Nicaragua and made him less sympathetic to the FSLN's explanation of events during his painful visit there--an explanation elaborated on and supported by a large number of Nicaraguan and foreign Catholic leaders shortly after that trip.

In May 1984, and not a month after being called to Rome for consultations with John Paul, Archbishop Obando led a Managua rally which "resembled an anti-government political rally" (NYT, 5-22-84). In July, Obando led twenty-seven priests and three hundred people in a march protesting the government's charges against Obando aide, Reverend Luis Amado Pena, of complicity with the counter-revolutionaries. Then, following his elevation to Cardinal in mid-1985 and during a period of increased church-state tensions Obando undertook a nation-wide tour which featured indirect political exhortations. These incidents left little doubt that the Pope had encouraged Obando's increasingly militant opposition to the government.

Finally, the very selection by the Vatican in 1985 of Obando for elevation to Cardinal from among many other Latin American clerics with broader experience or accomplishments, was taken in Latin America, the United States and elsewhere as a gesture of support for the Catholic opposition to the Nicaraguan government. Without making a public statement of support for the hierarchy's position, in other words, the Vatican sent a symbolic message both to the Sandinistas and to Catholics in the liberation theology stream. On the other hand, the Pope had earlier given his blessing to multilateral, regional peace talks and on one occasion in late 1984 offered the Vatican's mediation skills.

For their part, the FSLN extended congratulations to Obando and President Ortega personally visited Obando after the announcement. Yet, the Frente also took note of the lines that again had been drawn and pledged to continue church talks. Given the importance of the church issue to their public image and international solidarity during a period of military and economic emergency, they could do little else. However, in late 1985 and 1986 the FSLN also appeared to be losing patience with the hierarchy's persistent criticism. Sensing a heightened level of internal anti-Sandinista activity among vocal pro-US sectors in Nicaragua, the Frente broadened national emergency restrictions and took action against several unauthorized Catholic church activities which were perceived to be political in purpose.[18]


CONCLUSIONS

Using available channels of opposition the United States government and several other external actors sought to influence the course of the Nicaraguan revolution, the prospects for its survival and the distribution of political power among competing social groups. In so doing, these actors also narrowed political options for the Sandinistas and forced them to expend increasing energies on defusing domestic-conflicts-gone-international for the sake of national unity, defense and international image management. One of the United States' contentions about Sandinista rule, for example, was that it had alienated democratic, peace-loving constituents into spontaneously taking up arms against it. The FSLN used

international forums to refute this civil war thesis, insisting
instead that the United States both created anti-Sandinista forces
and used domestic class, ethnic and religious differences to
exacerbate tensions, giving them an international dimension in the
process.

US policy, bolstered by the political stance of conservative
church sectors, had the intended effects of: widening the scope of
defense concerns for the Frente; creating well-publicized bases for
domestic and international challenges to FSLN political legitimacy;
and necessitating the diversion of skills, resources and energies to
national defense. Opportunities for settling differences within the
Nicaraguan system were narrowed as the United States and other
foreign players offered domestic opponents of the FSLN alternatives
to negotiation and dialogue with the government. Already engaged by
the process of overseeing a revolutionary transformation of its
political and socioeconomic structures, the FSLN was additionally
pressed by armed, externally based and supported opposition groups.
By mid-1983, Nicaraguan domestic and foreign policy could be
characterized as survival politics; national reconstruction programs
had to be post-poned, but the foreign policy emphasis on winning
support from a wide range of states became even more important.

Ultimately, however, the United States was unable to create an
internal front capable of coordinating a war of subversion with the
contras in Honduras and Costa Rica. Indeed, the electoral process
of 1984 showed that the civilian political opposition, save for a
narrow bourgeoisie elite aligned with the United States, preferred
to influence the revolutionary process from within that system. For
their part, the Miskitos were internally split over alignment with
the contras and as it became clear that US and Miskito interests
were not necessarily complementary.

Militarily in disarray, major Miskito groups were participating
in talks with the Frente by 1984 and 1985. Although the Catholic
hierarchy continued to voice its political preference for a
Nicaragua without the Sandinistas, this opposition was significantly
blunted by continuing FSLN offers to dialogue and the existence of a
large popular church in support of the revolution. During 1985 and
1986 Cardinal Obando toured Nicaragua preaching reconciliation among
all Nicaraguans--a reference to the bourgeoisie and US demands for
FSLN - contra talks. Large turn-outs for his masses, notably, did
not immediately transfer into popular anti-Sandinista demonstrations
or activities. Whether Obando's campaign would stimulate mass
opposition to the FSLN in the second half of the 1980s depended,
among other things, on the FSLN's ability somehow to mitigate the
effects of socioeconomic hardships on the Nicaraguan people, and,
its willingness to tolerate what had become only thinly-veiled
anti-revolution messages during a national military emergency.

US policy, including its bolstering of the internal Nicaraguan
opposition, clearly put the Sandinistas on the defensive and slowly
drained the economy. But due to an activist Nicaraguan foreign
policy and adept FSLN political moves at home, US harassment was
unsuccessful in reversing the revolution. On the other hand, US
attempts to build an internal opposition front led to expanded
restrictions on civil liberties such as those announced by the FSLN

in October, 1985. While it did not immediately enforce the
restrictions in a rigorous manner, the FSLN established the legal
framework for confronting in the future anti-regime, subversive
groups linked to the armed opposition.

Experiences with the bourgeoisie, the Miskito Indians and the
Catholic Church nevertheless reminded the Sandinistas and other
Latin Americans of the means yet available to the local hegemon in
attempts at undermining a government that had been judged
ideologically aggressive or other-bloc. Especially in the case of a
dependent society where historical links of common interest existed
between powerful and weak state economic and political
sectors--sectors that in the weaker state were small and
internationalized or paternalistically colonized--the larger power
could maneuver to penetrate, influence events and significantly
raise the costs of nonconformity. It was just such a scenario of
external manipulation or political indebtedness that the Sandinistas
rejected for Nicaragua and hoped to change through their foreign
policy.

## NOTES

1. Gilbert (1985) notes the existence of four entreprenurial
strata on the eve of the revolution: 1)the Somoza group; 2)the Bank
of Nicaragua and Bank of America groups that accounted for
approximately 20 percent of the GNP; 3)the middle bourgeoisie,
represented by COSEP, the Superior Council for Private Enterprise
and 4)the small producers and merchants.

2. According to PCdN leaders Edwin Yllescas and Gustavo
Mendoza in an interview in August, 1985, Bergold told them they
should not go into the elections because Cruz was not participating.
They and their colleagues "turned down Bergold's offer flat",
preferring to work within the new system to check the FSLN and shape
the new constitution. The US Embassy in Managua denied all charges
that it tried to influence the behavior of political groups during
the electoral period, although one analyst suggested these
groups..."may have made decisions about participating based on what
they thought the US wanted them to do" (author interviews, Managua).

3. This was a not-so-veiled threat against the Contadora
process and other initiatives calling for dialogue. It also
reflected the discontent expressed by FDN and ARDE leaders in 1984
and 1985 that the United States treated them simply as agents of US
policy, disregarding the contras' ultimate raison d' etre: nothing
less than the overthrow of the Sandinistas. It was at this time
that the United States broke off the Manzanillo talks with the FSLN
(see Chapter 5).

4. Another "dissident" had been purged from the FDN in
November, 1984. Edgar Chamorro, an FDN leader and spokesperson was
expelled after he openly criticized the United States and CIA over
the now-infamous manuals for guerrilla operations which became
public that fall. Chamorro became outspoken against US contra
policy.

5. The document called for a "just and efficient mixed
economy"; a free press; a "real division of power"; an immediate

ceasefire and amnesty prior to the start of negotiations; the dissolution of most FSLN-created structures; a depoliticized army; the withdrawal of foreign military advisors; the release of the remaining National Guardsmen captured after July, 1979; a reduction in military capacity; and other things (NYT, 3-3-85; BI, 3-21-85).

6. An administration official noted that the plan put Nicaragua into a no-win situation and that Washington's reasoning could follow the strategy used earlier in the battle with Congress over the MX missile: if the FSLN refused to bargain, Washington would justify contra aid on the grounds the Frente was intransigent; if the FSLN gave no clear response, Washington would insist on maintaining its pressure through contra funding; and if the FSLN agreed to talks, Washington would argue that contra funding would keep the Sandinistas at the table (NYT, 4-7-85).

7. In this section on the Miskito Indians and their links to US policy, I draw from interviews with Norman Bent, a Moravian church pastor and church spokesman, in August, 1983 and August, 1985 in Managua; and from the Center for Research and Documentation of the Atlantic Coast (CIDCA) report "Trabil Nani", 1984. CIDCA is an autonomous social science research institute based in Managua.

8. The indigenous peoples viewed the world in ethnic terms after years of racism, exploitation and discrimination. The FSLN saw the world in class and nationalist terms, emphasizing first improvement in material conditions among the costenos and then giving attention to larger structures that imposed ethnocultural discrimination. As the CIDCA (op. cit.) analysis points out, however, the minorities suffer both class and ethnic oppression. FSLN and indigenous struggles were therefore linked. Stereotypes operating on both sides naturally tended to obfuscate common tactical and strategic interests.

9. The US experience during the Vietnam era with the Hmong peoples of Southeast Asia is a recent example. See Bourgois, 1985: 213.

10. Fagoth was a young, charismatic man who had worked as an informer for Somoza during his college days in Managua in the 1970s. A Pentacostalist, not Moravian, he nonetheless gained a Miskito following at the time of the revolution preaching a separatist message. Former colleagues such as Brooklyn Rivera, another Miskito leader, characterize Fagoth as "psychopathic", suffering from "persecution trauma", "totally blinded and sick with power and personal ambition" (Bourgois interview with Rivera, January, 1984). Fagoth was later to break with other Miskito leaders and by 1984 had lost the trust of many Miskitos who came to see him as not representing their interests.

11. On the Miskito and human rights issue see the 1982 and 1983 reports of Americas Watch; and the summary a report of the Inter-American Rights commission report in New York Times (6-8-84). CIDCA (1984) reports the difficulties from language, culture and psychological colonialism in investigating human rights charges. Many reports were found to be rumors, third-hand descriptions and otherwise unconfirmable--reports kept alive by anti-government sentiment.

12. Fagoth visited Washington in February, 1982 under the sponsorship of the conservative American Security Council. The

State Department arranged several meetings for him with Congressional sub-committees where he charged the FSLN with genocide. Freedom House and other conservative organizations funded another trip for Fagoth in December. He met with a range of US policy-making officials on both trips.

13. On church issues see the references in Chapter 2. In this section I also draw from interviews in 1982, 1983 and 1985 with Catholic and Protestant church leaders, workers and scholars in Nicaragua. A 1982 interview with Interior Minister Tomas Borge, in particular, shed light on the FSLN's perspective on the state and religion.

14. Catholic Church leaders equated Marxism with communism and therefore with atheism. Liberation theology was seen by the church hierarchy as 1)fueling class animosity rather than focusing on Christian unity and 2)engendering grass-roots church activism not always under the control of the bishops.

15. For example, see Hynds, 1982; Lernoux, 1984: 138; LASA, 1985: 18. In the 1978-1979 period Obando worked with bourgeoisie and professional groups in attempts at creating an alternative to Somoza or FSLN rule.

16. Jerez (1984: 16-17) argues that the document represented the first time a Marxist-inspired political movement in power contradicted the theoretical perspectives of traditional Marxism which paints religious belief as delusory and reactionary.

17. This nine-page memo from a John Meehan to W.P. Grace was reportedly leaked by a Grace Company employee and was circulated in 1984 by concerned US church-affiliated groups. The contents of the memo describing the meeting with Obando were consistent with public statements on Nicaragua by Grace officials and other media reports about Obando's planning of church-social networks in Managua in 1984. Giving evidence of the extent of preparations made, Obando was said to have referred to a spreadsheet of Managua broken down into small units and detailing specifics on costs and numbers of trainees.

18. In late 1985 the FSLN prohibited the further publication of a new and unauthorized (unlicensed) Catholic Church newspaper "Iglesia". The first issue had contained material openly attacking the military service law. In early 1986 the government shut down Radio Catolica for a period when the station failed to carry President Ortega's New Year message. As in many other Latin American countries, Nicaraguan law requires that the major media carry the leader's New Year message as a public service.

# PART 3

# International Constraints
# on Foreign Policy

# 5

## US Policy Toward
## the Nicaraguan Revolution

Global events, foreign powers and regional realities provide the context to a state's foreign policy. For a small, poor and dependent state in close geographical proximity to a traditional superpower, calculations of foreign interests and tolerance become even more important. For the small state in particular, it has been a fact of political life that foreign pressures will regulate or mitigate foreign policy objectives and behavior. Political, military and economic capacities of the large states, especially when they are highlighted by superpower philosophies of global bipolarity and spheres of influence, yield a continuing potential for direct influence over the affairs of smaller states.

The Sandinistas' foreign policy orientation after 1979 connoted a determination to accept the (inevitable) struggle for independence in foreign policy. Part of that struggle would involve asserting a new basis for relations with the local superpower and finding political and moral support for pursuing new policies from a Third World perspective. Increasing its independence vis-a-vis the United States also meant finding other sources of capital, raw materials, military hardware, etc., and creating new markets. FSLN leaders nonetheless recognized the continuing importance to Nicaragua's development of the United States' assistance, or barring that, of its benign neglect. Nicaragua's primary interest vis-a-vis the United States was in a discontinuation of historic patterns in US-Nicaraguan relations. It was this stance that the United States interpreted as a threat to its geostrategic interests. The US reaction to Nicaragua's foreign policy stance and the threats to the survival of the revolution resulting from that reaction constitute the central focus of Part Three. While US policy has been the single most important external factor shaping Nicaragua's foreign policy, other important factors include the disposition and policy of Nicaragua's Central and South American neighbors toward the revolution. As the United States looked to close off Nicaragua's options and undermine the revolution's survival, Nicaragua looked increasingly to its Latin American neighbors for political and economic support.

## US POLICY DIRECTIONS

Several inter-related themes had shaped US policy toward
popular movements in Latin America. First, in the interests of US
hegemony, succeeding presidents aimed at eliminating nonconformist
or revolutionary examples. The United States historically worked to
maintain its assumed right unilaterally to determine its rights and
interests vis-a-vis Latin America and often, from the Latin American
perspective, disregarding the sovereignty of small states in the
process. US administrations persisted in prescribing for Latin
America one formula for economic growth and development: the
capitalist model of free enterprise, which could be spurred in Latin
America by those states creating advantageous conditions for (US)
private investment.

A corollary to the emphasis on US regional hegemony existed in
the notion that the world was bipolar, pitting Western (US)
interests against Eastern (USSR) interests in a zero-sum game.
Washington came to expect calm and stable politics in its sphere,
particularly in the Caribbean-Central American "underbelly" region,
and, to assume control over events there (e.g., Hayes, 1984). In
the US view, ideological nonconformity, represented by popular,
anti-regime movements in Latin America, constituted a "vicarious
aggression" being waged by the other bloc--recall the Johnson
Doctrine at the time of the United States' 1965 military operation
in the Dominican Republic (e.g. Frank and Weisband, 1976). Popular
movements were not interpreted as having been precipitated by
economic bad times, world recession, high unemployment, unequal land
tenure structures, widening rich-poor gaps, changing class
alliances, government repression, or the like. Instead, political
unrest was explained as subversion instigated by the Soviet bloc.
Local unrest was defined as a threat to the political and economic
well-being of the entire Western Hemisphere.

Tied in with an East-West purview and a concern over spheres of
influence ("backyards") was the unwillingness of the United States
since the 1960s to accept the notion of a "third way" between
Western or Eastern alignment. Reflecting Henry Kissinger's notion,
enunciated during the Allende years in Chile, that nothing important
ever comes from the South, the United States generally denied
credibility to Third World concerns over superpower rivalry and
self-determination. US administrations preferred unrestrained
license for determining when or where Soviet influence needed to be
confronted.

Many of these themes came together in a policy of supporting
friendly (but non-leftist) governments, no matter their political
stripe, with military aid and economic support so long as US private
investment was facilitated there. Movements or governments defined
as hostile to US interests, i.e., as Soviet-instigated or
Cuban-supported, had to be confronted with strength--not
negotiation--and ultimately rooted out of the hemisphere.
Revolutionary movements, moreover, had to be made to look as
miserable alternatives to the status quo.

## The Carter Years

For the Carter Administration, Nicaragua became a test of both its "independent players" policy toward Latin America and its human rights emphasis. That both policies would be discarded for a more traditional stance toward "troubles in our backyard" became clear by the time the FSLN came to power in July, 1979. As it became obvious by 1977 that the authoritarian Anastasio Somoza faced opposition not only from the FSLN leftist guerrillas but also from the more conservative business sector, the Carter Administration pushed its traditional ally to negotiate a settlement with the private sector and thus stablize the political situation (e.g. Somoza, 1980). When instead, an obstinate Somoza unleashed his brutal National Guard to repress opponents, Carter cut back military--but not economic--aid and criticized Somoza's human rights practices. But it was soon clear that because Somoza refused to resign or share power with the traditional, pro-US political sectors, the prospects for an FSLN victory were improving. The FSLN was showing great success in directing and channelling the popular insurrection which arose spontaneously in the last half of 1978. (The FSLN had prepared for an insurrection through its political work in the 1970s; however the Sandinistas had assessed in 1978 that the time was not yet right for moving to that stage.) An August, 1978 letter from Carter praising Somoza's efforts that year to improve human rights in Nicaragua signalled a policy determination in Washington. Carter, spurred by traditionalists and a conservative lobby of Somoza supporters in Congress, would absorb the embarrassment of appearing to support a hated dictator and would press to keep the FSLN out of power. Barring that, the administration would work to limit strictly any FSLN influence in a new government (LeoGrande, 1982). Conservative groups in the United States had labelled the FSLN communist and Soviet-backed; others saw the FSLN as at least an unknown political quantity which might challenge US prerogatives. Pressed with such concerns, Carter worked through bilateral and regional channels in attempts to replace Somoza with a private sector government, and, after sponsoring elections and other efforts, to coopt growing popular discontent. However, Carter's attempts failed. US policy-makers had been blind to local realities that were to bring the Sandinistas to power in 1979.

First, the small private sector bourgeoisie that has been politically active during Somoza's time nonetheless had neither a broad popular base nor nation-wide organizational structure. The Somozas had effectively blocked real political competition from developing in Nicaragua (e.g. Cruz, 1984). The bourgeoisie, moreover, was not unified in its support in 1978 and 1979 for various plans offered by the United States for a mediated settlement with Somoza. For example, though most wanted Somoza himself ousted from power, the bourgeoisie was split over a role for the National Guard in a post-Somoza government. Similarly, they were split in their views of the FSLN. Additionally, to many poor Nicaraguans, the bourgeoisie was guilty for their oppression along with Somoza, the Guardia and their US backers. In sum, the organized political sectors as they existed under Somoza could not compete with the

FSLN.

By 1979 the Sandinistas had organized and waged political education throughout the country and among most social sectors, had supported a popular insurrection in a war of liberation, had offered a detailed political program and had organized themselves into a broad front organization in pragmatic efforts at bringing together all sectors open to social restructuring in Nicaragua (e.g. Booth, 1982). In the international arena, moreover, the Frente had wooed broad support--in the form of weapons and material--from Latin America and Europe. It had waged an international public relations campaign against the Somoza dictatorship. This, then, was the second reality Washington had ignored. The Sandinista Front would be one, if not the only, major political contender upon Somoza's ouster. Yet, the United States had not even made attempts to deal directly with the Frente until just prior to the July 19 Triumph. Washington held onto hopes that it would be able to negotiate a coalition government where FSLN influence would be slight or easily over-ruled (e.g. LAPR, 7-13-79).

Third, the United States was seemingly unaware of the broad support the Sandinistas had in Latin America and in the OAS for overthrowing the corrupt and bloody Somoza government. Although several states, including Venezuela, preferred a coalition government built around the FSLN and other sectors and initially worked with the United States to that end, when the choice came down to a Sandinista government or a US- and OAS-enforced coalition and an OAS military intervention, the Latin American states preferred the former. This situation occurred at a June OAS meeting, where, in an eleventh hour attempt by the Carter Administration to keep the Sandinistas from power, Secretary of State Cyrus Vance maneuvered to keep the FSLN representative from speaking. Vance proposed an OAS peacekeeping force be sent to Nicaragua to impose a cease-fire, block an FSLN victory, and install an interim government to prepare for elections.[1] The proposal was flatly rejected and Miguel D'Escoto, a Catholic priest representing the FSLN, was allowed to address the OAS meeting as part of Panama's delegation. The Latin American states blocked the US initiative, preferring that the Nicaraguans work out their own settlement.

Carter Administration policy toward Nicaragua after 1979 was very cautioualy accommodationist; in Trilateralist fashion,[2] the administration wanted to block "another Cuba" from forming, but wanted to keep Nicaragua open for investment, trade and financial links. For example, Nicaragua had a $1.6 billion debt, much of it owed to the United States or US banks. Carter policy aimed at encouraging "pluralism" in Nicaragua while, on the public level at least, maintaining friendly relations with the new government (e.g. NYT, 7-29-79; 8-17-79). The United States gave over $100 million in food and relief aid in the next year and a half to help Nicaraguans recover from the great destruction and loss due to the war. Ambassador Lawrence Pezzullo developed a positive working relationship with the Junta and the State Department and President Carter discussed sending development aid.

Other moves signalled Carter's caution and Brzezinski's preference for "containing" Nicaragua. First, while Washington generously provided humanitarian aid, it also did not make any gesture or commitment to Nicaragua, for example, in support of its sovereignty and right to self-determination. When the Frente asked for military aid, Washington took it under "further discussion" and in late 1979 provided an amount, $23,000, just large enough to cover field binoculars and a trip for several Sandinista Commandantes to tour military installations in the United States.

Moreover, tension was mounting in Nicaragua over Somocista National Guard training camps in Honduras (on Nicaragua's northern border) from which thievery and border raids were being launched. The Guardia in Honduras also warned of a counter-revolutionary movement to retake power, although the exiles were hardly capable of such an effort without foreign backing. The camps, as it turned out, were being run and coordinated by National Guard officers, many of whom had been given asylum in the United States at the time of Somoza's ouster. The FSLN asked the Carter Administration to use its influence in Honduras to get the camps dismantled. The Guardia continued to operate and, although the United States argued that it had no ties to these groups, a number of US politicians were calling precisely for US facilitation of such groups while withholding aid from the FSLN. Moreover, suspicion about the nature and direction of the FSLN government was aired regularly by a conservative bloc in Congress. Visiting Sandinista officials were at times grilled by US politicans (e.g. WP, 12-1-79). These things and earlier US-Nicaraguan history shaped the FSLN's own wariness of US motives.

US-Nicaraguan relations in 1980 were increasingly shaped by the perspectives of US conservative and traditional foreign policy sectors. The long, heated debate in Congress over Carter's proposed $75 million aid package to Nicaragua symbolized an underlying suspicion of the new leftist government. Reacting negatively to FSLN revolutionary and Marxist rhetoric, its mobilization methods of popular participation and its policy independence, Congress nevertheless finally approved the aid. But it did so only after placing a series of conditions on the aid[3] and after President Carter certified to the law-makers that Nicaragua was not exporting revolution. The aid was finally approved on East-West logic; the aid would help Nicaragua resist increased Cuban assistance while building up the pro-US, capitalist sector in Managua. Meanwhile, a $73 million aid package went to El Salvador to help prevent the conditions for a popular uprising there. Thus, despite cordial relations at the diplomatic level, US policy toward Nicaragua retained its interventionist element.

In Nicaragua, the nationalist FSLN watched the debate process and in September accepted the first installment of the grant, acutely aware of the anti-Sandinista sentiment on Capital Hill but dissuaded by the US Ambassador in Managua from criticizing the structure of the aid (NYT, 11-16-80). In the United States, meanwhile, the Republican Party and the Reagan team were posturing on the issues of Nicaragua's revolution and the United States' waning world power in preparation for the November presidential ballotting. The Frente braced itself for a Reagan victory at the polls, all the more determined to pursue its independence and its defense.

## Reagan and the Political Agenda of the Right:    Policy Directions in Central America

If Carter's policy toward Nicaragua (1978-1980) reflected uncertainty and suspicion about the nature of the revolution, the intention of the Reagan ideologues was clear:  the revolution had to be destroyed and the Sandinistas put out of power.  The foreign policy perspective of the "Conservative Revolution", heralded with Reagan's inauguration in January, 1981, had been clearly enunciated in the "Santa Fe Report" (drawn up by Reagan campaign aides), the 1980 Republican Platform and position papers of conservative think tanks such as the Heritage Foundation, the American Security Council (ASC), the Committee on the Present Danger (CPD), and the Council on Inter-American Security (CIS).  It is worth quoting from one early document, the Sante Fe Report on inter-American policy in the 1980s."[4]

> Containment of the Soviet Union is not enough.  Detente is dead.  Survival demands a new US foreign policy.  America must seize the initiative or perish.  For World War III is almost over.  The Soviet Union...is strangling the Western industrialized nations....Latin America and Southern Asia are the scenes of strife of the third phase of World War III....America is everywhere in retreat....Even the Caribbean, America's maritime crossroad and petroleum refining center, is becoming a Marxist-Leninist lake. Never before has the Republic been in such jeopardy from its exposed southern flank.  Never before has American foreign policy abused, abandoned, and betrayed its allies to the south in Latin America....The Americas are under attack....The Caribbean rim and basin are spotted with Soviet surrogates and ringed with socialist states (p. 1-3)....The Nicaraguan base on the American Continent will now facilitate a repeat of the new Nicaraguan revolutionary model.

The 1980 Republican Platform, negotiated at the Dallas convention several months later, reflected this policy agenda for Nicaragua and Latin America:[5]

> Overseas, conditions already perilous, deteriorate.... Marxist tyrannies spread more rapidly through the Third World and Latin America.  Our alliances are frayed.... These events are not isolated, or unrelated.  They are signposts....Latin America is an area of primary interest for the United States....We deplore the Marxist Sandinista takeover of Nicaragua and the Marxist attempts to destabilize El Salvador, Guatemala, and Honduras.  We do not support United States assistance to any Marxist government in this hemisphere and we oppose the Carter Administration aid program for the government of Nicaragua.  However, we will support the efforts of the Nicaraguan people to establish a free and independent

government...Republicans recognize the importance of our relations within this hemisphere and pledge a strong new United States policy in the Americas. We will stand firm with countries seeking to develop their societies while combating the subversion and violence exported by Cuba and Moscow. We will return to the fundamental principle of treating a friend as a friend and self-proclaimed enemies as enemies, without apology. We will make it clear to the Soviet Union and Cuba that their subversion and their build-up of offensive military forces is unacceptable....

That the conservative agenda for Central America would shape US-Nicaraguan policy after 1980 was assured by the influx of many conservative organization members into the Reagan Administration. For example, at least fifty members of the Committee on the Present Danger went into government service or policy posts; the authors of the Santa Fe Report went to work for the White House and the National Security Council; and persons with conservative and anti-Communist credentials were appointed to diplomatic and political posts in Central and South America and in State Department and Pentagon analyst positions. In addition, numerous ties existed between administration officials and the think tanks mentioned earlier.[6] The impact of so many ideologues in policy positions was to be felt throughout Reagan's terms in office.

The Perspective of the Right. In brief, the conservatives of the 1980s eschewed "liberal accomodationism" and detente, reinvigorated cold war, bipolar politics, communist conspiracy and roll-back communism themes, and introduced some new conceptualizations of the East-West struggle. Influential in policy circles through both their official or advisory positions and policy papers, these opinion leaders hoped to reestablish US hegemony in Latin America and in the world. In their view, the "Vietnam Syndrome" had immobilized the United States in the underdeveloped world, providing space for liberation movements in Africa in the 1970s (Ethiopia, Mozambique, Angola, etc.) and in Central America in the late 1970s and 1980s. To stop this trend, the United States had to return to earlier policy toward the Third World--bolstering friendly regimes and punishing enemies. Indeed, the post-World War II bipartisan consensus regarding US interests in the Third World put a premium on political stability and exerting US influence in the "periphery" of the bipolar world. "Friendly" regimes in this traditional foreign policy scenario referred to states open to US economic and military influence and with an anti-communist stance. They did not have to have democratic governments as a criterion for US aid; because they were not ideologically leftist there was every possibility for democratic politics to evolve in good time under US tutelage (e.g. Kirkpatrick, 1979). In these cases, and especially where popular movements threatened order, the status quo, and, US national interests, (El Salvador, Guatemala, South Korea, the Philippines, etc.), democratic niceties or greater socioeconomic equity could be deferred in the interests of (re-)establishing order, often with US military aid and training.

This national security doctrine, encouraged in underdeveloped states friendly to the United States, was rooted philosophically in anti-communism. It was facilitated physically by US military aid. The doctrine placed a premium on maintaining order when such regimes were being challenged by domestic insurgents. Endowing Third World national military organizations with renewed legitimacy, the national security approach was politically defended as a transitional phase of elite domination, to be replaced in time with, first, a restricted democracy and then full-fledged (Western-modelled) democracy. The beauty of this process in the view of its proponents was that reforms could be introduced slowly and in a manner which would not require structural or distributional change; traditional patterns of bilateral relations with the United States and the political dominance of Western-oriented elites could be maintained.

In practice, the reforms, along with economic sweeteners, constituted counterinsurgency in disguise.[7] The dual purpose of such "guns and beans" policies[8] -- policies devised and tested first by the Kennedy Administration in Latin America, then by Johnson and Nixon in Southeast Asia and being studied and improved upon by conservative think tanks in the 1980s -- was to defeat insurgents by robbing them of their domestic base (popular support) and to gain legitimacy for the national government by introducing moderate land, wage, or political reforms. Doing so demanded wariness, however, since such reforms could not be allowed to threaten the old order. Typically, reforms and the delivery of basic services, such as health, education, and water wells or electricity, were introduced following military sweeps in pursuit of guerrillas and were sometimes accompanied by search and destroy campaigns which razed villages suspected of guerrilla sympathies. Other programs which put the people into government-directed development or security projects, like village patrol or road-building, would follow. Thus were friendly regimes facing sociological strains and popular movements to be kept friendly and in the United States' sphere. Winning hearts and minds was key.

Enemy regimes, on the other hand, were those which expressed an aversion to US influence, were ideologically leftist, or declared a preference for socialist or Marxist models. In traditional and conservative thinking, such situations effectively placed these states in the Soviet camp. The socialism-equals-Sovietism thesis also held that such regimes by nature were: totalitarian; aggressive; in the business of exporting revolution (the domino theory), inimical to US business interests; part of the Soviet conspiracy to dislodge democratic regimes (through subversion or terrorism); and condemned to being irreversibly Marxist-Leninist once political structures were consolidated. Such regimes were typically characterized as irreconcilably opposed to US interests, untrustworthy and implacably hostile. US accommodation of such a regime would signal weakness and lack of resolve to the Soviet Union.

This global categorization, which also led to political polarization among political elites within the underdeveloped state, led to several tacit conclusions among the 1980s conservatives concerning the United States' relations with Third World states.

First, different yardsticks or standards of judgement could be employed vis-a-vis countries which were hostile to the United States and those which were not. For instance, Washington could legitimately hold Nicaragua to a higher standard of expectation than El Salvador, such as in human rights and democratization, because the government of the latter did not expouse Marxism or pose a security threat to the United States. Political or human rights abuses in friendly states would be underplayed in formulating US aid packages, for instance, while such abuses in an enemy state would be publicized and exaggerated in government reports. Second, there was no moral equivalence, and thus no legitimate comparisons, between the United States and the Soviet Union or between the United States' actions in the Third World and the USSR's actions there. While the United States operated in the Third World to instill democracy, development and freedom, the USSR operated solely to expand its empire and world control. No matter that the superpowers' means--manipulation, armed insurgency, intimidation, etc.--might be the same or appear so; their respective desired ends exonerated the United States and condemned the USSR. Both of these themes became explicit in Reagan Central American policy.

Recalling US practice in the 1960s and early 1970s, the conservative agenda for the 1980s called for the United States to recover its unquestioned leadership among its allies, to lead in the defense of the free world and to play an active role in stopping other-bloc subversion of friendly (or, traditionally US-influenced) governments in the South. Socialist governments and movements had to be rolled back, not simply contained. US control over the periphery states in its traditional sphere had to be reinforced. Thus, for example, the Heritage Foundation (1984:39) and other groups called for supporting anti-communist insurgency and paramilitary forces in order to serve notice that the United States "no longer will countenance the subversion or overthrow of friendly governments within the developing world." This policy position, which turned into Congressional legislation in mid-1985 for support to rebels in Angola, Cambodia, Nicaragua and elsewhere, stemmed from the widely-held conservative thesis that the most urgent foreign policy task for the United States in the 1980s was developing a method and shoring up the national will to stop wars of national liberation. Indeed, just as they worked to improve counterinsurgency in theory and practice as a key element of US foreign policy for the 1980s, conservative groups and the Reagan Administration moved to facilitate, or initiate and direct armed counter-revolutionary and anti-communist groups within underdeveloped states. Nicaragua was an immediate target.

Policy Prescriptions for Nicaragua. These positions shaped US policy objectives, rationalizations and actions in Central America in the 1980s. For Nicaragua after 1979 it meant that just at the time of its anti-imperialist revolution and its search for a new model of development, the local hegemon was reinvigorating cold war, bipolar themes -- themes which, in effect, delegitimized the very nationalist motives upon which Nicaragua's revolution was based. Similarly, as one of his first acts as Reagan's Secretary of State, Alexander Haig announced in 1981 that the anti-government guerrillas

in El Salvador -- the <u>Frente</u> <u>Farabundo</u> <u>Marti</u> <u>de</u> <u>Liberacion</u> <u>Nacional</u>,
the FMLN -- represented a "textbook case" of Soviet expansionism in
Central America. Nicaragua, in this scenario, had become (along
with Cuba) the local Soviet strategic base and its totalitarian
proxy intent on spreading Soviet-inspired communist revolution in
the region.

Popular movements elsewhere in the region, for example in
Guatemala, were interpreted as co-conspirators in this Soviet plot,
the end purpose of which was to gain a foothold in the United
States' traditional sphere of influence by establishing ideological
loyalists and military bases. With naval and air bases in the
Caribbean, the USSR would be in position to disrupt US oil
and shipping lines, distract US military energies from Western
Europe, the Middle East and elsewhere, and make direct attacks on
the US mainland. In order not to get tied down in this heretofore
militarily secure area and to be free to expend US energies rearming
and reasserting the US security apparatus around the world,
Washington had quickly to defeat regional insurgent movements and
rollback the Nicaraguan revolution. With its "soft underbelly" once
again secure, the United States could confront the Soviet Union in
more distant areas. And, in the optimism of many conservatives of
the 1980s, such confrontations with the Soviets in economic and
military spheres would ultimately lead to a "victory" for the United
States given its superior science and technology. In brief, popular
movements and dissent in the South were not indications of a need
for structural change in the world political economy or the result
of sociological upheavals rooted in large rich-poor gaps, inequality
or oppression. Movements led by labor, church, student, women and
peasant groups aiming at empowering ascending (or historically
suppressed) majorities were not forwarding democratic participation.
These and "nationalist" movements were agents of Soviet intentions.
The real battle to maintain US world leadership, to protect US
interests, and to secure world freedom and democracy had to be
fought against the USSR. Thus, the Reagan Administration
immediately elevated Central American events to a crisis situation
to get the new campaign off the ground.

Throughout the Reagan period and in building its case in
Central America the administration necessarily focused on:
1)proving the existence of clandestine military linkages among the
USSR, Cuba, Nicaragua and El Salvador (the FMLN); 2)characterizing
Nicaragua as totalitarian, Marxist-Leninist, and Soviet-aligned;
3)justifying a regional US military build-up; 4)characterizing US
friends, El Salvador and Honduras in particular, as moving steadily
toward democracy; and 5)presenting a US-modelled, capitalist, free
enterprise development strategy as the answer to both economic
underdevelopment and social unrest. The Reagan Administration
sought to make the case that the Soviet Union was working to disrupt
the normally pacific US-led inter-American order.

Flowing from this US world-view were policy prescriptions for
Nicaragua: this threat to US hegemony and to hemispheric
ideological consensus had to be eliminated, not accommodated.
Nicaragua's independent action threatened both US-created regional
military pacts like CONDECA (the Council for Central American

Defense) and the US-inspired CACM (the Central American Common Market) which had been set up in the early 1960s. Rather than negotiating with the FSLN, the United States had first to contain Nicaragua militarily and then eliminate this social, economic and political example, following the watchwords-turned-motto: "No second Cuba, no second Vietnam!" As one former Reagan Administration official laid out the scenario of US means vis-a-vis Nicaragua, the United States would use economic sanctions, military maneuvers and stepped-up paramilitary actions to bring about "negotiations" on US terms; then "...you get them in the groin and get them out" (quoted in Sanders, 1985). By 1983, and through 1985 the US military circle around Nicaragua was tightened, top policy officials and President Reagan were publically saying that the United States could not work with a Sandinista government and that the "internal structures" of Nicaragua had to be dramatically changed before the United States would halt its paramilitary war against Nicaragua. Nicaragua, in President Reagan's words, had to "cry uncle."

CONFRONTING THE REVOLUTION

Political-Diplomatic Policy:  Building a Domestic Consensus Against Nicaragua

Speaking in an August, 1985 interview about varying interpretations between the Reagan Administration and its critics of the political and economic situation inside Nicaragua, a US Embassy official in Managua noted: "This is an ideological administration....No matter who's right, the assumptions held at the top drive the policy" (author interview). Indeed, conservative ideologues held the Central America policy initiative from their center-front positions in the Reagan Administration; political and diplomatic appointees at the White House, within the National Security Council, at the CIA, at the State and Defense Departments and in regional diplomatic posts had the president's ear and a philosophical agenda prescribing preferred policy moves. They were aided by the fact that liberal, Democratic and other Central American policy critics in Washington failed to conceptualize or communicate an alternative agenda for US Nicaragua or Central American policy, one that, for example, assessed regional events from a North-South, dependency or interdependence perspective.
But, although the White House National Security Council ideologues (in particular) drove the policy and often set the limits of debate, they also had to work within a larger foreign policy sector where career diplomats, politically pragmatic Reagan conservatives, the Congress and public opinion also influenced policy. The conservative preference for rolling back communist insurgencies had to be pursued through the maze of domestic politics and inter-agency compromise. Moreover, United States experiences with Vietnam and unpopular regimes in South Korea, the Philippines, Iran, Nicaragua (under Somoza) and elsewhere left many Americans wary of supporting such regimes against domestic insurgency, or, of

undermining regimes that grew out of a popular response to repression. The public, as well as sectors within the US military also preferred short engagements with clear and uncontroversial objectives. The result was a relentless drive during the Reagan years to build a domestic political consensus to act against Nicaragua and, as part of that drive, to find a broad, politically acceptable rationale for a policy and a US involvement growing steadily larger at every level: military, paramilitary, economic and diplomatic.

Efforts to obtain a working consensus for encircling, containing and chipping away at the Nicaraguan revolution, or, at least for coopting or neutralizing policy dissenters, featured several major tactics. The first was to build and sell to relevant opinion sectors a negative image of the revolution, to pose it as a threat to US national security and to place the revolution and other events in Central America within an East-West crisis situation. Administration rhetoric regarding Nicaragua was sharp and heated and it escalated through the mid-1980s. A second effort was to list peace, negotiation, regional development and democracy as top US goals even while the conservative agenda required side-stepping or side-tracking opportunities for political solutions, and, while US military moves in the region, in effect, constituted a US invasion of Central America. As National Security Council and Administration leaks revealed, the ideologues defined peace and negotiations as militarily enforcing a Nicaraguan surrender on US terms ("peace through strength"). While stressing the goal of political stability and peace, therefore, initiatives proposing talks with the FSLN had to be coopted or discredited. Or, if they had to take place for reasons of domestic political expediency, they would not be pursued seriously.

When these tactics needed reinforcing, and particularly when political support for US regional activities was waning, the administration raised the stakes for the United States in the region by increasing its estimates of the size of the threat posed to US national security, and using ever more stark, forceful rhetoric. Especially in early 1983, when it became clear that initial estimates of the time and effort it would take to "secure Central America" were wrong the administration pressed a harder policy line with Congress and critics, took firmer control of policy, and increased the US military and CIA presence in Central America. But in order to maintain policy momentum in the face of Nicaraguan peace initiatives, Latin American peace efforts and Congressional or international pressures, the administration also had regularly to change or enlarge its policy rationale. For instance, US military policy against Nicaragua was initially (1981) justified as an effort to stop gun-running to the FMLN guerrillas in El Salvador. By 1985 the rationale had expanded to include, at various times, forcing the Sandinistas to change internal political structures toward centrist (pro-US) politics, to hold new elections, to break any ties with Cuba and the USSR, to negotiate with US-sponsored "freedom fighters" based in Honduras, to end their support of "terrorism", and the like. Thus, as the rationale expanded, so did the size of the effort required to meet it. And, not accidentally, the room for

administration maneuvering also expanded.  The conditions placed on
stopping the contra war and all other hostile policy against
Nicaragua were increasingly things open to US interpretation:  what
were acceptable Nicaraguan election results; what were acceptable
political structures; what were terrorist acts and when were they
facilitated by the Frente  -- all these things were left to
Washington to decide.
    Nicaraguan policy was very much a product of domestic US
politics and the struggle of conservative ideologues to impose their
foreign policy agenda.  As the ideologues maintained control over
policy and upped the ante in Central America, policy was less and
less a reflection of local (Central American) realities and more a
reflection of political conflict in the United States.  A review of
US policy will demonstrate these points.
    Policy Outlines:  1981.  Secretary of State Haig set the stage
and the momentum for US policy in Central America and Nicaragua in
the first months of Reagan's coming into office in January, 1981.
In public speeches and Congressional testimony Haig defined the
Nicaraguan revolution as the first part of a four-phase Soviet
operation to spread communist revolution in Central America.  That
operation, he charged, had already spread to El Salvador and was
being fueled by gun-running from Nicaragua.  Through its
Marxist-Leninist bases in Nicaragua and Cuba, the Soviets planned an
assault through to Mexico and the US border.  On the strength of
this argument, which was laid out in detail in an early White Paper
of proofs--a report which was shortly thereafter discredited in the
United States and abroad and parts of which the State Department
later was forced to recant --the Reagan Administration moved against
Nicaragua in economic and military spheres.  In February the United
States broke its contract to sell wheat to Nicaragua, citing the
gun-running charge.  Although the Sandinistas sent assurances to
Washington in March that they would do what they could to prevent
arms from passing through their territory and named Arturo Cruz as
Ambassador to the United States, the United States in April halted
payment of the $15 million remaining of the $75 aid package awarded
Nicaragua in 1980.
    Meanwhile, despite protests from Nicaragua and a call from
Daniel Ortega for friendly relations, the United States by April was
facilitating the training (on US soil) and organization of
anti-Sandinista groups (ex-Guardia groups, later called contras).
The contras were based in Honduras, but also had headquarters in
Miami (see Chapter 6).  In fact, plans were being made in April and
were approved by the president in November to provide $19 million in
support of paramilitary operations against the FSLN government.  The
existence of the training camps and US complicity seemed the more
menacing to the Frente when, in September, the United States
announced the Halcon Vista joint military maneuvers with Honduras,
exercises the United States called "routine."  That same month
Assistant Secretary of State for Inter-American Affairs, Thomas
Enders, travelled to Nicaragua and, according to reports from US and
Nicaragua officials interviewed later, with a heavy-handed approach
verbally made a series of demands on the Nicaraguan government.
With an imperious, "Attila the diplomat" attitude (according to US

140

officials), Enders warned Nicaragua of the United States' strength and demanded (among other things) that Nicaragua freeze its aquisition of heavy weapons such as armed or unarmed helicopters and planes and that they re-export to the country of origin--and in their original crates--heavy weapons that the United States named (Gutman, 1984). Nicaragua had to expel Salvadoran rebel leaders from their alleged command-control center in Managua and end arms flows to the FMLN. Enders, in essence, communicated the conditions Nicaragua had to meet before the United States would participate in serious talks. The Sandinistas, extremely sensitive to signs of traditional US imperialism toward Nicaragua, reacted with ideological rhetoric asserting the independence and sovereignty of Nicaragua. Cruz, a non-Sandinista government official, characterized the US demands as "the conditions of a victorious power" (quoted in Gutman, 1984). In the Sandinistas' view, the Reagan Administration was willy-nilly implementing the Santa Fe policy proposals.

At the UN in October, Junta leader Ortega attacked US policies in Central America and Deputy Foreign Minister Tinoco said progress in relations depended on the United States closing anti-Sandinista training camps in Florida. In this atmosphere of mutual suspicion, US officials in November publically characterized Nicaragua as quickly becoming totalitarian and communist. According to US officials, Nicaragua using Cuban aid, was building a military machine with Cuban aid. Haig, meanwhile, reported that the Pentagon was studying military options against Nicaragua and that he would not rule out the use of a blockade to contain the Nicaraguan threat. This prompted a warning to Haig from the Mexicans against any precipitous US action against Nicaragua. At the OAS meetings in December and afterward -- and, despite the fact that Nicaraguan Foreign Minister Miguel D'Escoto had met with Haig, expressed a desire for talks and discussed the bases of Nicaragua's foreign policy -- Haig continued his rhetorical campaign against the Sandinista government. Just as it had rejected a French-Mexican offer in August to mediate US talks with Nicaragua, in December the United States discounted a UN call for talks among the contending parties in Central America. In the US view, any talks had to be exclusively regional, that is, held in forums the United States traditionally controlled.

1982. The United States in 1981 laid the diplomatic and military foundation for an East-West, security-crisis campaign against Nicaragua and, using the "Nicaragua-Cuba-Soviet Union axis" argument, significantly increased its military involvement in El Salvador as well. In 1982 Washington expanded it regional political-military influence in Honduras and Costa Rica, widened the contra war of insurgency inside Nicaragua and maneuvered to avoid negotiations with Nicaragua.

Working through diplomatic channels, the United States sponsored efforts to build an anti-Sandinista bloc among Honduras, El Salvador and Costa Rica. This initiative got its first breath at a San Jose meeting in January, the purpose of which was to create a "Central American Democratic Community" where US definitions of regional events could be aired in a cordial forum as "regional" moves to counter the Nicaraguan threat were planned. But the CADC never got off the ground. This was undoubtedly due to the fact that: the initiative was not genuinely local; the largest state in the region, Guatemala, was hardly democratic; historical animosities left over from the 1969 "Soccer War" existed between Honduras and El Salvador; and the real regional power, the United States, did not reside in the region. Nevertheless, diplomatic contacts among the states remained open and US pressure continued.

The Reagan Administration was more successful in the military realm. In February the Defense Department revealed that it was keeping Nicaragua and Salvador under electronic surveillance from ships in the Pacific and in March the administration announced that it was considering new military bases in Honduras or Colombia (e.g. WP 3-2-82). At about the same time the administration began a campaign of formal proofs of the Nicaraguan-Cuban threat, complete with briefings and aerial photos. US-sponsored contras, meanwhile, escalated attacks inside Nicaragua, demonstrating their capacity by blowing up several bridges in the north, and later, killing 15 young people at San Francisco del Norte. As the CIA and US officials took more direct control over the contras, the number of men in arms also increased dramatically in 1982, far above the 500-man force approved by the president at the end of 1981. In the following months, US warships -- the USS Coontz and the USS Trippe -- patrolled the Nicaraguan coasts. In August the United States held another series of military maneuvers with Honduras, this time only twenty-five miles from the Nicaraguan border. The military situation around and inside its borders was made more tense for Nicaragua that same month when the mood of conservatives in Congress was expressed in the Symm's Amendment: the United States would use all necessary means to stop Cuban expansion in the hemisphere.

Given the regional situation and hostile US rhetoric, Nicaraguan leaders began fearing an imminent invasion; they moved to publicize their worries. In March, Nicaragua introduced a resolution in the UN Security Council prohibiting the use of force or intervention by one state into another. Condemning US actions against them, the FSLN hoped to bring world attention to their cause, something they felt they accomplished despite the US veto in April. At home, the Frente responded to Haig's renewed rhetoric by declaring a military emergency and increasing the size of its army, leading political opponents there to blame Washington for forcing a radicalization of the revolution.

If the United States passed up several opportunities to find a negotiated, political settlement with Nicaragua in 1981, in 1982 it became clear that the administration preferred to press and isolate the revolution until such time as Nicaragua would capitulate on a growing list of US demands. In February, Mexican President Portillo offered to mediate talks both between the United States and Nicaragua and the United States and Cuba. While the Nicaraguans accepted the idea of having a friendly witness to any talks with the United States, Washington rejected the offer, stating its preference for bilateral talks.

In March and April a new opening came. US Ambassador Anthony Quainton arrived in Nicaragua in March -- a post that had been left vacant for seven months -- and Nicaragua used the occassion to express its willingness to open talks with the United States at any time. The United States in April, and one week after vetoing the UN resolution, responded in writing with a list of eight points -- five demands and three contingent proposals for aid and cultural exchanges. According to Quainton, the United States felt Nicaragua had displayed inflexibility and insincerity after Ender's 1981 visit, had not moved in the military realm to reduce US concerns and had to be dealt with more sternly.[10] Other officials also confirmed that the United States in April shifted its terms vis-a-vis Nicaragua: now US concerns over gun-running and an oversized military structure were to be part of a larger set of demands that were expressed in the eight points. Addressing these concerns were said to be essential, the sine qua non for future relations with Washington. Nicaragua should: reduce the size of its military structure (personnel, weapons and Cuban advisors); permit regional verification of its borders and airports; pledge not to export its revolution (such as aiding the FMLN); pledge non-interference in its neighbors affairs; and observe what the United States now held to be the FSLN's pledge to the OAS in 1979 concerning the goals of the revolution -- primarily, in the United States' view, that Nicaragua pursue democratic pluralism in a way consistent with US values. The United States, in other words, had considerably broadened the scope of its bargaining position and had expanded its regional military presence at a time when a number of parties had offered to facilitate a political solution.

The objective of the administration was to avoid negotiations not controlled by the United States. A National Security Council report dated April, 1982 and entitled "US Policy in Central America and Cuba through F.Y. '84, Summary Paper" made that clear. Leaked in 1983 by someone in the White House, the paper focused on the effort to withstand domestic pressures to negotiate, to "step up efforts to coopt [the] negotiations issue to avoid Congressionally mandated negotiations which would work against our interests," and to wait for "negotiations and compromise on our terms." The other major focus of the report, one related directly to US efforts to isolate the Nicaraguan revolution, was on strengthening counterinsurgency capabilities in Salvador and Guatemala, improving military capacities, policy coordination and collective security among ally states, increasing covert pressure on Nicaragua and Cuba and improving intelligence collection in ally and other Central American states (NYT 4-7-83).

While Nicaragua felt the United States was stalling on talks, it accepted the US points and reponded with thirteen counter-proposals expressing Nicaragua's concerns about US military moves, and, detailing proposals for talks. Although several more exchanges of letters occurred, the process was side-tracked over the summer by the Falklands/Malvinas War. In the war between Argentina and Great Britain, the United States joined in Britain's cause and most of the Latin American states rallied behind Argentina. But in July when Quainton responded to Nicaragua's May letter it became clear that the United States was intransigent, particularly on its condition that Nicaragua stop supplying arms to the FMLN -- a US claim against Nicaragua that was being refuted by both Nicaraguan officials and US intelligence and diplomatic officials in the region. Moreover, it was clear that the Reagan Administration and the FSLN had different conceptions of democracy, and, that the Frente flatly rejected US attempts to influence its internal political structures.

In September another negotiation initiative was undertaken, this time by Mexico, Venezuela and Panama. These states offered to arrange bilateral talks between Nicaragua and both the United States and Honduras.[11] Enders countered this proposal saying that the democracies of the region, namely Nicaragua's neighbors, should define the conditions for peace in Central America; bilateral talks were not an acceptable alternative. A week later renewed US efforts to build a regional anti-Sandinista bloc seemed to pay off when its Central American allies agreed to try again at coordinating their Nicaraguan policies, this time in a new "Forum for Peace and Democracy". That this was not to be an opening for negotiations, however, became clear from the fact that Nicaragua was excluded from the meetings and that the Mexico-Venezuela-Panama plan for dialogues was not discussed. In fact, the "Forum" was to go the way of the CADC and for the same reasons. In the future the United States was forced to build its anti-Nicaragua policy separately with each of Nicaragua's neighbors. Yet, again, the United States was able to take momentum away from non-US initiatives and to insist that any movement had to take place in a US-controlled forum where US objectives could define the agenda and the terms of peace. In November Washington influenced a Honduran decision not to meet with Nicaragua over their border clashes, a meeting the Nicaraguans had proposed.

By the end of the 1982: no talks with Nicaragua were underway; the CIA informed Congress that the size of its rebel army had increased to 4000; Nicaragua declared its northern region a military zone in response to escalating fighting; Newsweek printed a detailed expose of the CIA's activities against Nicaragua and the contras' open intent of overthrowing the Sandinistas; and the USSR and both East and West European states were promising Nicaragua new economic aid and spare parts in response to further aid cuts by the United States in 1982. For its part, Congress, increasingly anxious about the administration's true objective vis-a-vis Nicaragua, now publicized the Boland Amendment which had been quietly written into law at mid-year. The amendment forbade the provision by the US government of military equipment, training, advice or other support for military activities intended for the purpose of overthrowing the Nicaraguan government or provoking an armed exchange between Nicaragua and Honduras. Yet, the initiative and the momentum in foreign policy remained with the president.

1983. By the end of the first quarter of 1983 the foreign policy ideologues decided to drive harder for a consensus that would allow them to pursue their agenda. Indeed, 1983 marked a turning point in US-Central American policy for a number of reasons. First, Haig and others had initially believed that the area could be "quickly secured"; instead, by 1983 the war in El Salvador (against the FMLN guerrillas) was going badly despite heavy US involvement,

144

and, the contras were not showing much success in winning political support or in sparking a mass uprising in Nicaragua. Congress and the public, meanwhile, were opposed to military aid requests and were increasingly critical of the Reagan Administration's apparent attempts to find a military solution. Nor were US allies in Latin America and Europe accepting the US interpretation of Central American events. Even containing the popular movements in Salvador and Nicaragua seemed an elusive prospect at the current rate.

In efforts to change the political tide in Central America and their own political prospects at home, policy leaders began a new campaign against regional leftists and domestic critics. First, control over regional policy was moved to the White House ideologues and away from the State Department pragmatists. Enders at State, who had basically overseen policy up to Spring, 1983, was removed from his post in May and policy initiatives became the domain of National Security Council members like Casey and Menges (CIA), Kirkpatrick (UN), Clark (National Security Advisor), and Sanchez and Ikle (Defense Department).[12] These policy-makers voiced a US "moral duty" to stop communist expansionism; ideologues were distressed by the pragmatists' "overemphasis" on negotiations and their failure to win more votes in Congress.

In conjunction with the change in policy personnel, the White House greatly stepped up its image-management, psychological warfare campaign against Nicaragua in 1983. Although the National Security Council had approved a disinformation campaign against the Sandinistas and the FMLN in Salvador in late 1981, efforts in 1981 and 1982 to portray Nicaragua as a threat to the region did not bear much fruit. Nor did efforts to paint the FMLN as extreme, radical leftists, and, to break the confidence of the FMLN by intimidating the Sandinistas meet much success (McConnell, 1983). Moreover, early 1983 State Department documents on weapons flows from the USSR to the FSLN and the FMLN were greeted with skepticism due to the highly speculative nature of much of the analysis and conflicting reports from intelligence and other officials. Now, White House policy-makers began a new effort by establishing the Office of Public Diplomacy on Latin America and the Caribbean (under the State Department) and a White House "outreach group" which held weekly meetings and published anti-Sandinista materials.

President Reagan also took up a new argument against the Frente. In a July speech the president claimed that at the OAS in 1979 the FSLN had "literally made a contract to establish a "true democracy" in Nicaragua. The argument, one that was now to become a major rallying theme for the administration, was that the Sandinistas had broken their "solemn promise" to the OAS to establish a Western-oriented democracy. Actually the Sandinistas had told the OAS that they planned to organize "the first free elections in this century" in Nicaragua; they offered no timeframe, nor did they discuss their conception of participatory democracy. Yet by July, 1984, Reagan was claiming that the FSLN had promised in writing to hold "genuinely democratic elections", implicitly suggesting that the United States would retain the right to decide what were proper political practices in Nicaragua. Until the FSLN changed its behavior accordingly, the United States would continue the contra war of attrition against Nicaragua.  As in earlier cases in US-Latin American history, the United States would try to install democracy by armed force.

So, the propaganda war accelerated in 1983; as Newsweek reported to the general public later in the year, the CIA was masterminding various propaganda activities to destablize the Sandinistas at home and abroad -- something which the Boland Amendment had aimed at preventing.  Issues which were raised repeatedly against the FSLN-- until they took on lives of their own -- included Miskito massacres, aid to the FMLN, persecution of the Catholic Church and anti-semitism.  Although the Sandinista government and independent groups presented alternative documented information on all of these issues, they remained potent weapons in the administration's campaign against the Frente.

In a second policy thrust in 1983, the president was encouraged to put himself personally into the political fray on Central America, thereby heightening attention to the issues and putting Reagan's popularity to work for the conservative agenda.  In major policy addresses in March, April, June and July President Reagan used strong images to raise the spectre of "the communist agenda striking at the heart of the Western Hemisphere" and the need to use US military means to "hold off the guerrillas and give democratic reform time to take root."  In the April 27 speech before a joint session of Congress the president for the first time claimed that unrest in Central America threatened US security interests worldwide.  In a move to evoke a crisis atmosphere and increase prospects for Congressional and public support, the president concluded:

> In summation, I say to you that tonight there can be no question:  the national security of all the Americas is at stake in Central America.  If we cannot defend ourselves there, we cannot expect to prevail elsewhere.  Our credibility would collapse, our alliances would crumble, and the safety of our homeland would be put in jeopardy. We have a vital interest, a moral duty and a solemn responsibility.

The language of urgency and national security was directed especially at Congressional critics who had been successful both in getting military budgets for Central America trimmed and in legislating restrictions on CIA military activities in Salvador and Nicaragua.  In this period, the president and his advisors directly challenged critics, took Congress publically to task for this hampering of regional policy and effectively used the traditional "soft on communism" charge against the critics.  Using a theme usually popular at home, officials argued that the United States was fighting (without using US troops) to protect incipient democratic structures by pursuing a "dual strategy":  using a "military shield" against foreign (other-bloc) influence while encouraging democratic development through economic aid.

Third, the US regional military presence was increased dramatically in 1983 through legislative and non-legislative avenues. The administration introduced ongoing joint military maneuvers with Honduras and large increases in military aid to ally states; reinvigorated CONDECA (the anti-communist Central American Defense Council, begun in the 1960s);[13] invaded Grenada; and instructed the contras to show some results in Nicaragua. In fact, contra raids seemed to be timed to coordinate with domestic political battles: at Congressional funding times, during contra policy debates on the Hill and when negotiation initiatives offered an alternative to the contra war. A second leaked NSC document dated July 8, 1983 again revealed White House policy objectives: the United States had the power and resources to limit Soviet and Cuban influence without introducing troops. But to be effective military budgets had to be increased about 40 percent, friendly local armies had to be upgraded, covert action against the FSLN had to be increased, FMLN rebel camps in Honduras had to be hit, etc. In short, while Congress tried to limit the growing US military presence in the region and stress instead economic aid, administration policy was characterized by military confrontation and hopes of victory over alien ideological influence.

A final policy thrust in 1983 centered on pressing harder to assert US political influence and its policy framework vis-a-vis Central American allies. Although two major efforts in 1982 (the CADC and the Forum For Peace and Democracy) failed to establish an institutional vehicle through which Washington could address its local allies collectively, the United States nevertheless pushed hard in 1983 for regional military coordination and contingency planning (through CONDECA) in the case of aggression from Nicaragua, the FMLN or other leftist movements. On the political and diplomatic levels, the United States after 1981 was left basically to puruse support for its anti-Sandinista policy in bilateral relations and through bilateral aid programs to local allies. The heavy pressure applied by the administration to influence anti-Sandinista policies in Costa Rica and Honduras (especially) was to produce destabilizing effects within both societies.

Political and diplomatic activity in 1983 centered on avoiding international (non-US) initiatives for a negotiated peace in the region, though doing so successfully required political concessions by the White House. The initiative that after 1983 was to present the largest threat to US influence in Central America was the Contadora process, begun in January 1983. Venezuela, Colombia, Mexico and Panama decided to take the lead in forging a regional agreement for peace among all contending parties and to that end held multilateral meetings in April, July, September and November. Real progress had been made by September when all five Central American states agreed to sign the 21-point "Document of Objectives" outlining agreements for mutual disarmament, reductions in numbers of foreign advisors, border supervision and the like.

Although the United States paid lip service to the process for reasons of political expediency at home, policy officials, and especially the hardliners, worried about its implications. As CIA analyst and National Security Council director for Latin American affairs, Constantine Menges argued: the Contadora countries were precisely those states which helped bring the FSLN to power in 1979 accepting Sandinista "democratic promises." How could these states put together a credible agreement when they had failed to bring Nicaragua into compliance with those promises? Contadora would be "wholly inadequate" if verification or implementation was to be left to these countries (Gutman, 1984: 18). But other aspects of the process were also troubling to the conservatives. The process legitimized the FSLN as a trustworthy negotiator for Nicaragua; a peace settlement would leave the leftist government in power and undermine US efforts to purge such elements from the region. In addition, an agreement would for the first time establish limits on US military activity in the Caribbean basin -- joint maneuvers with regional allies; providing US training and advisors. Moreover, to the Reagan Administration's surprise, Nicaragua had announced in May that it would work within the Contadora process. This image of a Nicaragua willing to negotiate and hear the concerns of its neighbors did not mesh with the administration's argument to the American public that totalitarian Nicaragua was acting unilaterally to build a military machine with which it would threaten its neighbors.

The United States let its local allies know its concerns and at the November Contadora meeting asked that more stringent verification measures be adopted. When, before the scheduled December meeting, the Frente offered to discuss an arms freeze, Nicaraguan-Costa Rican relations thawed, and the OAS formally endorsed Contadora, the United States (not an official party to Contadora) worked through Honduras and Salvador to stall and then delay the meeting until 1984. The White House strategy was to use the delay to campaign in Latin America for its own "bipartisan" plan for peace. The Kissinger Commission report was due out in January and paralled the administration's prescriptions for the region as well as its definitions of US security interests and prerogatives in Central America. Because this report did not gain legitimacy outside the United States, however, the administration was to find other ways in 1984 and 1985 to stall Contadora.

In fact, the appointments of both the Kissinger Commission (July) and a roving ambassador for Central America (April) were concessions made by the White House in 1983 to quell growing Congressional skepticism about the administration's interest in negotiations as a means to settlement. A number of events, and Nicaraguan moves in particular, had fed this skepticism. For one thing, US military involvement in Central America was growing even though US efforts in Salvador and Nicaragua appeared not to be yielding fruit. Additionally, US military officers in the field reported in February that arms flowing to the FMLN through Nicaragua amounted only to "peanuts"; those arms were said to be neither extensive, nor vital to the FMLN's effort. This contrasted sharply with the central rationale being used to justify large US efforts in support of the Salvadoran army and the Honduran-based contras. Such intelligence reports suggested the need to shift to a broader policy rationale emphasizing democratic reform in both Salvador and Nicaragua and regional allies' "fears" of Nicaragua. In mid-1983 officials were referring to Central American requests for a large US military presence and the need for "a certain level of comfort" for our regional friends. But it also became clear in March, after a week-long UN Security Council debate -- over the United States' role in Central America, and vis-a-vis Nicaragua in particular -- that the United States was isolated internationlly. Fifty-five states rose to condemn US paramilitary and economic aggressions against Nicaragua. In fact, only Honduras and Salvador stood with the United States. When the UN offered its offices for mediation, Ambassador Kirkpatrick rejected the idea. To many in Congress and the American public, these events in the UN suggested the need for policy reevaluation.

Nicaraguan moves also fed Congressional skepticism over Reagan's interest in negotiations. Briefly, Nicaragua repeatedly called for unconditional, open-ended talks with both the United States and Honduras. Nicaragua answered every major US policy statement with an explanation of events or a detailed refutation of US claims and a call for talks. In July, Daniel Ortega offered a peace plan including multilateral talks which addressed major US concerns and offered a non-aggression pact with Nicaragua's neighbors. In October foreign Minister D'Escoto presented four draft treaties to the State Department -- treaties the United States dismissed as full of hostile rhetoric, unserious and designed for propaganda purposes. It became more difficult to hold to policy rationales in November, December and January (1984), despite the public popularity of the Grenada action, when the Frente made a series of moves on issues raised by the White House. The FSLN relaxed censorship enforced under the State of Emergency; offered an amnesty to Miskito and other contra fighters; introduced an autonomy process for the Atlantic Coast; planned for sending over 1000 Cuban advisors (some military) home; sent FMLN personnel out of Nicaragua; rescheduled elections for 1984 (rather than 1985 as previously announced); and held talks with domestic critics.

Nevertheless, the United States' response at the end of the year and into 1984 was consistent. Initially surprised and sent into policy confusion by Nicaraguan moves, US officials publically maintained that these moves were insincere and did not suggest a change in Nicaragua's "Marxist-Leninist" philosophy. Actually, the events led again to redefinitions and shifts in emphases in policy rationale. Not the least of the White House's concern at this time: the war in El Salvador was going poorly; officials were reporting that army discontent there meant the army could collapse suddenly; heavy death squad activity threatened the administration's argument about democratic improvements there; and coup rumors were rampant. The United States, worried about an FMLN victory in the current situation, was said to be reviewing contingency plans for invading El Salvador (LAWR, 12-9-83.)

This was no time for a conciliatory US attitude toward Nicaragua; to the ideologues Nicaragua was both a source and a symbol of troubles in Central America. In this context, Washington added to its list of conditions for talks with Nicaragua that the Sandinistas institute "genuine" democracy and hold talks with the FDN, the largest, most important contra group dubbed by President Reagan that year as "Freedom Fighters". But this demand seemed strange in light of the fact that after more than two years of challenging the Sandinistas, the contras had yet to present any coherent political program. Frustration was running high among policy ideologues as 1983 came to a close. Despite the fact that they had aggressively pursued their policy agenda on many fronts, their efforts proved futile in turning the tide of public opinion at home. Polls in late 1983 (and again in 1984) showed that about 60 percent of the American public did not support President Reagan's Central American policies or the sending of US troops to the region. Nearly half of all respondents in a New York Times/CBS poll in early 1984 expressed the fear that current policy might lead the country into war.

1984. In 1984 a policy of paying lip service to Contadora was accompanied by frontal attacks on the process, while the policy of deflecting Nicaraguan moves and international opportunities for talks continued. As in the previous years, in 1984 the United States increased both its military pressure on Nicaragua -- by now becoming directly involved in attacks on Nicaraguan targets -- and its military presence in the region. In the face of a Congressional cut-off of funds for the contras, the administration also refashioned its Nicaragua policy rationale in efforts, once again, at forging foreign and domestic support for its growing military commitment to the region.

At the February inauguration of President Jaime Lusinchi in Venezuela, Secretary of State Shultz directly undermined Contadora in the eyes of the Latin American sponsors by labelling the process well-intentioned but ill-informed about the regional roles of the Soviets and Cubans. The Latin American presidents, Shultz argued, were not fully conversant with the real causes of conflict in Central America. He went on to discredit any future Nicaraguan elections. (The Nicaraguan Council of State had spent over a year preparing an electoral law and was to announce an election date and campaign rules that month). A few days later Shultz told reporters in Caracas that Nicaragua had reason to worry about a US invasion (LAWR, 2-10-84).

Meanwhile, the Kissinger Report had been released. It noted indigenous causes of local unrest but went on to indict the USSR and Cuba for upsetting the regional balance. The report identified the Nicaraguan revolution as an indispensible stepping stone for USSR-backed insurgency and expansionism. Essentially echoing the administration world-view and calling for massive new military and non-military aid programs, the report endorsed a continuation of support for the contras as an incentive to a regional settlement. Contadora, it argued, could not be a substitute for US policy. The report reflected Kissinger's view that the United States could and should manage Central America and the administration's view that Contadora, a Latin initiative, effectively robbed the United States of its traditional military free-reign. Contadora limitations on arms, advisors, maneuvers and the like would apply to the United States as well as to Cuba, the USSR and the Central American states. Further, Contadora recognized the sovereignty and legitimacy of the FSLN governemnt, something Reagan was not prepared to do.

The Latin American reaction to the United States' maneuvering around Contadora was strong, despite the fact that all the states

directly involved with or supporting Contadora were US allies in
good standing. At the February meetings facilitated by Lusinchi's
swearing-in and in response to Shultz's remarks, the presidents of
nine Latin countries--Argentina, Bolivia, Colombia, Costa Rica,
Dominican Republic, Nicaragua, Panama, Venezuela and Spain--signed a
declaration backing Contadora (LAWR op. cit.). The foreign
ministers of Mexico and Colombia, moreover, argued separately that
border clashes and US-sponsored (contra) attacks inside Nicaragua
appeared to be timed to hamper or interfere with Contadora's work,
and, that the United States had not discarded the possibility of a
military solution (Gutman, 1984: 22). Contadora insisted on both
the United States and the USSR and Cuba giving up that notion. The
direct clash in positions between the Contadora initiatives on the
one hand and the Reagan Administration and the Kissinger report on
the other had been openly aired.[14]

New proposals worked out with US officials and taken to
Contadora by Salvador, Honduras and Costa Rica in late April
(Guatemala refused to co-sponsor the proposal) appeared to be
designed to make security agreements difficult, if not impossible.
While Nicaragua had historical reason to be suspicious of forums
where the United States had inordinate influence--such as the
OAS--the US allies proposed turning over verification of Contadora's
security agreements to the Inter-American Defense Board (IADB), an
extension of the OAS which had been originally designed to root out
Marxist-Leninist insurgencies. As outlined by Motley in May, the
United States also wanted Contadora to include: an inventory of
each state's combat units (including reserves), principal weapons
systems, military treaties and numbers and locations of all foreign
military advisors. These inventories would be given to the IADB,
published, and become subject to on-the-spot verification by the
IADB. The proposal was rejected by Nicaragua as inappropriate and
illogical and was viewed with suspicion by other Contadora states.

Nicaragua's surprise offer on September 21 to sign Contadora as
it then stood, i.e., without the United States' verification
demands, and Ortega's call a few days later for Reagan to endorse
the treaty led to new US emphases for a regional peace settlement.
Working in conjunction with Nicaragua's domestic (pro-US)
opposition, the State Department argued that the upcoming Nicaraguan
elections had to be postponed and the rules revamped to allow
broader party participation. Internal reconciliation became the
test of a "real" settlement; the FSLN was called upon to hold talks
with the US-backed "freedom fighters" (NYT, 9-23-84). The United
States had been moving to make this condition central to bilateral
talks as well.[15] In the short term, Shultz charged the Frente with
insincerity and argued that the September 7 Contadora
agreement--which had been presented to the UN as an official
document, along with a request that Contadora be given legal
status--was merely a draft and not meant to be final. In the face
of new Nicaraguan political concessions at home and its public
relations coup in offering to sign Contadora immediately, the United
States emphasized conditions on which there was little hope of
compromise, and in the next weeks dropped references to Contadora.
The administration stepped up criticisms of the FSLN and the

upcoming November elections.

Contadora had been effectively stalled for the remainder of the year; hopes for new progress seemed dimmed by the US group's inflexible negotiating position. An October 1984 National Security Council document boasted that the administration had "effectively blocked" the Contadora process (IHCA, December, 1985).

In the wider diplomatic sphere, the administration had to work to counter conciliatory Nicaraguan moves--the FSLN was holding talks with Miskito leaders and other opposition groups, had loosened censorship and removed the ban on labor strikes had relaxed State of Emergency restrictions, etc. These moves were getting recognition by policy critics and the international media. More importantly, the administration had to justify to domestic and foreign critics its direct participation in the mining of Nicaraguan harbors, in several sea and air bombing raids directed at strategic Nicaraguan targets (the Managua airport and the main oil terminal at Corinto) and in writing and disseminating a handbook for the contras which referred to "neutralizing" Sandinistas and creating "martyrs" for the contra cause. Direct US participation in these activities, which came to light in the Spring and Fall of 1984, led to Congressional condemnations and hearings, public protests and charges that the US was blatantly violating domestic and international law. In an election year and with Central America the centerpiece of Reagan foreign policy, the administration had to turn the tide of public opinion. Rather than softening its tone and working for a quick "success" through a Contadora agreement or bilateral talks with Nicaragua, the administration decided to dig in its heels.

It did so by once more heating up the rhetoric of "communist expansionism" and "counterfeit revolutionaries" and by justifying US military moves as "collective self- defense." But a new "crisis" element was also introduced--one that in 1985 would become the major tact against Nicaragua. The administration introduced its foreign policy campaign against "state terrorism". Such "terrorism" as was being manifested in the Middle East, Central America and elsewhere, the administration argued, was sponsored ultimately by the USSR and motivated by "ideology and political hostility toward Western democracies" (Shultz, quoted in Dixon, 1985). Consistent with the conservative ideologues' explanation of political instability in the Third World, the campaign subtly identified political unrest, national insurgency, socialism, and Soviet alignment as parts of the the same reality: weapons of state-sponsored terrorism, or, "unconventional war against democratic societies." Battlelines were clear: states (or critics) not on the US side (the Reagan Administration side) were part of the problem. Elevating the argument used since 1981, but never adequately documented, that Nicaragua supported insurgency in El Salvador, Shultz in April and October, 1984 implied that Nicaragua--guilty by its association with the USSR and Cuba--supported state terrorism against US values, interests and allies. To counter this immediate threat the United States had to be prepared to use military force even if ..."few cases will be as clear or as quick as Grenada...." Nicarargua, "aligned" with other "terrorist states" like Iran and Libya

(Nicaragua had oil agreements with both countries) was a direct threat to Western democracy. In October, Shultz served notice to the public that the United States might have to act against cases of "terrorism" before each and every fact was in. Yet this campaign against Nicaragua was weakened by the fact that, besides the civil war in El Salvador, there was no major "insurgency" or terrorist activity in the region; evidence that weapons from Nicaragua supported or were critical to the FMLN cause was weak.

Behind Shultz's rationale that the United States and its allies were the real victims, not Nicaragua,[16] the White House pressed on with Congress to coopt or intimidate dissenters; took a hardline position on negotiations and the need for an active CIA; gave encouragement and advice to private US groups funding the contras; announced that the United States would not accept World Court jurisdiction for the next two years; intensified efforts to unite the contras; and increased the number of US personnel, warships and planes trained and ready for combat in Central America.

But the need for at least minimal policy concensus among Washington pragmatists and ideologues and for running room from Congress led the administration to hold a series of bilateral talks with Nicaragua at Manzanillo, Mexico. The administration also stressed that democracy--not purging leftists or toppling a sitting government--was the objective in Nicaragua (and Salvador). That the Manzanillo talks were motivated by US election and Congressional politics became clear in January, 1985 when they were broken off as "going nowhere" due to "Nicaraguan insincerity." Actually, participants in those talks argued privately that a framework had been established at Manzanillo for addressing US (and Contadora) security concerns (author interviews, Managua).

The "MIG crisis" of November represented a continuation of administration efforts to raise the stakes in Nicaragua and produce an opinion tilt toward a harder-line policy. To deflect both international media reports of clean elections in Nicaragua on November 4 and the continuing furor in Washington over the CIA manuals for contra sabotage, the White House announced on the eve of US elections that Soviet-made MIG fighter jets were en route to Nicaragua, thus highlighting arguments that Nicaragua was arming itself for aggressive purposes. Earlier, US officials had warned of surgical air strikes against any such weapons in Nicaragua. Now, officials did not wait to confirm the story with intelligence data but began a campaign of high rhetoric against Nicaragua, going so far as to equate the situation to the Cuban Missile Crisis.[19] Shultz announced that the United States would do whatever necessary to defend its allies against a Nicaraguan invasion and rumors floated in Washington about the United States using military force to curb the Soviet's arming of Nicaragua. In the week prior to the "MIG crisis" and on election day the United States sent SR-71 Blackbird spy planes over Managua on several runs a day, their sonic booms waging a kind of psychological warfare against a people already worried about a US invasion. At the same time twenty-five US warships were on maneuvers in the Caribbean and the 82nd and 101st Airborne Divisions held exercises in Georgia. Nicaraguan and US forces were on full alert.

It soon became obvious that no MIGs were on aboard the Soviet ship. But the United States had focused public attention on Soviet links to Nicaragua at a time when the Congress was calling for a reigning-in of the CIA. The administration was also trying to delegitimize Nicaragua's internal political consolidation. The early November episode, moreover, demonstrated how volatile the Nicaragua issue was in US domestic politics and how quickly officials could create a pretext for a US invasion. In fact, the White House decided to keep the pressure on, hoping to "...translate concern about the military build-up in. Nicaragua into support for renewed aid to the rebels" (Pentagon official, quoted in NYT, 11-15-85). As another administration official put it: "Some of those who want us to adopt a harder line have long wished that MIGs would be delivered because they know that would tilt the policy in their direction.... The next best thing to the delivery of MIG's was the possibility that they might arrive any day" (NYT, op.cit.). Thus, officials also accused the Nicaraguans and Soviets of violating the Monroe Doctrine by "heavily arming" Nicaragua in preparation for imposing their systems on neighboring states by force.[18]

In contrast, US military officers reported that newly-acquired helicopters and radar equipment would increase Nicaragua's defense, but not its offense capacity (see Chapter 8). In their opinions, the acquisition of MIGs would do the same, although Washington had already informed both Moscow and Managua that that event would spark immediate US retaliation. These and similar challenges to administration posturing, in turn, renewed charges in Congress, the public and among policy pragmatists that the Reagan team sought a military rather than a political solution to the situation. Policy disputes among the ideologues and pragmatists flared, effectively muddying statements of purpose and stalling policy momentum. At year's end, the administration announced that Nicaragua policy was under review.

1985. The deadlock that resulted from the administration's policy review ultimately produced the ascendancy of the ideologues' agenda for Nicaragua: to create the conditions for the FSLN's collapse, whether by direct or indirect means, and to prepare an alternative government to take its place. To these ends, in 1985 the administration fought successfully to maintain official, Congressionally-sanctioned links to the contras. It built increased momentum for a militarily-imposed "solution" in Nicaragua, added new economic and military pressures on Managua and consolidated the framework and leadership structure for a pro-US government for Nicaragua.

The Reagan Administration waged an all-out battle to win Congressional funding for the contras when the votes came up in the Spring. Beginning with his February 6 State of the Union address and in the next months the president equated the contra struggle against the FSLN with the United States' struggle for national security. Labelling the contras "our brothers", "the moral equivalent of the Founding Fathers" and "true champions of freedom and democracy," the president identified the FSLN as a "small communist clique" whose leader was a "little dictator in green fatigues." Shultz also contributed to the image-control campaign, arguing that it was the "moral duty" of the United States to help the people of Nicaragua who had fallen "behind the iron curtain." Both men charged Nicaragua with aggressive designs against its neighbors and with exporting Soviet-type revolution and insurgency. The other tact for winning contra funding involved a campaign to deride Congressional opponents, a campaign which heated up after Congress turned down military aid in April and was considering alternative "humanitarian" aid in June. In May and June, while Fred Ikle (Pentagon) indicted Congress for undermining the president's policy with "a policy of pinpricks" and raised the spectre of later having to send marines against a fully-armed, Cuba-like Nicaragua "hell-bent on pursuing their policy", Shultz chided Congress for acting as "apologists for communists", for "failing to see the Nicaraguan communists for what they are", for writing "Dear Commandante letters" and for "appointing themselves emmisaries to the communist regime." Reagan himself echoed these themes, blaming Congress ahead of time for communist expansion and further instability in Central America. Reflecting on the heated rhetoric and Congress' mood in the first half of the year, Senator Lugar (R-Indiana), Chairman of the Senate's Foreign Affairs Committee, noted that the issue of Nicaragua had divided the president and Congress like no other issue since Vietnam.

Congress' decision to deny military aid but grant $27 million in non-lethal aid in no small part reflected the president's campaign to place "the responsibility for Nicaragua" on Congress' shoulders. In granting aid for non-military supplies, Congress signalled its belief that the Nicaraguan government had to change and that paramilitary pressure would help that change come about (e.g. NYT, 6-14-85). For its part, the administration took the vote as running room for another year of paramilitary action against the FSLN. The White House continued to facilitate private US funding for the contras. Weeks later it was revealed that, in fact, even before Congress reestablished sanctioned links (cut off in June, 1984) between the US government and the contras, NSC staff, under National Security Advisor MacFarlane's direction, were counselling contra leaders. A Congressional investigation reported that technically the Boland Amendment and other Congressional restrictions had not been violated. But many members felt that, again, the spirit of Congressional restrictions had been disregarded.

Directly related to the campaign vis-a-vis Congress were administration efforts to block peaceful solutions and concomitantly to broaden the bases for a justification of US military action. Adminstration officials in March revealed the White House agenda when they defined US conditions for supporting Contadora: the only Contadora agreement acceptable to Washington was one where the FSLN renounced Marxist ideals, invalidated the 1984 elections and turned the country into a "pluralist democracy" with leaders acceptable to the United States. This switch from the 1983-1984 US emphasis on technical and verification issues became necessary precisely because the Manzanillo talks had shown that agreement on these issues between the two countries was possible. But a Contadora agreement on these terms would leave the 15,000 or so contras in Honduras--something Honduras would not stand for--and would leave the FSLN in power.  Thus, a September, 1985 State Department working paper at the time argued that a Contadora agreement would be "phony" if it did not include articles on "internal reconciliation."

Administration policy-makers thus appeared to be holding out for the Frente's total capitulation, hoping the FSLN would crumble from within, but preparing the way for direct assault if the rebels failed.  According to US Embassy officials in Managua in 1985, President Reagan himself believed not only that the rebels, with continued US support, would win soon against the FSLN, but also that this process would be speeded by internal Nicaraguan political conditions.  The president believed that internal support for the Frente was evaporating quickly, that the economy was about to collapse and that Nicaragua by 1985 was at a "pre-insurrectionary" stage.  When all these forces converged, the FSLN would crumble. Thus negotiations were seen as unncecessary and counter-productive. From the US Embassy view in Managua in mid-1985, bilateral diplomatic efforts were effectively dead and the Sandinista Army (EPS) and the contras --- who were said by one official to be "awash in money and heavily arming" -- would decide the future of Nicaragua on the battlefield "in the next year."  Providing the contras moral support and more time, therefore, were important aspects of the president's policy in 1985 and 1986.[19]

The Contadora states, meanwhile, distressed by the Washington's stonewalling tactics and preference for military pressure, were saying publically that there were no other choices for Central America but Contadora or war.  In an effort to increase Contadora's hemispheric and international prestige or moral weight and to express more emphatically a Latin American perspective within the multilateral process, four other major Latin American actors joined with Contadora as an official support group:  Peru, Brazil, Argentina and Uruguay -- all states that had recently introduced new civilian and democratic governments.  The "Lima Group" dedicated itself to being a catalyst to the peace process.  Latin American unhappiness with Reagan's position was again registered.

On a second front the Reagan policy team hit again on the terrorism theme.  The anti-terrorism campaign begun in 1984 was directed specifically against Nicaragua in 1985.  In a speech to the United States Bar Association in July, President Reagan developed the terrorist theme raised against Nicaragua in his State of the Union message.  Citing the existence of "new international version of Murder Incorporated" dedicated to committing "outright acts of war against the United States," the president labelled Nicaragua, Iran, Libya, North Korea and Cuba:  "...outlaw states run by the strangest collection of misfits, Looney Tunes and squalid criminals since the advent of the Third Reich."  Admitting political reasons for its exclusion, the administration left Syria off its list.

The US case against Nicaragua was built around a series of inter-related contentions:  that the war in Salvador was an outgrowth of Sandinista exportation of revolution; that Nicaragua was arming offensively and for purposes of attacking its neighbors; that Nicaragua was getting weapons from "the Soviets and their terrorist allies" who were "pumping in money to establish a beachead on our own doorstep"; and that Nicaragua had become, as US Attorney General Ed Meese claimed, "a countryclub for world terrorists." Reacting to a terrorist attack in San Salvador in June in which six off-duty US Marines were gunned down at a popular cafe, and, claiming guilt by association, the United States sent a terse note to the Nicaraguans warning that the United States in the future would hold Nicaragua responsible for any acts against Americans in Central America and retaliate when, where and how it chose. By declining to be more specific about which acts would be judged terrorism and given the level of political instability in the region, Washington effectively broadened the possibilities for justifiable military action against Nicaragua. Yet once again, El Salvador was the administration's best case against Nicaraguan "terrorism" in the region and that case had proven weak. The government's best evidence was contradicted by ex-CIA and ex-diplomatic corp personnel, by US military and intelligence people on the ground, and by the Nicaraguans who brought their evidence into their World Court case in 1985.

Evidence of the administration's linkage of the terrorism campaign to its hostility toward Nicaragua existed in the policy recommendations Vice President Bush presented in mid-1985 following his study of possible US responses to world terrorism. Part of a broad strategy of war against leftists in Central America, the options offered by Bush included: requesting Congressional funding for doubling the size of contra forces to 30,000; increasing police and military training to regional allies; moderating or eliminating presidential prohibitions against assassinations; and carrying out air attacks or commando raids against rebel and training centers in Salvador and Nicaragua (IHCA, August, 1985).

Military and economic pressure on Nicaragua was increased in 1985. The most dramatic action came on May 1 when President Reagan invoked the International Emergency Economic Powers Act, declared to Congress that US national security required action, and announced an economic embargo on Nicaragua. The embargo decision would be reconsidered only if the Frente opened talks with the armed opposition under the auspices of the Catholic Church hierarchy in Nicaragua. Part of a larger US program of economic strangulation, and coming just after Congress denied military aid for the contras, the embargo was actually intended for domestic and regional political consumption rather than as a move that could induce much more economic pain on Nicaragua. In line with the president's portrayal of Nicaragua, Congressional and conservative supporters demanded stronger measures be taken, including a break in relations or using US troops, to force the Frente into talks with the contras. Pressure mounted from the right to put US actions in line with the level of security threat said to be posed by Nicaragua. The embargo, aides determined, would also demonstrate to Congress the president's will prior to the June contra funding ("humanitarian") vote. Reagan officials privately rationalized the embargo as a way to send a message of reassurance to allies that the United States would not abandon them in the cause against Nicaragua.

The move itself, however, was counterproductive to US interests

as the administration defined them. Inside Nicaragua, the embargo
gave the Frente more evidence for blaming Nicaragua's economic ills
on US aggression, it fueled antagonism toward the United States and
further undermined the private sector which did the bulk of
Nicaragua's trading with the United States. The embargo also worked
to hasten Nicaragua's economic diversification away from the United
States and the West as the FSLN sought out new markets and sources.
In the international arena, the US move earned condemnations from
GATT, Western European governments, the EEC, the Non-Alignment
Movement, India, China and Latin America. Meanwhile, Canada, Sweden
and other states offered immediate new aid and trade (IHCA, June,
1985).

Finally, in 1985 the Reagan Administration carefully fostered
and coerced the unification of the various contra groups under a
"clean" political leadership and a "democratic program of
government" into the United Nicaraguan Opposition (UNO). (I discuss
this in detail in the next chapter.) It was this group with which
Washington coordinated its demands on the FSLN and its peace plans
for Nicaragua. And it was through this group that the United States
had strong[20] contacts with the CDN civilian opposition inside
Nicaragua. But because a number of independent human rights
groups and contra defectors had extensively reported both contra
atrocities against civilians and their attack strategy of targetting
social service, education, health and church centers, presenting UNO
as a good alternative to the Sandinista government remained a
political problem.


DISPUTES OVER NICARAGUA POLICY

Ronald Reagan was an ideologue who had shown on a number of
issues that he could be a pragmatist when his preferred option
proved too costly -- even if in giving up a position he claimed a
victory and went on to pursue his goals. A real test of his ability
to be a "consummate politician" developed for Reagan by 1983: the
president had become and remained personally identified with the
anti-Sandinista cause, a cause for which there was no national (or
conservative) consensus and which was failing in the field. Yet, he
and the conservative ideologues continued to pursue that cause,
bucking the political mood of Congress and the public on Central
America and working around obstacles put in their way to maintain a
low-intensity war of attrition against the revolution. Determined
to regain the prestige and military prowess he believed America had
lost under weaker presidents, Reagan surrounded himself with
conservative aides, some ideologues and other pragmatists. Though
there was generally a consensus among his top foreign policy-makers
around the conservative agenda on issues of leftist revolution and
the use of force as a primary policy instrument, the pragmatists put
more weight on what was politically possible at any given time.
Regarding Nicaragua, the consensus of the top policy- makers in 1981
was that the Sandinistas -- both as leftists with ties to Cuba and
as promoters of economic independence from Washington -- constituted
a national security threat to the United States that had to be

eliminated. That consensus also resulted in hard, negative rhetoric against the Sandinistas from all White House and other top policy makers, and, a general agreement that a US military presence in the region needed to be enlarged. However, it became clear over time that the Sandinistas were firmly in control of Nicaragua, and, that Congress would both create obstacles for an overt military action in Nicaragua and maintain financial and legal limitations on the president's covert war against the Sandinistas. As the political costs of toppling the FSLN government thus rose, it also became clear that there was no consensus among conservative policy-makers on the appropriate level of force to be used in countering that threat; specifically, whether a direct move to unseat the FSLN was politically feasible, or whether the United States could negotiate with a considerably tamed, militarily and politically contained FSLN government--the so-called "Yugoslavia solution."

By the end of 1984, dissensus among the White House policy-shapers had led to a deadlock over how to proceed vis-a-vis Nicaragua; as no new ground could be agreed upon, the White House policy team sought to maintain the political space for keeping military and economic pressure on Nicaragua. Yet, within the administration there was no agreement on whether this domestically controversial policy was achieving the stated objectives of changing the political reality inside Nicaragua. The policy stalemate in 1985 and 1986 amounted to buying time for the contras. But it also pointed to the inevitable policy crisis if the contra war failed: would the administration send in troops (even without public support) or would it recognize the legitimacy of the FSLN regime and work for the best possible political solution? The latter would be a bitter pill for President Reagan and the ideologues even if doing so was dictated by political necessity and could be made to look a victory. The president was betting that the US campaign would bring the FSLN to its knees. Yet, the inability of the conservative ideologues in top policy positions to rally support among conservative pragmatists, the Congress, and the public for a direct US military action to eliminate the FSLN as a power contender in Nicaragua while the necessary military infrastructure for such a move was in place, constituted an essential feature of regional policy-making under the Reagan Administration. Conversely, the inability of those who opposed the president's military and hostile policy to stop it, to force the president to the negotiating table, or to offer a coherent alternative to administration policy, characterized the politics of US-Nicaragua policy into the mid-1980s.

While only a few of the "hardliners" spoke openly in 1981 and 1982 of their belief that the FSLN government had to be eliminated, by 1983 and 1984, as I have pointed out, the president and other officals asserted that they could not and would not work with the "present structure" in Nicaragua. According to senior Reagan aides, removing the Sandinista regime had always been a major factor in policy deliberations and actions (e.g. NYT, 8-18-85). Nicaraguan policy after 1983 featured White House end-runs around Congress and Contadora, a pull-out-the-stops anti-communism campaign to intimidate critics, the continued militarization of Central America

and the Caribbean, and attempts to remake the Somocista contra force
into an acceptable alternative ("democratic" and pro-US) government
for Nicaragua. But where the policy was going remained unclear.
Through mid-1986 the contras and other US pressure had not affected
Nicaraguan concessions on the United States' major demand--FSLN
talks with the contras on a new form of government. In spite of all
US economic and military efforts up to that point, the Nicaraguan
revolution was being consolidated and internationally supported.
Attaining President Reagan's objective--rooting out "ideological
aggression" in the United States' backyard--appeared unachievable,
unless a direct and major US military move was undertaken. A
consensus for sending in US troops and destroying the revolution by
a massive military assault was an illusive prospect; nevertheless,
the White House team was able to establish the physical (military)
infrastructure to support such a move should it become "necessary"
or tenable. It was also able to keep the issue alive as the "only
alternative" to getting the Frente to "change its behavior" if other
attempts -- namely, support for the contras -- failed.
    Major elements of White House policy, then, were avoiding
non-US negotiation initiatives and painting the Sandinista
government as hostile, intransigent, aggressive and untrustworthy.
If no consensus for invading Nicaragua came together, US military
moves and heated rhetoric would keep the Sandinistas nervous, wear
down their domestic support or push them into making moves against
Honduras or Costa Rica. That in turn would justify a "defensive"
military move by the United States against Nicaragua under the Rio
Treaty. Despite the lack of consensus within top policy circles
over the amount of force necessary to neutralize the security threat
posed by the FSLN (i.e., in the absence of a national consensus that
a security threat was immediate or demanded a defensive military
action) and in spite of the policy-makers' disagreement with a
majority in Congress over the choice of policy instruments--force or
negotiation--the White House team was able to maintain the policy
initiative and momentum even as Congress placed obstacles in the way
of a military solution.
    Anti-Sandinista rhetoric, however, also closed off certain
policy options from a domestic politics point of view. The bigger
the security threat, the fewer the options available to a superpower
in dealing with it. Pragmatic options for US policy, such as a
political settlement, were being edged out. Threats against US
national security had to be neutralized or eliminated. So, the
White House, despite the policy stalemate over options other than
invasion, was actually creating a situation where force appeared to
be the only logical choice. To negotiate with a
"totalitarian-terrorist" government would appear to be conceding to
communism, to be dealing from a position of weakness. Conservative
constituents called for actions consistent with rhetoric condemning
expansionist communism, i.e., overthrowing the FSLN with US troops.
The pragmatists remained wary of an unpopular war at home, of major
confrontations with Congress which would ultimately hamper other
programs as well and of condemnations from Latin American and
European allies. Internationally, the United States was isolated in
its no-negotiation policy on Nicaragua.

## Administration Ideologues and Pragmatists

Two centers of policy disputes worked to rob the ideologues of
the consensus necessary for directly toppling the FSLN government.
One center of dispute existed among top decision-makers who
disagreed over how far to go in pursuing an ideological agenda and
at what point political costs demanded compromise. The ideologues,
bolstered by the president's support, the language of immediacy and
the similarity of their view to traditional US policy regarding
Latin America, maneuvered to predominate on Central American policy.
For example, by early 1983 when it appeared that Washington was
losing the military and diplomatic initiative in El Salvador and
Nicaragua, the policy power-axis ran among the White House National
Security Council, the Pentagon and the CIA. Although Secretary of
State Shultz worked to change the situation in 1983 and 1984, the
State Department, except for some of its hardliners, was often
outside the initial policy information loop. Instead, political
appointees of the NSC like William Clark, Jeane Kirkpatrick, William
Casey, Constantine Menges, Nestor Sanchez and Fred Ikle and their
officers and contacts in the field were prominent in setting and
implementing the policy agenda. The conservative "moderates" --
those who wanted to give negotiations more energy or time -- were
edged out and replaced with policy hardliners or Reagan loyalists.
Motley, Pickering and Schlaudeman replaced Enders (Assistant
Secretary of State for Inter-American Affairs), Hinton (US
Ambassador in Salvador), and Stone (roving ambassador) in 1983. In
1984 loyalist Harry Bergold replaced Quainton as Ambasssador to
Nicaragua (Quainton was reportedly not negative enough on the
Sandinistas when Kissinger visited Nicaragua in 1983), and, when
loyalist Motley, ideologue Kirkpatrick (UN), and moderate Mac
Farlane (NSA) left the administration in 1985, they were replaced
respectively by ideologue Elliot Abrams, loyalist Vernon Walters,
and loyalist John Poindexter.
Inevitably, policy disputes between ideologues and pragmatists
broke out, accompanied by inter-agency and intra-agency squabbles
over turf. Top Pentagon officials worried about the growing role of
the CIA in the contra war, while within the military community there
were policy disputes between political analysts like Ikle and
Sanchez, and, the Joint Chiefs of Staff, other top officers and
military and intelligence analysts. The latter argued for
accommodating a militarily contained FSLN. Similarly, the
diplomatic community envied the predominance of other agencies or
White House independence in agenda-setting, but was also split
between various "exterminate" and "accommodate" positions. These
realities contributed to deadlocks when policy options were
reviewed, such as at funding time, while day to day decisions and
(military) activities in the field were directed by those who
generally held the harder line, i.e., Pentagon, CIA and NSC
political appointees.
Policy perspectives among Reagan conservatives had come by the
end of 1984 to group around two poles. A number of officials
rejected the idea of a political settlement with the Sandinistas,
arguing that the FSLN could not be trusted to abide by any agreement

and that, in any case, such an agreement would amount to sanctioning
a Cuban and Soviet role in what was traditionally the United States'
backyard. Although the United States had been demanding that the
Frente send home its Cuban and Eastern bloc military advisors and
pare down its Soviet-supplied military arsenal, as US pressure
continued the Nicaraguans continued to rely on these sources. And,
they expanded trade with the Eastern bloc to include oil, machinery
and raw materials. Given this situation, top political appointees
(i.e., not the generals) at the Pentagon, the CIA, and on the NSC
staff argued for a change in policy: the United States should
withdraw diplomatic recognition from the FSLN government, recognize
the contras as the legitimate government of Nicaragua, use US force
(e.g., navy sea interdictions; increased US maneuvers) to stop arms
flows to Nicaragua and provide <u>overt</u> aid to the contras to
facilitate their military victory over a weakened FSLN. This group
appeared to be split on the issue of whether the contras were a
viable fighting force without US aid. Casey, for one, argued that
they were and the president reportedly took Casey's word on this
issue. But most argued along with a few Congressmen that the United
States should confront the Nicaraguan security threat openly and
thereby also circumvent the appearance of illegality surrounding the
"secret war" of the contras. It was clear to all that the contras
had made no territorial or political progress on the ground in
nearly five years of fighting. The United States needed to
demonstrate its sincerity with firm action. Secretary Weinberger
confirmed in November, 1984 that Washington was preparing for all
these contingencies.[21]

This hardline group, which ultimately wanted the Sandinistas
removed from power and felt that the president's reelection made
this the time to pursue a new policy thrust, argued that Nicaragua's
military posed a threat to the Panama Canal, to neighboring
countries and to US security. According to Weinberger in November,
offensive weapons flows from the Soviet Union had increased
tremendously. The weapons link with the Soviet Union could open the
possibility for the future of USSR military bases in Central
America. In sum, many in this group believed that Nicaragua had
become a "second Cuba" and that the United States could not allow
such a development in Central America. Such had also been the
themes of President Reagan since he personally entered the debate on
Nicaragua in 1983: there was no hope for peace in the region or for
a "Yugoslavia solution" so long as the FSLN was in power in
Nicaragua. The Sandinistas had shown that they did not respond to
US incentives. As policy options narrowed to exterminate or
accommodate, the ideologues easily preferred the former.

The second group within the top policy cadre also believed that
the Frente would respond only to force -- both groups strongly
supported the use of the contras in weakening the FSLN's political
and economic position in Nicaragua. But the second group tended to
see the contras as an alternative to the use of US troops and feared
that recognizing the contras as an alternative government and aiding
them would lead both to direct US involvement, and demands for a
declaration of war if and when the contras could not hold their own
militarily. The contras' poor military showing and Congress'

refusal to give more military aid to the contras made the
hardliners' policy recommendations untenable politically. On
another level Secretary Shultz and other top State Department
officials within this camp appeared less convinced in 1984 that
Nicaraguan political structures had become consolidated, or, on a
Cuban model. In their view, current US policy of attrition had made
new diplomatic moves possible; the earlier intransigent Sandinistas
had been convinced of Washington's depth of concern and were ready
for talks. This group generally accepted the Sandinistas' offers of
concessions, or, were willing to test their sincerity in bilateral
talks. Their bet was that the Nicaraguans were ready to comply with
a peace plan. As evidence of this, they pointed to the outline of
an agreement on security issues which emerged from the bilateral
Manzanillo talks.[22]   Shultz argued that bilateral agreements could
be incorporated into Contadora, an initiative which was supported by
Congress, the public, major international organizations and US
allies, thus giving the peace plan domestic viability and
international force. If the hardliners wanted to follow a rollback
strategy against the FSLN, the pragmatists argued that the political
costs of doing so were too high; US security concerns could be
addressed by a contained Nicaragua.

The policy review begun at the end of 1984 ended in a
deadlock.[23]  No consensus existed for an outright military invasion
or for direct US military moves of a lesser nature such as a naval
blockade or limited air or naval strikes. The White House, on the
other hand, was not prepared to probe the possibility of a political
settlement.

Once again in 1985 and into 1986 the president and the
ideologues preserved the momentum on Central American policy, aided
now by politics at home and events in the region. Owners of a
so-far-unsuccessful, stalled policy, the administration ideologues
were yet able to foist blame on a resource-cutting Congress, up the
political ante with the anti-terrorism campaign, characterize
Contadora as "sanctioning another Cuba" and gain time for the
"freedom fighters" -- their only alternative politically. Moderate
conservatives Shultz and National Security Advisor MacFarlane,
meanwhile, were prioritizing arms talks and a major summit meeting
with the Soviets in 1985 and appeared to give some ground to the
ideologues on Nicaragua in return for elbow room in establishing the
US framework for the arms talks. But another factor was the
conservatives' concern generally about the seeming success of the
post-election constitution-writing process underway in Nicaragua
after 1984; political consolidation of the revolution continued
under FSLN leadership. These things bolstered the ideologues'
position and over 1985 the moderates within the administration were
noticeably silent. The hardliners thus spearheaded the drive to
refinance the contras, newly united under an opposition front and
proposing a "democratic program". The president, recall, believed
in 1985 and 1986 that the contras could win against the Sandinista
army as a combination of US pressures converged to weaken the
Frente. If some results could be shown in Nicaragua, for example if
the contras could win internal support or take some territory, the
way might be clear for more direct US moves. Top officials,

sabre-rattling to warn both the FSLN and Congress, began talking openly about invading Nicaragua (e.g. NYT, 6-5-85).

At the same time, Congressional opposition had lost much of its momentum, having failed to offer alternative policy leadership or a different framework for debate. Public opinion -- running in February at 70 percent disapproval of Reagan's Central American policy -- was being largely ignored by policy ideologues or neutralized in its impact on the administration by the fervor of anti-communist, pro-Reagan interest groups. Still, no consensus existed in Washington for directly overthrowing the Sandinista government, even if no group in government would stand to support that regime. Military analysts and Pentagon generals, concerned about the public if the White House team was not, warned of the consequences of large military actions where there was neither popular support nor clear, noncontroversial objectives for such a move.

The consensus that did seem to exist in Washington by 1985 was that the Sandinista government was a bad government as it stood and was bad for the region. Yet, a majority did not believe Nicaragua posed a direct security threat to the United States. The evidence on claims against Nicaragua, on gun-running, aggressive intentions, human rights violations or support for insurgency or terrorism was just too inconclusive. Yet, as the administration continued to press its communist-expansionism and terrorism themes on Congress, its members increasingly declined to stand in the way of confronting these threats to US national security as the president defined them in Central America. For example, after a House vote that sparked the arrest of over a thousand protestors across the United States in June, 1985, Congress sent $27 million in "humanitarian aid" to the contras, whom, the president argued, were the only hope for moderating the Sandinistas. In a significant move, Congress also approved the sharing of US military intelligence with the contras. Shortly thereafter, the House debated conditions under which the president could strike or use troops against Nicaragua without Congressional approval, thereby sending a signal to the White House that actually enforced rather[24] than limited the president's initiative vis-a-vis Nicaragua;[24] the president would be left to define the security threat. The president, in other words, had kept the policy initiative and had put off, for at least another year, confronting stark, politically more costly choices on Nicaragua. Reagan also believed time and the internal situation in Nicaragua were on his side; chances were that the FSLN would collapse from within.

Policy disputes, the lack of broad policy consensus and the controversial nature of some of the administration's underlying objectives, however, did exact a toll on the president's policy and image. In deference to the lack of a national consensus, policy had to be couched in language that stressed Washington's preference for negotiation and political settlements. It had to include the appearance of political concessions to the domestic opposition or to regional peace initiatives. The policy language or image, however, was inconsistent with both stated and leaked objectives and national security rationalizations. The language of peace and negotiation, similarly, did not match actual policy (e.g., military) activities in the region. Nor was diplomatic and military policy always coordinated. For example, when domestic political considerations led the administration to go through the motions of pursuing talks, to tone down its rhetoric or work to present a bipartisan definition of regional realities, military expansion in the region continued apace. The president continued to deny that the United States aimed to overthrow the Sandinistas. The upshot was that policy appeared at times incoherent or confused and was always controversial due to the underlying ambivalence over administration actions within the wider Washington foreign policy sector. The president and his aides were imprecise in public statements about contra goals and US purposes in supporting them; the imprecision reflected both the controversial nature of US undertakings and conservatives' varying rationales for supporting the policies.

Moreover, when the Sandinistas or Fidel Castro responded to US military pressures by offering to talk with the United States, sponsor a ceasefire or make other concessions as they did in 1983 and 1984, administration officials had no plans on how to proceed. Disagreement existed over when the United States should negotiate with the FSLN, if ever. What negotiating "on US terms" meant shifted with what appeared politically feasible at the time. To the hardline ideologues, the phrase meant when the FSLN was effectively neutralized as a power contender. But the hardliners had also not expected concessions from "enemy" states and were suspicious of them; concessions represented insincere propaganda moves ("a Marxist government cannot reform") or were signs of weakness and called for increased pressure on the state to speed up the inevitable capitulation. The pragmatists were more apt to push for quiet diplomacy to feel out the sincerity of the gestures. But the policy stalemate meant a continuation with policy as it had evolved: discrediting peace gestures, avoiding movement toward negotiations and keeping up the pressure. Similarly, into 1986 Congress was yielding the president more time to demonstrate that military pressure would "produce results" in Nicaragua.

## Disputes With Congress

The other arena of dispute over policy was between the administration and Congress. Beginning in 1982 with public revelations about the depth and nature of US involvement with the counter-revolutionaries, Congress repeatedly investigated, publicized and constrained the administration's and the CIA's covert military operations against the Sandinistas. Congress expressed concern about the legality of the operation and the potential it presented for involving the United States in a Vietnam-like quagmire. The Boland Amendment, which banned the use of US weapons or training in efforts to overthrow the FSLN government, passed in a 411-0 House vote in December, 1982. In the next three years, repeated administration and Republican efforts to repeal or circumvent that amendment were defeated. In 1983, the House voted to cut contra funding altogether, an effort not accomplished until 1984 when funds ran out (in June) and the Democratic House refused

to join the Republican Senate on a request from the president for an
additional $21 million. By this time Congressional committees were
expressing deep skepticism about: 1)the contras' capacity to meet
the redefined objectives for them (they had not confiscated any
weapons en route to El Salvador and they were seemingly ineffective
in forcing the FSLN to change their internal political behavior);
2)the CIA's ability to control the greatly expanded militry force;
3)the methods employed by the CIA in the covert war; and 4)the
administration's circumvention of and apparent disdain for
Congressional actions and opinions.

Refusing military aid in 1985, Congress nonetheless provided
$27 million in "humanitarian aid" to the contras[25] and restricted
the CIA and the Pentagon from overseeing those funds. While
Congress' mood had shifted in the preceding year to a somewhat more
critical view of the Frente, Congress also made it clear that the
president's contra war and Nicaragua policy generally had to show
some results soon or face pressure for a new policy tact.

Although Congress forced the president to work with less money
and restricted objectives, it was not successful in stemming or
changing the administration's clear preference for military force as
the major instrument of foreign policy in Central America (see also,
Destler, 1984). Nor was Congress successful in arresting the growth
of US military activity in Central America or in offering a coherent
alternative to Reagan's policy of confrontation and East-West
posturing. Congress was successful, periodically, in forcing the
president to change his rhetoric and to talk about negotiations.
Moreover, Congressional activity forced the administration to spend
much energy explaining and justifying money requests. The
administration's range of policies was thereby laid open to public
inspection. It was this aspect of Congressional activity that led
to the greatest restriction on foreign policy ideologues into 1986:
they would have to pursue their objectives vis-a-vis Nicaragua
without using US troops. Indeed by late 1984 these policy
officials, frustrated by their failure so far to undermine the
Frente, were busy laying groundwork for new rationalizations for a
direct US military move on Nicaragua. Throughout 1985, the
ideologues continued to press their view that the United States
could not work with "self-described revolutionaries" in Nicaragua.
Working within the conceptual limits established over previous years
and expressed as "No second Cuba, no second Vietnam," policy shapers
"played the breaks" as events unfolded, hoping the FSLN would
collapse internally (NYT, 8-18-85). The conditions under which
President Reagan, backed to the wall by determined political
opposition at home and by continued Sandinista resilience in
Nicaragua, would have to show his pragmatism and survivor political
skills had not developed on the issue of Nicaragua. Whether such a
time would come before the end of his second term or whether he
would finally put together the consensus or the conditions necessary
to order an invasion remained to be seen. By 1986, both the FSLN's
staying power and Latin American opinion appeared to suggest that
the "problem" of Nicaragua might well be left for another US
president. Contra leaders, on the other hand, insisted that they
would induce major changes in Nicaraguan politics in the next year

or two.

## CONCLUSIONS

As the Reagan Administration's preferred policy options vis-a-vis Nicaragua became articulated it also became clear that Reagan policy was motivated more by ideology than reality or long-term considerations. Spurred by a preference to defeat rather than negotiate with "enemies" and to make Nicaragua a test case in the global confrontation with the USSR, the White House adjusted its rationale and grounds for a direct military move against Nicaragua from things it could not directly control, such as Nicaragua obtaining advanced fighter jets or allowing a Soviet base in its territory, to things more maneuverable or open to administration interpretation, such as when or where Nicaragua was behind an act which constituted terrorism or an act which constituted aggression against its neighbors. For instance, with the FMLN guerrillas in Salvador returning to urban sabotage and assassination tactics in 1985, and, with an increasing number of border incidents with Costa Rica and Honduras in the same year that Nicaragua initiated an effort to inflict a decisive blow on the contras, many opportunities existed for an administration judgement that the conditions justifying a military response were present. Meanwhile, administration rhetoric maintained the volatility of the issue as its campaign against Congressional critics raised the political costs to any obstructionists in a moment of "national security crisis." In less than a crisis situation, the White House had found, it could not organize a public -- or administration-wide -- consensus directly to overthrow the FSLN government. Manipulation of the evidence became crucial to maintaining the military options as the only possible options. Indeed, Reagan ideologues after 1983 successfully shifted the debate on Nicaragua to whether the United States would or should invade.

Yet, enough counter-evidence and alternative regional scenarios existed to suggest that support for a crisis-sparked invasion would be shortlived, and, that a military solution to the problem of Nicaragua (or of the FMLN) was no solution at all. A number of realities poignantly demonstrated the ill-conceived nature and the short-term view of Reagan's policies, among them: 1)the inability of the contras in five years of fighting to spark an uprising in Nicaragua, or, to coordinate with or create an internal front; 2)the continued military strength of the Sandinistas and the FMLN in Salvador after years of hostile US policy and regional militarization;[26] 3)the increasingly polarized nature of politics in Central American states and the accompanying loss of motivation for compromise; 4)the inability of the Reagan Administration to obtain international or allied support for its Central American policies; and 5)the continued determination of Latin American states to reserve political initiative in South American affairs, or, to insist on cooperative solutions rather than Washington's imposed solution. Latin American states challenged both US attempts to maintain the political initiative in the Western Hemisphere and US suggestions that US-USSR relations -- not the UN, the World Court, the OAS, or Contadora -- would establish the framework within which hemispheric relations or political problems would be addressed. Nevertheless, President Reagan again showed his proclivity for viewing world affairs exclusively through an East-West prism when he decided to place "Third World trouble spots" or regional security issues as a top agenda item for the late 1985 summit meeting with Soviet leader Gorbachev. Taking attention away from nuclear arms negotiations, Reagan suggested that a solution for Nicaragua and for Central America would ultimately come through talks with the Soviets.

That suggestion reflected, too, the Reagan Administration's realization by 1985 that the war in El Salvador could not soon be won on the ground by either side. Increased shipments of helicopter gunships and counter-insurgency training there in 1985 amounted to short-sighted US posturing; besides maintaining ground, the Salvadoran government needed to broaden its support from (and control over) civilian population in order to narrow bargaining room for the FMLN in the future. Again, military programs were offered as fostering democracy.

Regional realities in the mid-1980s suggested that the United States' military solutions would be costly in the short- and long-term for relations with Nicaragua and Central America. They also symbolized the inappropriateness of pursuing US hegemony as a long-term posture vis-a-vis a Latin America increasingly insistent on its policy independence, and, over a continent bound to experience other reforms and revolutions not approved by the United States. If the United States was to learn these lessons at a later time, it remained for revolutionary Nicaragua to formulate a foreign policy for survival in the face of immediate threats posed by the local superpower.


NOTES

1. The United States had not recognized even by this time the deep hatred felt by most Nicaraguans for the Guardia and Somoza structures. As late as May, 1979 the United States backed a $66 million IMF loan to Somoza's politically and morally bankrupt government (Stepan, 1981: 29).
2. This is a reference to the Trilateral Commission. On its philosophy and structure see Holly Sklar (1981).
3. The Senate allocated 60 percent of the funds for the use of the private sector. The House listed sixteen other conditions, for example, that no money could go into health or education programs in which Cubans were involved and that 1 percent of the funds were to be used to publicize the United States' aid to the Nicaraguan people. See Jonas (1982) and Mathews (1985).
4. Referred to by Central Americans and others as the "Sante Fe Document" the report's complete title is "A New Inter-American Policy for the Eighties", and was written by five men, four of whom joined the Reagan Administration to help implement their own recommendations. The report was published in Washington

D.C. in May, 1980 by the Council for Inter-American Security.

5. The platform text was published by Congressional Quarterly in its July 19, 1980 edition, page 2030ff.

6. Sanders (1985) cites numerous examples.

7. On this topic see Richard White (1984) and Jorge Nef (1984).

8. "Guns and beans" was the name given to President Efrain Rios Montt's counterinsurgency campaign in Guatemala in 1982 and 1983, a policy continued by General Mejia when he became President after Montt's overthrow in 1983. Peasants in the affected zones were promised food and other services if the men joined the military in patrols or in hunting down "insurgents." The alternative to joining the military's campaign was often death. This phase of the operation followed military burn-and-raze sweeps through areas where insurgents had been active. Homeless peasants and campesinos were then relocated into "protected" villages of the strategic hamlet variety (Vietnam vintage) and introduced to "guns and beans". By 1984 the United States was joining the Guatemalan government in calling these military-secured villages "development poles" and in 1985 US AID monies went to support development projects in the same villages.

9. The Washington Post and the Wall Street Journal each reported on inconsistencies, poor or faulty documentation, inaccurate translations of documents, deletions and purposefully misconstrued passages used in the White Paper. See WP, 6-8-81; 6-9-81.

10. Author interview with Ambasssador Quainton in Managua, August, 1982. On this period, also see Gutman, op.cit.

11. Border clashes between Honduras and Nicaragua had been occurring, sparked by contra raids into Nicaragua originating from Honduras. The FSLN and some Honduran leaders feared war would break out (see Chapter 7.)

12. For an expanded discussion of this and other personnel changes in this period see Vanderlaan (1984).

13. The prospects for the usefulness of this military organization in service of US anti-communism were mixed, at best. While Guatemala's military participation was strategically vital if a successful regional war were to be waged against leftists in Salvador or Nicaragua, President Mejia tried to steer an independent path in regional politics -- preferring that to US orchestration of regional politics. Guatemala preferred maneuvering room vis-a-vis Nicaragua.

14. Also in February, roving Central American Ambassador Stone resigned reportedly after a series of disputes with Motley (State Department) over the US position on negotiations in general (LAWR, 2-24-84). Stone, who had been working in the region and with the Contadora states, advocated a stronger US emphasis on negotiations. Stone was replaced by Harry Schlaudeman who had had diplomatic experience in other Latin American "trouble spots", notably Chile in 1973 and the Dominican Republic in 1965.

15. The urgency of this condition for the United States becomes clearer when put into context. The contras had been having few battlefield or political successes. Congress had been moving to

cut funds for them in the wake of revelations about CIA and contra human right abuses. The Hondurans had been threatening to push the contras out of Honduras.

16. In April UN Ambassador Kirkpatrick argued that the United States would not unilaterally obey international law that adversaries violated "with impunity", and, that for critics of US policy to portray Nicaragua as the victim was "...a complete Orwellian inversion of what is happening in Central America" (NYT, 4-13-84). In another US-as-victim scenario, one raised by the president himself in 1983 and 1984, CIA's Casey said in April, 1984 that he believed US citizens were more concerned about waves of immigrants that would follow Soviet gains in Latin America than about reports of CIA-supervised harbor-mining in Nicaragua (NYT, 4-16-84).

17. In the Cuban case, the Soviets were sending over forty ships a month to Cuba with arms and support material. In the Nicaraguan case, Soviet shipments were irregular and nowhere near the level of military support given Cuba. The "MIG Crisis" involved one Soviet freighter.

18. The revival of the Monroe Doctrine was part of a larger administration effort to establish grounds for "collective self-defense" against alleged Nicaraguan support of the FMLN in El Salvador. At the World Court in October, 1984, State Department lawyers defined US-Nicaraguan policy as self-defense against "armed attack", as recognized in the UN charter.

19. By early 1985, the administration was involved in a third round of talks with the Honduran army which was increasingly wary of a large contra presence in their territory at a time when Congressional funding had been cut.

20. US Embassy officials in Managua confirmed that the contra (UNO) leaders had multiple and regular contacts with the civilian opposition in Managua. According to one analyst there, UNO's cause was the CDN's cause.

21. Secretary Weinberger also held that Vietnam had taught that large military actions had to have public support behind clear and limited military and political objectives (NYT, 11-29-84).

22. Interviews with US Embassy and Nicaraguan foreign ministry officials in Managua in August, 1985 confirmed that the Manzanillo talks held between June and December of 1984 had made room for agreements on all the United States' major security concerns: armaments, advisors, insurgency and the like. However, the US position was to continue US pressure until the FSLN agreed to internal political reforms which would include FSLN recognition of the contras as legitimate, Nicaraguan political opposition.

23. Indicative of the pragmatist-ideologue split among conservatives are contrasting statement of US purpose vis-a-vis Nicaragua made by high level officials in mid 1984. Some argued that the United States would be happy with or settle for a system in Nicaragua similar to the one-party (PRI) dominant system in Mexico. Others held that, as one official put it referring to the leftist FSLN and FMLN in Salvador, "Why bother if after November 6 [and Reagan's reelection] we'll role up the bastards with everyone else," (LAWR, 8-3-84).

24. Just prior to the June contra vote, President Ortega took a trip to the USSR -- this just after Congress had voted no <u>military</u> funding for the contras. Many Congress members who were <u>opposing</u> the president on his contra policy felt betrayed by Ortega's trip. The Nicaraguans countered that the trip had been one month in the planning; that Nicaragua was down to one month's oil supply, and that they needed to negotiate new oil and economic aid to shore up an ailing economy (author interviews).

25. Though labelled "humanitarian aid", the money did not qualify as such under the Geneva Convention. Under the Accords, such assistance could go only to civilians and noncombatants and was to be doled out to both sides by neutral states accepted by both parties to the conflict. In the case of the US-supported contras, the integrity of humanitarian aid under the Accords was in jeopardy; the US national security establishment was giving nonmilitary aid to facilitate a group involved in combat aimed at getting political concessions from a third party (the FSLN).

26. As the Salvadoran army began to implement US-inspired reforms in its command and combat practices and to work more effectively against the guerrillas in 1984, the guerrillas in turn changed tactics, returning to earlier methods of urban warfare, constant mobility and sabotage. Nevertheless, the overall strength of the FMLN did not appear to have diminished, nor did its force level fall from the 1983-1984 levels of about 9-10,000 fighters (e.g. <u>CARIN</u>, June, 1985).

# 6

## US Economic and Military Policy: Low-Intensity Attrition Warfare

> We must remember that if the Sandinistas are not stopped now, they will, as they have sworn, attempt to spread communism to El Salvador, Costa Rica, Honduras and elsewhere....America may never have been born without the help and support of the freedom-loving people of Europe, of Lafayette and von Steuben and Kosciusko. And now the free people of El Salvador, Honduras and, yes, Nicaragua ask for our help. There are over 15,000 freedom fighters struggling for liberty and democracy in Nicaragua and helping to stem subversion in El Salvador. They are our brothers. How can we ignore them? How can we refuse them assistance when we know that ultimately their fight is our fight?
>
> Ronald Reagan
> February, 1985

If the political support structure for President Reagan's agenda vis-a-vis the Sandinista government was not yet together by the second half of the 1980s, his military policy was in place well before that. Owing to political constraints on the use of a major military assault to topple the Frente, the Reagan Administration greatly expanded programs of economic pressure on Nicaragua begun under Carter and added its own paramilitary actions in Nicaragua. To support those efforts, Reagan undertook a major militarization of Central America and the Caribbean that amounted to a US invasion of the region. The president's economic and military policy toward Nicaragua took the form of low-intensity attrition warfare.

## ECONOMIC AGGRESSION

Following precedent set by US economic destabilization policies against Brazil (1964), Chile (1973), Bolivia (1971) and elsewhere, the Reagan Administration enacted a series of policies after 1981 to disrupt the economy of Nicaragua. White House purposes appeared to be threefold: 1) to make the revolutionary model of a progressive mixed economy fail; 2) to undermine popular support for the Frente by inducing economic hardship; and 3) to undermine world economic confidence in the Sandinista government. The economic changes being

171

pursued by the revolution's leaders were interpreted as a threat to US economic and security interests; the model and the revolution itself had to be discredited.

United States economic policy against Nicaragua was coherent rather than ad hoc; it followed a wider strategy of economic aggression that the United States had earlier developed as a tool of its foreign policy. As it has been applied, this form of aggression has several consistent characteristics: 1)it is articulated through policies linking interests of international institutions (e.g. IMF) with economic interests of local elites who claim representation of broader social groups; 2)destabilization programs are developed gradually, then are escalated "...with deliberately misleading demagoguery to justify increasingly open economic aggression"; 3)a campaign to delegitimize the government includes demands for change that are as great as possible, while the opposition is linked to "private enterprise"; 4)"campaigns of fear about the future are created that encourage destructive behavior on the part of business people in the country...inflationary pressures are brought to bear and domestic production suffers from the climate of uncertainty, international finance is increasingly blocked..."; 5)the coordinated policies become open, public, international economic aggression (Vuskovic, in Conroy, 1985a:50).

US efforts were both bilateral and multilateral and were justified by the same arguments given for US pressure in other spheres: Nicaragua supported terrorism and insurgency in El Salvador and was intent on spreading communism through Latin America. Nicaragua's external dependence and its reliance on a narrow export sector as its major source of foreign exchange and economic growth meant that Nicaragua was quite vulnerable to such aggression. US efforts focused on undermining Nicaragua's export production and squeezing off its markets and credit, despite the fact that the FSLN in 1979 had offered to guarantee private, small business credit and to renegotiate and pay off Somoza's debt.

Table 6.1 gives evidence of the success with which the United States after 1980 pursued its policy of undercutting Nicaragua's agricultural, industrial and social development programs. Using its voting strength, veto powers and political influence, the United States shut off major multilateral development funds to Nicaragua. The Reagan Administration used its influence to delay vital loans and to reduce aid to Nicaragua, while at the same time working to increase aid available to other Central American states. In 1981, for example, the United States blocked a $30 million fisheries loan from the Inter-American Development Bank and officials later privately admitted political rather than technical reasons. Around the same time, the United States vetoed road construction funding from the same source. A month earlier, Washington influenced the World Bank to impose lending cutbacks -- the IBRD cited US displeasure with Nicaraguan politics among its reasons -- even though the Bank had earlier endorsed Nicaragua's reconstruction plans (CARIN, November, 1983; IHCA, September, 1985).

The table does not reflect the additional loss of credit and production Nicaragua suffered due to other US government actions, such as its pressuring private US and foreign lending institutions and banks not to make loans to Nicaragua, and, ending Export-Import

Table 6.1
Aid and Credit Monies Blocked by the US, 1981-1984

(US $Millions)

| | Value of Project | Probable Disbursements 1981 | 1982 | 1983 | 1984 | Blocked or Cancelled |
|---|---|---|---|---|---|---|
| **Bilateral US/Nicaragua** | | | | | | |
| -Partial blockage of already approved $75 million loan | 15.0 | | 15.0 | | | 15.0 |
| -Suspension of already approved wheat credits | 10.0 | 5.0 | 5.0 | | | 10.0 |
| -Rural development program, education and health | 11.4 | 2.2 | 2.3 | 2.3 | 4.6 | 36.4 |
| Bilateral subtotal | 36.4 | 7.2 | 22.3 | 2.3 | 4.6 | 36.4 |
| **Multilateral** | | | | | | |
| Inter-American Development Bank (IDB) | | | | | | |
| -Abisinia - Cua valley (agriculture) | 2.2 | | | | 2.2 | 2.2 |
| -Monte Galan-San Jacinto Tizate Basin (energy) | 15.0 | 1.0 | 7.0 | 7.0 | | 15.0 |
| -Global Agricultural Program II (agroindustry) | 55.0 | | | 8.0 | 11.0 | 19.0 |
| -Livestock Development Program Boaco-Chontales | 50.0 | | | 10.0 | 15.0 | 25.0 |
| -Agroindustrial Rehabilitation Program | 98.0 | | 6.0 | 23.0 | 28.0 | 57.0 |
| -Potable water, public service and sewage program for intermediate cities and rural communities, stage II | 21.0 | | 3.0 | 9.0 | 9.0 | 21.0 |
| -Preinvestment Program | 5.3 | | | 2.0 | 3.3 | 5.3 |

Table 6.1 (cont.)

| | | | | | | |
|---|---|---|---|---|---|---|
| IDB subtotal | 246.5 | 1.0 | 16.0 | 59.0 | 68.5 | 144.5 |

World Bank

| | | | | | | |
|---|---|---|---|---|---|---|
| -Agricultural Credit Program | 50.0 | | | | 10.0 | 10.0 |
| -Support to food production and export | 90.0 | | | | 9.0 | 9.0 |
| World Bank subtotal | 140.0 | | | | 19.0 | 19.0 |
| Multilateral subtotal | 386.5 | 1.0 | 16.0 | 59.0 | 87.5 | 163.5 |
| TOTAL | 422.9 | 8.2 | 38.3 | 61.0 | 92.1 | 199.9 |

Source:  Instituto Historico Centroamericano, Envio, Vol. 4, No. 51, (Sept. 1985), Managua.

Bank guarantees (in 1981) to finance US exports to Nicaragua.  In 1982, for example, Nicaragua was excluded from Caribbean Basin Initiative aid monies for Central America, and in March the Reagan Administration pressured US banks to withdraw from a London-based consortium pledging $130 million to Nicaragua.  The 1982 year-end report from the US Embassy in Managua claimed that the healthy markets and receptive political climate necessary for investment did not exist in Nicaragua and noted a Nicaraguan "preference for non-US sources for imports" (CARIN, op. cit). While the report did not cite major reasons for economic difficulties in Nicaragua -- such as the Ex-Im Bank credit cut-off, the fact that the Commerce Department regularly held up licenses for exports to Nicaragua, and that the resulting foreign exchange crisis forced Nicaragua to trade where it was given credit -- it worked to discourage international financiers and US firms operating in Nicaragua.  In 1983 the State Department discouraged US banks from participating in a $30 million credit line organized by the Bank of America and later closed all Nicaraguan consular offices in the United States, cutting commercial import operation and exacerbating liquidity problems for Nicaragua.  The economic noose was being tightened, even though US business people in Nicaragua at the time had found they could work with the Frente. The US government more so than FSLN policy was making it tough to operate in revolutionary Nicaragua (e.g. NYT, 8-15-83).  It was also in 1983 that the United States cut its sugar quota to Nicaragua by 90 percent, amounting to a $14 million loss for Nicaragua.  In 1985, the year of Reagan's economic embargo on Nicaragua, the United States blocked another multilateral loan for $58 million for agricultural development.

Together with the widespread damage to Nicaragua's economic infrastructure resulting from the war against Somoza and contra sabotage, the loss of US and multilateral credit profoundly affected Nicaragua's development plans (see Tables 6.3 and 6.4).  The FSLN's development strategy involved transforming the agricultural and natural resource sectors into the key sources of accumulation both to assure sufficient food production, thereby improving the standard of living of most Nicaraguans, and to earn foreign exchange. Social welfare development was the other aspect of its strategy. US pressures, however, slowed such infrastructural development by blocking monies for projects essential to the stable development of the economy. Pursuing the same strategy, the contras targetted social and cultural services, machinery and personnel. The contra war additionally led the Frente to redirect large portions of the national budget from development to defense. The results were a lowered standard of living for Nicaraguans and declines in production.

On another level, however, the United States did not accomplish its purposes: while the economic squeeze caused suffering and some social tension in Nicaragua, the blame for the dislocations for the most part was laid, in international circles and in Nicaragua, on the United States and not on the FSLN. The Frente retained the bulk of its popular support at home and US allies, Latin American and Soviet bloc states alike provided Nicaragua alternative aid, credit, and -- just as important to a beseiged Nicaragua--moral support (see Chapters 7 and 9).


US REGIONAL MILITARIZATION

The most important aspect of the United States' military aggression against Nicaragua and its most destructive policy effort--the organization and support of the contras--is discussed in detail in the next section, although it must be considered as part and parcel of wider US diplomatic, economic and military policy in Central America. First, I discuss the outlines of the broader, regional military policy of the United States, aimed as it was at blocking leftist movements and "neutralizing the Nicaraguan threat."

US military strategy in Central America in the 1980s reflected the United States' renewed commitment to military expansion and increased capacities for US military presence in the Third World generally. Renewed emphasis on developing rapid deployment forces, special forces (e.g., Green Berets), air and sealift capacities and light infantry divisions, as well as augmenting these efforts with mercenary and private (anti-communist) organizations, have all been visible in the US military presence in Central America since 1981. US philosophical motivation has been counterinsurgency. As manifested regionally, counterinsurgency has meant 1)using US-supported economic and social programs to pursue military objectives, thereby eliminating popular movements that threaten traditional politics or US hegemony and 2)establishing permanent military infrastructure to facilitate a long-term US presence. Thus, in El Salvador, Honduras and Costa Rica the United States expanded military bases and training, implemented continuous military maneuvers, stationed troops and advisors, and assumed key roles in directing the wars in Salvador and Nicaragua. In these states and in Guatemala civic action programs, greatly increased military aid supported efforts to win the hearts and minds of rural peasants. Reinforcement of these programs to counter perceived

Soviet influence was provided by a large increase in CIA presence
and activity in the entire Caribbean Basin, pursuant to a National
Security Council decision in 1981 to deal with local opposition to
US policy through covert paramilitary, intelligence networking and
propaganda actions (McConnell, 1983; WP, 2-14-82). By 1983, El
Salvador was the base of an extensive spy network and the center for
many covert actions in Salvador, Nicaragua, Honduras and elsewhere
(e.g. LAWR, 3-25-83). Most CIA activity centered on using the
contras to create an internal front and to undermine the FSLN
government. The contra program was coordinated and supported from
San Salvador, Tegucigalpa and Washington. In brief, the United
States expanded its potential for projecting US power "where the use
of conventional forces would be premature, inappropriate or
unfeasible" (Defense Department document on unconventional warfare
quoted in NARMIC, 1985:3).

## The Military Isolation of Nicaragua

The isolation of Nicaragua was overseen by an enlarged Southern
Command (Southcom) headquartered in Panama and serving as a command
center for all army, navy, and air force activities in Latin
America. In 1983, under the direction of four-star General Paul
Gorman, Southcom's mission was widened from defending the Panama
Canal area to countering "Soviet and Cuban militarization and other
destabilization undertakings" (mission statement quoted in NYT,
6-4-85). With approximately 10,000 troops in Panama and 1,500 in
Honduras, Southcom was to oversee the increasingly sophisticated US
military apparatus in Central America, plan military contingencies
and coordinate preparedness through stepped-up foreign officer
training. An ongoing task was the coordination of a continuous
series of war games with allied armies.[1] Further preparations aimed
at mobilizing the US Readiness Command, based at MacDill Air Force
Base in Florida, and the US Atlantic Command, based at Norfolk,
Virginia, for services in Central America. Having disbanded the
Canal-oriented mechanized infantry unit, Vietnam-experienced Gorman
brought in intelligence, communications, aviation, construction and
other experts. He oversaw the installation of the US National
Security Agency's most advanced electronic eavesdropping equipment
at listening posts around Nicaragua and Salvador, such as at Tiger
Island in the Gulf of Fonseca (NYT, 6-4-85).

Reflective of the military nature of US Central American
policy, General Gorman was influencial from 1983 to 1985 in shaping
US policy and in pursuing US military objectives. Gorman worked
closely with the CIA and Honduran and Salvadoran political and
military leaders. He personally pressed President Monge of Costa
Rica, officially a neutral state, to allow the US military to build
roads and airstrips near Nicaragua's southern border. His active
role in local affairs led critics in Congress to charge that Gorman
was providing policy leadership, and at times preempting US
ambassadors in the region, because there was no defined diplomatic
strategy from a president who believed in a military solution (e.g.
NYT, 5-19-84; Newsweek, 3-19-84). Close to White House policy
makers ideologically, Gorman testified before Congress during
several contra-funding debates, labelling Nicaragua a "militarist

behemoth" in the image of Cuba and lamenting the "...tragedy that many in North and South America are prepared to tolerate the consolidation of a Marxist-Leninist garrison state in Nicaragua" (NYT, 6-30-84). Such testimony in 1984 and 1985 left Congressional and other Washington critics like House Speaker Tip O'Neal and (ret.) Admiral Eugene Carrol charging that Southcom's purpose was not just to improve regional capacities, but explicitly to invade Nicaragua (NYT, 6-4-85).

Honduras. Illuminating US objectives in the region was the activity of the United States in Honduras. The poorest country in all of Latin America and manifesting all- the problems attending such underdevelopment, Honduras had been largely ignored by the United States until the 1979 Nicaraguan revolution. Honduras became the central focus of US militarization efforts in 1981 in addition to its already serving as the contras' main base of operations. Overseen by General Gorman, and later (1985) Lt. General John Gavin, new military bases and training centers were built; road, airport and other infrastructure construction was undertaken; and US permanent personnel expanded from about two dozen in 1980 to 500 by 1985. Military aid zoomed from $4 million in 1980 to $77.5 million in 1984 and President Reagan was requesting a much larger figure for the future (see Table 6.2). Several sizeable US bases grew up at San Lorenzo, Puerto Castilla and at Palmerola, the operating arm of the US military in Honduras and the home of Joint Task Force Bravo which coordinated the ongoing joint military maneuvers with Honduras. Although Congress prohibited the storage of bombs and rockets at Palmerola and San Lorenzo, Southcom had stored 100 percent of its oil requirements for a major military operation at those bases. Absorbing larger and larger military aid packages from the United States, Honduras: built the largest airforce in Central America and airstrips to facilitate both light supply planes and US C5A's -- the biggest plane in the US force; modernized its armed forces; and made them compatible with US and other US-supplied forces in the region.

Much of this development was facilitated by joint military maneuvers, which after 1983 were continuous. Only Guatemala was hesitant about coordinating regional military commands or appearing united against the "threat" from Nicaragua. As senior Reagan Administration officials noted about the maneuvers, they were designed as part of the administration's perception-management campaign to intimidate and scare the Nicaraguans into concessions. During maneuvers, American troops "...push very close to the border, deliberately, to set off all the alarms" (official quoted in NYT, 3-30-85). At the same time, Honduras, in particular, was receiving the training to affirm its central role in future US regional military activities.

To Nicaragua in the south, Honduras appeared to have become a US military base, ready to move against Nicaragua at any time and with great air, land and sea force. The FMLN in Salvador similarly believed that the United States was preparing for a major operation to end the civil war there. Indeed, in 1983 top-level discussions of war scenarios and invasion contingency plans, including options for assaults in both Salvador and Nicaragua which incorporated US allies' armies under CONDECA or the Rio Treaty, were being reported

Table 6.2
US Military and Economic Assistance to Central America and the Caribbean (millions of dollars)

| | FY80 | FY81 | FY82 | FY83 | FY84 | FY85[1] | FY86[2] |
|---|---|---|---|---|---|---|---|
| **COSTA RICA** | | | | | | | |
| Military Assistance | 0.0 | 0.03 | 2.1 | 2.6 | 9.2 | 9.2 | 2.725 |
| Economic Support Funds | 0.0 | 0.0 | 90.0 | 157.0 | 130.0 | 160.0 | 150.0 |
| Economic Assistance | 14.0 | 13.3 | 30.6 | 55.4 | 47.9 | 48.0 | 37.35 |
| **EL SALVADOR[3]** | | | | | | | |
| Military Assistance | 6.0 | 35.5 | 82.0 | 81.3 | 196.5 | 128.2 | 132.6 |
| Economic Support Funds | 9.1 | 44.9 | 115.0 | 140.0 | 210.5 | 195.0 | 210.0 |
| Economic Assistance | 48.7 | 68.7 | 67.2 | 91.1 | 120.65 | 131.1 | 140.8 |
| **GUATEMALA[4]** | | | | | | | |
| Military Assistance | 0.0 | 0.0 | 0.0 | 0.0 | 0.0 | 0.3 | 10.3 |
| Economic Support Funds | 0.0 | 0.0 | 10.1 | 0.0 | 0.0 | 12.5 | 25.0 |
| Economic Assistance | 11.1 | 16.6 | 13.8 | 17.6 | 33.3 | 61.3 | 52.2 |
| **HONDURAS** | | | | | | | |
| Military Assistance | 4.0 | 8.9 | 31.3 | 37.3 | 77.5 | 62.5 | 88.25 |
| Economic Support Funds | 0.0 | 0.0 | 36.8 | 56.0 | 112.5 | 75.0 | 80.0 |
| Economic Assistance | 51.0 | 33.9 | 41.2 | 45.2 | 96.5 | 63.9 | 77.9 |
| **PANAMA** | | | | | | | |
| Military Assistance | 0.3 | 0.4 | 5.4 | 5.4 | 15.5 | 20.0 | 19.05 |
| Economic Support Funds | 0.0 | 0.0 | 0.0 | 0.0 | 30.0 | 20.0 | 40.0 |
| Economic Assistance | 2.0 | 10.6 | 13.0 | 7.2 | 15.9 | 20.3 | 22.6 |
| **BELIZE** | | | | | | | |
| Military Assistance | 0.0 | 0.0 | 0.026 | 0.066 | 0.6 | 0.6 | 1.1 |
| Economic Support Funds | 0.0 | 0.0 | 0.0 | 10.0 | 10.0 | 4.0 | 4.0 |
| Economic Assistance | 0.0 | 0.0 | 0.0 | 6.7 | 4.0 | 6.0 | 6.8 |

| | | | | | | | |
|---|---|---|---|---|---|---|---|
| **DOMINICAN REPUBLIC** | | | | | | | |
| Military Assistance | 3.5 | 3.4 | 5.5 | 5.6 | 5.7 | 8.8 | 10.8 |
| Economic Support Funds | 0.0 | 0.0 | 41.0 | 8.0 | 34.0 | 45.0 | 50.0 |
| Economic Assistance | 54.3 | 36.0 | 38.3 | 51.8 | 50.7 | 54.9 | 61.8 |
| **EASTERN CARIBBEAN [5]** | | | | | | | |
| Military Assistance | 0.0 | 0.0 | 0.0 | 2.27 | 7.4[6] | 5.36 | 10.4 |
| Economic Support Funds | 4.0 | 0.0 | 20.0 | 35.0 | 15.0 | 20.0 | 35.0 |
| Economic Assistance | 41.8 | 27.0 | 29.95 | 23.1 | 29.5 | 32.13 | 31.1 |
| **HAITI [7]** | | | | | | | |
| Military Assistance | 0.13 | 0.4 | 0.5 | 0.7 | 0.8 | 0.0 | 0.975 |
| Economic Support Funds | 1.0 | 0.0 | 0.0 | 10.0 | 5.0 | 5.0 | 5.3 |
| Economic Assistance | 25.9 | 33.7 | 34.2 | 35.8 | 41.5 | 49.1 | 50.7 |
| **JAMAICA** | | | | | | | |
| Military Assistance | 0.0 | 1.7 | 2.1 | 2.4 | 4.2 | 5.3 | 8.275 |
| Economic Support Funds | 0.0 | 41.0 | 90.5 | 59.4 | 55.0 | 70.0 | 70.0 |
| Economic Assistance | 12.7 | 30.0 | 46.4 | 42.3 | 53.3 | 58.1 | 54.4 |
| **TOTAL [8]** | 289.03 | 406.03 | 846.976 | 989.24 | 1,142.6 | 1,371.53 | 1,489.425 |

Sources: US State Department and Congressional documents; NARMIC/American Friends Service Committee, 1985, INVASION: A Guide to the US Military Presence in Central America (by permission).

NOTES

1. FY 1985 Figures are those appropriated by the US Congress. Each year since 1981 actual spending in the region has outstripped the funds Congress initially approved, as a result of presidential authority, military supplementals and reprogramming, and the Caribbean Basin initiative; it is impossible to project accurately the actual cost of US policy for FY 1985.

2. Reagan Administration Foreign Aid requests.

3. FY 1985 and FY 1986 military assistance to El Salvador was supplemented by an estimated $6 million each year in Commercial Sales. Commercial Sales in the region generally run less than $1 million to any country in a fiscal year.

180

Table 6.2 Notes (cont.)

4. In FY 1977 Guatemala refused to comply with US human rights legislation and rejected US government military assistance. Until FY 1985 the US Congress maintained the cut-off. Between FY 1977 and FY 1985 Guatemala was able to purchase military equipment, weapons and training through Commercial Sales, Foreign Military Sales cash programs and the Commerce Department.

5. In this table the Eastern Caribbean includes: Antigua, Barbados, Dominica, Grenada, Montserrat, St. Kitts-Nevis, St. Lucia and St. Vincent.

6. As part of the Peace Keeping Operations budget in FY 1984, an additional $5 million went to the Eastern Caribbean countries to train special paramilitary units which made up the Caribbean Peace Keeping Force deployed to Grenada following the October 1983 US-led invasion.

7. FY 1985 assistance to Haiti was conditioned on a halt to illegal immigration to the United States, and improvement in human rights conditions and on the management of Agency for International Development programs.

8. This table is necessarily an understatement of levels of US support because it includes only a) military assistance: government-to-government grants for military equipment, weapons and/or training; government-to-government credit or loan guarantees for the purchase of military equipment, weapons and/or training; and government-to-government grants for training military and related civilian personnel; b) economic support funds: monies for governments of special political or security interest to the US; and c)economic assistance: programs administered by the Agency for International Development and increasingly directed toward the private sector and coordinated with military programs; and Public Law 480--food provided for domestic resale. The table excludes: Foreign Military Sales cash programs (government-to-government sales for cash payments), funds allocated by the Pentagon for military maneuvers, training and construction; Commercial Sales (military sales by companies directly to foreign governments, individuals or organizations), sales through the Commerce Department of equipment used by the military and police, assistance through the CIA and private programs, and some bilateral economic assistance programs and multinational lending programs.

in US and Latin American media. Such plans fueled even greater regional anxiety after the October invasion of Grenada.[3] Belying public claims in Washington that Nicaragua was arming in preparation for aggressive assaults against its neighbors, US military officials in Honduras and State Department officials speaking in private argued that Nicaragua would not venture a major military assault against Honduras and was not preparing for that, but, that in such an event, Honduras was prepared to defend itself. Rather, US Embassy and military officers in Honduras in 1985 justified a large US presence as an effort to assure the Hondurans who feared "ideological aggression" and insurgency from Nicaragua; two isolated cases of "Nicaraguan-backed insurgency" in 1982 and 1983 were cited as evidence of Nicaragua's aggressive intent (author interviews).

Whatever the official explanations of US military expansion in Honduras, El Salvador, Costa Rica and Guatemala -- and they usually included the argument that such activity was to prepare the way for or enhance incipient democracy -- the evidence of the amounts of money spent and the types of programs in place confirmed other objectives: 1)the short-term elimination of the FMLN in Salvador and the FSLN in Nicaragua; and 2)the long-term security of the region for pro-US governments. Table 6.2 highlights the mushrooming growth of US military attention to Central America and the Caribbean, although it underestimates actual spending on military preparedness. For example, military aid figures do not include costs of the joint and extraordinary military maneuvers that have been continuous after 1982 and that have meant additional equipment and infrastructure for local armies, including the contras.

Military assistance figures indicate huge increases to Nicaragua's neighbors, El Salvador, Honduras and Costa Rica, from 1980 to 1981--that is, well before the Nicaraguan military build-up and Soviet weapons importation, the grounds on which the United States later indicted Nicaragua and justified its own regional military presence. The 1981 aid levels, moreover, increase by about three times in 1982. While the aid to these states holds at about the same levels for fiscal year 1983, the Reagan Administration's renewed determination in 1983 to overcome domestic (political) and regional obstacles to a solution to the "Nicaragua problem" on US terms is reflected in the 1984 aid figures. Military aid to Nicaragua's neighbors, and by this time to the Caribbean, Jamaica, and Panama as well, again doubled or tripled.

Policy Debates. As White House rhetoric heightened tensions, debates among and within the military, intelligence and diplomatic communities concerning the political and economic feasibility of invading Nicaragua spilled over into the public arena in 1985 and 1986. Top intelligence and policy officials were arguing that while an invasion would be "undesirable from a propaganda point of view", if a consensus came together for doing so it would be like "falling off a log" (NYT, 6-4-85). Intelligence reports trusted by the White House argued that Nicaragua lacked the military skill, the popular base and supply lines to fight an effective guerrilla war against US forces should they enter Nicaragua; a US move, then, would not lead to a quagmire. Principal targets in Nicaragua, according to the reports, were so lightly defended that with minimal risk the United States could neutralize Nicaragua's small air force, command

centers, radar, artillery and the like. The military commander of
US forces in Honduras, Col. William Comee, moreover speculated that
the United States could control 60 percent of the Nicaraguan
population within two weeks after heavy air strikes against major
targets. In this scenario, after about a month of heavy air strikes
with minimal troop actions on the ground, and, with a new government
(UNO) put into place in Managua, the new government's army -- the
contras, presumably -- could pursue FSLN remnants. White House
intelligence also reported: that the FSLN would find little popular
support in the mountainous hinterlands; that the Nicaraguan people
would rise up to support the US action; that Nicaragua's neighbors
would eagerly assist the United States; and that Washington would
only need supply the new government and army with heavy aid, weapons
and advisory support along the lines of US involvement in Salvador
through 1985. In this view, the United States could easily enough,
and without committing US troops, absorb the costs of finally
eliminating the "Sandinista threat."

Top Pentagon generals, the Joint Chiefs of Staff and other
intelligence and diplomatic officers in the field subscribed to
another view. This group regarded the White House scenario as
politically unfeasible and too optimistic militarily. For example,
General Wallace Nutting, who had headed Southcom prior to Gorman's
appointment, argued on the eve of his retirement from active service
in 1985 that the United States should isolate Nicaragua politically,
not militarily, by encouraging democracy in the region, by helping
to build political stability through political reform and economic
development and by presenting successful and contrasting models to
Cuba and Nicaragua (NYT, 6-30-85). In this view, current US policy
only spurred increased militarization. Nutting's views, reportedly,
reflected those of other senior Pentagon officials as well.

Bolstering this thinking was a Joint Chiefs report to the
Secretary of Defense outlining the costs to the United States of an
invasion of Nicaragua. According to the Joint Chiefs, not only
would an invasion require an offensive force three times the size of
Nicaragua's defensive force (estimated at 119,000 potentially
armed), it would also drain US resources from other parts of the
world, jeopardize US-Latin American and US-Western European
relations and encourage military thinking rather than a new social
conscience among Latin militaries. The Pentagon view was that given
Latin American animosity toward the United States over its activist
role in South America during the last fifty years, the rule for the
1980s should be "the less visible the US military, the better."
Moreover, the generals contended that in countries like Honduras,
the last thing the United States or Honduras should be doing was
spending money for arms. The generals, in other words, defined both
the problem and its solution in Central America differently than did
the White House, the NSC and President Reagan himself.

It was in this context, in 1985 and 1986 for example, that
Shultz, Ikle and the president were warning that if current policy
toward Nicaragua -- the contra program -- failed due to lack of
Congressional funding, an invasion by US troops was the only answer.
Having rejected negotiations as "sanctioning another Cuba," the
White House, in effect, admitted having no other policy options.
For its part, in 1985 Congress accepted that policy framework and

the argument that the contras could or would shortly force political change in Nicaragua. But it was on just these claims -- the contras' battlefield prowess, their domestic support inside Nicaragua and their democratic and political potential -- that the White House scenario was vulnerable. The continued strength of Sandinista support, the contras' political and military failures into 1986, the belated contra (UNO) efforts to present a political program, and the legacy of hatred among Nicaraguans for Somocista-identified forces were factors working both to make a contra victory less probable and to increase the costs to the United States of an invasion. These 1985 and 1986 realities, however, did not figure in setting US policy options. The White House and NSC policy leaders pressed ahead to create the opening for the military solution. By 1984 and 1985, although public, Congressional and US military opinion created obstacles to a military solution, the administration had nonetheless successfully built the infrastructure for such a move should opinion turn or a security-threatening "crisis" emerge.


## THE UNITED STATES AND THE CONTRAS

Given the Reagan Administration's determination to stem Soviet influence and revolutionary fires in Central America, and, Congressional wariness about direct US military involvement, Vietnam-style quagmires and public opinion, the covert war waged by the CIA and anti-Sandinista counter-revolutionaries quickly became the key element of US Nicaraguan policy. Assured by the administration that its goal was simply to change the behavior of the Sandinistas, not overthrow them, Congress sanctioned the covert paramilitary force by voting about $80 million in military and logistical aid by 1985. At the same time Congress put restrictions on how the CIA could use the money and in 1985 called on the president to find a way to pursue US objectives openly and without the stigma which had become attached to the CIA's program. The result by 1984 and 1985 was that the administration had expended much energy attempting to build a democratic case for the contras, to preen a clean political leadership as an alternative to the Sandinistas and to argue to Congress that this "democratic" force -- the best hope for Nicaragua and for peace in the region -- was the only alternative to preserving US security without introducing US troops. Privately, administration officials and President Reagan himself were betting that the contras would spearhead a convergence of events that would shortly lead to a toppling of the FSLN. Meanwhile the administration waited for Congressional opinion to change -- i.e., toward supporting more direct moves against Nicaragua -- or, for the Sandinista government to be weakened to the point of collapse by the United States' low-intensity attrition campaign. Given its importance to US regional policy and to Nicaragua's survival strategy in the 1980s, then, an analysis of the contras' origin, development and impact is necessary.

## Origin and Mission

According to several contra leaders, the Reagan team made contact with ex-Somocista Guardia exiles in Miami and Honduras prior to Reagan's inauguration, promising them aid if they would organize into a unified force.[4] The incoming Republican Administration, having addressed the issues of leftist movements in Salvador and Nicaragua as textbook cases of Soviet expansionism, now argued that Honduras might be the next target for leftist insurgency. In March, 1981, President Reagan sent a finding to the Congressional Intelligence Oversight Committees that the United States should organize political propaganda campaigns and increase intelligence gathering in the region, and, that it was considering a paramilitary operation to interdict gun flows between Nicaragua and Salvador. As presidential assistant Vernon Walters consulted with Guatemala, Honduras and Argentina on the possibility of joint covert activities against Nicaragua, the CIA in August recruited willing anti-Sandinista fighters in the form of the 15th of September Legion and other Somocista exile gangs. These gangs had been operating in Central America since 1979 and had acquired a reputation as thieves and murderers (Newsweek, 11-18-82; 4-11-83). The Legion itself included sixty top Guardia personnel who had headed intelligence, logistics, special warfare, and key combat and training units under Somoza. These men were anxious to reclaim power in Nicaragua, settle scores with the FSLN and, in their words, cause "heads to roll" in Managua. By September of 1981 these men had formed into two bands under the banner of the Fuerza Democratica Nicaraguense, the Nicaraguan Democratic Force (the FDN), and began receiving US aid and training in Argentina (and later in Honduras), paid for by the CIA (NYT, 3-18-85). Arguing that these were the only people willing to fight against the Sandinistas, the CIA had hired unemployed Somicistas whose battlefield experience under Somoza had earned them a reputation as one of the world's most corrupt and brutal forces. It was this group that was commissioned to carry out a ten-point covert plan worked out by the National Security Council in November, 1981 and signed by the president in December. According to the "scope paper" on permissible operations accompanying the finding, the president allocated $19.9 million to train a 500-man interdiction force, with the Argentinians training an additional 1000 men.

As it was explained publically -- but not until after news about the paramilitary force got out in February, 1982 and was widely reported to the US public by Newsweek in November -- the purpose behind the operation was to interdict arms shipments to Salvador. Yet it was not long before a picture of a broader purpose emerged. According to numerous reports and Washington leaks, the original purposes were to harass and punish the FSLN for allegedly aiding the FMLN, to draw the FSLN into reprisal actions which would paint them as repressive rulers, and, if possible, to take a piece of territory into which a new government could be interjected and quickly recognized by the United States. The contras themselves were open from the beginning about their own motivation -- overthrowing the FSLN. And, it was on that basis that they were recruited by the CIA. Several contra leaders, including Edgar

Chamorro who left the FDN in 1984, have said that the CIA lured them into service with promises of helping them overthrow the Sandinistas "within a year" (NYT, 11-1-84). As one senior State Department officer who worked on Nicaraguan policy put it: "The idea that the rebels have been armed and equipped initially so they could intercept arms shipments was ludicrous. That would be an extraordinary way to use them. It would be a fool's errand" (NYT, 3-17-85).

Decision-makers in 1981 fully discussed possible secondary and tertiary effects of the paramilitary program, including the toppling of the FSLN government. The latter option in fact, was openly advocated by some policy makers in 1981, though politically it was not feasible to assume responsibility for that consequence until 1985. The administration attitude was that it would press Nicaragua to the extent that it could, publically claiming a limited purpose, but letting the chips fall. By 1985 the administration had silenced those within the administration who argued for learning to live with a contained Nicaragua -- the "Yugoslavia solution" -- and many in Congress had become unwilling to continue challenging the president on Nicaragua. Top administration officials spoke openly of not being willing to make an agreement with the Sandinistas and of the need for a new government based on "national reconciliation." In the intervening years from 1981 to 1984, officials had continued to refer to arms interdiction and Congress tried to hold the administration to that narrower purpose. Yet, by 1983 other rationales were being added and justified before Congress, such as putting pressure on Nicaragua to get the Frente to the negotiation table.

## Proliferation and Changing Tactics: 1982 and 1983

The first hints that the Reagan agenda included more than arms interdiction came early on. Reports at that time (and confirmed later) were charging that the United States had planned a "Red Christmas" operation to take Nicaraguan territory in December, 1981 -- a plot that failed -- and, that the CIA had set up a government-in-exile, housed in Miami and made up of wealthy Nicaraguan business people who were now on the CIA payroll. Moreover, Congressional committees had learned that the contra force of 500 had grown to 4,000 by the end of 1982 and to 7,000 by mid-1983, though the administration still spoke only of the interdiction purpose and could provide no intercepted arms caches.[5] The reports of a wider covert operation took on credibility and initiated public concern and Congressional inquiries when the November, 1982 Newsweek expose detailed a complex and rapidly expanding US-controlled and financed operation in which the combatants' purpose, at least, was to topple the Managua government. A review of the development of the covert program after 1981 confirms both the depth of US involvement and the widening objectives of the Reagan Administration as it built its case against a "totalitarian" Nicaragua.

1982. In early 1982 and with the operation formally approved, the CIA relied on Argentinian and other foreign military personnel to train and directly oversee the contras in Honduras while it worked to enlist into its service groups known to be unhappy with the FSLN. Miskito Indians, ex-<u>Guardia</u> soldiers, exiled businessmen and foreign mercenaries were all wooed, given supplies and came to account for the large increase in fighters in 1982. The effects of this broad recruitment, however, were continuously to plague the contra operation and act to curb its development as a unified political or combat force with unanimous purposes and vision. For example, though two groups of Miskitos -- Misura, under Steadman Fagoth and Misurasata, under Brooklyn Rivera -- came to be dissatisfied with the FSLN and were willing to take up the CIA's arms to fight, the groups were also split due to personal rivalries and differing opinions about: the appropriate approach to the FSLN, being tied to the CIA and/or to Somocista forces and optimal governing structures for the Atlantic Coast.

Meanwhile, former Sandinista hero Eden Pastora, whom the United States initially tried to woo as a leader of the armed opposition and, ultimately, a replacement for the FSLN, rejected the CIA's offer to join the FDN on the grounds that he would never align with Somocistas or take CIA money. Pastora formed his own operation in Costa Rica. Joining Pastora in a southern contra force were Alfonso Robelo, Fernando Chamorro and Brooklyn Rivera, each with their own small opposition groups (the MDN, UDN/FARN, and Misurasata respectively) but none with a significant following of fighters. Yet, this group, known as <u>Alianza Revolutionaria Democratica</u> (ARDE), would eventually disband (1984) amid disputes over strategy and linkages with the FDN and the CIA. The Reagan Administration, however, made attempts from 1982 to 1984 to put Pastora's fame, charisma and political acceptability -- i.e., to anti-Somoza, anti-Sandinista Nicaraguans and to Congress -- at the disposal of US objectives in Nicaragua. But as time wore on and it became clear Pastora was a man that could not be controlled, US officials from 1984 onward tried to discredit him as a political force. Although they accepted his help in lobbying Congress for contra funding in 1985 and 1986, Pastora's refusal in early 1985 to join UNO essentially condemned him to working without US support.

Deep political divisions and jealousies within and between the Honduran- and Costa Rican-based contras were manifested in constant leadership squabbling, contra indiscipline and independent group actions. Such factors also led to a large and permanent planning, coordination and enforcement role by the CIA, US officials in the region and the US National Security Council.

The assumption of direct control and ownership of the contras by the CIA (or the United States) appeared more a result of these realities and of the Falklands/Malvinas War in June, 1982 than of original policy design. The United States' siding with Britain in its war with Argentina resulted in the latter severing the bulk of its ties to the US contra effort. At a time when aid for the contras was also being increased and when Honduras was officially implementing a civilian political system, Secretary of State Haig sent Southeast Asia-experienced John Dimitri Negroponte as new US Ambassador to Honduras to run the anti-Sandinista operation "without qualms of conscience" (US official quoted in <u>Newsweek</u>, 11-8-82). The White House was pressing for results which would demonstrate to Congress the operation's success. Aided by an expansion in the number of CIA agents sent to Tegucigalpa, Negroponte established an elaborate US command incorporating not only the CIA but the Honduran military, Honduran political leaders and US military special forces (e.g., Green Berets). Operations in Honduras were also coordinated with the Southern Command in Panama. Contra training camps were set up in both Honduras and Nicaragua, and US operatives took over not only the training and command but also logistics, intelligence and equipment repair for the contras. By 1983 Negroponte had established a clear chain of command over contra operations: Negroponte, along with US CIA and military officers, developed day-to-day strategy at the top level of decision-making; at the next level Honduran military chief General Gustavo Alverez and the Honduran High Command, the CIA station chief in Tegucigalpa and contra military leader Col. Enrique Bermudez--a top intelligence officer under Somoza--coordinated implementation; and at the third command level FDN officers, all ex-Guardia, directed action in the field. According to independent accounts, the latter groups also pursued their own "fanatic" agendas.

Beginning in 1982, then, the Honduran military was pressed into service to help Negroponte and the CIA show some results against Nicaragua. Also a base for US destabilization efforts against Guatemala in 1954, Honduras now provided bases for US operations against Nicaragua. The Honduran army became the main link for transfers of small arms to the contras and was the United States' link to other Latin American armies. Honduran military and intelligence personnel were trained to provide logistical support for the contras' raids into Nicaragua and joined the CIA and remaining Argentinian personnel in training the contras for sabotage. Honduran army intelligence agents became an important liaison to the contras. General Alverez, meanwhile, acted on Negroponte's instructions regarding the contras, only too happy to help fight "communism" in return for increasing military aid packages from Washington. Indeed, by 1983 US journalists and Nicaraguan army sources confirmed that the Honduran army was regularly providing covering fire into Nicaragua for retreating or returning contra fighters.

Land operations against Nicaraguan villages, border posts and infrastructure were greatly expanded in 1982, leading to a growing number of deaths and the first reports back in the United States of the contras' methods and tactics. Kidnap, murder, torture and rape were commonly reported as contras attacked unguarded villages or Sandinista youth and government workers. The July, 1982 attack at San Francisco del Norte, for example, where contras killed and brutally mutilated the bodies of fifteen young militia volunteers, created a national outrage in Nicaragua and drew attention to the tactics which were used in contra raids. This began to reflect poorly on the CIA operation, close as the CIA was to the contras through its advising of the rebels and through its weekly meetings with both General Alverez and Col. Bermudez, the contras' top military leader and strategist. In addition, reports on the unsavory conduct of many ex-Guardia contra leaders started filtering into US media. To create the appearance of some distance between itself and the FDN, to forge some unity among contra groups and to present a clean contra face to Congress and the public, therefore, the CIA handpicked six men to act as the FDN directorate and to speak publicly for it. But Congress was also now expressing doubts about the actual agenda of the contra operation; the contras had moved camps into Nicaragua, had blown up bridges, and had carried out other operations unrelated to interdicting arms. Some members voiced concerns that the contras could spark hostilities between Honduras and Nicaragua.

By the end of 1982, the administration, through Negroponte's command structure, force enlargement and direct collaboration with the contras, had circumvented at least the spirit of Congressional (mid-1982) restrictions on contra aid and had greatly exceeded the small operation approved in December, 1981. In fact, several reports indicated that the United States had helped coordinate ex-Guardia placement into the military police structures of several states in the region in the hopes that these men, and some from the states they worked for, would come to the contras' aid within a few hours notice of a major operation against the FSLN. For example, 1000 former Guardia were said to have joined the Salvadoran army and 200 others reportedly had joined Guatemala's security police (CAU, December, 1982). Separate anti-Sandinista training activities were reportedly going on in Venezuela and Mexico. (Newsweek, 11-8-82; BI, 6-18-84).

Not all of these events or undertakings had been revealed to Congress during 1982. Congressional intelligence committees were surprised and Congress itself became wary when the CIA reported in December that the contras now numbered 4,000. The Miami news conference of the FDN that same month was also discomfitting; the contras claimed they would topple the FSLN within the next twelve months. Congress responded by making public and formally passing the Boland Amendment. The Boland bill outlawed the use of US monies for any activities that aimed at overthrowing Nicaragua's government or sparking hostilities between Nicaragua and Honduras.

Despite contra activity, the continuous presence of US warships off Nicaraguan coasts and intelligence over-flights by US planes, the administration was unable to produce tangible results in 1982 toward either its public objective, interdicting arms, or its broader objectives of forcing the FSLN to change its structure and politics. In Nicaragua, revolutionary social and economic programs were being implemented and popular political organizations were growing. In the international arena, Nicaragua was establishing multilevel contacts with a broad range of states, including US allies, and was playing a leadership role among Third World states. Moreover, in response to the contra threat and larger concerns about direct US military actions, Nicaragua expanded its army and militias and increased its efforts to find military suppliers in Europe and Latin America. US policy appeared counterproductive when assessed in the light of the policy's public objectives.

1983. During 1983 when the White House had stepped up its campaign against Nicaragua and had raised the political stakes for the United States, the contra operation proved even more problematic. While Congress and the White House continued to press for results, the contras appeared to be increasingly inept, disunified and corrupt. In order to fend off Congressional restrictions and funding cuts and to preserve time for the

president's agenda in Central America, the CIA and the Pentagon
increased their roles in Honduras and in the region generally.
Meanwhile, US policy officials and FDN leaders publically maintained
that the contras were being successful in gaining popular support
and territorial control inside Nicaragua. FDN political leader
Edgar Chamorro announced at mid-year that the contras would defeat
the Sandinistas by November.

In fact, the contras were increasing activities in Nicaragua's
northern coffee regions of Nueva Segovia, Madriz, Esteli, Jinotega
and Matagalpa. In March and April they penetrated deep into
Nicaragua to carry out sabotage and ambush operations. FSLN militia
losses were increasing as about 1500 contras moved into Nicaragua in
groups of 200, were well equipped and received intelligence on FSLN
positions from the CIA. Following CIA sabotage instructions, and
though their ultimate goal remained taking territory, the contras
targetted schools, factories, machinery and equipment. They avoided
direct engagements with the FSLN militias which were carrying
Nicaragua's defense burdens at that time. Expecting a Nicaraguan
reaction to the increased attacks, the Honduran army was also
mobilized. By June, the Nicaraguan army did send its first regular
units to pursue the contras in the northern regions and along the
border with Honduras.

As reports of military activity and contra attacks increased
and reached the US public, US officials announced that the number of
contras had increased to nearly 8000 and estimated that the contras
would control half Nicaragua's territory and one-third of its
population within the year (NYT, 6-13-83; 6-14-83). The FDN's
Chamorro used the opportunity of heavy and positive publicity to
call for a dialogue with the FSLN on the issues of elections,
"revising" FSLN structures, Cuban advisors and ending the "civil
war" (LAWR, 7-15-83). At the same time, FDN leader Calero announced
a large new military offensive -- an offensive which never got off
the ground.

These events only served to point up critical contradictions in
the contra program. First, although they were causing deaths and
some damage in the field, the contras were not severely threatening
Nicaraguan security as such. While they attempted strikes against
major Nicaraguan infrastructure, such as its only petroleum refining
facility, many of these efforts were foiled by Nicaraguan defense
forces or botched by the contras themselves. Meanwhile, Nicaragua
reinforced defense structures and Nicaraguan citizens volunteered to
help in village defense. Notable because of FDN claims to the
contrary, few Nicaraguans were joining the contras. Rather the
contras were finding it difficult to wage a guerrilla war without
popular support, and, with the conventional warfare skills many of
them had learned as cadets under Somoza. The CIA, for example, had
to air-drop supplies to the contras inside Nicaragua because the
contras were not successful in building support among rural
Nicaraguans. Ironically, it was US citizens through their tax
dollars and later, private US funders who provided the military base
and lines of support (cargo planes) for the contras in their fight
against the Frente. Nicaraguan citizens, in whose name the contras
said they were fighting, essentially denied the contras an
indigenous base and organized themselves to defend against contra

attacks. Nor were contra tactics winning them the image in Nicaragua as a popular democratic force. Instead, questions about their purposes and methods, as well as about CIA complicity, were again being raised in Congress. In August, 1983, the House voted to block contra funding.

A major indication that the contra operation was assessed by US policy makers in 1983 as failing to move sufficiently toward administration objectives was the start-up in mid-year of what were to be massive and continuous joint military maneuvers near Nicaraguan borders. The Big Pine II maneuvers of 1983, which lasted eight months and involved 10,000 US troops, left up to 5,000 US troops in Honduras at one time and ran contemporaneously with US naval deployments of two battle groups on Nicaragua's Pacific and Atlantic coasts. Reminiscent of US gunboat diplomacy of an earlier era, the United States' fire-power display was explained by officials as both a warning to the FSLN and as "routine" military preparation with US allies.

The maneuvers were more than routine, however. According to Honduran sources, for example, beginning in 1983 the United State regularly left equipment behind for the contras as maneuvers ended. In addition, the US military resupplied the Honduran army for large quantities of supplies it gave to the contras. In this same period US and Central American media were reporting that Israel, itself a major US arms recipient, was sending weapons captured in Lebanon to the contras at the United States' request -- a charge the Israelis denied. In any case, the new influx of material to the anti-Sandinista fighters was more than the contras could handle at the time. In the words of a top FDN military leader: "In 1983 we felt like one who had won the lottery. We lacked soldiers to carry all the weapons we got" (NYT, 3-18-85). The maneuvers, besides preparing the region for any future major US assault, prepared Honduras to act as a major US staging arena and provided a cover for aiding the contras with supplies, intelligence and moral support. As new and continuous maneuvers were planned for 1984 and beyond, in August President Reagan talked about increasing contra numbers to 20,000; in October the United States invaded Grenada; and in the same month the United States re-established the CONDECA military pact among its Central American allies. Invasion fears were strong among Nicaragua's citizens as it became clearer that the contras were only one aspect of the United States' unfolding military strategy.

Another attempt to cover up the contras' inept performance and to create the impression that they were being effective in Nicaragua involved a further expansion of the CIA's and Washington's role in contra activities. Given Congressional wariness, the House vote to cut funding and growing public concern over the not-so-covert war, the CIA set out in August, 1983 to provide evidence of contra successes and thereby influence continuing Congressional debates over contra funding. The CIA directed a series of dramatic raids against Nicaraguan infrastructure using its own experts and trained Latin American commandos rather than relying principally on the contras. CIA planes flying at different times from Costa Rica, Salvador and Honduras bombed Sandino International Airport in Managua as well as oil and chemical storage facilities at several

locations.  In October and November, CIA personnel launched rocket
attacks by speedboat on the Corinto and Puerto Sandino oil storage
and pipeline facilities and made other shelling attacks in the Gulf
of Fonseca.  All of the attacks were credited to the FDN or to ARDE,
which was now operating on a limited basis out of Costa Rica under
Pastora and with CIA aid.  At the same time, FDN forces themselves
were instructed to step up their attacks against coffee centers,
border posts and the like to, among other things, provoke a
Nicaraguan military response against its neighbors.  In October,
however, at least two contra resupply planes crashed in Nicaragua
and investigations later revealed that Salvadoran pilots in
Salvadoran planes--purchased with US aid monies--were flying about
twelve supply sorties per week from El Salvador deep into Nicaragua.
Contra operations, in other words, were being facilitated from three
regional states.  Also in October two attempts to take the city of
Ocotal failed, as did efforts to destroy major bridges.
     These FDN setbacks and others at the hands of Nicaraguan civil
defense units led the FDN and the CIA to put major emphasis on an
insurrectional strategy, thus switching from the earlier major focus
on seizing territory for a provisional government, a plan which had
proven unachievable.  The war of attrition aimed at wearing down the
FSLN through economic sabotage and intimidating politically
organized campesinos.  It reflected CIA and White House realization
that the contras alone could not defeat the FSLN.
     Simultaneously, the CIA acted to cleanse the image and
leadership of the contras.  Several commanders who had extorted or
mis-used CIA funds, resold US weapons on the black market or been
involved in other illegal activity were purged.  The CIA also
instructed the FDN to end human rights abuses in the field.  For
example, three FDN fighters were reported executed by FDN commanders
for having gone on a killing spree in Nicaragua.  Yet it would prove
difficult to curb atrocities given the nature of contra tactics from
the beginning.  It had been policy among the contras not to take
prisoners, but to execute them.  Moreover, killing villagers had
become a tactic of terror and warning to Sandinista sympathizers.
Nevertheless, recognition of abuses and formal commitments to reform
were presented to Congress as an improvement in the situation.
     In an ironic twist, only two months later a CIA manual was
distributed by hand and hot-air balloon to FDN fighters.  It
instructed them on creating "martyrs for the cause", "neutralizing"
Sandinista officials and sympathizers and hiring criminals to
perform special jobs. Entitled "Psych Operations in Guerrilla War",
several thousand copies were distributed.  Despite public and
Congressional outrage when the manual's dissemination was publically
revealed in late 1984, President Reagan came to the defense of CIA
director Casey and subsequent investigations resulted in only the
firing of two lower-level CIA personnel.  As revelations uncovered
the wider aim of the contra war and the central role of US agencies,
the administration countered criticism with stepped-up
anti-Sandinista rhetoric and greater efforts to sell the contras to
the US public as the democratic alternative to the Sandinista
"communists."  In the "no moral equivalence" theory of the Reagan
ideologues, contra terrorism and atrocities were unfortunate, but of
less importance than alleged Sandinista human rights abuses.  This

was held to be so because, according to US officials, the US-backed contras were pursuing democracy while the FSLN was implementing totalitarianism (author interviews).

The Foot Soldiers. A brief word is in order about who the contra fighters were and where new recruits came from as the operation expanded in 1982 and beyond. While the military command structure remained Somocista and ex-Guardia, as the contra force was enlarged Somocista foot-soldiers were quickly outnumbered by rural peasants. These peasants came mainly from north, central Nicaragua where the Somozas had traditionally recruited for the Guardia. In the period of 1981 to 1986, for example, there was only narrow support for the contras and that support was limited socially, to isolated and poor peasants, and geographically, in the north. Many joined the contra forces voluntarily, but other peasants were kidnapped or terrorized into joining by threats against their families or belongings. Contrary to their initial expectations, the contras did not get defectors from the Sandinista army.

Based on reports from those working in the field and who have had contact with the contras, motivations among the volunteers varied greatly. Many were angered by economic hardship and rationing and feared Sandinista socialism. Others condemned the military draft law of 1983, Sandinista regulations concerning agricultural production and pressures to join popular organizations. On the other hand, some fighters exhibited ideological confusion and fuzziness about what they were fighting for. Some believed they were fighting for Jesus Christ and the Virgin Mary and against communists. Others believed they were fighting Yankee imperialism. Few contras in the field had a political direction or goal, save to overthrow the Sandinistas (e.g. NYT 3-18-85). Among poor isolated peasants, especially, the goal in joining the contras was to be on the winning side; the contras worked in isolated areas to foster perceptions that they would soon be victorious over the FSLN. In these cases there was little depth of loyalty to the contras. Among the fighters, generally, morale seemed to rise and fall with abundance or scarcity of supplies. Very few of the foot soldiers had any contact with the top FDN, and later, the UNO leadership.

## From Interdiction to Removing the "Present Structure" of the Sandinista Government: The Contras in 1984 and Beyond

More than interdicting arms now, the contras by 1985 were said to be the means for getting the FSLN to "cry uncle" and for bringing "genuine democracy" to Nicaragua. US officials were saying they could not work with a Sandinsita government.

Congressional Cuts and Administration Responses. Contra attacks increased in the first half of 1984 as did CIA coordination and oversight of FDN and ARDE hit-and-run and air operations. While there were about seven hundred contras estimated to be inside Nicaragua in November, 1983, by May of 1984 there were about five thousand contras operating inside the country. The heavier fighting and new coordinated sea and air attacks, again, were aimed at demonstrating increased contra skills to a reluctant Congress. US military operations provided intelligence and logistics support to the rebels under cover of military maneuvers in Honduras and US advisory support in Salvador. That the United States was providing such aid became public over time and with a series of incidents. For example, in January, 1984, a US serviceman was killed when his army helicopter was forced to the ground by Nicaraguan fire as it flew in Nicaraguan airspace. In September, 1984, two private US citizens were killed at Santa Clara when the Nicaraguans shot down a CIA helicopter that was part of an aerial attack against a military training school. Though the CIA claimed that the two mercenaries -- members of the Alabama-based, anti-communist Civilian Military Assistance -- did not work for them, CMA officials confirmed that some of their members were working with the FDN. ARDE attacks in the south of Nicaragua, meanwhile, were supported by US C-47 supply flights from Ilopango, El Salvador. During 1984, moreover, FSLN units shot down a number of supply planes from Honduras and Salvador. In other attacks CIA agents clashed directly with Nicaraguan troops. In January and March, in sea attacks against Potosi and San Juan del Sur, CIA operatives flew Hughes-500 helicopters in air support of Latin commandos attacking by boat and exchanged fire with Nicaraguan forces.[6]

The most dramatic military activity against Nicaragua in 1984, however, was again carried out by CIA operatives acting independently of the contras. In early spring the CIA planted mines in three key ports -- Sandino, Corinto and El Bluff -- causing Japanese, Dutch and Soviet ships to be damaged. In the United States a public outcry condemned the mining as an act of war and a violation of the Neutrality Act. The House Judiciary Committee requested an investigation by the US Attorney General. Nicaragua brought its case against the United States to the World Court. The Reagan Administration justified the mining as collective self-defense and later announced that the United States would not recognize the jurisdiction of the World Court on issues pertaining to Central America for the next two years.

Expressing fears that the contra program verged on the edge of legality, that it would soon draw the United States into an unpopular war or that the United States should pursue negotiations rather than military solutions, Congress in June, 1984 effectively cut funding for the contras when the Senate, for the first time, shelved Reagan's request for new funds. The administration nevertheless maintained that it would continue its moral support for the contras; in a statement foreshadowing the administration's defiance of Congressional moves, Secretary of State Shultz said that Congress' votes would not shut the contras down. Adolfo Calero of the FDN similarly pledged to find alternative funding.

The administration's moral support for the contras, in fact, translated in 1984 and 1985 alone into about $25 million in aid from private individual and corporate sources in the United States and elsewhere. Encouraged by administration verbal and advisory support, as well as by information from the Pentagon and other agencies, retired US General John Singlaub, for example, used his post as head of the World Anti-Communist League (WACL) and of the US Congress for World Freedom to raise money for the contras from a number of US and foreign organizations. Spearheading the fund-raising from the United States, General Singlaub closely coordinated his work with FDN leaders in Honduras and with anti-communist and other conservative groups around the world. The bulk of the money raised came from US groups that a Congressional Arms Control and Foreign Policy Caucus report labelled "ultra-conservative or paramilitary groups on the fringe of American political opinion" (Congressional Record, 4-23-85). Among these groups giving civilian and military assistance were WACL, the Soldier of Fortune Defense Fund, Civilian Military Assistance and Reverend Sung Myung Moon's (of the Unification Church) International Relief Friendship Foundation. But groups from South Korea, Taiwan, Israel, Argentina and elsewhere also contributed monies which allowed the contras to maintain supplies and operations, though without direct CIA coordination after October, 1984. Another form of aid in this period involved private US soldiers sent to the region by anti-communist groups such as the Civilian Military Assistance, a practice endorsed by President Reagan in October, 1984 when he characterized such activities as part of an "honorable tradition" of helping foreign friends struggling against communism.

Without official US backing which Congressional funding had earlier provided, however, and with the loss of the major portion of CIA direction, the contras' fighting capacity and international standing was reduced.[8] Moreover, much of the private funding came through in the spring and summer of 1985, leaving the contras with a reduced flow of goods from October, 1984 up to that time. In that period the critical role of US moral and logistical support to the contra effort again became obvious.[9] Particularly acute were problems of coordinating and distributing supplies to the fighters, although a number of local observers pointed out that the contras were probably better supplied than the FMLN in El Salvador. Contra deserters nevertheless reported low morale, drug use and criminal behavior among contra fighters. Moreover, contra links to the Honduran army and intelligence services continued and a secure supply line to the main training base on the Honduran-Nicaraguan border existed. Yet the loss of direct CIA coordination, the reduced flow of weapons and ammunition and the reduced accessibility of supply aircraft meant that contras operating deep inside Nicaragua were effectively cut off and had to be withdrawn in late 1984. By the spring of 1985, the contras in Nicaragua were being out-gunned and out-fought; they were in strategic decline, owing both to the US funding cut-off and to a new FSLN military offensive aimed at routing the contras in 1985 (see Chapter 8). In Congressional hearings on new funding in February, 1985, US General Gorman testified that there was no prospect in sight that the contras would be able to "march into Managua" or be victorious over the Sandinistas, despite contra claims to the contrary.

Just as important to the contra effort as the logistical problems, however, was the reduced legitimacy and confidence lent the operation by countries that were vital to its existence and success. As I detail in the following chapter, both Honduras and Costa Rica feared being left with large foreign armies within their borders should the US Congress permanently abandon the contras. The contra program by early 1985 reflected both Congressional doubt about its purpose and prospects and the policy stalemate within the administration at that time.

Convergence Theory in Practice. The $27 million in non-lethal assistance awarded the contras by Congress in June, 1985, and, Congressional determination that US military intelligence could be shared with the contras, represented both a reaction to President Ortega's May trip to the Soviet Union and a change in attitude among some members toward giving the contras and the president another chance to pressure the FSLN into letting the contras into the government. This attitude change, moreover, reflected the effectiveness of the administration's anti-Nicaragua, anti-communism campaign in Congress. It signalled Congress' willingness, in the absence of a coherent policy alternative from administration critics, to continue the drive for a· military solution of the Nicaraguan problem. Yet, information challenging presidential claims existed. Several things, for example, suggested that the contras were not the organized, democratic group the president said they were. During this period separate human rights reports cited atrocities still being committed by the contras,[10] and, leadership squabbles among the contra organizations continued. In addition, the contras practice of not engaging FSLN troops but instead targetting civilians and services was damaging their image. According to US Embassy officials in Managua in 1985, some in the administration had been trying to get the contras to change this tactic, to engage troops, and generally to improve their control and command over their fighters (author interviews). Nor did Congress pay much attention to the administration's increasingly open assessment that the Sandinistas themselves had to go. It had become politically feasible for administration aides to talk about getting rid of the Sandinistas. The emerging consensus in Washington -- that the FSLN was a bad, undemocratic government -- provided space for the president's "convergence theory" of a pre-insurrectionary Nicaragua ripe for a US-sponsored change to a "genuine democracy."

The private funds, which had peaked by summer, and the assurance of new money and intelligence support for the contras in the fiscal year beginning October, 1985, rejuventated the contras. So did the administration's recommendation that, to fight terrorism, the contra force should be doubled to 30,000. The contras, according to US Embassy sources in Managua, were "awash in money" and significantly upgrading their arsenals with helicopters, surface-to-air missiles and the like (author interviews). Under heavy pressure from Washington and private donors to show some results soon, the contras also began a new recruitment drive.[11] Resupplied contras moved back into Nicaragua. The contras' military plan, Operation Roundup '85, aimed at taking the important city of Esteli around the time of the sixth anniversary of the revolution (July 19), as well as attacking other central Nicaraguan strategic targets such as the Sebaco agro-industrial project. To that end 3,000 contras entered Nicaragua and about 1,200 infiltrated south from Jinotega to the Esteli area. Others made attacks in the Matagalpa region. The Nicaraguan Defense Ministry reported forty-two contra-Sandinista confrontations in July, 1985 alone -- few of them stemming from contra attacks on military units as such. However, the operation was unsuccessful in causing major infrastructural damage; nor did the contras take a city or a village. The contras again failed to produce a significant sign of progress. At the July and August battles at La Trinidad outside Esteli, for example, local villagers and milicianos held off 200-500 contras for four hours until the Sandinista army could arrive and help in defense. At that battle, the FSLN introduced Soviet MI-24 Hind helicopters into combat for the first time.

The 1985 contra military offensives were significant in demonstrating once more the lack of reality-based evaluation in Washington regarding the contras' actual military and political capacity. Given the FSLN's preparations in the field to deal a military blow to the contras, its successes earlier in 1985 in incapacitating the contras and the continued unpopularity of the contras among the great majority of the Nicaraguan people, Operation Roundup '85 had little chance for success. Nor were the Nicaraguan economy and popular support for the Frente deteriorating as quickly as President Reagan believed they were. At the same time, the contras' military command and control remained poor, leading a senior US analyst in Nicaragua to label them a "hillbilly army" (author interview). Washington's demands upon the contras for convincing results thus forced them into missions doomed to failure. Not able to penetrate to major targets and unwilling to confront the Sandinista army directly, the contras continued the operations they did best: hit-and-run attacks in isolated and agricultural areas in which government workers, services, Sandinista sympathizers, small economic intrastructure and export crops were targetted.

Creating An Alternative Government: 1983 to 1986. Major administration efforts beginning in the fall of 1983 and continuing into 1986 centered on creating a clean and united political leadership around the FDN, the largest and most responsive contra force. Such a leadership and organizational image was necessary for pacifying domestic critics of the contra program and justifying the large US role in it. Moreover, as the United States raised the demand that the FSLN hold talks with the counter-revolutionaries on the future of Nicaragua, more attention was focused on the nature and make-up of that group. The difficulty for the United States came in that although the FDN was its best hope for effective military operations, it was heavily Somocista-led, operated and identified. Anti-Sandinista Nicaraguans who could fill the bill as nationalist, anti-Somoza and "centrist" politically were scarce in 1983; that is, those with acceptable qualifications and who were well-known or respected -- Eden Pastora and Alfonso Robelo -- were in 1983 refusing to associate with the FDN. Pastora was politically independent and resented US efforts to identify him with objectives--although he did begin accepting CIA money in late 1983. Pastora and Robelo's ARDE had only a few men under arms-- ranging from 100 to about 1,500 at different times--and shaky international support. Moreover, alliances within both the FDN and ARDE were shifting and fleeting as sub-groups vied for US money and recognition, or, for personal and political power within the organizations. These inter-and intra-group strains were initially exacerbated by US pressure to unify, and later, to develop a political program.

A good example of CIA manipulation of anti-Sandinista fighters to bring them in line with US objectives is the CIA's (and the administration's) relationship with Eden Pastora and ARDE. Because

of Pastora's nationalist and anti-Somoza credentials, US officials
sought to enlist him in their paramilitary campaign from the time he
announced his taking up of arms against the Sandinistas. Alfonso
Robelo, who later joined ARDE, was also attractive to the United
States for his anti-Somoza and business background. Together, these
men made ARDE a choice political alternative to the Sandinistas in
the US view. Yet, Pastora and Robelo initially and publically
rejected US financial aid in their struggle. Both rejected an
alliance with the FDN, which in Robelo's words, sought to retake
power rather than "rechannelling the revolution" as ARDE aimed for.
However, by mid-1983, the first year of ARDE's existence, and
without resources necessary for a prolonged struggle, ARDE was in
trouble. One ARDE sub-group, UDN/FARN, had decided in March to join
with the well-endowed FDN in Honduras. ARDE also was not drawing
the international support or the Sandinsta army defections it had
counted on. By late spring Robelo was in Washington asking for
$300,000 per month funding from the Reagan Administration, a request
initially denied because, as roving Ambassador Stone explained, it
would be difficult to fund ARDE in Costa Rica as part of the arms
interdiction campaign. New US pressure on ARDE to join with the FDN
in Honduras was thus brought to bear. In June, and for the second
time since the start of the year, Pastora announced the suspension
of ARDE's guerrilla campaign.

Within a few days of Pastora's June announcement, however, arms
and support started coming in, reportedly from groups organized in
Panama and including US private donations. Although Pastora denied
that any of the new funding came from the CIA, there was already
speculation at that time that unofficially, and to retain ARDE's
image as a nationalist force independent of the United States,
Washington had provided funding to the politically more suitable
(i.e. than the FDN) ARDE. Between October, 1983 and April, 1984
reports of increases in ARDE strength and activity in southern
Nicaragua credited ARDE's new ability to the CIA. The link became
public when in March, 1984 a CIA DC-3 supply plane carrying weapons
from El Salvador to ARDE base camps in northern Costa Rica crashed.
The weapons salvaged from that wreck along with other air-supply
drops by the CIA, in fact, made possible ARDE's most dramatic action
inside Nicaragua: in April ARDE troops captured San Juan del Norte.
Because it was the first town ever taken by contra forces and
because Pastora, in a media fanfare, claimed ARDE would set up a
provisional government there, establish relations with other states
and begin a march on Managua, this event received major media
attention. Actually, ARDE forces managed to hold the previously
abandoned and militarily unimportant town for only a short period.
But ARDE had scored a public relations coup. The event also served
to highlight the United States' link to ARDE. Reports based on
interviews with ARDE officials in Mexico and Costa Rica revealed
that the CIA was directing ARDE military strategy and prompting
actions by ARDE, threatening at the same time to withhold aid if
ARDE did not pursue CIA goals. The event also a served, then, to
point up Pastora's dependence on the CIA at a time when the CIA--and
the Honduran army--was working behind the scenes in renewed efforts
to unify the three contra forces operating at the time: the FDN,
the Miskito Indians and ARDE. Pastora, nonetheless, held out,

198

refusing to be associated with the heavily Somocista FDN.

Within ARDE, meanwhile, a split had developed between Pastora, the military leader, and Robelo, the political leader. Robelo, whose cousin Alfonso Callejas was with the FDN, had come to believe that ARDE's cause could only be achieved in alliance with the Honduran-based rebels. Pastora refused to join the FDN, which Adolfo Calero had been promoted to head, unless ex-<u>Guardia</u> members were purged. The FDN and CIA, however, found the demand impossible given the key military positions held by the Somocistas. The split became public in May, 1984 as did the CIA's demand to ARDE that it join the FDN. Meanwhile, FDN leaders were condemning Pastora as an FSLN agent out to keep the contras divided. At the end of the month, a bomb attack on Pastora's headquarters killed several reporters and badly wounded Pastora. While the United States blamed the FSLN for the attack, Pastora labelled it an assassination attempt on him by the FDN and the CIA.[12] According to Pastora, the CIA had not given his forces funding since the San Juan attack in efforts to force him over to the FDN. In the end the attack served to punctuate the break-up of ARDE; under Robelo's leadership, ARDE voted in June to expel Pastora and to join with the FDN. While Robelo brought few troops with him, the United States happily promoted Robelo to the FDN's political leadership alongside Adolfo Calero, one of the few non-Somocista, non-<u>Guardia</u> FDN members. Pastora and his few loyal troops were left to shift for themselves. What was left of Pastora's ARDE managed only small and isolated military campaigns in the next years. According to Pastora, "We have just been instruments of US policy and for that we are dying. They were wasting our people. We call this the Doberman policy. The US has a dog in the north and a dog in the south" (<u>NYT</u>, 2-29-85).

As Pastora proved unpredictable and uncooperative, the United States supported Adolfo Calero, Alfonso Robelo and Arturo Cruz, a late-comer to the armed opposition, as the top contra leaders from 1984 onward. Top <u>Guardia</u> members, like director of the military Col. Enrique Bermudez, were demoted from visible leadership positions in 1984 and Edgar Chamorro, a political leader who publically criticized CIA methods and contradicted US statements, was purged from the FDN. Calero, a former Managua businessman, was promoted earlier (1983) under CIA pressure in efforts at winning new US and international aid for the FDN. As an ex-<u>Guardia</u> military leader of the FDN commented on the CIA's political leadership recruitment for the FDN: "The benefactor had to find something to guarantee his investment. The people in the directorate were chosen because in reality we had no political charisma" (<u>NYT</u>, 3-18-85).

With Pastora edged out in 1984, and, after a successful FSLN military campaign to push remaining ARDE forces back into Costa Rica in early 1985 the Reagan Administration worked in mid-1985 to re-establish a US-controlled anti-Sandinista force in Costa Rica. This move was necessary to the administration's continuing objective of creating a two-front war against the FSLN government. Because Congressional restrictions disallowed direct CIA contact with the rebels, the administration coordinated and facilitated the organization of the new FDN-allied force through the offices of the National Security Council. Arms and supplies were air-dropped to northern Costa Rica, reportedly again from El Salvador, and logistics and other aid was provided by people in Costa Rica who had cooperated with the CIA contra operations in previous years. Cruz and Robelo were provided monies to conduct related "political work", undoubtedly aimed at recruiting members for the Costa Rican-based force (NYT, 8-25-85). According to contra officials, the plan was to expand "greatly" an initial 300-400 man force during 1985 and 1986, drawing from ex-ARDE and other anti-Sandinista ranks. As part of the overall US strategy, this southern force -- the Southern Opposition Front -- was officially under the Calero-Cruz-Robelo political leadership along with the FDN and was to operate in conjunction with US-FDN objectives.

Meanwhile, inside Nicaragua the United States was working through embassy, FDN and other contacts to influence the political and civil opposition to drop out of and condemn the political processes of elections and constitution-writing. The problem for US policy regarding Nicaragua's internal politics in 1984 onward was precisely that a viable non-Marxist opposition had chosen not to take up arms but to work within the system as it had been organized by the Frente since the revolution. The political directorate of the FDN, on the other hand, although it consisted of men who were pro-US and who owed their organizational existence to the United States, nevertheless represented a narrow strata of people in Nicaragua, had not tested their political following there and had only a tenuous hold over the military wing -- the original and operational core of the FDN. Few in or out of Nicaragua accepted the FDN political directorate as representing an indigenous, independent basis for centrist democratic politics. Rather, many saw it as a group dependent on the United States and/or a Somocista military organization that continued to use brutal tactics.

A Congressional caucus report in April, 1985 again confirmed such fears about the FDN. While the State Department itself did not publish information on the FDN leadership until 1986 but quoted "FDN reports" that Somocistas were not prominent in the FDN, this report found that forty-six of forty-eight positions in the FDN military command structure were held by ex-Guardia members (see Figure 6.1). The key military strategists, the general staff, four of five central commanders, six of seven regional commands and all thirty task force commanders were found to be former members of Somoza's Guardia. The report, which also investigated the political nature of the FDN's private donors, lent credibility to the argument that the creation of the United Nicaraguan Opposition (UNO) in 1985 was a US attempt to present a clean and "democratic" political contra leadership to domestic critics in the United States. Promoting Calero, Robelo and Cruz as UNO's leaders would disassociate UNO somewhat from its actual base, the FDN's military leaders and fighters, as well as from the FDN's poor image.

In fact, throughout 1985 and 1986 US efforts focused on uniting the contra forces under one banner and one political directorate with a program of government. To that end the political directorate published initial documents calling for changes in Nicaragua. But besides appearing late in the contra effort, the broad political objectives enunciated in 1985 failed to paste over differences on political and military strategy among the top three political

Figure 6.1
FDN Military Command (as of April, 1985)

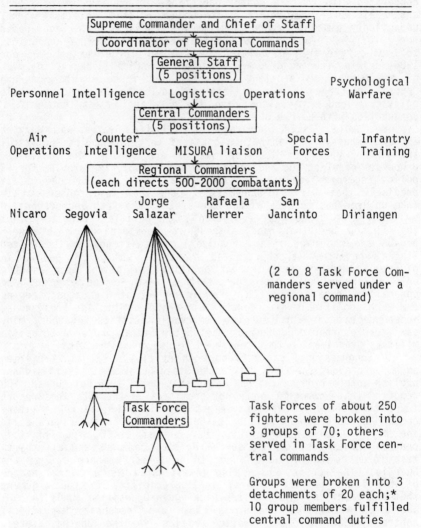

| Supreme Commander and Chief of Staff |
| Coordinator of Regional Commands |
| General Staff (5 positions) |

Personnel  Intelligence   Logistics   Operations   Psychological
                                                    Warfare

| Central Commanders (5 positions) |

   Air         Counter                      Special      Infantry
Operations   Intelligence   MISURA liaison  Forces       Training

| Regional Commanders (each directs 500-2000 combatants) |

Nicaro   Segovia    Jorge      Rafaela    San
                    Salazar    Herrer     Jancinto    Diriangen

(2 to 8 Task Force Commanders served under a regional command)

Task Force Commanders

Task Forces of about 250 fighters were broken into 3 groups of 70; others served in Task Force central commands

Groups were broken into 3 detachments of 20 each;* 10 group members fulfilled central command duties

*While 46 of the top 48 military commands were held by Somocista Guardia exiles, approximately 80% of field group leaders had no Guardia experience.

Source:   Based on information from the Arms Control and Foreign Policy Caucas, in Congressional Quarterly, 1985.

leaders. This, in turn, made it difficult for UNO to win political support in Nicaragua and in Congress. Political disputes into 1986 centered on how UNO should be structured, who should be appointed to key positions, how rights abuses should be punished and what specific objectives the contras were fighting for -- i.e., to negotiate with or to overthrow the FSLN. The latter issue was spurred by differences between public and private administration statements and by conflicting signals to UNO from the CIA, the NSC, the State Department and the White House, according to UNO officials. In addition, UNO leaders were split on tactics. Adolfo Calero, who represented the most conservative wing of the contras, got his international and private backing from anti-communist groups, was the leader and patron of the majority FDN military forces and of Somocista elements within the contras, handled most of the contra army's supplies and aimed at overthrowing the Sandinistas. Calero also had the strongest and most developed ties to the Reagan Administration; the CIA instructed other UNO leaders not to disrupt Calero's "existing structure" lest his supporters -- who represented the bulk of the contra fighters and private funders -- became demoralized (NYT, 11-4-85; 5-20-86). Ideologically, Calero was closer to Reagan ideologues. Cruz and Robelo, who reportedly often felt out-gunned by Calero, were ideologically more liberal and were inclined to negotiate with the FSLN if the Frente did not eventually collapse under pressure. Both men had worked in the Sandinista government until they realized that the revolution was to extend beyond the system reforms they preferred. Being somewhat distanced from Somocista forces, however, these men could potentially draw wider political support in the United States and elsewhere at some future time and if they were not displaced by the Calero's contingent.

Another sticky problem for UNO leaders was changing its international image by effectively curbing systematic human rights abuses. Under heavy pressure from Washington, in August and September, 1985 UNO leaders formed their own human rights commission to prosecute the "few violations" uncovered by their investigations. A Red Cross unit was started in an effort to bring money and services to people inside Nicaragua, a direct attempt to improve their image among rural Nicaraguans. That these would be difficult areas in which to show improvement, however, became clear almost immediately. For example, in August atrocities continued as the contras pursued Operation Roundup. At least eleven Sandinista army prisoners were executed in central Nicaragua, and near Esteli and La Trinidad unarmed workers and children were killed in contra ambushes. The political directorate itself had no proven authority over fighters in the field; even within the military command structure cases of insubordination and the use of separate task forces--which were in the field for up to five months at a time--weakened command and control among the forces. Contra tactics made it difficult to honor human rights or to take prisoners. Arturo Cruz noted in August that it was "a delicate thing" to persuade the fighters to respect the lives of prisoners and pro-Sandinista civilians without demoralizing them, and, when medical and transportation facilities were scarce (NYT, 8-24-85). Though contra military commanders continued to argue that they could not take prisoners because they had no secure means for holding or caring for them, Cruz and the other UNO political leaders referred to the need to follow President Reagan's guidelines when he promised Congress in June that the rebels would improve their rights practices. According to US and contra officials in the field, administration pressure on the contras in this period to "clean up their act" was intense. Given the animosity and fear with which most Nicaraguans viewed the contras, however, improvement in public relations or increasing rural peasant support appeared far off. A lack of progress on such issues through early mid-1986, however, was not to weaken the administration's political support for or defense of the contra program. During the first six months of 1986 the Reagan Administration waged a fierce political campaign to win new military funding for the contras.


## THE ECONOMIC IMPACT OF THE CONTRA WAR

Together with the economic sanctions, and later, an official embargo placed on Nicaragua by the United States in mid-1985, the contra war exacted an enormous toll on Nicaragua. If the contras were not successful politically or militarily, the damage they inflicted on Nicaragua's economic infrastructure was great -- especially after 1983 when contra strategy changed from trying to win a military victory, to targetting economic infrastructure in an attrition campaign. While in Part Four I discuss how the contra war and resulting economic hardship shaped Nicaragua's military and foreign policy, here I review briefly the economic and human impact of the war on Nicaragua.[13]

The most severe economic damage and the most direct impact of the war was seen in primary production, or, on the macro-economy of national-level production, investment and consumption. The destruction of capital assets and infrastructure, such as buildings, machinery, livestock or bridges, was also enormous and costly to the small economy. Yet these losses were secondary to losses of coffee, lumber, fish and mineral production in the war zones. It was from these export products that Nicaragua traditionally earned its foreign exchange. And it was the export sector that the contras began targetting. In the years of fighting up to 1985, for example, losses in primary production alone (i.e., not factoring in related infrastructural losses, losses of human services facilities, or other human costs) amounted to approximately one year's worth of exports. Half of that total loss came in 1984 alone (see Table 6.3). For example, forestry, fishing and mining--activities carried out in areas that have become war zones--were hit hard. These activities traditionally accounted for about 14 percent of Nicaragua's total primary production. By late 1984, moreover, up to 50 percent of Nicaragua's maize and bean crops--staples of the local diet--were lost because they were grown in areas most affected by contra attacks (LASA, 1985). Actual fighting and fear of attacks kept peasants from sowing and harvesting.

Losses in exports led to large balance-of-payment deficits and to the unavailability of foreign exchange for purchasing production materials and inputs from abroad. Secondary production, in other

Table 6.3
War-Related Losses in Exports and Domestic Production

| | (US$ millions) | | | | | |
|---|---|---|---|---|---|---|
| | 1980 | 1981 | 1982 | 1983 | 1984 | Total |
| Agricultural Export Production | 0.9 | 3.5 | 6.1 | 65.3 | 102.8 | 178.6 |
| - Coffee | - | - | - | 32.1 | 37.0 | 69.1 |
| - Tobacco | - | - | - | 1.9 | 1.6 | 3.5 |
| - Livestock | - | 0.1 | 0.2 | 1.0 | 3.3 | 4.6 |
| - Lumber | - | - | - | 25.0 | 52.2 | 77.2 |
| - Fishing | 0.9 | 1.2 | 2.8 | 4.0 | 6.6 | 15.5 |
| - Mining | - | 2.2 | 3.1 | 1.3 | 2.1 | 8.7 |
| Production for Domestic Consumption | - | - | 15.0 | 32.1 | 56.9 | 104.0 |
| - Basic Grains[a] | - | - | - | 0.4 | 11.3 | 11.7 |
| - Other Crops[b] | - | - | - | 1.7 | 0.6 | 2.3 |
| - Construction | - | - | 15.0 | 30.0 | 45.0 | 90.0 |
| Total | 0.9 | 3.5 | 21.1 | 97.4 | 159.7 | 282.6 |
| Exports | 451.0 | 499.8 | 405.8 | 428.6 | 381.6 | |
| Losses of Exportable Production/Exports (in percentages) | | 1% | 2% | 15% | 27% | |

Source: IHCA, September, 1985, Managua.

[a]Lost production of basic grains is calculated as a negative effect on the export sector because it must be replaced through imports.

[b]Coconuts, cocoa, cassava and other root crops.

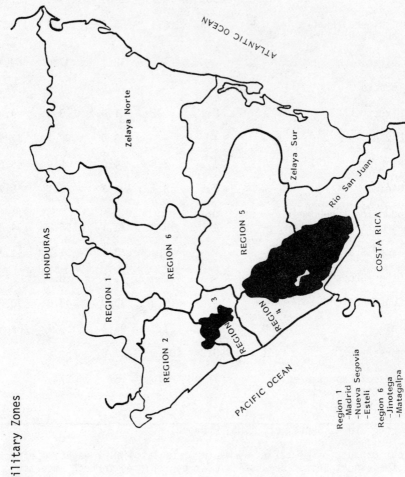

Figure 6.2
Nicaraguan Military Zones

Table 6.4
Calculated Direct Losses in External Sector Due to Aggression

| | (US$ millions) | | | | |
|---|---|---|---|---|---|
| | 1980[a] | 1981 | 1982 | 1983 | 1984 |
| Increase in Commercial Deficit (for imports) Due to Aggression | 0.9 | 3.4 | 17.4 | 100.1 | 99.0 |
| Loss of Capital Goods | - | 2.2 | 8.9 | 66.9 | 22.6 |
| Total | 0.9 | 5.6 | 26.3 | 167.0 | 121.6 |
| Percent of Exports | - | 1% | 7% | 39% | 32% |

Source: IHCA, op.cit., p. 4B.

[a]The 1980 figure estimates costs from Honduras-based ex-Guardia thievery and cattle-rustling, activities carried out by Somocista gangs prior to their organizational affiliation with the CIA.

words, was also directly affected by the attrition strategy. Losses or slow-downs in industrial activity, in turn, affected other parts of Nicaragua's economy: industrial exports, employment, debt repayment, and the like. Nicaragua's Secretariat for Planning and Budget estimated that in 1984, had there been no contra aggression, secondary production would have been 10 percent higher, exports would have been 32 percent greater, imports would have been 6 percent higher and payment of debt services could have been met. In order to calculate estimated costs to Nicaragua's export sector, these costs must be added to the costs of increased imports to replace lost domestic production, such as grains for local consumption, and to the costs of lost or replaced capital goods. Table 6.4 displays these losses by year. But the magnitude of direct financial losses to Nicaragua from US activity to undermine Nicaragua's already vulnerable economy is only seen by adding the totals in Table 6.4 to the yearly totals of aid and credit monies blocked as displayed in Table 6.1. In 1984 for example, that total--$213.7 million--represented 56 percent of Nicaragua's export income that year.

The Human Impact. The nature of contra attrition tactics and the correlary aim of undermining the citizenry's faith in the government meant that human (noncombatant) suffering would also be high. In the zones of heaviest contra attacks and fighting, Zones 1, 5, 6 and the Special Zones of the Atlantic Coast and Rio San Juan (along the Costa Rican border), the social and human impact of the war was highest (see Figure 6.2). It was in these zones, where one-third of Nicaraguans lived, that attacks on social services, including health, welfare, education and human development projects and facilities, were concentrated. In these zones (updating the data in Table 6.5 through August, 1985) 25,680 primary students and 10,095 adult education students were left unattended due to contra attacks, the murder or kidnapping of teachers, or the destruction of schools. In 1984 alone the contras killed 98 teachers and kidnapped 180 others; 24 schools were destroyed; 360 rural schools were forced to close and hundreds of adult education programs were forced to close (INSSBI, 1985). Health care and health brigadistas also became casualties: one-fourth of the population in these zones were left without stable health care; the extension of prevention services was hampered; epidemiological advances, such as with malaria and poliomielitis, stopped. Many health and nutrition facilities for infants and children were destroyed.

Contra attacks also affected other aspects of rural life. New housing and electricity, telephones and transport systems became targets of sabotage. More importantly, the traditional peasant economy was disrupted in the war zones. Small producers of coffee, grains and livestock faced contra attacks and a scarcity of labor power as young men went to war or as families relocated to larger towns or cities. The deterioration of commercial networks compounded problems as fighting kept merchants or marketing agents from storing crops, providing credits or selling production inputs. Similarly, planting and harvesting for commerce fell as peasants relocated or moved to subsistence planting. Indeed, as Table 6.6 shows, eleven percent of the residents in the zones of heaviest fighting were displaced by the contra war by 1984 and before the FSLN relocation programs began in 1985. According to the Minister of Social Welfare, the government had to reroute critical development funds to his ministry which in turn provided basic health, nutrition and education services to displaced persons. In one six-month period over 1984-1985, for example, $2.3 million was used by the ministry to provide staple food items for over forty-six thousand displaced persons. By mid-1985 7,000 orphans and 180,000 homeless were under the care of a ministry which had to abandon new programs to address war needs. While 12 percent (or $9 million) of the Social Security budget was spent on new resettlement camps in 1985, $54 million total from various government agencies was being spent to provide a basic living to displaced and relocated persons.[14]

Deterioration in living conditions was experienced by city dwellers whose average per capita consumption of basic items was down 20 percent in 1984 from 1982. Declining living standards accrued from both the stagnation of industrial production and the reassignments of quotas (of provisions) to defense and to those hit hardest by the fighting. Meanwhile, real salaries for workers fell up to 50 percent between 1982 and 1984. The lack of spare parts led to deterioration in services, many of which people had only begun receiving after Somoza's overthrow. Similar to the situation in many Latin American states in this period, inflation in Nicaragua was spiralling. The consumption of rice and beans was down 15 percent nationally, but this amounted to a 30 percent decrease for the cities due to the priorities given to feeding those in arms and those in rural war zones. The availability of powdered milk in Managua fell 20 percent from 1983 to 1984 for similar reasons. Defense forces, meanwhile, were designated up to 40 percent of Nicaragua's industrial production in 1985, according to Planning Minister Henry Ruiz (NYT, 10-27-85). Forty-five percent of shoe

Table 6.5
Human and Infrastructural Losses Incurred Through December, 1984

| | |
|---|---|
| Total deaths | 7,430 |
| Children and adolescents killed | 3,346 |
| Private farm-owners killed | 190 |
| War orphans | 6,339 |
| Campesino and Indian population displaced | 150,000 |
| Health centers destroyed or damaged | 41 |
| Health workers killed (including 2 European doctors) | 28 |
| Health workers kidnapped or injured | 41 |
| Schools destroyed | 14 |
| Schools forced to close | 359 |
| Child care centers destroyed | 10 |
| Teachers killed | 170 |
| Adult education collectives forced to close | 840 |
| Members of these collectives killed | 247 |
| Civilian communities attacked | 97 |
| State-owned cooperatives and enterprises attacked | 80 |
| Total economic losses | US$1.1 billion |

Losses inflicted during the coffee harvest

(January-March 1985)

| | |
|---|---|
| Private farms destroyed | 17 |
| Coffee pickers killed | 39 |
| Material losses | US$1 million |
| Rural population displaced | 50,000 |
| Cost of resettling population | US$50 million |

Source: Nicaraguan National Emergency Committee; cited in Barricada International, 4-4-85.

208

Table 6.6
Population Displaced from the War Zones, as of May 1984

| DEPARTMENT | Total Pop. | Displaced Pop. | Percent Pop. Affected |
|---|---|---|---|
| Region 1: | | | |
| Esteli | 110,076 | 7,060 | 6.5% |
| Madriz | 72,408 | 11,334 | 15.7 |
| Nueva Segovia | 97,765 | 11,736 | 12.0 |
| Region 2: | | | |
| Chinandega | 228,573 | 13,097 | 5.7 |
| Region 6: | | | |
| Jinotega | 127,159 | 14,120 | 11.1 |
| Matagalpa | 220,548 | 11,076 | 5.0 |
| Special Regions: | | | |
| Zelaya Norte y Sur | 202,462 | 35,682 | 17.6 |
| Rio San Juan | 29,001 | 16,567 | 57.1 |
| TOTAL | 1,087,992 | 120,672 | 11.1 |

Sources: Nicaraguan Institute of Social Security and Welfare, 1984; Cited in Barricada International, 3-28-85.

manufacturing, 24 percent of textiles and clothing and about 10 percent of basic consumer items -- sugar, rice, corn, soap, oil, salt -- went to the armed forces (IHCA, September, 1985). All of these provisions were extracted from quotas which previously went to Pacific Coast cities; the needs of rural civilians and war zone inhabitants were assigned top priority in terms of delivery of basic provisions, supplies and social services infrastructure.

All of these dislocations existed alongside constant regional tension and a fear that US forces were preparing for imminent attack. Psycho-social costs of US pressure rose as the contra war continued and as Nicaragua moved officially to a war-time footing. The contras targetted precisely those things which were associated with revolutionary social and redistributive programs; agrarian reform, cooperatives and government extension workers, for instance, were all targets of contra sabotage, assassination and terror.

Moreover, as the war continued, as villagers were called upon to defend local targets and as a military draft was imposed, defense became a way of life for every Nicaraguan. The FSLN stressed the obligation of each citizen to defend the revolution. At the same time, the Frente was unable to continue many popular social service programs. In this situation, and though the majority of Nicaraguans in fact took up voluntary militia or civil defense training, many professional and technical people left the country to escape economic hardship or military service.

Defense as a way of life had to take a toll. Education for a generation of children would be set back as some schools in rural areas and as about half of all males and many women between ages 17 and 25 had their work or studies disrupted by military or emergency tasks such as harvesting crops in the war zones. At the same time, those in regular, militia or voluntary defense duties were not economically productive and had to be supplied and cared for. Constant defense concerns, in sum, drained and redirected creative energies so badly needed in an underdeveloped country. For its part, the Sandinista government focused on redirecting the economy to address the immediate needs of producers who supported the war effort and who constituted the pillars of the Nicaraguan economy: workers in agriculture and industry. Simultaneously, the FSLN had to enlist the continued support of Pacific urban dwellers, who made up a "rearguard economy", and had to justify continued austerity measures. Although most families in Nicaragua had lost a relative or acquaintance in the contra war by 1986, the government also ceaselessly stressed struggle, sacrifice and US complicity in their suffering. Other efforts went into finding alternative international support to replace losses in commercial relations with the United States, or, into securing arms and moral support to bolster defense. The measure of their success in all these areas would be continued popular support at home and enough international support to counter external, hostile pressures. Through the mid-1980s the Frente had demonstrated the resilience and policy flexibility necessary to succeed in these areas. In that context, the United States talked of increasing the contra force and of introducing US military training of the force, introduced its state terrorism campaign and moved to encourage popular discontent inside Nicaragua.

UNO AND THE FUTURE OF US POLICY

Refusing a "passive" stance of coexisting with the revolutionary government, and being held back by domestic and world opinion from direct military moves, Reagan ideologues opted for a covert, paramilitary operation aimed at not simply containing the leftist government, but at rolling it back. Simultaneously, the administration worked to build an anti-Cuba, pro-US, nationalist opposition in Central America generally. As a White House aid explained policy intent in 1985: "If the Soviet Union metaphysically is equated to an ancient, evil empire, then to the extent we can, we ought to attack it by going at the colonies. We don't do it well now. Central America is the first opportunity to do it right" (NYT, 8-9-85).

This "win one for Reagan" push against Nicaragua, however, relied on a force of fighters and on military threats which could only spell long-term US policy failure. Nicaraguans, and Latin Americans generally, resented the United States' use of a Somocista force and its constant threats of outright intervention in Nicaragua. Ingnoring these local realities, the Reagan Administration continued to press for new contra monies from Congress as the only alternative to the use of US troops against "communist" Nicaragua. During the 1985 and 1986 contra funding debate, both supporters and critics of current US policy argued that without the contra program, US policy in Central America would unravel. The contra program had become the essence of US Nicaraguan policy and the largest element of its low-intensity, attrition warfare strategy against the Sandinista government.

Although there were signs that their analyses might be problemmatic, the White House ideologues in 1985 and 1986 believed the internal situation in Nicaragua was one of irreversible deterioration entering into a pre-insurrection period where economic decline, contra military actions and opposition to the FSLN would soon converge to topple the Frente without the need for US troops. This convergence theory led the White House and private funders to demand convincing military blows from the contras. The result in the field was stepped-up fighting, but contra losses in 1985. The losses stemmed from military planning based on United States domestic political needs and from attempts at forging compliance with US foreign policy goals rather than planning based on assessments of local Nicaraguan realities. Additionally, the convergence theory led to a scramble in 1985 and 1986 finally to establish a united and clean political leadership for the US-backed contra forces, one which could be emplaced as an alternative Nicaraguan government when the Frente fell.

The signs that the convergence theory was wrong, or at least premature in 1985 and 1986, were many. Foremost among the contradictory evidence was the feeling among the top US military brass that the contras could not win against the FSLN soon or alone and that the attrition campaign still required years and heavy military aid to produce changes in Nicaraguan structures (e.g., General Gorman, NYT, 2-28-85). Whereas, "containing" Nicaragua through regional militarization was costing the United States over $1 billion per year by 1985, an active campaign to roll back or defeat the leftist government, as well as regional leftist movements, could well cost several times that figure in the second half of the 1980s. Indeed, top military people with experience in Central America pressed the administration to consider political solutions. But another sign that US involvement could not be minimized soon was the very dependence of the contras or UNO on US logistical, moral and political support and pressure. Even with alternative (non-Congressional) funding in 1985, for example, the contras lacked their own logistical capacity. Without US pressure, the contras lacked unity and political direction. Without the United States' wooing or maneuvering of Calero (in 1983), Robelo (1984) and Cruz (1984-1985), the contras lacked a viable political leadership. Without official US backing of the contras, international support faltered. Adolfo Calero's claim in 1985 that UNO and the contras were an indigenous force and not a US creation fell under inspection. Indeed, deprived of US support, the contras comprised a homeless army without a plausible goal and a new force for regional destabilization.

Despite these signs, and consistent with administration behavior since 1981, as the contras failed militarily and politically, Reagan Administration policy-makers in 1985 and 1986 asked Congress for more of the same: more money and more time. As the contras failed with guerrilla or unconventional military strategies, the United States moved to facilitate more conventional warfare, providing military infrastructure in neighboring countries for back-up and supply and moving the contras toward heavier, less-than-mobile weapons, artillery and combat air support. White House and contra officials also continued to expand the contra effort. And, in 1985 these officials spoke of increasing the force to 20-25,000 in Honduras and coordinating 5-10,000 fighters to operate from Costa Rica under a new Southern Opposition Front aligned with the FDN and UNO--neither of which proved possible by mid-1986. Along with increased Nicaraguan military preparedness, these plans suggested a long-term US military role in the region. The US contra program also bore significant implications for regional politics and stability.

The possibility of military imbroglios between Nicaragua and its northern and southern neighbors was also increased by the United States' sponsorship of armed groups in these countries. As I noted earlier, US-contra strategy involved trying to create border incidents for which Nicaragua could be blamed. Between 1983 and 1986, for example, hundreds of border attacks and crossings were reported by the three governments. Not only did Honduran military forces provide cover fire for the contras, but the Sandinista Army also pursued contra fighters into Honduras and Costa Rica and used cross-border bombardments to hit contra base camps. For example in May, 1985 the Sandinista army waged a coordinated assault on a large contra camp in southern Honduras and in March, 1986 undertook a somewhat larger campaign (with about 900-1000 troops) against the main contra training camp about 10 miles into Honduras. The later assault, coming as it did during the Reagan Administration fight on Capitol Hill for $100 million in new contra military funding, led to: White House charges of a Nicaraguan invasion; an emergency $20 million military aid package to Honduras; and the use of US helicopters and crews for transporting Honduran troops to the border zone.[15] Meanwhile, cases of downed aircraft along the Nicaraguan-Honduran border increased through 1985, as did population relocation along both sides of the border. The repeated US warning that it would retaliate under the Rio Treaty against an attack on its allies, and, contra efforts to get Nicaragua to retaliate against Honduras or Costa Rica for contra attacks launched from those states greatly increased regional tensions (e.g., WP, 5-21-84; NYT, 3-27-86).

The United States' proxy war against Nicaragua had various effects on the internal situation there. Not the least of these was the Frente's determination to increase its arms and preparedness to defend against contra attacks, a possible regional assault under the

auspices of CONDECA or a direct military strike or invasion by the
United States. While US officials argued that one purpose of the
contra paramilitary operation was to get Nicaragua to reduce its
armed forces, US policy had the effect of doing the opposite (see
Chapter 8). By 1985 over 50 percent of Nicaragua's national budget
and 40 percent of its productive output went to the war effort.
Early in that year the _Frente_ had officially put the economy on a
war footing. But the costs of militarization were also high for the
FSLN; not only did it reduce monies for socioeconomic development
and play into the US portrayal of a militarist Nicaragua, it also
led the _Frente_ to impose an unpopular military draft law in 1983.

In economic terms and in conjunction with US economic
sanctions, the contra war diverted development funds, damaged
economic infrastructure and created a foreign exchange crisis
through destruction of export crops. It induced scarcity, rationing
and labor discontent. These things acted to undermine support for
the revolutionary government in some quarters. On the other hand,
some effects of the contra war worked to errode the potential for US
economic influence in the future. The Nicaraguans were quite
successful in finding alternative sources, markets and aid monies.
Another side effect of the economic damage was widespread hatred of
the contras and animosity toward the Reagan Administration,
attitudes which would factor in any post-Sandinista regime and
affect the course of Nicaraguan politics far into the future. This
political polarization was exemplified by the Sandinistas' refusal
to lend any legitimacy to the contras or their UNO political
directorate and by the contras' stance toward the "rabid dog"
Sandinistas. The military commanders of the contras similarly
rejected any dialogue with the Sandinistas.[16]

Despite US efforts, the Sandinistas proved resilient and
responsive to major citizen concerns in wartime. Improving their
own defense prospects and wooing public opinion, the FSLN adopted
and changed a number of policies to meet citizen demands. Land
reform was quickened and, in 1985, changed to reflect rural
families' desires for private plots. Social services were expanded
or redirected to aid victims of the war or families of combatants.
Several amnesties allowed contra fighters to return home. An
autonomy plan was being developed in consultation with Atlantic
Coast citizens. Food distribution and subsidy programs aimed at
assuring basic diets for those most affected by the scarcity brought
on by US sanctions and contra crop damage. Thus, on top of the
improvements in education and health care since 1979, these policies
limited the United States' and the contras' prospects for creating
social disaffection toward the _Frente_ in the short-term. At the
same time, the Sandinistas' social and human services record greatly
raised expectations of the populous, expectations that any new
government would have to meet.

Other questions about the future of US policy and whether, in
the long-term, it could yield greater regional stability arose from
the nature of the contra group itself. It remained to be seen
whether the civilian leaders in the new political directorate could
take over power from the military leaders and effectively address
human rights abuses or insubordination in the field. For example,
the political leaders had to rely on the Somocista military command

to uncover and handle abuses and troop discipline. In nearly six years of fighting, the contras had shown little concern for human rights; they had maintained the brutal tactics institutionalized under Somoza and in their struggle against the Sandinistas. Nor by mid-1986 had the Reagan Administration directly engaged its influence over the contras in a serious attempt to move them away from systemmatic atrocities in the field -- something Congress had forced the president and his staff to pursue vis-a-vis the army in El Salvador. But it was also unclear whether, in a victory over the Sandinistas, the UNO political directorate would be able to wrest power from the Somocista military command which had made the victory possible. That the Reagan Administration denied the existence of leadership squabbles and downplayed the possibility of such a problem emerging is clear from the fact that in 1985, the State Department's publications on the "top leaders" of the contras gave biographical data on only one person in the military command (e.g. DOS, September, 1985). Nevertheless, those persons in the military command structure, the Somocistas, were the initial CIA recruits and remained the backbone of the new UNO. Sharp political and attitudinal differences existed, for example, both between and among military leaders Bermudez and Lopez and political leaders Calero, Cruz and Robelo. And the political program of the latter came very late (1985) both to the contras and to the struggle against the Sandinistas' political program. Just what kind of government the contras would establish was not clear to the Nicaraguan people. Nor did those in Nicaragua who disliked the FSLN welcome the contras; the contras remained identified with Somocismo in the minds of most Nicaraguans in the mid-1980s. According to several sources, including US Embassy personnel in Managua, most people in Nicaragua who were disenchanted with the Frente were fence-sitters who would not cast their lot with the contras, who doubted that UNO's political directorate could control its Somocista military structure, and who were also not happy with US policy. This group hoped for a lowering of tensions to allow more political space and inter-party bargaining within the Nicaraguan political system and among Nicaraguans. As it was, the FSLN's legislative opposition was participating in the 1985-1986 constitution-writing process.

What popular resistance a new US-backed government would face also remained to be seen. Judging from the mass politicization of the Nicaraguan citizenry, the expectations raised by the FSLN's redistributive policies, Sandinista pledges to fight a guerrilla war against such a government and the like, there is little doubt that resistance would exist and that the new government's dependence on the United States for economic and military security would be great.

US policy vis-a-vis revolutionary Nicaragua was at a crossroads in the second half of the 1980s. Congress appeared unwilling to go on for several more years giving unlimited funding to a covert paramilitary operation that was producing heightening regional tensions and threats of war, but none of the political changes sought in Nicaragua. New military aid (narrowly) voted in mid-1986 was couched in language of restrictions and progress toward negotiations. Alternatively, Washington preferred not to break relations, close its[17] Managua embassy and lose an important intelligence source.[17] A naval blockade, funding the contras openly or similar military acts, on the other hand, would be difficult without a declaration of war -- something the American public was in no mood for. Yet, the ideologues agenda of purging leftist movements had narrowed the options for US Nicaraguan policy.

If and when 1)the contras failed to induce an anti-Sandinista insurrection or 2)Congress rejected further US sponsorship of the contras and 3)US and world opinion continued to reject direct US military moves as legitimate behavior, the United States -- under Reagan or his successor -- would have to reassess policy assumptions and come to terms with realities on the ground. The most salient reality, undoubtedly, would be the continuing political power of the Sandinistas and their revolutionary objectives for Nicaragua. Another Nicaraguan reality would be the continued existence of political opposition -- to the left and to the right of the FSLN -- within the body politic, as well as unanimous hatred of Somocista elements. The United States would have to reassess what roles the contra force could realistically play, if any, in forwarding US objectives. And the future of a heavily-armed exile force would have to be addressed whether or not UNO's political leadership rejoined the political process in Nicaragua. But regional political disarticulation due to ideological polarization and militarization would also need to be addressed if immediate and long-term stability in Central America was of priority to US policy makers.

If Washington, under the above conditions, decided not to use military might to force a solution of its choosing, negotiations to reduce regional tensions and to get recognition of US national interests -- i.e., interests defined more narrowly than conservative ideologues had defined them -- constituted the only feasible future for US policy toward Nicaragua. The Contadora process and the Manzanillo (bilateral) talks had, by 1985 provided frameworks for addressing United States security concerns, at least insofar as the US did not insist on controlling all political initiatives in the Western hemisphere in the 1980s and beyond.[18]

On a broader level was the question of what lessons Latin American states would ultimately draw from US paramilitary activities against revolutionary Nicaragua, or , from a direct US military action to overthrow the Frente. Only two states in the hemisphere openly supported the United States' contra program, by 1986: Salvador and Honduras. Support for Contadora, on the other hand, was strenuous and reflected the mood of Latin Americans for independence from US dictates and political maneuverings. In fact, the Nicaraguan revolution and the local superpower's reaction to it spurred Latin American diplomatic activity, feelings of interdependence and expressions of solidarity in search of political solutions like few other hemispheric issues. There was little doubt that a direct US move against Nicaragua would spark near-universal condemnation and would have negative repercussions in US-Latin American relations for years to come. The decline in US influence, for example on the Latin American debt issue or through joint economic or military programs, would be precipitous. On the other hand, demonstrating a US willingness and commitment to working out political settlements in bilateral and multilateral settings would go far in both improving a tarnished US image in Latin America and in encouraging the recent movements toward civilian and participatory governments there.

NOTES

1.  Until 1983 Southcom held only one sizeable exercise each year, Kindle Liberty, which practiced the defense of the Panama Canal. A main focus of the post-1983 exercises was to give US and local troops practice in working in tandem in any large US military undertaking.

2.  By 1986 Southcom planned to increase its air force holdings to include small supply planes that could use the 900 tiny airships in Central America. Thirty airfields in the region could accommodate US C-130s transport planes.

3.  From 1982 to 1985 contingency plans focused on involving regional armies under US coordination against the FMLN and "their Nicaraguan suppliers", thus raising local fears of a regionalization of the Salvadoran civil war. Joint military maneuvers near Nicaraguan borders and the training of Salvadorans by US teams in Honduras gave credibility to the ideas of a regional war.

4.  After the FSLN military victory in July, 1979 a number of top _Guardia_ leaders were permitted exile in the United States. Many more ex-_Guardia_ fled across the border to Honduras and began plotting to retake control, though they were disorganized, demoralized and without a central or political leaders. Several thousand more were captured and imprisoned by FSLN fighters. According to several contra members, they met with Reagan aide Vernon Walters in 1980 to discuss paramilitary action against the FSLN government (e.g. NYT 3-17-85).

5.  After 1982 it became difficult to assess the actual size of contra forces since US and FDN officials regularly overestimated the number of active troops in efforts to demoralize the FSLN and to depict the contras as successful in recruiting support. Ex-FDN official Edgar Chamorro reported that he was routinely instructed to double actual figures in citing contra strength.

6.  According to numerous reports, the CIA was paying mercenaries, such as Malvinas-experienced Argentinian officers and Israelis, from $5-10,000 per month to fight with the FDN or to carry out special operations.

7.  Singlaub was relieved of his South Korean command by President Carter after he publically disagreed with Carter's military policy there. In his work in support of the contras General Singlaub claimed to have received help and encouragement from Fred Ikle and Nestor Sanchez at the Pentagon and the National Security Council, from the White House and from the State Department. In 1984 and in 1985 moreover, President Reagan sent messages of greetings and his personal support to the World Anti-Communist League on the occasions of its fund-raising conventions in San Diego and Dallas.

8.  In August, 1985 it was revealed that National Security Council members working under NSA Mac Farlane had been advising the contras on their operations despite the Congressional aid cut-off in effect after October, 1984. Acting on the premise that the NSC is an instrument for enforcing the president's will, NSC members kept

216

in touch with the CIA and the State and Defense Departments on contra activities and visited contra camps. US military officers interviewed in Honduras in August, 1985 denied having any contacts with the contras after the aid cut-off went into effect (author interviews).

9. General Singlaub noted that after the CIA was forced to pull out of the contra operation in 1984, "...these guys didn't know how to buy a Bandaid" (NYT, 8-13-85).

10. A report by US lawyer Reed Brody detailed a series of atrocities. America's Watch similarly noted the persistence of contra abuses.

11. Rural farmers reported in this period that the contras carried large amounts of money with them to buy food from farmers and local merchants, offering twice the amounts the Sandinista army could pay for pigs, chickens or other food it needed to sustain itself.

12. According to the report of a 16-month investigation by two North American journalists in Costa Rica, one of whom was injured in the bomb attack, this may well have been the case. Martha Honey and Tony Avirgan reported that the bomber, a right-wing Libyan national, was contracted by the CIA in Chile and was hired for the assassination attempt against Pastora by the CIA and the FDN. The bombing, they charge, was intended to be blamed on the Sandinistas and to raise tensions between Nicaragua and Costa Rica. See ICAS, October, 1985.

13. In this section I draw from the Instituto Historico Centroamericano's publication, September, 1985. Unless otherwise noted, the data are from the UN's Economic Commission for Latin America and from the Nicaraguan government.

14. Interview with Reinaldo Antonio Tefel Velez, Minister of INSSBI, Managua, August, 1985. A corresponding figure of displaced persons in the United States would be over 14 million.

15. The Hondurans were reluctant to acknowledge the 1986 Sandinista incursion, did not view it as anti-Honduran in intent and only acknowledged the territorial crossing under US pressure to do so (e.g. NYT, 3-29-86; 4-2-86).

16. Contra military strategist Enrique Bermudez, for example, held that the Sandinistas had "absolutely not" produced any positive changes in Nicaragua since Somoza. His second-in-command Armando "Tono" Lopez argued that, "He who speaks of dialogue with the communists speaks of wasting his time" (NYT, 3-18-85). These attitudes appear to limit the potential for reconciliation in the near future.

17. According to US Embassy analysts in Managua (1985), the primary function of that embassy was to gather intelligence.

18. For discussions of possible negotiation positions see: Farer (1984), Wiarda (1984); LeoGrande (1985); and PACCA (1984).

# 7

## Latin America and Europe
## View the Revolution

CENTRAL AMERICA AND THE SANDINISTA REVOLUTION

Historic patterns of conflict and cooperation among the Central American states influenced their bilateral and multilateral policies toward Nicaragua. Just as historic animosities interfered with US efforts to form a cohesive anti-Nicaragua bloc in Central America, common economic concerns lead to ongoing interaction that often transcended political conflicts. For example, all the states expressed desires to keep common market mechanisms alive, to extend regional fiscal incentives to industry and to establish a new regional tariff scheme. In 1983 and 1984 the states acted as a bloc in arranging negotiations with Western Europe on economic aid. While the reconstruction of the old CACM was unlikely and overall regional trade was declining, common concerns over high external debt, oil dependency, balance-of-payments problems and new aid increased the potential for cooperation on global economic questions. Fears that Nicaragua might not be able to meet payments, more so than differences in political orientations, seemed to shape regional decisions regarding exports to that country. Despite US economic hostility and a 1985 embargo, its neighbors continued to import Nicaraguan products, including staple food items. Central American states recognized that they could not economically survive apart from one another, even if current economic interaction remained limited.

Yet the effect of US policy was precisely to heighten tensions among these states; US intent was to isolate Nicaragua from its neighbors. Washington worked to confound economic (and diplomatic) initiatives that included Nicaragua, while at the same time emphasizing military over socioeconomic development. Despite the large US regional presence in the 1980s, and, in no small part due to the nature of that presence, regional economic decline continued apace. The bases for actual regional economic cooperation dwindled as local economic dependence and political polarization grew; as El Salvador, Costa Rica and Honduras became more dependent on the United States, Nicaragua--shut off from the United States--became more dependent on Eastern Europe. Among US allies, Reagan Administration policy undergirded traditional, security-minded sectors.

Political tensions among the Central American states were a

218

more salient feature of regional relations in the 1980s. Above and beyond intense US pressure on these states to reject the Sandinista regime, traditional political sectors had their own reasons for fearing the Nicaraguan revolutionary model of popular hegemony and non-alignment. Regional oligarchs and militaries had usually usurped or maintained power with US aid. Similarly, small new middle classes had developed close links to US capital. In an era of increasing social tension and economic dislocation, US aid would be necessary for successfully repressing or coopting popular challenges to badly skewed distributions of wealth and power. The Sandinistas, by contrast, represented the ascendance of popular rule and a successful example for those wishing to challenge traditional social structures. The Sandinistas' vocal support of national liberation movements elsewhere in the world added to the concern of local traditional elites. Not long after the 1979 Triumph, Guatemala and Salvador charged Nicaragua with assisting anti-government groups in their countries. Honduras and Costa Rica later made similar charges. Though few of these links were ever convincingly documented, this charge was a common one levelled against the FSLN. The Frente's reliance on popular mobilization for defense and its use of Cuban advisors and Soviet-made equipment again worried local militaries which had long before adopted anti-communist, national security mentalities and US training programs. These forces were more accustomed to confronting their own populations rather than relying on them for military preparedness or development campaigns. Competing worldviews added to suspicions and mistrust of the Sandinista revolution among groups anxious to maintain the status quo.

Although various strains of thinking developed among and within these states on the issue of whether they could work with a leftist neighbor which challenged US predominance, the hardline and pro-US sectors worked to narrow room for debate. Simultaneously, US pressures mounted on those governments and sub-groups that supported Nicaragua's demand for non-interference and self-determination. Ultimately, the Central American states' dependence during a period of economic decline and political conflict limited opportunities for independent behavior in the short term. Nevertheless, nationalist sentiments were also being aroused; they would have consequences in the long term.

## Honduras

For the military regime in Honduras, the Sandinista revolution came at a time when it was also facing potential economic and social crises at home. While the economic decline which began around 1970 continued, the social strains produced by rural landlessness and underdevelopment were exacerbated by the reluctance or incapacity of traditional elites to sponsor structural change. At a time when the United States was seeking a replacement for Somoza's Nicaragua--heretofore the regional US bulwark against communism--and for bases from which to contain the leftist revolution, Honduran elites needed economic and other aid in order to confront and contain social movements there. The scene was set for a large Honduran role in US policy not only toward Nicaragua and El Salvador in the 1980s but also in longer-term US military planning for Latin America and the Caribbean. The great amount of attention given Honduras in US policy after 1979 seemed more awkward given Honduras' status as the poorest state in the region after Haiti.

Although Honduras' official reaction to the revolution was one of "neutrality," the presence of some 5-6,000 Somoza Guardia exiles there was an immediate and constant source of tension between the neighboring states. Cross-border attacks by Somocista bands into Nicaragua as early as August, 1979 led to Sandinista protests and cross-border chases, as well as to the deployment of some Honduran troops along the border to regulate Guardia activity. While the Honduran government initially claimed it was in strict control of the Guardsmen, the attacks continued through 1980 to provoke border clashes and to demonstrate the Honduran army's inability or unwillingness to stop anti-Sandinista forces. Aware that they had the support of at least some in the Honduran military command, the contras were interested in involving the Honduran army in their cause. By November, 1979, the FSLN was considering a break in relations with Honduras. As the Honduran government reiterated its neutrality stance, the foreign ministers met to defuse tense relations. But Honduran elites' wariness over leftist politics and Cuban teachers and doctors in Nicaragua continued. Through 1980, contra raids, Nicaraguan reprisals and trade issues prompted protests from both sides, but also spurred several high-level meetings to address concerns.

At this critical time in Nicaraguan-Honduran relations and in Honduras' own political evolution, the United States acted upon its new assessment of Honduras as "the ham in the sandwich" between leftist elements in Nicaragua and El Salvador.[1] According to senior Honduran army officials, the Carter Administration held secret talks with them in Washington and Miami in 1980 to discuss Pentagon plans to arm Honduras as the main military force in Central America (e.g., FBIS-LAM, 1-21-81). Days prior to Reagan's inauguration in January, 1981, thirty-six US military advisors--experts in counterinsurgency, logistics and communications--arrived in Honduras, along with several ships and planeloads of weapons (FBIS-LAM, 1-23-81). The new administration was prepared to use the Honduran connection in an ever-widening agenda. In February, both Secretary of State Haig and US Southern Command head General Nutting went to Tegucigalpa to discuss US interests, US aid and joint military operations. By March, Honduran officials, repeating Haig's claims in the United States, openly identified Nicaragua with the Soviet Union and Cuba, raised the issue of Nicaraguan arms trafficking and accused "foreign interests" of fomenting inter-state tensions (FBIS-LAM, 3-4-81). Meanwhile, US officials and US policy encouraged anti-Sandinista, anti-FMLN elements in the Honduran military; influenced the ascendance of staunchly anti-communist Gustavo Alverez Martinez to Commander-in-Chief of the armed forces in early 1982; rapidly established the groundwork for making Honduras the local gendarme of US policy; and pushed the Honduran elite to adopt formal democratic institutions befitting Honduras' new relationship with Washington.

Military Predominance. Buoyed by new US military aid and tough anti-Sandinista rhetoric from the Reagan Administration, the Honduran army effectively prepared for war with Nicaragua in early

1981. Waging an anti-Nicaragua press campaign, giving the Somocistas free reign and putting the armed forces on full alert, the army command reported that war was "70 percent likely." According to the Honduran army colonel in charge of the contested border region, Nicaragua was the "pawn of international communism" and was "trampling" Honduras' integrity by its cross-border pursuit of the Somocistas (LAWR, 5-22-81). In the view of many in the army command, the Somocistas were a first line of defense against the Sandinistas and were preferable to the FSLN. The FSLN, meanwhile, charged that Somocistas in Honduras were coordinating an anti-Sandinista front with groups in Guatemala and Miami and presented a security threat to Nicaragua from bases in Honduras (NYT, 4-21-81). On numerous occasions after July, 1979, the Frente had called on Honduras to disarm the Guardia exiles. Yet Honduran elites had been split on the question of how to deal with Nicaragua; the army in particular feared the spread of popular movements. Now in the midst of a tense situation and with the Honduran army opting for a confrontation with Nicaragua, Reagan Special Envoy Vernon Walters flew to Honduras in May, 1981 to avert war and to establish US policy predominance in the new US-Honduran relationship. At the same time, however, Walters announced a doubling of military aid to $10.5 million.

The early episode was indicative of the effect US policy was to have on Honduran politics and on its military policy. As US military aid to Honduras doubled, then tripled and later doubled again; as Washington sponsored continuous joint military maneuvers in Honduras; and as the United States took on a broad military infrastructure development program there, Honduras and the Honduran army came to act as Washington's regional proxy and policy arm. With about 1,500 permanent US military advisors, seven new or rebuilt airstrips that could accommodate C130 or larger craft, two radar posts, and several training camps and fuel depots, Honduras was provided the military infrastructure capable of facilitating any Washington policy decision regarding Nicaragua or El Salvador. Militarization had the inevitable effect of making a military solution to the "Nicaraguan problem" seem plausible to many Honduran military leaders.

The Honduran army was a proxy for US regional military policy in several ways. For example, despite continuing disputes with El Salvador, the Honduran army--under US encouragement-- coordinated with the Salvadoran army in sweeps against FMLN guerrillas or Salvadoran refugees suspected of being guerrilla supporters. In a hammer and anvil pattern of military cooperation, the Salvadoran army typically pursued guerrillas or suspects to the border where the Honduran army was waiting to hold them from fleeing into Honduras; unseasoned guerrillas and noncombatants, unaware of the tactic, were often caught in the middle (see White, 1984: 191). The Honduran army joined the Salvadoran action at La Virtud in March, 1981 which resulted in the killing of Salvadoran war refugees (e.g., LAWR, 4-3-81). In mid-1982, 3,000 Honduran troops were sent to the Salvadoran border area where they clashed with FMLN units and went on to fight alongside the Salvadorans in Morazan province in El Salvador.[2] Although the larger action spurred public protest demonstrations in Tegucigalpa in July, 1982, joint operations by the two US-supported armies against leftist guerrillas continued. In early 1985, for instance, it was again reported that Honduran soldiers were sent to the northern Salvadoran border.[3]

More important in Nicaraguan concerns, the Honduran army played the role of local facilitator for the US contra program. As I discussed in Chapter 6, Honduran Commander-in-Chief Alverez took orders regarding the contra campaign from US Ambassador Negroponte and held regular meetings with the contra military command. In late 1981, the Honduran army cooperated with US, Somocista and Miskito forces in the "Red Christmas" plot and in other attacks in northern Nicaragua. Besides providing training, intelligence and arms-ferrying in the next years, the Honduran army became involved against FSLN troops by providing cover-fire for contras crossing the border. Although military complicity with the contras was officially denied, numerous border clashes involving FSLN and Honduran forces occurred and increased in intensity in 1985 (see Chapter 8). Such clashes, when they resulted in the destruction of Honduran aircraft or loss of lives, also led to Honduran diplomatic or military retaliation against Nicaragua. In May, 1984, for example, the Nicaraguan ambassador was expelled from Honduras after the Nicaraguans downed a Honduran military helicopter that was flying over Nicaraguan territory. In September, 1985, Honduran warplanes strafed army positions in Nicaragua after the Nicaraguans pursued 800 retreating contras with cross-border artillery fire (ICAS, October, 1985).

While the Honduran military command was willing to facilitate local US military designs in return for increasingly larger military aid packages, it was also interested in expanded military capacity for its own sake. Not only did Honduran military leaders view Nicaragua as a security threat, they retained suspicions (from the 1969 Soccer War) about El Salvador's military intent and worried about heavy US military aid and training in that country. The thought in some military sectors was that if or when the FMLN was defeated, the large Salvadoran army would turn against Honduras. At the same time, Alverez publically echoed the US administration's view that if the Salvadoran government fell to the FMLN, Honduras would be the regional leftists' next target. In Alverez's view, Salvadoran refugees themselves were subversives. So the number of perceived military threats increased. Thus, in addition to US aid, and, in an attempt also to limit somewhat US influence over his military plans, Alverez sought more military hardware and training from Israel, West Germany and others. He increased the Honduran army to 20,000 during 1982 alone and established more military commands. In 1981 and 1982 Alverez tried to provoke war with Nicaragua by encouraging expanded contra activity; in 1983 he told the Honduran legislature that there could be no neutrality against communism (NYT, 9-9-82, 6-29-83). Shortly after the US-sponsored revitalization of CONDECA, Alverez declared: "War with Nicaragua is an option to consider for resolving the crisis" (IHCA, January, 1984). As his political power quickly overshadowed that of the civilian president, Roberto Suazo Cordova, Alverez became the Honduran negotiator in relations with the United States. From that position he asked for ever-larger aid commitments. In mid-1983, for instance, Alverez lobbied Washington for $400 million in military aid over the next three years. And, it was Alverez, not the Honduran president and legislature, that in 1983 initially approved major US military construction projects, new advisors and plans for US training of Salvadoran troops at Puerto Castilla, Honduras.

Consistent with the worldview of Alverez and the Honduran right, the Hondurans created a large paramilitary, security apparatus to counter what was said to be an expanding threat of internal insurgency encouraged by regional leftists. In July, 1982 Alverez publically lauded Argentinian anti-insurgency methods, declared war on the FMLN and on the undeveloped and fractionated Honduran left and defined the new anti-insurgency forces' purpose as fighting "...not a war with a physical frontier, but a war in which the frontier is our liberty, our democracy, our Christian values and our social harmony" (LAWR, 7-23-82). Pointing to sabotage acts against two Tegucigalpa power plants and Honduran airline offices in San Jose and Guatemala City, the military charged Nicaragua with sponsoring terrorism and training Honduran subversives. That the FSLN in 1981 had publically rejected requests for aid and training from Honduran leftists and that Nicaragua now denied such connections made little difference to the army's plans. In the next months and years, new anti-terrorism laws were generously applied against suspected Honduran and foreign leftists as well as against peasant and union leaders, land squatters or other political activists. In 1983 and 1984 military and social counterinsurgency programs were carried out in conjunction with or under the guise of joint military maneuvers. The anti-insurgency military sweep in Olancho province during the Big Pine II maneuvers in 1983, for example, involved four military units and US helicopters ferrying counterinsurgency units. Twenty-six suspected guerrillas and a Canadian priest were killed in the operation (LAWR, 9-30-83).

By 1983, human rights abuses were being reported regularly in a country that had had comparatively few such occurrences in earlier years. In 1983 rights groups cited 145 disappearances and the death or disappearance of another ten opposition leaders in the previous twenty months (author interviews). Complicating the Honduran civil rights situation, the contras were also reported to be targetting Salvadoran or Honduran leftists in Honduras, acting both independently and under contract with government officials. In Honduras, church and rights organization leaders were indicting General Alverez and US policy for the worsening state of affairs.

Civilian-Military Tensions. Even as the military came to control policy toward Nicaragua, the Foreign Ministry and other government officials feared a military confrontation. In something of a power struggle with the military top command, they tried to build on the official position of neutrality toward the revolution and normalized relations with the FSLN. The result in 1981 and afterward was a series of public clashes between policy statements from Alverez or the military command and the Foreign Ministry under Minister Paz Barnica. Though it was usually Paz Barnica or other civilian government officials who met with Nicaraguan counterparts when border tensions led to bilateral meetings, it became increasingly evident that US objectives and the Honduran military's stance shaped policy in practice. On a number of occasions from 1980 to 1983 the Honduran Foreign Ministry officially pledged to

Nicaragua that Somocista camps would be moved away from the border, that Honduras would enforce strict measures to control the contras and that Honduran territory would not be used as a staging area for an invasion of Nicaragua.[4] Yet, at the time of each announcement, the military responded with anti-Nicaragua statements or its own announcements of new maneuvers. In 1981, the military responded to government pledges simply by moving the contras to less visible camps--closer to the border. In late 1982 Alverez responded to Paz Barnica's reiteration of the pledges by repeating his charge that the nine FSLN commandantes were enemies of the Honduran people. Also, at an OAS meeting in 1982, Paz Barnica offered a peace plan with Nicaragua, which, according to a government official, "...aimed less at our neighbors than at our own hardliners" (LAWR, 4-2-82). Further, Paz Barnica asked the UN High Commission on Refugees to relocate the contras out of Honduras.[5]

In May and November of 1982, President Suazo Cordova--who tended to align politically with Alverez--rejected a bilateral peace plan and refused a meeting with Nicaragua's Ortega. Honduras' involvement with the contras and with US military plans was growing. In March, 1983, when the Foreign Ministry announced it would look for a new peace tact in conjunction with Contadora initiatives, the United States also announced the installation of a new radar tracking station near Tegucigalpa[6] and by the end of the month the army had called a "red alert" in response to continuing border clashes. By June the military had used artillery fire both to cover retreating contras and to shell Nicaraguan positions. Nicaragua charged the Honduran army with aiding the contras and sent its first regular army units to its border zones. Again, the Honduran (civilian) government had proven ineffectual.

As Honduras continued to be a loyal US proxy in the diplomatic and military realms, concern grew among domestic critics about Honduras' international image, the loss of its sovereignty, the growth of military power (and budgetary predominance) and continued economic underdevelopment. In the view of many civilian politicians, the US presence in Honduras strengthened traditional authoritarian sectors and hampered civilian democratic development. This sector believed in a negotiated settlement with Nicaragua.

Limitations on US Policy. According to the civilian critics, US encouragement of Honduras' military and anti-communist elements led to growing political polarization after 1980, and, to the creation of a domestic atmosphere in which those with dissident views were labelled "communist" or "subversive." Rather than bolstering democratic pluralism, anti-Nicaragua posturing discouraged political leaders from openly confronting the government. Instead, the civilian opposition argued, Honduras was an "occupied country" housing US, contra, Salvadoran and Honduran troops; its foreign policy was made by the Honduran military command in consult with Washington. Honduras was becoming inextricably linked the US process of regionalizing local wars. Constitutional requirements regarding presidential or legislative consultation were repeatedly violated.

Among the major issues raised by critics was Honduras' continuing economic decline in a period of large military budgets and US military aid. By 1985: unemployment and underemployment stood at 29 percent and 50 percent respectively; 50 percent of Hondurans were illiterate; 30 percent of school-aged children were not in school; 73 percent of children under age five were malnourished; skewed land owning patterns left many landless or without fertile land; one-third of the population was without even minimal healthcare; and 56 percent of the four million Hondurans lived below the governments' conservatively estimated poverty line. Meanwhile, military necessities and IMF austerity requirements had led to severe budget cuts in health, education, public works, housing and agrarian reform (ICAS, December, 1984; November, 1985). Complicating the skewed budget, a large proportion of US economic aid after 1980 had gone to military-related projects; of $102.7 million total economic aid in 1983, $84.4 million was spent on military projects. Export earnings--which were steadily declining--were eaten up by debt servicing (on a $2.3 billion national debt) and petroleum import requirements. On top of these difficulties, farmers in southern Honduras staged protests at the US Embassy in 1985 over economic losses caused by contra activity and retaliatory shelling from Nicaragua. According to this group, the contras ruled border areas as "war-lords" and "cold-blooded killers" (NYT, 11-16-85). Underlining the economic hardship facing the majority of Hondurans, a Honduran Bishops pastoral letter in 1984 held US policy and Honduran military spending responsible for the conditions of the poor. In 1985, Archbishop Hector Enrique Santos warned that the stage was set for civil war; as the GNP had fallen 12 percent, a majority of the population had insufficient income for meeting basic daily requirements (CAU, February, 1985).

These issues, and, General Alverez's preoccupation with internal security and confronting Nicaragua had led, by late 1983, to concern among other top armed forces commanders. Military disenchantment, however, also had to do with Alverez's closeness to US officials, his circumventing of the consultative Military Defense Council and the feeling that Honduras was not adequately rewarded for the role it was playing in US policy. Many in the military believed that the United States would once again ignore Honduras when the Nicaragua issue was "solved." These officers feared that Honduras would be left with a large, well-armed and uncontrollable contra force inside its borders, and, that by allowing the US training of Salvadoran officers in Honduras, Honduras was training its own enemies.

In late March, 1984 military dissatisfaction -- centered especially among younger, more nationalistic officers -- culminated in the surprise ouster of[7] Alverez. His replacement was Air Force head Walter Lopez Reyes.[7] Though the military command remained suspicious of the FSLN, Lopez softened the stance toward Nicaragua, expressed concern about socioeconomic development and[8] made moves to decrease the contras' operating room inside Honduras.[8] In mid-1984 some contra camps were closed, the contra command near Tegucigalpa was shut down and the fighters themselves were pushed out of Honduras. Maneuvering for greater bargaining room with the United States, Lopez expressed the fear that Honduras was becoming another Lebanon (LAWR, 7-13-84) and demanded that many fewer Salvadoran and more Honduran officers be trained in Honduras. Although the contras were allowed to return when the US Embassy interceded, the military command had made points; the United States would have to negotiate now with a somewhat less servile Honduras.

Arguing that Honduras could deal with Nicaragua's military, Lopez lobbied Washington for greatly increased economic aid. But Lopez and President Cordova also pressed the United States for a military commitment that, in their view, would reduce the size of the risk Honduras was taking by facilitating US objectives in the region. In return for a bilateral defense treaty, Honduras was willing to allow a permanent US base in its territory to replace US bases in Panama. In addition, Honduras sought: 1)assurance that the contras would be relocated if Congress ended funding; 2)US mediation in the continuing Honduras-Salvador border dispute; and 3)a clarification of the diplomatic status of US advisors in Honduras.

In early to mid-1985 high level Honduran officials met with Pentagon and State Department officials to work out conditions under which Honduras would continue to promote US policy. It was soon obvious, however, that although the United States sought to reduce tensions with the Honduran leadership and keep its options open regarding new bases, it was not prepared to make extraordinary military or economic commitments to Honduras or go beyond commitments it had with other regional allies. Instead the United States: reaffirmed its mutual defense responsibilities under the Rio Treaty and the OAS Charter; issued a joint Reagan-Cordova statement which stated that "Honduras is a friendly nation facing a serious threat of communist aggression and subversion"; and updated the 1954 Honduran-US Assistance Agreement to cover contingencies brought about by much-increased military cooperation (NYT, 5-2-85; BI, 5-23-85). Thus, the new military command was able to win slightly improved terms for its cooperation with Washington. Honduras' role in US policy, however, remained pivotal. As a US Embassy spokesperson in Tegucigalpa put it in 1985, Honduran stability was the bottom line for the United States (author interview).

While the military command was somewhat reassured of the US commitment to them by the mid-1985 US Congressional allocation of $27 million for the contras, both the late 1984 US decision thereafter to train Salvadorans in Salvador and the 1985 constitutional crisis that arose over the planned electoral process in Honduras eroded potential bargaining chips for the military command. What also remained clear after the 1985 talks was the window-dressing nature of Honduras' civilian government. Not only was it the military that again dealt with the United States and set the limits for policy vis-a-vis Nicaragua, it was also by the military's influence that the electoral process--so necessary to maintain both the image of democratic development in Honduras and the US rationale for its aid activity there--proceeded in 1985. As the formal process went on, however, neither of the two leading candidates offered strategies for dealing with the two key issues facing Honduras: economic deterioration and Honduras' status as the centerpiece in US anti-FSLN policy.

That the latter issue would continue to be a point of contention between the two governments after 1985 was suggested by the fact that late in the year and into 1986, the Honduran military confiscated US government aid shipments to the contras. By March,

1986 only half of the $27 million voted by Congress for the contras
had actually reached them. (Honduras aimed to use the contras as
another bargaining chip.) In so doing, the military command
registered its insistence that it be accorded greater control over
US-sponsored activities on its territory. The Hondurans were yet
interested in asserting sovereignty and maintaining the public
posture that they were not complying in anti-Sandinista military
activities (e.g., NYT, 11-23-85). Nevertheless, the military and
civilian leaders knew only too well the price Honduras was paying
for continued US economic and military aid. Differences among
Honduran politicians over the appropriate course for the future
continued to manifest themselves in fractionated politics where the
military was the final arbiter.

Yet that body too was experiencing a political crisis by 1986.
Reflecting both internal power conflicts between younger and senior
officers and CIA moves to isolate the younger, nationalist officers,
in January, 1986 Lopez was dismissed from his post (NYT, 1-31-86).
The dismissal followed the purge of several younger officers from
key army posts in late 1985, a purge carried out by senior officers
aided by CIA intelligence. Washington's interests in internal army
disputes had to do with its (faulty) assessment that the younger
officers and Lopez represented the last obstacles to getting US aid
to the contras (e.g. ICAS, February, 1986). (At mid-year the US
Government Accounting Office reported that Lopez had received a
$450,000 payment -- money taken out of the $27 million US grant --
from contra officials in January, presumably to buy his
cooperation.) The younger officers had also been involved in
disputes with the US Embassy.

Older officers, by contrast, were both more pliable and more
supportive of a military drive against the FSLN. Whether the Lopez
dismissal signalled continued policy dominance of the more pro-US
forces, however, was unclear. New Chief of Honduran Forces,
Humberto Regalado Hernandez, was reported to be closely identified
with the policies of (former Chief) Alverez. But Regalado also
appeared to wield less political clout than his predecessors (e.g.
IRTFCA, March, 1986; ICAS, March, 1986). It was clear that US
policy had sparked political polarization within both civilian and
armed forces sectors, and, that resulting political conflicts could
produce new obstacles for US policy.

Events of 1986 demonstrated the decision of top Honduran
officials to continue facilitating US policy. US aid to the contras
resumed under new President Jose Azcona Hoyo. Under heavy US
pressure, the Hondurans reluctantly cooperated with Washington
during and after the Easter "Nicaraguan invasion" crisis of March.
Meanwhile, nationalist and developmentalist sentiments continued to
spur debate within the limited political arena.

## Costa Rica

Similar to Honduras in its level of dependence upon the United
States, Costa Rica was also to come under severe pressure to
formulate a policy of hostility vis-a-vis its northern neighbor.
Yet, historical realities were to complicate US efforts to
"Honduranize" Costa Rica: Costa Rica had disbanded its army in 1948

and had declared itself a neutral state. Costa Ricans had sought to avoid the internecine bloodshed--so typical to the region--which resulted from oligarchs calling out the army to repress social movements. In fact, Costa Rica had earned a reputation for maintaining among the most open political systems in Latin America. Moreover, under President Rodrigo Carazo Odio (1978-1982) Costa Rica had facilitated the Sandinista struggle against Somoza by providing sanctuary to FSLN and other anti-Somoza leaders and by channeling weapons to the revolutionary fighters. Willing, unofficially, to violate neutrality to aid in the overthrow of the brutal Somoza, President Carazo, and Costa Ricans generally, warmly embraced the new FSLN government. In the first two years of the revolution at least eight high-level discussions occurred between Costa Rican and Sandinista officials on issues of trade, aid, the revitalization of the CACM and border security. (The unchartered border had led to smuggling and illegal migration.)

Carazo's preference for policy independence from the United States yielded the FSLN an early regional ally and a temporarily secure southern border--a situation unlike the one on Nicaragua's northern border. In 1981 Carazo refused US offers of military aid and rejected US UN Ambassador Jeane Kirkpatrick's suggestion that Costa Rica establish an army. Carazo went only so far as to allow the training of twenty rural guardsmen at US Fort Gulick in Panama; this represented the first US military aid to Costa Rica in fourteen years. But by 1981 pressure on Costa Rica to assume Washington's "communist expansion" thesis was mounting, as was Costa Rica's economic crisis and its need for new infusions of US aid. Carazo and earlier presidents had over-borrowed to hold off the inevitable socioeconomic difficulties related to low export earnings. Costa Rica's debt hovered at $4 billion and was to serve as its Achilles heel in the next years.

While for the most part Carazo did not accede to US pressure to militarize in return for new economic aid, he did move to distance himself from the FSLN by late 1981 when Costa Rica's business sector began raising concerns about the future of Nicaragua's business bourgeoisie. The continuing presence of Cuban technicians in Nicaragua worried President Carazo, who warned that both superpowers were trying to manipulate the revolution. In early 1982 as his term was ending, Carazo hosted the US-inspired (but ill-fated) Central American Democratic Community. Yet he also maintained contact with the Frente and refused fully to endorse US policy.

Monge's Balancing Act: A Precarious Neutrality. Carazo's successor in May, 1982 -- Luis Alberto Monge -- faced rising social tension from the worsening economic crisis. Heightening inflation, growing unemployment, labor strikes, peasant land invasions and lowered credit-worthiness in 1982 and 1983 meant that Monge could not ignore US aid offers, which were increasingly couched in regional security language. Nor did Monge relish the idea of implementing the austerity conditions that went with acquiring IMF loans. Though Monge too preferred to maintain neutrality status and tried to avoid the militarization the United States sought, he nevertheless went some distance in yielding to pressures from Washington and the increasingly vocal Costa Rican right to enlarge Costa Rica's security apparatus in return for US aid commitments.

Publically declaring Costa Rica's external neutrality, Monge worked delicately to balance competing demands on his administration without directly confronting US policy. The Costa Ricans' historical preference for demilitarization had to be balanced with the business sectors' increasingly hostile attitude toward the FSLN, as well as its preference for relinquishing neutrailty for an armed anti-Nicaragua stance. This sectors' control over the media and its traditional ties to the US right ensured a process of political polarization in Costa Rica similiar to that going on in other parts of the region in reaction to the Nicaraguan revolution. Not-so-subtle economic, diplomatic and military pressures by the United States had to be balanced with Costa Rica's neutral, peace-loving image and its concern about sovereignty and alignment. The result was inconsistant behavior and a Costa Rica which appeared to wax hot and cold over Nicaragua. In general, while Monge sought to maintain military neutrality and to limit contra operations from his country, in the political and diplomatic spheres Monge gave the appearance of being closer to US positions on Nicaragua and the regional leftist threat. As a party to Contadora, Costa Rica joined Honduras and El Salvador in trying to shape a document to the United States' liking, or, barring that, to stall the process. Concurrently, Monge maintained relations and trade with Nicaragua and established a border commission with the Sandinistas in 1984 when contra attacks on Nicaragua escalated. In 1983 and 1984 Monge made attempts to diversify Costa Rica's financial dependence and to expand its space for diplomatic maneuvering by turning to Western Europe, Mexico and South American states for aid and support. Nevertheless, by 1984 the scale was clearly tipping in favor of rightist, pro-US and militarist forces. In fact, the Reagan Administration had targetted Costa Rica's historic neutrality in its efforts to turn that country into the southern perimeter of the US military encirclement of Nicaragua. A leaked May, 1984 State Department policy memorandum, for example, advocated US military assistance as a means to prevent Costa Rican "backsliding" into non-belligerence (COHA, 5-29-84). Under US and domestic pressure, the position of the "neutralists" in Costa Rica was a tenuous one after 1981.

Increased US interest in Costa Rica was palpable by 1982: economic aid to Costa Rica increased several times from 1981 to 1982, again rose significantly in 1983 and stayed at relatively high levels through 1986 (see Table 6.2). Even larger increases occurred in economic support funds for Costa Rica--monies stipulated for governments of special security interest to the United States. Such funds rose from zero in 1980 and 1981 to $90 million in 1982, $157 million in 1983 and $160 million in 1985. Coupled with US economic aid and Costa Rica's reliance on loans from private US banks, these figures reflected Costa Rica's growing financial dependence on the United States in the 1980s. By 1983, Costa Rica was second only to El Salvador in the hemisphere as a recipient of US economic aid. With the world's second highest per capita debt in the world (after Israel), with 70 percent of its population by 1984 at or below the poverty line, and with 20 percent of the work force unemployed, Costa Rica was necessarily mindful of Washington's policy preferences. In the economic realm, the United States used its aid leverage from 1982 onward to demand denationalization of Costa Rican enterprises and a larger role for private banks in the local economy. Economic pressures on Costa Rica paralleled those on Honduras in the same period; there, Ambassador Negroponte submitted to the government a "Reagonomics" plan for economic reorientation. Austerity measures enforced by the IMF and the United States as a loan condition, moreover, exacerbated already severe social tensions and discomfort. The manifestations of these tensions--strikes, work-stoppages, rallies, etc.--in turn spurred demands from the right for increased anti-insurgency and security forces.

Simultaneously, US diplomatic efforts to enjoin regional allies in anti-Nicaragua initiatives persisted. Because of its democratic tradition, Costa Rica figured prominently in US planning. During an increasingly tense period in regional politics, President Reagan sent ultra-conservative Curtin Winsor as Ambassador to Costa Rica to maintain US pressures on Monge to arm his country. Known for his vocal hardline tact, Winsor waged a public campaign against Nicaragua, in 1983 chiding Costa Rican officials for being "overzealous" in enforcing neutrality (they had arrested several contra leaders) and in 1984 comparing Nicaragua to "...an infected piece of meat that attracts insects" (NYT, 10-5-84). Although he also drew criticism for his undiplomatic statements, Winsor nonetheless was successful in manipulating local opinion regarding the Sandinistas and their revolution. The campaign yielded results. Pressed to maintain aid flows, President Monge met on numerous occasions with President Reagan or his representatives; he cited communist expansionism as a threat to Costa Rica; and he slowly but steadily allowed security reinforcements and infrastructure development.

The Growth of Security Forces. The quantitative and qualitative growth of Costa Rica's security apparatus began in 1982. Not only were many more officers trained in Panama in the next years--600 of them between 1981 and 1985--but in 1982 Monge's party formed an "anti-terrorist" paramilitary force (OPEN) which rapidly expanded to 10,000 members. The force was later employed against strikers, land squatters, demonstrators and the like, in coordination with the national Civil Guard. The Guard itself received improved weaponry, intelligence and related training from Israeli and US advisors, in effect, tp prepare it to respond more like an army. In 1985, Costa Rican officials acknowledged that US military engineers were advising Costa Rica on the conditioning of a future military base at Punta Castilla near the Nicaraguan border. A "reaction battalion" was also being trained by US forces in Honduras and Costa Rica to operate on the border (BI, 4-25-85). And, according to US military personnel in Honduras in 1985, Costa Rica had agreed for the first time to participate in 1986 joint military maneuvers in Honduras, along with other US regional allies. Although Monge turned down a repeated US offer to send 1000 US army engineers to speed up the construction of a network of roads and bridges along the Nicaraguan border, a project underway by the US AID, his government did contract with the Israelis to build an "electronic defense line" in the northern regions. Adding to the preparation of Costa Rica's unmapped and sparsely populated northern frontier for possible military use was a $19 million US AID project begun in 1982 for, ostensibly, agricultural settlements. Coordinated with the Israeli project, the AID land development project included building new roads, bridges and airports in this strategic (in the US view) jungle area and settling farmers in the region. Not coincidentally, the project forced Costa Rica to plan for defending the new settlements and infrastructure--facilities which also amounted to a platform for deploying forces against Nicaragua.[10]

US military aid also escalated after 1981. First, working around the 1974 Congressional limitations on US security aid to Latin American police forces, the Reagan Administration reinstituted such aid in the form of training for Costa Rican security forces in 1981 and a $2 million grant for "non-lethal" military assistance to its police forces in 1982. While such aid in 1981-1983 represented the first US military aid to Costa Rica in well over a decade, in each of 1984 and 1985 that aid quadrupled to $9.2 million--huge figures for a small country of 2.4 million people without an army or a history of unrest.[11] Indicative of the Unites States' role in deciding the amount of military aid "requests" from Costa Rica, and, of US pressures to create a regional military response to leftist challenges to ally governments there, in 1984 the US Embassy in San Jose unilaterally reactivated and increased an earlier Costa Rican request to Washington for military assistance. This move followed a Nicaraguan-Costa Rican border skirmish sparked by contra attacks from Costa Rica. Hours after the limited skirmish, the United States responded with offers of arms deliveries and 1,500 combat troops (CAU, August, 1984).

In 1984 and 1985 Costa Rica's weapons arsenal grew qualitatively as well as quantitatively. While the security forces had previously been armed with World War II vintage rifles and about one thousand machine guns, in 1984-85 the Pentagon delivered four thousand M-16s and new machine guns. Helicopters, observation aircraft, jeeps and patrol boats were also delivered as US Green Berets began a five-month training program for security forces at a field school ten miles from the Nicaraguan border. The program carried added significance beyond possibly jeopardizing Costa Rica's neutrality status and establishing the precedent of US military stations in Costa Rica; the new program violated the spirit of Contadora which aimed to reduce the number of foreign military advisors in the region. The United States appeared determined to involve Costa Rica in its conflict with Nicaragua. In the meantime, the United States was gaining useful intelligence on the unchartered northern Costa Rican region.

Further evidence on the nature of US objectives existed in the United States' financial and logistical complicity with ARDE and other small anti-Sandinista forces operating out of Costa Rica. As discussed earlier, US plans for the contras included sparking border incidents between Nicaragua and Costa Rica in order to justify a US reaction and increased Costa Rican militarization (e.g., WP, 5-21-84; ICAS, October, 1985). The Reagan Administration and conservative sectors in Costa Rica sought to galvanize public opinion against the FSLN, thereby erroding support for continued neutrality. To these ends, Washington-allied forces introduced large amounts of CIA and other illicit funds into Costa Rica for purposes of buying operating room for the contras (e.g., NYT, 4-23-84; 7-8-85). According to local reports from 1983 to 1986, corruption was becoming endemic as pro-US sectors sought to circumvent the goverment's official neutrality position by facilitating US regional policy. But rightist security force commanders also had their own ideological motivation for facilitating contra operations, sharing intelligence on Nicaraguan army movements and turning blind eyes to CIA supply air-drops to the contras. Such complicity on the part of the Civil Guard continued into 1986.

A Resurgent Right. Such activity by 1984 had made it difficult for President Monge, who repeatedly ordered the arrest of contra combatants or the dismantling of camps, to maintain his neutrality status. Reports of contra activity in Costa Rica, moreover, embarrassed Monge, who was a rather unwilling--if not sometimes unwitting--participant in this aspect of US policy. Monge publically complained about the anti-Nicaragua hysteria being created in the Costa Rican media and in 1983 and 1984 he sought alternative foreign support for Costa Rica's neutrality in order to counter or evade US pressures. In 1983 and 1984 Monge participated with the other Central American states--including Nicaragua--in aid talks with the West European EEC. The following year Monge toured eleven European states in search of new aid. Also demonstrating Costa Rica's independence, in October, 1983 the Monge government voted at the UN to condemn the United States' invasion of Grenada--a move which led to the resignation of the anti-Sandinista foreign Minister Volio. In November Monge declared his country's "perpetual" neutrality. On the day of that announcement, which included a rejection of the US offer to send 1000 army engineers to Costa Rica, Washington cancelled $60 million in aid to Monge's government. In February, at Venezuelan President Lusinchi's inaugeration, Monge joined eight other Latin American presidents in signing a document supporting Contadora. The United States at that time was publically distancing itself from that peace process.

But even at home it was increasingly difficult for Monge and other neutralists in his government to hold their own against outspoken pro-US, anti-FSLN politicians who were posturing to keep the neutrality declaration out of the constitution. This group had adopted the position that Costa Rica could not live with a "Marxist-Leninist" neighbor. In early 1984, for example, the local Chamber of Commerce demanded that Costa Rica break relations with Nicaragua, pull out of Contadora and arm itself. The Free Costa Rica Movement associated with the extreme right-wing, meanwhile, was becoming more vocal and active, training its own paramilitary force. Monge nevertheless agreed in May, 1984 to work under the aegis of the Contadora group to form a Mixed Commission with Nicaragua for monitoring and responding to border incidents. This became part of what Monge called a period of "dis-tension" with Nicarauga.

The degree of political polarization caused by the Nicaraguan and security assistance issues became more apparent in August and September, 1984 when rightist elements, hinting at a coup, claimed Monge had too many "leftists" in his administration. In the cabinet shake-up that followed, Monge signalled increased deference to the anti-Nicaragua position. Anti-Nicaragua politicians replaced neutralist ministers in several important ministries, including the Public Security Ministry. The new Public Security administrator, Benjamin Piza did not support Contadora, was against negotiations with Nicaragua and did not support Monge's neutralist stance. Piza reportedly made arrangements with the United States in 1985 for Green Beret trainers despite Monge's own misgivings (CAHI, 7-11-85). Monge's position on Contadora also hardened at that time, though he did not change his public stance of neutrality. Shortly thereafter, the political parties began candidate-selection processes for the early 1986 presidential elections. Monge, who may have harbored thoughts of a re-election bid in 1990 (a president by law cannot serve consecutive terms), took note of the fact that the front-running candidates were more pro-US than neutralist on the key foreign policy issues.

Costa Rican-Nicaraguan Relations Sour. As pressures on the government mounted, it became increasingly difficult for Monge to steer a center course or to lend Sandinista initiatives credibility. The Frente, for instance, had been anxious to invigorate the 1984 border commission and create a demilitarized zone on what had become its southern war front. To undermine potential bilateral cooperation, however, rightist elements in Costa Rica--now well-represented in government--looked for ways to discredit and condemn the FSLN. When, in late 1984, the FSLN arrested a draft dodger who had been seeking asylum inside the Costa Rican embassy, the Costa Rican media had an anti-Nicaragua heyday. Despite the fact that the initial Costa Rican response was mild and that the circumstances surrounding the arrest were fuzzy, the issue was blown to such major proportions by the local media that Monge was led to denounce the FSLN and to call for an OAS investigation (CAR, 1-25-85). Along with continuing tensions caused by the contra presence at the border and FSLN anti-contra operations there, this issue led to Costa Rica's boycott of an important Contadora meeting, to Monge's threat in January, 1985 to invoke the Rio Treaty and to Costa Rica's order to Nicaragua in March that it reduce its embassy staff in San Jose. Bilateral tensions were only somewhat reduced when Nicaragua, under international pressure, released the draft dodger; Costa Rica agreed to return to the Contadora process despite US support for its earlier moves to stall the process.

But relations with Nicaragua soured even further after a May, 1985 border incident at Las Crucitas. There, two Costa Rican Guardsmen were killed when they were fired on from Nicaraguan territory. The Costa Rican media, charged to hysteria, initially claimed six were dead and that Nicaraguan forces were invading Costa Rica. The Monge government itself blamed Nicaraguan forces for the attack and called on the OAS--not Contadora, the group which had helped establish the border commission--to investigate. Nicarguan leaders denied that the attack was perpetrated by their forces; the FSLN interpreted the event as another contra-US effort to spark a border incident.[12] They blamed ARDE forces under Tito Chamarro for the shootings. Yet the competing claims were difficult to prove. FSLN forces at that time were engaged in "Operation Sovereignty," a military effort to push all remaining contra forces out of southern Nicaragua in early 1985. The border area, in other words, was populated by Nicaraguan, contra and Costa Rican armed groups.

Costa Rica's position toward Nicaragua, Contadora and the OAS hardened significantly when the OAS report on the incident--written under OAS consensus by four Contadora state ambassadors to the OAS--failed to indict Nicaragua, but held that the origin of the shots could not be traced. Instead, the OAS called for Nicaraguan-Costa Rican talks. Undoubtedly embarrassed by international recognition of a contra presence in Costa Rica, and, demanding an apology from Nicaragua as a precondition for any talks, Monge charged the bodies of bias in favor of Nicaragua. In September he announced a possible "freeze" on relations with both Contadora and the OAS. During the remainder of 1985, Monge downplayed initiatives from Nicaragua, Panama, France and Contadora to get new talks underway. On the grounds that Costa Rica was already neutral, Monge rejected new Nicaraguan offers to create an internationally supervised de-militarized zone. Simultaneously, the Monge government talked to Venezuela and Panama about security issues; the Green Berets continued their training of a 750-man border force in the northern frontier; and Monge began interpreting border incidents as part of a larger FSLN offensive against Costa Rica. But, typical of the Monge Administration's ambiguousness regarding US intentions and Costa Rica's role in them, tensions within the government over its relations with the contras also remained.

The Reagan Administration, nevertheless, was clearly pleased by Monge's apparent change of heart. As the United States and the Honduran-based FDN contras worked in late 1985 and early 1986 to replace ARDE forces in Costa Rica with new contras loyal to the United Nicaraguan Opposition (UNO), Costa Rica's neutrality was eroded even further. Instead, Costa Rica had actually become involved in the regional conflict. However, this reality coexisted with another, namely, strong public antipathy against involving Costa Rica in a regional war. Although anti-Sandinista sentiment was strong, the February, 1986 presidential elections appeared to affirm those supporting Costa Ricas' military neutrality. Moreover, president-elect Oscar Arias Sanchez publically questioned US support for the contras, suggesting that aid might better be awarded to regional governments for economic development. Thus, though he was not to assume office until May, 1986, Arias signalled an interest in avoiding further US pressure on Costa Rica to help facilitate an anti-Sandinista military policy devised in Washington.

Meanwhile, contra-related border tensions with Nicaragua, and, a carefully worded statement from President Ortega in February regretting the Las Crucitas incident created an opening for a Costa Rican-Nicaraguan border pact. Assessing public sentiment and the real possibility of heightened border tensions or an actual armed confrontation, Costa Rican officials accepted Ortegas' message as meeting their earlier conditions for any rapproachment. New ambassadors were exchanged. More importantly, Costa Rican officials agreed to work with FSLN counterparts, under the auspices of Contadora, to establish "a permanent force of inspection and vigilance" on the border, charged with keeping peace. Under the terms of the pact, the two countries expressed a commitment to assure the integrity of the border and "to prevent it from being used to carry out destabilizing actions in other countries."

According to Deputy Foreign Minister Frejos, the decision to join in the border pact reflected Costa Ricas' desire to "comply with the obligations of neutrality" (NYT, 2-26-86).

Though it remained to be seen whether the joint border force would be effective in inhibiting contra activities inside Costa Rica, the pact potentially threatened the US-FDN military pincer strategy against Nicaragua. US-sponsored contra organizing continued. Similarly, just as it pressed the Monge government into compromising the neutrality doctrine, the Reagan Administration would work to influence more compliant (anti-Sandinista) policies from the Arias government. Arias himself announced plans to seek incresaed US aid (ICAS, February, 1986).

## Other Central American Actors

El Salvador. Because of their critical dependence on the United States in the civil war against FMLN guerrillas, Salvadoran government and military also supported and facilitated US policy vis-a-vis Nicaragua. For example, CIA operations and contra supply flights often originated in El Salvador and Salvadoran pilots regularly flew supply missions over Nicaragua. Salvadoran military people joined in a number of CIA activities in Nicaragua. Moreover, because the United States saw the FMLN and the FSLN as intimately related and as parts of the same problem of communist expansionism, US policy toward Nicaragua--especially from 1981 to 1984--was greatly influenced by how well or how poorly the war was going for the Salvadoran military. The Reagan Administration blamed the FSLN for Salvadoran army failures and for guerrilla successes. Central to the US argument was its claim that the FSLN supplied the FMLN with significant amounts arms and facilitated the guerrillas by offering them training, Managua offices and advice. Charging the Frente with exporting revolution to El Salvador, the Reagan Administration justified its own support of the anti-Sandinista contras in Nicaragua as a response of "collective self-defense," one which would give the Sandinistas a "taste of their own medicine." On these grounds, in 1983 and 1984 Washington promoted the notion that there was a "symmetry" between the Nicaraguan and Salvadoran cases; the Salvadoran government should only negotiate with the FMLN if the FSLN negotiated with the contras; the United States would only withhold military aid to its clients if Cuba and the USSR did the same (e.g., LAWR, 3-18-83).[13]

The FMLN in Salvador had thus become the nemesis not only of the Salvadoran army, the Honduran army and the Honduran left, but also of the FSLN. Although Washington held the FSLN responsible for FMLN activity, the bulk of the evidence suggested that the FSLN had limited influence over the Salvadoran group beyond being an example and offering political solidarity or advice. (See Chapter 9). Nevertheless, the United States' insistence on linking the FMLN and the FSLN meant that any settlement or reduction in tension between Nicaragua and the United States would have to be part of a wider regional settlement; that was only possible if the United States gave up the idea of the total defeat of regional leftists.

While the FSLN would not condemn the FMLN or its cause, it maintained diplomatic relations with the Salvadoran government and in 1985 quietly offered the Duarte government a bilateral peace treaty when Contadora appeared indefinitely stalled. Yet, for the Sandinistas, the FMLN represented a regional ally at a time of increasing regional isolation. For that reason and given the military stalemate that had developed on the ground by 1984, the FSLN hoped for a political settlement in Salvador that would allow FMLN representation in a new government. In the long view, however, the FSLN saw leftist, revolutionary or popular movements in the region as the inevitable response to historical oppression. The FSLN's political links to the FMLN were rooted in that belief. At the same time, the FSLN itself had found that political negotiation was more expedient than inflexible confrontation in the face of powerful status quo forces. The Sandinistas attempted to influence the FMLN in that direction, for example, in 1983 when US Roving Ambassador Stone put out feelers regarding meetings with the guerrillas. The FSLN, aware that negotiations in El Salvador could mean a lowering of US pressure on Nicaragua, apparently urged the FMLN to lower tensions in order to give the negotiation idea some time and space (LAWR, 7-29-83). The fact that in 1983 and 1984 Reagan ideologues were working in the domestic political arena to close off the option of negotiations with regional leftists, however, meant that the FSLN was using up its political capital with the FMLN in an effort doomed to fail.

Events surrounding the negotiation issue and others demonstrated that, as in the Honduran case, the Salvadoran civilian government itself had little influence over how the conflict with the guerrillas or claims against Nicaragua would be settled. The United States and the Salvadoran right (the army and conservative political and business sectors) held the cards. For example, an opening in El Salvadoran-Nicaraguan relations appeared in early 1984 when Jose Napolean Duarte told visiting US Congresspeople that as the elected president he would seek negotiations with Nicaragua. Shortly thereafter, Duarte announced that he would send a delegation to the fifth anniversary celebrations in Nicaragua in July. These attitudes worried a US administration which had been arguing that Nicaragua sought to overthrow the Salvadoran government. Pressed by Salvadoran rightists and, no doubt, the US Embassy in San Salvador, Duarte reversed his decision to send a delegation to Managua. Determined at that time to work toward ending the war through negotiations, President Duarte met with FMLN leaders in October and November, 1984 amid mounting pressures from the right to reject any further dialogue.[14]

Meanwhile, however, the United States: stepped up its delivery of sophisticated fighter aircraft to the Salvadoran army; continued to provide intelligence for Salvadoran pilots on bombing runs against "guerrilla concentrations"; included the Salvadoran army in joint maneuvers with Honduras (Granadero I); and increased military aid. Together with the United States' new anti-terrorism push, Salvadoran army successes against the FMLN, rightist pressures and guerrilla terrorist attacks in 1985 (including the kidnapping of Duarte's daughter), these events both produced a harder line in the Duarte government and reflected the ineffectual nature of the civilian regime. After the release of his daughter in October, Duarte immediately flew to Washington and there in an emotional speech denounced Nicaragua as the "...Central American source for totalitarianism and violence." Linking terrorism in Salvador to "the terrorist dictatorship in Nicaragua" which gave "support, direction, approval and timely protection" to guerrilla terrorists, Duarte squarely aligned his policy statements on Nicaragua with those of President Reagan (NYT, 11-1-85). The army agreed to join the United States and Honduras in new military maneuvers in 1986, despite the continuing presence of tensions between the two Central American countries on territorial and other issues. In fact, the stepped-up US campaign against the FSLN in 1985 was reflected locally in a joint Honduran-Salvadoran statement in July which characterized Nicaragua as the "...principal factor of political and military destabilization in the area" (BI, 7-18-85).

Although Duarte warily raised the issue of negotiations with the FMLN again in mid-1986, it was also evident that, as in Honduras and Costa Rica, the political space for independent foreign and domestic policy was limited.

Guatemala. Guatemala's leaders pursued an independent and neutralist policy toward revolutionary Nicaragua and conflicts in Central America. Though Guatemala had four different presidents between mid-1979 and mid-1986--Lucas Garcia, Rios Montt, Mejia Victores and elected civilian Marco Vinicio Cerezo Arevalo--its neutralist stance on regional issues remained basically unchanged. Desirous of not becoming entrenched in regional conflicts, preferring to act independently rather than in concert with neighboring states and interested primarily in politically stable neighbors, Guatemala chose to work pragmatically with the FSLN government. The operative theme was that Guatemala could live with a leftist and even a Marxist-Leninist Nicaragua.

In the first months after the FSLN Triumph, Guatemalan President Lucas Garcia extended credits and food aid to Nicaragua, signed agreements to expand mutual cooperation and received several high level delegations from Nicaragua. Although in 1981 the two countries traded similar charges that the other was involved in training and aiding insurgents, the charges did not lead to a break in relations or an end to trade. While in 1983 and 1984 Guatemala expressed concern that Nicaragua might not be able to repay its import bill to Guatemala, in 1985 the two countries worked out an arrangement for continuing trade. Compared to its relations with other Central American neighbors, Nicaragua's relations with Guatemala after 1979 were normal and uneventful.

A major factor influencing Guatemala's independent behavior was its determination to avoid US dictates on human rights issues. After Congress cut military aid to Guatemala in 1977 based on the military government's poor rights record, Guatemalan leaders chose--for the time being--to seek aid elsewhere rather than answer to the United States. From 1982 to 1985 Presidents Montt and Mejia followed the Lucas Garcia example and employed ruthless military sweeps, widescale peasant massacres and counter-insurgency "development" programs to wipe out what they saw as renewed leftist challenges to the political status quo and military rule. The Guatemalan army, rather than joining in US-led regional efforts to isolate and condemn Nicaragua, was preoccupied at home with the objective of defeating its "communist" rebels.

Deemphasing the Guatemalan human rights situation, President Reagan sought to enlist that country in his anti-communist cause in Central America. For example, in his late 1982 tour of the region, Reagan met with President Montt, expressed confidence in Montt's integrity and commitment to restoring democracy, and tried thereby to interest Congress in exploring renewed relations with Guatemala. By early 1983, however, the US media was confirming what human rights groups had been saying at the time of the Reagan-Montt meeting: Rios Montt's government had carried out thousands of killings in an attempt to pacify the countryside of suspected communists (e.g., White, 1984). Montt himself had already reiterated Guatemala's preference for policy and military independence. In the next year and until his August, 1983 overthrow by General Mejia, Montt largely ignored Reagan Administration overtures.

Just as it had embraced Montt in 1982, the United States was optimistic that new President Mejia would be more sympathetic both to US-inspired regional initiatives and to rights concerns. In fact, Mejia's government did join other traditional US allies in the October, 1983 meetings to reinvigorate CONDECA. In the hope of continued regional cooperation from Guatemala, in 1984 US economic aid to that country nearly doubled--from $17.6 million in 1983 to $33.3 million in 1984. Yet, while Mejia proved to be less outspoken than his predecessor, he too maintained policy independence from Washington; nor did he act to end army atrocities. In 1984 Mejia declined US offers to join Honduras and Salvador in US-coordinated joint maneuvers. Even when military aid to Guatemala was restarted by a counterinsurgency-minded President Reagan in 1984 and 1985--$.3 million and $10.3 million respectively--and, when economic aid again nearly doubled (see Table 6.2) it did not spur greater cooperation with US policy. Guatemala did not join with other US allies in Central America to stall Contadora. Instead Mejia angered other regional leaders in 1985 when he again stated that Guatemala could live with the Sandinistas.

Civilian President Cerezo, inaugurated in early 1986, promised to maintain this policy stance toward Nicaragua. To Cerezo, the danger of US policy regarding Nicaragua was that it emphasized military problems and solutions. His administration preferred to respect Nicaragua's "own way" and seek political settlement through Contadora. Nor did he fear the Cuban presence in Nicaragua; Cerezo instead stressed pragmatic cooperation in an "inter-related world" (Cerezo interview; McNeil-Lehrer Report, 12-17-85). Cerezo, labelling himself a nationalist, announced that he would try to reduce Guatemala's traditional dependence on North America by building stronger relations with other Western states. He also signalled a new willingness to enter the peace dialogue on Central America when he travelled to Central American capitals in late 1985 and proposed a regional parliament within which regional settlement could be addressed. But just how much room for maneuvering the civilian president would have in Guatemala was unclear. The Guatamalan right had campaigned during the electoral period for a pro-US, anti-Nicaragua stance that in essence would have meant an end to Guatemala's regional neutrality. The Guatemalan military and rightist businessmen had supplied anti-Sandinista contras with weapons and other aid (e.g. NYT, 3-23-86). This group, moreover, was interested in acquiring new and large security aid packages from the United States. Cerezo's meeting with Daniel Ortega shortly after his election did not sit well with rightist sectors. Guatemala's history of right-wing politics and power transfer by coups d'etat suggested that Cerezo would have carefully to balance competing interests as he formulated his foreign policy. Meanwhile, though the United States continued to try to enlist Guatemala in its cause, Nicaraguan leaders hoped at least for the maintenance of that country's neutrality.

Panama. While Panama's behavior after 1979 demonstrated some ambiguity over regional issues and its search for a comfortable role in the region, Panamanian leaders appeared united in their fear that Central America might become the scene of an East-West confrontation. That possibility had to be avoided. In the Panamanian view, peace could best be preserved in a Central America with stable governments which did not provoke US security concerns. Thus, though General Torrijos aided the FSLN in their struggle against Somoza, he expressed "friendly" concern in 1980 over the Frente's use of Cuban military-security advisors. Similarly, in the next years Panama both promoted Latin American initiatives and concerns for non-intervention and sovereignty, and, maintained fruitful economic and military relations with the United States. US interest in and aid to Panama jumped significantly after 1982. Military aid, especially, registered this reality, increasing from $.4 million in 1981 to $5.4 million in 1982 and 1983, and increasing to $15.5 million and $20 million in the following years. In addition, despite the fact that Panama was one of the co-founders of the Contadora peace process--a process which aimed at demilitarizing the area--Panama's military forces joined the United States' in major joint maneuvers in 1984 and 1985. These maneuvers went beyond the joint canal-defending training agreed to under the Carter-Torrijos pact in 1977. This position of balanced engagement, in brief, differentiated Pananamian from Guatemalan policies.

That the most powerful sectors in the Panamanian military would opt to maintain the flexible middle course in the face of US pressure became clear in 1983 and 1985. In 1983, National Guard leader General Ruben Dario Paredes' pro-US stance was becoming increasingly overt and compromising to Panama's middle course. In mid-year Paredes warned Cuba and Nicaragua that Panama might break relations with them. Arguing that Panama's security was on the Costa Rican-Nicaraguan border, General Paredes reportedly discussed sending arms to contra leader Eden Pastora and proposed an armed peace force to back up Contadora (LAWR, 7-15-83). His comments were not well-received at home or in the region. When an opportunity arose, therefore, Parades was edged out by new strongman General Manuel Antonio Noriega. Taking the hint, president de la Espriella reshuffled his cabinet, replacing the ministers known to sympathize with Paredes' pro-US line.

General Noriega, the real power behind civilian presidents, sought alternative military aid from Israel, France and Britain as part of his general policy of greater independence from the United States. Similarly, in Contadora Panama maintained some distance from the United States' Central American allies, preferring to consult with all sides and opinions. In 1985 Noriega tried to assert regional leadership when the Las Crucitas incident threatened permanently to stall Contadora. Consulting with both Costa Rican and Nicaraguan leaders, Noriega offered mediate border talks. In an effort to move Costa Rica from its no-negotiation position, Noriega assured that country of Panama's continued support for its security. Nicaragua accepted and applauded Noriega's offer. At home, meanwhile, Noriega pushed the resignation of civilian president Ardito Barletta whom Noriega believed, among other things, was not strong enough to stand up against US economic pressures.[15]

Although the Panamanian power elite remained somewhat divided on the questions of relations with the United States and with leftist governments, the balanced engagement approach appeared to facilitate Panama's regional interests as they were being defined in the 1980s. Panama maintained normal relations with Nicaragua.


OTHER LATIN AMERICAN STATES

Mexico

Under Presidents Portillo and de la Madrid, Mexico was revolutionary Nicaragua's most faithful supporter and ally in the hemisphere. Mexican leaders acted out of an inter-related set of motivations. Mexico, along with other Latin American states, wanted to avoid a US-USSR confrontation in Central America, already the least developed area of Latin America. Instead Mexico sought the further strengthening of Latin American solidarity and increased independence vis-a-vis the United States. According to President de la Madrid in 1982, the promotion of regional integration in Latin America and the Caribbean would be a major foreign policy thrust of his administration (LAWR, 10-22-82). Both Portillo and de la Madrid held that the isolation of Cuba from Latin America and the United States' rejection of rapproachment with that country was a stumbling block to peace in the region. In the larger context, Mexico was vying with Venezuela for regional leadership. Both states worked after 1980--and often, together--to create Latin American initiatives for political settlements of regional conflicts. In the Mexican view, US military pressure only served to strengthen Leninist elements in the Sandinista leadership and to provide justification for restrictions on civil liberties there.

Mexican leaders, while they noted ideological differences between the two countries, saw the political defense of Nicaragua as key to their own national security. As de la Madrid put it in 1983, "Our existence as a nation had been threatened from the first moment of our independence by struggles for conquest, by acts of aggression and by open and covert intervention" (LAWR, 12-2-83). Mexico's southern orientation on international relations and issues of economic expansion led its leaders to promote the development of an independent and progressive Nicaragua. Mexico encouraged increased non-aligned behavior among Latin American states and hoped that Sandinista Nicaragua would present a model to other underdeveloped states of development without alignment. The destruction of Nicaragua's revolution by a US intervention, on the other hand,

could spark a leftist backlash and increasingly polarized politics
not only in Mexico, but throughout Latin America. In such a
scenario, Mexico feared, continued pluralistic political development
and incipient Latin American non-alignment would become casualities.

Limitations on Mexico's Independent Action. Although Mexico
maintained an activist role in the region and on issues pertaining
to Nicaragua, its relative power or bases for action were noticeably
narrowed by 1983 by economic and social factors. Whereas President
Portillo had promised to defend Nicaragua's cause "as our own", de
la Madrid faced the task of adjusting Mexican foreign policy to its
economic difficulties. Most significantly, Mexico's economic
crises--related to the world oil glut and its huge foreign
debt--left Mexico especially vulnerable to US pressures. US
officials related to their Mexican counterparts the US preference
that Mexico take a lower-key approach in criticizing US policy, and,
that Mexico reconsider its attitude toward the FSLN and the
Salvadoran FMLN. Given its weakened economic position and its
significant economic ties to US capital, Mexico was also concerned
about possible US retaliatory moves in other areas under discussion
by the two governments: immigration, investment practices, trade
and tariffs. Nor did Mexican officials want to jeopardize US
backing of IMF credits to Mexico, an issue which arose in 1983 when
$3.92 billion in credits was pending.

But Mexican policy-makers also worried about the potential for
social tensions in their own country as the peso was devalued and
austerity measures reduced the overall standard of living. Economic
hardship reduced Mexico's resources for aiding a beseiged Nicaragua.
The concern about social tension cut another way as well: Mexico
sought a settlement of Nicaraguan and Salvadoran conflicts lest
violent outbreaks spurred by large rich-poor gaps spilled over into
Mexico itself.

Mexico's Nicaragua Policy. Mexico's solidarity with Nicaragua
was initially demonstrated by its aid commitments. By early 1980
President Portillo had offered aid in the areas of communications,
medicine, literacy training, agriculture, transportation and fishing
industries. In the next years, Mexico extended millions of dollars
worth of credit for Mexican imports; offered loans for mining and
other industries; gave advice in the areas of economic planning,
food distribution and finance; sent helicopters and doctors for
literacy and vaccination campaigns; and greatly expanded trade with
Nicaragua. By early 1981, Mexico had provided 16 percent of all
support loans to Nicaragua up to that time, a figure which
represented 42.5 percent of total loans from all of Latin America
(LAWR, 4-3-81). More important to the FSLN's sense of security, in
April, 1981 Mexico with Venezuela pledged economic and political
support for Nicaragua in the face of Reagan Administration cut-offs.
By September, 1983, Mexico had replaced the United States as
Nicaragua's main trade partner and was Nicaragua's largest supplier
of manufactured goods (LAWR, 9-9-83). Though the flow of Mexican
aid was somewhat reduced after 1983 primarily for economic reasons,
Mexico had been a primary source of economic support for Nicaragua
during the period in which US economic ties to Nicaragua were cut.

The most crucial aspect of Mexico's economic support for
Nicaragua was its willingness to supply oil on concessionary terms

after 1979. Under the San Jose oil agreement, Mexico and Venezuela extended these terms--discounted rates, with a portion of repayments covered by long-term loans--to ten Central American and Caribbean states. Mexico and Venezuela each provided half of Nicaragua's oil needs until 1983. At that time Mexico assumed the total 1500 bpd requirement when Venezuela stopped sales to Nicaragua due to the latter's inability to maintain the contracted pace of repayment. Yet Mexico was under mounting pressure by the IMF and oil shippers like the US Esso Company to cease its shipments to Nicaragua. At the end of 1983 Mexico did reduce its concessionary sales, though in mid-year Mexico had renegotiated Nicaragua's $300 million oil and credits debt.[16] During 1984 oil supplies to Nicaragua were largely provided by the USSR. However, after the US embargo was imposed on Nicaragua in May, 1985, Mexico resumed oil shipments and filled 45 percent of the trade gap created by US sanctions. By mid-1985, Nicaragua's debt to Mexico hovered at $500 million. Again, Mexico absorbed added economic burdens in order to increase Nicaragua's capacity to survive in the face of US hostility.

In the political-diplomatic sphere Mexico led Latin American initiatives for a political settlement among contending forces. In 1981, Mexico with France offered a formula for US-Nicaraguan talks. When the US ignored that offer and other Latin States expressed discomfort about a non-hemispheric actor becoming involved in regional disputes, in early 1982 President Portillo offered Mexican mediation alone, and, in late 1982 made a new proposal with Venezuela for talks between Nicaragua and the United States and Nicaragua and Honduras. But because the United States successfully stalled, circumvented or outrightly rejected these overtures, in 1983 Mexico decided along with Venezuela, Panama and Colombia, to initiate exclusively regional talks toward finding a formula for peace. The Contadora process became Mexico's primary diplomatic avenue after 1983 for pursuing its regional objectives. As a leader of the peace process, Mexico played undoubtedly the most vigorous role in keeping Contadora alive; Mexico also proved to be somewhat less vulnerable to US anti-Contadora pressures and in 1985 worked successfully to counter (initially successful) US efforts vis-a-vis Colombia, Panama and Venezuela to keep Contadora from being presented formally to the UN. In that role, Mexican officials after 1983 repeatedly cited US intransigence and Reagan Administration militarism as major obstacles to a settlement.

Mexico's work in Contadora did not preclude it from continuing bilateral efforts to bring the United States and Nicaragua together. On a number of occasions after 1980, Mexican officials--acting sometimes on Nicaraguan requests--interceded for the Nicaraguans, asked the Reagan Administration to hold talks with the Frente or called on the United States and Nicaragua to temper their statements. In 1984, Mexico provided a place--Manzanillo--for US-Nicaraguan talks, though the United States, as it had in the past, rejected Mexican offers to mediate such talks. When the United States refused to renew those talks, Mexico warned the Reagan Administration of continent-wide political repercussions from a US decision to invade Nicaragua. Nor by 1986 was there any indication that Mexico was prepared to forsake either multilateral or bilateral efforts in its search to avoid what it saw as the only alternative to Contadora--region-wide war in Central America.

## South America

While Mexico was the least faltering in its support for Nicaraguan self-determination and the most willing openly to challenge US policy, there was a generalized fear among other South American states that US policy was both making war inevitable and turning back the clock in US-Latin American relations. Though less vocal about their positions than Mexico, many Latin American leaders agreed with new Peruvian President Alan Garcia who argued in 1985 that "Nicaragua stands for the sovereignty of the Latin America continent;" and had earned its right to establish "...its own destiny and the right to defend itself, to develop its own path toward democracy" without conditions being imposed from outside. "We are supporting Nicaragua because it is a symbol of an independent sovereignty and destiny for the continent" (IHCA, August, 1985). Despite varying levels of enthusiasm for the Sandinista government itself, South American states generally promoted the concepts of non-intervention and self-determination; they developed pragmatic, if not supportive, relationships with the FSLN. In part, these stances were reflective of the wide popular support and positive image the FSLN government had among Latin American peoples generally. For example, on visits to Brazil and Uruguay in 1985, President Ortega was greeted by throngs of enthusiastic crowds. Similar receptions in other South American states for Vice-President Ramirez confirmed the lingering popularity of the revolutionary leaders and their message in the mid 1980s.

Although the majority of Latin American states with supportive or benign policies toward Sandinista Nicaragua faced US pressures similar to those placed on Mexico, room for independent policies was also provided by multilateral initiatives and joint action. Common preferences to avoid both a rejuvenation of the inter-American security era and a return to the exclusive reliance upon regional forums where the United States was dominant motivated regional support for 1)negotiated settlements; 2)the recognition of the FSLN government as the legtimate government of Nicaragua; and 3)attempts to mitigate or moderate US policy in Central America. Nor did the OAS through 1985 endorse US regional policy or its war against Nicaragua. When it did comment on regional conflicts heightened by US policy, such as in the 1985 Las Crucitas dispute, it called for dialogue between parties, support for Contadora and a shift in US policy emphasis away from a military solution. Although talk about creating an exclusively regional forum (i.e. not including the US) remained only an undercurrent in the mid-1980s, Latin American states publically rejected US policy or proposals on a number of occasions (e.g. LAWR, 10-22-82). Policy differences reflected differences in priorities and in perceptions of security threats or the purposes of North and South American cooperation. Regarding Nicaragua, Latin American states independently and jointly called for US non-intervention; worked to moderate the Nicaragua policies of US Central American allies; refused to accept or employ conditions on relations with Nicaragua suggested by the United States (e.g., LAWR, 10-8-82); encouraged pluralist and non-aligned politics; and included Nicaragua in bilateral and regional aid packages. In 1985 nearly all the Latin American states, including most of the US regional allies, condemned or refused to join in the US economic embargo on Nicaragua. Instead, the eight South American states which by that time were co-sponsoring Contadora began a new diplomatic effort to restart US-Nicaraguan talks.

The policies of Brazil and Venezuela typified considerations of regional governments in establishing relations with Nicaragua. Vulnerable to US pressure due to their reliance on US markets and US help toward economic recovery, both nations nonetheless maintained regular relations with the Sandinistas and actively worked to forward Contadora--Venezuela as a founding member and Brazil as part of the Lima Support Group, established in 1985. Brazil's interest in trading with and aiding Nicaragua was affected by its growing concerns by 1984 about Nicaragua's capacity to repay loans. Yet Brazil sent aid and opened lines of credit in 1979 and 1980; greatly expanded trade to Nicaragua in 1980 and 1981; contracted with Nicaragua to explore for oil in 1982; and provided a low-interest, long-term $30 million loan for roadbuilding and agricultural development the same year. Brazil's exports to Nicaragua by 1980 rose to $17.9 million--a figure greater than all sales to Nicaragua in the previous sixteen years. In the next years to 1986, trade and aid were further expanded, especially in the energy-related and cultural fields. Though in 1984 Brazil, in the Nicaraguan view, dragged its feet in negotiating $600 million in credits for equipment for energy transmission, and, in 1985 banned arm sales to Nicaragua (as part of its policy not to sell arms to nations in conflict), bilateral relations remained normal. Brazil's Foreign Ministry--Itamaraty --characterized its policy as practical, pragmatic, and without ideological implications (LAWR, 5-14-82). During his term, President Figueiredo publically aligned Brazil with Mexico against US policy and against an East-West conceptualization of regional conflicts (e.g., LAWR, 5-6-83). Brazil pursued an independent policy despite the fact that the Reagan Administration had helped Brazil through liquidity crises in the preceding years. While rejecting US policy, Brazil in 1983 also disallowed planes carrying Libyan weapons to transport their cargo to Managua after refueling in Brazil. But as US anti-Sandinista action heated up thereafter, Brazil increased its trade with that country and, under civilian President Sarney, joined the Contadora Support Group in 1985.

While political groups within Venezuela were more openly polarized on the issue of Nicaragua than were groups in many other Latin American states, Venezuela consistently supported negotiated settlements and offered Nicaragua alternatives to socialist-bloc aid in the face of US cutoffs. Working through the Socialist International and Latin American forums, Venezuela worked to influence domestic Nicaraguan politics toward pluralism and away from what it feared were externally-reinforced tendencies toward Marxism-Leninism. From 1979 onward Venezuela couched its aid in calls for FSLN ideological tolerance and pluralistic development (e.g., LAWR, 10-19-79). At the third anniversary celebrations in Managua in 1982, President Campins called on the FSLN to maintain an independent revolution and a pluralist polity as part of a moral

244

commitment to Latin America and as a basis for continued Venezuelan aid. Under those conditions, Venezuela would not be a "fickle ally" (LAWR, 7-23-82). With some dissent from rightist political sectors, the Campins and Lusinchi governments pursued a regional power role for Venezuela on Central American issues, a role which demanded distance from US policy and the political will to lead in offering Latin American alternatives to US policy. This Venezuela did in conjunction with Mexico in 1982 and through Contadora after January, 1983. Although in 1981 and 1982 evidence surfaced that some Venezuelan officials--if not the Venezuelan government itself--were supporting Costa Rican-based rebels[17] in performing counter-revolutionary acts inside Nicaragua, Venezuela continued after 1979 to provide aid to Nicarauga and to warn the United States against moving militarily to oust the Frente (e.g., NYT, 11-18-81; CAU, April, 1982; NYT, 12-5-84). Venezuelan technicians helped create the Nicaraguan Ministry of Energy in 1979 and Venezuela, with Mexico, provided oil to Nicaragua under the San Jose Oil Accords through early 1983. Other aid, including a $14 million grant for the reconstruction of businesses destroyed in the war, was awarded Nicaragua during the critical early years. In 1984 and 1985 Washington tried to link Venezuela's position on Central American issues Washington's help in addressing its debt problem and to the United States' willingness to encourage US banks to renegotiate part of Venezuela's debt (e.g., LAWR, 6-8-84). Though for a period in mid-1984--when he was talking about economic issues with Washington--President Lusinchi appeared cooler in his support for a Contadora peace plan at the end of the year Lusinchi used a state visit to Washington publically to warn against military actions in Nicaragua, to refer to bilateral tensions over the US rejection of Contadora's proposals and to distance Venezuela from the hostile US stance.

Yet, Venezuela's interest in 1)a centrist or moderate political regime in Nicaragua (and in El Salvador); in 2)not adding to its own economic hardship; and in 3)not alienating its own business sectors or its economic ties to Washington meant that it could best pursue independent policy in conjunction with other large Latin American states. Those objectives also dictated that relations with Nicaragua be measured. President Lusinchi remained reluctant to accept soft refinancing of Nicaragua's oil debt for political and economic reasons. At the same time Venezuela's position in Contadora allowed it to retain a regional leadership position.

Nicaragua Seizes Opportunities. As US diplomatic efforts increasingly targetted Nicaraguan internationalism, the FSLN actively pursued openings and opportunities for expanding support in Latin America. At the time of the 1982 Falklands/Malvinas War Nicaragua publically championed the cause of Latin American solidarity and, in siding immediately with Argentine at the OAS, the UN and in the Non-Aligned Movement, effectively broke Argentinian military support for the Honduran-based contras. Latin American resentment toward the United States turned into new support for Nicaragua among some states. Argentina and Chile, which earlier had voted with the United States to stop an Inter-American Development Bank loan to Nicaragua, in September supported the $34 million loan for a hydroelectric power project (NYT, 19-17-82). Besides withdrawing its advisors and military-logistics support team from Honduras, Argentina also later supported Nicaragua for a UN Security Council seat and began considering expanded relations. After the inauguration of civilian Raul Alfonsin in 1984, relations became noticeably warmer. Alfonsin publically supported Nicaragua's self-determination. A $45 million credit and food aid package for Nicaragua was announced in April, 1984. In 1985 Argentina joined the Contadora Lima Support Group, thereby also rejecting US pressures made possible by Argentina's huge debt and domestic financial difficulties. Similarly, President Betancur's Colombia assumed a key role in Contadora after 1982. Colombia's policy toward Nicaragua reflected a change in presidents in 1982 and the new president's hopes for renewed Latin American solidarity: that multilateral action could improve the chances for negotiated settlements, while stemming momentum toward increasingly polarized politics throughout Latin America.[18]

Similarly, the _Frente_ sought to get political mileage out of the near universal Latin American condemnation of the United States' October, 1983 intervention of Grenada. Nicaragua's references to US lawlessness in that case were also later cited by other alienated governments in warnings to the United States regarding Nicaragua. Another opening was produced, in the Nicaraguan view, by the democratization movement in Latin America after 1982. The ascendency of civilian governments in Argentina, Brazil, Uruguay, Peru and Guatemala suggested room for greater policy independence from the United States in these states as well as for the airing of the FSLN's or of pro-Sandinista group's concerns. Indeed, the relative visibility of Nicaraguan leaders at inaugural celebrations in these countries and the favorable receptions given the FSLN delegations served to highlight the differences between North and South American perceptions of the Nicaraguan revolution.

Finally, the FSLN sought and won important support--material and psychological--from South American states after the May, 1985 US economic embargo. Responding to visits by Vice-President Ramirez and others, Latin American states condemned the embargo. Members of the Latin American Economic System (SELA), pledged to counteract US policy with new aid commitments--a pledge more significant to Nicaragua politically than economically. Meeting FSLN officials in June, SELA's Secretary General prepared a list of Nicaragua's raw material, spare parts and production-input needs for distribution among member countries and as part of SELA's resolution to collaborate with Nicaragua in a period of new economic hardship (_BI_, 7-4-85). Nicaragua's participation in the Contadora process reinforced continental cooperation with the FSLN.

Contadora

If Contadora has proposed anything, it is to cooperate to make the solutions to the Central American problem Latin American and to have them depend on the will and the political decision of the region's governments, in order to put them out of reach of the direct East-West confrontation.

246

Luis Herrera Campins
Venezuelan Ex-President
(IHCA, November, 1985)

Motivated by growing fears of a direct US military intervention in Nicaragua--or elsewhere in Central America--and by Reagan Administration East-West posturing, the presidents of Mexico, Venezuela, Colombia and Panama took an historically important step in January, 1983 when they initiated a Latin American peace process for Central America. These leaders sought to find a negotiated settlement among conflicting parties in Central America by formulating agreements and regulations on issues related to regional security: the size of armed forces and arsenals; the presence of foreign military advisors; military maneuvers involving extra-regional forces; national reconciliation; and the like. The initial action and the Contadora process represented not only a shift away from traditional acquiescence to US policy, but also a distinct Latin American assertion of will. Mexico determined to work in concert with other potential regional power rivals. Venezuela's participation indicated a move away from its earlier qualified support for US policy in Salvador. New Colombian President Betancur signalled his governments' decision purposely to create some distance between Colombian and US policy and to assume a higher profile in regional affairs (e.g., LAWR, 1-21-83). Panama responded to Reagan Administration pressures to support US regional policy by opting to co-sponsor a Latin American formula for conflict resolution in Central America. Panama's and Colombia's decision to align with the Mexican-Venezuelan peace initiative dealt a blow to the October, 1982 US-sponsored Forum For Peace and Democracy which the two states had earlier joined. Fearing a US militarily-imposed solution, key Latin American leaders and traditional US allies worked to create a framework for peace through autochthonous means. A second emphasis was on winning broad support among fellow Latin American leaders.

But the political will for the Latin American initiative also came from a view of regional conflict that differed dramatically from the prevailing US view. In contrast to the Reagan Cold War perspective and the United States' clear preference for an end to the FSLN regime, Latin American leaders saw regional conflicts as a direct by-product of socioeconomic change and dislocations, of incipient political transformations and of lingering rich-poor gaps reinforced by oppressive rule. While these leaders hoped to contain armed popular movements, to discourage foreign support of local insurgents and to encourage open, democratic institutions for the resolution of domestic struggles, they also did not subscribe to the US notion of the usefulness of insisting upon an immediate adoption of a particular brand of pluralism. Nor did they believe with US officials that democratic, open systems would naturally result after a military defeat of organized leftist groups such as the FSLN or the FMLN (e.g. Farer, 1985: 65, 68). Rather, pluralism would only evolve over time, as politics were de-polarized, as democratic ideas and practices spread and as power distributions within societies shifted. Concerned about US attempts to limit or circumvent Latin American sovereignty and to maintain a hegemonial prerogative in

Latin American affairs, the Contadora states were predisposed to accept the legitimacy of the FSLN leadership and to recognize its right to self-determination. As for the Soviet threat, the Contadora leaders believed that traditional allegiencies, nationalism, cultural proclivities, and US power made the growth of USSR influence in the hemisphere improbable.

The fear of a US military move was thus tied to these leaders' own instinctive preference for centrist politics and ideological neutrality given the real possibility that an intervention in Nicaragua would spark a new cycle of oppression - opposition - repression in Central and South America. As Nicaraguan leaders publically warned in 1984 and 1985, Latin American governments also predicted that leftist and popular groups throughout Latin America would explode in reaction to a US intervention. Fragile centrist coalitions and tenously balanced interests in many Latin American states, including the Contadora and newly democratizing countries, could well be undermined as politics became polarized between leftist and rightist groups (Farer, op.cit.: 60). Mexico and Colombia had warned the Reagan Administration of such repercussions among leftists in their countries. According to Nicaraguan Defense Minister Humberto Ortega: "A direct intervention by the United States would be very difficult to confine to our territory. It would logically have to extend itself to neighboring countries. Popular forces in Latin America will unleash their violence. The outcome will not be determined only by military power" (NYT, 6-30-85).[19]

Latin American leaders worried that such an intervention would be difficult to contain--e.g., the US project would undoubtedly include requests for logistical aid or supply routes and refueling stops from South and Central American states. Moreover, they feared that if leftist movements or the Sandinista model were militarily destroyed, traditional rightist forces and historical intransigence on the issue of sharing power and wealth with the disinfranchised would be reinforced. The problems of political refugees and instability in Latin America would proliferate. Numerous Latin American officials warned of the dangers of increasing resentment of the United States among South American peoples. A negotiated settlement, on the other hand, would reinforce momentum for democrateic compromise among competing interests.

Given these motivations, the Contadora states by 1985 were openly angry with the United States' tactics for blocking and supplanting a Contadora treaty. One Latin American response during 1985 was the creation of a support group for Contadora which enlarged the number of Latin American states associated directly with Contadora. The Lima Support Group consisting of Peru, Uruguay, Brazil and Argentina was formed in July shortly after the inauguration of Peru's new, young president, Alan Garcia. Garcia's outspoken support for Nicaragua's sovereignty, in fact, reflected both growing Latin American disappointment over US policy intransigence and feelings that time for Contadora was running short. Further, the states hoped to broaden the scope of their influence by preparing to bring the peace draft before the United Nations.

In the face of Latin American solidarity, the United States

worked through its regional allies to confound a final agreement
(see Chapter 10). In another direct move, the Reagan Administration
planned for undermining united Latin American pressures to move
Contadora forward. In a leaked September, 1985 State Department
document which outlined policy directions for Central America,
policy officials argued that the United States:

> ...must develop an active diplomacy to neutralize the
> Latin American solidarity efforts directed against the
> United States and its allies, whether they are sponsored
> by the Support Group, the Cubans or the Nicaraguans. We
> must find the way to turn the pressures being directed
> against us and our friends to our advantage. We need to
> find a way to deflect the pressure they impose on us.
> (IHCA, October, 1985).[20]

Reflecting the US attempt to act as the final judge of what would be
a bad Contadora peace agreement, the document further contended "We
have the eight [Contadora and Support Group states] maintaining
strong pressure on the United States and our friends to accept any
accord rather than a good accord...The collapse of Contadora would
be better than a bad accord" (IHCA, op.cit.).[21]

The Reagan Administration also moved in 1985 to coopt the
process by trying to bring it under the domain of the OAS--where the
United States was not only a member, but the dominant one--and, by
attempting to move the discussion of solutions out of Latin America
and direclty onto the US-USSR negotiating table during the 1985-86
summit diplomacy period. The resentment in Latin America and
Nicaragua over the latter move was palpable. Co-founder of
Contadora, Herrera Campins of Venezuela, reflected Latin sentiments:
Washington was trying to supplant Contadora, and doing so by
inviting the Soviet Union to play a role (IHCA, November, 1985).

Through Contadora--the vehicle of its unity and the symbol of
its will--Latin America challenged the United States to redefine its
security interests in Central America and hoped to blunt the effect
of any US retaliation for southern independence. As they tried to
woo US allies in Central America from political dependence on
Washington, the Contadora states also appeared interested in
creating longer-term bases for multilateral action vis-a-vis the
United States. These developments were helpful to revolutionary
Nicaragua; but, to some extent, such solidarity also shaped the
foreign policy context for the FSLN.

Cuba

> Cuba has been profoundly respectful of our decisions and
> has helped us beyond its international commitments.
>
> Tomas Borge
> Interior Minister
> (FBIS-LAM, 6-29-83)

A natural affinity existed between the Latin American
revolutionaries in Nicaragua and Cuba. According to Nicaraguan

Alfonso Robelo (who later joined the US-backed contras), the Nicaraguans and Cubans were "brother peoples" who would continue to have a special relationship. For Cuba, so long isolated by the United States and many Latin American states, there was joy and satisfaction over the triumph of another anti-imperialist revolution in the region. Cuba's aid to Nicaragua immediately after Somoza's overthrow signalled the Castro government's eagerness both to assist materially and to advise the new revolution's leaders. But to focus on that linkage of mutual support between the two countries as representing a uniform identity or social vision is misleading. Leaders in both countries stressed that development policy must address local realities and that lessons from history--i.e., from Cuban development attempts, from US-Cuban and USSR-Cuban relations--should be heeded by the Sandinistas. Nevertheless, a significant factor shaping opportunities for the FSLN leadership in foreign affairs was precisely this--that the Reagan Administration closely identified Nicaragua and Cuba, set them up as the twin threat to US regional security and charged that both sought to forward Soviet goals in Central and South America. Thus, in 1981, Secretary of State Haig threatened to "go to the source"--Cuba--to extinguish leftist movements in Central America, whereupon Cuba mobilized and braced for an imminent US military attack (see Smith, 1983). US policy toward the two countries in the 1980s shared many common features, including US refusals seriously to pursue talks aimed at defusing tensions.

Fidel Castro offered the FSLN political solidarity and warnings, before and after the US invasion of Grenada in 1983, that Nicaragua had to be prepared to defend itself against military aggression. This posture was in contrast to Castro's interpretation of Cuba's foreign policy of proletarian internationalism vis-a-vis Angola in 1975; at that time he argued that Cuba had a duty to help defend Angola's incipient socialist government regardless of price. Mindful of the counter-revolutionary threat posed to Nicaragua by a conservative US administration, Castro warned the FSLN of the costs of being over-identified with Cuba and cautioned moderation to avoid US retaliation against Nicaragua or Cuba. Because he was interested in helping the Nicaraguan revolution become consolidated and shared the Sandinistas' hope of greater Latin American solidarity in the future--both events which would also raise Cuban prestige and influence in the region--Castro played a generally moderate diplomatic role in the region after 1979, yet maintaining with the FSLN that revolutions would naturally spread in Latin America.

In 1981 Castro joined Mexico, Venezuela, France and others in calling for open discussions between the United States and Nicaragua, the United States and Cuba, and among contending parties elsewhere in the region. In the following years Castro maintained that position, in 1983 calling for "a clean slate" with Washington over regional issues and for all-party support for Contadora (e.g., LAWR, 4-15-83). Continuing military aid to Nicaragua for its war against the contras, Castro also supported a negotiated settlement between the government and FMLN guerrillas in Salvador, stressed the necessity of avoiding a regional war in which the United States would be heavily involved and held talks--mediated by Mexico--with ARDE contra officials in efforts at creating space for negotiations

250

among contending parties in Nicaragua (NYT, 10-6-83; LAWR, 6-24-83 and 10-14-83). Rejecting a neutralist stance, however, Castro labelled the United States as the aggressor state and demonstrated his willingness to increase the costs to the United States of its military campaign against Nicaragua. That a good deal of common perspective on Central American issues existed among Cuba and other states in the Latin American system became increasingly evident in the period. Cuba's traditional isolation from continental Latin America also continued to errode. One indication of this was the expansion of Cuban-Latin American ties from 1984 and 1986: among other things, Cuba received a $600 million loan from Argentina, which had become along with Mexico, a major Latin American supplier of goods to Cuba; the President of Ecuador made the country's first official visit to Cuba since 1960; Uruguay, Brazil, and Peru were considering full diplomatic relations with Cuba; and Cuban aid and gifts (of medical buses) were received in Guyana and Bolivia (NYT, 5-19-85). Cuba was increasingly acting within, and being seen by fellow Latin Americans as part of, the Latin American system.

Non-Military Aid to Nicaragua. Although Cuba purposefully played a low-key role in aiding the FSLN during its war against Somoza, within the first month after the July 19 Triumph Castro established full relations with Nicaragua, sent about two dozen military and security advisors to aid in establishing defense institutions there, sent forty medical doctors to help with the war-related health crisis and offered to send teachers according to Nicaraguan need. While the FSLN avoided full identification with Cuba and sought to balance Cuban ties with ties to other regional states (particularly Mexico, Panama, Costa Rica and Venezuela), it also praised Cuban assistance as among the most bountiful and forthright assistance they had received. Only one week after their victory, an FSLN delegation travelled to Cuba to thank Castro for his support and to discuss broad strategies for reconstruction and survival. Likewise, in the next years Sandinista officials and technicians from many areas of government frequently consulted with their Cuban counterparts, just as they utilized Cuban technicians and other foreign "internationalistas" in the reconstruction drive which dominated Sandinista energy and policy to about mid-1983. Foreign policy issues such as appropriate responses to regional peace initiations, were also matters of mutual discussion (e.g., FBIS-LAM, 9-22-82).

By November, 1980, Cuba had provided $10 million in emergency relief and economic aid and had signed an economic and technical accord with the FSLN. This was followed in April, 1981 with a $64 million economic cooperation agreement. All toll, by early 1981 Cuba had provided 2.2 percent of total support loans to Nicaragua to date (i.e., compared to Latin America's provision of 42.5 percent and the US provision of 26.4 percent of total support loans). As the US response to the revolution took shape, Cuban economic and development aid increased. By the end of 1982 the total was $286 million, including $80 million in relief assistance following the devastating floods in Nicaragua in early 1982. Cuban development assistance, most of it free according to Nicaraguan Interior Minister Borge, was notable in the areas of health, education, radio and telecommunications, agriculture, sugar industries, road-building, fishing, hydro-electricity and shipping. Of probably greater importance than material assistance, however, was the breadth and depth of skilled human assistance provided by Cuba. For example, by 1983 nine hundred medical workers--doctors, nurses, administrators, etc.--served in Nicaragua as had several thousand Cuban teachers since 1980. Cuban construction and industrial technicians worked on development and reconstruction projects in Nicaragua; Cuba loaned equipment and workers for other special projects provided for in the reconstruction budget to mid-1983. Hundreds of Nicaraguan doctors, teachers and technicians studied in Cuba as part of broad cooperation pacts between the two countries. By 1983 Nicaragua leaders Daniel Ortega and Bayardo Arce were calling relations with Cuba permanent and non-negotiable (Schwab and Sims, 1985: 452).

Beyond revolutionary bonds, practical realities also contributed to Nicaragua's expansion of economic relations with Cuba. While Central America was experiencing recession in the 1980s, Cuba was experiencing sustained growth and had a per capita production output three times that of the Central American states (Brundenius, 1982: 39). Cuba was thus a good candidate for advising Nicaragua in its drive for new industrial development. At the same time, however, trade remained limited. Nicaragua had few industrial goods that Cuba needed. Yet Cuba was willing to explore expanding trade, for example, by buying Nicaraguan cotton to replace its import of synthetic fibers for its textile industry.

US policy was also to affect the relationship between the two revolutionary states. Cuban military assistance--material and advisory--grew as the contra war heated up in 1983 and thereafter. Cuba determinedly stood by Nicaragua as other sources of military aid dried up. After 1983 and up to 1986, military support was undoubtedly Cuba's largest and most important contribution to the survival of the Nicaraguan revolution. The contra war, US pressure regarding Cuban personnel in Nicaragua and the shifting of Nicaragua's national budget toward defense, moreover, combined to reduce the number of non-military Cuban nationals in Nicaragua. In November, 1984 Nicaragua announced the end of the use of Cuban teachers in primary schools since, particularly in rural areas, Cuban teachers, doctors and other personnel had become primary targets of the contras.

The Example of Cuba. Common experiences with US-backed dictators and with restructuring society suggested that Nicaragua might well benefit from the successes and failures of the Cuban case. In fact, FSLN leaders studied the Cuban revolution at its various levels, with a special focus on Cuban mobilization techniques. Cuban experience with cooperative agriculture, labor laws, labor unionization and popular organization influenced FSLN policy and shaped its objectives of avoiding excessive dependence by mobilizing voluntary labor and self-help projects. The Frente also took note of production problems accruing from Cuban nationalization of most productive sectors. The Sandinistas, rejected that path for Nicaragua. In the mid 1980s, socialist development remained an ideal, not a reality in Nicaragua.

In the political realm, Nicaraguan and Cuban leaders had many similar aspirations regarding such issues as socioeconomic redistribution, Third World liberation and self-determination. In a 1981 letter to Castro, for instance, FSLN Directorate member Jaime Wheelock noted the common role played by Nicaragua and Cuba in holding out hope for oppressed peoples in Latin America (FBIS-LAM, 12-14-81). Yet their political development and preferred domestic political methods differed.[22] Nicaraguan economic policy remained primarily reformist rather than revolutionary. More important in terms of political method, the Frente--though it restricted and sometimes harassed its political opposition--did not systematically attempt to break the organization of the domestic opposition. In contrast to political development in Cuba, the FSLN in practice rejected the idea of a revolutionary vanguard with a monopoly on power.

The leaders of the Nicaraguan revolution readily accepted Cuban aid and advice; they came to depend on its military assistance and politicl solidarity. Nor was it a secret that deep fraternal ties existed between the Cuban and Nicaraguan revolutionaries, ties that dated back to early Cuban support for the incipient FSLN organization as it evolved under Fonseca and others. In a tribute to Cuba's help and its cancellation of $73 million of Nicaragua's debt, in January, 1985 President Daniel Ortega awarded Fidel Castro Nicaragua's highest honor--the Augusto C. Sandino Order (BI, 1-17-85). But other notable features of the special relationship were Castro's preference and work for a negotiated settlement of regional tensions; the Sandinistas' acknowledgments of differences between the development paths of the two countries; the sensitivity of the two states to US security concerns; and the FSLN's attempts to balance its ties to Cuba and the Soviet bloc with ties to other Latin American, and Western European states (see Chapter 9).


WESTERN EUROPE

The latter point highlights a significant difference between the international opportunity structures facing Nicaragua in 1979 and Cuba in 1960. The twenty years separating the two revolutions allowed the development of greater policy independence from the United States in both Latin America and Western Europe, thus opening to the Nicaraguan leaders greater potential for non-alignment or diversified relations. Working to diminish those opportunities in the 1980s, however, was the US-led resurgence of the Cold War. These realities combined to shape Nicaraguan-West European relations.

Western Europe's interest in Nicaragua was motivated not so much by its level of economic investment there--which was low--but by its concern that Central America not become enmeshed in an East-West conflict, and, that the United States not become bogged down there to an extent that its capacity to carry out its NATO obligations was diminished. Moreover, like their Latin American counterparts, European observers identified the root causes of Central American tensions in regional socioeconomic and political oppression. More so than the Reagan Administration, the European leaders appeared to have a clearer vision of the necessity for structural change in Latin America. Nor were they motivated to crush leftist movements. Rather, such movements had been facts of European political life since World War II, just as communist parties in Latin American had been considered a minor problem there and one related to US intrusion in local affairs (e.g., Oduber, 1985: 138). In the view of Western European leaders, the Reagan Administration's heavy-handedness in Central America hurt both East-West and North-South relations, increasing the likelihood that Third World states would turn to the Soviets for aid. European leaders generally argued for: providing Nicaragua and regional liberation groups alternatives to USSR support; drawing popular governments or movements into political dialogue with Western groups concerned with social justice or political pluralism; encouraging regional economic integration and development; and working toward a negotiated settlement of conflicts.

## Themes in Western European Policy

Taking pains to avoid the appearance of directly challenging US-Nicaragua policy, Western European states offered bilateral development aid packages and continued or expanded trade with Nicaragua. In the first year and a half of the revolution, for example, West Germany had provided $50 million in aid or soft loans to Nicaragua and the Swiss had given a long-term loan of $2.6 million for rural health clinics. Western Europe provided the bulk of the $20 million financing for Nicaragua's heralded literacy campaign in 1980. By the end of 1982 many more governments had made commitments to Nicaragua and the EEC and the Socialist International (SI), in particular, aided and communicated with the FSLN. Western European donations to Nicaragua by this time amounted to 32.5 percent of total gifts to that country. Swedish aid in 1981 amounted to 9 percent of all Nicaragua's loans that year while the $93 million in bilateral loans provided by Western Europe represented 18 percent of all such loans to Nicaragua up to 1983. In 1982 Sweden provided another $14 million loan for forestry and mining projects and Holland awarded the FSLN a $24 million grant for port modernization. Besides providing $80 million in development assistance to Central America as a whole, in 1982 the EEC donated millions of dollars to Nicaragua under various food and finance programs.

Some open criticism of US policy was also emerging in the early 1980s as Reagan policy took on an increasingly hostile tone. Vowing not to allow East-West conflict overly to influence Nicaragua's development, in early 1982 France announced its military aid package to Nicaragua. In February, 1982 France joined West Germany and Latin American states in pledging to offer Nicaragua alternatives in the face of US economic cut-offs. Shortly thereafter, the EEC pledged more aid for the entire Central American region. Similarly, the Socialist International criticized the Reagan Administration for excluding Grenada and Nicaragua from its Caribbean Basin Initiative aid package. At a Bonn meeting the SI condemned the destabilization of Nicaragua and called for support of the Sandinistas on the basis of political pluralism and a mixed economy (NYT, 4-3-82; LAWR, 3-3-82; 4-9-82). At the end of the year, European Social Democrats joined their Central American counterparts in condemning US policy, but without unconditionally supporting Nicaragua.

Yet polarization over Nicaragua -- due in part to US pressures and perception-management in Europe -- had also come to characterize West European politics by this time. Citing "a lack of democratic credibility" and militarization in Nicaragua, the West European Parliament in mid-1982 recommended a suspension in aid until "free elections" were held (LAWR, 6-25-82). Though that suggestion did not immediately affect aid to Nicaragua, it signalled both European dissatisfaction with FSLN political development and the failure of the Frente effectively to have made its case before European governments. For example, in 1982, the Thatcher government in Britain had objected to the inclusion of Nicaragua in EEC plans for a cooperative development project in Central America. Nicaragua was therefore not included in the program (Malley, 1985: 487). In late 1982 and 1983 France and West Germany--for different reasons--put some distance between themselves and Nicaragua. France, busy trying to contain Libyan moves against Chad in northern Africa, was dismayed by Libyan-Nicaraguan ties. (These were exemplified by the Libyan offer in 1981 of $100 million in credits and a joint Nicaraguan-Libyan agricultural development project in Nicaragua.) Rumors of Libyan military aid to Nicaragua added to French caution, as did Nicaragua's criticism in 1983 of the presence of US and French forces in Lebanon. In Germany the more conservative and pro-US Christian Democratic party had made headway against the Social Democratic Schmidt government. The new Kohl government proved less sympathetic to the Sandinistas' anti-imperialist stance. While Germany did agree to nearly double aid to Nicaragua following talks with Nicaraguan officials early in 1983, that aid--which rose from $10 million to $16 million--was targetted for the private sector and non-government cooperatives (LAWR, 2-15-83).

By the end of 1983 France, West Germany and Spain--who alledged FSLN support for Basque revolutionaries--had each expressed its opinion that Nicaragua[23] rather than being non-aligned, was leaning toward to Soviet bloc. The fact that European opinion of the FSLN was split, however, was evident in continued support from the governments of Holland and Sweden. While Sweden provided another $23 million in aid in 1983, at the end of the year the Netherlands provided Nicaragua $2 million in road-building monies to replace an Inter-American Development Bank grant for that purpose which had recently been vetoed by Washington. The Mitterand government itself--always more supportive than West Germany--granted Nicaragua a new loan in September. Yet political differences within the European systems as well as US pressure to end aid to Nicaragua continued to make aid to the FSLN a potentially controversial subject. In efforts at circumventing US and other political pressure and ensuring continued aid flows to the Frente, supportive groups in France, Italy, Holland, Britain and Scandinavia formed five non-governmental consortiums in early 1985 through which additional aid could be channelled (BI, 4-4-85).

Despite varying opinions about the FSLN, European states continued to express concern about US policy in Central America and to promote economic cooperation and development there on a regional basis. In March, 1983 France and Spain floated the idea of their sponsoring talks among contending parties with Spanish President

Felipe Gonzalez acting as mediator (LAWR, 3-18-83). Because the new
Contadora process had not yet had time to develop, this European
idea never got off the ground. But the persistence of European or
EEC support for a negotiated settlement in Central America became
evident in 1983 onward. Attitudes regarding Central America
expressed by the ten EEC leaders at their July, 1983 meeting found
an avenue for concrete action at a September Brussels meeting which
was jointly sponsored by the EEC and the Inter-American Development
Bank for the purpose of raising European funds for Central American
development. Initiated on the notion that economic development
could facilitate regional political solutions, the meeting was
important in signalling both Central American willingness to
cooperate in economic aid requests or in joint development projects
and the fact that US policy of isolating Nicaragua had few European
adherents.[24] Although the meeting generated few new loans, it
established the basis for future meetings and for Central
American-West European dialogue. For Nicaragua the meetings yielded
a new $120 million loan from France and a $20,000 grant and promise
of a $5 million loan from Finland (LAWR, 9-30-83).

The September, 1984 meeting of the group in San Jose resulted
in an announcement of all-party support for Contadora and a $500
million aid grant to the region. The grant included Nicaragua
despite a blunt US request that Nicaragua be excluded. The final
communique called for regular meetings, dialogue and European
support in the implementation of any regional peace agreement (IHCA,
October, 1984; Council on Foreign Relations, 1985: 149). Also in
1984 and 1985 Western European actors demonstrated a willingness to
counter or respond to hostile US acts against Nicaragua.
Condemning--along with the other European states--the US mining of
Nicaraguan harbors, France in April, 1984 offered to help in
sweeping the harbors for mines. Later, after the US-inspired MIG
scare, France responded with a token $1.73 million aid package,
intended to help Nicaragua "...assure its own development, make its
own choices and determine the environment in which its people live"
(NYT, 11-25-84). To support the 1984 electoral process in
Nicaragua, moreover, Norway, Sweden and Finland donated $800,000,
$400,000 and $450,000 respectively in paper and other
election-related materials. France and other states consulted with
Nicaraguan officials on election methods and models. In addition to
Scandinavian election-related aid, the Socialist International
worked with FSLN and CDN opposition leaders to counter US attempts
to limit the number of participants in Nicaraguan elections.
Although SI official Willy Brandt and others ultimately failed to
get the CDN candidate--Arturo Cruz--to participate, SI efforts
marked the distance it had come in the last decade at influencing
Latin American politics.

Though few European governments, save Sweden and Norway,
publically praised the Nicaraguan elections and while most declined
to send high-level delegations to Ortega's January, 1985
inauguration, a number of governments did respond to the United
States' May 1, 1985 embargo announcement with new promises of aid to
the FSLN government. Vice-President Sergio Ramirez's three week
tour of Austria, West Germany, Belgium, Holland and Spain, and,
President Ortega's visit to five other West European states in May

yielded Nicaragua $200 million in new aid commitments for 1985. Included was a $25 million credit from Italy for work on the Momotombo Geothermal Project, part of Nicaragua's drive for energy independence, and $10 million in aid from Finland. Around the same time France approved $30 million to fund a series of industrial, agricultural, energy and other development projects (CAR, 5-3-85). In May, Sweden announced that it was cancelling the debts owed it by Nicaragua, Tanzania and several other underdeveloped states (IHCA, May, 1985).

In addition, Ramirez's talks with EEC representatives in Brussels--which he labelled "extraordinary"--yielded unspecified agreements for assistance and bilateral cooperation and reinforced the EEC's commitment to include Nicaragua in regional aid projects. Shortly after the US embargo was announced, the EEC approved a special $200 million, 5-year regional aid package (IHCA, June, 1985). Given its public positions in 1984 and 1985, it appeared that the EEC had decided against pursuing a neutral stance on the issues of Nicaragua and US Central American policy. The Socialist International, which had maintained ties to the FSLN, also expressed increased concern about US policy in 1985. The June meeting in Sweden reflected growing preoccupation in Europe with US Nicaraguan policy and was, according to the Brazilian representative, the most Latin American of SI meetings (IHCA, July, 1985). Not only did the SI Executive Bureau reject the US embargo and call for the signing of the September, 1984 Contadora draft, it also called for continued technical-economic assistance to Nicaragua and support for the Nicaraguan constitution-writing process; the bureau agreed to a Nicaraguan request to send a fact-finding commission to the region. Placing their criticisms of Nicaragua within a framework of support, SI representatives from Europe discussed with their Latin American counterparts strategies for unifying to counter US policy (BI, 7-4-85; IHCA, op.cit.).

## Untapped Potential For Nicaragua?

Compared to their efforts in Latin America and in regional and international forums, Nicaraguan leaders expended lesser efforts and energies to develop sturdy relations with major Western European governments. Though FSLN links to European Social Democrats date to 1978 and were maintained after the Triumph, the Frente did not systemmatically or effectively campaign among Western European governments to present its case, to counter US claims, or to explain its political-military strategy for national defense. Nor were its development philosophy and accompanying projects lobbied for effectively.

As US policy edged the FSLN into more hardline stances at home and toward a greater dependence on Eastern bloc military aid, European leaders became more suspicious of the FSLN's political intentions. The Nicaraguan model of pluralism with "popular hegemony" was either misunderstood, i.e., as to how it differed from European Social Democratic models, or was held to the criteria of Western democratic models. Indeed, a belief on the part of FSLN leaders that closer ties to Western European governments would constitute added pressures against their mass mobilization methods and for early Western-styled elections may have been what led to a weaker FSLN drive in Western Europe. As Tomas Borge noted in the early years of the revolution, the Nicaraguan leaders were after something more than European-style social democracy (Black, 1981: 171).

Yet, given its stance of promoting a new foreign policy and its need for international legitimacy, a more activist role in Western Europe may have netted the FSLN greater political support there. As it was, the Sandinistas usually approached Europe with systemmatic appeals only as part of their strategies to counter new US cut-offs or hostilities. In those instances, the FSLN was usually rewarded with both material assistance and European cautions to the United States.

THE USSR AND EASTERN EUROPE

On the first day after the victory of FSLN forces in Nicaragua in 1979, Soviet President Brezhnev declared his country's willingness "to develop multifaceted ties with Nicaragua" (quoted in Rothenberg, 1984: 133). The Sandinistas' victory in Central America prompted renewed Soviet interest in Latin America generally, suggesting as it did to the Soviets at the time that there might be greater potential for anti-imperialist movements in Latin America than they had earlier estimated.

Yet, actual Soviet commitments and ties to Nicaragua were measured, stemming from the USSR's determination 1)to avoid aiding in the creation of another regionally isolated, dependent regime like Cuba; and 2)to avoid a direct confrontation with the United States in the Western Hemisphere. Soviet ties to Nicaragua developed proportionately in response to increasing US hostility in economic and military spheres. While the Soviets demonstrated a willingness to help facilitate the revolution's survival, they showed no willingness to shape Nicaragua into a vested interest which could require direct Soviet military or economic intervention. For example, hard currency requests from Nicaragua were ignored and commitments for long-term development assistance were not made. Soviet military aid, as I point out in Chapter 8, came along with warnings that the FSLN had to defend itself. A consideration of Soviet and Eastern European aid patterns, moreover, suggests that much of the aid was intended for filling Nicaragua's emergency needs accruing from US cut-offs and aggressions. The USSR and Bulgaria donated 30,000 tons of wheat to Nicaragua in 1981 to compensate for the US cut-off of $9.6 million in wheat credits to Nicaragua. Later, the USSR purchased wheat from Canada to subsidize Nicaragua's needs. In 1983 nearly two-thirds of Nicaragua's wheat needs were filled by Soviet donations and this aid continued through the next year as well. As the contra war was heating up, in early 1984 Moscow signed its third cultural and scientific agreement with Managua in a show of solidarity. Similarly, aid and lines of credit from Eastern Europe only reached significant and steady levels after US and other Western aid dropped off.

In 1984, the Soviet Union took over supplying 25 percent of Nicaragua's oil needs in response to repeated Nicaraguan requests and after Venezuela and Mexico eliminated their oil-on-easy-terms program to Nicaragua. Though Mexico, Algeria, Libya and Iran all made commitments in 1985 to supply some of Nicaragua's future oil needs, the USSR's continuing commitment to ensure that Nicaragua's needs would be met provided Nicaraguan leaders the added security they sought. That this and other Soviet aid decisions were influenced by Nicaragua's security situation was clear. The Soviets responded to new Nicaraguan requests for energy-related support in 1984 after contras destroyed oil storage facilities at Puerto Sandino. According to Nicaraguan Planning Minister Ruiz who was in Moscow to sign aid contracts, "By destroying our storage of oil in Puerto Sandino, the US imperialists forced us to request help; now we will reconstruct the same storage deposits and build a pipeline that will extend all the way from the port to Managua" (quoted in Sims, 1984: 11). Symbolic of the events which were strengthening Nicaraguan-Soviet ties, as Ruiz and the Soviets were negotiating the 1984 oil, textile and communications aid, a Soviet ship was damaged by a CIA-planted mine in Nicaraguan port waters; five Soviet sailors were injured. Similarly, after the announcement of a 1985 US embargo on Nicaragua, the Soviets officially responded that they would "...continue giving fraternal assistance to Nicaragua to help overcome urgent problems of economic development as well as political and diplomatic support in its struggle to preserve sovereignty" (IHCA, May, 1985).

The Soviets did not give the FSLN a blank check regarding assistance. Rather, their aid was meant to increase the odds for the survival of the Sandinista revolution and to increase the costs of a US intervention. Unwilling to underwrite the FSLN government, the Soviets did not want to alienate other potential sources of aid or spark a total cut-off of Western aid to Nicaragua. According to a 1984 US Department of State report, "...in the context of her overall aid to the Third World nations, Moscow's commitment to Nicaragua is modest" (NYT, 3-13-84). USSR influence in Central America, the report noted, was limited by the presence of the Catholic Church and crucial aid from Western European and UN agencies. Nor was there much potential for mutually beneficial economic ties among the parties. The Soviets and Eastern Europe had no need for Nicaraguan exports like coffee, sugar and cotton. Their ability and willingness to subsidize Nicaragua's export sector over a long term was limited. The fact that Nicaragua and other Latin American states were so heavily connected to the United States in financial investment, markets and spare parts areas meant that a close relationship would require retooling Nicaraguan industry and reorienting its economic system. That course of action was the preferred route of neither Nicaraguan or Soviet leaders (see also Chapter 9).

The Soviets had not assessed that Nicaragua was a Marxist-Leninist state or that objective conditions necessary for a transition to socialism were existent there. Nor, according to Western diplomats in Managua, did Moscow consider Nicaragua vital in terms of its global strategy (e.g., NYT, 3-28-84).[25] One indication of Nicaragua's lower priority among Soviets' ties to the Third World is the fact that by 1986 the Soviets had shown no interest in signing a friendship treaty with Nicaragua like those it had with

Afghanistan, Angola, Ethiopia, India, Syria and others. Undoubtedly because of the heterodox nature of <u>Sandinismo</u> and the revolution itself, Nicaragua ranked below these African and Middle Eastern states pursuing a socialist orientation (Edelman, 1985: 40).

Soviet interest in Nicaragua appeared to lie in encouraging anti-imperialism rather than in trying to enforce Nicaraguan ideological or policy deference to Moscow. Anti-imperialism, in the Soviet view, carried with it a potential for socialist development and by its nature weakened capitalism (e.g., Valenta 1984; Armstrong, 1985). Soviet trade, aid and diplomatic or military support, then, aimed toward enabling system transition to socialism or, lacking that, increasing the bases for Soviet political influence. Hostile US policy in the 1980s appeared to facilitate these Soviet aims in Nicaragua, and perhaps, in Latin America generally.

## NOTES

1. This characterization of Honduras was made by US Embassy analysts in Tegucigalpa during interviews in August, 1983. In this section on Honduras I draw heavily from interviews with US and Honduran political and military officials, and with social, political party and economic leaders in Honduras during 1983 and 1985.

2. Though denied by the Honduran government and played down in the United States, the Morazan action was confirmed by two London papers, the <u>Times</u> and the <u>Guardian</u>. Joint Salvadoran-Honduran actions against suspected leftists dated back to the May, 1980 Rio Sumpul massacre where the armies together killed 600 unarmed and fleeing peasants at the river boundary.

3. In retaliation against Honduras, the FMLN coordinated isolated actions with the Chinchoneros (Honduran leftists). In 1981 the Chinchoneros hijacked a Honduran flight to Nicaragua, demanding the release of FMLN-FDR prisoners. In 1982 the Chinehoneros performed a media-event kidnapping of businessmen in San Pedro Sula. The Honduran army cited such instances as evidence of Nicaraguan attempts to export revolution.

4. Although from 1979 to 1981 the Honduran government acknowledged the presence of anti-Sandinista Somocistas in Honduras, by late 1981 the government referred only to "delinquents" operating along the border. As Honduras came to play an important role in the US contra program, it refused publicly to admit their presence in Honduras.

5. The UNHCR ignored this request interpreting it as a reflection of an internal Honduran power struggle.

6. The $5 million radar base had a 230 mile detection radius and allowed monitoring of events in both Nicaragua and El Salvador.

7. US officials in Honduras were reportedly not too upset about Alverez's replacement. The general's outspokenness, had caused concern among officials who publically denied US intent to overthrow the FSLN. The CIA, however, was reportedly embarrassed that the young officers had been able to initiate and carry out the purge of such a close CIA ally. The CIA had been monitoring the

young officers who, they suspected, were leftists (NYT, 1-31-86). President Suazo Cordova himself accused Alverez of meddling in politics.

8. In the United States, Congress had turned down new contra funding.

9. After being posted for fifteen months in Costa Rica, in February, 1985 Winsor was reassigned and left San Jose.

10. The US's strategic intentions for the AID project were first reported in the Mexican daily Excelsior in mid-1982 and were reported by Jack Anderson in the United States in February, 1983. The potentially strategic nature of the construction projects had become visible in Costa Rica by 1984. See also CAU, August, 1984.

11. In this period Costa Rica received additional military assistance from Israel, Taiwan, South Korea and Argentina. All but Argentina were themselves recipients of large US military aid packages.

12. Contra bands were operating regularly along both sides of the border and had earlier admitted that they hoped to lure Costa Rica into their conflict with the FSLN. The Frente, moreover, produced a tape of a Chamorro radio communication to prove their claims.

13. The symmetry argument was vulnerable on several counts. First, US actions made it clear that Washington preferred the total surrender or defeat of the FMLN; power-sharing suggestions by the FMLN were rejected out of hand. Second, though the administration labelled the Nicaraguan conflict a genuine civil war, i.e., with an indigenous and self-propelled opposition, it rejected that labelling for Salvador. Third, as a Republican critic (Jim Leach-Iowa) of symmetry put it: "US actions against Nicaragua undercut the moral imprimateur upon which US policy in El Salvador is based. In El Salvador we stand foursquarely against those who are armed and financed from abroad and who would shoot their way into power. In Nicaragua we stand foresquarely with such forces and in fact are the financiers of anarchy" (NYT, 6-15-83).

14. Apparently sensing that US officials would create obstacles to such a meeting were they aware that he planned such talks, Duarte announced his plans before the world body at the UN in the fall, 1984 and without having consulted the United States.

15. Noriega was simultaneously pursuing his own personal agenda. Deeply involved in drug trafficking and money laundering schemes, Noriega had, according to US intelligence, ordered the assassination of vocal political activist and opponent Dr. Hugo Spadafora in 1985. President Barletta, under pressure from civilian parties, had just ordered an investigation into Spadafora's death. Another motivation for Noriega in regional affairs was his arrangement with US intelligence to supply them with sensitive information on Nicaragua and Cuba. (Noriega was also supplying Cuba with information on the US military -- another side to his "balanced engagement" stance.) However, by 1986 Noriega was reportedly being less cooperative with US agencies; in mid-1986 these agencies released their intelligence on Noriega's dealings dating back to the 1960s (e.g. NYT 6-12-86; 6-13-86, 6-14-86).

16. Nicaragua's oil debt to Venezuela--$20 million--was minimal in comparison.

17.  Nicaraguan officials decided in 1982 to play down any Venezuelan government role in such acts, preferring to keep aid and relations flowing (e.g., LAWR, 1-22-82).

18.  In the early years of the revolution, Nicaragua pursued a territorial dispute with Colombia over the San Andres and Providencia Islands.

19.  Some US officials interpreted Ortega's comments as an FSLN admission that it had helped organize terrorist rings in other parts of Latin America.  This scenario fit nicely into the Reagan Administration's campaign to label revolutionary Nicaragua a terrorist state.

20.  At the March, 1985 OAS meeting, US Ambassador Middendorf said of the Contadora process that it was "...only a piece of paper until it is put into practice."  He went on:  The US "is not prepared to let this organization neglect its responsibilities in this respect and reserves the right to introduce a motion in the future that will lead to the satisfactory resolution of Nicaragua's problem if the aforementioned process is not successful" (BI, 4-4-85).

21.  The document was dated September 4, 1985 and had been prepared for meetings held in Panama that month between Assistant Secretary of State for Inter-American Affairs, Elliot Abrams, and US regional ambassadors.

22.  On this topic see, e.g., Azicri, 1982; Chilcote and Edelstein, 1986.

23.  Earlier in 1983, Spain agreed to provide Nicaragua credits for a cross-country railroad project.  Spain was thereby joining Argentina, Cuba and Bulgaria in committing to the project (LAWR, 7-23-83).

24.  Nicaraguan representatives, who had become experienced lobbyists since 1979, were the only delegates to meet with virtually all the states and agencies represented.

25.  These diplomats reported that the Soviet ambassador in Managua was not known to be particularly close to the FSLN leadership and that generally, the USSR "has been pretty cautious here."  They reported little evidence that the Soviets were "pushing the Sandinista to greater radicalization."

# PART 4

# Patterns in Revolutionary Nicaragua's Foreign Policy

# 8

## Nicaraguan Military
## and Defense Policy

> Our military doctrine is based on the moral strength
> of our people, who have en masse taken up arms to defend
> their homeland and revolution.

> Defense Minister Humberto Ortega
> April, 1985

Just as economic and development strategies in revolutionary
Nicaragua were products of Sandinista philosophy, historical
realities and actual exigencies, defense and security institutions
were shaped by these factors. Stressing popular mobilization for
the defense of the revolution, the FSLN sought to eliminate
inordinate US influence over Nicaragua's security apparatus and
nationalize defense institutions. The defeat of Somoza's brutal and
corrupt Guardia and the physical destruction of much of Somoza's
defense apparatus during the popular insurrection in 1979 thus
presented the Sandinistas with both a problem and an opportunity.
The problem stemmed from the fact that the FSLN came to power by
means of a small core of disciplined, but not professionally
trained, guerrilla fighters. Their efforts had been broadly
supported by loosely coordinated streetfighters and independent,
popular sabotage activities. Having relied during the struggle on
an assortment of donated, homemade, black market and international
arms market weapons, moreover, the Frente in 1979 faced the
immediate issue of creating long-term structures for the defense of
the nation. At the same time, however, the situation provided the
opportunity for leaders of the revolution to extend new values,
objectives and roles where a vacuum had been left by the collapse of
the Guardia.


THE EVOLUTION OF NICARAGUA'S DEFENSE STRUCTURES

As in other spheres of Nicaraguan life after the 1979 Triumph,
external pressures and mitigating factors profoundly affected the
pace and nature of the development of defense institutions there.
Again, US military pressure was a key factor influencing the size of
and the role played by the armed forces in the revolutionary
process. Washington's low-intensity attrition campaign affected

266

Nicaragua's international linkages and the pace of its socio-political and economic development. In a context of increasing regional hostility, the Sandinistas came to the conclusion early on that since they could not hope to defeat US military forces, their best strategy was to raise the military, diplomatic and political costs to the United States of invading Nicaragua or undermining its revolution. By 1983 Nicaragua began moving from social reconstruction to survival planning. In the defense sector this meant defeating US-backed insurgents while preparing for a US invasion--fears of which US officials purposely kept alive. In other sectors and among the populous the watchwords became constant vigilance and self-sacrifice.

Defense thus came to be the responsibility of every Nicaraguan, just as it demanded the bulk of Nicaragua's political and physical energies after 1983. Defense criteria became central to policy-making in every sphere--from agrarian reform to production for local consumption, and from electoral laws and civil liberties to international relations. Most immediately, external threats shaped defense structures, military policy and the role of the armed forces in Nicaraguan life.

## Initial Directions

The struggle against Somoza was significant in establishing the bases for post-Somoza defense structures. The FSLN was able to gain the military initiative against a highly trained Guardia, mobilize or direct decisive popular participation, raise political consciousness and gain military and political control. Its popularity and moral authority in 1979, in turn, allowed the FSLN to assert control, maintain order after Somoza's fall and ask cooperation and disciplined behavior from citizens (Gorman, 1982: 115, 119). This process and concurrent regional events reinforced Sandinista beliefs that any new army should coexist side-by-side with the people; that maintaining order would discourage foreign (US or OAS) intervention to quell disintegration; and that "...the dominant factor in establishing political guidelines is in the international correlation of forces, ...the influence that imperialism and its allies exercise on the continental level" (FSLN, 1979: 13).

Interested in disallowing even a modicum of US influence in Nicaragua's military forces, the Frente envisioned security built on broad political organization at all social levels under the "vanguard" FSLN (FSLN op.cit.: p. 35-36). According to the document from the national meeting of the FSLN two months after Somoza's overthrow, the Sandinistas saw victory as only the first step in gaining security for the revolution. The next step entailed political education, isolating anti-revolutionary forces within Nicaragua, and cultivating loyalty to the revolution among those selected to defend it militarily. Warning against dogmatism or following a strictly theoretical line, the FSLN nevertheless planned to utilize "vanguard activists of recognized revolutionary qualities" to pursue continual political education of the armed forces and a sifting out of members not loyal to the peoples' revolution (p. 37). Overall, however, the document notes the FSLN's

"instinctively rather defensive and more conservative posture
instead of pursuing a clear-cut policy for this stage..." (p. 13).
The Sandinistas sought to maintain defensive flexibility in
fitting new structures to Nicaragua's situation.  Though the FSLN
Directorate was intent upon domestic reconstruction and in
September, 1979 saw "no clear indication of an armed
counter-revolution" threatening stability at that time (p. 14), the
Sandinistas had taken note of the US record of promoting economic or
political destabilization in "nonconformist" Latin American states.
They took the lessons of Mexico, Guatemala, Cuba, Chile and similar
cases to be that the United States and Nicaraguan sectors tied to it
were not to be assumed friendly to the revolution (e.g., Walker,
1982: 4,8).  According to Defense Minister Humberto Ortega, the
Frente in 1979 operated on three assumptions in planning for the
armed forces: 1)that Nicaragua would be surrounded by neighbors
undoubtedly opposed to the FSLN's political philosophy; 2)that the
army would have to be created out of paramilitary guerrilla columns;
and 3)that internal security would be necessary to protect the
revolution, owing to the geographical proximity of the United States
and its history of intervention in Nicaragua's internal affairs
(King, 1985: 5).  Given its own reading of continental history and
planning assistance from Cuban, Soviet and other foreign officials,
the FSLN believed long-term defense required:  mass volunteer
militias to support a limited regular army;  non-military
mobilization at the grassroots; and rapid social progress (Walker,
op.cit.; King, op.cit.; Gorman, 1982: 124).
Despite early confidence expressed at the September meeting, a
series of events in 1979 and early 1980 shaped Nicaragua's defense
strategy and encouraged renewed wariness among the FSLN over
"counter-revolutionary circles" with possible links to the United
States.  Shortly after the July 19th victory, Sandinista military
leader Luis Carrion warned of new kinds of aggression from Somocista
forces reorganizing abroad--in Honduras and in the United States.
While in August, 1979 rumors of impending counter-revolutionary
actions were rampant in the capital, in November a Somocista force
of sixty men crossed from Honduras and attacked Nicaraguan outposts.
Inside Nicaragua, meanwhile, pockets of resistance from both the
right (Somocista and bourgeoisie) and left (Marxist-Leninist and
Trotskyist) led to ambushes and armed exchanges.  In October, twenty
militia members died in such an ambush.  During the nation-wide
literacy campaign in 1980, several teachers were killed by Somocista
forces in the north.  Cattle-rustling and thievery raids were being
launched from Honduras.
US attitudes about the revolution also prompted FSLN wariness,
although this did not prevent the Frente from requesting
unconditional military aid from Washington in 1979.  A source close
to FSLN decision-making in that period cites "the steady right-wing
drift" in the United States and "the resurgence of the Cold War in
the months following the Nicaraguan victory" which "made the task of
consolidation and reconstruction all the more difficult" (Bandana,
1982: 322).  Arturo Cruz (1984) notes both the high priority the
FSLN placed on military preparedness against any US intervention and
the Frente's recognition of the real possibility for US
collaboration with Nicaragua's neighbors.  Cruz argues that at the

time the FSLN saw only two options in Central America during a Cold War period: total regional revolution, or, the military defeat of revolutionary Nicaragua. For this reason, according to Cruz, the FSLN decided early on to arm at a level commensurate with the combined capacities of US regional allies. Initial US dubiousness (under Carter) about the revolution and the subsequent US-sponsored military build-up on Nicaragua's borders influenced Sandinista planning. Moreover, a late 1979 article by former-CIA operative Philip Agee which speculated on how the CIA might attempt to destabilize the revolution was published in Covert Action and reprinted in La Prensa in January, 1980. That article also served to fire Sandinista suspicions of US intentions (Walker, 1981).

Local realities also shaped early Sandinista security decisions. While some debate took place about whether Nicaragua's army should be small, professional and equipped with sophisticated equipment, or, large, based on popular mobilization and utilizing less sophisticated, less expensive equipment, the latter approach quickly won out for pragmatic reasons. Nicaragua's economic underdevelopment, minimal foreign exchange and great development needs dictated an army drawing on mobilized masses rather than on the most modern or costly equipment (LARM, 3-19-82). Moreover, Somoza's defense structure had been built on the first model. It had become elitist and dependent on the United States, and had come to represent repression to the majority of Nicaraguans. The FSLN preferred to trace the origins of its army to Sandino's anti-imperialist, populist and nationalist army of the 1930s (IHCA, October, 1983). That army had organized in regions and by column to defend itself, while also performing social tasks and raising popular consciousness. By contrast, most Nicaraguans viewed the Guardia as a force occupying its own country. It had protected US rather than Nicaraguan interests, had collaborated with US forces against other Nicaraguans, and had enforced a corrupt and ruthless dictatorship. Rather than being a Nicaraguan force, the Guardia was created, trained and equipped by the local superpower; it operated as the Somoza family's private militia.[1] The FSLN chose to create an armed force that alternatively would defend Nicaragua and the revolution as well as participate in the rebuilding of the country according to revolutionary values. The Popular Sandinista Force (EPS) was officially enjoined on September 2, 1979, the date on which fifty-two years earlier Sandino had formed his army.

Early Structures. The new armed forces were to be organized by a subcommittee from the Sandinista National Directorate, the group of nine commanders of the revolution which set policy outlines in conjunction with the ruling Junta after July, 1979. That committee, made up of Tomas Borge, Luis Carrion and Humberto Ortega, also assumed the key positions in the armed forces and security structure: Borge served as Interior Minister; Ortega became Defense Minister and Carrion served as the Vice Minister of Defense and the second in command of the EPS. (Carrion later became Deputy Interior Minister.) Structurally, the police, under the Interior Ministry, were separate from the other armed forces, though in practice the popular militias served with both forces and effectively formed an integrative security link among the groups (Gorman, op.cit.: 120; Booth, 1985: 42). Moreover, coordination of all people under arms was facilitated by Borge's and Ortega's common membership in the National Directorate and by the representation of Interior officials on the General Staff at the Defense Ministry (see Figure 8.1). Such integration was intended for coordinating and streamlining defense and social tasks and tightening state security.[2]

Though the security apparatus aimed at coherence in a period of social rebuilding and political transformation, the new system was nevertheless more decentralized and broadly focused than the security apparatus under Somoza. For example, in the earlier system the Guardia--which operated under the dictator's command rather than as a national army--controlled the police; the armed forces in general assumed no social function. In revolutionary Nicaragua by contrast, and as a result of the armed insurrection which brought the new system into existence, military structures underpinned the majority of state institutions as Nicaragua prepared for rebuilding. People trained in defense skills and/or who fought during the civil war were now commissioned to carry out social and economic tasks (LARM, 3-19-82). The 15,000 combatants (of all types) under the FSLN at the time of the victory were disarmed and some from among these forces--those with proven combat experience or with a history of association with Sandinista forces--were selected for the EPS. Veteran FSLN guerrillas, about 1,300 of whom remained after July, 1979, made up the core of the EPS.

The idea in 1979 was to form the army into small mobile forces which would coordinate with militia forces. The infantry was to remain the primary arm of the military because manpower was the least costly and most readily available security resource. To support the infantry the FSLN created two tank brigades to provide mobile defensive firepower; gun and rocket field artillery battalions for long-and short-range defense of the infantry; and gun and missile anti-aircraft units to protect the infantry, airfields, installations and logistics capacities (King, 1985: 6). This development in 1979 and 1980 was facilitiated by the importation of light and generally upsophistocated weapons from the Soviet Union during a period in which the US first hesitated over an arms request and then offered weapons with stipulations including US training of Nicaraguan troops.

According to Defense Minister Ortega, the FSLN foresaw a regular force of about 30,000 people and an additional 25,000 member militia which could serve during security emergencies. Additionally, reserves would be trained through universal military training. But emphases remained on keeping the armed forces low-cost and relevant to Nicaragua's situation: military people and reservists assumed civic responsibilities, worked in literacy and health campaigns, harvested coffee for export, joined labor brigades and construction projects, and the like. During the first year of the revolution the army and militia were often organized and trained side-by-side and both performed economic and social projects; defense was not a daily priority, save for the border patrols. A system of ranks was not introduced until 1980, with the highest rank being Commander of the Revolution--a rank held by those who were top guerrilla leaders during the war against Somoza.

According to Commandante Luis Carrion, recruits were attracted mainly through moral incentives. Their training consisted of three

Figure 8.1
Sandinista Military-Security Structures

========================================================

FSLN National Directorate
Commission For Military Reorganization
       /                              \

Ministry of Defense                    Ministry of Interior
(Minister:  Humberto Ortega            (Minister:  Tomas
Saavedra)                              Borge Martinez)

1.  Sandinista Peoples Army        1.  State Security (DGSE)
    (EPS)
    A.  Infantry                   2.  Sandinista Police
        (regular EPS and               (PS)
        draftees)
        - Border Patrol Troops     3.  Support Organizations
          (TGF)*                       (immigration, fire-
        - Irregular Fighting           fighters, etc.)
          Battalions (BLIR)*
          - Tank Units
          - Artillery Units
          - Infantry Troops

    B.  Sandinista Air Force
        and Anti-Aerial Defense
        (FASDAA)

    C.  Sandinista Navy (MGS)[a]

2.  Sandinista Peoples Militia
    (MPS)[b] (volunteer)
    A.  Reserve Infantry Bat-
        talions (BIR)*

    B.  Territorial Battalions

3.  Civil Defense[c]
    (volunteer, unarmed)

_____

Sources:  Gorman (1982); IHCA (October, 1983); CAHI (12-3-84;
          2-28-85); NYT (5-25-86).

*Groups most active in combat against the contras.

a  In 1985 Nicaragua had approximately 62,850 persons under arms
   on active duty:  60,000 EPS and MPS; 850 MGS (navy); and 2000
   FASDAA (airforce).
b  In 1985 there were approximately 20,000 MPS on active duty,
   coordinated with TGF and BLIR units of the EPS.
c  Civil Defense activities were coordinated in support of EPS
   and MPS actions.

to six months of basic drills under veteran troops and Cuban trainers who numbered from 200-300 in 1979-1980 (Gorman, op.cit: 123, 125). The militia (MPS), officially organized in February, 1980, served mainly at the neighborhood level in unarmed capacities as extensions of the army and the police. Again, the military strategy was to have people organized and responsible for their own defense in the case of a major military (or another) emergency.

Political training of the recruits was viewed as central to the overall preparation for military service. Keen to the lessons from other revolutionary struggles and Latin American experience with military divisiveness, coups or insubordination, the Frente stressed national unity, loyalty to the revolution and responsibilities to the people. Such training focused on the history of Nicaragua, the development of the FSLN and its role as the philosophical and political guide for Nicaragua's reconstruction along socialist lines. The armed forces were thus initially conceived as the armed extension of the revolution which would guard against both the return of the old order and foreign intruders. Introducing the recruits to a socialist philosophy that did not reject private property or directly adhere to Marxist-Leninist principles, the Frente was interested in putting at its service the nationalist fervor awakened during the war against the Somoza regime. Acknowledging the explicitly political nature of the new armed forces, Tomas Borge pointed out: "There are no apolitical armies: every one serves some determinant political purpose. In the case of Nicaragua, the EPS is a Popular and Sandinista Army. It is not by accident that we call it such" (quoted in Gorman, p. 23).

Early Problems. The early vision of an army at the service of national reconstruction soon was blurred by local realities. Probably foremost among these was the low level of education among the armed forces--the illiteracy rate for the army was 45 percent in 1979--and the lack of technicians or skilled recruits. Such a force could not spearhead the broad reconstruction task Nicaragua faced. Moreover, the social dislocation that accrued from the insurrection period in 1978 and 1979, and, the heterogeneous make-up of FSLN combatants meant that much energy had to be spent in demobiliizing undisciplined fighters, re-establishing social cohesion or law and order and pacifying political reactionaries on the left and the right (e.g., LARM, 3-19-82). Complicating these immediate tasks, Nicaragua lacked both money for reconstruction tasks and professionally trained officers. It relied for security on a diverse array of poor quality weapons--of US, Belgium and Israeli origins--which made up the Sandinista arsenal. As the US State and Defense Departments reported in 1981: "the Nicaraguan defense establishment was swept away. Nothing remains except for some small arms and the battered remnants of other equipment, all of it battle-scarred and most of it fit for little more than salvage. The armed forces of Nicaragua must be entirely rebuilt, both its personnel and equipment...."[3]

By 1980, the tasks assigned to the armed forces were already taxing its physical and educational capacities. The nation-wide literacy campaign, for example, required from the army: military protection, transportation and supply coordination and members' participation as students and teachers. But the mobilized cadres

were also assigned to perform community service and emergency
production tasks in the industrial and agricultural sectors.
Meanwhile, from 1980 onward security needs greatly expanded. Border
raids had begun in 1980 and a larger threat appeared to loom for the
future; Argentinian military personnel were training some of the
3,000 ex-Guardia exiled in Honduras (e.g., FDN testimony in NYT,
3-30-85).

As duties thus proliferated, the FSLN formed the Sandinista
militia (MPS) in February, 1980 and put some volunteers on the
northern border alongside regular border patrol troops. Reservists
were called to take on more military duties. The growing need for
more sophistocated EPS training meant that in 1980 and into 1981 the
militia was allowed to grow; it took on the bulk of social duties
and played an ever larger role in irregular and border defense as
regular EPS troops were put into training for conventional or larger
military assaults. By February, 1981, for example, sixty-seven
Nicaraguan soldiers had died in cross-border attacks and the Frente
had announced its intent to expand the civilian militia. As the new
(Reagan) administration in Washington introduced its bipolar
assessment of events in Nicaragua and Salvador, Nicaraguan leaders
were re-evaluating military strategies and defense structures.

Popular Mobilization

Mobilizing its population for defense and providing at least
rudimentary organizational and weapons training became a central
feature of Nicaragua's defense establishment after 1980. Emphasis
on vigilance and citizen participation was renewed with each contra
campaign and as perceptions grew after 1981 that a US invasion was
imminent. In 1984 a campaign was begun in Nicaragua for handing out
guns to families or persons who lived in zones where contras were
active and who had organized for local defense. By 1986 nearly
300,000 rifles had been dispersed in this program as communities in
the war zones created their own first line of defense against the
contras. As veteran guerrilla commander Omar Cabezas pointed out in
1985, a war against Nicaragua would mean war not just against the
army, but against the Nicaraguan people who had mobilized for
national defense. Cabezas, reflecting the FSLN's defense strategy,
argued that the 300,000 figure should be multiplied six to eight
times to get an estimate of the force an invading army would face;
other family members, he argued, would in turn take up the rifle if
a loved one fell during battle.[4] The FSLN government, besides
depending on its trained military forces, was clearly relying on the
willingness of the Nicaraguan people to defend the revolution
against a much larger and stronger enemy. Based on its assessment
of the peoples' support for the revolution and for
self-determination, the FSLN promised Washington a Vietnam-style
quagmire should it launch an invasion.

The Militia. According to the FSLN, contra methods dictated a
popular defense strategy in Nicaragua. But popular mobilization for
"conquest" had also been the salient feature behind other major
revolutionary efforts, such as in the literacy, health, nutrition,
production and other campaigns after July, 1979. Since the
insurrection, moreover, popular familiarity with military practice

and high levels of politicization had contributed momentum for the
Frente's position that broad military preparedness was the only hope
for the revolution's survival in the face of US hostility. Arguing
that the people should defend themselves, the FSLN characterized the
army as the spearhead of defense and the militia as the spear. On
that philosophy, and unlike military practice elsewhere in Latin
America, the FSLN handed out guns to civilians and encouraged the
organization of local militias based on local needs or the presence
of critical economic infrastructure.

In 1980 militia membership was opened to any
volunteers--workers, women, children, students, older people--aged
16-60 who were willing to go through weekend drills, guard
infrastructure like factories and bridges or take turns doing
neighborhood night watch. Whereas the EPS was strictly controlled
by the FSLN, the MPS was open to anyone who wanted military training
or was willing to participate in defense-related activities at the
workplace or barrio levels. By 1982 and 1983, however, the need for
nationwide self-defense training increased along with contra attacks
on isolated villages, schools, coops and development projects. In a
short time the nature of the militia changed from marching clubs,
where elderly women or young boys waved sticks in the air, to more
highly trained combat battalions which served as back-up to regular
military forces. The first such voluntary combat battalion formed
in 1981 and initiated the practice of serving in defensive actions
for up to six months at a time. When a state of military emergency
was announced in March, 1982, 70,000 militia were mobilized for
building defensive barriers and training new members. The militia,
growing in direct response to counter-revolutionary threats from the
United States and the contras, was by 1982 taking up a larger
portion of the national budget than the government preferred (e.g.
Booth, 1982: 210).

Militia infantry battalions were initially formed from
volunteers who showed special aptitude during weekend militia
training. These volunteers were given several weeks of full-time
training and then awaited the call to active duty. As the regular
army trained for conventional warfare and resisted being lured away
from major installations, the militia in 1982 and 1983 carried a
large portion of the defense burden in the contra war. In the
absence of a military draft, the militia became a vital defense
force. And, the militia was taking heavy casualties due to contra
ambush methods and the milicianos' the poor training and weapons.
In early 1983, for example, militia troops outnumbered regular army
troops by five to one in the northern war zones and were being
commanded by EPS officers in those areas. The military strategy up
to this time had been: to reserve the regular army for larger-scale
defense operations by using the local militias for chasing guerrilla
bands; to maintain EPS strength at major military bases; and to
involve citizens in their own defense rather than leaving defense to
an isolated, professional army. In fact, as funerals for militia
volunteers became common in Managua and other urban areas in 1983,
popular awareness of and support for the war against the contras
grew (NYT, 4-10-83). The militias were serving an important
political function as well.

Although local militias were to continue in their original

mission as the "strategic base for the defense of the revolution," a re-evaluation of defense needs and structures led to their reorganization in 1983 in conjunction with the introduction of a military draft under the Patriotic Military Service law. The changes were a response to several factors. First, defense planners could no longer justify the heavy defense burden placed on the milicianos while the army remained in its barracks. As the contra war intensified, families of the militia volunteers were asking for more intensified training and better military back-up for the volunteers. Meanwhile, the high level of awareness about the war and its costs allowed for a step-up in military preparedness as well as a re-routing of energies and material to the war effort. Second, while military planners continued to believe that Washington might launch a direct invasion at any time, they began to see the contra offensive as a first step in the invasion process. In that case the United States might be holding off on a full assault to give the contras time to weaken FSLN structures. As contra attacks increased and were coordinated with more dramatic CIA bombing and sabotage, the EPS was increasingly sent into the field. A proportion of EPS and MPS soldiers were put into specialized training to serve as "irregular" forces which directly targetted the contras.

The militia was also reorganized in 1983 to meet intensified defense requirements. The emphasis was on preparing local volunteers to act as "the first ring of defense" in the cities, rural areas and factories.[5] Civil defense training in preparedness, construction of bomb shelters, first aid, fire-fighting, child care and the like aimed at integrating and implementating earlier militia planning. Residents were educated in guarding local infrastructure and were generally impressed with a responsibility to defend their own neighborhoods.

The armed militia was meanwhile reorganized into territorial battalions. These units operated with old rifles, machine guns, grenade launchers and light mortars. Mobilized in the regions in which they lived, these defense forces were generally highly motivated (e.g., King, 1984: 18). Smaller or less coordinated workplace militias were integrated and organized by geographical location into more effective fighting units. Militia preparation now involved training in defensive and offensive actions, column, squadron and company formations and periodic intensive training under seasoned EPS soldiers. Workshops provided instruction in making contact bombs or other homemade weapons found effective in the war against Somoza. Some militia units began receiving field training in battle zones in late 1984 (BI, 2-28-85).

In addition, agricultural cooperatives and independent farmers were given land and guns with which to defend it in a stepped up agrarian reform program in the war zones. These new land owners, who were now called both to produce food for consumption or export and to defend their land, proved to be highly motivated fighters. As Defense Minister Ortega challenged in 1983: "The counter-revolution will find the country 'mined' with better organized and better armed militia in specific places of the military theatre" (IHCA, October, 1983).

By 1985 the number of volunteers who had received some form of military training reached 250,000. These volunteers--35 percent of

them women--would use AKA rifles, rocket launchers and mortars in
the event of attack. With three to six weeks of rudimentary
training, some militia members were prepared to serve as light
infantry units if called to active service. Others continued to
serve in infantry reserve battalions which sought out and engaged
contra units. Now better trained and equipped, the militia was also
increasingly specialized into artillery, explosives, anti-aircraft
and telementry and computation units (BI, 7-25-85). These units
provided support to select army ("irregular") units, which after
1983, were specially trained in guerrilla warfare. In early 1985,
the number of militia mobilized in active infantry units were
estimated at 100,000 (King, 1985: 6). According to the Defense
Ministry, in some regions the militia represented 60 percent of
mobilized forces and had as their main function the protection of
rural communities.

Summing up the FSLN's view of the militia's importance to
Nicaragua's defense apparatus, Brigadier Commander Hugo Torres, head
of the political section of the EPS, characterized the MPS as "a
fundamental echelon in the current irregular battle against the
aggression, which will become the principle force in the peoples'
active resistance in the event of invasion" (BI, 2-28-85). As the
US campaign of low-intensity attrition intensified in 1983, the
Nicaraguan Defense Ministry came to rely heavily in its defense
planning on popular voluntarism as a critical supplement to its
armed forces.

Civil Defense. Instituted officially in 1981, Nicaragua's
civil defense program had its roots in civil defense committees that
were formed during 1978-1979 the insurrection period. While civil
defense volunteers were active principally in implementing
nutrition, vaccination, sanitation, emergency care or similar
campaigns after 1979, during 1981 and 1982 organizational emphases
began shifting toward military defense. Civil defense program
development paralleled that of the militia; as the MPS prepared to
assume the first line of local defense, civil defense training
increasingly focused on: protecting or administering to the
population in the event of attack; assuring basic services during
emergency or war times; and coordinating defensive activities with
EPS and MPS forces.

The most sophistocated civil defense system developed in
Managua, home to 30 percent of Nicaragua's population. Reacting to
invasion scares emanating from Washington, civil defense planners in
the capital prepared to respond to a rapid deployment war featuring
massive air raids and airborne troop assaults. Believing that
Managua--the hub of the revolution and the symbol of its
power--would be the main US target in an invasion, civil defense
plans aimed at coordinating popular action with EPS defensive
actions. Indeed, as civil defense training expanded in Managua
during and after 1984, volunteers were effectively paramilitary.
Though unarmed, volunteers were trained in first aid, disease
control, air-raid shelter construction, food and medicine
distribution and population control (CAHI, 12-3-84). Coordinated by
the EPS, civil defense was organized by barrio and at local,
regional and national levels. Government agencies and popular
organizations participated by providing training or the use of their

276

offices. For example, INSSBI, the Institute of Social Security, trained housewives in caring for the elderly, pregnant women and children. Others were trained in firefighting and burying the dead.

Civil defense involved whole communities and families in planning for war-time contingencies. For example, in one Managua neighborhood of 4000 residents, El Riguero, one-half were in the militia, two-thirds were active in civil defense preparation and eighty-four bomb shelters had been build by the end of 1984. Reenforcing a sense of urgency, a full alert for the EPS and national civil defense was issued in response to the US-created "MIG Crisis" of November, 1984. While the T-55 tanks that had been stationed around Managua were withdrawn two weeks after the alert, the civil defense campaign continued and involved most large population centers in Nicaragua. By the mid-1980s, a majority of Nicaraguans had some training in survival skills. A good proportion of the civilian population had additional instruction in sabotage, insurrection methods or weapons handling (e.g., BI, 7-4-85). The voluntarism exhibited in these campaigns--whether it reflected depth of ideological conviction or simple nationalism--suggested that the cost of attempting to topple the FSLN government would be higher than that estimated by calculations based only on neutralizing Nicaraguan military targets.


MILITARY BUILD-UP: 1981 AND BEYOND

While establishing adequate security was a priority concern, the new leaders initially laid plans for committing the bulk of national energies to reconstruction and social programs. The process of building a structured defense force and standardizing its weapons was begun in 1979. That it was conceived as a longer-term project was clear both from the armed services' first missions--social and reconstruction tasks--and from the low levels of new arms acquisitions in the first two years of the revolution. External threats posed by irregular armed attacks and hostile rhetoric in 1980 and 1981, however, spurred a defensive reaction in Nicaragua. Wary of a shift in US policy away from Carter's careful tolerance to US support for counter-revolutionary activities, the FSLN re-emphasized international solidarity and popular mobilization as critical means for the defense of the revolution. After 1980, the Reagan Administration's language of urgency and crises in Central America, together with its escalating involvement in destabilization efforts, sparked an escalation in Nicaraguan military preparedness that continued through the mid-1980s.

Assessing the External Threat.

In the first year and a half of the revolution the FSLN government pursued security through international activism: increasing Nicaragua's diplomatic contacts; joining the Non-Aligned Movement and other Third World groups; and approaching a wide variety of governments, including the United States and the Soviet Union, with requests for economic and military aid, credits and loans. High level officials visited Europe, the United States and

Latin America. In March, 1980, after the US Congress had frozen foreign aid appropriations which included a proposed $75 million aid package for Nicaragua, Nicaraguan officials made a first visit to the Soviet Union, a move viewed with much scepticism in Washington. In Moscow, Defense Minister Ortega, Planning Minister Ruiz and others met with technical experts, party officials and military representatives in efforts to assess the Soviet's disposition toward aiding Nicaragua. According to Agriculture Minister Jaime Wheelock, the trip was an effort to "feel out" what help Nicaragua could get for it "strategic development"--defined in economic and security terms--then and in the future (FBIS-LAM, 12-23-80; 12-30-80). Rebuffed by the Soviets on requests for economic aid, the Nicaraguans' major achievement consisted of eight scientific and cultural trade agreements. Military aid was undoubtedly explored, though no heavy Soviet weapons were approved for Nicaragua until mid-1981.

In early 1981, the Defense Ministry anticipated wider contra attacks and the possibility that the Somocistas would get support from the United States and others fearful of Nicaragua's revolution. In March, press reports in the United States revealed that Nicaraguan and Cuban exiles were training in both Honduran and US camps with the expressed purpose of overthrowing the FSLN government. Apparent US complicity and administration posturing about Nicaragua worried the Frente. Shortly thereafter, the year-old militia was expanded, army recruits (pre-draft) began receiving more rigorous military training and the Nicaraguans imported their first heavy weapons: Soviet-made, World War II-vintage T-54 and T-55 tanks. Prior to this time, according to the US Defense Department, Nicaragua had been acquiring only light artillery and small arms. The US cancellation of its wheat credits and other aid to Nicaragua in early 1981 were cited by Daniel Ortega when he was asked about this first significant shipment of Soviet military aid (NYT, 5-9-81).

By the end of 1981, security threats had become a major concern; defense became the FSLN's priority. Not only was US Secretary of State Haig speaking publically about military contingency plans against Nicaragua ("not ruling out" a naval blockade in the near future), but contra insurgents had taken Bluefields (on the Atlantic Coast) for a day and reports of CIA coordination with the contras had begun circulating. In the Atlantic Coast region armed opposition to the Sandinistas was being organized and encouraged by CIA operatives among Miskito Indians. Ex-CIA agent Agee, moreover, warned that a step-up in CIA subversion usually preceded a direct invasion (FBIS-LAM, 12-1-81). In November, the Junta sent Defense Minister Ortega to the Soviet Union to discuss military aid with three top Soviet military heads, Ustinov, Ogarkov and Yepishev.

The FSLN's earlier fears of US preparations for a wider military move appeared to be confirmed by events in December. Tensions were heightened when a Costa Rican newspaper quoted a Nicaraguan "defector" who charged that Cuban MIG 21 fighter planes were in Nicaragua at a secret airstrip--a report which proved untrue. Around the same time the CIA launched the "Red Christmas" operation and other attacks in northeastern Nicaragua (e.g.,

FBIS-LAM, 12-7-81; 12-29-81). The FSLN began calling on all Nicaraguans to be prepared to defend themselves against imperialism: Bayardo Arce called on a Sandinista Youth Assembly to study with their rifles nearby; popular and union organizations called for national unity and preparedness in every field; and Interior Minister Borge promised that the contra attacks which were killing Nicaraguans would not go unpunished (FBIS-LAM, 12-22-81; 12-23-81; 12-29-81). Sandinista officials warned that a state of emergency would become necessary if attacks continued. In the international arena that month: Foreign Minister D'Escoto acknowledged that Nicaraguan pilots were training in Bulgaria and he later visited Soviet Foreign Minister Gromyko in Moscow; the Nicaraguan government sent official protest notes to Honduras over contra attacks from that country; Junta leader Daniel Ortega called for open and improved relations with Washington; and National Directorate member Jaime Wheelock called for a mediated settlement of disputes along the lines being proposed by France and Mexico.

As Reagan Administration charges against Nicaragua were levelled with increased intensity from 1982 onward, the Frente also broadened its diplomatic activism and its military preparedness at home. Using the expansion of Nicaragua's militia and its importation of tanks and trucks from the Eastern bloc as evidence, the US State Department in early 1982 began a campaign labelling Nicaragua militarist and Soviet-aligned. Meanwhile, the US contra operation and US military activity in the region were steadily expanding. Inside Nicaragua, internal security was tightened by a March, 1982 imposition of a State of Emergency. Under that act, constitutional guarantees were suspended and press censorship was imposed in the name of national security. While FSLN officials, including Ramirez and Wheelock, addressed US claims point by point, Nicaragua also brought charges of US aggression to the UN--something Nicaragua was to do many times in the following years. At the same time the FSLN continued its drive for international solidarity by increasing contacts in Western Europe, among US allies and in the Third World. In May, 1982, and as Washington was being more-or-less successful in applying pressure on Western and Third World allies not to sell weapons to the Nicaraguans, Daniel Ortega travelled to the Soviet Union to sign economic agreements, discuss regional events and consolidate fraternal ties with the Soviets. As tension mounted between the United States and Nicaragua, by mid-1982 many in Nicaragua feared that the United States was about to spark a Gulf of Tonkin situation in Nicaraguan waters or provoke a border dispute with Honduras and follow up with an invasion. The fact that the Reagan Administration had rejected Mexican and UN initiatives for peaceful settlement that year convinced many Nicaraguan policy makers that US intent was nothing less than the destruction of the revolution. In that context, the FSLN justified its arms acquisitions as well as it purchases from the Eastern bloc as the right of a sovereign state to defend itself.

## Military Reorganization

Shaken by new wide-scale contra attacks in the north, the start-up of the ARDE contra campaign in the south, the apparent relentlessness of the United States in isolating Nicaragua and the accumulating economic and human losses accruing from contra incursions, the FSLN in 1983 reorganized and strengthened its armed forces. It also greatly increased its arms acquisitions, though Sandinista forces hardly constituted an aggressive offensive force. In 1983 the EPS was organized into:  twelve multi-objective, motorized infantry battalions; two or three armored brigades, equipped with about fifty aged tanks and thirty to sixty used PT 76 amphibious tanks and armored personnel carriers; and several field artillery and anti-aircraft battalions, armed with older Soviet guns and supported by rocket launchers and heavy mortar companies (King, 1984: 18). The air force and navy remained small, antiquated and ill-equipped. The military defense of Nicaragua thus rested primarily on the infantry-heavy EPS and variously trained militia units.

To no small extent, it was the contras' strategy and tactics-- i.e., low-intensity, attrition warfare aimed at undermining Nicaraguan's faith in the FSLN government--that guided the military reorganization in 1983 and beyond. The contras, in small-group cross-border raids from Honduras and Costa Rica, attacked civilians and civilian and military outposts, committed sabotage acts against economic infrastructure and violated Nicaraguan airspace in reconnaissance and re-supply missions. Between 1981 and 1983, the Nicaraguans documented in a report to the UN 400 ground attacks from Honduras, 34 occasions when the US Navy entered Nicaraguan waters and similar violations by Honduran and Costa Rican craft on 24 and 31 occasions, respectively (Goldblatt and Millan, 1984: 534).[6] Such events led Defense Minister Ortega to call on the international community to help Nicaragua assemble the military means to defend its coasts and airspace.

Another important factor shaping FSLN thinking in 1983 was the realization that its territorial defense was up to Nicaragua itself; the Soviets and the Cubans had made it clear to the Frente that though they could provide aid and political solidarity, they would not or could not (Cuba) come to Nicaragua's aid in the case of a US invasion. Nicaraguan defense would ultimately depend on its building an international consensus against US policy, and, on preparing Nicaragua for a major assault and prolonged attrition warfare against the occupying force in the aftermath. Yet, rather than saving the EPS for responding to such an assault, in 1983 the FSLN began shifting tactics from a militia-based defense against the contras to regular army involvement. The FSLN began rotating large battalions among villages to support local militias and assigning crack army units (irregular warfare specialists) to the war fronts.

In addition to reorganizing the militia into territorial battalions, in 1983 Nicaragua introduced its first military draft. The draft was designed to address a continuing problem for the EPS, the low levels of education and training among most recruits. It was to allow a consolidation and strengthening of the army by obliging young men to register and be trained for two years of active service when called.[7] Although implementing the draft incurred political and social costs for the FSLN -- the political opposition cited it as an attempt to integrate all social sectors into the FSLN (LAWR, 9-9-83), some draft evasion occurred in all parts of Nicaragua (e.g., <u>NYT</u>, 6-26-84), and several public protests erupted over the law--by 1985 the military rewards of better organized, trained and educated recruits replacing pre-draft reserve battalions and volunteers were being reaped in the war against the contras (CAHI, 11-22-85).[8] Militia battalions were relieved of the primary defense burden in the war against the contras.

The Sandinistas sought now to institutionalize a military organization which allowed for participation at different levels and which took account of regional defense needs and economic or military capacities. Popular mobilization and preparedness among all citizens remained an important aspect of national defense. But now greater emphasis was placed on specialization, decentralization and local responsibility for the defense of strategic targets. In rural villages and agricultural cooperatives, campesinos were organized for self-defense. In October, 1983, for instance, Commander Carrion announced that thousands of AK-47 rifles had been handed out to militia members in the Jinotega area where a year earlier the contras had met little armed resistance when they attacked. As defense was organized in these areas, local militias would take over secondary defense as regular army troops moved to new locations. Local peasant militias took on duties in hunting down and routing the contras in their locales (<u>LAWR</u>, 10-7-83). Within the EPS, irregular fighting battalions were given special training for combatting and pursuing the contras, while regular (non-draft) army recruits were stationed along the border with Honduras and at strategic posts. When the military situation demanded it, as in October and November, 1983, EPS and MPS reserve infantry battalions were mobilized to fight alongside both regular and irregular army units (IHCA, October, 1983).

In 1983 and through 1985, however, improvements in combat readiness and performance were limited by the lack of professionally trained and experienced officer cadres, the lack of field and long-range communication equipment and overlaps in jurisdiction among the various active military units. FSLN guerrilla veterans trained junior officers and non-commissioned officers. Required to remain in active duty, this leadership cadre directed the armed forces against the contras who had logistical and intelligence assistance from the CIA and the Honduran army. Compared to the armies in Salvador and Honduras, the young Sandinista army lacked experience in command and control, was dependent on not-yet-standardized (and many outdated) weapons and had yet to develop a high level of military coordination. Nevertheless, the armed Nicaraguan units were now more than a match for the contras when they met in combat. In addition, popular mobilization and national vigilance campaigns denied the contras success in establishing popular support or an underground communications and supply system so crucial to guerrilla armies. While the Defense Ministry was determined to resist letting forces be drawn into a major clash with the Honduran army, Nicaraguan forces in late 1983 destroyed a major contra base in Jinotega and disallowed the taking of territory. The EPS also introduced the use of its surface-to-air missiles (SAMS) in October, downing a US-registered DC-3 from Honduras just ninety miles from Managua (<u>LAWR</u>, 11-25-83).

Nicaraguan diplomatic and political moves in 1983 also focused

on defense and defusing military-security issues between Nicaragua
and the United States and Honduras.  In May, FSLN political
coordinator Bayardo Arce responded to President Reagan's fiery April
speech to Congress (on the security threat posed by Nicaragua) by
proposing negotiations, an end to the US contra program and the
signing of peace treaties between Nicaragua and its neighbors. Arce
also asserted Nicaragua's right to seek defensive weapons from any
nation, while he denied that Nicaragua would allow USSR missile
installations there.  In late 1983 Nicaragua presented an amnesty
for contra fighters and offered to stop buying arms and to send home
its foreign advisors if its neighbors did likewise.  For its part,
in the last months of 1983 the United States invaded Grenada,
re-invigorated CONDECA, stepped up arms shipments to allies and
increased its hostile rhetoric vis-a-vis Nicaragua.  Conciliatory
gestures were ignored.  The nature or depth of Nicaragua's
committment to a regional peace settlement, thus, was not tested.

## Defense Replaces Reconstruction

Rather than simply maintaining its state of military
preparedness in 1984, Nicaragua continued to brace itself for a US
military move.  This meant both the continued strengthening of its
armed forces in a context of popular mobilization and the
importation of more weapons to increase, for example, Nicaragua's
air defense systems.  In dollar terms, the Nicaraguans increased
arms purchases (by some accounts spending almost double the 1983
amount in 1984) acquiring more Soviet-made tanks, helicopters and
anti-aircraft guns.

For the contras and the CIA, on the other hand, 1984 was
probably their most successful year--i.e., in terms of the damage
done to Nicaragua's infrastructure.  The CIA's mining of Nicaragua's
harbors, its aerial bombings and increased hit-and-run attacks from
Honduras and Costa Rica exacted a large toll on Nicaragua's economy
and productive capacity.  The Sandinistas in turn, rushed to
consolidate the military reorganization of 1983.  In the economic
realm the Frente began shifting to a war economy.  Yet the armed
forces remained defensive and geared to counter the contras.
Deployment and training in 1984 was defensive in nature; regional
EPS units did not display a high degree of wartime preparedness;
supply stock-piles were scattered around the zones of heaviest
fighting; and the EPS was spread out in guerrilla formations (King,
1984: 18-19).  Logistics remained a problem for the armed forces;
the EPS spent a large amount of time seeking out provisions.
Confirming these observations, FDN (contra) leader Calero reported
in November, 1984 that his troops saw little evidence in the field
of the major USSR arms build-up the Reagan Administration claimed
was taking place in Nicaragua (NYT, 11-22-84).  Lt. Col. King
(US-ret.), one of the few Americans who spent time in the field with
Sandinista forces, noted the high morale and confidence among troops
and officers and their in-depth talk about waging guerrilla warfare
against US forces should they invade Nicaragua.  Both the EPS and
the MPS had absorbed the FSLN's short-term defense strategy:  to
rout the contras while preparing for attrition warfare against an
invader.

Several political-military offensives against the contras were initiated by the FSLN in 1984 as a prelude to what would be a major offensive in 1985. In June, the Defense Ministry sent 2,000 EPS troops armed with heavy artillery to attack ARDE rebel camps and columns along the Rio San Juan. The campaign was effective in pushing ARDE back and demoralizing its forces. In the north-central region of Matagalpa, meanwhile, Commander Wheelock worked full-time wooing local support in areas under contra attack (LAWR, 6-22-84). Together with the armed forces' defensive posture, these coordinated efforts effectively kept the northern-(Honduran) and southern-(Costa Rican) based contras from seizing territory or joining forces inside Nicaragua, a situation which could have created a military line disecting Nicaragua. By the end of 1984 Defense Minister Ortega reported that there had been 1,500 armed encounters between FSLN forces and the contras that year; 3,000 contras had died and 1,000 had been wounded and captured (BI, 1-10-85).

The 1985 Anti-Contra Offensive. While through the mid-1980s the contras did not pose a strategic menace to the revolution, contra sabotage attacks were disrupting socioeconomic development plans and thus the course of the revolution. In early 1985, Defense Minister Ortega announced a major, year-long offensive to deal the contras a "strategic blow" and rout them from Nicaragua. Made possible by the 1983 military reorganization and the military draft which were beginning to yield new capacity in the field, the FSLN military campaign of 1985 also demonstrated the extent to which Nicaragua's defense apparatus and institutions were shaped by and geared for addressing the contra threat. As EPS Chief of Staff, Joaquim Cuadra, noted in an October 1985 "60 Minutes" interview, the FSLN had taken advantage of "the US's war" as a "laboratory" and "testground" to make Nicaragua stronger. President Ortega also shed light on FSLN strategy when he said in March and in October that he hoped an FSLN military victory over the contras in 1985 would not only force Washington to the negotiating table, but would also allow Nicaragua to negotiate peace with dignity (IHCA, March, 1985; NYT, 10-21-85). By 1985 the stabilization of the territorial militias and their active coordination with the EPS's anti-contra-oriented irregular infantry battalians and border guards allowed the EPS greater military initiative. It also acquired greater control over inacessible areas where contra regional commands had been located. Improved militia training, organization and weaponry allowed the EPS's crack units to concentrate their efforts in Military Region 6 where contras had been most active. Meanwhile, in Region 1, for example, defense rested almost entirely on militia forces (see Figure 6.2). By August, the Defense Ministry claimed that because of such shifts in duties among FSLN armed units, 90 percent of all confrontations with the contras ended in the Sandinistas' favor (IHCA, August, 1985).

To support the 1985 military campaign, the Defense Ministry initiated its fourth and fifth draft call-ups and required men 25 to 30 years of age to register for reserve service. Trained in short courses and given experience in combat zones, these men were used to fill out Nicaragua's infantry battalions as part of the strategy of inflicting long-term damage on the contras (BI, 2-21-85). From early 1982 to mid-1985, EPS forces increased from 25,000 to 40,000 and were supported by 20,000 active-duty militia. The EPS also moved heavy artillery to the north central combat zones and permanently stationed highly trained combat brigades there. These forces' mission was to push the contras back into Honduras and break up the contras' early 1985 "generalized offensive" in Matagalpa and Jinotega. A related FSLN effort involved specially- trained border patrol battalions and planting a portion of the Nicaragua-Honduras border with land mines. This concentrated effort in the northern zones of heaviest fighting resulted by May in the retreat of about 90 percent of the contras back into Honduras for resupply and regrouping. The contras also moved their camps deeper inside Honduras (NYT, 5-19-85).

Nor were new contra incursions later in the year successful at meeting the objective of taking over important northern towns. From August to September, 1985 FSLN forces disarticulated two main contra campaigns inside Nicaragua, again chased the contra over the border into Honduras and followed up with cross-border bombardments and Sandinista patrols of the poorly marked border area. However, the FSLN's determination to push the contras back from the border frontier, and, the Honduran army's practice of providing covering-fire to retreating or attacking contra forces led to border clashes involving the Honduran army and air force. These clashes, the largest ones in May and September, led to the downing of Honduran and Nicaraguan support helicopters, FSLN saturation shelling of suspected contra camps just inside Honduras and the removal of Honduran peasants from these zones. (Nicaraguans living near border areas had been evacuated in 1983.) Defending its moves as inevitable so long as Honduras provided sanctuary to the contras, the Nicaraguan Defense Ministry promised a continued border presence and strikes against border sanctuaries (NYT, 6-4-85).

EPS tactics also represented the FSLN's decision by early 1985 to begin shooting at unmarked supply aircraft -- so important to the contra effort. Up to that time, the EPS had been under orders not to down these aircraft, some of which were on reconnaissance missions, for fear of creating greater tensions with the United States and Honduras. But the fact that so many of the overflights represented supplies for contra units inside Nicaragua led the FSLN to use its anti-aircraft rockets against planes violating its airspace. In April, 1985 Humberto Ortega reasserted the Sandinistas' intention of improving its rapid-interception, anti-air defense force as part of Nicaragua's anti-contra defense. He alluded to the acquisition of aircraft with air-to-air interception capacity, a possibility which worried officials in Washington (BI, 4-25-85). The FSLN pointed out that supply planes from Honduras were allowing the contras to carry on campaigns deep inside Nicaragua.

US officials, meanwhile, were calculating that Nicaragua's offensive would lead it to blunder or miscalculate and to move too aggressively in Honduran territory. The United States repeated warnings in 1985 and 1986 that it would come to Honduras' aid if it was attacked. Honduran officials, fearing a widening of the border incidents and somewhat embarrassed both by their role in the contra attacks and their inability to control contra moves, were hesitant to react against the FSLN's hot pursuit and cross-border shelling tactics. Nevertheless, encouraged by the Reagan Administration to react firmly, in September (1985) six Honduran fighter jets attacked Nicaraguan military positions (inside Nicaragua), shot down a Nicaraguan helicopter and recalled its ambassador to Nicaragua (ICAS, October, 1985). In reaction, President Ortega protested Honduras' complicity with the contras, charged the Honduran government with supporting a recent attack by 800 contras and called for a meeting with Honduran President Suazo Cordova. The meeting proposal was rejected by Honduras and the United States (NYT, 9-13-85; 9-15-85). Reflecting US attitudes, the Honduran president responded to Ortega's proposal for discussions saying it "...would only serve propagandistic purposes" (COHA, 9-24-85).

In late May the EPS had begun a similar rout-the-contras campaign in the south. Named "Operation Sovereignty", the campaign aimed at pushing ARDE and small contra groups over the Rio San Juan into Costa Rica and destroying ARDE bases in Nicaragua. By early August, the FPS had taken over ARDE's last supply and air bases in Nicaragua--at La Penca and Saripiqui--and thus had effectively cut the southern contras' supply lines to Bluefields and Nueva Guinea in Zelaya as well (IHCA, July, 1985; August, 1985).[10]

In coordination with EPS strategic defense moves in the primary areas of contra activities in 1985, in March the government announced plans for the forced evacuation of peasants and small farmers into resettlement villages. By the end of 1985, about 50,000 Nicaraguans in north central and southern war zones had been moved into new villages where the government provided protection and social services. Although President Ortega emphasized that the program was designed to address the defense and welfare needs of already displaced farm families, and, that people were moving on their own to more secure areas, the FSLN had other intentions as well. At least three military-defense objectives were being pursued by the relocation program during the 1985 military campaign against the contras: 1)the movement of peasants to more secure areas would deny the contras local support, material and intelligence; 2)the relocations gave the armed forces a free-fire zone where they could operate freely against the contras and, for example, use aerial bombardment without hurting civilians; and 3)in areas where peasants were resettled in protected (coffee or other) export-production coops, production could continue and vital lands were denied to the contras.

Together with the continuing campaign to hand out rifles to peasants and to organize local self-defense militias, these military campaigns put the contras into strategic decline during 1985. Not only were contra fighters outfought by apparently highly motivated EPS and militia forces, but the contras proved logistically weak and unable to counter the EPS's heavy artillery. According to US Embassy sources, moreover, the Sandinistas by 1985 had the contras deeply penetrated with intelligence agents. With the introduction into combat of the Nicaraguan's sophistocated Mi-24 Hind helicopters in August, intelligence on rebel locations could be acted upon quickly; flying at a maximum cruise speed of 183 miles per hour (199 m/h attack speed), the Hind aircraft would be dispatched to bombard rebel bands (author interviews; NYT, 10-27-85).[11] The aircraft made an impact on the war in 1985. FDN contra leader Calero testified to the effectiveness of the Sandinistas' (eight to twelve) Hind helicopters in October: the contras could no longer move across open territory and had to adopt new strategies. US officials confirmed that the contras were at an "economic disadvantage" because of the aircraft (NYT, 12-6-85). Nicaraguan sources also noted the helicopters' effectiveness in convincing rural peasants that the FSLN government would defeat the contras; peasants who before only heard far-off artillery fire now saw visible signs of FSLN strength. In some areas, this led to contra sympathizers turning in their weapons to the EPS under the FSLN's continuing amnesty offer (e.g., IHCA, September, 1985).

In response, the contras were gearing up for heavy fighting in 1986 and were acquiring anti-aircraft weapons. In late 1985 the FDN -- in a Soldier of Fortune magazine ad -- offered $1 million to any Sandinista pilot who would fly a Hind helicopter out of Nicaragua. And in December, the contras successfully employed a SAM in downing an FSLN helicopter--an event which sparked public glee in Washington. Yet, along with Congressional restrictions on the level and nature of US aid to the contras, the EPS campaign in 1985 put the contras in the position, according to the political head of the Sandinista army, Commander Hugo Torres, of "...trying desperately not to die as a political and military option" (IHCA, August, 1985). At the same time FSLN leaders believed it was probable that regrouped and newly supplied contras would pose a military threat again in 1986. In Washington and in Managua US officials were openly predicting that renewed US financial backing for the contras in addition to private funding would mean heavy fighting and contra successes in 1986. Citing in late 1985 what it said was an increase in the Cuban role in the FSLN armed forces, the Reagan Administration also began a new campaign to win new military (i.e., lethal) aid for the contras from Congress in 1986. UNO leader Arturo Cruz, meanwhile, predicted that 1986 would be the determinative year for the FSLN; speaking in November, Cruz implied that if the FSLN was still in power by the end of 1986, the contra war would have to be replaced by other US moves, presumably a direct invasion or a political solution. By mid-1986, however, contra leadership squabbling, supply problems, and corruption contributed to a stalled contra effort. President Reagan and contra officials extended their timeframe for a contra victory (or, an FSLN capitulation) into 1987 and 1988.

## Internal Security

On a related battle front, in 1985 the Interior Ministry stepped up intelligence work with the purpose of uprooting any contra- or CIA-inspired internal front. FSLN intelligence reported several uncovered CIA plans to discredit their government or to create opposition political cells or networks inside Nicaragua. As politics became increasingly polarized after the 1984 November elections, the Sandinistas became more suspicious of their oppositions' activities. In July and October the FSLN reported that it had broken up at least seven FDN-related "political cells" in the Western departments, including the Managua area, had confiscated hundreds of pounds of plastic explosives traced to the CIA, and had captured FDN operatives who planned to commit sabotage and bombing in the capital and other large cities (BI, 7-25-85; NYT, 10-19-85).

To undergird what it saw as the imminence of a strategic victory over US-supported rebels, in October the Frente announced widening of curbs on civil liberties. The 1982 State of Emergency was extended and broadened. According to President Ortega, such curbs were necessary to keep "desperate" US-aligned and US intelligence groups from aiding contra efforts or from regrouping when the contras were on the verge of being eliminated (NYT, 10-18-85; 10-21-85). The right curbs thus were presented as another aspect of the Frente's war against US efforts to undermine its rule. Yet they also reflected the Frente's fears that continued economic decline left Nicaraguans increasingly vulnerable to overtures from anti-Sandinista elements. Although the announcement of the curbs was not accompanied by a sweeping crackdown and opposition groups continued to meet and even issue denouncements of FSLN policy, the FSLN government clearly was expecting that Reagan ideologues would soon react to contra military failures. Willing to accept the political costs of negative world opinion, President Ortega argued that failure to curb opposition activity might prolong the war. As the FSLN saw US intentions, the Reagan Administration would rebuild the contras and was already planning new offensives in the north. Interior Minister Borge characterized the move as a display of the FSLN's will to halt US destabilization and to warn the internal opposition against turning political criticisms into anti-system activities--moves the US Embassy was encouraging among Nicaraguan political parties during the November, 1984 election period.


ARMS, SOURCES AND THE QUESTION OF ALIGNMENT

The Sandinistas' determination to reduce US influence over Nicaragua, to diversify its dependence and to renounce membership in military pacts meant that the historic military relationship between the United States and Nicaragua would be changed. The Frente's stance, however, did not necessarily consign Nicaragua to military dependence on the Soviet Union and its allies; many Latin American states had similarly been working to reduce their dependence on the United States' military establishment and had broadened military contacts in the preceding decade. But the early US reluctance to support the revolutionary government in Nicaragua and its direct efforts after 1980 to isolate and destabilize it made weapons acquisition and broadening military ties problemmatic for the FSLN. By influencing Western or friendly states not to sell arms to Nicaragua, while simultaneously increasing pressure on the FSLN, Washington ensured Nicaraguan military linkages to the USSR. The Reagan Administration fed its own predictions that Nicaragua was becoming a "Soviet proxy force."

In the Reagan State Department view, Nicaragua had quickly moved into the communist and Soviet camps and was serving as the Soviet's proxy force in supporting regional sabotage, terrorism and the spread of communism. US officials publically interpreted Nicaragua's weapons shipments from the Eastern bloc as offensive in nature and excessive given Nicaragua's defense needs. According to

President Reagan, the Sandinistas were building a "...war machine that dwarfs the forces of all their neighbors combined." Other officials, including Vice President Bush, insisted that the FSLN had "extraterritorial ambitions" and was "rushing pell-mell" towards an arms build-up even prior to the start-up of US support for the contras (e.g., NYT, 3-17-85). Nor was the "Nicaraguan threat" limited to the Central American region in the administration's public posturing.[12] Dating from President Reagan's April, 1983 speech, Nicaragua was presented publically as a direct security threat to the United States and its Western alliances. US officials argued that a Nicaragua with long-range jet fighter planes, or, which allowed Soviet bases or submarine pens would threaten: the Panama Canal; the 45 percent of US trade that entered through Gulf of Mexico ports; the 55 percent of US crude oil imports which passed through the Caribbean; US resupply lines to European allies during any West European-Soviet conflict; US sea lanes of communication (SLOCs), and the like.[13] That Nicaragua by mid-1986 had neither obtained sophisticated jet fighters nor conceded territory for USSR military installations did not dampen US rhetoric.

In the Nicaraguan view, Nicaragua's sovereignty and military threats from the United States justified its military links and its military build-up. Although the FSLN maintained that its foreign policy stance was non-alignment, and, that Nicaragua would join no military pact nor allow foreign bases on its soil, Defense Minister Ortega and others also continued to assert Nicaragua's right to obtain jet fighter planes if its defense so required. The issue of fighter jets soon came to symbolize concerns on both sides regarding the others' aggressive intent. For their part, Nicaraguan officials focused more on the immediacy of defense requirements and preparedness than they did on possible long-term implications of an Eastern bloc-dependent military. On the diplomatic-political front, Nicaraguan officials worked with determination to balance international ties. That foreign policy stance characterized Nicaragua's broadly conceived defense strategy.

## The Early Years

Given the diverse array and low quality of weapons in the FSLN's arsenal, a first order of defense business was to obtain military hardware and training -- at low or no cost. In the first months, the FSLN decided to approach the United States and other major arms suppliers even while it welcomed technical and military advisors from Cuba. FSLN officials Pastora, Borge and D'Escoto talked to US officials about military aid in August 1979, reporting to the media that both nations wanted to forget the past. Yet, some tension accompanied these meetings. D'Escoto, for example, cautioned that the United States should keep a low profile when making suggestions to Nicaragua--clearly a reference to the history of US-Nicaraguan relations. Pastora, in an apparently unauthorized statement, warned that Nicaragua would go to the socialist states if Washington did not give military aid. Pastora's superior at the Interior Ministry, Tomas Borge, immediately clarified Nicaragua's position, when he responded the next day that Nicaragua preferred US aid but would seek arms from all states, save Israel and Chile.

While not ruling out purchases from communist states, Borge left the impression that these would be approached as a last resort, specifically to avoid a "pretext to feelings that we are aligning ourselves with them politically." If both East and West denied Nicaragua arms, Borge said, the Nicaraguans would defend themselves with arrows (NYT, 8-12-79; 8-13-79; WP, 8-12-79). Arms aid was raised again in September when Daniel Ortega, Sergio Ramirez and Moises Hassan visited Washington and talked to President Carter.

US critics of the revolution, however, raised strong opposition to arming the FSLN. First, many believed the FSLN was Marxist-Leninist and would soon show its true totalitarian colors. This group saw the Sandinista requests as merely baiting the United States before they turned to the Soviets, their real choice for such aid. Others argued, contrary to official Pentagon reports, that the FSLN had enough arms, or, that the Frente would transship weapons to the FMLN or other regional popular movements. Newly concerned about US influence in the Third World, i.e., given the recent overthrow of the Shah in Iran, the Panama Canal Treaties and Cuban activism in Africa, these voices prevailed in the brief debate about arms aid to Nicaragua. In the fall of 1979 the United States offered Nicaragua: $3,000 for binoculars and compasses; $20,000 to fund the visit of a small team of FSLN army officers to US military bases; and FSLN army officer training at Fort Gulick, Panama--where Somoza's Guardia had been trained. The latter offer amounted to a somewhat cynical Carter Administration "good faith test" of the FSLN's requests for aid. It was an offer the Frente immediately turned down on moral and political grounds.[14] Nicaraguan leaders simultaneously increased their efforts to obtain aid elsewhere, although again in late 1980 the FSLN approached Washington for aid, this time presenting a lengthy document detailing spare parts it wished to obtain.[15]

Other governments, too, proved reluctant to provide military aid to the FSLN in the first years of the revolution, awaiting evidence of the new regime's political and economic credit-worthiness. In September, 1979 Foreign Minister Bernardino Larios came home empty-handed from an arms purchase mission to Belgium, West Germany, Spain, Mexico and Brazil.

Complicating the FSLN's problem was its economic situation, US pressure on allied states not to sell arms to Nicaragua and the presence of Cuban advisors in Nicaragua's developing armed forces system. First, because the promise of the revolution involved bringing socioeconomic benefits to Nicaraguan citizens, the Frente was determined in 1979 not to divert resources for the purpose of military development. In fact, in its first forays abroad, FSLN officials sought arms donations and gifts or easy-credit sales; Nicaragua was not prepared to pay market rates. Second, besides refusing to provide Nicaragua large amounts of aid or sophisticated and lethal weaponry, the United States, especially under the Reagan Administration, also dissuaded other states from doing so. The most clear example of US pressure and of its ability to establish limits on Nicaraguan moves involved the French arms sale to Nicaragua in December, 1981 worth $15.8 million. The sale included the future transfer of two patrol boats, two Alouette helicopters, several dozen lorries, about one hundred rocket launchers (with 7,000 rocket rounds) and training for ten naval officers and ten pilots. The sale was the largest aid package acquired by the Frente up to that time (LAWR, 1-3-82; NYT, 1-8-82; 1-9-82). Although the French characterized the weapons sale as one adding only to Nicaragua's defense, and, as an effort to keep Nicaragua non-aligned, US Secretary of State Haig publically characterized the sale as a "stab in the back." Others in the United States credited the French with doing the Soviets' job and helping Nicaragua export revolution. Likewise, some officials in Spain and Mexico criticized the sale as extra-continental meddling and a contributing factor to military tensions in Central America. Ultimately, the Mitterand government informed Washington that it would delay the sale. Despite its history of defiance toward US foreign policy, its activist stance vis-a-vis Third World politics and its status as the Third World's third largest arms supplier, France capitulated to US pressure and withdrew as a potential FSLN source for future military aid (Mathews, 1985; 29).

Similarly, a combination of US pressure, the leftist nature of the FSLN revolution and Western European unwillingness to get drawn into a military conflict in the Western Hemisphere kept Thatcher's United Kingdom, Schmitt's (and later Kohl's) West Germany and several Italian governments from selling arms to the Sandinistas. With US-Western Europe relations already strained by Ronald Reagan's tough anti-Soviet and military build-up stances, by US pressures on Europe to assume greater responsibility for the West's nuclear defense, and by cross-Atlantic economic competition, the European allies did not want to oversee a further deterioration in relations with the United States.

A country with greater latitude from the United States, Cuba represented to the FSLN a Latin American country which had successfully tackled US imperialism and historic domination and gone on to build a modern army in the context of a social revolution. Indicating that it did not want similarly to come to rely on the Soviet bloc for military equipment, the Sandinistas nevertheless hoped to use Cuban advisors (in addition to Western advisors) to organize its armed forces from variously-experienced FSLN guerrilla columns. As I noted earlier, the Frente was all too aware of potential ramifications of an army not loyal to the revolution and its leaders; in a period of widespread social and economic transformation and given the presence of domestic and international anti- or counter-revolutionaries, a loyal army was a necessity. Its revolutionary stance thus also limited the FSLN's choices of states from which to seek help in building its military apparatus. US trainers and strategists were out of the question.

The problem for Nicaragua, however, was that in an historical period when the local hegemon was emphasizing a bipolar vision of global politics, Cuban aid served to alienate other potential aid donors. Whereas Panama sent officers to Nicaragua in August, 1979 at Nicaragua's request to train the Sandinista police, the Panamanians were wary about the presence of Cuban advisors there and unhappy about the fact that they were given no role in army intelligence--an area in which the Cubans were working. The FSLN had been worried that due to close US-Panamanian ties in the military sphere--Panamanian officers were trained by the United

States at Fort Gulick and Panama was home to the US Southern Command--the Panamanian advisors might serve as a cover for US intelligence (LAWR, 12-21-79). The Panamanian role, then, was limited by Nicaraguan efforts to ensure distance from US military influence as well as by Panama's preference for a larger role in Nicaragua, and, some hesitancy about Cuba's influence there. Around the same time Venezuela cited the Cuban presence as its reason for refusing a joint Costa Rican-Panamanian request that it train the Sandinista Air Force. The few other Latin American states with the capacity to offer military aid--Brazil and Argentina, for example--were hesitant to do so for a variety of reasons related to the fragile relations in their own countries among left, center and right political elements, or, to their own military (and economic) linkages to the United States. Some Latin American politicians also voiced concern about any appearance of military or diplomatic imbalance between themselves and states (or factions) in a region experiencing sociopolitical tensions and conflict.

While these factors limited Nicaragua's arms and military sources, the US and its regional allies began their own military build-ups. Not only did the United States under Presidents Carter and Reagan sharply increase military aid to, and show increased political interest in, Nicaragua's neighbors after July, 1979. The rightist, military governments in El Salvador, Honduras and Guatemala on their own also acquired new high performance aircraft and other weapons from Israel and Brazil. As Washington set aside its concerns over human rights abuses in El Salvador, and later, Guatemala to allow new military aid to these governments facing popular resistance, US officials also decided in 1979 that Honduras would now replace Nicaragua as the US regional bulwark. Topmost on Washington's list of regional security concerns was the swelling popular resistance to the brutal and bloody government in El Salvador and the effects that the Nicaraguan revolution would have on an armed guerrilla movement there. Particularly after the inauguration of Ronald Reagan, the civil war in El Salvador became a key determinant of US-Nicaraguan relations: when the war went badly for the Salvadoran army and its US advisors, Washington increased pressures on Nicaragua. The FMLN and the FSLN were increasingly tied together in US foreign policy as the (Soviet-aligned) enemy which had to be militarily isolated and destroyed.

The Reagan Administration's charge by 1982 that Nicaragua had begun an unprovoked, offensive military build-up, and, its claim that the FSLN purposely sought to establish exclusive military links to the Soviet bloc obscured important regional political realities in the 1979 to 1982 period. It was in this period that the boundaries of Nicaragua's military relationships were set.

## Soviet Bloc and Cuban Connections

The Sandinistas faced the post-Triumph task of building military institutions and a defense arsenal, basically, from the ground up. When early requests for major arms purchases from the West appeared to be bearing little fruit, the FSLN in 1980 and 1981 continued probing Western sources, but also put out feelers to the Soviet Union, its East European allies and, later, to Third World states like Vietnam, Algeria and North Korea which were receiving arms from the Eastern bloc. That the Soviets and their allies moved cautiously in providing military aid to Nicaragua, however, is clear from the timing and the nature of such aid. Heavy Eastern-bloc aid arrived only after a clear counter-revolutionary security threat had developed, and, after the new US administration's position on Nicaragua and the revolution had been enunciated. US intent was reflected in increased US military aid to regional clients and US aid cut-offs to Nicaragua. Significantly, Eastern bloc military aid shipments after 1980 came in response to US regional military activities: with each major escalation in US rhetoric or military presence new shipments of arms arrived in Nicaragua. Arms shipments followed: revelations in 1981 about US support for the contras; the start up of continuous military exercises in Honduras in 1983; the escalations in the contra war in late 1983 and 1984; US contra aid renewal in 1985 and 1986; and US predictions (in 1985 and 1986) of heavy fighting in 1986 and 1987. Notably, the acquired weapons provided Nicaragua defensive, not offensive, capacities and were accompanied not by the signing of a military pact or a large influx of Soviet advisors, but by promises of "political solidarity", by cautions that Nicaragua's defense was Nicaragua's task alone, and by calls for a negotiated peace in Central America (e.g., Duncan, 1984; NYT, 6-20-84; 6-27-86).

Table 8.1 highlights the trends in Soviet-made weapons deliveries to Nicaragua. Several points give context to these data. First, while the table is based on US government information and is the data considered by US policy-makers, the Pentagon regularly cited larger numbers regarding Nicaragua's military capacity than did other independent and institutional sources. For example, at the end of 1984 the Pentagon claimed Nicaragua had 150 tanks, 45 aircraft and 17 helicopters. The Reagan Administration also stressed Nicaragua's aggressive intent in its briefings. Meanwhile US military intelligence, other officials and independent experts argued that Nicaragua's arsenal was defensive in nature. In March, 1985, the US Department of State claimed Nicaragua had "at least" 340 tanks and armored vehicles and that the delivery of the Hind helicopters in 1984 introduced further offensive capacity and added a "new dimension of warfare" to Central America. Commenting on the same late 1984 helicopter (and other weapons) deliveries, US military officers in the field claimed that the new weaponry added little to Nicaragua's overall capacity (e.g., NYT, 11-10-84).[16] Also indicative of US uses of the data to build its case against a "militarist" Nicaragua, US officials focused variously on dollar values or metric tonnage in citing Nicaragua's build-up or capacity, without giving a broader assessment of the actual capacities or usefulness of the weapons involved or of the Nicaraguan's ability and training to employ the weapons. One independent source argues in detail that Sandinista armed forces were over-equipped and undertrained: the EPS in 1985 was "unprepared" or incapable of professionally using Soviet-supplied weapons in an effective way (King, 1985: 16). This condition was spurred by FSLN security concerns and the lower prices and easier terms of Soviet weapons; Soviet weapons were cheaper than Western weapons and were provided to the Nicaraguans as donations, through barter agreements or on

Table 8.1
Soviet-Bloc Military Deliveries to Nicaragua 1979-1984

| | Approximate Dollar Amount ($US Millions) | Metric Tonnage | Types of Weapons Transferred |
|---|---|---|---|
| 1979 | 5 | n.a. | Light anti-aircraft guns; SA-7 surface-to-air missiles |
| 1980 | 6-7[a] | 850 | Several hundred East German trucks; AT-1 and AT-3 anti-tank missiles |
| 1981 | 39-45 | 900 | About 25 T-54 and T-55 tanks[b] |
| 1982 | 80 | 6,700 | About 20 T-54 tanks; 12 BTR-60 armored personnel carriers; 6 105mm howitzers; about 38 ZIS-2 37mm anti-aircraft guns; SA-6 GAINFUL surface-to-air missiles, SA-7 GRAIL light anti-aircraft missiles;[c] small transport and trainer planes |
| 1983 | 113 | 14,000 | Additional trucks, tanks; AN-26 transport planes and spare parts;[d] 2 MI-8 helicopters (NYT, 8-2-83); artillery pieces |
| 1984 | 112-250[e] | 18,000 | 30 PT-76 light tanks; 6-12 MI-24 helicopters; 12-MI-8 helicopters; minesweeper patrol boats; radar-controlled anti-aircraft guns |

Sources: US Department of State (March, 1985); Edelman (1985); Sims (1984); Buchanan (1982).

a. This compares to $36.3 million in US military aid to its regional allies that year.
b. At 32 tons apiece, these World War II vintage tanks made up the bulk of 1981 aid.
c. In late 1982, Nicaragua received its first sophisticated Soviet electronic gear.
d. After early 1983 the inflow of key items like trucks and tanks was reported to be at a much reduced rate.
e. Western analysts in Managua put the figure at 100-150 and estimated a 25 percent increase over 1983 in the value of arms shipped in 1984 (NYT, 3-28-84).

easy credit. Nevertheless, US officials tended to emphasize their dollar estimates of weapons transferred to raise complaints of large military build-ups. For example, President Reagan and others cited the dollar increase in acquisitions from 1980 to 1981 in that context, whereas the metric tonnage increased only slightly. In 1984 Reagan and Shultz raised the issue of increased arms shipments with Soviet Foreign Minister Gromyko, citing a 50 percent increase from mid-1983 to mid-1984. Later in the year some US policy makers were using a 100 percent increase figure for 1983-1984. Other observers regarded these figures as inflated. Similarly, in mid-1986 the Pentagon claimed that Soviet weapons shipments that year were already double those of 1985.

A second point in assessing Nicaragua's military capacity regards the quality and appropriateness of the weapons transferred, particularly in view of the much superior weaponry being supplied to US allies--Nicaragua's neighbors. Evidence suggests that the Eastern bloc included outdated and less-than-efficient weapons in its sales and shipments to Nicaragua. For example, in late 1980 the Nicaraguans learned from the Cubans that the East German trucks they had agreed to purchase were both unreliable and short of spare parts. The Germans refused to let Nicaragua out of the deal (WP, 11-9-80). The T-54 and T-55 tanks shipped to Nicaragua, moreover, arrived there only after Honduras acquired 16 amphibious Scorpion tanks built in the 1970s and capable of traveling at 48 miles per hour. The Soviet tanks, on the other hand, were of 1948-1963 vintage, topped out at 30 miles per hour, were fuel-inefficient, were not amphibious and could travel only over flat land. Much of Nicaragua's territory, like that among its northern border, is hilly or mountainous; rivers mark much of the border separating Nicaragua from its northern and southern neighbors. Both the defensive and offensive capacities of the Soviet-made tanks were thus limited. The PT-76 tanks Nicaragua received in 1984 had amphibious capabilities, but had only half the speed of Honduran tanks. Nicaragua's helicopters, the key element of its airforce, were also matched or surpassed by its neighbors' aircraft: when Nicaragua received its Hind helicopters in late 1984, El Salvador already had 15 combat helicopters with 9 more enroute, Guatemala had 50 similar craft and Honduras had use of 15 US combat helicopters (e.g. Edelman, 1985: 51). Given the contras' reliance on air resupply and intelligence gathering in Nicaraguan airspace, the FSLN focused in 1984 on obtaining anti-air systems that could respond to the contra-related overflights. Indicative of that concern was the increase in the sophistication of weapons delivered to Nicaragua in 1984 and 1986: Hind helicopter gunships and radar-controlled anti-aircraft guns.

This ties into a third point: as suggested earlier, increases in military acquisitions noted in the table reflect Nicaraguan responses to US military moves in the region and to expansions in contra forces or attacks. After early 1982, most of Nicaragua's military hardware and supplies were of Soviet origin and were often sold or shipped by a third party. Although Nicaragua's military preparedness increased significantly from 1982 to 1984, from November 1984 to November 1985 US intelligence observed a sharp reduction in arms shipments. According to a number of FSLN officials, Nicaragua by the end of 1984 had the heavy equipment and ammunition it felt it needed both to eliminate the contra threat in 1985 and to increase military costs to the United States of an invasion. Additionally, the Frente had given some consideration to US concerns about Nicaragua's continued build-up; the FSLN was hoping to move bilateral and multilateral negotiations forward in 1985 and sought to reduce its image as a provocatuer in Central America. Thus, the reduction in arms acquisitions. By the end of 1985, however, Nicaragua perceived a renewed determination on the part of the United States to empower the contras and raise the level of military pressure on Nicaragua during 1986. As before, Nicaragua responded to the perceived increased threat. Replacement helicopters were delivered by the Soviets in May. According to the Pentagon, an estimated ten additional Mi 17 helicopters were acquired by mid-year.

In November, 1985 the Reagan Administration cited evidence that new shipments including more T-54 tanks were on their way to Nicaragua through Cuba. Defense Minister Ortega responded that Washington was sending small, armored, high powered speed boats to the contras and that Nicaragua would obtain any air, land and naval material needed to counter what were expected to be decisive confrontations with the contras in 1986. Defense Minister Ortega also announced that Nicaragua would seek Soviet MIG fighter jets in light of the fact that the US had plans to ship F-5 fighters to Honduras in the future--a charge US officials confirmed without giving a timeframe (NYT, 11-13-85). The F-5's would introduce a new level of military sophistication into Central America and represented another threat to the Nicaraguans. They had been warned by the United States not to acquire such aircraft. Again, domestic political pressure on the Reagan Administration and the contras to produce results against the FSLN had led in the fall of 1985 to US talk about wider contra assaults or a US military move in 1986. President Reagan began a new campaign for Congressional approval of military aid to the contras in 1986. In turn, the Nicaraguans sought new arms and braced themselves for new CIA-supported sabotage inside Nicaragua.

The MIG Issue. Although the US sharply criticized each new weapons delivery to Nicaragua and used the deliveries to renew arguments of Nicaragua's unprovoked aggressive intent, there was one major limit beyond which the US consistently warned the Sandinistas not to go: acquiring MIG or similar jet fighter planes. On several occasions from 1983 to 1985, the Reagan Administration warned the USSR, Nicaragua and Cuba that it would immediately retaliate, possibly with surgical air strikes, to knock out such planes. Top officials warned that the United States would not allow sophisticated air-to-air or air-to-ground capacities in the arsenal of the leftist government. According to US policy makers, MIGs would allow Nicaragua to threaten the Panama Canal, to damage Honduras' edge against Nicaragua (i.e., its air force superiority) and to attack US planes in an area traditionally open to US security activity. Fueled by repeated rumors from 1981 onward that Soviet MIGs or French Mirage jets were on order, en route or secretly housed in Nicaragua, the issue of jet fighters with air intercept capacity in Nicaragua festered through the mid-1980s. The Reagan

Administration used the MIG issue as a political weapon in its efforts to convince Congress to continue funding the contras.

Despite Nicaragua's complaints that Washington had no right to impose such restrictions over another sovereign state, both Moscow and Paris--the two governments Nicaragua repeatedly approached with requests for jet fighters--declined to extend credit for such a sale. For its part, the Kremlin apparently assessed, in the absence of similar jet fighters elsewhere in Central America, that MIGs would do more to harm Nicaragua's defense than to aid to it. The result was that through mid-1986 Nicaragua lacked air intercept capacity even while the contras continued to rely heavily on air supply and aerial intelligence. Throughout the period US violations of Nicaragua's airspace increased.

Nicaragua continued to claim its sovereign right to obtain any weapons system necessary to its defense. In the event of a direct US military move, the Frente expected massive air strikes against Managua and EPS installations. Defense Minister Ortega asserted on several occasions in 1984 and 1985 that Nicaragua would obtain such planes, that Nicaragua had several dozen trained pilots ready to fly the aircraft and that Nicaragua had no intention of ceding its right to obtain these fighters. Ortega also claimed Nicaragua was willing to buy Northrup F-5 fighters and other US combat aircraft if the US would extend credit. In Nicaragua, construction of a new military airport at Punta Huete continued, though construction was interrupted for periods by war-time shortages and lack of funds. The airport, which was only in preparation stages during Somoza's last years, had a 10,000 foot runway and aircraft revetments (protective earthen mounds) for facilitating MIG or Mirage fighter jets.

That US policy regarding Nicaragua's acquisition of jet fighters had less to do with a concern about increased weapons sophistication in Central America and more to do with the success of its contra program (and winning Congressional and public backing of that program) became clear in late 1984 and 1985. For example, when FSLN leaders, acknowledging that they would have to do with lesser jets, announced that they would acquire Czech L-39 Albatross subsonic trainers and made arrangements to take delivery of L-39s from Libya, the US broadened its restrictions on Nicaraguan aircraft to include these 2-seater planes. Although US restrictions on these jets had a lesser basis for justification--the US A-37 Dragonfly, similar to the L-39, was used widely in El Salvador--the administration announced that such planes would also be considered a security threat to the US (e.g., WP, 4-13-85). The "threat" apparently rested in the fact that the L-39s could be equipped with counterinsurgency capabilities which the Sandinistas could then use in their war against the contras. Nevertheless, the Soviets and the Nicaraguans again heeded the warning and the L-39s were not delivered.

Shedding further light on US policy, US officials admitted during the November 1984 "MIG Crisis" that such periodic crises and charges of Nicaragua's aggressive intent worked to increase public awareness of Soviet arms shipments generally--i.e., even though MIGs were not being delivered--and added to public and Congressional support for the president's contra program (NYT, 11-8-84). Finally,

in November, 1985 Nicaragua cited US intentions to deliver
MIG-comparable F-5 fighters to Honduras. US officials confirmed
that several years earlier the Honduran army had been told that its
Super Mystere jets would eventually be replaced with sophisticated
F-5 fighters. The United States itself, in other words, had
intentions of introducing more sophisticated jets into Central
America, albeit into ally arsenals. The effect of the revelation
was that the United States, under penalty of losing its moral
authority on the issue of Nicaraguan aggressiveness, would either
have to refrain from sending F-5s to Honduras or drop its
restrictions on Nicaragua. In the case that Honduras received F-5s,
the Soviets could reconsider and accede to Nicaragua's long-standing
request for MIGs.

    Soviet-Bloc Advisors. Cuban advisors arrived in Nicaragua
shortly after the 1979 Triumph. According to US intelligence
reports, several dozen Cuban military advisors were working in
Nicaragua by mid-1980. In late 1979, twenty Nicaraguans who would
later train and lead militias received military training in Cuba.
As Eastern bloc equipment began arriving after 1981, and, as the
nature and extent of the external military threat became clear, the
need for technicians to service the equipment and to train
Nicaraguans in their use grew. The pace of military development
also quickened as the Nicaraguans geared their forces toward
confronting the contras in the field. In the area of state
security, moreover, Soviet-bloc and Cuban advisors assisted the FSLN
in creating intelligence, anti-subversion and internal security
units. According to one Nicaraguan defector who told his story to
Washington officials in 1983, 70 Soviet, 100 Cuban, 40-50 East
German and 20-25 Bulgarians worked in Nicaraguan state security.
Whatever the numbers, the Cubans in particular came to predominate
in key military advisory positions in Sandinista defense and
security institutions as the contra war intensified. In June, 1983,
Cuba's top combat commander -- general Armando Ochoa Sanchez -- made
the first of several visits to Nicaragua (NYT, 6-19-83).

    But the presence of Cuban and Eastern bloc advisors soon became
a political problem for Nicaragua. The Reagan Administration
pointed to Cuban, Soviet and East German advisors as proof of
Nicaragua's political alignment with the Soviet Union. Washington
defined the presence of Eastern bloc advisors as a security threat
to the United States and to Nicaragua's neighbors. As the
administration's public campaign accelerated in 1983 onward, US
estimates of the number and role of Nicaragua's foreign advisors
also expanded. What amounted to a numbers war developed as a key
element in US charges against Nicaragua. Ignoring earlier US
intelligence reports of dozens of Cuban advisors in Nicaragua in the
first years of the revolution, the United States later claimed two
hundred Cuban advisors arrived shortly after the July, 1979 FSLN
takeover. By 1983 the administration claimed that there were 6000
Cuban troops and personnel in Nicaragua as well as 7,000 Soviet and
Eastern-bloc personnel in all fields (e.g. NYT, 7-27-83). In the
latter group, there were said to be 30-40 Soviet and 50-60 East
German military advisors in Nicaragua, numbers which remained
relatively constant through 1985.

    The administration also tried repeatedly to link the

Sandinistas with a long-term US enemy and a group publically associated in the United States as anti-US , anti-Israel and terrorist--the PLO. In 1983, for example, President Reagan publically claimed that there were fifty PLO pilots in Nicaragua, a charge which was disputed at the time by another administration official who said there were maybe twenty-five PLO people there, a few of whom were pilots. By 1985 however, and because there was no evidence that the PLO figured significantly in FSLN military or foreign policy decisions, the role of the PLO was downgraded to "minor" in a joint Department of State and Defense publication (DOS-DOD, 1985).

Similarly, the estimated number of Cubans working in Nicaragua changed over time and did not match independent or Nicaraguan figures on foreign advisors. In the 1985 publication, for example, the administration claimed that though there had been upwards of 9,000 Cubans in Nicaragua earlier, in 1985 there were 7,500 Cubans there--3,000 in the military and security field alone--all of whom had some military training. These figures were significantly higher than the 6,000 figure used in 1983, though they again stressed the potential military role played by all Cubans in Nicaragua, no matter their field. US claims rested on the fact that many Cuban civilians received some militia reserve training in Cuba. The extrapolation that any Cuban in Nicaragua could therefore double as an additional FSLN fighter, or, that such limited training in Cuba made Cuban teachers and doctors potential military advisors, though far-fetched, again forwarded objectives of the US image-management campaign begun earlier.

The Nicaraguans themselves claimed that in 1985 there were 786 Cuban military advisors and trainers in their military establishment. Similarly, independent sources estimated these Cubans to number under 1,000 (e.g., King, 1985). More important than numbers to the Nicaraguans, however, was that the revolution's defense be secured. Expressing a sentiment heard widely in Nicaraguan government circles, Nicaraguan economist-priest Xabier Gorostiaga commented in 1982: "Some people here say Cuban assistance is an excuse to maintain a Sandinista dictatorship. But in Nicaragua we say this is the only way to survive" (Newsweek, 11-8-82). According to Defense Minister Ortega, "...hundreds of Cuban instructors, professors and experts have helped in tasks of military organization, structure and science," but "...US intelligence knows there are no Cuban or other fighting forces here" (BI, 4-25-85). Cuban advisors assisted in individual training and instruction in small unit tactics, while the relatively few Soviet military personnel provided technical assistance on Soviet bloc weapons.[17] There was little evidence that foreign advisors had given training in armed forces command and staff control procedures, nor that they had commanded EPS units in combat. Indeed, the shortage of officers and of training in control over coordinated offensive operations remained into 1986 as a critical problem for the Sandinista army (King, 1985: 18; author interviews). Although Cuban advisors were reported in late 1985 to be regularly accompanying EPS units in operations against the contras, the Sandinistas did not rely solely on the Cubans or the Soviets as irregular warfare experts, an area in which both these groups had little experience. Instead, the EPS relied on its own guerrilla-experienced FSLN cadres to train special anti-contra units.

Contentions over just what role the Cubans were playing in Nicaragua flared again in late 1985 when a contra SA-7 anti-aircraft missile downed a Nicaraguan MI-8 helicopter carrying four Cubans among its fourteen passengers. Using the incident to bring new charges of Cuban interventionism and a regional security threat, the Reagan Administration alleged that Cuban advisors had become the "backbone of the Sandinista army" and had come to assume actual combat roles (NYT, 12-6-85). Moreover, the administration cited increasing reports of Cuban pilots flying Nicaraguan helicopters and spotter planes in the war against the contras. Indeed, administration officials used the incident to renew calls for continued US military support for the contras, indicating also that the presence of Cuban advisors in Nicaragua would be a key argument in their 1986 bid to Congress for lethal aid.

The greater visibility and combat involvement of the Cuban advisors--said by US officials to number 2,500 in late 1985--actually reflected the EPS 1985 campaign to deal the contras a strategic blow. There were no Cuban combat units in Nicaragua, nor had the number of Cuban advisors there increased. Rather, to compensate for the lack of highly trained or experienced EPS cadres, the roles played by the Cubans were expanded as the contra war heated up. There were no indications that the FSLN had given over leadership roles to Cubans. But the US again got political mileage out of the communist-expansionism argument. As Assistant Secretary of State for Inter-American Affairs Elliot Abrams put it in testimony before the House Foreign Affairs Committee. "You now have Cubans fighting not just in Africa, but on the mainland of North America" (NYT, op.cit.).

Denying that Cubans were significant in combat roles in Nicaragua, the Frente instead emphasized the danger of the escalation in the fighting represented by the contras' acquisition of sophisticated anti-aircraft missiles. Charging that the CIA had provided the weapons in violation of US Congressional restrictions, the FSLN called for a UN Security Council meeting to discuss a heightening of tensions by US-backed forces in Nicaragua.

The presence of non-Western, foreign military advisors in Nicaragua lingered as a point of contention among the FSLN, the United States, its regional allies and the FSLN's domestic opposition. It was an issue addressed by Contadora and the bilateral (US-Nicaragua) Manzanillo talks. Nicaragua's position remained essentially the same: Nicaragua would send all of its foreign advisors home if the US simultaneously withdrew the bulk of its advisors from Central America and withdrew its support of the contras. From 1983 to 1985 Nicaragua offered unilaterally to begin the phase-out process. The Contadora draft also required advisor withdrawals by both Nicaragua and the United States, a position that offended Washington's sense of historical prerogative. The United States ignored such offers as "FSLN propoganda." At the Manzanillo talks, moreover, the US position was that Nicaragua should send its advisors home over a period of months, in return for which the United States would consider a pull-out of its advisors from Central

America. According to US and Nicaraguan sources close to these talks, however, there was room for a settlement of this issue. But the Manzanillo talks, having met their domestic political purpose for the Reagan Administration, were suspended by the United States in January, 1985.

Soviet Perspectives and Nicaragua's Defense. Clearly wanting to avoid the economic burden of another Cuba, the Soviets nonetheless showed that they were willing to increase the costs to the United States of any drastic military action against Nicaragua. While the Soviets demonstrated a willingness to commit themselves to supplying Nicaragua when other states could or would not offer military aid, Soviet leaders in 1982 (Brezhnev), 1983 (Andropov) and 1984 (Chernenko) also stressed the great distance between the states and the political nature of Soviet support. The USSR had not shown a desire or a willingness, for example, to sign any military pact with Nicaragua. Moreover, the timing of shipments and, in some instances, the nature of the weapons involved suggested Soviet circumspection about going too far to challenge the United States in its immediate "backyard." Soviet aid was modulated, with an eye toward avoiding either direct confrontation with Washington or a military-economic imbroglio. Nor did the Soviets want to spur a US retaliatory move against Cuba. Rather, the Soviets pursued a low-cost strategy for creating political space in Central (and South) America in the post inter-American security era. At the same time, the Soviets were not unhappy about the diversion of US interest and resources to Central and South America and away from Europe or elsewhere. Through their aid, the Soviets contributed to a narrowing of US policy options on Nicaragua to negotiating or invading. They had not chosen to pursue a high-profile policy in Nicaragua.

Nicaraguan leaders maintained that they would not allow foreign military bases in their country, and, that their military development and Soviet (military) dependence more a function of US policy than of an FSLN desire to align with the Soviet Union. Yet, whereas basing rights in Nicaragua would enhance the Soviet's surveillance of the United States, it seemed doubtful that the Soviets would risk placing nuclear weapons there--sparking an immediate "missile crisis." Nor did it appear likely that the Soviets and Cubans would risk a retaliation against Cuba or USSR facilities elsewhere by interrupting or interfering with US shipping and communications lanes in the area (e.g., Cirincione and Hunter, 1984). As US military experts pointed out during the short-range nuclear missiles debate of the early 1980s, a more likely nuclear challenge than nuclear-capable MIGs or nuclear missile basing in Cuba or Nicaragua was the possibility of a Soviet deployment of strategic nuclear submarines off the United States' Atlantic Coast as a response to US Pershing missiles in Europe.

By 1984 the FSLN was aware that neither Cuba nor the USSR would come to Nicaragua's aid in the event of a US invasion. After his talks with Soviet leader Andropov in March, 1983, for example, Daniel Ortega said that Nicaragua had "all the necessary resources to defend the motherland" (quoted in Rothenburg, 1984: 140). This followed Andropov's statement that he was convinced that Nicaragua could uphold its own independence. Later Soviet statements

300

continued to assert political support for Nicaragua. Nor was there ever mentioned a need for a Soviet role in Nicaragua. In October, 1983, moreover, Fidel Castro gave a long press conference in Havana in which he said that Cuba would not be able to assist Nicaragua if the United States invaded. Cuba lacked the air transport and amphibious assault landing craft to move large numbers of troops or heavy armor (e.g., Cirincione and Hunter, op.cit.; DOS Bulletin, September, 1982). According to political leaders of the Contadora states who met with Castro, the FSLN leadership and the political arm of the FMLN in Salvador, the Soviets' position offering only moral and political support (i.e. not direct military assistance) was clear to both Managua and Washington (LAWR, 6-24-83). It appeared to be this knowledge, along with increased contra-related economic damage in 1983-1984, that motivated the FSLN's continued military build-up through 1984, its strengthening of the armed forces through EPS expansion and reorganization and the activation of reserve forces in that period.

## A Defensive Posture

Despite its military build-up and weapons purchases from the Soviet bloc, Nicaragua's military posture remained defensive and ill-suited for any offensive actions against its neighbors. As Defense Minister Ortega pointed out in a military assessment in 1985, economic and material conditions severely limited an offensive capacity (BI, 4-25-85): 1)Nicaragua was dependent on imported oil; an enemy could quickly neutralize the one main port at which Nicaragua received its crude and thereby effectively cut the vital supply route. Nicaragua's main military weakness was its lack of fuel supplies; in early 1985 the EPS had only a few days-worth of reserve fuel; 2)Nicaragua had a limited number of military vehicles--50 percent of the vehicles the army was currently using belonged to other government ministries or agencies and all vehicles were affected by the scarcity of spare parts; 3)Nicaragua had limited air transportation and a small airforce: MI-8 helicopters were the mainstay of its force and its few Hind helicopters were underutilized and potentially vulnerable to contra anti-aircraft weapons (e.g. King, 1985; NYT, 10-27-85); 4)Nicaragua lacked strategic reserves to supply the army; 5)Nicaragua had no military medical systems; Nicaragua's medical care was focused upon the civilian population; 6)Nicaragua had no military industry; and 7)Nicaragua lacked back-up support for offensive moves -- its industry was heavily dependent on imports; Nicaragua had no capacity to produce rations or canned goods for its troops; and a naval blockade would mean the end of clothes and uniform production, of medical supplies and of arms and supply importation. The fact that 90 percent of imports and 80 percent of exports flowed through the port of Corinto exemplified Nicaragua's vulnerability.

Yet another weakness in Nicaragua's military structure: Nicaragua had a shortage of military officers and professionally trained officers. Again according to the Defense Minister, the EPS command structure did not permit the execution of complex military missions. It focused on sustaining organization and discipline among the permanent, reserve and militia forces. Five years

was not time enough to have graduated and given field experience to
officers.  Defense Minister Ortega argued that it would take ten to
fifteen years to obtain a sufficient general staff.

Heavily dependent on infantry battalions, the EPS air force and
navy were small and under-equipped.  Through 1985, for example, the
"incipient" navy depended on twelve French and Soviet patrol boats,
a few coast guard units and some mine-sweepers obtained after the
US-CIA harbor mining in 1984.  Nicaragua had no naval combat forces,
no disembarkment craft and no air support system.  Although the
Sandinistas' early Belgian FAL, US M-16 and Israeli Galil rifles had
been replaced by Eastern bloc AK-47s and Czech BZ-52s, the FSLN's
"arms to all the people" campaign was slowed by the limited number
of these weapons in Nicaragua.  Nor did the Sandinistas have large
ammunition caches in the countryside (e.g. NYT, 6-4-85).  According
to a 1985 US intelligence report, the EPS was defense oriented,
though it was improving its irregular warfare capacity (WSJ,
4-3-85).

Tanks.  A key piece of evidence the United States used against
Nicaragua after 1981 was its Soviet-built tanks.  Yet, according to
Nicaraguan and independent US military analyses, Nicaragua's 150
tanks--most of which were aged T-54 and T-55s--hardly provided
Nicaragua an offensive capacity.  Moreover, while Honduras and
Salvador had many fewer tanks -- 12 each -- their tanks were of much
more recent vintage and had advanced technological capacities.  Nor
did either of these states have reason to fear attack from the
United States; rather, Washington promised these states back-up
support in the event of regional war with Nicaragua.  According to
State Department military advisor Colonel Lawrence Tracy and others,
the Sandinistas' tanks could not survive against US or Honduran
anti-tank weaponry; nor were the tanks suited for Nicaragua's
mountainous northern regions.  Such tanks "would have to be loaded
on flatbed trucks and driven up the Pan American Highway..." in
order to be used against Honduras.  More likely, Honduras' modern
air force would "easily put them out" (NYT, 3-30-85).  A single US
SR-71 surveillance plane could "map" most of Nicaragua in about an
hours' time, its infra-red and other high-tech capacities noting the
location of Nicaraguan tanks (and other equipment) prior to a US or
Honduran bombing raid.  The Sandinistas' forty Soviet-supplied
flatbed trucks and six amphibious ferries were likely acquired to
tailor the tanks to meet road conditions inside Nicaragua rather
than in an effort to introduce tanks into Honduras in support of an
FSLN attack.  Nicaragua's roads and bridges could not support the
weight and tread damage of the tanks (author interviews).

A similar assessment was given in Congressional testimony by
Lt. Colonel John Buchanan (USMC, retired) who concluded about the
Reagan Administration's claims: "...a smokescreen is being laid and
a military debacle is in the offing" (Buchanan, 1982).  Regarding
Nicaragua's tanks, Buchanan argued: "The Nicaraguans do have a lot
of tanks, but they're not in very good condition.  The gun is so
bulky and the crew is so cramped that their lives are endangered.
Mechanically they're not reliable, and they're easily turned into a
pyre.  Moreover you don't make a tank attack without massive
supplies of fuel to sustain the attack, and without the mobile
infantry accompanying the tanks, they're dead ducks...." (CAHI,

302

2-28-85).
Regional Comparison. A brief comparison of regional military
systems puts Nicaraguan military capacity into perspective. Total
armed forces in the region grew significantly after 1979 and in 1985
compared as follows: Nicaragua - 62,850, including about 20,000
militia; Honduras - 16,600, and a 4,500-strong paramilitary force;
El Salvador - 41,650, and a 9,500-strong paramilitary force (and a
70,000-strong "civil defense" force--Orden); Guatemala - 31,700, and
a large rural paramilitary force; and Costa Rica - 8,000 Civil
Guard, plus a 10,000-member paramilitary force (International Institute for Strategic Studies, 1985; NYT, 11-18-84; 3-30-85; 5-25-86).
While Nicaragua had the largest armed forces, its neighbors had
larger and more modern air forces. Honduras in early 1985 had over
70 jets and combat aircraft, including 15 Super Mystere
fighter-bombers, 10 Huey UH1H helicopters, 10 A37B Dragon Fly attack
planes and about 14 transport aircraft. El Salvador had over 60
combat aircraft, including 40 Huey UH1H helicopters and 9 A37B
Dragon Fly attack planes, in addition to about 14 transport
aircraft. El Salvador had more aircraft on order from the United
States. Nicaragua's air force, again, was heavily dependent on its
8-12 Soviet Hind combat helicopters; its aged T-28 and T-33 trainers
were no match for its neighbors' newer craft. Moreover, US capital
expenditure for airport expansion and military infrastructure in US
major regional ally states far outstripped similar Soviet investment
in Nicaragua.[18] Nor was Nicaragua protected from external
aggression by membership in any military pact or defense treaty.
Besides being members of the (multilateral defense) Rio Treaty with
the United States, the other Central American states had also
tentatively committed themselves to the CONDECA pact. Nicaraguan
leaders interpreted these realities as representing a combined
regional threat to Nicaragua's security. They acted on this
perception in the military and diplomatic-political spheres.


DEFENSE AND SURVIVAL

"Everyone to the defense, everything for the war fronts!" Such
slogans in Nicaragua succinctly characterized both the Sandinistas'
charge to fellow citizens and the socioeconomic reality there from
1983 onward. By 1985 the Frente had officially confirmed what had
been the direction of domestic policy: Nicaragua moved from
national reconstruction to a war economy for national defense.
As dislocations occurred and were exacerbated by the continuing
contra war and external economic pressures, the FSLN's defense
strategies had to be geared toward mobilizing economically pressed
citizens to support Nicaragua's defense structures. Defense came to
be broadly defined. These developments hold long-term implications
for the future of Nicaragua. Defense institutions had come to play
a key role in the revolutionary process and defense considerations
became the primary criteria influencing domestic and international
policy. New political and social institutions were being developed
in a context of a national security emergency and during a period in
which national reconstruction essentially came to a halt. The
danger was that the emerging socio-political and defense

institutions might not suit the Nicaraguan situation in peace-time; that, for example, larger-than-necessary state regulatory or armed forces institutions might use up limited national resources well into the future, or, as a national security mentality became a government characteristic.

A related issue--one raised by US charges against Nicaragua--involved the possibility that continuous security threats or US attempts to spark an anti-Sandinista rebellion inside Nicaragua might encourage the FSLN to use its tanks against its own people. President Reagan began making claims in 1983 and 1984 that the "totalitarian" Sandinistas were "waging war on their own people." Although that rhetoric amounted to hyperbole, history suggested that militarized societies do not encourage pluralism. Moreover, a national security state could well develop in Nicaragua should future US presidents and Congresses maintain a permanent stance of hostility vis-a-vis that state.

The military-security situation in Nicaragua in the mid-1980s appeared to remain fluid. Significantly, a sizeable part of Nicaragua's defense and of its military apparatus remained in the hands of the Nicaraguan people themselves. The nearly 300,000 rifles distributed to individuals and families by 1986, and, the rural, locally controlled and organized community defense programs represented forces that could just as well be employed against the FSLN government were widespread anti-Sandinista sentiment to develop. Yet, contradicting US claims of anti-government feelings in Nicaragua, by 1986 there had not been large public rallies or spontaneous anti-government mob behavior. Moreover, as the draft was instituted, Nicaragua's regular defense came to depend on a much wider assortment of young men, not just on FSLN faithfuls and volunteers. As training time shortened or was focused on the immediate contra threat, so did opportunities narrow for ensuring that all recruits were politically trained and loyal to the FSLN itself. Nicaragua, in sum, was years away from having a highly centralized, tightly controlled military apparatus typical of the totalitarian or national security state. Nor, by FSLN accounts, did the _Frente_ prefer to move in that direction at the expense of national economic development.

At the same time that defense relied a great deal on voluntarism, the military draft begun in 1984 met much criticism and was probably the issue on which the FSLN was the most vulnerable among Nicaraguan citizens. The idea of a draft was foreign to the Nicaraguan people; the Somozas and the political factions that ruled before had relied on their own private armies rather than on universal conscription. Moreover, as the contra war led to more and more deaths, some mothers and families of young recruits protested the idea of their sons being sent to the war zones. The criticism peaked in 1985 along with the government's anti-contra campaign and appeared to ebb as the level of fighting also fell at late year and into 1986. The political opposition, on the other hand, resented a legal draft for an army that was tied to the Sandinista political organization rather than to the state as such. Many young men went into hiding or into exile to escape the new draft. And, the nature of the army and the draft itself became the topic of much inter-party political debate. Certainly the inter-related issues were ones on which the FSLN would have to come to terms with its domestic opposition. According to a number of FSLN and opposition leaders in 1985, the odds were that the majority FSLN would be flexible on the issue of a national army in response to public sentiment, but that the circumstances of the continuing security threat and contra war discouraged constitutional development in this area. A regional peace agreement, on the other hand, would allow demilitarization, a normalcy in Nicaraguan national legislative politics and increased political space there.

Development was postponed for defense and most economic infrastructure was geared to support military development. As part of this dislocation, the work force was increasingly recruited into regular or militia forces or asked to give time to help harvest vital export crops or to aid in community preparedness programs. Economic decline continued as a source of FSLN vulnerability. Students, meanwhile, lost study time to the same efforts as new land ownership and militia duty increasingly absorbed the traditional export crop harvestors. Human energies which had been successfully mobilized for popular development in the first years of the revolution and which represented one of the important resources of otherwise-poor Nicaragua now were being put to military development. The armed forces were not economically productive, yet they had to be supported with food, clothing, transportation and weapons. The arms themselves represented another problem for the future: most of Nicaragua's weapons came on a pay-later basis and amounted to a debt against Nicaragua's future.

Survival planning introduced yet another irony. Although increasing Nicaragua's independence and diversifying its dependence were priority goals of the FSN, the international linkages made during the security crisis raised the possibility that Nicaragua was incurring political debts, and, that dependence on economic aid and donations was actually increasing. In the military-security realm, Nicaragua had become dependent upon not only the willingness of its people to defend themselves, but also upon Soviet-bloc weapons. The virtual shut-off of Western arms sources made this dependence inevitable. Similarly, the extent of Nicaragua's relations with the Eastern bloc increased at a quickened pace; as President Ortega argued repeatedly, Nicaragua would obtain weapons wherever it could in order to meet the security threat. The political solidarity, weapons and oil commitments offered by the Soviet Union in the 1980s suggested a long-term relationship between the two nations. How exclusive that relationship would become, however, appeared to depend more on future US policy than on any other single determining factor.

As matters stood by the mid-1980s, the FSLN had successfully built a defense force, which in turn involved many of Nicaragua's people and effectively denied any national territory or large public support to the US-sponsored forces. Nor had armed Miskito Indian groups come to represent the majority opinion in the Atlantic Coast regarding the appropriate methods for finally addressing ethno-cultural differences between Eastern and Western Nicaragua. By 1986 many Miskitos who once had been armed turned to searching out political solutions in dialogue with the FSLN government. These defense successes for the Sandinistas also yielded them renewed respect in international circles; the FSLN's legitimacy as the representatives of the Nicaraguan people was expanded. It was also on the basis of their continued political and military viability that Latin American recognition and solidarity prevailed. For the FSLN, its defense strategy was based on the recognition that given its ultimate inability militarily to defend the revolution against a hostile US, it had to wage its defense and ensure its economic and political survival in the political-diplomatic realms.


NOTES

    1. The United States had created and trained the Guardia during the years of its military occupation of the country. In 1933, when US Marines left Nicaragua, the Guardia became the military enforcer of the Somoza regimes. US aid and training maintained the force and it represented probably the strongest link in the US regional military presence. For example, after 1944, all National Guard cadets did their final training at US Fort Gulick in Panama. From 1949 to 1973, 4,119 Guardia received counterinsurgency training in Panama; from 1959 to 1976, 4,897 Guardia officers and personnel were trained by the United States. These numbers exceed those for any other Latin American army in that period (IHCA, October, 1983).
    2. State Security Forces (DGSE) operated internally as a third branch of the police. According to the US State Department, the DGSE was modelled after Cuban Intelligence structures and was run by a former Cuban citizen. The State Department, which has used inflated figures on foreign advisors (i.e., compared to independent and Nicaraguan sources) in other instances, reported in 1984 (DOS, October, 1984) that no fewer than 400 Cuban, 70 Soviet and other East German and Bulgarian advisors work for the DGSE. US figures were based on the testimony of a Nicaraguan intelligence defector, Miguel Bolonos Hunter, published by the Heritage Foundation in its pamphlet "Inside Communist Nicaragua" (September, 1983).
    3. This is an excerpt from the "Congressional Presentation Document," on security assistance programs for fiscal year 1981, p. 419.
    4. Author interview. Cabezas, who served as a deputy Minister of the Interior, also repeated Defense Minister Humberto Ortega's claim that a US invasion of Nicaragua would spark armed rebellions by popular groups throughout Latin America.
    5. Usually, arms were distributed to militia members only at the time of attack or to volunteers doing patrol or guarding harvesters, bridges and the like. On the other hand, many isolated villages and farmers had been given rifles outright in the "arms to all the people" campaign.
    6. Between March and August, 1982 there were 75 airspace violations over Nicaragua, 29 by the US Air Force, according to Nicaraguan officials. In 1983 the Nicaraguans counted 200 US reconnaissance flights over their territory.
    7. Registration, recruitment and training occurred on the regional level and calls to service went out according to national military need. While peace-time exemptions existed for the sick,

sole supporters of families, those in the last year of high school or college, etc., mental or physical incapacity was the only exemption guaranteed in wartime. According to a Defense Ministry spokesperson in 1985, local recruiters had quotas to fill during recruitment campaigns and would listen to the cases for exemptions as draftees presented themselves for service. He suggested some local flexibility even in wartime in who was selected to serve (author interview). While the law originally allowed for consciencious objectors, as hostilities increased, these too were drafted and put into noncombat positions. Failure to register was punishable by 3 months to 2 years in prison and failure to show for service could bring 2 to 4 years in prison (e.g. CAHI, 11-22-85).

    8.  In 1983 Nicaragua was alone in Central America in instituting a legal draft, although in February, 1984 Honduras also legislated military conscription. Honduras, Guatemala and Salvador all used forced recruitment to build their armies. The majority of the young men pulled into service in this manner were taken in military sweeps in poor rural areas.

    9.  The contras' July-September "Plan Round-Up" aimed at taking regional capitals after attacking major infrastructure in the vicinities. Esteli had been targetted in early August, but the contras were less than successful in taking La Trinidad just outside Esteli or in destroying the nearby agricultural project at Sebaco. The contras' "Plan September," meanwhile, focused on attacking Sumu and other Indian villages in Zelaya in efforts at derailing the FSLN's political autonomy process there. This effort too failed. Earlier, the EPS routed the contras from the important cattle-raising areas of Boaco and Chontales where the contras had hoped to establish a bridgehead between Honduran- and Costa Rican-based forces (BI, 7-25-85).

    10.  The size and nature of the La Penca base on the Rio San Juan and the existence of the contra camps just inside Costa Rica suggested that Costa Rican officials had allowed or ignored their existence and had actually complied in contra attacks. Nevertheless, at the close of Operation Sovereignty individual Costa Rican Civil Guard units met with EPS officials and pledged to prevent contras from firing on FSLN positions. These agreements were not formalized by the Costa Rican government which was pursuing an anti-Sandinista campaign at that time in response to shooting incidents at Las Crucitas in May (see Chapter 7).

    11.  In 1985 Nicaraguan pilots did not have the training or experience to use the Hind helicopters to their full potential. Nicaraguan pilots were not trained in using the aircraft's capability to shoot down other aircraft. To avoid losing one of these expensive aircraft, pilots generally flew them at high altitudes.

    12.  In private, US officials recognized the role of US policy in fueling Nicaraguan military build-up and gave much lower assessments of Nicaragua's military capacity (author interviews).

    13.  For an assessment of these claims see: Rothenberg; Cirincione and Hunter; Wiarda, all 1984; and King, 1984 and 1985.

    14.  Mathews (1985: 26) notes that the Nicaraguans did not want to offend their earlier benefactor, Panamanian leader Omar Torrijos, who had just negotiated with the United States to phase out the

military School of the Americas in Panama. Pastora said as much in October, 1979.

15. Nicaragua also had difficulty obtaining arms in US commercial arms markets and, apparently out of frustration, the FSLN government sought help from the Miami mafia in late 1980. In January, 1981, in an event which embarrassed the Nicaraguan government, two Sandinista Air Force officers tried to smuggle two US Huey helicopters--an item on the US Munitions Control list--out of Texas. They were caught by US officials and the aircraft and the money for their payment were confiscated.

16. Similarly, administration officials cite much higher figures than do independent and media' sources in detailing the numbers of arms shipments arriving in Nicaragua each year. For instance, while the New York Times reported one shipment about every three months, for a total of 5, in 1982, US officials cited a total of 14 in 1982 and 11 by mid-1983 (NYT, 7-27-83; 11-10-84).

17. King (1985) and media sources reported that Soviet advisors were perceived by EPS military officers as arrogant and disdainful of Nicaraguan culture. Cuban advisors, fellow Latins, were preferred.

18. Guatemala had 16 combat planes, 4 combat helicopters and 43 other helicopters (IISS, 1985). For further comparisons see NARMIC (1985); King (1985).

# 9

# Nicaraguan Internationalism:
# Principled Pragmatism and Survival

The Sandinistas' policy of internationalism grew out of their conceptualization of the Nicaraguan revolution as one part of the world struggle for liberation from foreign domination or socioeconomic oppression. Among its first official acts in the international arena, the government joined the non-aligned movement to confirm its commitment, FSLN leaders said, to struggle alongside other oppressed peoples in the Third World. But the policy of internationalism also reflected the FSLN's recognition of the role of international support in the war against Somoza and the ancien regime. Getting the revolution underway after the Triumph and defending Nicaragua's independence into the future would require continued broad international support; neutralizing counter-revolutionary tendencies was one objective behind Nicaragua's policy of seeking broad diplomatic relations. The policy of international activism was simultaneously a strategy for the defense of the revolution and a means of signalling the FSLN's radical shift away from Somoza's US-aligned foreign policy. The FSLN made it clear immediately that its primary foreign policy orientation would be toward promoting self-determination, policy independence and national liberation.

The contexts within which the Sandinistas' internationalism had to be pursued have been outlined in Parts Two and Three. Among other things, the earlier discussion enumerates the obstacles which had to be circumvented, overcome or adapted to in the Frente's efforts to develop a new foreign policy. A major theme has been the emergence of military security and economic survival as key determinants or shapers of Nicaraguan policy. As defense requirements grew, domestic and foreign policy options narrowed.

In this chapter, I focus on foreign policy patterns which have emerged in the first six years of Nicaragua's revolution. Having considered major policy environments and the development of the FSLN's military defense policy, here I discuss the political and economic ties forged by the Nicaraguans within those constraints. The FSLN government's behavior in the international arena is examined.

NICARAGUA'S POLITICAL-DIPLOMATIC RELATIONS

The Sandinistas' pre-and post-Triumph foreign policy consistently called for an independent policy vis-a-vis the superpowers; for non-alignment based on anti-imperialism, nationalism and self-determination; and for political alignment and fraternal collaboration with oppressed peoples around the world. According to the FSLN 1969 "Historic Program," the Sandinistas would "...put an end to Yankee interference in the internal problems of Nicaragua and practice toward other countries a policy of mutual respect...," accepting "...economic and technical aid from any country as long as it did not imply political commitments" (quoted in Edelman, 1985). In its early post-Triumph internal document (FSLN, 1979), FSLN leaders reflected their concern about securing the revolution through broad international ties and supporting other liberation movements. The FSLN pledged to "chart and pursue a nationalistic, anti-imperialist and democratic policy", to "develop the political and diplomatic relations that will further our military consolidation and economic independence"; and to "help further the struggle of Latin American nations...for democracy and national liberation" (p. 30-31).

These objectives were to be simultaneously pursued through an activist and internationalist stance. Revolutionary internationlism in practice required active membership in major international forums, solidarity with other liberation movements and increasing Nicaragua's own visibility and influence capacity. Just as Nicaragua's history with US intervention led the FSLN to identify its struggle against Somoza with the struggle against US imperialism, so the FSLN's victory in 1979 led it to identify Nicaragua's struggle with other anti-dictatorial and anti-imperialist struggles in Latin America and the underdeveloped world. The FSLN clearly saw the Nicaraguan revolution as a model for other underdeveloped states seeking national sovereignty and independence from the superpowers. According to Sandinista leaders, although revolutions were not exportable, more revolutions were inevitable; moreover, revolutionary and reformist movements alike would benefit from Nicaragua's policy innovativeness in forging an independent path and its insistence on relations based on mutual respect. Sandinista leaders maintained that revolutionary internationlism did not connote a proclivity for sponsoring subversion in others countries, but referred to the usefulness to other poor states of the Nicaraguan experience. Aware of their role as a test case and their position on the "front lines of Latin American sovereignty," Nicaraguan leaders claimed to be ever conscious of the implications of their policies for the Third World generally. So Tomas Borge argued in 1981, "This revolution goes beyond our borders."

But if philosophical orientations established a broad framework for the Frente's foreign policy, geopolitical and defense considerations yielded more specific requirements. Securing defense and economic reconstruction -- the early priority tasks -- while also pursuing reduced dependence upon and challenging the historical hegemonic prerogative of the local superpower, however, meant that the Frente had to take care to avoid sparking a

counter-revolutionary effort. Just as they had to garner
international support in 1979 to block US plans at the OAS for
denying an FSLN victory, in the following years the Sandinistas
pursued the revolution's defense in the international area by:
drawing support from the broadest array of states; balancing
relations among the West, the East and the underdeveloped states;
opening relations with the Arab states; and maintaining a realistic
perspective about why various states offered help. Although they
were in no position to apply an ideological test in establishing
foreign relations, the Sandinistas emphasized ties with states that
could provide appropriate economic assistance -- without attaching
conditions -- or that operated from. similar philosophical or
objective conditions. Reducing Nicaragua's economic vulnerability,
for example, required building sound relations with a variety of
states offering materials or markets. Thus, within its first year
in power the FSLN nearly doubled the number of states with which
Nicaragua had formal relations; by 1985 Nicaragua had relations with
110 states. It did so while remaining vocal in international forums
about the broader goals of the revolution. The FSLN established
financial or economic relations with thirty of these states, seven
of which were socialist. This record, according to the FSLN
leaders, both demonstrated diplomatic acumen and flexibility and
denied the United States international support for its campaign
against the revolution.

Yet, the Sandinistas were also under great pressure to refute
US claims that the revolution was a threat to regional peace and
pluralistic development. Maintaining Western European and Latin
American support required constant refutations and demonstrating
interest in political pluralism. On the other hand, keeping
important economic or military support from progressive or
anti-imperialist quarters and maintaining broad and non-Western
contacts required continued visibility in promoting Third World and
liberation themes. Doing so and projecting Nicaragua as a model for
other states, in turn, fueled US concern and military responses; the
FSLN's call for policy independence was interpreted in Washington as
a frontal assault on US regional and global interests.

In the context of new Cold War politics in the 1980s,
Nicaraguan leaders had to be dexterous in devising their non-aligned
foreign policy. Few models existed for the revolution; while the
leader of the Western world denied the FSLN legitimacy and labelled
its project communist, the Frente rejected the Soviet model for
Nicaragua and was wary of rejecting one dependence for another --
something Cuba and other states had been forced to do. The
socialist states had both the experience and the political will to
help in key areas of social mobilization and socioeconomic
restructuring. Balancing that aid and influence with Western and
non-Western models of democracy in the midst of a US-led campaign to
isolate them became the foreign policy task of the FSLN. The
Sandinistas claimed they had accepted this historical challenge of
melding a democratic, economically viable, soverign and non-aligned
state. According to the Frente, its method would be principled
pragmatism.

Diplomatic Relations and Political Affiliations

In the months after the Triumph the Nicaraguans relied on
international gifts of food, emergency relief, and cash from Sweden,
Mexico, the United States, Holland and other Western states. Latin
American countries and banks provided loans and lines of credit and
the World Bank provided a $50 million soft loan (e.g. NYT,
11-29-79). This response again impressed upon the Sandinistas both
the potential in and the necessity of maintaining relations with a
range of states. One of the first economic tasks, for example, was
renegotiating Nicaragua's (Somoza's) debt, establishing the new
government's credit-worthiness and thereby winning new loans from
old and new creditors. At the same time, the FSLN was aware of
early Western and Latin American concern over the role being played
by Cuban advisors in the military-security fields.

Diversity in relations was an aspect of FSLN foreign policy
pursued in the first months of the revolution. According to a
Foreign Ministry official: "The point was not merely to prove that
Nicaragua was now free to establish relations with any nation, but
more importantly to use old and new diplomatic ties to encourage a
genuine and independent understanding of the Nicaraguan and Central
American reality on the part of other governments and political
forces" (Bendana, 1982:323). The fact that 1) Nicaragua was not an
island -- in both geographic and political senses -- and, 2) that
this was not the 1950s was cited by the Frente as a premise in
foreign policy decision-making. Similarly, the notion that, as one
official put it in 1983, "We can't allow any doors to be closed to
us" grew in importance as a decision factor as the
counter-revolution developed under Washington's direction.

Employing state-to-state, party-to-party and people-to-people
contacts and giving "strategic weight" to relations with the United
States, Latin America and socialist states, the Frente quickly
expanded Nicaragua's official and fraternal relations. Western
European support and aid was considered vital to diversifying
Nicaragua's dependence, and, significant levels of aid were
forthcoming in the next years. At the same time, the FSLN
apparently chose to put less "strategic weight" on expanding (i.e.
as opposed to simply maintaining) their relatively good relations
with Western Europe. More energy was to go into exploring new
relationships with states similarly interested in distancing from
the United States or in promoting the causes of the underdeveloped
states. Seeking to reflect its non-aligned stance, the FSLN
established relations with both North and South Korea and both East
and West Germany. Establishing relations with both China and Taiwan
proved more difficult. According to FSLN officials, the Frente was
prohibited from doing so by the fact that China conditioned
relations with Nicaragua on the FSLN's breaking relations with
Taiwan. The Frente's position was that it would not accept
conditions in opening relations. Taiwan had long had relations with
Nicaragua and expressed a willingness to aid and trade with the new
government. Through 1985, Nicaragua had formal relations only with
Taiwan, though China had become an important importer of Nicaragua's
cotton. By the end of 1985, however, the FSLN's position on China
appeared to have changed. Responding along with other Latin

American states to a continent-wide diplomatic offensive from
Peking, the Nicaraguan leaders negotiated with a Chinese trade
delegation greatly to expand commercial ties in conjunction with
opening formal relations. In turn Nicaragua would break relations
with Taiwan, while$_2$ allowing that government to maintain a trade
mission in Managua.
    South American solidarity was an early goal which took on new
importance to the Sandinistas when Latin American peace initiatives
appeared to be the only factor confounding United States policy.
Confirming that in early 1985, President Ortega said that
Nicaragua's physical defense rested on the shoulders of the
Nicaraguans themselves. Although Nicaragua would not be a member of
a military pact, it nonetheless recognized the role to be played by
other Latin American states in securing its ultimate defense: "We
seek our security in the moral support of Latin America." Thus, the
democratization process underway in Latin America in the
1980s was also seen by the FSLN as an important opening for
Nicaragua. The move away from military or military-dominated
governments to electoral and civilian systems in Argentina, Brazil,
Uruguay, Peru, Panama and Guatemala meant that an important source
of traditional US influence -- through military ties or a common
anti-communist, national security state mentality -- would be
diminished. Indeed, though the Reagan Administration took pride in
the move toward democracy in Latin America, the new civilian
governments were significantly more vocal in calling for
independence, self-determination and a lessened US political and
military role. The civilian leaders in each of these states,
moreover, called on the United States to recognize Nicaraguan
sovereignty, actively supported Contadora and aided and traded with
the FSLN government. Referring to the impact of these events on US
policy generally, a US Embassy analyst in Managua noted in 1985 that
the new democracies "will be pesky as hell for the United States!"
(author interview).
    Recognizing the potential in this opening, the Frente placed
renewed emphasis in its diplomatic efforts on Latin American
nationalism, on common economic (e.g., debt) problems and on a
vision of increased continental independence through Latin American
solidarity. As FSLN leaders, especially after 1984, placed
Nicaragua's survival and conflict with the United States into a
broader north-south context -- for example, by arguing that
Bolivarism was being reborn in Sandinista foreign policy during a
period when Washington was reviving the Monroe Doctrine -- they
reinforced among Latin American peoples Nicaragua's image as a
regional leader in the drive for sovereignty. Similarly, the FSLN
sought to make Nicaraguan survival a Latin American project, thereby
enlarging the scope of the conflict for the US. As Vice President
Ramirez argued before the Latin American Conference on External
Debt in Havana in August, 1985:

    The contradiction between the imperial interests of the
    United States and the interests of Latin America for its
    sovereignty and its independence is being played out today
    in a dramatic and crucial way in Nicaragua....all people
    of good will must be called to the defense of Nicaragua,

314

> because this is the hour of the continental test....the
> more arduously we are called upon to struggle, the more
> will we be the voice of Latin America, the more will we be
> identified with the interests of democracy on the
> continent, for change, for justice, for full
> independence...We are proud to defend, as Latin Americans,
> the vital interests of Latin America (IHCA, August 1985).

The general success of this tactic was reflected during 1985 in the
reception of Ramirez at the debt conference; in the response of
Latin American states to the US embargo; in the popularity of
Sandinista Nicaragua among Latin American masses; and in the US
State Department's recognition that it would have to find new ways
of circumventing Latin American unity and pressure if it was to keep
the costs of pursuing its regional policy at acceptable levels.

The Sandinistas' philosophical orientation and history of
struggle for liberation led them to feel a special affinity for
other oppressed or struggling peoples and movements. A natural
affinity also existed for other states or groups which had struggled
against US domination or northern imperialism. Thus
anti-imperialist states like Algeria and Libya -- states which could
also provide oil, technical aid and Third World solidarity -- seemed
natural friends for the FSLN. In fact, both states came to provide
important credits and some military material even though the FSLN
did not acutally develop close relations with either state or
politically align with, for instance, Libyan initiatives. Likewise,
Iran was sympathetic to the FSLN's continuing struggle against US
dominance.

The FSLN established relations with Vietnam in September, 1979
and formalized contacts with the Palestinian Liberation Organization
in July, 1980. Relations with the PLO dated to the late 1960s when
the FSLN supported PLO efforts to undermine Israel and when a few
FSLN fighters trained with PLO forces. The Israelis had provided
Somoza's National Guard its armored force and later supplied Somoza
with nearly all the military material used in the war against FSLN
guerrillas (e.g., Edelman, 1985:37). This reality led to the early
FSLN-PLO connection. Geographical distance, Western antipathy
toward the PLO, and differences in objective realities between
Nicaragua and the FSLN and the PLO, however, meant that the FSLN's
ties to that group would be of lower priority. Historical factors
were also to shape Nicaragua's relationship with Israel. For
example, though the FSLN assumed the rest of Somoza's debt, it
refused to assume the military-related debt incurred with Israel in
the last months of Somoza's rule. In 1982, moreover, Nicaragua
broke relations with Israel over the latter's invasion of Lebanon.
Shortly thereafter Israel's role in supplying weapons and training
to US Central American allies -- including weapons for the contras
-- became public. Yet by 1984 the FSLN showed interest in
re-establishing relations and maintained contact with Israeli
parties through the Socialist International and other forums (e.g.
LAWR, 12-14-84).

FSLN moves to investigate the potential for economic and
strategic ties with the Eastern bloc in 1980 corresponded not only
to the _Frente's_ non-aligned stance and its interest in financial

diversification, but also to the tenuous future of US aid given the conservative surge in US Congressional and domestic politics. While the Eastern bloc extended no credits or major aid to Nicaragua in 1979,[3] in 1980 the FSLN negotiated scientific, cultural and technical agreements with the Soviets. In mid-1980, the Soviets opened an embassy in Managua, and established regular Aeroflot flights between the two states. Also in 1980, Bulgaria and Czechoslovakia extended industrial credits on soft terms for hydroelectric and textile projects in Nicaragua and discussed with the FSLN delegation the possibility for joint investments where the investment would be paid off by Nicaraguan production.[4] Hungary, East Germany and Poland, meanwhile, provided Nicaragua nearly $35 million in loans and additionally sent food, clothing and medical donations to the Nicaraguan people.

The FSLN's early thoughts regarding ties with the USSR and Eastern Europe were reflected in a December, 1980 Barricada (the official FSLN newspaper) interview with FSLN Directorate member Jaime Wheelock. According to the Agriculture Minister, the FSLN's first official trip to Moscow and other eastern capitals in March, 1980 was intended as a step toward sounding out Eastern bloc willingness to aid Nicaragua, given Nicaraguan reconstruction needs and growing indications of a counter-revolutionary potential. It was also part of the FSLN's "broad plan of support and solidarity with the world's progressive peoples," one that, according to Wheelock, paralleled the Sandinistas' efforts vis-a-vis the Socialist International. Nicaragua had recently enjoined a support and solidarity committee with SI leaders Olaf Palme and Willy Brandt "to reinforce collective actions of democratic socialist peoples" amidst "threats from imperialist, reactionary sectors." Stressing both the Frente's desire to cooperate with all states willing to extend fraternal support for Nicaragua's reconstruction task and the US conservatives' call for the Sandinistas' overthrow, Wheelock went on:

> We are not going to fan the hope or the illusion that the socialist countries are going to present gifts to the Nicaraguan people because socialist countries...do not practice extortion of nations. It is a matter of mutual cooperation in which we are going to acknowledge the credit somehow. But credit is unconditional...We are not trying to create false expectations in this sense. [We will] open and expand economic and trade relations with these states and maintain traditional ties...We are not trying to replace our economic sector. This is not the most advisable course for us...(FBIS-LAM 12-23-80).

Calling these new contacts "highly positive for Nicaragua's strategic development," Wheelock noted the FSLN's post-trip feeling of enhanced security: "We truly do not feel we are alone, but rather have more support since this tour of the socialist nations" (FBIS-LAM, op. cit.). Wheelock also noted the beneficial aspects of easy and unconditional industrial credit offered by Bulgaria and Czechoslovakia. At the same time, however, the FSLN asserted its independence. Speaking before Soviet leaders in Moscow during the

316

March, 1980 trip, delegation leader Tomas Borge declared that Nicaragua..."has taken the irrevocable decision to be free and Nicaraguans will go on being masters of our destiny...We are the ones who decide and it's for that reason we are here" (LP, 3-20-80).

Further evidence of the FSLN's early caution and attempts to balance relations exists in the fact that even as this delegation was in Eastern Europe, another high level delegation headed by Junta member Sergio Ramirez, Nicaragua's Finance Minister Joaquin Cuadra and FSLN Political Secretary Bayardo Arce, was touring Western Europe. Moreover, while Nicaraguan officials made a number of high level contacts with Western and Third World governments in 1980 and 1981, it was to be another year and a half before a second high level delegation visited Moscow. In November 1981, Defense Minister Humberto Ortega went to the USSR with requests for military aid.

The pattern of balancing trips to the Eastern bloc with similar campaigns for aid in Western Europe, Latin America or Canada remained a noticeable feature of Nicaragua's foreign policy into 1986. The year 1984 provides an example. That year FSLN officials made five trips to the Soviet Union -- one for Andropov's funeral and two each for purposes of discussing economic relations and military aid. Included in these Eastern European itineraries in 1984 were three visits to East Germany (one visit appeared to be ceremonial in nature), two stop-overs in Bulgaria and one in Czechoslovakia, all in pursuit of more economic aid. By this time, the United States' unofficial economic boycott of Nicaragua had deprived the Sandinistas of major Western bilateral and multilateral aid; moreover, many of Nicaragua's resources were being directed to the war effort. Eastern bloc aid was becoming crucial to Nicaragua's continued economic survival.

Yet, during 1984 Nicaraguan leaders busily pursued new or continued economic aid and political support from Western Europe and the Third World. In 1984 the FSLN government received high level delegations, including the Prime Minister, the Foreign Minister or the Economic Minister, from Sweden, France (two visits), Canada, Holland, Denmark and Australia (two visits). Nicaraguan economic leaders met with EEC officials on two occasions and FSLN leaders met with or hosted SI representatives on three occasions. While officials from the Ministry of Health undertook an aid mission through Western Europe, Minister of Foreign Trade Alejandro Cuenca sought trade assurances on trips to Canada, Spain and Sweden. Many other less formal contacts were made with major Western powers on the issues of Contadora and Nicaraguan elections. Several US Congressional delegations visited Managua.

Similarly, in 1984 Nicaragua pursued strengthened ties with Third World supporters. High level economic or political delegations travelled to Ecuador (two visits), Venezuela, Panama (two trips), Argentina, Mexico (three trips outside the Manzanillo talks), Colombia, Costa Rica, Cuba, Algeria (three trips, one regarding trade), Libya (a ceremonial visit by Borge), Ethiopia, Mozambique and Iran (two trips regarding trade). New economic exchanges were negotiated with Colombia, Argentina, and Iran. Political affiliations were renewed with the Latin American Commission of Political Parties (COPPPAL) and with the Algerian FLN. In the area of labor organizations, unions and aid, in 1984

Nicaragua made technical and advisory exchanges with Mexico and Canada and in April hosted the First International Trade Union Conference for Peace, attended by 125 labor organizations from sixty countries. The labor ministers from the Non-Aligned countries also met in Managua in May (BI, 4-30-84; 5-15-84; 5-22-84; 11-3-84).

The picture that emerges, in brief, is of an activist FSLN leadership which purposely pursued relations and foreign policy objectives in numerous arenas and among a broad spectrum of states.

Nevertheless, Eastern bloc willingness to respond to Nicaraguan needs became an important source of economic and psychological security to the Frente. As aid links grew, so did Nicaraguan sensitivity about not directly confronting the Soviets on controversial international issues such as Soviet troops in Afghanistan, Soviet policy regarding the Polish Solidarity union and the USSR downing of the Korean Air Lines 007 flight in 1983. Of priority importance to the Nicaraguans, the Soviets offered political solidarity, military aid and support for a negotiated settlement in Central America through Contadora. That solidarity was fostered after 1981 through: regular visits to the USSR and Eastern Europe by Nicaraguan Planning Minister Ruiz; six visits to Moscow by Daniel Ortega between 1981 and 1986 -- including three trips to attend the funerals of Brezhnev, Andropov and Chernenko; and several visits to Moscow by Defense Minister Humberto Ortega and Foreign Minister D'Escoto.

Political and Cultural Affiliations. The FSLN sought to affiliate its revolution with what it saw as other progressive, anti-imperialist and pro-liberation groups. At the same time, the priority objective of non-alignment and the eclectic, non-Western nature of Sandinismo dictated balancing ties among a variety of groups which accomodated Third World perspectives.

The Sandinistas' political orientation and their international contact before and immediately after the Triumph influenced revolutionary Nicaragua's socio-political ties. Links to the Socialist International, for example, were considered key to maintaining the solidarity and support of Western European (and other) Social Democrats forged by Nicaraguan delegations during the struggle against Somoza. Acknowledging the many common political aspirations between the revolution and the Social Democratic body, the FSLN joined the SI as an observer, consolidating the association both by attending its meetings and cultivating ties with SI-affiliated parties in Europe and Latin America. That Nicaragua's affiliation was active and considered important to the SI group as well was reflected in the amount of time given at meetings to considering Central American and Nicaraguan-US issues. The SI supported Nicaragua's goal of non-alignment; on that basis the SI criticized US policy. From a position of general support, SI leaders pressed the FSLN to accommodate its business bourgeois opposition and worked as mediators between the FSLN and the Coordinadora in 1984 (see IHCA, November, 1984). Although there were at times heated debates among constituent delegations about the direction of the Nicaraguan revolution and the orientation of the FSLN, they did not lead to an SI rejection of Nicaraguan affiliation. In a less tense situation, SI members believed, efforts and influence toward pluralism had a much better chance to succeed (IHCA, July, 1985).

Affiliations to the SI also existed through the Nicaraguan women's group AMLAE (FSLN-affiliated). A Women's Socialist International meeting, for instance, was hosted by the Nicaraguan group in December, 1983 (BI, 12-12-83). Meanwhile, links to the Liberal and the Christian Democratic Internationals also were cultivated. Both groups issued statements in the early 1980s calling for support of the revolution on the basis of pluralism, a mixed economy and non-alignment. In 1982, Junta member Sergio Ramirez addressed an LI seminar and FSLN Political Coordinator Arce met with LI delegates to discuss Nicaraguan politics. The latter meeting resulted in a joint call for promoting social justice, human rights and non-alignment and included praise for Nicaraguan efforts at pluralism and social progress (FBIS-LAM, 9-2-82; CAU, November, 1982). These associations, then, represented pressures for pluralistic development in post-Somoza Nicaragua.

FSLN ties to Social Democratic parties in Latin America were solidified through its membership in the Permanent Conference of Latin American Political Parties (COPPPAL). Though affiliated with the SI, COPPPAL was an independent regional body which was strengthened and fostered in the early 1980s by Mexican efforts to better represent Latin American concerns. Spurred both by Mexico's support for the Nicaraguan revolution and the Sandinista's interest in FSLN association with major Latin American parties, Nicaragua assumed an active role and one of the vice-presidencies in COPPPAL. Nicaragua hosted its meetings in February, 1982. The FSLN used the forum presented by its membership in COPPPAL to explain its policies, to increase its regional visibility, and to win Latin American support for the revolution. COPPPAL provided Nicaragua another avenue for identifying its revolutionary cause with Latin American struggles for greater independence and sovereignty. Its work paid off in COPPPAL statements of support and calls for US restraint. At its 1981 Santo Domingo meeting, COPPPAL called for political solutions to regional conflict and for unconditional economic cooperation with Nicaragua. Calling for solidarity with Nicaragua, the body also condemned the "despotic" regimes in Guatemala, Chile and Argentina, thereby reflecting especially Nicaragua's and Mexico's support for liberation and civilian movements in Latin America (LAWR, 5-29-81). At the 1982 meetings, the FSLN hosts used the forum to forward initiatives which could provide bases for a rapproachment with the United States and the Reagan Administration. According to Tomas Borge, COPPPAL's support for such peace initiatives would add necessary momentum to so-far-unsuccessful efforts at getting negotiations underway (BI, 2-27-82). In the following years Nicaraguan activism in this and other Latin American forums aimed at preserving room and garnering support for Nicaraguan positions.

The invitation to Nicaragua to join the Latin American legislative association, Parlatino, in 1985 was similarly heralded in Nicaragua both as evidence of regional support for Nicaraguan elections in late 1984 and as a forum within which Nicaragua would meld regional solidarity on issues of common concern (BI, 1-23-84; IHCA, July, 1985). Pursuing the same visibility on the world level, in October, 1985 a multi-party delegation from Nicaragua's National

Assembly attended the 74th conference of the World Interparliamentary Union in Ottawa, Canada. There the Nicaraguans denounced US policy, aligned Nicaragua with Third World aspirations for a New International Economic Order, and addressed the Third World debt problem. The Nicaraguan delegation also made bilateral contacts with sixty-five of the ninety country delegations present. In part reflecting Nicaragua's activism at the WIU meeting, the 1986 meeting agenda was set to deal with the themes of Central America and nuclear disarmament (IHCA, November, 1985).

The political affiliation which received wider attention in the United States was the FSLN's party-to-party accord with the Communist Party of the Soviet Union. That agreement was made at the time of the March, 1980 trip to the USSR and was formally implemented after a June, 1983 trip to Moscow by Bayardo Arce (Rothenberg, 1984: 134; NYT, 3-23-85). The agreement implied that FSLN representatives would be invited to CPSU party congresses and meetings and provided for purchase of Soviet literature. However, this Nicaraguan move appears to have been designed originally to demonstrate Nicaraguan independence from the United States and the FSLN's shift away from Somoza's policies. US State Department officials, for instance, viewed the accord as more show than substance (see Edelman, 1985:40). That assessment is reinforced by the fact that whereas CPSU meetings rarely touched on issues immediately pertinent to Nicaragua, Nicaraguan concerns were regularly aired at SI and COPPPAL meetings. Third World and Latin American forums better facilitated Nicaraguan foreign policy objectives. Ties to Western European parties, moreover, balanced FSLN ties with the CPSU. Further, though the CPSU apparently advised the FSLN on mobilization and organizational methods -- Political Coordinator Arce met with CPSU officials twice in 1981 and several times in the next years (Schwab and Sims, 1985) -- the FSLN in 1983 and again in 1985 initiated decentralization and grass-roots efforts in representational and neighborhood organizations. Soviet party and state structures were neither reproduced in Nicaragua, nor were they judged by the FSLN leadership to be appropriate in the Nicaraguan situation. Nor was Soviet literature used in FSLN political training. Similarly, the old pro-Moscow communist party of Nicaragua had little influence in the leadership ranks of the FSLN.

Soviet influence in Nicaragua was nonetheless evident by 1981 and 1982. Besides military aid, economic aid and cultural exchanges were growing. Moreover, Marxist-Leninists within the FSLN were encouraged by the new level of fraternal ties with the USSR, openly to discuss their orientations and, at times, to identify the revolution with Marxism-Leninism. In 1982, for example, political leader of the Sandinista army, Hugo Torres, declared his Marxist-Leninist commitment just as an FSLN delegation was set to leave for Moscow on an aid-seeking trip (Schwab and Sims, 1985). Daniel Ortega returned from Moscow with new economic agreements and credits from the Soviets worth $166.8 million. Also in 1982 the FSLN affiliated its mass organizations with respective Soviet-sponsored international bodies and joined a number of other Third World States in affiliating with the Intersputnik telecommunications organization. According to a Radio Sandino announcement at the time, by the end of 1983 Nicaragua would have direct satellite communication with the Eastern bloc, Asia and Africa through the Intersputnik system, thanks to Soviet provision of project financing, equipment, training and ground station equipment (LAWR, 10-1-82). Strengthening these ties was the fact that a growing number of Nicaraguan students and technicians were being trained in Eastern Europe and Cuba in conjunction with technical and economic aid packages.[5]

There is little doubt that Soviet willingness to aid Nicaragua was promoted by both the FSLN's willingness to associate with some Soviet organizations or causes as well as by the Sandinistas' commitment to some form of socialism. On the other hand, there is little evidence that the Soviets applied pressure on the Nicaraguans to pursue particular policies or a particular brand of socialism. According to Nicaraguan officials, Soviet aid and friendship was offered without conditions and was accepted by the FSLN in the context of its own development planning (e.g., FBIS-LAM, 12-23-80; Conroy, 1985). This stands in contrast to SI support which, though it remained relatively constant to 1986, was couched in the context of continued FSLN commitment to pluralism, a mixed economy, and the like. Indeed the debates within the SI over Nicaragua centered around various members' interpretations of Nicaraguan policies and their own conceptions of appropriate political and economic models. While the FSLN sought out and cultivated SI support, it also insisted on defining its own political path which, it said, would not be identical to European Social Democratic models.

## Participation In Multilateral Organizations

The FSLN strategy in multinational arenas involved optimizing its chances for diplomatic success by committing its greatest energies to forums where revolutionary Nicaragua could get the most sympathetic hearings or support, and, where majorities held similar foreign policy objectives. Especially as the war situation came to dominate Nicaraguan life, the Sandinistas used international or regional organizations to forge a broad condemnation of US policy and to build momentum for a negotiated settlement. Additionally, the FSLN saw multilateral forums as potential avenues for avoiding the constraints upon its independence posed by traditional US hegemony.

The UN. The international forum in which Nicaragua was most visible was the United Nations. The FSLN used that forum repeatedly as a platform to give its analysis of US policy, to warn of US intentions to invade Nicaragua and to report the costs and implications of the contra war. Even before it won a seat on the Security Council beginning January, 1983, Nicaragua requested and received that body's consideration of charges of US aggression -- moves Nicaragua claimed were in violation of UN Charter restrictions on foreign intervention. Nicaragua's success in campaigning for the Security Council seat, in fact, foreshadowed the success it was to have in isolating the United States at the UN on votes regarding US regional policy. Western European states, which three years earlier had voted against Cuban representation on the Security Council, backed Nicaragua's candidacy despite heavy US lobbying and US arguments that Nicaragua was incapable of reflecting Latin American views (NYT, 10-20-82; LAWR, 10-29-82). Contrary to expectations in the United States, on the third round of balloting, Nicaragua gained the two-thirds majority it needed to win the seat. Washington's preferred candidate, the Domincan Republic, could not garner the necessary votes (LAWR, 19-29-82; NYT, 10-20-82).

By 1986, Nicaragua had successfully convened nine Security Council sessions to denounce US-backed contra attacks, to offer peace proposals, to call for UN support for negotiations and to counter US charges against Nicaragua. One of the most successful sessions for Nicaragua took place in March, 1983 when the Council spent five days considering Nicaragua's complaints against the United States. During the debate, in which many states rose to speak, it became clear that only the Salvadoran and Honduran representatives would stand with the United States; none of the other US allies supported the US position that the war in Nicaragua was essentially an internal matter. In this visible world arena Nicaragua's position was largely affirmed, while the United States was isolated. Although the final resolution employed mild language about the US role in Nicaragua, it commended Contadora efforts toward regional peace, called on regional actors to dialogue and instructed the Secretary General to keep the Security Council informed of events. Hailing the Council activity as a victory for Nicaragua and a defeat for the Reagan Administration, Nicaraguan officials were pleased that the UN had been assigned a role in the region (NYT, 3-23-83; 5-6-83; 5-14-83; 5-20-83). They took special satisfaction in Secretary General deCuellar's statement that the FSLN was the legitimate government of Nicaragua.

At other times as well, the Nicaraguans used the Security Council or the General Assembly to create momentum against hostile US actions or to call on the United States to abide by international law. Shortly after the US military move into Grenada in late 1983, for example, Nicaragua played a key role as drafter of a General Assembly resolution condemning the act. Interpreting the Grenada events as a dry run for a US invasion of Nicaragua, Nicaraguan delegates worked to push the resolution to its final 108 to 9 passage (27 abstentions). In November, 1984, for the eighth time, the FSLN initiated Security Council discussions concerning US policy. On that occasion, Nicaragua was responding to the heightened US-Nicaraguan tensions brought on by the "MIG crisis". Citing US overflights, military maneuvers close to Nicaraguan borders and the presence of twenty-five US warships near Nicaraguan waters, the Frente warned that the United States was about to attack Nicaragua. In May, 1985 Nicaragua called a Security Council meeting to criticize the new US embargo. After two days of debate, a Security Council resolution, sponsored by 36 states -- 13 of them Latin American -- was offered condemning the embargo (ICAS, June, 1985; NYT, 5-6-85; 5-10-85). Another resolution, vetoed by the United States, called for a return to the bilateral Manzanillo talks. The document -- which did not specifically mention the United States, but called for the immediate revocation of economic sanctions against Nicaragua -- passed 91 to 6 (with 49 abstentions) in a December vote (ICAS, January, 1986). Finally, in another 1985 diplomatic initiative before the UN, President Daniel Ortega used

Table 9.1
A Comparative Perspective on Nicaragua's UN Voting, 1979-1985

| | | Average | GENERAL ASSEMBLY SESSION (% Common Votes) | | | | | | |
| | | | 34 | 35 | 36 | 37 | 38 | 39 | 40 |
|---|---|---|---|---|---|---|---|---|---|
| Nicaragua | US | 5 | 4 | 0 | 5 | 4 | 14 | 5 | 3 |
| | USSR | 84 | 96 | 82 | 84 | 87 | 67 | 86 | 86 |
| majority Latin America | | 83 | 92 | 75 | 84 | 83 | 92 | 76 | 78 |
| | Mexico | 90 | 92 | 82 | 84 | 91 | 97 | 92 | 89 |
| | Venezuela | 84 | 96 | 82 | 74 | 83 | 92 | 78 | 81 |
| | Costa Rica | 76 | 83 | 80 | 76 | 82 | 83 | 68 | 58 |
| | Panama | 82 | 84 | 90 | 77 | 82 | 92 | 76 | 75 |
| | India | 93 | 100 | 100 | 100 | 96 | 83 | 86 | 86 |
| | Tanzania | 90 | 92 | 90 | 98 | 87 | 94 | 84 | 83 |
| Mexico | US | 9 | 4 | 9 | 5 | 13 | 14 | 8 | 11 |
| | USSR | 82 | 96 | 75 | 79 | 87 | 69 | 84 | 86 |
| Costa Rica | US | 12 | 8 | 18 | 11 | 14 | 14 | 11 | 8 |
| | USSR | 71 | 88 | 82 | 61 | 82 | 61 | 62 | 58 |
| Venezuela | US | 14 | 4 | 17 | 21 | 17 | 14 | 8 | 14 |
| | USSR | 79 | 96 | 83 | 74 | 83 | 67 | 68 | 81 |
| Cuba | US | 2 | 0 | 0 | 0 | 0 | 8 | 5 | 3 |
| | USSR | 94 | 100 | 100 | 100 | 96 | 78 | 89 | 94 |

Based on a variety of thirty-six votes recorded during the September to December sessions in each of the seven years; Session 34: September, 1979-December, 1979; Session 40: September to December, 1985. Data are from the UN Department of Public Information, Press Section.

the fortieth anniversary General Assembly session to challenge
President Reagan to make his case against Nicaragua before the UN,
or, to make peace, recognize the orders of the World Court and
normalize relations with Nicaragua: "This is the challenge of peace
that Nicaragua puts to him. The peace of Central America depends
upon his answer (IHCA, November, 1985).[6]
    In its voting behavior at the UN Nicaragua tried to avoid
ideological identification with the USSR or as a radical
pro-revolution actor. FSLN delegates consistently expressed
opposition to imperialism and voted in accordance with national
security or foreign policy objectives.. Nicaragua distanced itself
from states or causes considered by a majority of states to be
radical or outlaw (see also Queiser-Morales and Vanden, 1985).
Nicaraguan delegates to the UN were activist and cultivated the
image of flexible spokespersons for Third World causes.
    Table 9.1 presents data comparing Nicaragua's General Assembly
voting with that of the superpowers, several of its Latin American
neighbors and two leaders in the Non-Aligned Movement -- India and
Tanzania. While these data are limited, they present an initial
comparative picture of Nicaragua's UN record through 1985. Several
trends seem clear. First, Nicaragua's vote behavior most closely
resembled that of two states with established records of
non-alignment. As Nicaraguan officials have contended, Nicaragua
appears to take a cue from India in deciding its UN vote. Moreover,
Nicaragua voted with Tanzania and Mexico around 90 percent of the
time. Second, Nicaragua voted with the USSR about as often as it
voted with Venezuela and the majority of Latin American states.
Overall, Nicaragua voted with the Soviet Union about as often as
Mexico did. Its pattern of common voting with the USSR is closer to
Venezuela's than it is to Cuba's. Third, while Nicaragua voted with
the United States only on rare occasions, averaging 5 percent of
common votes, regional US allies like Mexico, Venezuela and Costa
Rica averaged common votes with the United States only 9 percent, 14
percent and 12 percent of the time, respectively. Cuba voted with
the United States about 2 percent of the time. Fourth, Nicaraguan
vote behavior generally reflected a policy congruence with Third
World states. These data point up the fact that Third World and
Latin American voting has closely resembled USSR voting. That
pattern reflects shifts in the character of UN politics in the
post-World War II era of decolonization. Emphases have been on the
issues of imperialism, underdevelopment, Western economic dominance,
and the like. The differences between Nicaragua and other Latin
American states in common voting with the USSR can be accounted for
by a number of inter-related factors: Nicaragua's more vocal
and activist non-aligned stance; its greater propensity to champion
liberation causes; its growing aid ties to the USSR beginning in
1982; and its greater mistrust of Washington.
    These FSLN foreign policy orientations were reflected in
Nicaragua's controversial UN votes on two highly charged issues
involving the USSR -- the invasion of Afghanistan in late 1979 and
the downing of the Korean Air Liner flight 007 in 1983. Nicaragua
abstained on repeated General Assembly votes condemning the USSR
over its moves in Afghanistan and on the Security Council vote
condemning Soviet actions in the KAL 007 incident. The Reagan

Administration referred especially to the Afghanistan votes to argue
that Nicaragua had become incorporated into the Soviet camp.
Nicaraguan foreign ministry officials gave a different explanation:

> Although not in agreement with the presence of Soviet
> troops in Afghanistan, Nicaragua took the position, shared
> by India, that a punitive resolution alone would not
> contribute to peace in the area. A concern...was that
> condemnation of the Soviet Union would provide a rationale
> for the escalation of the US military presence in
> Southeast Asia; subsequent events bore that fear out
> (Bendana, 1982: p. 324).

Likewise, Foreign Minister D'Escoto voiced Nicaragua's support
for Afghan self-determination at the UN in 1981 and called for
regional negotiations. Later, D'Escoto referred to Nicaragua's
condemnation of "intervention and interventionism" by both the USSR
and the United States (i.e. US military presence in the Indian Ocean
and Pakistan) in the region (quoted in Edelman, 1985:40). Rather
than adopting the USSR line, in other words, the Nicaraguans pursued
what they saw as a non-aligned position which would not contribute
to East-West posturing or regional escalations. In other ways and
on other votes the Nicaraguans expressed support for
non-intervention -- an issue central to their own survival!

Independence in the face of heavy US pressures to join in
condemnations of the USSR was also the path Nicaragua followed on
the KAL 007 Security Council vote. Arguing that not all the facts
were in regarding the circumstances surrounding the airliner downing
incident, Nicaragua -- along with China, Guyana and Zimbabwe --
abstained.

The Non-Aligned Movement. Joining the Non-Aligned Movement
(NAM) just six weeks after the Triumph, the Sandinistas signalled
their determination 1) to avoid international isolation -- a fate
Cuba had suffered after 1960 -- and 2) to work in concert with
similarly-oriented states. But joining the Non-Aligned Movement was
also a natural or rational response to Nicaragua's history of
foreign occupation and domination. Yankee imperialism was both an
historically and psychologically potent image for revolutionary
Nicaragua; joining the ranks of NAM affirmed the Sandinistas' stance
for national liberation. Concerned about the development of US
hostility and new counter-revolutionary threats, the FSLN saw in NAM
an arena in which its assertion of independence would be supported,
where it could gain support somewhat protected from East-West
pressures and where its foreign policy aspirations would be
understood. NAM membership, thus, was an extension of Nicaragua's
new internationalism. It was consistent with the FSLN's drive to
add to its security by garnering international solidarity and by
avoiding charges of Eastern alignment -- a tactic used by the United
States in the past to isolate nonconformist states in the region.

Rather than representing neutrality or equidistant stances
between the "two imperialisms" of the United States and the Soviet
Union, the Non-Aligned Movement had come by the 1970s to represent a
forum within which Third World states could pursue independent paths
(e.g. Queiser-Morales and Vanden, 1985: 477). What drew the members

together were common concerns over global economic reform and Western economic and political hegemony. They shared a desire to provide support to national liberation struggles. Within this framework, member states differed in their tendencies toward the Soviets or the United States. Indeed, the Yugoslavian - Algerian position in NAM -- that equidistance was required for non-aligned status -- had become a minority view within the movement, taken over by greater affinity with the Cuban view -- that the socialist bloc was a natural ally to NAM members (Armstrong, 1985:15). That latter view was reinforced, in effect, by differences between the superpowers in how they viewed the Non-Aligned Movement. The United States preferred to interact with loyal or proven allies and historically saw NAM as irrelevant, or worse yet, as a proxy for the USSR. The Soviets, by contrast, lent NAM credibility and verbal support, believing that NAM's colonial experience and anti-imperialist orientation might work in their favor.

The five conditions for NAM membership were: support for anti-colonial liberation; independent foreign policies based on peaceful co-existance; committing to no formal military treaties; allowing no foreign military bases in national territory; and belonging to no world military alliances. Nicaraguan policy objectives, then, were considered mainstream. In fact, Nicaragua again avoided identifying with extremist groups within NAM. Instead, Nicaragua argued for conciliatory flexibility except where its national security appeared to be on the line. Consistent with its post-Triumph international activism, Nicaragua became a visible and outspoken advocate of NAM and a leader among its Latin American members.[8]

The FSLN's activism in the movement again yielded rewards in the area that quickly became the Frente's greatest concern: US hostility toward the revolution. At NAM meetings in New Delhi (1981) and Havana (1982) the body condemned US hostility and reasserted support for Nicaraguan self-determination. In 1983 the FSLN hosted a well-attended NAM meeting and used the occasion to raise discussion of the US role in the contra war, and, to focus meeting attention on Latin and Central American issues. Although NAM-member friends of the United States (Seaga's Jamaica and Egypt among them), worked to soften the final language, the meeting communique called for a peaceful solution to regional conflict and noted the large role being played by the United States. The Managua NAM meeting was considered by the FSLN as another diplomatic victory against Reagan Administration attempts to reassert hegemony in Latin America. The fact that Colombia and Panama left the US-sponsored Forum for Peace and Democracy to join both the Contadora and this NAM meeting -- where they voiced condemnation of US destabilization efforts -- sweetened that victory for the Sandinistas (e.g. LAWR, 1-21-83).

Although after 1983 Nicaragua devoted most of its multilateral diplomatic efforts to pursuing peace and survival initiatives through the UN, the Contadora process and other regional forums, Nicaragua retained an active membership in NAM and relied on NAM support in maintaining the momentum against US policy. Again at the 1985 Luanda, Angola meeting, for example, NAM expressed concern about Nicaragua's situation and reiterated support for Contadora.

The Non-Aligned Movement represented for the FSLN a forum within which it did not have to prove its motives.

The OAS. The FSLN was somewhat less inclined to view the Organization of American States as a sympathetic forum. Unlike at the United Nations, at the OAS the United States retained considerable influence. When OAS initiatives ran counter to US policy or its preferences, moreover, the United States -- as it did several times on issues pertaining to Nicaragua and Contadora -- declared that it retained the right to act unilaterally to pursue its interests (e.g. IHCA, December, 1984). The Sandinista government thus assessed that it could best pursue its goals of independence and security in forums where the odds were better for avoiding US dictates. The FSLN supported the Latin American idea -- which predated the revolution -- of creating an exclusively Latin American forum. Taking note of the "positive experiences" of Contadora, the Cartagena Group (formed to address the debt issue), Latin American responses to the US embargo and OAS support for Costa Rican-Nicaraguan border talks in 1985 (all discussed in Chapter 7), the Nicaraguan government worked in the region to build a consensus against "being continual victims of US political pressures and blackmail." According to Deputy Foreign Minister Jose Talevera, there were advantages to: "dealing with strictly Latin American issues without the participation of countries that have a much higher level of development and whose problems are completely different than those of our undeveloped nations." Latin Americans needed to solve common issues, employing mechanisms which avoided "disproportionate" US pressure or influence (BI, 8-1-85).

Despite its wariness, the Frente played an active role in the OAS as well. Encouraged by the fact that the OAS had not supported the US effort in July, 1979 to send an OAS peace-keeping force to Nicaragua, the Frente aimed at influencing greater Latin American independence in that forum in the future. In the early years the FSLN worked behind the scenes at the OAS to preserve maneuvering room for itself and the FMLN in Salvador and worked formally to build credibility and support for the Sandinista revolution. As the contra war heated up, its efforts turned to building momentum for a negotiated settlement through Contadora and to short-circuiting US initiatives which were interpreted as harmful to Nicaragua's interests. A major tactic employed by the Frente at the OAS was appealing to Latin American nationalism, to aspirations for greater independence and to common economic concerns.

Nicaraguan efforts to maintain a sizeable base of support at the OAS paid off on several important votes in the 1980s. In April, 1983 the OAS voted to refer all questions regarding peace in Central America to the Contadora group, rather than to debate proposals before the entire OAS body. The importance of that move to Nicaragua lay in the fact that the United States was not a member of Contadora; the peace process thus was in the hands of fellow Latin Americans who identified more easily with Nicaraguan positions. Nicaraguan officials hailed the vote as the second major OAS victory for the Sandinistas after the July, 1979 vote (IHCA, May, 1983). When the Contadora process appeared to be stalled due to the "Tegucigalpa draft" counter proposals brought by US regional allies in late 1984, the OAS proclaimed support for the Revised Act of

September 7 and called on parties to sign an agreement. It was that Act which the FSLN -- surprising the United States and its allies -- had offered to sign (see Chapter 10). The later counter-proposals were much less satisfactory to the _Frente_. For that reason, Nicaraguan officials had gone to the November OAS meeting charging the United States with "torpedoing Contadora" and supporting contra "terrorism." The leaked US National Security Council document which referred to US efforts to block Contadora worked in Nicaragua's favor; the OAS acted to lend further legitimacy to the Contadora process (e.g. IHCA, December, 1984). Finally, as I noted in Chapter 7, in 1985 the OAS refused Costa Rica's request that it interject itself into the Nicaraguan-Costa Rican Las Crucitas border dispute, instead referring the issue to Contadora and calling for bilateral talks. The OAS had essentially adopted Nicaragua's position.

Just as Contadora came to symbolize differences in the North and South American worldviews regarding the Nicaraguan revolution, OAS politics in the post-Triumph period reflected deteriorating US-Latin American relations and an increased capacity or willingness among Latin American states to act in concert to check US policy. The FSLN took every opportunity to use this political dynamic to its own best interests. Nor were the Sandinistas alone in considering Nicaragua a test case for intra-hemispheric relations.

## Nicaraguan Support For National Liberation Movements

> This revolution goes beyond our borders.

> Nicaragua will not export revolution. Our best support for change in Latin America and the world will be to advance our revolution. Our neighbors can rest assured of this.

> Interior Minister Tomas Borge
> 1981

Rather than being contradictory, Borge's two often-quoted comments reflect the Sandinistas' view that socio-political revolution or popular liberation will inevitably spread in the Third World; that counter-revolutionary interventions from outside will "...not quench revolution but will spread it throughout Central America"; and that because national situations differ, revolution is not an exportable item (Humberto Ortega, FBIS-LAM 12-24-80). In victory, the FSLN remained committed to the cause of the poor and the weak in underdeveloped areas. In its international diplomacy, the FSLN propounded the thesis that in unity the weak would constitute a moral and compelling cause; only through Latin American or Third World unity could common continental or global issues effectively be addressed. The Sandinistas consistently expressed their opinion that consolidating their revolution would be their most important contribution to the struggle for self-determination and sovereignty taking place both in the field and in diplomatic arenas.

As revolutionaries and internationalists asserting their independence in the "backyard" of the United States, the Sandinistas considered themselves and their new government to be a test case not only for the cause of liberation, but also for the cause of economic independence and self-propelled growth. The Nicaraguan struggle, in their view, offered hope, example and diplomatic space for other armed and unarmed groups engaged in battle with repressive forces. In diplomatic arenas and through interparty contacts the FSLN demonstrated its political solidarity. FSLN material support for regional liberation movements, however, quickly became a key contested issue between Washington and Managua. Citing Sandinista internationalism and FSLN philosophical affinity with other guerrilla movements as proof of the Frente's commitment to overthrowing regional governments by force, the US government after 1980 carried out a major international campaign against Nicaragua on this issue. The FSLN, not denying its identification with popular movements in neighboring states, nevertheless consistently denied charges of official Nicaraguan material aid for these insurgent groups. Yet the Sandinistas also publically linked their destiny to the destiny of the Salvadoran peoples' struggle against an oppressive military and corrupt elites there. In the FSLN's view, a common correlation of international forces had shaped the histories of Central American peoples. Moreover, between 1981 and 1984 in particular, the Reagan Administration's policy toward Nicaragua was shaped by the status of the civil war in Salvador.

The importance to US policy of gun-running and material aid charges against the Sandinistas lay in the fact that building an "externally-supported subversion" case for Central America (recall Haig's conceptualization of a four-stage Soviet plan for spreading subversion) was key to winning Congressional support for US regional military expansion. Arms interdiction was the singular justification given in the early years for the Reagan policy to undermine the leftist and troublesome FSLN government. In later years the material-aid-to- regional-guerrillas charge became the foundation for the Reagan Administration's campaign to identify Nicaragua as a terrorist state, a "cancer" which had to be "cut out." According to the administration, Nicaragua was a key supplier of weapons to terrorist groups, including the PLO, the Italian Red Brigade and the autonomy-minded Basques of Spain which allegedly took sanctuary there. Though little evidence was offered to support President Reagan's claim that Nicaragua ranked alongside Libya in facilitating terrorism,[10] support for the contras was depicted as collective self-defense where the United States and its regional allies were the victims of Nicaraguan subversion and terror.

Reagan Administration officials had a difficult time through 1985 presenting convincing evidence of any sizeable or determinative role by the FSLN in supporting the FMLN guerrillas in El Salvador -- the administration's "best case" for proving Nicaraguan aid for insurgency according to senior US analysts in Managua. Indeed, the best evidence suggested that Nicaragua had allowed or facilitated arms transports through its territory in late 1980 and early 1981, but that after US warnings the weapons trafficking was slowed to what US agents in the field variously labelled "a trickle" and "peanuts". The inability of the contras from 1981 onward to capture even one arms shipment from Nicaragua seemed to confirm those assessments. The Honduran army reported in 1982 that it had not intercepted any major gun shipments since January, 1981 (NYT, 2-5-82). Meanwhile, the FMLN complained of weapons and ammunition shortages. Nor was there consensus among top US policy makers on the size of the role Nicaragua could be charged with playing. Although US National Security Council and Pentagon political appointees termed the FSLN-FMLN weapons link "vital" in 1982, the State Department at the time was saying that the FMLN guerrillas captured many of their weapons, that they bought others from Salvadoran army officials and that US-made M-16s had become the FMLN's standard weapon (e.g. LAWR, 5-27-82). Shortly thereafter, Fred Ikle at the Pentagon confirmed a much lesser FSLN role.

Another weakness in the administration's case against the "outlaw regime" of Nicaragua accrued from the obvious fact that outside of the civil war in El Salvador, there were no other successful insurgencies being waged at the time in Central America, or, in countries President Reagan claimed had received FSLN arms or training -- Honduras, Costa Rica, Guatemala, Ecuador, Brazil, Chile, Uruguay and the Dominican Republic. Interestingly, a number of these governments countered Washington's allegations, arguing that they had no knowledge of such insurgencies or of local leftist's military links to the FSLN. The day after President Reagan's vitriolic anti-Sandinista speech of March 16, 1986, for instance, the Brazilian government denied having knowledge or evidence of any FSLN-backed insurgent group there. The governments of Brazil and Argentina demanded an apology from Washington; instead President Reagan repeated the charges several days later (NYT, 3-18-86; ICAS, May, 1986). Coming shortly after Colombia's withdrawal of similar (Washington-inspired) accusations against the FSLN (NYT, 1-23-86), these counterclaims added to skepticism regarding Reagan Administration evidence, timing and motives.

US officials close to the scene also publicly challenged Reagan Administration claims and several ex-CIA agents -- David MacMichael and John Stockwell -- testified to the nature of US claims in Nicaragua's behalf at the World Court in 1985. According to MacMichael, the CIA's information about gun-running from Nicaragua to other Latin American states was distorted by the administration in its public campaign; there was no credible evidence that the FSLN supplied significant amounts of arms to insurgents. Nor, according to MacMichael, was there proof that the Nicaraguan government itself had ever been involved with supplying arms. Instead evidence suggested no significant weapons trafficking had occurred since 1981 (e.g. NYT, 6-11-84).

Calling such testimony and Nicaraguan denials "outright lies," the new Assistant Secretary for Inter-American Affairs, Elliot Abrams, began a new campaign of proofs against Nicaragua in September, 1985. Hoping to counter media coverage of Nicaragua's World Court case and to push off the 1986 campaign for Congressional (military) funding for the contras, the State Department issued a number of documents accusing Nicaragua of overseeing the distribution of weapons and explosives among FMLN units according to FSLN assessments of the soundness of FMLN plans.[11]

While US embassy analysts in Managua and Tegucigalpa in 1982 and 1983 explained the lack of evidence against Nicaragua by arguing that arms were shipped in small, undetectable amounts in dug-out canoes across the Gulf of Fonseca and on mule-packs across narrow mountainous passage through southern Honduras, by 1985 top analysts in Managua were acknowledging an apparently minor role for Nicaragua (author interviews). In 1985 the analysis of the US Embassy in Nicaragua was that the gun-flow had dropped off after 1981, that "Nicaragua is a supermarket of last resorts" for the FMLN and that the FSLN itself was not moving any guns for the FMLN. Instead, the FSLN allowed "safe houses" inside its territory for FMLN leaders and allowed small FMLN units to use Nicaraguan training facilities. According to this analysis, corrupt Honduran officials were selling weapons to both the FMLN and to the contras; however, the black market remained the FMLN's vital source of weapons (author interviews). In early 1986, moreover, new charges surfaced that the contras themselves were illegally shipping weapons out of the United States. Thus, the evidence of Nicaraguan gunrunning, even in the "best case," was weak or discredited.

Other evidence, such as testimony by guerrilla desertees, suggests that the FSLN had contacts with FMLN leaders and strategists and that Cuban advisors in Nicaragua were known to have met with FMLN leaders as well (e.g. NYT, 7-12-84). In 1983 a Salvadoran army official charged that the FSLN met regularly with both the FMLN high command and top Guatemalan rebel leaders. Little supporting evidence was available (NYT, 1-23-83). Other reports suggested that the FSLN provided the FMLN with both advice on methods for lobbying the US Congress and (in the early 1980s) intelligence on the Honduran and Salvadoran armies and regarding arms transshipments (NYT, 4-16-86). But evidence as to the importance, nature and timing of these contacts was scarce. Few US officials after 1982 argued that the FMLN depended on the Sandinista government for crucial logistical or tactical planning.

Neither the FSLN nor the FMLN kept it a secret, however, that there was a feeling of comradeship between the groups. Daniel Ortega, noting the Nicaraguan people's support for the FMLN's cause in Salvador and their desire, after the Triumph in 1979, to assist the FMLN, revealed that on several occasions the government had stopped gun-carrying Nicaraguans headed for El Salvador. Moreover, FSLN Directorate member Bayardo Arce acknowledged the FSLN's help in introducing the FMLN to the world arms market (WP, 2-21-83). At least up to 1984, the FMLN openly had offices in Managua as well as in Mexico City. The FMLN leadership took R and R in Nicaragua, Mexico and elsewhere and FMLN leaders often appeared at early FSLN national celebrations. According to several former FSLN guerrilla leaders, the FSLN was repaying a debt to the FMLN; in 1978 Salvadoran guerrilla organizations had donated $10 million in to the Sandinista revolution (NYT, 4-6-86). But even these nonmilitary contacts were reduced as US charges of FSLN-FMLN complicity were expanded. For example, FMLN offices and FMLN leaders living in Nicaragua were officially relocated to Mexico. The FMLN became less visible and had lesser diplomatic status in Nicaragua by 1984. Not the least of the factors binding the FMLN to the FSLN, they shared a common threat in the military policy of the Reagan Administration.

For its part, the Sandinista government argued that any popular movement had to be viable and self-reliant enough to command an arm its combatants using its own resources. The FSLN, nevertheless, continued to offer moral and political support; it publically denied shipping arms to El Salvador. Privately, FSLN officials argued to the United States that they had ceased facilitating Cuban arms shipments in 1981. Other officials claimed that if guns were flowing through Nicaragua, it was without the governments knowledge or support. The FSLN, in other words, claimed quickly to have learned the impracticability of supporting anti-government movements in the region with arms.

Charging the United States with fabricating evidence against them, the FSLN expressed their willingness to come an agreement with the United States on security issues. And, acknowledging regional realities, the Sandinistas reiterated their support for inter-party dialogue and power-sharing in El Salvador. For example, speaking before the UN, in October, 1981 Daniel Ortega presented an FMLN-formulated proposal for dialogue in El Salvador. Coming after the Mexican-French initiative of August which had referred to the political representativeness of the FMLN, the Frente's decision to speak for the FMLN in the UN reflected its judgment that a negotiated end to the Salvadoran war was in its own best interests. An end to the civil war there would significantly reduce regional tensions and eliminate a major US argument against Nicaragua. The FSLN maintained this public position thereafter, even though in 1983 and early 1984 the FMLN forces were gaining ground in their war against the Salvadoran army. In January, 1984 the FSLN endorsed an FMLN-FDR proposal for power-sharing in Salvador which the Salvadoran Catholic Church labelled an "important alternative" to the current situation (ICAS, March, 1984). And in March, 1984, the FSLN called on the Contadora States to address the civil war in Salvador as a major source of regional tension: "The Civil War of our sister Salvadoran nation has been unfortunately absent from the agenda of the Contadora peace process, weakening the chances that this initiative will react the core of the regional crisis" (ICAS, op. cit). In January 1984, the FSLN repeated to Senator Moynihan (D-New York) its recognition that the FSLN and the FMLN had to come to an accommodation with Washington. Again at the Manzanillo talks in 1984, the FSLN expressed a willingness to pledge not to assist regional leftist groups.

This Nicaraguan stance, however, remained unacceptable to the Reagan Administration into 1986. Not yet ready to give up on a military solution, and having made too large an investment in the Salvadoran military and government to concede to talks, the administration harbored hopes of yet defeating both the FSLN and the FMLN (e.g. LAWR, 8-12-83). The Nicaraguan response to US sabre-rattling also remained the same: maintaining high levels of military preparedness, the FSLN (along with other Latin American leaders) warned of widespread uprisings in Latin American in the case of direct US intervention into Nicaragua. Although increasingly preoccupied with its own survival, the FSLN yet maintained high visibility on Third World issues, employing its international activism in pursuit of solidarity and offering its experience as a model for others seeking liberation. But the FSLN had also shown that its affinity for liberation movements would not be allowed to become an obstacle to a regional peace settlement or to a rapprochment with the United States.

DIVERSIFICATION:  NICARAGUA'S ECONOMIC TIES

The Sandinistas' policy of expanding international ties was manifested in the economic sphere in policies aimed at market and financial diversification.  Unable in the short run significantly to reduce Nicaragua's agro-export and financial dependence, the FSLN sought to diversify that dependence among Western, Asian, other Third World and Socialist bloc states.  Such a strategy would reduce Nicaragua's vulnerability to any one state or bloc and could open new financing possibilities which would not restrict economic planning for structural change at home.  For example, the FSLN rejected IMF austerity conditions which inevitably placed the economic burden of underdevelopment on the poorest sectors of society.  Nor did the Frente want to exacerbate the economic dislocations Nicaragua had already experienced by suddenly shifting to new suppliers of materials, machinery and technology.  Hard currency shortages, large trade imbalances, a large national debt and the objective of greater economic sovereignty all worked to shape early trade and foreign economic policy.  Particular emphases were placed on a gradual realignment of economic ties toward a more balanced, non-aligned position.

External pressures, however, significantly constrained actual opportunities and behavior in the trade and financing areas.  Most importantly, US policy targeted Sandinista development strategy and, by closing off important sources to Nicaragua, forced an acceleriton of the process of diversification and of Nicaragua's reliance on non-Western actors.  Contra attacks, war damage and defense needs effectively skewed Nicaraguan economic priorities and necessitated a reliance on states willing to make medium-and long-term commitments.  Economic hardship in the Third World similarly worked to shape FSLN policy outcomes.

## Trade Patterns

With an eye toward achieving national autonomy in the trade sector and thereby "rationalizing trade", the FSLN largely nationalized foreign commerce.  By 1985 the Ministry of Foreign Trade and other state-run enterprises handled 90 percent of exports and 65 percent of imports.  According to Foreign Trade Minister Alejandro Martinez Cuenca, nationalization allowed for dealing in volumes, avoiding fragmented purchasing and the like, yielding a small, poor country like Nicaragua a stronger position in negotiating prices, shipping and insurance costs (author interview, Managua, 1985).  Centralized management of foreign trade had the added benefit of allowing Nicaraguan leaders to react quickly to hostile US economic moves such as the US sugar quota reduction in 1982, the regular delaying of import/export trade licenses by the US Commerce Department and the May, 1985 US embargo.  Although "managing exports is a learning experience" according to Cuenca, state goals of social transformation, "making the people part of the process" of production and accumulation, diversifying links and markets, and expanding export revenues, in the FSLN view, made nationalization of foreign commerce a rational response to Nicaragua's situation.  Socioeconomic dislocations after the

Triumph, bourgeoisie reluctance to support FSLN economic plans and market situations, moreover, made central regulations over foreign commerce necessary if the new government was to be successful in translating export profits into benefits for a majority of Nicaraguans.

The process of diversifying trade patterns, however, was hampered by a number of regional realities. As earlier discussions have noted, US economic hostility and, to a lesser extent, pressures directed (by Washington) at Latin American and West European states, narrowed opportunities for the Frente. The results of the latter pressure was most notable in the area of arms transfers. But across the entire US-tooled Nicaraguan economy, the effects of US hostility toward the revolution were quickly felt. To minimize dislocations the Frente sought comparable markets, materials, parts and technologies from other Western or industrialized states. But as Nicaragua's ability to pay -- e.g. its export earnings and production levels -- was reduced by the contra war and a US-induced shut-off of multilateral credits, the willingness of many Western states to extend long-term credits and loans was reduced. Its hard currency shortage and growing oil debts with Venezuela and Mexico, for example, also affected Nicaragua's trade relations. Nicaraguan leaders had to find sympathetic and dependable oil and technology suppliers which were willing to delay payments or extend low-cost credits, but which would also not attach political conditions.

Regional realities, such as the economic retraction within the Central American Common Market and large foreign debts, and the similarity in products produced by many Latin American states meant that significantly expanding trade in the region would also be difficult. Nor did many fellow Latin American states have replacement technology for a Nicaragua cut off from traditional US sources. Within these constraints, the FSLN tried to move toward its objective of "walking on four legs."

Table 9.2 displays patterns in Nicaragua's commercial trade relations from 1976 through 1984. Immediately noticeable is the decline in Nicaraguan-US trade relations. Imports from the United States dropped from consisting of nearly one-third of Nicaraguan imports in the pre-revolution period to approximately one-fifth of Nicaragua's imports after 1981. This pattern reflects several things: Nicaragua's determination to diversify sources and to create a trade surplus with and reduce its dependence upon the United States; its inability to continue making cash purchases; and United States' reluctance even prior to the official embargo announcement of 1985 to facilitate Nicaraguan needs. But the precipitous nature of the decline, according to Nicaraguan officials, reflected more the latter reality than it did any determination or ability on Nicaragua's part to do without US chemicals, spare parts, etc., or, to commit to retooling Nicaraguan industry -- a sizeable and expensive project. Though Nicaragua obtained only 19-20 percent of its imports from the United States by 1983 and 1984, those imports accounted for 64 percent of the raw materials needed for Nicaraguan production, 31 percent of its machinery and equipment and 42 percent of its imported chemicals for cotton production (CAHI, 1-16-84). Agricultural and industrial production continued up to 1985 to depend on US goods and reflected

Table 9.2
Nicaraguan Trade Patterns:  1976-1984

| EXPORTS | 1976 | 1977 | 1978 | 1980 | 1981 | 1982 | 1983 | 1984 |
|---|---|---|---|---|---|---|---|---|
| United States | 30 | 23 | 23 | 36 | 27 | 22 | 17 | 20 |
| Western Europe | 15 | 28 | 28 | 33 | 19 | 23 | 26 | 27 |
| Central America | 22 | 21 | 22.5 | 17 | 14 | 13 | 8 | 9 |
| Other Latin America | - | 3 | 0.5 | 0 | 4 | 6 | 4 | 2 |
| Japan | 3 | 11 | 9 | 3 | 11 | 11 | 15 | 25 |
| CMEA Countries (Cuba) | - | 1 | - | 3 | 6 | 5 | 13 | 6 |
| Other | 30 | 13 | 17 | 9 | 18 | 19 | 17 | 9 |
| Total | 100% | 100% | 100% | 100% | 100% | 100% | 100% | 100% |
| Total Dollar Amount (millions) | 541.9 | 636.9 | 645.9 | 450.4 | 508.2 | 405.5 | 428.8 | 374.0 |

| IMPORTS | 1976 | 1977 | 1978 | 1980 | 1981 | 1982 | 1983 | 1984 |
|---|---|---|---|---|---|---|---|---|
| United States | 31 | 1 | 31 | 28 | 26 | 19 | 19 | 20 |
| Western Europe | 11 | 14 | 9 | 10 | 10 | 14 | 10 | 21 |
| Central America | 26 | 21 | 23 | 34 | 21 | 15 | 15 | 11 |
| Other Latin America | - | 14 | - | 20 | 30 | 31 | 30 | 14 |
| Japan | 8 | 10 | 7 | 3 | 3 | 2 | 2 | 3 |
| CMEA Countries (Cuba) | - | 0.3 | - | 0 | 3 | 11 | 17 | 26 |
| Other | 24 | 9.7 | 30 | 5 | 4 | 7 | 7 | 3 |
| Total | 100% | 100% | 100% | 100% | 100% | 100% | 100% | 100% |
| Total Dollar Amounts (millions) | 532.1 | 761.9 | 593.9 | 887.2 | 999.4 | 775.6 | 806.9 | 790.0 |

| TRADE BALANCE | 9.8 | -125.1 | 52 | -436.8 | -491.2 | -370.1 | -378.1 | -416.0 |

Sources:  Nicaraguan Central Bank; Ministry of Foreign Trade.

FSLN attempts to maintain production in key sectors even while diversifying in other areas.

US purchases from Nicaragua dropped as well after 1981, foiling Nicaraguan plans to increase hard currency reserves by concommitantly and strategically reducing imports from and increasing sales to the United States. From making up over one-third of Nicaraguan sales in 1980, by 1984 the United States purchased only about one-eighth of Nicaraguan exports. The steepest one year decline came in 1980-1981 with the change in US administrations. Declines of 5 percent occurred in each of the following years until the May 1985 cutoff of all trade. Traditionally the United States imported Nicaraguan bananas, beef, sugar and shellfish and in 1982, for example, purchased about $90 million worth of these products -- $32 million of it in beef and veal, $14.5 million in shellfish and $1.5 million in bananas. By 1984 and 1985 bananas had come to make up the bulk of US purchases. Of the $45 million in Nicaraguan goods purchased by the United States in 1984, $23.5 million went for bananas and $9.7 million went for beef.[12] In 1985 the United States accounted for 3 percent of total Nicaraguan trade, all of it contracted prior to the May embargo announcement.

EEC, Japan and Canada. Beginning in the late 1970s, Western European states had begun taking up a larger share of Nicaraguan exports. Though EEC purchases were down in 1981, the year that the United States began its rigorous anti-Sandinista campaign and a year in which the FSLN itself was wooing as yet untapped markets, from 1982 onward EEC purchases increased each year. As US claims of Nicaraguan-USSR alignment became louder and as fears of a US intervention increased, EEC purchases of Nicaraguan products grew to a record level in 1984. Similarly, after 1981 Nicaragua increased its imports from Western Europe and by 1984 had doubled its imports from these states as US sources were closing down. The increase in trade activity was maintained to 1986. According to mid-1985 (post-embargo) Foreign Trade Ministry projections, Western European states would account for 32 percent of Nicaragua's total trade in 1985 compared to the United States' 3 percent (author interview).

Very similar patterns of strengthening trade links with non-US, industrialized states emerged with regard to Japan and Canada. In the case of Japan, its share in Nicaragua's exports grew dramatically by 1984. Meanwhile, Nicaragua's Japanese imports remained constant after the Triumph. In 1985, Japan's share of Nicaragua's total trade was 12 percent (Ministry of Trade Projection). Canada also increased its traditional 2 percent share of total Nicaraguan trade to 5 percent in 1985.

Nicaragua's strengthening trade ties with these US allies again reflected political and economic realities. First, FSLN leaders by 1982 were putting more sustained efforts into finding alternative Western, industrial suppliers for their slated project of rebuilding industries which, in the pre-revolution period, produced export products for Europe. Second, by 1984 the Sandinistas had recognized the need for greater diplomatic efforts among Western European states. The FSLN worked in Europe, Japan, and Canada to use opportunities created by disapproval of US policy to open new markets and supply links. Meanwhile, motivated by an interpretation of regional events that differed from the United States', the EEC offered Central American states new economic aid. Japan and Canada were interested in developing their shares of the Latin American market which traditionally had been preserved for the United States. These interests came together in a pattern of increased Western commercial interactions with Nicaragua and Central America even while the leader of the Western bloc was consolidating its policy of hostility against the FSLN government.

Latin America. Nicaragua's trade with the Central American Common Market countries by 1981 led to a deficit situation, prompting a government decision in 1982 to restrict luxury imports from these states. Imports from the CACM therefore fell 6 percent in 1982 and another 4 percent in 1984. Declining exports to CACM states after 1979 reflected three factors affecting Nicaragua's trade relations generally: first, industrial and economic dislocation due to the war and to the implementation of new policies; second, recession and debt problems throughout the region; and third, regional political tensions. Because of old and new political tensions among Honduras, Nicaragua, El Salvador and Guatemala, revolutionary Nicaragua was more active (economically and diplomatically) globally than regionally. Internationalism afforded greater political solidarity and visibility from which to withstand hostile external pressures. Nor did the Central American states have technology or materials needed for Nicaragua's reconstruction tasks. Nicaragua trade officials maintained, however, that Nicaragua desired normalized regional relations, increased regional trade and a reinvigoration of the CACM on new bases which would enable it to support greater regional self-determination. Contrasting Nicaragua with Cuba, for instance, Trade Minister Cuenca noted "Nicaragua is not an island. We have to relate to the world."

Although movement toward political rapproachment was slow or at a standstill in the first half of the 1980s, economic transactions and exchanges among the states continued and remained economically important to Nicaragua. At the height of political tensions in 1982 and 1983, for example -- when its neighbors, backed by Washington, made several attempts politically, diplomatically and militarily to isolate Nicaragua -- Nicaragua was exporting staple diet items like beans and corn to Salvador and Honduras. Similarly, while Nicaragua traditionally sold 76 percent of its industrial exports to the Third World, its neighbors traditionally absorbed a good share of that. Ironically, though the United States had shepuarded -- and benefitted economically and politically from -- CACM integration in the 1960s, in the 1980s the United States tried to work through the same allies to isolate Nicaragua. Yet it was that very economic integration which stood in the way of US attempts completely to isolate Nicaragua economically. As Costa Rican Central Bank President Manuel Castillo argued in 1983: "We cannot cut Nicaragua off because it is a matter of our own survival" (CAHI, 1-16-84).

In the overall picture, however, the CACM in the 1980s was experiencing its sharpest declines in twenty years. By 1984 intraregional trade was 40 percent below 1980 levels. Nicaragua's CACM imports, for instance, had fallen off by two-thirds and Costa Rica's CACM imports were off by 50 percent in that period. Guatemala's 1984 imports were down 17 percent from the previous year alone (CAR, 4-19-85). Although Nicaragua's CACM deficit was shrinking, it remained large. Meanwhile, no new credits had been extended under the pact. Highlighting both the CACM's decline and its reduced overall economic importance to Nicaragua, by 1982 CACM trade accounted for 13.2 percent of total Nicaraguan trade -- down from 26 percent in 1970.

Patterns of trade with other Latin American states reflect revolutionary Nicaragua's Third World stance and beginning efforts at diversifying sources of raw materials. Imports, up significantly from the Somoza years, also reflect oil purchases from Venezuela and Mexico -- trade with these two states made up a significant share of Nicaragua's total Latin American trade -- and the signing of medium-term trade agreements with several states including Mexico. Conversely, the drop in regional imports in 1984 reflected Venezuelan and Mexican decisions to suspend concessionary oil sales to Nicaragua in the face of Nicaragua's inability to repay past oil debts. Increasing exports to the Latin American states which produced similar products was and will continue to be difficult unless Nicaragua can expand its export sector in the future. Yet exports to fellow Latin American states were up from the Somoza period.

Nicaraguan activities from 1983 to 1986 indicated that commercial linkages to Latin America would receive renewed attention as a way to balance US hostility and new economic credits from the Eastern bloc. In 1984 and 1985 Nicaraguan delegations toured Latin America in efforts at strengthening economic ties. This activity paralleled FSLN diplomatic efforts at aligning Nicaragua's cause with the cause of all Latin America. Among other transactions, this Latin American campaign paid off in 1983 with an agreement on commercial relations and cooperation with Argentina; in 1982 with a $50 million trade package with Columbia; and in 1985 with a $15 million credit line from Venezuela for raw materials and spare parts. Condemning the United States' embargo, the Latin American states urged economic cooperation with Nicaragua. Mexico also resumed oil shipments to Nicaragua.

CMEA. Although Nicaragua was not alone among Latin American states in trading with the Eastern bloc, trade with the Council for Mutual Economic Assistance (CMEA) countries was new to Nicaragua and was a result both of government policy to diversify and Cuban and Eastern bloc responses to the Nicaraguan revolution. For example, in the immediate post-Triumph period Cuba responded generously, and at levels that could not be sustained over a long period, to FSLN requests for international support and aid for reconstruction tasks. Likewise, according to the Foreign Ministry the Soviets and Eastern Europeans responded "most aggressively" in offering financing and credit lines to Nicaragua when Nicaraguan leaders expressed need. The CMEA states offered Nicaragua 2- to 12-year loans, credits at low interest of 2.5 to 7 percent and grace periods of up to 5 years. These long-term agreements provided price stability on CMEA products which were already competitively priced on the world market. Attractive in comparison to loans from Western Europe or Latin America, these long-term credit arrangements provided Nicaragua some marketing stability and the ability to plan for resource management in a period of economic crisis. Other CMEA trade accords provided for payment in kind (i.e. barter) rather than in hard currency. For example, Nicaragua traded cotton, sesame and coffee for oil and contracted to pay for CMEA-constructed factories with products from those new facilities (Edelman, 1985: 423).

These arrangements encouraged new levels of exchange between Nicaragua and Eastern Europe, the Soviet Union and Cuba. Trade figures in Table 9.2 show significant increases in imports from CMEA states; CMEA imports more than doubled between 1981 and 1982 and again from 1982 to 1984. By comparison, however, CMEA imports by the end of 1983 were still only half the value of imports from Mexico (CAHI, 1-16-84). Yet, more than one-fourth of Nicaragua's imports, worth about $210 million, came from CMEA states in both 1984 and 1985 (Foreign Trade Ministry, author interview) and may reflect the fact that in 1983 Nicaragua joined Mexico as an observer in CMEA. Imported items included: equipment and machinery for agriculture, mining, the petroleum industry, communications and fisheries from the Soviet Union; textiles-related equipment from Czechoslovakia; sugar refinery, fishing, poultry and livestock equipment from Cuba; medical equipment from Hungary; buses and food processing and hydroelectric equipment from Bulgaria; trucks and construction equipment from East Germany; and steel industry construction and production equipment from North Korea.

While imports from capitalist or mixed-economy states still provided about 75 percent of Nicaragua's imports in 1985, CMEA trade terms suggested that its percentage of Nicaragua's total trade -- 25 percent in 1985 -- could well increase in the future, especially if US hostility continued or if a regional peace agreement was not signed. Indeed, the patterns in Nicaraguan - CMEA trade parallel patterns in US economic hostility (see also Chapter 7). Nicaraguan CMEA purchases in 1981 came as Bulgaria, Cuba and East Germany offered credit in response to Reagan Administration credit cancellations. In 1982, not only the Soviets but also Algeria, Libya, Iran and Mexico offered to buy Nicaraguan sugar after the US preferential sugar quota to Nicaragua was cut. Similarly, as multilateral funding was reduced, CMEA states opened new credit. In 1983, as the contra war and US pressure intensified, Nicaragua-CMEA trade grew by about 80 percent over 1982 levels. Nicaragua, in dire economic straits, was to expand its reliance on CMEA easy credit in the next years even though its export production overall was not improving.

Export figures for CMEA states give a picture of growing Nicaraguan deficits and unbalanced trade between the parties. Nicaraguan debt to the Eastern bloc was growing and would continue to do so unless Nicaragua could increase its exports to CMEA, something the Trade Ministry was looking to negotiate. The fact that Nicaragua had little that the CMEA states needed, however, suggested that this would be a continuing problem. Nor were Eastern bloc imports sold to Nicaragua on concessionary terms. Instead, the added costs of transport over long distances had to be absorbed in the transactions and translated into worsened terms of trade. Moreover, though some barter was arranged and payment was on soft terms, most of Nicaragua's payments -- including those for arms -- were in hard currency.

Nicaraguan officials, in explaining the growth in financial

relations with CMEA since 1981, acknowledged the accumulating indebtedness and the fact that, according to Cuenca, trade with CMEA "is not modulated as a business transaction, but on political considerations; they respect Nicaragua's goals and self-determination" (author interview). For that reason, Nicaraguan officials have preferred to draw on credit from that quarter rather than relying on US-dominated international loan bodies or US banks, where assets were more apt to be frozen or loans denied for political reasons. A clear and recent example of that reality for the FSLN was Washington's blocking in early 1985 of the $58.4 million Inter-American Development Bank loan slated for agricultural development. The loan monies were to have financed: the reconditioning of coffee farms; land clearance for cotton cultivation as well as for rice, beans, sorghum and sesame projects; erosion-protection projects; pasture preparation; 28 new poultry farms, increased cattle herds; and the like (BI, 3-28-85). Again, political pressures hampered vital agricultural development and demonstrated the importance to Nicaragua of establishing alternative and reliable financing sources.

Yet, while FSLN officials considered CMEA "less dangerous", they also pointed to the fact that with US diplomatic efforts working against them, they had few options. As Minister Cuenca put it in 1985, "We take what we have."

Balanced Trade Relations. By 1984 and 1985 Nicaragua had not only spread out its trade relations over a greater number and variety of states, but also had balanced its trade a little more among its partners while moving -- and being pushed -- away from a predominant dependence on the United States and US finance. Total trade shares for Nicaragua's primary partners in 1984 broke down as follows: EEC and Japan - 37 percent; Latin America - 21 percent; the United States - 17 percent; CMEA states - 20 percent; Canada and others - 5 percent. Corresponding figures projected at mid-year for 1985, i.e., after the May, 1985 US embargo, showed that the decrease in US trade was compensated for in part by a 7 percent increase in total trade with the EEC and Japan (44 percent), by a five percent increase in trade with CMEA (25 percent), and an increase in Canadian trade from about 2 percent of Nicaragua's total to 5 percent (author interviews; BI, 7-25-85; CAR, 5-10-85). Meanwhile, Nicaragua aimed to expand commercial ties with Latin American states to compensate for declines in both US and CACM trade. The pattern that emerges from a consideration of the type and variety of trade links the FSLN maintained is one of activism and a commitment to diversification.

That pattern is demonstrated as well by FSLN policy regarding suppliers of Nicaragua's critical import, oil, and by the Sandinistas' response to the US embargo. In the latter case, as I discussed earlier, FSLN delegations visited Eastern and Western Europe, Latin America and elsewhere in search of new or alternative markets and suppliers. Within 48 hours of the US May embargo announcement, Nicaragua had arranged for a new banana market in Belgium and by July the Trade Ministry announced that Nicaragua had all its financial foreign exchange needs covered through early 1986. Markets in Europe, Canada and Mexico replaced the US market for Nicaragua's meat, seafood and bananas, though at higher shipping and administrative costs. Japanese technology would, in part, replace that earlier imported from the United States. Taiwan and China were buying Nicaraguan cotton (e.g. LAWR, 5-10-85; BI, 7-25-85). New credits and loans from Eastern Europe worth $202 million -- made up largely of USSR oil commitments worth about $130 million -- were matched by $200 million in commitments from Western Europe. Canada and several Latin American states increased their trade with Nicaragua. Yugoslavia offered to open trade relations with Nicaragua (BI, 6-20-85; 7-25-85). The effects of the embargo, in brief, were blunted both by Nicaragua's earlier attention to diversification and to widespread international condemnation of that US policy.

The FSLN similarly looked to spread out its oil dependence and its oil debt. Its yearly oil import bill alone, nearly $200 million, consumed almost half of Nicaragua's yearly export earnings. By 1985, Nicaragua's oil debt to Mexico and Venezuela stood at $1 billion and made up the largest single portion of Nicaragua's total external debt. When concessionary oil sales (under the San Jose Accord) from Venezuela were withdrawn in 1982, and again in 1984 when Mexico withdrew its concessionary pricing, FSLN delegations sought oil deals with Iran, other Middle East suppliers, the Soviet Union, Ecuador and Brazil. The Soviet Union became a major supplier in 1984 after the CIA harbor-mining incident and after Mexico's oil shipments stopped. The high-level trip by Ramirez, D'Escoto and Cuenca to Iran in March 1984 and Cuenca's fifth trade-related visit to Iran in July, paid off in a January 1985 oil sales agreement when Iranian Prime Minister Moussavi visited Nicaragua. Besides buying Nicaraguan sugar, a deal struck between the states after the US sugar quota reduction, Iran would now buy beef and cotton (LAWR, 2-8-85).

Preferring to open similar reciprocal trade agreements with other Middle Eastern states as well, in 1983 Nicaragua had begun an export drive to market its coffee, beans, and sugar there. An exchange agreement worth $25 million was signed with Algeria and signalled Algerian concern over Nicaragua's situation. Earlier, Algeria and Libya had offered to guarantee Nicaraguan oil needs should other sources dry up. But FSLN officials continued to probe other closer possibilities, again preferring greater Latin American support and imports which could be balanced by exports. For example, in March, 1985 President Ortega announced that both Brazil and Ecuador had offered to help Nicaragua in its critical oil situation.[13]

Though they had not come to a decision to rely exclusively on non-hemispheric, anti-imperialist producers, Nicaraguan officials kept open lines of trade and communication to Algeria and Libya in particular. During 1985 the USSR, Mexico and Iran provided the bulk of Nicaraguan oil needs and as of 1986 Nicaragua stood prepared to approach other producers as well. The FSLN had kept options open. The development of Nicaraguan energy production facilities (hydroelectric and gasohol plants), meanwhile, was being supported by financial and technical help from Italy, the CMEA countries and Brazil. The FSLN's ultimate goal was to cut Nicaragua's oil imports, harness its resources and actually export energy.

On the larger scene, the prospects for Nicaragua diversifying much further were limited. In the context of a war economy, hard currency shortages and a growing debt, Nicaragua was quickly becoming dependent on states willing to extend credits or soft-term loans. This alone had affected the timing and depth of Nicaragua's trade relations. Nicaragua's industrial development, moreover, was affected by the rapid decline in relations with traditional partners like the CACM and the United States and by the fact that CMEA economies were less compatible with Nicaragua's. As Nicaragua's markets and suppliers changed, so did the direction of its production. The question was whether relatively rapid changes in direction would pay off economically in the longer-term. By 1986 it was clear that CMEA (and Arab) trade and assistance, at first circumstantial, had become important to Nicaragua's development of a solid foundation for capital accumulation and production, at least to the end of the decade. At the same time, however, Nicaragua remained aware of limitations on Eastern bloc aid that stemmed from Soviet reluctance to carry Nicaragua. To the extent that Nicaragua retools its industry, moreover, space for US influence in the future will be limited.

## Economic and Technical Assistance

Diversification was also the early objective in seeking financial assistance for rebuilding Nicaragua's productive capacity, reactivating its economy and financing imports. Utilizing bilateral and multilateral openings and using debt renegotiations as proof of their credit-worthiness, FSLN officials began in 1979 to woo new monies to Nicaragua. Their efforts paid off in a wide variety of potential creditors, the ability to survive declining terms of trade and the capacity to replace credits and aid withdrawn or vetoed by the United States. For example, in the first 18 months after the Triumph Nicaragua attracted over $100 million each in loans from the United States and the World Bank. The Inter-American Development Bank provided nearly $200 million. By early 1981, the FSLN had obtained bilateral loans from Mexico, Sweden, West Germany, East Germany, Libya, the USSR, Bulgaria, Costa Rica, Brazil, Cuba, Venezuela, Holland, France, Spain and others. The bulk of that early aid came from capitalist states and nearly half of the total came from Latin America (e.g. LAWR, 4-3-81). Until mid-1982, aid from the USSR and the Eastern bloc (usually in the form of credits) was only at moderate levels, despite many requests from the Sandinistas. External military and diplomatic pressures and a disastrous flood in the Chinandega region during 1982, however, spurred a strong response from the CMEA states in the form of new assistance offers and pledges. For the 1981-1982 period, 49.4 percent of total loans and grants dispersed to Nicaragua came from Third World and non-aligned Third World states; 32.1 percent originated from developed capitalist states and 18.1 percent came from the socialist bloc. The FSLN government was careful only to draw on foreign credit lines when these could facilitate Nicaraguan development plans or priorities. The FSLN aimed to minimize imports or balance imports with exports. It also sought geopolitical balance among donors. Further, the FSLN preferred not to retool its industry with socialist bloc equipment. But many credit lines were also medium-to-long term and could be drawn on over a number of years. For example, of $486.1 million granted by international organizations between July, 1979 and march, 1982, $296.6 million had been dispersed. Of total bilateral funds, $721.8 million had been granted and $380.7 million had been dispersed (LAWR, 11-12-82). Of the bilateral loans received, 44 percent came from Third World states; 28 percent came from capitalist developed states; and 18 percent came from the socialist bloc (Managua, 1981).

By 1983, though Nicaragua's debt had climbed to one of Latin America's per capita highest and US diplomatic efforts to isolate Nicaragua were underway, Colombia, Peru and Argentina had joined Nicaragua's Latin American creditors, while earlier creditors like Spain, Bulgaria and Sweden were extending new lines of credit. In the second half of 1983, the FSLN announced other new aid commitments from West Germany, Austria, North Korea, Mexico, Holland, Canada and Denmark (e.g. CARIN, September, 1983; IHCA November, 1983). As Nicaragua's economy began showing appreciable signs of deterioration due principally to the contra war, and, as its debt climbed in 1984 and 1985, Nicaragua's financing options also narrowed (e.g. see Conroy, 1985a). In 1984, fewer new loans were available from capitalist and Third World countries. The Frente still aimed to balance its needs for easy CMEA credits with its desire to retain the flexibility and balance afforded by diversifying assistance sources. But, as the contra war continued, Nicaragua and the FSLN looked less and less creditworthy to states already economically pressed, or, to states which did not want to rile the United States or appear to take sides in the region.[14]

The striking feature about Nicaragua's aid situation through 1985, however, was that influential capitalist and mixed-economy states maintained economic or assistance links to the FSLN government and confirmed those links with new commitments after the May 1985 embargo. Although a number of Western European states voiced concern about the growing economic and military role of the CMEA countries in Nicaragua, they decided to reinforce the FSLN's commitment to a mixed economy by funding development projects. The successful May-June 1985 diplomatic efforts by the FSLN government to assure their financial situation into 1986 -- i.e., despite the embargo -- and their ability to garner support from among the Eastern and Western blocs and Third World states, again demonstrated FSLN political skill, flexibility and a commitment to retaining diversified and active relations. It also reflected an acceptance of the Sandinista government's legitimacy and viability. The FLSN's task had been to find credits and loans worth nearly two times the value of their exports. The amounts and types of aid offered to 1986, moreover, suggested that donors were not merely registering their disapproval of US policy.[15]

Yet, overall assistance levels were down in subsequent years from their high in 1981 of $687.1 million. Total multilateral and bilateral aid commitments in 1982 and 1983 were $541.1 million and $425.1 million, respectively (Conroy, 1985a: 60). One important factor was the decline in assistance which related to US diplomatic efforts to isolate Nicaragua. Over the 1979 - 1983 period, world scale and regional multilateral aid organizations -- where the US had predominant or significant influence -- drastically cut aid commitments to Nicaragua (see Chapter 6). The FSLN was increasingly dependent on negotiating bilateral aid commitments. Its success in drawing aid from a variety of states is reflected in Ministry of Foreign Trade statistics on actual assistance for 1984. In that year 25.3 percent of assistance drawn came from multilateral organizations; 11.3 percent from Western Europe; 3.3 percent from North America; 30.3 percent from Latin America; 5.6 percent from Africa and Asia; and 24.2 percent from CMEA states. Of all bilateral assistance, however, a large bulk came from CMEA states -- 50 percent according to one political source (LARM, 5-3-85). Yet, at that time, the United States remained Nicaragua's most important trade partner.

Likewise, the international private banking community, to which Nicaragua owed $1.5 billion of its $4.5 billion external debt, noted the FSLN's attempts to honor its obligations and remain in good standing with its US, Canadian, Japanese and Western European creditors. In June, 1985, the Committee of Creditor Banks negotiated with the FSLN to reschedule its debt on favorable terms through June, 1986. The IMF and the World Bank also agreed in 1985 to send delegations to study the situation in Nicaragua. Meanwhile, the FSLN made token payments on its debt principal and interest and continued to communicate with its creditors, both attempts at keeping Western credit lines open. In November, 1985 the FSLN government decided to take advantage of loan offers from friendly Latin American governments in order to meet debt interest payments due by the end of the year. That left Nicaragua up to date on its debt interest payments to its Western commercial creditors, as well as to the World Bank and the Inter-American Development Bank (ICAS, December, 1985). At the same time, the FSLN was among the leaders of a Latin American drive to forge a continental approach to Latin America's $400 billion debt. While the FSLN thus demonstrated its pragmatism regarding immediate issues of international finance, it also signalled continued activism on and adherence to Third World debt objectives.

The other striking features about the assistance situation were that Nicaragua was becoming heavily dependent on donations and other forms of foreign aid, and, that the CMEA countries were becoming Nicaragua's most important assistance source. Again, a hard currency shortage and political factors shaped financial decision making. In 1984, Nicaragua's GNP fell 3.1 percent and in October, 1985 it was projected that the GNP would fall by 2.5 percent during 1985 (NYT, 10-27-85). Of about $300 million in export earnings in 1985, the equivalent of one-third was needed to import basic production materials, while the year's oil bill was nearly $200 million. Servicing at least part of its debt, however, was another priority. With export earnings -- depleted by war damage and reduced production -- falling short of covering already-reduced imports, Nicaragua was left to drawing on lines of credit and rescheduling a growing debt. Nor was drawing on the CMEA credit lines the preferred route for the FSLN, despite the easy terms offered. Sandinista development planning called for limiting imports overall, while increasing exports. But as terms of trade and export production fell, the FSLN increasingly relied on bilateral treaties, lines of credit, donations and other import-financing schemes to maintain basic economic activity and to pursue foreign exchange-generating development projects.

CMEA Economic Links. Economic ties to CMEA states were cemented by regular visits to Eastern Europe and the USSR by Planning Minister and later Minister of Foreign Cooperation, Henry Ruiz.[16] Though the Soviet bloc states informed the FSLN that they could not provide for all Nicaragua's needs, they continued to send aid and remained a principal supplier into 1986. According to Trade Ministry and other sources, the bulk of CMEA aid came in the form of medium-to-long-range concessionary trade credits and development-related economic aid. Lesser amounts were provided as donations, non-trade related loans and technical assistance. CMEA aid sources were the USSR ($443.7 million in aid from 1979-1983), Cuba ($286 million), Bulgaria ($232.5 million), East Germany ($103.3 million) and Czechoslavakia ($75 million). Hungary, Yugoslavia, North Korea, Poland and Romania provided significantly lesser amounts of aid through 1985 (e.g. see Schwab and Sims, 1985; BI, 10-1-84; 7-18-85). By 1986 approximately one-third of Nicaragua's $4.5 billion debt was owed to CMEA states. Although CMEA assistance continued despite the growing debt, new long-term commitments were reduced after 1982.

Nor did Nicaragua's observer status in CMEA after 1982 spur large new aid offers. Although Minister Ruiz signed a cooperation agreement with ten CMEA states in 1983 when Nicaragua was first seated as an observer, Nicaraguan proposals for new bilateral and multilateral cooperation made at the 1984 Havana meeting bore less fruit (LAWR, 11-9-84; NYT, 10-27-85; BI, 7-4-85). No agreement was announced at the end of the meetings. And in 1985 the CMEA countries -- not ready for a permanent commitment and unwilling to coordinate their 5-year plans with one from Nicaragua -- resisted Nicaragua's request for full membership (Edelman, 1985; BI, 7-4-85; NYT op. cit.). In line with its emphasis on the necessity for Third World states to shape their own economic stability through sound economic policy, the Soviets were also not as forthcoming with economic aid as the FSLN hoped. In both 1982 and 1984 Daniel Ortega left Moscow with much less in economic commitments than he had requested. In 1982 an agreement was signed for Soviet repair and use of the Pacific fishing port at San Juan del sur and the Soviets extended $150 million in economic credits.[17] This offer came at a time when the FSLN was seeking hard currency aid and was trying to limit, not increase, imports. In 1984, apparently disappointed with aid negotiations in the USSR, Ortega announced in Moscow that he would go on to visit Eastern European states in the next days.

A number of factors worked to limit the fruitfulness of CMEA - Nicaragua economic ties. Most important among these, Nicaragua's economy remained mixed, with about 60 percent of production activity in private hands and with approximately half of the economically active population employed in the informal petty commerce and service sectors. CMEA states preferred agreements with public sector bodies. Moreover, Nicaragua's industry remained primarily US- and Japanese-tooled and the FSLN remained committed to a mixed economy developed in the context of Nicaraguan -- not Eastern bloc -- realities. Nor did the Sandinistas have the technical or personnel resources for managing a larger state sector; Nicaragua's bureaucracy was already heavily taxed managing the state sector as it existed by the mid- 1980s. CMEA state and foreign trade institutions and practices, in addition, were unfamiliar to the Nicaraguans, who also suffered from the Soviet bloc's lack of understanding of the FSLN's development strategy (e.g. see Edelman, 1985; Conroy, 1985). Finally, not only was CMEA trade not yielding hard currency earnings, but the prospects for increased Nicaraguan exports to CMEA states were also dim. CMEA economies themselves, meanwhile, were showing little or no growth. According to Trade Minister Cuenca, expansion of Eastern bloc trade and assistance in the future would be difficult.

At least until Nicaragua moved out of a war economy and was able to redirect resources and manpower once again to developing production and exports, it would have to rely on actors willing to absorb varying levels of economic and political costs to help the FSLN government survive. The FSLN maintained its commitment to diversifying and balancing its dependence as much as was feasible given the exigencies brought on by the contra war and a hostile superpower. Assistance from all quarters, meanwhile, had lessened, apparently reflecting both the donors' willingness to help Nicaragua barely survive, but also their assessments that under an emergency situation the Nicaraguan economy would not grow and might collapse. Uncertainty about US intentions vis-a-vis the FSLN government undoubtedly affected potential donors' decisions in various ways. For the future and if they were to keep assistance pipelines open, FSLN leaders had to maintain their international activeness, fiscal flexibility, responsibility regarding Nicaragua's debt and realism about why various governments lent aid. At home, meanwhile, the FSLN directed citizens' attention to the economic costs of the contra war and US sanctions. Citing these factors as the principal causes of their hardship and national austerity measures, the FSLN government called for sacrifice and vigilance. For the time being, national economic and military survival would be the top priority and the salient consideration in policy making. In this context, tough questions concerning longer-term strategies for reducing dependence and stimulating economic growth were put aside.


NOTES

1. Author interviews with Foreign Ministry officials, Managua, 1985. Domestic and US critics of the FSLN argued that the FSLN did not establish relations with the Chinese in the early years in deference to the Soviet Union. Foreign Ministry officials denied this.

2. Bolivia and Grenada had broken relations with Taiwan and opened relations with China at mid-year. Mexico and Venezuela were expanding commercial ties with China.

3. From July 1979 to November 1980, USSR aid to Nicaragua basically consisted of ten cars, 1.5 million each pencils and exercise books, 1,000 transistor radios and 30,000 pairs of boots. Cuba was the only communist state providing significant amounts of aid in the first 10 months of the revolution.

4. Actual use of these credits was delayed both by the

Sandinistas' judgement to move forward slowly in the area of Eastern economic relations and by the lack of inter-state mechanisms or offices to implement Nicaragua's new ties to these countries with very different economic systems and methods.

5. The Soviets offered 195 university scholarships in 1980 and 320 in 1981 -- many for engineers and veterinarians. In 1982, 1,260 Nicaraguans were studying in the Eastern bloc, while 1,240 were studying in the US. The Bulgarians, East Germans and Cubans have trained Nicaraguans in technical and agricultural areas, in industrial production and in health and medicine (see e.g. Edelman, 1985). Although Nicaragua maintained educational ties to the West, through bilateral exchanges, membership in the Latin American Student and Medical School Organizations, and attendance at education conferences, there were fewer education-related opportunities offered to and/or pursued by the Nicaraguan government (e.g. BI, 9-13-83; BI, 2-21-84).

6. In his UN speech President Reagan did not respond to Ortega's challenge. Instead he focused on US-USSR differences and the upcoming superpower summit at Geneva. He raised the issues of Nicaragua, Afghanistan, Angola, Cambodia and Ethiopia as East-West problems which the superpowers should address. Reagan did not mention Contadora.

7. Significant questions about the US explanation of events were also raised in the United States. See Pearson (1984) and Kang (1985). In retaliation against Zimbabwe for its vote, the US reduced its foreign aid appropriation by one half.

8. Other Latin American members were (with year of entry): Cuba (1961), Guyana (1970), Jamaica (1970), Trinidad-Tobago (1970), Argentina (1973), Chile (1973), Peru (1973), Panama (1976), Bolivia (1979), Grenada (1979), Surinam (1979), Bahamas (1983), Barbados (1983), Belize (1983), Colombia (1983), Ecuador (1983), and St. Lucia (1983). Other states were permanent observers: Antigua, Brazil, Costa Rica, El Salvador, Mexico, Uruguay and Venezuela. A number of other Latin American states were petitioning for full legal status.

9. One indicator of its activism in inter-American forums was Nicaragua's elections in 1985 to the presidency of the American Air Forces Cooperation System, a position it would hold at least to 1986. The inter-American group, which held its 1985 meeting in Texas, focused on cooperation in the case of disasters, in telecommunications and in accident prevention.

10. When pressed for evidence of Nicaraguan links to terrorism, one US Embassy analyst in Managua in 1985 referred to "reported citings" of Arab and foreign-looking men in southern Nicaragua especially around the fishing port of San Juàn del Sur -- a port used by the Soviets. Another analyst suggested that while Nicaragua did not "pull the trigger" in terrorist acts, the FSLN helped terrorist groups by supplying them weapons and safe haven (author interviews).

11. Two new cases against Nicaragua were raised in late 1985. One involved the confiscation by Honduran authorities of a Soviet-built automobile carrying weapons, cash and personal letters to guerrillas with the FMLN. Washington charged that the auto had passed through Nicaragua with full FSLN knowledge and support. The

second case involved US and, later, Colombian allegations that the FSLN had supplied weapons and other aid to Colombian guerrillas who carried out a brutal and deadly raid in November on the Palace of Justice in Bogota. Nicaragua denied both charges. Colombia accepted the FSLN's explanation for the presence there of rifles registered to Nicaragua and considered the case closed (NYT, 1-6-86; 1-23-86).

12.     An irony existed in the fact that the reduction of US purchases particularly affected the very bourgeoisie private sector that it hoped would take over power from the FSLN. For example, cattle-raising and beef production in revolutionary Nicaragua largely remained in the hands of traditional large cattle-raisers. Similarly, this sector utilized much of the production material imported from the United States and was hurt most by the 1985 embargo.

13.     In late 1985 Ecuador's new conservative and increasingly pro-US President Febres abruptly broke relations with Nicaragua, making any oil deals in the immediate future doubtful.

14.     Assessing that Nicaragua would not be able to pay its back debt and interest totalling $4.4 million, Spain, in March 1985, suspended its 1983 $34 million credit line to Nicaragua which was to have extended to 1986. Spain offered to reopen credit when Nicaragua paid $2.05 million in overdue interest. Spanish officials said there were no political reasons for their move (BI, 12-5-83; LAWR, 3-29-85).

15.     Among the projects being funded and technically assisted between 1983 and 1986 were the following: a Corinto to El Bluff (Pacific to Atlantic) rail link funded by Spain, Argentina, Bulgaria and others; a deep water port on the Atlantic at Bluff Island in the geothermal projects at Mombotombo funded by Canada, Italy, Brazil, the USSR and Bulgaria; an oil storage facility at Puerto Sandino, funded principally by the USSR; the Timal sugar mill, donated by Cuba; the Sebaco vegetable farm, a livestock/dairy farm in Matagalpa, and a large irrigation network from Lake Managua to large grain farms, funded by a CMEA consortium; and a palm oil production facility, funded by Holland (e.g. IHCA, June, 1985; LARM, 1-12-83; BI, 6-13-85; LAWR, 7-23-83; CAU, June 83; NYT, 10-27-85).

16.     Though he also made visits to other states, it was Ruiz who most often led delegations on ceremonial or economic aid-seeking trips to CMEA states. Trade Minister Cuenca, President Ortega, Vice President Ramirez or Foreign Minister D'Escoto usually led aid-seeking delegations to Western Europe, Latin America, Asia and elsewhere. Delegations led by President Daniel Ortega or Defense Minister Humberto Ortega negotiated military assistance.

17.     The San Juan del sur port was to be used by the Soviets' tuna fleet. As repaired, the port facility consisted of a 7000 ton dry dock and a 60 foot long floating pier. The Soviets had built a similar facility in Peru years earlier (CAU, 6-8-83).

# 10

## Nicaragua's Regional Negotiating Positions

Everytime you see the phenomenon of nationalism in Latin America and the recovery of a nation's own resources it has provoked confrontation with the United States. Ronald Reagan is nothing more than heir to the historical relationship of the United States with Nicaragua, except he uses the Soviet Union as a justification.

> President Daniel Ortega
> April, 1985

The present-day Monroists [i.e. Monroe Doctrine], who understand that there is something new and hopeful here, are attempting to discredit and vilify us, to distort our identity with the aim of isolating and crushing us in the short run. Perhaps at no other time in the history of the United States has a country so small and underdeveloped been treated with such importance and hostility. The terms they use to describe us almost make us appear to be a power; if we were a power, it would only be from the perspective of morality.

> Bayardo Arce
> FSLN Political Coordinator
> February, 1985

As fears of a US intervention grew, the Sandinistas expended increasing amounts of their foreign policy resources responding to the United States' anti-FSLN policies and creating maneuvering space for the revolution in the region--where security issues would ultimately be addressed. In the last chapter, I examined the nature of Nicaraguan internationalism and the degree to which a stance of global activism was both a means and an end. In this chapter I discuss Nicaraguan foreign policy objectives as they related to regional peace and security issues after 1979. I outline FSLN strategies and negotiation positions vis-a-vis the United States, bordering states and the Contadora peace process.

FOREIGN POLICY OBJECTIVES AND REGIONAL SECURITY CONCERNS

The FSLN's anti-imperialist philosophy translated into intransigence on the issue of Nicaraguan self-determination and respect for Nicaraguan sovereignty. As a senior FSLN foreign policy official put it following Thomas Enders' historic ultimatum to the Sandinistas in 1981: "A state that agrees to negotiate on internal matters wounds its substantive reason for being a state. It is the only point on which we are intransigent" (quoted in Gutman, 1984:11). The FSLN, according to Deputy Foreign Minister Tinoco, preferred to fight rather than once again have a government imposed upon Nicaragua by foreigners; the scope of the revolution would be determined by the Nicaraguan people, not by conditions imposed on them by foreign powers (King, 1984:28). Regarding domestic institutions, the FSLN rejected what it saw as United States' attempts to impose a Western-styled capitalist and pro-US model on Nicaragua. On similar grounds, the FSLN rejected the key US condition for a cessation of hostilities and the re-opening of talks with the Sandinista government -- i.e. that the FSLN hold "national reconciliation" talks on power-sharing with the contras. In the Sandinistas' view, both the Carter Administration's moves in June and July, 1979 and the Reagan Administration's contra policy after 1980 aimed less at Nicaraguan power-sharing than at eliminating the FSLN altogether as a power contender.

The FSLN saw US imperialism as its primary security threat. Rather than consisting of an indigenous, representative opposition such as the one posed by the FMLN in El Salvador, the contras were the United States' proxies in a counter-revolutionary war of aggression. In the FSLN view, the contras were defended by President Reagan, funded by Congress, totally dependent on US policy and only viable to the extent that they fit into the broader strategy of the United States. Moreover, though Honduras and Costa Rica individually did not pose a security threat to Nicaragua, to the extent that they facilitated US military and contra policies these states compounded Nicaraguan security problems. The FSLN position, therefore, was that, unlike the situation in Salvador, the military conflict in Nicaragua was not a civil war but a blatant, US-backed, aggression. For that reason, the FSLN, though it offered amnesty to contra fighters, stood firm in refusing to negotiate with contra (UNO) leaders. The Sandinistas called instead for unconditional bilateral talks with the United States on security issues. According to President Ortega, the FSLN wanted "...to talk with the owner of the circus, not the acrobats" (NYT, 3-29-85). Failing that, the FSLN insisted upon United States' assurances under a protocol to a Contadora peace treaty. Arguing that the United States' historical regional prerogative needed to be reassessed in the light of the revolution and Latin American nationalism, the Sandinistas called for a clarification of the United States' regional role and US recognition of Nicaragua's inalienable right to exist. In the FSLN view, the United States had to be considered along with Cuba and the USSR as an extra-regional actor in regional agreements pertaining to limits on foreign advisors, troops, maneuvers and bases. A major factor shaping the FSLN's position on the Contadora process was its fear that the United States -- the regional antagonist, but not a party to Contadora -- would try to circumvent a regional accord and continue support for a contra army under the Kissinger Commission thesis that Contadora could not be a substitute for US policy. The FSLN, concerned about the lack of progress to 1986 in reaching a Contadora agreement, also sought a resumption of the Manzanillo bilateral talks with the United States. The immediate and pressing issue for the Nicaraguan government remained negotiating an end to the contra war.

Meanwhile, the Sandinistas' position regarding a settlement of the conflict in El Salvador was to change over time. The FSLN originally argued that regional peace ultimately depended not only on resolutions to issues festering among Nicaragua, the United States and US regional allies, but also on a resolution of the Salvadoran civil war through a power-sharing formula. In the 1983 and early 1984 period, during which the FMLN appeared capable of a military victory over the demoralized and corrupt Salvadoran army, the Sandinistas worried that the Salvadoran situation would spur escalated US hostility toward Nicaragua. Therefore, the FSLN insisted that FMLN-Salvadoran government talks be incorporated into a broader Contadora settlement. But in 1984, as US pressures on Nicaragua mounted and as greatly increased US military aid to the Salvadoran army improved that government's military posture vis-a-vis the FMLN guerrillas, the FSLN dropped references to the Salvadoran situation and pushed harder for a treaty addressing security issues of immediate concern to Nicaragua.

While the FSLN came to accept regional arms reduction under Contadora as the only means to long-term peace, it remained suspicious of the United States' and its allies' intentions vis-a-vis a revolutionary Nicaragua. Both as a matter of principle and as a matter of security, therefore, the FSLN government refused US demands dating from 1981 that Nicaragua unilaterally disarm to levels on par with its individual neighbors in a demonstration of good faith before region-wide limitations -- including limitations on the United States' military presence and its support for the contras -- were fully developed and enforced. The FSLN rejected the notion of negotiating under overwhelming military pressures. In the Sandinistas' view, the regional military threat had actually increased significantly during the years of Contadora negotiations. Honduran and Salvadoran air and land forces had been greatly enlarged and upgraded. Costa Rican officials had become increasingly anti-Sandinista and appeared more willing to facilitate a US policy of militarization. A large US military presence at Honduran bases and in continuing military maneuvers, as well as Reagan Administration pledges to continue aiding the contras bespoke the United States' continued determination to undermine the FSLN government.

The FSLN negotiating stance was that military reduction formulations had to reflect the size of the threat that each state faced. To Nicaraguan leaders, the size of its defense forces had to be assessed in the light of the threat posed by the combined forces of the United States' regional allies. (Recall that in 1983 a revitalized CONDECA considered military contingency plans for dealing with "the Nicaraguan threat.") For similar reasons, the FSLN held that the verification and implementation of any treaty had

352

to be overseen not by a regional body in which the United States was traditionally dominant, such as the OAS, but by a broader collection of states acting independently, such as the Contadora group itself, the United Nations, or a group of Latin American and Western European states. Just as the FSLN's critical objective in the international diplomatic arena was to avoid political isolation, in the regional setting the FSLN jockeyed to maintain policy options and to resist US pressures.


CREATING MANEUVERING SPACE

The Sandinistas' strategies for reaching a negotiated settlement of regional conflict and avoiding a US militarily-imposed "solution" grew out of these concerns and objectives. First, by bringing its case to the international community, the FSLN sought effectively to broaden the scope of the conflict and to bring world pressure or international law to bear against US policy. The Sandinistas, keenly aware of the need to administer their international solidarity adroitly, aimed at employing their alignment with Latin American and international progressive forces to block or to mitigate the effects of US influence and power. The FSLN's two Western European diplomatic tours in 1985 -- in February and in May -- and their May to July tour of every Latin American state save Chile and Paraguay the same year were designed to clarify for these governments the FSLN's negotiating position on Contadora and on US demands. FSLN delegations pressed these states not only for political and economic displays of support in the post-embargo period, but also for their diplomatic help in urging the United States back to the Manzanillo talks (e.g. LARM, 2-25-85).

In addition to utilizing international forums and multi-nation diplomatic tours for such purposes, the FSLN government took its case against the United States' support for the contras and the CIA's mining of its harbors to the World Court in 1984 and 1985. There the FSLN regarded as a foreign policy victory the Court's May, 1984 restraining order against the United States and its November, 1984 decision (in a 15-1 vote) that the Court had jurisdiction in the Nicaragua-United States dispute.[2] The United States' announcement in 1984 that it was withdrawing from cases pertaining to Central America for a period of two years gave the FSLN another opportunity to argue that while it respected and abided by international law, the Reagan Administration did not. Nicaragua called on the Reagan Administration to bring evidence of its charges of Nicaraguan terrorism and subversion to the World Court. According to Foreign Ministry officials, the FSLN hoped that the authoritative prestige of the Court and media attention to Nicaragua's case as it was presented in 1985 would both deepen international awareness of the need to deter US acts and influence the US Congress and public opinion.

Ironically, the Court's ruling (12-3) against the United States came one day after the US House of Representatives voted $100 million in new contra funding, $70 million of it for military aid. The late June, 1986 ruling rejected the US "collective self-defense" argument and strongly condemned US complicity in the contra program (including the US mining of Nicaragua's harbors). The court found The United States guilty of eleven violations of international law and ordered Washington to pay reparations to Nicaragua. Reacting to the US administration position that its policy was within international law, Nicaragua -- in a tactical move to maintain issue momentum -- called on the UN Security Council to enforce the ruling.

A second FSLN strategy was to eliminate possible pretexts for invading Nicaragua by responding to US charges and initiatives. Thus, for example, in response to the United States' January, 1982 sponsorship of the Central American Democratic Community -- an effort labelled by Panama's president as "an arrow aimed at Nicaragua's heart" (IHCA, June, 1984) -- Nicaragua offered to negotiate and sign non-aggression mutual defense pacts with its neighbors. In April, 1982 the Frente offered a seven-point peace plan to Honduras and offered a point by point response to a US eight-point communication from the new US ambassador. In September Nicaragua agreed to the Venezuelan-Mexican initiative for bilateral talks among Nicaragua, Honduras and the United States. Also in September, the FSLN requested D'Escoto-Shultz talks at upcoming UN meetings and in October Daniel Ortega made another peace proposal in his UN General Assembly address.

After President Reagan's fiery anti-Sandinista speech of April, 1983 the FSLN repeated a request for dialogue with Washington (e.g. NYT, 4-29-83) and followed that up with new international diplomatic efforts to present the Sandinista view of local realities. In his fourth anniversary speech on July 19, 1983, Junta leader Ortega announced a Nicaraguan peace plan which, while it laid out Nicaraguan concerns, also built on agreements the Contadora states sought at that time. In October, 1983 Nicaragua offered four draft peace proposals to the United States and Contadora in which the FSLN said, among other things, that its sovereignty was incompatible with housing foreign bases and that its territory would not be used to threaten or attack the United States or other states. The FSLN made negotiating proposals concerning foreign advisors and regional weapons build-ups. And, as discussed in Chapter 5, the FSLN took a series of conciliatory steps in late 1983 and 1984 to reduce domestic tensions and/or to address issues the United States had raised against Nicaragua. Meanwhile, Nicaraguan leaders maintained a good working relationship with the Contadora states.

Again in 1984 the FSLN proposed unconditional talks with US officials regarding the latter's security concerns. At home, the FSLN government was overseeing an electoral process under the scrutiny of the international media. Yet, the United States responded consistently to each of these FSLN initiatives over several years by labelling the Sandinistas "propagandists" who were totally "without honor", or, by shifting or expanding policy demands and rationalizations. While it was true that the FSLN's moves were designed as much for international image management as for lowering local tensions, the Sandinistas were nevertheless demonstrating flexibility and a willingness to negotiate during a period of intense US regional military build-up. The Frente played upon this contrast in the international arena to sew doubts about US policy premises.

354

## Bilateral Border Talks

Another FSLN strategy for avoiding intervention and geopolitical isolation involved pursuing bilateral agreements with its neighbors. Such a strategy aimed not only at confounding US attempts to coordinate a regional anti-Sandinista bloc, but also at circumventing US intransigence while addressing Nicaragua's most immediate security threat -- the contra war. This top priority concern shaped the FSLN's pre-July, 1983 position that bilateral talks with the United States and Honduras should precede discussions on wider regional issues. The same concern shaped its position at Contadora.

First, hoping to elicit international pressure against these states, the FSLN publicized Honduran, and later, Costa Rican complicity -- direct or indirect -- in the contra effort. In November, 1982 the Sandinistas lodged their fiftieth protest note against the Honduran government over cross-border contra raids and increased the pressure by issuing a document from the Nicaraguan Embassy in Washington detailing, with photos and maps, 429 acts of contra aggressions staged from sanctuaries in Honduras. Such publicity of the Honduran role in US policy exacerbated already festering conflicts within Honduras over that country's relationship to the United States. Honduras' official position remained that its government had nothing to do with the contras or their war. In 1983 and 1984 the FSLN similarly distributed evidence of ARDE's presence in Costa Rica to counter Costa Rican denials and claims of complete neutrality. In fact, the embarrassment over contra activities inside their borders spurred Costa Rican officials into agreeing in 1984 to join with Nicaragua in creating a bilateral Mixed Commission for addressing border violations.

But more intensive diplomatic efforts went into Nicaraguan proposals for bilateral talks, non-aggression agreements or border pacification pacts. These efforts predated the Contadora process and continued thereafter. Nicaraguan interests were clear. A pact with Honduras in particular would greatly reduce Nicaragua's regional isolation as it eliminated much of the military pressure the United States was bringing to bear on the FSLN. While critics in the United States argued that Nicaragua pursued such talks in order to circumvent Contadora, its provisions for arms reductions and the US allies' stance on specific forms of pluralism or internal reconciliation, FSLN officials argued that any bilateral pacts could be brought under the sponsorship of Contadora and would be incorporated into a larger Contadora treaty.

FSLN efforts aimed at creating demilitarized border zones and signing individual peace pacts with neighbors stepped up in 1985 -- i.e., after the Manzanillo talks had been suspended and while Contadora appeared to be stalled. Employing government-to-government, leader-to-leader and less usual military-to-military appeals, the Sandinistas requested Panamanian- or Contadora-mediated bilateral talks. This diplomatic campaign paralleled EPS campaigns to push the contras out of Nicaragua.[3] In a May, 1985 diplomatic note to Honduran Foreign Minister Paz Barnica, Nicaragua outlined a plan for joint Nicaraguan-Honduran efforts at disarming and removing the contras based at 84 camps inside Honduras. Under the plan, the

355

contras would be relocated from border areas with the help of the Red Cross and/or the UN High Commission on Refugees, while those willing to lay down their arms could return to Nicaragua under amnesty. According to Defense Minister Ortega, this plan both took into account Honduran military and civilian resentment against the presence of a large, foreign armed force inside Honduran territory and expressed Nicaragua's attitude that the threat to its security originated in Washington, not Tegucigalpa (BI, 5-23-85). Reinforcing that diplomatic effort, Defense Minister Ortega proposed to Honduran Armed Forces' Commander Walter Lopez that the two armies, under third-party auspices, mediate recurring border conflicts. Proposals for a border commission and mediation were made public later in the month. Such offers were repeated over the next year in response to intermittent border clashes.

Sweetening the peace proposal, the FSLN later offered permanently to resettle (in Nicaragua) pro-FMLN Salvadoran refugees, who were currently residing in Honduran camps near the Salvadoran border. These refugees, considered by the Salvadoran and Honduran armies to be FMLN guerrillas, had become a security problem for the Hondurans as well as a point of contention between the Salvadoran and Honduran governments. The issue flared whenever Salvadoran army troops crossed into Honduras in hot pursuit of refugees.

Similarly, the Nicaraguan military commander in the region bordering Costa Rica, Luis Calderon, established contacts with local Costa Rican Civil Guard officials in hopes of establishing joint border patrols. In June and August, 1985, President Ortega wrote to President Monge asking him to reconsider talks on the establishment of a demilitarized zone. Ortega emphasized French willingness to facilitate such talks. In the FSLN's view, talks with Costa Rica would also get Contadora moving again (e.g. ICAS, September, 1985). Although the Panamanian military offered to mediate Nicaraguan talks with Honduras or Costa Rica, and though the OAS and Contadora supported Nicaraguan-Costa Rican talks, pressures from the United States and local right-wing sectors effectively doomed the initiatives in 1985. The public US position was that such bilateral pacts would undermine a coordinated regional peace agreement. Actually, Reagan Administration ideologues would not countenance agreements which left the FSLN in power. Reflecting these views, Honduras rejected Nicaraguan overtures on the grounds that solutions had to be multilateral (i.e. US-approved) not bilateral. Still bitter about the events following the Las Crucitas incident, Costa Rica responded in 1985 by arguing that no conditions existed at that time for formalizing bilateral talks with Nicaragua. Rather than rejecting the idea of establishing a border commission with Nicaragua, Costa Rican officials, in August, set preconditions for further talks: Nicaragua had to apologize for the Las Crucitas deaths -- effectively, then, accepting blame for the incident -- and Contadora (which President Monge had earlier accused of a pro-Nicaraguan bias) had to inspect the Costa Rican border to confirm Costa Rica's claim that there were no contras operating there.

An apparent shift occurred in Costa Rican policy direction, however, after the early 1986 presidential elections in that country. As I noted in Chapter 7, president-elect Oscar Arias

Sanchez's public criticism of US contra policy and Daniel Ortega's careful letter of regret over the Las Crucitas incident created a window of opportunity for Nicaragua's border pact initiative and encouraged neutralist elements in Costa Rican politics. The border agreement drawn up by the Nicaraguan and Costa Rican Foreign Ministries in February, 1986 aimed at disallowing contra activities in the tense region. If it was effectively implemented, the pact would not only improve Costa Rica's international image as a neutral and independent state, but would also allow the Sandinista Armed Forces to concentrate their efforts along the northern border with Honduras. The border talks and the exchange of new ambassadors, moreover, signalled somewhat improved bilateral relations. The Sandinistas hailed the rapproachment with Costa Rica as evidence that regional peace was achievable.

Once again, Nicaraguan diplomatic efforts and local nationalist sentiment threatened to hamper US regional policy. Costa Rica's adherence to the border pact would create obstacles for the United States' two-front, pincer military strategy agianst Nicaragua just as a Nicaraguan-Costa Rican rapproachment would further stymie a US-sponsored anti-Sandinista bloc. In the same period during which he was lobbying hard for new contra military funding from Congress in February and March, 1986, therefore, President Reagan also renewed efforts to influence the Costa Rican stance vis-a-vis the Sandinistas. In early March a senior American military official, Deputy Secretary of Defense William Howard Taft the 4th conferred with President-elect Arias in Costa Rica on regional security issues and Costa Rican defense. In the weeks following, both Roving Ambassador Harry Schlaudeman and Special Presidential Envoy Philip Habib travelled to Costa Rica to press Arias not to repeat his earlier public criticism of US contra policy (NYT, 5-9-86).

## The Manzanillo Talks

Domestic political pressures in the United States led to the June, 1984 agreement on the part of the Reagan Administration to open bilateral talks with the FSLN. The Sandinistas saw the talks as an opportunity directly to address both US security concerns and US backing for the contras. The FSLN saw greater opportunity for progress on security matters in bilateral talks with the United States than through the Contadora process. Again, this posture followed from the FSLN view of the United States as the regional antagonist, and, from its position that the US role had to be addressed directly if peace were to be achieved. Thus the FSLN delegation, headed by Deputy Foreign Minister Victor Tinoco, came to the talks with concrete proposals on security matters related to Nicaraguan military size and strength, foreign advisors, Nicaraguan pledges not to support subversion, and the like. Consistent with their insistence on political self-determination, however, the delegation refused either to address internal structures or to agree to a dialogue with contra leaders.

FSLN Foreign Ministry officials argued that an agreement at Manzanillo would secure and reinvigorate Contadora by providing a formula for agreement between the two main contenders. From the Sandinistas' perspective Contadora only indirectly addressed the contra war situation and could not guarantee US compliance. Nor had US Congressional restrictions regarding both the CIA's involvement with the contras and acts intended to overthrow the FSLN been effective. Even prior to its repeal in the fall of 1985, the Boland Amendment was being violated inadvertantly since: 1) there was no real auditing of the end-use of US weapons left behind for the contras at the close of US military maneuvers; 2) private US monies were flowing to the contras; and 3) US National Security Council advisors continued working with the contras. Bilateral talks would allow face-to-face discussions of the interests and concerns of both Nicaragua and the United States. An agreement would insure US compliance. The Contadora states, on the other hand, preferred at that time not to alienate the United States by acknowledging openly its regional role. This was a critical issue to the FSLN.

However, as I argued in Chapter 5, the Manzanillo talks were intended by the Reagan Administration to be nothing more than an election year ploy to appear reasonable on the Nicaragua issue. The US delegation, according to Tinoco, offered no substantive counter-proposals on security matters. Not only did the Reagan Administration withdraw from the talks in January, 1985, it also had no intention of returning to serious bilateral talks at a later date.[5] This decision did not result from a lack of progress at the talks. Though the first three meetings dealt largely with procedural matters, the next three meetings were exploratory and included discussions on: 1) the relationship of the Manzanillo talks to the Contadora process; 2) which security matters could be dealt with in a bilateral setting; and 3) a substanative agenda. Discussions also focused on conceptual differences between the states regarding the issues of foreign advisors and technicians and means for withdrawing foreign personnel from the region.[6] Differences on the issue of maneuvers were aired. Members of both delegations privately reported that the Manzanillo setting demonstrated the potential for coming to agreement on bilateral security issues. According to a senior US Embassy analyst in Managua, the Manzanillo discussions were "good talks," "sufficiently good that Nicaragua preferred them to Contadora." Meanwhile, US participants "began to see room for agreements." A US participant in the talks noted: "We made progress if what we had wanted was pledges for halting insurgency and a bilateral arrangement to reach a deal on limiting advisors, the numbers of armaments and of armed men."[7]

According to US officials in Managua and Washington, pressures against continuing such talks had come from US hardliners and Central American allies concerned about the effect on their relations with the FSLN government should the United States make a separate deal with the Nicaraguans. According to US Embassy officials, Nicaragua had acted imprudently by claiming publically that real regional progress was to be made at Manzanillo and not through Contadora. This worried US allies according to US officials. Yet the ultimate reason for suspending bilateral talks had to do with the United States' insistence, in President Reagan's words, on a change in the "present structure" of the Nicaraguan government. In fact, the US allies themselves were persuaded by fellow Latin American states in early 1986 to support a regional

call for Washington to return to bilateral talks. The United States
continued publically to insist on FSLN-contra talks and privately to
prefer the elimination of the FSLN. The Sandinistas' refusal to
acknowledge the contra army as a legitimate opposition force and the
contra war as a civil war, meanwhile, highlighted the extent to
which the United States and Nicaragua were at loggerheads.

Nevertheless, in 1985 the FSLN, supported by the Contadora
states, worked to press the United States into returning to
Manzanillo. In February President Ortega issued an invitation for a
bipartisan Congressional delegation to tour Nicaraguan military
installations for purposes of assessing the nature of Nicaraguan
military capability. In April, President Ortega pledged to call an
immediate cease-fire, restore full civil liberties and end press
censorship if the United States ended its support for the contras
and resumed bilateral talks. The same month, Deputy Foreign
Minister Tinoco said Nicaragua was ready to discuss Reagan's April
peace plan if the talks were rejoined (BI, 5-23-85; LAWR, 4-19-85;
CAR 4-26-85). And, in May Vice President Ramirez invited US
Congressional delegations to visit the Nicaraguan-Honduran border
area for on-site inspections and verifications of the nature of the
conflict with the contras and between Honduras and Nicaragua.

Yet, the regional political fallout over Manzanillo and the
Reagan Administration's larger agenda vis-a-vis the FSLN worked
effectively to kill the bilateral option. By mid-1985 US officials
were saying that the Manzanillo effort was dead.


NICARAGUAN POSITIONS AT CONTADORA

Just as the FSLN rejected Washington's symmetry argument that
the situations in Salvador and Nicaragua were identical and could
be "solved" in similar ways, the Sandinistas were initially wary
about the potential of a broad, regional approach to peace -- an
approach the United States was publically advocating in 1982 in
response to FSLN appeals for bilateral security discussions.
Because the United States 1) had been calling for unilateral
Nicaraguan disarmament as a precondition for bilateral negotiations,
2) had defined the contra war an "internal problem" and 3) had
labelled Nicaragua the source of all regional subversion, the FSLN
from 1982 to mid- 1983 worried that region-wide talks might be used
by US allies as a vehicle for delegitimizing or overriding
Nicaragua's security concerns. In a speech before the United
Nations in October, 1982 Foreign Minister D'Escoto charged the
United States with trying to avoid direct peace talks which would
address its backing of the contras (e.g. NYT, 10-11-82). Indeed, at
early Contadora meetings and until mid-1983 -- despite the FSLN's
April announcement that it would also cooperate with Contadora in a
multilateral setting -- the Frente continued to demand bilateral
talks with Honduras and the United States over the immediate
security threat posed by the contras. As Nicaragua's OAS Ambassador
Edgar Parrales argued, "A Central American agreement wouldn't be
worth anything if the United States doesn't make any commitments"
(LAWR, 4-15-83). Establishing effective limits on the United
States' regional presence and directly addressing the US role in the

contra war, therefore, were to remain top Sandinista priorities within Contadora.

## Agreeing to Multilateral Talks

By July 1983 a number of factors influenced a shift in the FSLN position regarding the efficacy of multilateral talks as a means for addressing security concerns. Not only were United States-Nicaraguan relations at their lowest point, but the escalating contra war was taking a significant toll on the Nicaraguan economy. The United States and Honduras continued to reject bilateral talks, while the US build-up of Honduran and Salvadoran military capacities continued. The Sandinistas feared an imminent US invasion. The Contadora states and the Socialist International, meanwhile, were encouraging the FSLN to demonstrate flexibility on the issue of negotiations and Cuba and the Soviet Union publically endorsed the idea of a regional negotiated settlement. Just as important to an FSLN worried about a solution on US terms, the Contadora states at mid-year had moved to counteract US pressure and create some distance between themselves and the United States. To reinvigorate a process which appeared to be faltering in the face of hostile rhetoric emanating from Washington, Tegucigalpa and Managua, Mexico -- at Nicaragua's urging -- convened a July meeting of the Contadora presidents at Cancun, Mexico. From Nicaragua's perspective, the meeting was an important signal that the peace initiative was in the hands of Latin American -- not US -- officials. But the Cancun meeting also demonstrated to the FSLN that important security proposals could emerge from the process. For example, the Contadora states: called on the leaders of the United States and Cuba to join in efforts at averting a war between Honduras and Nicaragua; called for the withdrawal of all foreign advisors from the region; and called for international border supervision.

In the same period the FSLN National Directorate had been holding urgent discussions on how best to eliminate possible US pretexts for invading. What resulted was an FSLN decision in July, 1983 to drop its condition of bilateral talks within Contadora and to join multilateral security negotiations. In a move designed both to spur new Contadora momentum and to influence the framework of future discussions, Daniel Ortega (speaking at the July 19th anniversary celebrations) outlined a six-point regional peace plan which built on the Cancun communique and addressed the FSLN's main security concerns. The plan called for 1) a Honduran-Nicaraguan non-aggression pact; 2) a halt in arms supplies to conflicting parties in El Salvador; 3) an end to the sponsorship of any regional force fighting to unseat a regional government; 4) the right to self-determination and non-intervention; 5) an end to policies of economic discrimination; and 6) a halt to the establishment of foreign military bases and to military exercises in the region.[8] In the next month both the FSLN and Cuba offered incentives to get negotiations moving. On July 29 Castro offered to halt military aid to Nicaragua if all countries similarly ended arms shipments to the region (NYT, 7-29-83). In August, the FSLN offered to send home all its Cuban military advisors and accept no further Soviet military aid if the United States would end its militarization of Honduras (NYT, 8-15-83). Nicaragua was anxious to come to an agreement on security issues, but only if the United States agreed to end its military campaign against Nicaragua and to respect Nicaraguan self-determination. The FSLN did not consider the nature of internal structures open for multilateral negotiating, though it did join in a call for the establishment of democratic and pluralistic systems in the region.

The FSLN's diplomatic efforts within Contadora in the second half of 1983 aimed at giving favorable concrete expression to the Contadora Document of Objectives (the "21 points") which was signed by all five Central American States in early September. That document emphasized: the observance of international law; the right to national self-determination; a halt to foreign intervention; the peaceful resolution of conflicts; non-aggression; a regional arms freeze; a prohibition against the installation of foreign military bases; a reduction in foreign military advisors; negotiations over regional arms control and reductions; regional economic integration; and the development of pluralistic institutions with social and economic equality and respect for human rights (e.g. CAHI, 7-9-84). Yet, little progress had been made in agreeing on actual measures to avoid war. When, in the Nicaraguan view, the Contadora process was threatened by the US invasion of Grenada and its reinvigoration of CONDECA in October, 1983, the FSLN offered the four draft peace treaties discussed earlier. Calling on the United States to recognize "Nicaragua's inalienable right to independence and self-determination as a sovereign state" the FSLN argued that Nicaragua did "not constitute a strategic or aerial base for the influence of foreign powers" and that allowing such was... "contrary to and incompatible with Nicaragua's sovereignty..." (IHCA, November, 1983). Trying to influence the shape of regional security agreements in the absence of other progress, Nicaragua again offered to sign mutual non-aggression pacts; to follow international law; to pledge not to promote the destabilization of neighboring states; to support a negotiated settlement in Salvador; and to abide by UN or Contadora verification.

In November, 1983 the Sandinistas reiterated earlier offers regarding foreign advisors and Soviet military aid. And in December the FSLN offered Contadora officials what amounted to a draft peace agreement. In that draft the FSLN offered to discuss: an arms freeze; the immediate withdrawal of foreign advisors; limitations on the size of regional standing armies; and measures for forwarding "...democratic, representative and pluralist systems which guarantee the effective participation of people in the decision-making process and insure the free access of different currents of opinion to honest, periodical elections based on the full observance of civil rights" (Gutman, 1984: 18; IHCA, December, 1983). The draft reflected FSLN responses to US concerns and pressures and, along with other 1983 gestures, constituted a conciliatory stance. At the same time, however, the FSLN restated its position that the United States was a party to regional conflict and had to commit itself to ceasing regional "belligerent conduct." Signalling its willingness again to work within the process, in January 1984, Nicaragua joined the other Central American states in signing three Contadora accords on implementation. The accords established sub-commissions to work out details regarding regional military inventories, irregular military forces, national reconciliation and regional integration.

## Responses to US-Inspired Delays

Due largely to United States and Honduran, and later, Costa Rican delay tactics, the Contadora process was slowed down and stalled during 1984. The US allies worked to include formulas for detailed military inventories and for verification which were to the United States' liking, or , which preserved US oversight and its option of a regional military presence. An April, 1984 proposal from Honduras, El Salvador and Costa Rica, for instance, called for an OAS group -- the Interamerican Defense Board -- to verify military inventories, though Nicaragua earlier had enunciated its concern that any agreement be verified by a group which did not include the United States (WP, 5-2-84). In the context of continued military build-up in Honduras and dramatic CIA sabotage acts against Nicaraguan infrastructure, the FSLN rejected the proposal and countered that the Contadora states or a UN group should verify any agreement. Yet, despite their concern 1) that the Contadora states were avoiding tackling the central issues (i.e. US regional hegemony, its role as a main actor in regional tensions and the need for structural change in the region) and 2) that US regional militarization was changing the geopolitical situation for Contadora, the FSLN continued working and exchanging views within the process.

The FSLN's ability successfully to promote its position, to offer alternatives to proposals made by US allies and to maintain respect or legitimacy within the Contadora group -- despite US pressures on those states -- was reflected in the fact that in September, 1984 Contadora produced a draft treaty which Nicaragua, with some wariness, agreed to sign. The draft called for an indefinite arms freeze; offered firm timetables for the departure of foreign military advisors and the removal of foreign military bases or schools; and proscribed foreign or provocative military exercises. Disputes among the Central American states were to be appealed to the Contadora foreign ministers, while verification and control would be carried out by an independent commission coordinated by Contadora. The US-sponsored demand that internal reconciliation with insurgent forces be undertaken was eliminated, thereby avoiding a requirement the FSLN feared would be used by the United States to impose on Nicaragua its particular vision of what constituted a "genuine democracy." Finally, a protocol attached to the treaty called on Cuba, the Soviet Union and the United States to refrain from interferring in the region and to support the elements of the agreement. That protocol could also be signed by other states willing to help facilitate the treaty.

Although the US allies initially indicated their willingness to join Nicaragua in signing the treaty as drafted, the United States moved quickly to instruct its allies to offer new counter-proposals. In October, the allies met in Tegucigalpa and produced proposals which both reflected mistrust of Nicaraguan compliance and maintained the space for a future US military presence in the region. The Tegucigalpa draft limited the arms freeze to sixty days, presented no timetables for military reductions and permitted "regulated" foreign military exercises. Appeals from disputes moveover, would be taken to a body of Central American and Contadora representatives, while an Ad Hoc Disarmament Group, made up of the five Central American states and four other unspecified states (i.e., not Contadora) would verify and control regional military build-down. The new proposals, in brief, additionally provided greater opportunity for the United States' allies to settle disputes with Nicaragua in their own favor in forums where they could more readily control the outcome. A US National Security Council Background Paper leaked to the press in late October noted the Reagan Administration's satisfication over its success at stymieing a Contadora agreement in 1984:

> We have effectively blocked Contadora Group efforts to impose a second draft of a revised Contadora Act. Following intensive US consultations with El Salvador, Honduras and Costa Rica, the Central American (sic) submitted a counterdraft to the Contadora states on Oct. 20, 1984...[that] shifts concern within Contadora to a document broadly consistent with US interests (IHCA, December, 1985).

Both because the Contadora states did not welcome the Tegucigalpa proposals and because Costa Rica refused to participate (due to tense relations with Nicaragua over the Urbina Lara asylum case), the February Contadora meeting was postponed. Meanwhile, the United States used the delay to increase diplomatic and military tensions with Nicaragua (e.g. the "Mig Crisis"; major new military exercises), to suspend the Manzanillo talks and to work to improve the contras' political image.

Nicaragua's response in the first half of 1985 was again conciliatory: by offering new initiatives for peace and seeking Western European and Latin American help in pressuring the United States to reconsider its position, the FSLN hoped to get both the Manzanillo and Contadora talks back on track. In February, President Ortega announced that Nicaragua would: concede to Costa Rican demands regarding the asylum case; send home 100 Cuban military advisors; suspend all new weapons acquistions, and host a US Congressional military inspection group (CAR, 3-8-85). Meanwhile, Vice President Ramirez took advantage of the Contadora delay to present Nicaragua's case to Western European leaders. Expressing Nicaragua's willingness to talk with the United States and its acceptance of US concerns over treaty verification, Ramirez asked European leaders to intercede with Washington on Nicaragua's behalf (LARM, 2-15-85).[9]

## A Hardening of the FSLN Position and the Caraballeda Response

Although Contadora discussions were reconvened in March and April, 1985, little significant progress was made in bridging differences between Nicaragua and the US allies on verification and control issues. The FSLN responded to the delay in talks by pursuing bilateral initiatives in the region. That the Contadora states themselves were feeling heavy pressure from Washington in this period was evidenced by the fact that the group did not enunciate a common position on President Reagan's April "peace plan," his May embargo, or his early 1985 efforts to win from Congress new military funding for the contras. Differences in approach between Venezuela and Mexico, for example, also meant that Contadora as a group did not immediately call on the United States to return to Manzanillo, and, that it agreed to make some changes in the 1984 treaty despite the fact that earlier Contadora heads had said they would accept only minor modifications or refinements (IHCA, December, 1985; CAHI, 6-27-85). In September, 1985 the Contadora states offered a new draft treaty to Central American leaders.

Given the May embargo and the June "humanitarian" aid (for the contras) vote in the US Congress, however, Nicaragua's position in Contadora hardened at mid-year. Arguing at the June Contadora meeting that Nicaragua could not ignore the intensifying war to join in elaborating abstract formulas for future peace, Deputy Foreign Minister Tinoco demanded that the group deal with specific problems aggravating the regional crisis -- namely, hostile US economic and military pressures on Nicaragua. New contra money, in the FSLN view, meant an escalated contra war and new obstacles to a negotiated settlement under Contadora. It was imperative, therefore, that Contadora take steps to contain current military action (BI, 6-20-85). The US allies responded by accusing Nicaragua of boycotting the meetings.

On the diplomatic front the FSLN launched a new drive in June to garner support for Nicaragua's concerns about the direction of Contadora. In June and July Ramirez toured Contadora and other Latin American capitals calling on leaders there to take a firm and public stand against the United States' embargo and support for the contras.[10] The Contadora states were asked specifically to become active on demilitarized zones on the border with Costa Rica. Ramirez aimed to woo support for the revolution and new momentum for the Contradora process from the new governments in Brazil, Uruguay, Argentina, Peru and Ecuador. This diplomatic effort paid off in the short-run with the creation in July, 1985 of the Lima Support Group to Contadora (Peru, Argentina, Brazil and Uruguay) and in the long-run -- by the end of 1985 and into 1986 -- with direct pressures (by the eight Contadora and Lima group governments) on the Reagan Administration to return to Manzanillo and end support for the contras.

In February, 1986, the Foreign Ministers of the eight countries met with US Secretary of State Shultz and other officials in Washington to emphasize their strong support for a Contadora treaty and direct Managua-Washington talks. The meeting with Shultz was arranged to express "the voice of Latin America" which had solidified during several meetings in January, 1986. Although Contadora had been formally suspended for a five-month period at Nicaragua's request to allow for government transitions in Guatemala, Honduras and Costa Rica, the Contadora and Lima Support Group states met at Caraballeda, Venezuela to reaffirm the basic principles of the original Contadora proposal, to call on the United

364

States to reopen talks with Nicaragua and to call on all states to refrain from supporting anti-government forces. At Vinicio Cerezo's inauguration in mid-month, Guatemala, Panama, Honduras, Nicaragua and El Salvador signed a pledge to support the Caraballeda document.[11] Other Latin American states joined in declaring support for renewing Contadora in line with the Caraballeda message. By the time of the February meeting in Washington, nearly all of the Latin American states stood behind the request for a change in US policy, and specifically, away from supporting the contras and toward bilateral talks between Managua and Washington. Reflecting the sentiments of many signers, Colombian Foreign Minister Augusto Ramirez echoed the Sandinistas' concerns: "As long as the United States is asking for aid for the contras, there is not a political climate for national reconciliation" (ICAS, March, 1986).

This early 1986 Latin American move, in effect, to identify US policy and the Reagan Administration as the major obstacle to a negotiated solution symbolized growing Latin American concern about the continent-wide destabilizing effects a US military intervention or a US- orchestrated anti-Sandinista insurrection would produce. Significantly, this Latin American movement away from earlier oscillation and hesitancy directly to address the United States' regional role was spurred in part by Nicaragua's security concerns, its diplomatic lobbying for an independent and united Latin America and its rejection of the September, 1985 Contadora draft. In November, 1985 the FSLN government had formally announced its rejection of the new draft and had outlined conditions under which it would sign a treaty. The FSLN interpreted the new draft as removing important restrictions on a future US-military regional presence and, according to President Ortega, as threatening "...to leave Nicaragua defenseless in the face of the declared desire of the United States government to destroy the Nicaraguan revolution" (NYT, 11-12-85). Moreover, the FSLN feared that if the new draft won widespread international support -- the Contadora process qua process was widely supported -- the United States would gain a diplomatic instrument for justifying military actions. Meanwhile, Nicaragua would be isolated and deprived of its diplomatic maneuvering space in Latin America and Europe. To preclude that possibility, the Sandinistas emphasized their reasons for rejecting a treaty under the prevailing circumstances. Noting bottom-line security concerns, the FSLN argued that signing the new draft would be an act of "suicide."

The September, 1985 draft contained changes influenced by the US allies' Tegucigalpa draft of October 1984. For example, rather than proscribing international military maneuvers in the future, the 1985 draft called for allowing regulated exercises until such time that regional arms reductions were agreed upon and achieved. Because the Nicaraguan government interpreted the continuous joint US-Honduran maneuvers as ..."preparatory steps for real and concrete future acts of aggression against Nicaragua," Nicaragua, as a "position of principle," called for a complete ban on regional maneuvers involving foreign troops (President Ortega, NYT, op. cit). In the absence of such a ban, Nicaraguan officials argued, Nicaragua would be kept in a continual state of military alert and tension (IHCA, December, 1985). Similarly, the Sandinistas argued that

formulas to limit national armies and arsenals should not be based
on population size -- the US allies' position -- but should reflect
the level of threat each nation faced, a position the 1984 draft
also took into account. In President Ortega's words: "For
Nicaragua, the level of armament necessary to defend national
sovereignty is determined by its need to resist United States
aggression." Nor would Nicaragua disarm or limit the size of its
military before the United States halted its support for the
contras, or, in Ortega's words, ..."until basic minimum security
conditions" were guaranteed (NYT, op. cit). Thus, the FSLN argued
that the United States should sign a protocol to the Contadora
treaty promising neutrality toward Nicaragua.[12]

On the other hand, Nicaraguan leaders signalled continued
willingness to negotiate by offering again to join other Central
American states in sending home foreign advisors, and, by expressing
a willingness to begin a process of "national reconciliation" that
had an "internal character" compatible with "the sacred principle of
nonintervention in affairs reserved to national jurisdiction" (NYT,
op. cit). The Mexicans and Colombians publically recognized this as
a positive and conciliatory sign on the part of the Sandinistas, one
which preserved momentum and space for Contadora (ICAS, March,
1986).

The FSLN position remained that differences (e.g. with the
bourgeoisie) should be worked out within the framework of domestic
political structures; the Sandinistas continued to argue, for
example, that a cessation of US backing for the contras would mean
the re-establishment of civil liberties in Nicaragua and a more
conducive atmosphere for pluralistic political development. As
matters stood, however, the FSLN government remained convinced that
for the United States, its allies and the contras, "internal
reconciliation" was a code-phrase for eliminating the revolutionary
government and replacing it with a pro-US government. The FSLN
looked for a sign from Washington that its interest in a negotiated
settlement was genuine -- i.e., that it was not premised on the
political elimination of the FSLN and that it excluded a resorting
to military means.

## Policy Disputes in Washington

Such a sign was not forthcoming. Rhetoric from the White House
in late 1985 and 1986 indicated instead a deep cynicism among
administration ideologues about negotiating with "communists." The
disputes within the Reagan Administration which in 1984 and 1985 led
to policy reviews and policy statements, by mid-1986 had surfaced as
public inter-agency disagreements regarding the legitimacy of the
Contadora process. The State Department and new Special Envoy
Philip Habib appeared willing to settle for less than a
restructuring of the Nicaraguan government which would undermine the
FSLN's political hegemony there. A "contained" Nicaraguan -- the
"Yugoslavia solution" -- would secure US interests. In conjunction
with a tour of the region, in April, 1986 Habib stated that the
United States would end its support to the contras if the Contadora
Treaty were signed. Habib's position that Washington would abide by
Contadora (e.g. abandoning the contra effort) was interpreted in

Latin America as new US flexibility. Likewise, a bipartisan majority in Congress appeared to support a shift in policy emphasis toward greater administration efforts to strengthen the regional negotiation process. (Habib and most Congressmen continued to view the contras as an important bargaining chip in securing Nicaraguan compliance with the Contadora treaty.)

In the context of a new push by the Contadora states to get a treaty signed by mid-year, conservatives in the administration and Congress moved to check this pro-negotiation momentum. Conservative Congressmen called for Habib's resignation on the grounds that he had no policy authority (e.g. NYT, 5-23-86). Then, in late May a newly-released Pentagon study (carried out under Fred Ikle) predicted war if the Contadora Treaty were signed. According to the report, "...the Sandinistas likely would conclude that a Contadora-like peace accord would provide them the shield from behind which they could continue their use of subversive aggression to impose Communist regimes throughout Central America" (NYT, 5-20-86). Because the FSLN would cheat on treaty provisions, the report argued, the United States would be forced -- in the assumed absence of a Latin American will to act -- to intervene to implement the pact. Such a move would require 100,000 US troops and an estimated $9.1 billion in first-year costs. Reflecting the administration ideologues' belief that negotiations did not constitute a viable path to regional peace (or, to securing US interests broadly defined), and coming shortly before a scheduled vote in the House over contra funding, the report's release appeared timed to regain the policy initiative for this group.

The official State Department reaction to the report's release was as quick and firm as it was unusual. Spokesmen contended that the report had no standing as an official US government document. Yet, divisions within the State Department between ideologues and pragmatists also remained visible. For example, the public statements of Assistant Secretary For Inter-American Affairs Elliot Abrams clearly identified him with administration ideologues such as Casey, Ikle and top NSC members. President Reagan, meanwhile, contributed further to the policy confusion by reaffirming Habib's role as his special envoy, but continuing his personal campaign for $100 million in new contra funding. Although the president did not comment on the Pentagon report or publically question Contadora's viability, he continued to call for change in Nicaraguan political and military structures as a precondition for US cooperation. In addition, the White House reported its intention to use Special Forces military units to train the contras on Honduran soil if Congress passed new contra aid. In the same period, Washington was exerting heavy pressure (in public and in private) on its regional allies not to be "forced into action" on an unacceptable or "unverifiable" peace treaty (NYT 5-29-86). Important as a signal to policy-makers in Managua, then, was the fact that while the White House refused to formulate or endorse a coherent US strategy for negotiations, US military policy was well articulated through words and actions.

Taking their cue from these events, the Sandinistas continued in 1986 to assess a US military intervention as the greatest threat confronting Nicaragua. Though urged by Peru, Guatemala and then

Contadora participants to sign the treaty without solid US assurances that it would discontinue support for the contras, the FSLN government reiterated its concern that Contadora could become "an instrument of the aggressive United States policy towards Nicaragua" (NYT, 5-12-86). The FSLN essentially maintained its November, 1985 position that it would not reduce the size of its armed forces nor its defensive capacity unless or until the US ceased all hostile actions against Nicaragua. Nevertheless, Nicaragua continued its negotiations within Contadora and in late May -- one week after the release of the Pentagon study -- President Ortega offered a proposal to open talks on region-wide offensive weapons reductions. Unwilling in the face of a consistently hostile US stance to specify what military curbs it was willing to accept under a revised Contadora treaty, but under intense pressure from other Latin American states to forward a treaty, the FSLN offered to negotiate reductions on a list of weapons which included aircraft, airfields, tanks, heavy mortars and artillery. Standing in contrast to US actions to delay a Contadora treaty and to isolate Nicaragua, the Nicaraguan proposal represented a compromise gesture which maintained negotiation momentum. (Ortega's proposal was discussed by Contadora diplomats in early June.)

In Sum. The Contadora process during 1986 was characterized by sparring among the United States and its allies, the Contadora states and Nicaragua. While a public Latin American consensus emerged by early 1986 identifying US policy as the central obstacle to a Contadora treaty (i.e., Carabelleda events), many Latin American leaders -- citing US intransigence -- were unsure about Contadora's future. As Venezuelan Foreign Minister Simon Alberto Consalvi argued early in the year: "If Congress approves US contra aid, it may well choke the final gasp of air out of Contadora and finish off the last of its many lives" (ICAS, March, 1986). Their frustrations, however, did not dampen the determination to forge a regional solution to Central American tensions. Rather, in the first half of the year the Contadora heads made a strong coordinated effort to secure the signatures of the five Central American governments on a basic treaty, even if disputed sections had to be left open to later negotiation. Spurned by the United States on their request that Washington end its contra support and reopen security talks with the FSLN, the Contadora states sought to move ahead without US assurances. The Latin Americans were no doubt hoping thereby to reaffirm their insistence on a regional role in any solution and/or to push Washington into compliance by presenting it with a signed treaty. In the latter case, pro-negotiation sectors within the United States would gain momentum and world opinion would point up Washington's isolation on the Contadora issue.

To counter Latin American moves, the Reagan Administration continued its campaign against Nicaragua. The 1986 Easter "invasion" crisis, the "emergency" military aid to Honduras, the extreme rhetoric about Nicaragua during the new contra funding campaign and new charges at mid-year concerning increased Soviet military assistance to Nicaragua all aimed at influencing both regional and domestic political debates on Nicaragua and Contadora. While new economic and security aid to Honduras and Costa Rica was pending, US officials pressed Presidents Azcona and Arias to back US objections to the current draft treaty. Meanwhile, US officials expressed doubts that the Latin American states could or would verify and enforce a peace treaty. Refusing to allow Nicaragua's sincerity to be tested, Washington preferred to delay a peace treaty. Such a delay would yield time for the contras and for the president's "convergence theory." The 1986 Congressional renewal of contra aid produced a new test for Contadora.

Nicaraguan officials too had doubts about the ability of the Latin American states to ensure a lessening of tensions under Contadora. The Sandinistas feared that Latin American efforts (or world opinion) would not be sufficient to deter the Reagan Administration agenda vis-a-vis the revolution. Yet, they also saw Contadora and Latin American solidarity as the only hope for peace. Again in 1986 it became clear that the United States and Nicaragua were the principal antagonists in the Central American peace process. Without the resumption of bilateral talks on security issues or a clear signal from the Reagan Administration that it would abide by the Latin American treaty, movement toward peace would be difficult.


PRINCIPLES AND PRAGMATICS

In the context of multilateral peace negotiations, Nicaraguan leaders maneuvered to avoid an agreement which undermined Nicaraguan self-determination or which challenged the legitimacy of the Sandinista government. The FSLN, while it was willing to negotiate regional military limitations and to pledge its support for pluralist political structures, stood firm on insisting that verification and control be the duty of a group free from dominant US influence. Nor did the FSLN back off from its original position that the United States' regional role had to be addressed directly. Demonstrating its distrust of the Reagan Administration, the FSLN came to demand as a pre-condition for settlement that the United States adopt a position of neutrality vis-a-vis Nicaragua and end its support for the contras. The Sandinistas also continued to reject US pre-conditions for bilateral talks or for the withdrawal of contra support -- that the FSLN unilaterally undertake the first steps in a military build-down, or, that the FSLN open talks with UNO leaders under the mediation of the Nicaraguan Catholic Church hierarchy. Meanwhile, the Nicaraguan government maintained its maneuvering space through an activist diplomatic stance, by constantly jockeying to preserve a Nicaraguan initiative in the Contadora drafting process, and by seizing opportunities provided by Latin American inclinations for independence from US dictates. Notably, the Sandinistas remained conciliatory on security issues in the face of both an escalating regional US military presence and repeated US efforts to undermine a Contadora settlement. Keeping open the channels of communication to their neighbors and to the Reagan Administration was an objective rigorously pursued by Sandinista leaders. To that end, and though some observers deemed such behavior inconsistent or contradictory, the FSLN utilized every possible avenue -- through Contadora, bilateral and other contacts

-- for pursuing security agreements which would reduce the size of its external threat.

From the Nicaraguan perspective, the future of Contadora depended on Latin American willingness and ability to address the United States' regional role and to confront the Reagan Administration. The election of new presidents in Honduras (Azcona), Guatemala (Cerezo) and Costa Rica (Arias) by early 1986, moreover, raised the possibility of increased momentum for Contadora, or, of somewhat decreased influence for the Reagan Administration in those countries. The new presidents had not yet developed personal political debts to Washington and their terms of office by law were to run beyond Ronald Reagan's presidency. Though they were not overly optimistic about major shifts in the US allies' policy positions, the FSLN pursued openings to each of these new leaders. In addition, issues of regional war and inordinate US influence had come to dominate local political life in all three US ally states. Heightened levels of political polarization in turn produced new momentum for demonstrably independent policy. Meanwhile, the Latin American states associated with Contadora were applying pressure on Honduras and Costa Rica, particularly, to work for a peaceful settlement despite US pressures.

Judging by the continued resilience of the Contadora states after repeated US attempts to block an agreement, by the expansion of support for Contadora represented by the Lima group and by continued Contadora momentum into mid-1986, Latin American states believed not only that there was room for a negotiated settlement, but that such an agreement was the only alternative to regional war and continent-wide instability. Issues raised by Nicaragua's revolution generated renewed Latin American determination to press their independence vis-a-vis Washington. Thus, two critical factors shaping the Contadora process generally were 1) the Latin American governments' acceptance of the sovereignty and legitimacy -- if not of the political direction -- of the sitting FSLN government in Nicaragua and 2) the FSLN's increasing political alignment with and reliance upon Latin American states. Indeed, these patterns -- more so than the FSLN's reliance on Eastern bloc aid in the face of US hostility -- constitute striking features of Nicaraguan foreign policy after 1979.


NOTES

1. In arguing that the FMLN in El Salvador was representative of the Salvadoran people, the FSLN and others referred to the FMLN's ability to hold and govern large portions of Salvadoran territory, its capacity to maintain its own media and radio station (Radio Venceremos) there, and its ability to garner international recognition. For example, France, Mexico and other states referred to the FMLN by 1982 as a legitimate political force in Salvador. The US-backed contras in Nicaragua, on the other hand, had little support inside the country, never held territory and had, basically, only US support in the international arena. No state labelled the contras a viable political alternative.

2. The Court rejected arguments brought by the Salvadoran

370

government that Nicaragua was not a victim of aggression because the mining of its harbors was a defensive measure to counter the Sandinistas' backing of the FMLN. This was a reiteration of the United States' "collective self-defense" justification. The Reagan Administration responded to Nicaragua's arguments before the Court in 1985 by labelling them "lies" and a "good propaganda show" for the Sandinistas.

3. In this section I draw from interviews with Nicaraguan Foreign Ministry personnel in August, 1985.

4. In 1984 France had helped facilitate the Mixed Border Commission. During 1985 both the EEC and the SI expressed interest in helping to further a Contadora agreement or regional bilateral cooperation.

5. According to senior US Embassy analysts interviewed in Managua, the president's letter to Congress in 1985 -- promising to return to Manzanillo if Congress passed aid for the contras -- was written in such a way as to avoid a commitment to more than one more meeting with the FSLN.

6. Author interviews, Managua, 1985. Recall that the United States' public position was that the talks were going nowhere due to FSLN intransigence.

7. Though the FSLN continued to deny arms links to the FMLN, it included the issue as one it was willing to discuss and thereby recognized the importance of the issue to the United States at a time when the FMLN appeared to be winning against the US-backed Salvadoran army.

8. In response, the United States indicted Nicaragua for not addressing the issue of verification and for not acknowledging its own military build-up. On July 21 the United States raised the argument that the FSLN was not living up to pledges made to the OAS in 1979. Likewise, rather than responding diplomatically to the FSLN's initiatives, on September 8 and 9, CIA-backed forces bombed the Managua airport and attacked Corinto. In October, these forces badly damaged Nicaragua's main oil storage facility at Corinto. According to Secretary of State Shultz, the intent of US policy was to influence a "greater openness" among the Sandinistas toward negotiations (LAWR, 8-12-83). Yet, it was also on September 9 that Nicaragua joined the other Central American states in signing the Contadora Document of Objectives.

9. The FSLN maintained this position of willingness to hold talks with the United States despite its deep suspicion about the motivations of the US diplomats with whom they had to deal. In the FSLN view, Reagan Administration officials such as Harry Schlaudeman, with experience in Chile, and Vernon Walters, with experience in Brazil and with the contras, were experts in toppling governments and were motivated by an ethics-of-power diplomacy. These men were seen as willing and anxious to use force to stifle revolutionary models. According to Nicaraguan Foreign Ministry officials, moreover, the Kissinger Commission -- which spent one day in Nicaragua in 1983 -- was not only poorly briefed on Nicaraguan realities, but its members were also rude and disrespectful toward Nicaraguan officials. According to FSLN officials, for example, commission members interrupted FSLN speakers or walked out of the meeting during FSLN presentations (author interviews, 1985).

10. The FSLN had its own reservations about the prospects for a Contadora treaty. First, the FSLN knew well the pressures the United States could bring to bear on these states to influence greater attention to the US position. Second, the Sandinistas were aware of variations among the four Contadora states in their proclivities to give weight to US or US allies' concerns, or in their distance from US policy. FSLN officials privately noted Panamanian and Venezuelan offers to reinforce Costa Rican security in 1985. Panama, militarily close to the United States, offered Costa Rica aid in the form of military and counterinsurgency training in 1985 and, according to these officials, President Lusinchi of Venezuela argued within his own government that Costa Rica should be supported in its diplomatic conflict with Nicaragua. Publically, Venezuela supported private sector, union and church groups inside Nicaragua which were often at odds with the FSLN (author interviews with Nicaraguan Foreign Ministry officials, 1985). The FSLN, however, did not air these issues publically and in 1985 accepted Panamanian offers to mediate between Nicaragua and its neighbors.

11. President Monge of Costa Rica was unable to attend the inauguration due to a domestic political scandal. However, President-elect Arias' comments in February that the United States' support for the contras was counter-productive, and, that aid monies could better be spent for regional economic development put him in line with the message of Carabelleda.

12. Other differences also existed between the 1984 and 1985 drafts. For instance, the 1984 draft called for a moratorium on arms acquisitions once national inventories had been enumerated i.e., within 30 days of the signing of the treaty. The 1985 draft put the moratorium into effect at the moment of signing. The period for increasing military personnel was extended from 30 (1984 draft) to 90 days (1985 draft). Moreover, the 1985 sections on what foreign advisors would be included in limitations on "foreign military advisors" appeared vague and imprecise to the Nicaraguans. The new draft included "other foreign elements capable of participating in military, paramilitary or security activities" among those advisors which would have to be withdrawn from the region. The FSLN felt that this addition would lead to confusion, contradictions and implementation delays given, among other things, the fact that a large number of Cuban technicians worked in a wide variety of fields in Nicaragua. The 1984 treaty, by contrast, specified "military advisors and other foreign elements, which includes the immediate withdrawal of those advisors working in operations and training" (IHCA, December, 1985).

# 11

## The Sandinista Record:
## "No Longer a Banana Republic"

> We feel that this revolution doesn't belong only to
> Nicaragua...Every single country in the developing world
> has a contribution made in this country and whatever we do
> here we view it not only having an impact on the social
> transformation that we are trying to carry out here, but
> in setting up a kind of experience that can be useful for
> other developing countries....We have interpreted that
> whenever [the United States] brings up that issue [that
> Nicaragua is a security threat] the US government sees the
> security issue in terms of the example that is being set
> up here that might lead other countries to ask the United
> States 'Please relate to us the way you relate to
> Europeans, with respect and understanding.'

> Alejandro Martinez Cuenca
> Minister of Foreign Trade
> August, 1985

From the vantage point of history, six years is not a long
enough period from which to note definitive foreign policy
methods--although to Nicaraguan policy-makers overseeing a
revolution under seige, the 1979-1986 period undoubtedly seemed like
an eternity. Nevertheless, some early observations and concluding
comments are in order. A consideration of Nicaraguan foreign policy
suggests that the FSLN government has responded flexibly enough to
external pressures that scenarios for the future remain open; in the
context of a struggle for survival, the policy process remains fluid
and dynamic. Contrary to Reagan Administration-inspired images of
the Sandinistas as ideological, intractable "self-made
revolutionaries," for example, policy behavior during the first six
years of the revolution cannot be characterized as programmatic.
Working through a time of transition for which there was no clear
model--i.e., moving away from Somoza's United States-centered
linkages toward greater independence, the Sandinistas nonetheless
established a clear foreign policy record.

Acknowledging critical domestic constraints mitigating against a
direct transition to socialism and adapting to geopolitical
realities, the Sandinista government forged a foreign policy which,
though increasingly focused on survival, eschewed East-West

373

alignment. Behaving more or less like the Coleman and Quiros-Varela "reformist" state, revolutionary Nicaragua successfully wooed Western and Eastern (as well as Third World) support and aid. In diplomatic exchanges with the East and the West, however, the FSLN also repeatedly stressed Nicaragua's right to policy independence and sovereignty. Preferring an informal political alignment with Latin American and world progressive forces, the FSLN worked to counter what it saw as the United States' domineering will and US attempts to destroy the Nicaraguan revolutionary example. If their Marxist or anti-imperialist rhetoric alienated the United States and the region's conservative and military governments, the Sandinistas' policies of capital generation and broad international contacts, as well as their continued political strength inside Nicaragua, yielded them alternative Western and Third World support and thereby the means to resist US pressures. Eastern bloc aid, though it bore economic and political costs, similarly yielded economic and military maneuvering space. The Sandinistas' internationalism, activism and sensitivity to concerns of external actors worked to compensate somewhat for Nicaragua's actual powerlessness in the international arena by increasing its capacity for not giving in to counter-revolutionary pressures. The FSLN government forged a foreign policy and a political stance acceptable to a critical majority of states. It was this reality, and in particular Latin American and Western European acceptance of the legitimacy of the Sandinista government, that US policy-makers had to face in assessing their options regarding revolutionary Nicaragua. That same reality, along with US domestic politics, accounted for the vigorous anti-Sandinista campaign waged by the Reagan Administration.

At home as well, the intangible resources of revolutionary fervor, energetic leadership and national will allowed the FSLN to sustain the participation of a majority of the population in productive and defense activities on the basis of what the FSLN referred to as "political co-responsibility" for the revolution. In terms of theory development, the Nicaraguan case provides insight into alternative internal strategies for weathering the adaptation-transformation process (i.e., of forging new international linkages) where internal socio-political structures themselves are not strife-free. As the discussions in Chapters 3 and 4 make clear, there is an organic link between domestic and foreign policies in Nicaragua. For example, the necessity of maintaining an internal political situation regarded as viable to outside supporters led to the tailoring of FSLN ideological commitments as well as to some economic accommodation and political concessions to the domestic opposition. Both geopolitical requirements and domestic realities have shaped the revolution and affected the evolution and practice of Sandinismo. A salient theme in the preceding chapters has been the interaction between the FSLN government's capacity to generate support abroad and its proclivity to maintain or alter domestic policy in the pursuit of projecting a credible image. Among international observers interested in applying labels to the Nicaraguan process--even if such labelling requires procustean feats--the question debated is whether FSLN domestic and foreign policy represents short-term accommodationism or long-term intent and ideological change.

Adaptation theory and the Nicaraguan case, however, suggest that foreign policy-making will continue to be a dynamic process, one where leaders' political projects and ideological orientations--though important in shaping an overall approach to international relations--are not necessarily the best predictors of specific policies. Although the Sandinistas supported the notions of Third World liberation and structural revolution (economic, social and political) in Latin America, for instance, anxiety among regional militaries and practical considerations of finance and state security inveighed against the FSLN's taking too active a role in forwarding these causes. In the case of the future of the Atlantic Coast, the FSLN gave up the notion of integration for an autonomy plan that aimed, among other things, at increasing internal security. Likewise, the FSLN appeared willing to dialogue and compromise with internal opposition groups, such as the pro-United States private sector and the traditional Catholic Church hierarchy, so long as those groups recognized the legal authority of the revolutionary government and refrained from calling (or working) for its overthrow. Diplomatic moves from 1983 to 1986 designed to address regional security concerns and to keep the Contadora peace process alive exemplified both the FSLN's willingness to make (a few) strategic and (more) tactical concessions and its capacity for resisting pressures to compromise domestic revolutionary structures. The Sandinistas demonstrated a willingness to strike bargains and to make concessions if and when by so doing the revolution at home was further secured or consolidated. In this sense foreign policy facilitated internal changes.

FSLN foreign policy makers worked to establish new bases for Nicaragua's international relations. Nicaraguan leaders characterized their approach "principled pragmatism." Rather than acquiescing to US demands of internal structural change and a break in relations with the Eastern bloc, for example, the FSLN coped with the international environment by seeking alternative political support, reducing ties to the United States and diversifying its economic--particularly its trade and finance--dependence. Membership and active diplomatic roles in Third World and regional forums, meanwhile, afforded the Sandinistas increased economic and political maneuverability as well as progress toward their objective of expanding and balancing their international contacts. The FSLN generally responded to external pressures by mobilizing internal support, resorting to new linkages and/or offering to negotiate new premises in inter-state relations. In so doing, the FSLN insisted upon mutual respect, non-intervention in internal affairs, recognition of Nicaraguan sovereignty, and the like. The FSLN opened relations with states willing to do so on these grounds. The Sandinistas' foreign policy, thus, was also designed to shape external environments and opportunities.

Under great military and economic pressure, the FSLN did not bargain with domestic structures in return for foreign aid or US promises to end its support for the contras--paths more acceptable to regimes interested in preserving the status quo or in acquiescing to a local hegemon. Their survival threatened, the Sandinistas rejected capitulation to US demands and aimed to avoid US pressures

by invoking anti-imperialism, Latin American solidarity, Third World
unity, and international law. In meeting immediate defense and
economic needs, however, the FSLN was also willing to assume a
growing dependence on and debt with the Eastern bloc in return for
the shorter-term capacity to resist US imperialism. Sustained over
the long-term in response to continued US hostility, such linkages
could threaten the FSLN's capacity to maintain balance in their
foreign relations. From 1981 onward, moreover, the United States
used the Soviet alignment argument against Nicaragua in efforts at
eliminating Western ties or aid to the Nicaraguan revolutionaries.
Aware of possible consequences of these realities, Nicaraguan
leaders renewed efforts to preserve their options. Yet they were
also keenly aware that they were working in an increasingly
polarized international environment. Nicaraguan foreign policy
after 1979 was forged in the contexts of both East-West and
North-South conflicts and confrontation. Their foreign policy was
therefore also apt to change paths or appear contradictory in the
short-term as leaders forged compromises in response to demands from
both arenas.


POLICY MOTIVATIONS

The United States' resistance to negotiation with the Sandinista
government--reflected both in US circumventions of Contadora and in
the CDN-La Prensa-church hierarchy oppositions' attitudes concerning
a coming-to-terms with the FSLN government--meant that the
Sandinistas' opportunities were limited for proving their sincerity
or trustworthiness as negotiators. Countering the US-inspired image
-- of inflexible, Soviet-aligned revolutionaries interested not in
serious dialogue but in buying time -- became an important
Sandinista foreign policy objective. Other FSLN motivations were
clear. The Sandinistas, unwilling to compromise on the issue of
self-determination by acceding to US demands for structural change,
nevertheless continued to assert: 1)that the revolution posed no
security threat to the United States; 2)that revolutionary Nicaragua
was willing to coexist with the United States on the basis of
cooperation and mutual respect; and 3)that they were willing to
conform to a regionally-negotiated peace and security formula so
long as the United States made assurances that it would cease
backing armed counter-revolutionary groups. Although they demanded
that the United States reappraise its policy of regional hegemony
"in the light of the Sandinista revolution" and refused to accept
"an open-ended exercise of United States' hegemony," Sandinista
officials maintained that they recognized the United States'
historical influence, Nicaragua's hemispheric situation, and
"limited" but legitimate US interests in the Caribbean basin (author
interviews, Nicaraguan Foreign Ministry). The FSLN position in the
mid-1980s was that the Nicaraguan revolution, though it represented
a different social and economic system, was not at odds with either
US national interests or recent Latin American developments such as
the return to civilian and pluralistic government in Argentina,
Brazil and Uruguay.
In the face of early counter-revolutionary threats and

escalating US hostility, however, the Sandinistas also demonstrated a determination to wage diplomatic campaigns and pursue military development for the defense of the revolution. Foreign policy was soon dictated by what the FSLN saw as the requisites of survival: forging alternative political and economic commitments; obtaining the necessary military hardware; avoiding US-dominated forums; circumventing regional isolation; and maintaining credibility at home and abroad. All of these required sensitivity to foreign--including US--concerns, ideological and economic flexibility and skillful handling of foreign support. As the discussion in Chapters 8 and 9 suggests, defense was broadly defined and vigorously pursued in every available forum. For the Sandinistas, preserving Nicaraguan sovereignty and self-determination became nearly synonomous with avoiding direct US pressure. Among the means employed by the FSLN for achieving these objectives were increasing Nicaragua's visability, pursuing economic diversification and achieving a conspicuous balance in relations among Western, Eastern and Third World--particularly Latin American and Arab--states. It became evident soon after the Triumph that the Sandinistas perceived Latin American solidarity to be critical to the revolution's survival, especially given US efforts to reassert its traditional continental hegemony.

## A Latin American Context

Continued Mexican support and the emergence of the Latin American Contadora peace effort were two factors reinforcing the Sandinistas' proclivity for Latin American alignment. The Sandinistas asserted not only that the revolution was consistent with Latin American aspirations and developments, but also that Nicaragua's struggle was representative of--and indeed, a model for--the struggle of all Latin Americans for independence from the local superpowers' dictates. On these grounds, Nicaraguan leaders called for continent-wide support for their peace and defense efforts and empathy regarding their security situation.

But more that this, the Sandinistas were increasingly aware of Mexican, Honduran, Costa Rican and others' concern about the nature and direction of the revolution, and, of the relevance of this concern to Nicaraguan security. The FSLN's heightened sensitivity to regional attitudes was due, in no small part, to the fact that US policy worked to exacerbate national tensions in the region and, ultimately, to internationalize Nicaragua's domestic conflicts. Yet even prior to the full implementation of the Reagan Administration's anti-Sandinista campaign, the FSLN recognized certain obligations to these states and to Venezuela and Panama, all of which helped facilitate the 1979 Triumph. Mexico's help in acting as a mediator with the United States in the post-Triumph period and the Contadora states' willingness to coordinate a regionally-mediated settlement of tensions also impressed upon the FSLN how vital Latin American solidarity was to the survival of the revolution. Ignoring or downplaying the US allies' concerns about regional stability, for example, would undermine both the prospects for a regional settlement and Latin American efforts to influence a change in US policy. As a British advisor to the FSLN government noted:

> You need to recognize that this is a very small, vulnerable country, in the backyard of the United States, with long land borders which are very hard to police--not an island like Cuba. The Nicaraguan Revolution can survive only with the support of its Latin American neighbors....The Mexicans and the Costa Ricans are not starry-eyed radicals. They want a stable Central America. This requires Nicaragua to adopt certain strategies. These geopolitical realities are more important [as predictors of the future] than the Sandinistas' intentions.... They have not yet fixated on a single model of the future; this is constantly being debated within the government (LASA, 1985: 41).

As the FSLN looked into the future of regional politics it also considered optimal strategies for preserving political space for other revolutionary groups such as the ones in El Salvador and Guatemala. The FSLN was aware that its behavior could well affect the prospects for these groups exerting influence in their own societies in the future. On the other hand, prolonged or escalated guerrilla war in El Salvador translated into increased US military or counter-revolutionary pressure on Nicaragua. Thus, rather than having an interest in expediting or enabling a leftist victory there, the FSLN from 1981 onward was on record calling for a negotiated settlement and power-sharing in Salvador. The Sandinistas continued to maintain that revolutions were not exportable, and, that strategies for change had to grow out of local realities and opportunities.

The Nicaraguan revolutionaries chose to pursue a non-aligned stance for philosophical and practical reasons. Given their geopolitical situation in the Western hemisphere, demonstrating non-alignment and a willingness to negotiate inter-state security concerns was key to national security and to the maintenance of new socioeconomic institutions. Procuring a negotiated lessening of tensions, in turn, was essential if the Sandinistas were to get back to the pressing tasks of national reconstruction and economic development. Regional history suggested, moreover, that both national security and long-term economic stability required at least moderate levels of cooperation or consultation among the Central American states. Similarly, a non-aligned stance by the FSLN would reinforce Latin American determination to offer a regional alternative to solutions devised in Washington.

Whether Latin American states had the political will or capacity to challenge US hegemony, to forge Latin American unity behind a regionally-enforced negotiated settlement, and to confront head-on contradictions between Latin American and North American priorities and interests in this case remained to be seen. Latin American leaders, cognizant of increasing anti-American grafitti in their cities and the popular appeal of the Sandinista revolution, feared the political polarization and instability that could result from the imposition of a US military solution in Central America (e.g., NYT, 6-30-85). Nicaraguan Deputy Foreign Minister Jose Leon Talevera noted the political dynamic accruing to Contadora and Nicaragua from the hostile US stance:

> The conflict through which the United States intends to overthrow the revolutionary government and do away with the phantom of "Sandino-communism" in Central America, looms over the Latin American countries as a catastrophy of unforeseeable dimensions. This reality has made it possible for the nations of the subcontinent to go beyond their specific differences and speak a common language, which is quite different from the Reagan Administration's war rhetoric. Growing support for Contadora is a political manifestation of this phenomenon which has made it possible to overcome the systematic sabotage by the United States (BI, 8-1-85).

At the same time Latin American leaders sought to influence pluralistic, stable governments which did not support insurgents or encourage instability, which did not constantly provoke the United States and which did not align exclusively with the Eastern bloc. It was within this framework that the FSLN had to garner regional support. The revolutionary government's success in influencing more than a modicum of continental solidarity and in identifying its cause with the larger causes of Latin American peoples depended upon its ability to demonstrate sensitivity to, if not support for, these objectives.

It was the unacceptability of this Latin American framework to the Reagan Administration, however, that lead Washington in 1985 specifically to target Latin American unity and regional peace initiatives. By 1986, the question of the survival of the Nicaraguan revolution had precipitated a diplomatic confrontation between the United States and Latin America, one symbolized in the Contadora process. If progress under Contadora was made possible by periods of indecision in Washington, long-term peace yet required bilateral lessening of tensions between Nicaragua and the United States.


## THE NICARAGUAN EXAMPLE

Revolutionary Nicaragua stood as an example to other small and underdeveloped states which were willing or able to assume the risks, benefits, and costs associated with pursuing sovereignty and self-determination in foreign affairs. Through their internationalist stance, and, spurred to creativity by threats to the revolution's survival, the Sandinistas demonstrated a capacity for innovativeness which yielded the small state new options, increased alternatives and, thereby, greater policy freedom. The Nicaraguans' activism, in fact, resulted in a visibility and global presence more akin to that of larger powers.

Nicaragua's example to other small states consisted of its experience and noteworthy success in creating alternatives to economic, military and political reliance upon one superpower or one superpower bloc. Targetting Nicaragua's economic dependence, social inequities and traditional outward-directed development model, the Sandinistas set out explicitly to diversify foreign relations and to reduce Nicaragua's dependence on the United States. Non-alignment

and Third World unity were embraced as principal means to
facilitating a development model which placed a premium on
self-determination and achieving adequate resilience to counter
northern hegemony. The FSLN's success in forging broad
international links, its propensity to seek help from non-Western
sources and to employ Marxist or revolutionary rhetoric and its
improved ability to circumvent US pressures, indeed, narrowed the
chances that Nicaragua's future would be strife-free. Yet, while
they were determined to break the United States' political hegemony
over Nicaragua the Sandinistas continued to maintain that their
stance did not pose a security threat to the superpower or to
neighboring states.

The view from Washington, however, was that Nicaragua's example
of political defiance and economic independence signalled the
emergence of an unacceptable political reality in the US "backyard".
The fact that Nicaragua was not operating from within the Eastern
bloc, that it did not pose a hard-line, orthodox Marxist-Leninist
economic or political model, but instead offered a nationalist,
Third World-oriented example of independence from Washington
appeared to account for the US bipolarists' high degree of anxiety
over Sandinista Nicaragua. It served US interests to characterize
post-1979 Nicaragua as Soviet-aligned and to create pressures which
would inevitably compel the FSLN toward obtaining commitments from
the USSR. A Moscow-aligned FSLN government would frighten other
Latin American governments, provide a rationalization for any US
intervention and discredit the Sandinista example for other Third
World states contemplating policy independence. This stance was
consistent with the position traditionally assumed by US
administrations: that non-alignment was impossible or unfeasible,
and, that it served as a cover for the expansion of Soviet
influence. The Reagan Administration objective of reasserting the
United States' continental hegemony, moreover, required that the
Nicaraguan model be destroyed; this was an issue separate from the
security arguments raised publically by the Reagan foreign policy
sector. This US objective pursued vis-a-vis Nicaragua in turn
raised the possibility that other poor or underdeveloped states in
the future might devalue the Sandinista model of mixed economy
reforms and popular hegemony in favor of more rapid, violent
revolutionary change.

It was because the Sandinistas also saw the conflict with the
United States as one centering on the issue of superpower hegemony
in the Western Hemisphere that they stressed the role Nicaragua was
playing in the larger North-South struggle. FSLN leaders presented
Nicaragua as a symbol and test case in the Third World's historical
battle against imperialism. The Nicaraguan struggle to survive in
the face of US hostility was posed as encompassing the Third World's
struggle for sovereignty, legitimacy and respect. Therefore, the
Sandinistas argued that there was a "convergence of interests" among
Third World and progressive developed states in promoting world
peace, an end to the arms race, nuclear disarmament, a restructured
international economic order and Nicaraguan survival (e.g., BI,
7-25-85). Making a "third Way" possible, according to the
Sandinistas, required a minimum of Third World unity and Latin
American solidarity on the issue of independence from Washington.

Such solidarity would significantly increase the costs to the United States of destroying the Nicaraguan example or of putting down future revolutionary experiments.

But as their experience had also taught them, evidence of real policy independence and responsiveness to neighboring states' concerns had to be forthcoming. Unable to demonstrate either balanced relations or an attitude of non-intervention in the affairs of other countries, a state's leaders would similarly be unsuccessful in garnering the diversified support necessary to assuring greater policy independence. It was precisely on these points that the FSLN was vulnerable. As FSLN economic and military links to the Eastern bloc grew in response to US pressures, US claims about a Moscow alignment were lent new credibility. Presenting itself as conciliatory and open to negotiations became the FSLN's paramount foreign policy task from 1984 onward. The FSLN's diplomatic activity aimed at achieving a careful balance between the requirements of survival and not provoking a US military response. Its activity within Contadora and its persistence in pushing for improved bilateral communication in the region, from the Latin American perspective, improved the prospects for a negotiated settlement. The Sandinistas were well aware that increased ties to the Eastern bloc, or, an intransigent stance on security issues could also undermine those forces in the United States which were working to block a military solution. To the extent that the FSLN was able to succeed in efforts at lowering tensions with its neighbors, moreover, US policy options in the region were narrowed.

Another lesson from the Nicaraguan case was that a successful change in foreign policy direction required that neighboring states' security interests be respected. Achieving mutual understanding, or, avoiding interstate suspicion during a period of policy change, then, required consultation and compromise. Major policy shifts when pursued dogmatically or when accompanied by high rhetoric or fanfare, would likely spur regional anxiety, inter-state tension and challenges to state security. Regional realities, thus, presented critical constraints on the state pursuing new international linkages. Nicaragua's geographical location insured that local realities would also be affected by and manipulated according to the local superpower's assessment of independent foreign policy initiatives within its traditional sphere of influence.

The Nicaraguan example did not involve a coherent or proven method of economic survival in the case of a unilateral withdrawal of traditionally important economic linkages. Nor did Nicaragua have a socialist economy by 1986. Rather, the Sandinistas' example consisted of pragmatism and a willingness to negotiate new linkages and to be flexible and creative in devising proposals for development aid from a broad range of potential donors. As the revolution encountered increasingly hostile challenges, the FSLN was also willing to absorb added but calculated development costs in order minimally to preserve the revolution's promise. For example, despite their preferences not to do so, and, in the interest of economic planning to the end of the decade, by 1985 the Sandinistas had begun retooling some industries to accommodate Eastern bloc aid and trade. At the same time, the Sandinistas chose to work within the Western world's finance system when doing so did not compromise

principles central to the revolution. The FSLN worked to repay its
debt on renegotiated terms and to maintain a creditworthy image; it
chose not to compromise redistributive economic programs by
complying with IMF austerity preconditions for loans and drawing
rights. Meanwhile, emphasizing the United States' role in their
economic predicament and their own interest in a regional approach
to development, the Sandinistas were able to secure aid and loans
from other Western and Third World states. Keeping these supply
lines open, however, again hinged on demonstrating sensitivity to
these states' preference for pluralistic, non-interventionist
political structures. Yet, US economic and military pressure
successfully curtailed Nicaragua's economic growth and induced
economic exigency after 1983. Revolutionary Nicaragua's experience
demonstrates the obstacles to structural change created by export
dependence and the vulnerability of economic growth or development
to political pressures exerted by international capital or the
traditional hegemon.

Nicaragua thus came to represent a test case of the potential
for and limitations of pursuing an independent foreign policy in the
"backyard" of the United States some twenty years after the Cuban
revolution. Its experience was therefore also most pertinent to
other Latin American and revolutionary governments (or movements)
interested in asserting independence or nationalist aspirations.
Without question the United States continued to present a major
obstacle to, and could, by defining its interests broadly, exact a
high price for successful independent action by Latin American
states. Yet, in the intervening twenty years the bases for Latin
American solidarity and for independent foreign policy behavior had
also expanded. These were related both to political and economic
developments across the continent--e.g., the expansion of
participatory institutions; the decreased legitimacy of military
rule; and an increased reliance on non-hemispheric markets and
suppliers--and to challenges to global bipolarity emanating from
developed and underdeveloped states alike. Taking advantage of such
openings, however, required international activism and a willingness
to absorb inevitable costs--those imposed by the locale hegemon and
those that arose from maintaining diversified foreign relations.

Whereas Nicaragua's experience was bound to enlarge the scope
for independent action and Third World solidarity for reformist and
revolutionary states in the future, whether Nicaragua would
ultimately serve as a "reference point" (Bayardo Arce's
characterization) for developing states depended upon the type of
political structures institutionalized there. The explosion of
participation accompanying the revolution under the banners of
"popular power" and "popular hegemony" translated into work-place
organization, neighborhood commities, womens organizations, and the
like. On the institutional level a multiparty system
operated--under FSLN hegemony--in the National Assembly and through
national dialogues. Importantly, an electoral system and a
constitution-writing process was initiated in revolutionary
Nicaragua despite the imposition of the war-related State of
Emergency. Yet these very developments exemplified the problem of
political development Nicaragua faced: whether viable participatory
structures and norms could develop in an atmosphere of

externally-supported security threats and nation-wide defense mobilization.

To ensure the future of popular government in Nicaragua popular interests would have to prevail over those of state bureaucrats and technicians. Institutionalized channels or access to government would have to be guaranteed to allow organized groups of workers, peasants or voters at large to present themselves as a check on the state or the currently-dominant party (FSLN). The incipient constitution provided for such access and checks. Revolutionary policy had mobilized and empowered -- e.g., through land reform, redistribution of access to national surpluses, etc. -- the (majority) underclasses. And, the FSLN, as "vanguard of the revolution," did not have or insist upon a monopoly of power in the first six years of the revolution. However, external pressures threatened to provide an impetus and a rationale for a more closed, less responsive political system as the price to be paid for securing the revolution. By 1985 the Sandinistas were displaying some cynicism about the prospects for a peaceful regional settlement. The political test for the Sandinistas involved balancing these competing forces.

To the extent that the revolutionary process produced responsive government and an atmosphere of open political debate, Sandinista Nicaragua would provide a compelling model for other Third World states. Alternatively, continued rights restrictions and economic austerity, if they were not deemed justifiable by a majority of Nicaraguans given the level of national security threats, could lead to popular disaffection. The "Nicaraguan model" would be delegitimized. Again, the peace process was important in this regard. A lowering of regional tensions under a Contadora Treaty or a bilateral (US-Nicaragua) security agreement would improve the prospects for the development of pluralistic structures not only in Nicaragua, but also elsewhere in the region.

## The Limits of the Nicaraguan Model

A consideration of regional politics in the 1980s, however, also suggests that for other Central American states foreign policy independence was still assessed as too costly. To the extent that El Salvador, Honduras, Costa Rica, and to a lesser extent, Guatemala and Panama, were dependent on the United States for critical military or economic support, they were vulnerable to pressures to follow the United States' policy lead regarding Nicaragua. Although nationalist sentiments and fears of regional war led to political polarization over the issue of facilitation of US policy and created some obstacles for US policy, traditionally powerful elites in the region feared the implications for their own (already waning) power of Nicaragua's revolutionary model. Evoking anti-communist and national security passions, these sectors of Central American society yet had considerable clout to wield in efforts at forwarding anti-Sandinista policy. The potential and prospects for independent policy in these states was tied in with the prospects and futures of the new civilian governments in Salvador, Honduras and Guatemala in particular, as well as with the further development of nationalist tendencies within regional militaries and among middle class business sectors. Admiration for or satisfaction taken from the Sandinistas' policy independence was more apt to be expressed in South American states. Nevertheless, by early 1986 all five Central American states had endorsed the Contadora-backed idea of creating a Central American parliament for purposes of negotiating regional solutions to regional tensions. This reality, among others, pointed up the (slowly) expanding bases for nationalist or independent policy making even in the traditional US "back patio" area. The Sandinista revolution and US reactions to it had the effect of highlighting both obstacles to a reassertion of unchallenged US regional prerogative and factors--political, economic and military--compelling greater regional cooperation. Although other Central American regimes could not (or chose not to) emulate revolutionary Nicaragua's policy independence, they were bound to accrue greater maneuvering space vis-a-vis the United States in the wake of post-1979 events and as a result of Latin American reactions to those events.

Other factors limiting the applicability of lessons from Nicaragua's experience have to do with historical realities. Much of the Sandinistas' determination to reduce US influence over Nicaragua was born from a history of US domination and interventionism. Much of their political and military resilience grew out of the national experience of a popular revolution and the political mobilization and popular organization that occurred thereafter. The energies or momentum unleashed for defense, development and structural change by such methods are not easily replicated in non-revolutionary settings. The Nicaraguan people by 1986 had absorbed heavy costs for the state's policy independence.

Moreover, its geostrategic location assured that revolutionary Nicaragua's foreign policy would be shaped by global power realities and the nature of superpower politics during the 1980s. The ascendency of activist, bipolar-minded conservatives in the Washington foreign policy sector by 1981 quickly translated into a narrowing of options for the FSLN and signalled a new level of US cynicism regarding the concept of non-alignment. Western Europe, Japan, Canada and other traditional US allies--themselves concerned about maintaining some distance from Washington's heightened anti-USSR, anti-communist stance--were interested in offering anti-imperialist Nicaragua an alternative route between US or USSR alignment. However, global and local political considerations limited their capacity or willingness to commit themselves fully to assuring Nicaragua's survival in the context of the United States multifaceted campaign of low intensity attrition warfare against the FSLN. Again, US policy established critical limits for Nicaragua's mixed economy, non-aligned model. As I suggested in earlier chapters, Latin American solidarity in the second half of the 1980s and into the next decade will be crucial for moving regional issues out of East-West decision arenas. Western European, Canadian and Japanese support for Latin American initiatives could improve prospects for making military reactions or "solutions" (to economic or political independence) unfeasible.

The Sandinistas' commitment to anti-imperialism and socioeconomic restructuring, meanwhile, led to USSR willingness to commit enough aid or resources to Nicaragua to raise the stakes for the United States in the region. Given th vigorous anti-USSR rhetoric emanating from the White House and the heightening of superpower tensions in the first half of the decade, the USSR appeared to have little reason easily to defer to the United States on Nicaragua. Instead the USSR took advantage of opportunities to increase its influence in Latin America and among states interested in escaping US hegemony. As I have noted, however, the Soviets' circumspection about underwriting the troubled Nicaraguan economy suggests that Moscow was similarly unwilling or unable to commit its resources to guaranteeing the revolution's survival. Nor did the Soviet Union appear interested in creating a "second Cuba" in Nicaragua, despite Reagan Administration claims to the contrary. The USSR knew what limits had been established by US definitions of its national security interests in Central America; the Soviets were not willing to accept the military costs of directly assuring Nicaragua's military security or of provoking US security concerns in the area. Indeed, in the midst of the heated 1986 White House campaign to win new military funding for the contras, some US State Department Soviet experts expressed their assessment that Nicaragua did not represent a Soviet security challenge to the United States (e.g., NYT, 3-16-86).

Yet, in the Reagan Administration's continuing drive to build an anti-Sandinista consensus, communist expansionism continued as a central theme. US national security became identified with getting rid of the Sandinistas. Calmer analyses suggested that Moscow's interests in Latin America generally were being pursued cautiously and on a relatively low budget. Nevertheless, Soviet commitments to provide oil and arms aid had become key to FSLN planning for its own military and economic survival. To the extent that the FSLN could thereby avoid US dictates or pressures, Washington had difficulty imposing its political will or traditional hegemony in the area. It was this reality, again, which spurred the Reagan Administration's anti-Sandinista fervor. Yet it was also increasingly clear given the Sandinistas' political resilience that to impose its will in Central America, the United States would have to introduce troops. Governments with even the passive support of their people are not easily overthrown; the US contra effort (at its mid-1980s levels) was proving counter-productive in forcing change in the "present structure" of Nicaraguan politics.

Aid from Western Europe and the Eastern bloc was both motivated and limited by the fact that the US had interpreted the continuation of the Sandinista revolution as a direct threat to US security. If the United States (or the Soviet Union) looked to Nicaragua's strategic location or political significance in an East-West contest, Western European and Latin American interests laid in facilitating a non-aligned Nicaragua and avoiding an East-West confrontation in Central America. But the priority assigned to the Nicaragua issue and the high level of resources committed to the anti-Sandinista objective by Washington meant that a "third way" for Nicaragua could only be facilitated at significant economic or political costs. Latin American leaders tried to avoid or lessen these costs through multilateral initiatives and united front actions. Western European leaders lent political support to Latin

American initiatives and further pursued a lessening of regional tensions by encouraging economic integration and offering economic aid on a regional basis.

Given their public commitment to non-aligned diversified relations, their insistence upon self-determination and the partial effectiveness of President Reagan's campaign to isolate Nicaragua internationally, the Sandinistas' foreign policy method necessarily involved wooing support from East, West and South, meeting at least minimal political tests from each, stressing negotiated solutions and maintaining a visible, activist role in international affairs.

At home the Sandinistas were overseeing a weakening economy and were ever wary of CIA plots to create an internal front aimed at undermining their government. National defense rather than socioeconomic development remained the foremost priority. The United States, though unsuccessful in routing the FSLN, had successfully targetted the Sandinistas' development strategy; US economic warfare purposefully undermined FSLN initiatives for increasing Nicaraguan self-sufficiency. Although the Sandinistas' original popularity had narrowed somewhat over time, most Nicaraguans continued to believe that the United States, more so than the FSLN itself, bore the greatest responsibility for their hardship. Nor had war weariness and economic austerity translated into active opposition among average Nicaraguans. Senior Sandinista leader Jaime Wheelock arugued in early 1986 that the FSLN government grew stronger every day it remained in power:

> As long as people perceive that we are on the side of the poor and dispossessed, and as long as they perceive that we are victims of a foreign aggression, they will be with the revolution. In this sense, it may even be that the aggression helps us. If we were at peace, it would be harder for us to explain the causes of economic problems. Thousands of [skilled] people are still here working, even though they may disagree with our policies. Every one working in this society is within the political framework we have established, and that in itself is a measure of our success (NYT, 3-16-86).

The most vocal and organized opposition--which was also anti-system in character--continued to be that of the pro-US and US-cultivated La Prensa-CDN-Catholic Church hierarchy group. Among rural and poor inhabitants or marginalized workers who had benefitted from the revolution's land reform, education, health and price subsidy programs, meanwhile, support for the Sandinista government remained strong. Similarly, revolutionary socioeconomic and political structures were being consolidated; the vast majority of Nicaraguans lived and worked within the system. Political consolidation of a revolution-inspired constitutional system continued in the wake of the 1984 national elections, in spite of the military emergency and US rejections of the Sandinista model. This staying power and the Sandinistas' continued political viability was facilitated ultimately by a program which balanced flexibility, pragmatism and an internationalist stance with a dogged insistence on self-determination and mutual respect among nations.

# References

Ambursley, Fitzroy and Robin Cohen (1983) "Crisis in the Carib-
    bean:  Internal Transformations and External Constraints,"
    in Ambursley and Cohen [eds.] Crisis in the Caribbean.  New
    York:  Monthly Review Press.
Armstrong, Robert (1985) "Nicaragua:  Sovereignty and Non-
    Alignment."  Report on the Americas.  North American Con-
    gress on Latin America (May/June).
Atkins, G. Pope (1977) Latin America in the International Politi-
    cal System.  New York:  The Free Press.
Audett, Rose Marie and David Kowalewski (1983) "Nicaragua Debates
    New Rules for Foreign Companies," in Peter Rossett and John
    Vandermeer [eds.] The Nicaragua Reader:  Document of a Revo-
    lution Under Fire.  New York:  Grove Press.
Azicri, Max (1982) "A Cuban Perspective on the Nicaraguan Revolu-
    tion," in Thomas W. Walker [ed.] Nicaragua in Revolution.
    New York:  Praeger Publishers.
Barry, Tom, Beth Wood and Deb Preusch (1982) Dollars and Dicta-
    tors.  Albuquerque:  The Resource Center.
Bendana, Alejandro (1982) "The Foreign Policy of the Nicaraguan
    Revolution," in Thomas W. Walker [ed.] Nicaragua in Revolu-
    tion.  New York:  Praeger Publishers.
Black, George (1981) Triumph of the People:  The Sandinista Revo-
    lution in Nicaragua.  London:  Zed Press.
Booth, John A. (1982) The End and the Beginning:  The Nicaraguan
    Revolution.  Boulder:  Westview Press.
_____ (1985) "The National Governmental System," in
    Thomas W. Walker [ed.] Nicaragua:  The First Five Years.
    New York:  Praeger Publishers.
Borge, Tomas, et.al. (1982) The Sandinistas Speak.  New York:
    Pathfinder Press.
Bourgois, Philippe (1985) "Ethnic Minorities," in Thomas W.
    Walker [ed.] Nicaragua:  The First Five Years.  New York:
    Praeger Publishers.
Braveboy-Wagner, Jacqueline A. (1981) "Changes in the Regional
    Foreign Policies of the English Speaking Caribbean," in Fer-
    ris and Lincoln [eds.] Latin American Foreign Policies.
    Boulder:  Westview Press.

Brundenius, Claes (1984) "Industrial Development and Strategies in Revolutionary Nicaragua." Lund, Sweden: Research Policy Institute (Research Paper no. 160).

Buchanan, Lt. Col. John H. (1982) "Testimony Before the Subcommittee of Inter-American Affairs." US House of Representatives (September).

Center for Research and Documentation of the Atlantic Coast (1984). Trabil Nani. Managua: CIDCA.

Cirincione, Joe and Leslie Hunter (1984) "Military Threats Actual and Potential," in Robert Leiken [ed.] Central America: Anatomy of Conflict. New York: Pergamon Press.

Chilcote, Ronald H. and Joel C. Edelstein (1986) Latin America: Capitalist and Socialist Perspectives of Development and Underdevelopment. Boulder: Westview Press.

Cochrane, James D. (1978) "Characteristics of Contemporary Latin American International Relations." Journal of Interamerican Studies and World Affairs 20 (November).

Colburn, Forrest D. "Rural Labor and the State in Post-revolutionary Nicaragua." Latin American Research Review 19, no. 3.

Coleman, Kenneth M. (1984) "On Comparing Foreign Policies: Comments on van Klaveren," in Heraldo Munoz and J. Tulchin [eds.] Latin American Nations in World Politics. Boulder: Westview Press.

Coleman, Kenneth M. and Luis Quiros-Varela (1981) Determinants of Latin American Foreign Policies: Bureaucratic Organizations and Development Strategies," in Elizabeth G. Ferris and Jennie K. Lincoln [eds.] Latin American Foreign Policies: Global and Regional Dimensions. Boulder: Westview Press.

Conroy, Michael (1985a) "External Dependence, External Assistance, and Economic Aggression Against Nicaragua." Latin American Perspectives 12, no. 2 (Spring).

_____ (1985b) "Economic Legacy and Politics," in Thomas W. Walker [ed.] Nicaragua, The First Five Years. New York: Praeger Publishers.

Coraggio, Jose Luis and George Irvin (1985) "Revolution and Democracy in Nicaragua." Latin American Perspectives. Beverly Hills: Sage Publications.

Council For Inter-American Security (1980) "A New Inter-American Policy for the Eighties." Washington, D.C.

Council on Foreign Relations (1985) "Communique of Meeting of European, Central American and Contadora Foreign Ministers in San Jose, Costa Rica (September 28-29, 1984)" in Europe-America: Third World Instability as a European-American Issue. Chicago

Cruz Sequeira, Arturo (1984) "The Origins of Sandinista Foreign Policy," in Robert Leiken [ed.] Central America: Anatomy of Conflict. New York: Pergamon Press.

Dealy, Glen C. (1985) "The Pluralistic Latins." Foreign Policy 57 (Winter).

Department of State (1985) "Revolution Beyond Our Borders: Sandinista Intervention in Central America" (September). Washington, D.C.

Department of State and Department of Defense (1985) "The Soviet-
    Cuban Connection in Central America and the Caribbean"
    (March). Washington, D.C.
D'Escoto Brockman, Miguel (1983) "Nicaragua: An Unfinished Can-
    vas." Sojourners 12 (March).
Destler, I.M. (1984) "The Elusive Consensus: Congress and Central
    America," in R. Leiken [ed.] Central America: Anatomy of
    Conflict. New York: Pergamon Press.
Dixon, Marlene (1985) "Overview: Militarism As Foreign Policy -
    Reagan's Second Term. Contemporary Marxism 10. San
    Francisco: Synthesis Publications.
Dodson, Michael and T.S. Montgomery (1982) "The Churches in the
    Nicaraguan Revolution," in Thomas W. Walker [ed.] Nicaragua
    in Revolution. New York: Praeger Publishers.
Dodson, Michael and Laura O'Shaunessy (1985) "Religion and Poli-
    tics," in Thomas W. Walker [ed.] Nicaragua: The First Five
    Years. New York: Praeger Publishers.
Duncan, W. Raymond (1984) "Soviet Interests in Latin America:
    New Opportunities and Old Constraints." Journal of Inter-
    american Studies and World Affairs 26 (May): 163-198.
Dunkerly, James (1983) "Class Structure and Socialist Strategy in
    El Salvador," in Ambursley and Cohen [eds.] Crisis in the
    Caribbean. New York: Monthly Review Press.
Edelman, Marc (1985) "Lifelines: Nicaragua and the Socialist
    Countries." Report on the Americas. North American Con-
    gress on Latin America (May/June).
Europa Yearbook (1979-1984) Europa Publications Limited. London:
    England.
Fagen, Richard (1983) "Revolution and Crisis in Nicaragua," in
    Martin Diskin [ed.] Trouble in Our Backyard. New York:
    Pantheon Books.
Farer, Tom J. (1981) "Reagan's Latin America." New York Review
    of Books (March).
_____ (1984) "At Sea in Central America: Can We Negoti-
    ate Our Way to Shore?" in Robert Leiken [ed.] Central Amer-
    ica: Anatomy of Conflict. New York: Pergamon Press.
_____ (1985) "Contadora: The Hidden Agenda." Foreign
    Policy 59 (Summer).
Feinberg, Richard (1982) "The Recent Rapid Redefinitions of US
    Interests and Diplomacy in Central America," in Richard
    Feinberg [ed.] Central America: International Dimensions.
    New York: Holmes and Meier Publishers.
Feinberg, Richard and Robert A. Pastor (1984) "Far From Hopeless:
    An Economic Program for Post-War Central America," in Robert
    S. Leiken [ed.] Central America: Anatomy of Conflict.
    New York: Pergamon Press.
Ferris, Elizabeth G. (1981) "Toward A Theory for the Comparative
    Analysis of Latin American Foreign Policy," in Ferris and
    Lincoln [eds.] Latin American Foreign Policies: Global and
    Regional Dimensions. Boulder: Westview Press.
FitzGerald, E.V.K. (1982) "The Economics of the Revolution," in
    Thomas W. Walker [ed.] Nicaragua in Revolution. New York:
    Praeger Publishers.

390

Foreign Policy Association (1979) Great Decisions '79. New York:
Foreign Policy Association, Inc.
Fox, Annette B. (1977) The Politics of Attraction: Four Middle
Powers and the United States. New York: Columbia Univer-
sity Press.
Franck, Thomas M. and Edward Weisband (1979) Word Politics:
Verbal Strategy Among the Superpowers. New York and London:
Oxford University Press.
FSLN (1979) Analysis of the Situation and Tasks of the Sandinist
People's Revolution. Managua, September 21-23. Reprinted
and distributed by the US Office of Public Diplomacy for
Latin America and the Caribbean. Washington: Department of
State.
Galtung, Johan (1981) "The Politics of Self-Reliance," in Heraldo
Munoz [ed.] From Dependency to Development: Strategies to
Overcome Underdevelopment and Inequality. Boulder: West-
view Press.
Gilbert, Dennis (1985) "The Bourgeoisie," in Thomas W. Walker
[ed.] Nicaragua: The First Five Years. New York: Praeger
Publishers.
Goldblat, Jozef and Victor Milan (1984) "The Honduras-Nicaragua
Conflict and Prospects for Arms Control in Central America."
SIPRI Yearbook. London: Taylor and Francis.
Gonzalez Casanova, Pablo (1984) "Intervention and Negotiation in
Central America," Contemporary Marxism 8 (Spring).
Gorman, Stephen M. (1982) "The Role of the Revolutionary Armed
Forces," in Thomas W. Walker [ed.] Nicaragua in Revolution.
New York: Praeger Publishers.
Gorman, Stephen M. and Thomas W. Walker (1985) "The Armed Forces,"
in Thomas W. Walker [ed.] Nicaragua: The First Five Years.
New York: Praeger Publishers.
Gutman, Roy (1984) "America's Diplomatic Charade." Foreign Pol-
icy 56 (Fall).
Hall, Kenneth and Byron Blake (1981) "Collective Self-Reliance:
The Case of the Caribbean Community (CARICOM)," in Heraldo
Munoz [ed.] From Dependency to Development. Boulder: West-
view Press.
Harris, Richard (1985) "The Revolutionary Process in Nicaragua."
Latin American Perspectives. Beverly Hills: Sage Publica-
tions.
Haq, ul, Mahbub (1981) "Negotiating A New Bargain with the Rich
Countries," in Heraldo Munoz [ed.] From Dependency to De-
velopment: Strategies to Overcome Underdevelopment and In-
equality. Boulder: Westview Press.
Holsti, Ralvei J. (1978) "A New International Politics? Diplomacy in Complex Interdependence," International Organization 32 (Spring).
House Committee on Foreign Affairs (1980) Assessment of Conditions in Central America. Washington, D.C.: US House of
Representatives (May).
Hynds, Patricia (1982) "The Ideological Struggle Within the Catholic Church In Nicaragua." Instituto Historico Centroamericano. Managua (September).

Jerez, Cesar (1984) "The Church and the Revolution In Nicaragua."
    London:  Catholic Institute for International Relations.  22
    Coleman Fields, London N1 7AF.
Jonas, Suzanne (1982) "The Nicaraguan Revolution and the Reemerg-
    ing Cold War," in Thomas W. Walker [ed.] Nicaragua in Revo-
    lution.  New York:  Praeger Publishers.
Kang, Sugwon (1985) "Flight 007:  Was There Foul Play?"  Bulletin
    of Concerned Asian Scholars (April/June).
King, Lt. Col. Edward L. (1984) Out of Step, Out of Line:  US
    Military Policy in Central America.  Boston:  Universalist
    Unitarian Service Committee.
_____ (1985) The Nicaraguan Armed Forces:  A
    Second Look.  Boston:  Universalist Unitarian Service Com-
    mittee.
Kirkpatrick, Jeane (1979) "Dictatorships and Double Standards."
    Commentary (Fall).
LaFeber, Walter (1983) Inevitable Revolutions:  The United States
    in Central America.  New York:  Norton Press.
_____ (1984) "The Burdens of the Past," in Robert
    Leiken [ed.] Central America:  Anatomy of Conflict.  New
    York:  Pergamon Press.
Lagos, Gustavo (1981) "The Revolution of Being:  A Preferred
    World Model," in Heraldo Munoz [ed.] From Dependency to
    Development:  Strategies to Overcome Underdevelopment and
    Inequality.  Boulder:  Westview Press.
Latin American Studies Association (1985) Report of the Delega-
    tion to Observe the Nicaraguan General Election of November
    4, 1984.  LASA Forum 15 (Winter).
LeoGrande, William M. (1982) "The United States and the Nicara-
    guan Revolution," in Thomas W. Walker [ed.] Nicaragua in Re-
    volution.  New York:  Praeger Publishers.
Lernoux, Penny (1984) "Revolution and Counterrevolution in the
    Central American Church," in Donald Schulz and Douglas Gra-
    ham [eds.] Revolution and Counterrevolution in Central
    America and the Caribbean.  Boulder:  Westview Press.
Lieuwen, Edwin (1967) US Policy in Latin America:  A Short His-
    tory.  New York:  Praeger Publishers.
Lincoln, Jennie K. (1981) "Introduction to Latin American Foreign
    Policy," in Ferris and Lincoln [eds.] Latin American Foreign
    Policies:  Global and Regional Dimensions.  Boulder:  West-
    view Press.
Malley, Nadia (1985) "Relations with Western Europe and the So-
    cialist International," in Thomas W. Walker [ed.] Nicaragua:
    The First Five Years.  New York:  Praeger Press.
Managua, Nicaragua Libre (1982) "The Philosophy and the Politics
    of the Government of Nicaragua" (March).
Matthews, Robert (1985) "The Limits of Friendship:  Nicaragua and
    the West."  Report on the Americas.  North American Congress
    on Latin America (May/June).
Maxfield, Sylvia and Richard Stahler-Sholk (1985) "External Con-
    straints," in Thomas W. Walker [ed.] Nicaragua:  The First
    Five Years.  New York:  Praeger Press.

McConnell, Jeff (1983) "Counterrevolution in Nicaragua: The US Connection," in Peter Rossett and John Vandermeer [eds.] The Nicaragua Reader: Document of a Revolution Under Fire. New York: Grove Press.

McGowen, Patrick J. and Klaus-Peter Gottwald (1975) "Small State Foreign Policies," International Studies Quarterly, Volume 19, no. 4 (December).

McShane, John F. (1981) "Emerging Regional Power: Mexico's Role in the Caribbean Basin," in Ferris and Lincoln [eds.] Latin American Foreign Policies. Boulder: Westview Press.

Milenky, Edward S. (1977) "Latin America's Multilateral Diplomacy: Integration, Disintegration, and Interdependence," International Affairs 53 (January).

Ministry of Foreign Trade (1984) "The Economic Strangulation of Nicaragua." Contemporary Marxism 8 (Spring).

Munoz, Heraldo (1981) From Dependency to Development: Strategies to Overcome Underdevelopment and Inequality. Boulder: Westview Press.

National Action/Research on the Military Industrial Complex [NARMIC] (1985) "Invasion: A Guide to the US Military Presence in Central America." Philadelphia: American Friends Service Committee.

Nef, Jorge (1984) "Political Trends in Latin America: A Structural and Historical Analysis," in Jan Knippers Black [ed.] Latin America: Its Problems and Its Promise. Boulder: Westview Press.

Nicaraguan Institute of Social Security and Welfare (1985) Maryrdom of the Nicaraguan Children Under the Aggression of the Reagan Administration. Managua: Nicaraguan Government Publication.

Nye, Joseph S. Jr. (1976) "Independence and Interdependence," Foreign Policy 22 (Spring).

Oduber, Daniel (1985) "A Central American Perspective on European and American Roles in the Region," in Council on Foreign Relations, Europe-America: Third World Instability As A European-American Issue. Chicago.

Ortega Saavedra, Daniel (1983) "Inauguration of 4th Legislative Period on the Day of National Dignity," Speech to the Council of State. Managua: Nicaraguan Government Publication (May).

O'Shaughnessy, Laura Nuzzi (1985) "Beyond Rhetoric: Political Evolution in Nicaragua." Paper presented at the XIth International Congress of the Latin American Studies Association, Alburquerque (April 18-20).

Pearson, David (1984) "The K.A.L. 007: What the US Knew and When We Knew It." The Nation (August 18-25).

Petras, James (1981) Class, State and Power in the Third World. London: Zed Press.

Pittman, Howard T. (1981) "Geopolitics and Foreign Policy in Argentina, Brazil and Chile," in Ferris and Lincoln [eds.] Latin American Foreign Policies. Boulder: Westview Press.

Poitras, Guy (1981) "Mexico's Foreign Policy in an Age of Interdependence," in Ferris and Lincoln [eds.] Latin American

Foreign Policies: Global and Regional Dimensions. Boulder: Westview Press.

Policy Alternatives for the Caribbean and Central America (PACCA) (1984) "Changing Course: Blueprint For Peace in Central America and the Caribbean." Washington, D.C.: Institute for Policy Studies.

Queiser Morales, Waltraud and Harry E. Vanden (1985) "Relations with the Nonaligned Movement," in Thomas W. Walker [ed.] Nicaragua: The First Five Years. New York: Praeger Press.

Ramirez Mercado, Sergio (1983) "The Unfinished American Revolution and Nicaragua Today," speech of July 14, 1983 to the Conference on Central America, Managua. Reprinted in Contemporary Marxism 8 (Spring).

Rosenau, James N. (1980) The Scientific Study of Foreign Policy. New York: Nichols Publishing Co.

_____ (1982) "National (and Factional) Adaptation in Central America: Options for the 1980's," in Richard Feinberg [ed.] Central America: International Dimensions. New York: Holmes and Meier Publishers.

Rothenberg, Morris (1984) "The Soviets and Central America," in Robert S. Leiken [ed.] Central America: Anatomy of Conflict. New York: Pergamon Press.

Sanders, Jerry (1985) "Terminators." Mother Jones (August-September).

Schulz, Donald E. and Douglas H. Graham (1984) Revolution and Counterrevolution in Central America and the Caribbean. Boulder: Westview Press.

Schwab, Theodore and Harold Sims (1985) "Relations with the Communist States," in Thomas W. Walker [ed.] Nicaragua: The First Five Years. New York: Praeger Publishers.

Selcher, Wayne A. (1981) "Brazil in the World: Multipolarity As Seen By A Peripheral ABC Middle Power," in Ferris and Lincoln [eds.] Latin American Foreign Policies. Boulder: Westview Press.

Serra, Luis (1982) "The Sandinist Mass Organizations," in Thomas W. Walker [ed.] Nicaragua in Revolution. Boulder: Westview Press.

Sims, Harold (1982) "Sandinista Nicaragua: Pragmatism In A Political Economy In Formation." Philadelphia: Institute for the Study of Human Issues.

_____ (1984) "Nicaragua's Relations With the Communist Party States During 1984." Austin: Central America Writers Clearing House.

Sklar, Holly [ed.] (1980) Trilateralism: The Trilateral Commission and Elite Planning for World Management. Boston: South End Press.

Slater, Jerome (1984) "United States Policy in Latin America," in Jan Knippers Black [ed.] Latin America: Its Problems and Its Promise. Boulder: Westview Press.

Smith, Wayne (1982) "Dateline Havana: Myopic Diplomacy." Foreign Policy 48 (Fall).

Somoza Debayle, Anastasio (1980) Nicaragua Betrayed. Boston: Western Islands.

394

Stavenhagen, Rodolfo (1981) "The Future of Latin America: Between Underdevelopment and Revolution," in Heraldo Munoz [ed.] From Dependency to Development: Strategies to Overcome Underdevelopment and Inequality. Boulder: Westview Press.

Stepan, Alfred (1981) "The United States and Latin America: Vital Interests and the Instruments of Power," in Ferris and Lincoln [eds.] Latin American Foreign Policies: Global and Regional Dimensions. Boulder: Westview Press.

Tancer, Shoshana B. (1976) Economic Nationalism in Latin America. New York: Praeger Publishers.

Tinbergen, Jan (1981) "The Need For An Ambitious Renovation Of the World Order," in Heraldo Munoz [ed.] From Dependency to Development: Strategies to Overcome Underdevelopment and Inequality. Boulder: Westview Press.

Valenta, Jiri (1982) "Soviet and Cuban Responses to New Opportunities in Central America," in Richard Feinberg [ed.] Central America: International Dimensions. New York: Holmes and Meier Publishers.

Vanderlaan, Mary B. (1984) "The 'Dual Strategy' Myth in Central American Policy." Journal of Interamerican Studies and World Affairs 26 (May).

van Klaveren, Alberto (1984) "The Analysis of Latin American Foreign Policies: Theoretical Perspectives," in Munoz and Tulchin [eds.] Latin American Nations in World Politics. Boulder: Westview Press.

Walker, Thomas W. (1982) "Images of the Nicaraguan Revolution," in Thomas W. Walker [ed.] Nicaragua in Revolution. New York: Praeger Publishers.

Wallerstein, Emmanuel (1981) "Dependence In An Interdependent World: The Limited Possibilities of Transformation Within the Capitalist World Economy," in Heraldo Munoz [ed.] From Dependency to Development: Strategies to Overcome Underdevelopment and Inequality. Boulder: Westview Press.

Weber, Henri (1981) Nicaragua: The Sandinista Revolution. London: Verso Editions-NLB.

_____ (1983) "Nicaragua: The Sandinista Revolution," in Ambursley and Cohen [eds.] Crisis in the Caribbean. New York: Monthly Review Press.

Wheelock Roman, Jaime (1984) "You Cannot Overthrow a People," an interview with Commandante Jaime Wheelock Roman, October 1983. Reprinted in Contemporary Marxism 8 (Spring).

White, Richard Alan (1984) The Morass: United States Intervention in Central America. New York: Harper and Row Publishers.

Wiarda, Howard J. (1974) "Corporatism and Development in the Iberic-Latin World: Persistent Strains and New Variations," in Pike and Stritch [eds.] The New Corporatism. South Bend: University of Notre Dame Press.

_____ (1984) "At the Root of the Problem: Conceptual Failures in US Central American Relations," in Robert S. Leiken [ed.] Central America: Anatomy of Conflict. New York: Pergamon Press.

# Newspapers and Periodicals Cited

| | |
|---|---|
| BI | Barricada International (Managua) |
| CAHI | Central America Historical Institute (Washington) |
| CAR | Central America Report (Guatemala City) |
| CARIN | Central America Research Institute (Berkeley) |
| CAU | Central America Update (Toronto) |
| COHA | Council on Hemispheric Affairs (Washington) |
| FBIS-LAM | Foreign Broadcast Information Service, Latin America |
| FBIS-SU | Foreign Broadcast Information Service, Soviet Union |
| ICAS | Institute For Central American Studies (San Jose, Costa Rica) |
| IHCA | Insituto Historico Centroamericano (Managua) |
| IRTFCA | Inter-Religious Task Force on Central America (New York) |
| LAPR | Latin American Political Report (Great Britain) |
| LARM | Latin American Regional Report (Great Britain) |
| LAT | Los Angeles Times |
| LAWR | Latin American Weekly Report (Great Britain) |
| LNSN | LASA-Nica Scholar News |
| LP | La Prensa (Managua) |
| MH | Miami Herald |
| Newsweek | |
| NYT | New York Times |
| WP | Washington Post |
| WSJ | Wall Street Journal |

# Index

398

Carter, President Jimmy, 288
Casey, William, 144, 160,
161, 169 (n16), 366
Castro, Fidel, 20, 164, 249,
251, 252, 359
Catholic Church (Nicaraguan),
39, 40, 108-119, 123
(n18)
hierarchy, 39, 60, 86, 90,
96, 108, 110, 112, 113,
114, 115, 256, 368,
375
Central American Common Market (CACM), 61, 62, 64,
69, 137, 217, 333, 334,
336, 341
Central American Democratic
Community (CADC), 141,
143, 146, 353
Central Intelligence Agency
(CIA), 98, 107, 113,
138, 141, 143, 144,
152, 165, 176, 183,
184, 185, 186, 188,
190, 191, 196, 213,
230-231, 234, 259 (n7),
298, 329, 361, 386
manuals for contra sabotage,
151, 152
harbor mining, 169 (n16),
193, 258, 281, 340, 352-
353
Cerezo Arevalo, Marco Vinin-
cio, 237-238, 364, 469
Chamorro Barrios, Pedro Joaquin, 97
Chamorro Coronel, Edgar, 121
(n4), 184, 189, 215
(n5)
Chile, 244, 267, 287
Christian base communities
(communidades de base),
39, 40, 109
civil defense, 274, 276
Civilian Military Assistance
(CMA), 194
Clark, William, 144, 160
"collective self-defense",
151, 234, 352, 370 (n2)
Coleman, Kenneth C., 5, 16,
17
Colombia, 245
See also Contadora States

Comee, Col. William, 182
Committee on the Present Danger
(CPD), 132
Central American Defense Pact
(CONDECA) 4, 25, 136-137,
144, 177, 190, 212, 221,
237
Congress (US), 93, 97, 131, 138,
148, 152, 153, 163, and contra program, 154, 164, 176,
183, 186, 188, 193, 210,
213
constitution drafting process,
55, 56, 199, 386
Contadora, 19, 121 (n3), 147,
149, 150, 154, 158, 162,
167, 228, 231-232, 239,
241, 243, 245-248, 298,
321, 325, 349, 350, 351,
354, 355, 357, 358, 359,
365, 366, 376, 368, 375,
379, 381, 383
"Document of Objectives", 146,
360, 370 (n8)
1983 Draft, 360
1984 (Sept. 7) Draft, 150,
256, 361, 371 (n12)
1985 Draft, 364, 371 (n12)
Tegucigalpa Draft, 326, 361,
362, 364
Lima Support Group, 155, 363,
369
Nicaraguan positions at 358ff.
verification and implementation issues, 351, 360,
361, 362, 368,
Contadora States, 99, 146, 155,
233, 246, 353, 357, 358,
359, 361, 362, 363, 366,
371 (n10), 377
contras (counter-revolutionary
fighters), 153, 155, 158,
166, 183-202, 257, 259
(n4), 274, 281, 350, 357,
358, 364, 366, 369 (n1)
Alianza Revolucionaria Democratica (ARDE), 91, 106,
186, 191, 192, 196, 197,
232, 233, 278, 282, 284,
354
United Nicaraguan Opposition
(UNO), 95, 96-98, 157,
182, 183, 192, 199, 201,

404